THE CELTIC CONSCIOUSNESS

IV

THE CELTIC CONSCIOUSNESS

Edited by

ROBERT O'DRISCOLL

GEORGE BRAZILLER   NEW YORK

First published in Canada in 1981 in a limited edition of 500 copies by McClelland and Stewart and The Dolmen Press.

First published in the United States in 1982 by George Braziller, Inc.

For information address the publisher:
George Braziller, Inc.
One Park Avenue
New York, NY 10016

Library of Congress Cataloging in Publication Data
Main entry under title:

The Celtic consciousness.

   Papers first presented at a symposium held in Toronto, February, 1978.
   Includes index.
   1. Civilization, Celtic—Congresses.
I. O'Driscoll, Robert.
CB206.C44   1982   909'.0974916   82-1269
ISBN 0-8076-1041-0   AACR2

The Celtic Consciousness, edited by Robert O'Driscoll, is designed by Liam Miller and photoset in Berner typeface by Kornagraphics in Toronto.

Typeset with the assistance of a grant from Wintario and the Multicultural Development Branch, Ministry of Culture and Recreation, Government of Ontario.

Printed in the United States of America
First printing.

vi

CONTENTS

FOREWORD

What is a Foreword and who writes it? In this case, a Foreword can only be a statement by an interested, involved, but a peripheral participant in an event; moreover, the statement is made by a novice who got caught up in, and was swept along by, the ebb and flow of the Celtic tide from which the event emerged, a tide which offered no release.

The papers in this book are the fabric of the event which took place in Toronto in February of 1978: a major Symposium on the Celtic Consciousness. That it happened in Canada is proof that Canadians can, if challenged, do worthwhile things on a worthwhile scale. That the theme was *consciousness* ensured the catholicity of subject matter. After Jung, who can set limits to consciousness? Consciousness, however, can be dormant. It needs a gadfly — a spark to awaken it — an artist to organize it and a producer to put it on the stage. Robert O'Driscoll was all of these rolled into one. The Celtic Arts organization was his creature and, for two years, the creature tried to limit the passion and the enthusiasm of its creator. After all, it was the fiscally responsible agency. On the campus of the University of Toronto, O'Driscoll is the proof that only that which is a contradiction in terms is impossible. The Celtic Consciousness event was deemed impossible by all program organizers save O'Driscoll and those who caught the fever of his infectious spirit.

The event was explosive: it lasted for weeks and played to full houses in the largest auditoria on campus. Moreover, the explosion has had a fallout, one which improves the academic ecology on campus. In 1981, as this book goes to press, there begins at the University of Toronto a full Major Programme in Celtic Studies, the emergence of which Dean Kruger calls a miracle. New programmes are impossible in an era of cutbacks, impossible save in the Celtic world. The Symposium on "The Celtic Consciousness" was but the dawn of the day of revival.

2 September 1981   *John Kelly*
St. Michael's College   *Chairman*
University of Toronto   *Celtic Arts Board*

INTRODUCTION

ROBERT O'DRISCOLL

I

The cauldron, or, in Christian terms, the Grail, is a central recurring motif in Celtic mythology: the vessel is a symbol of the inexhaustible resources of the spirit, forever renewing itself, whether it be the hidden spirit that animates all matter, or, in modern psychological terms, an energy in the depths of the mind that, if developed, can free man from dependence on the body and the tyranny of historical fact. On a more literal level, the cauldron seems an appropriate image to represent the fate of the Celts in the Western world. They seem to have emerged from the east; then, for almost a thousand years, they dominated the centre of Europe, stretching from the Black Sea to Iberia and from the Mediterranean to the North Sea and Ireland. Two thousand years later they survive on the western periphery of Europe, having been pushed to the extreme edge of the cauldron.

Was the construction of Dún Aenghusa on the edge of Aran, with its stylized suggestion of heroic defiance at the limits of the known world, a symbolic representation of the movement of history and the fate of human life, the physical movement from circumference to centre to circumference? Once the vital energies of a civilization have been exhausted, is there an instinctive return to the spiritual values initially displaced by that civilization?

> On their own feet they came, or on shipboard,
> Camel-back, horse-back, ass-back, mule-back,
> Old civilisations put to the sword. . . .
> All things fall and are built again,
> And those that build them again are gay.[1]

Does the resurgence of the Celtic spirit in the twentieth century, and the reappearance of mystics and visionaries, suggest that Vico, Spengler, and Yeats were right in their contention that history moves in cycles? Do perceptions and ideas which have been pushed to the periphery in one cycle become the spiritual nucleus of the next? In any case, contemplation of the Celtic experience forces one to look backwards and forwards at the same time, and an appropriate image of that experience seems to be one of those ancient Celtic faces carved in stone, looking simultaneously in many directions.

II

To understand the Celtic consciousness, the peripheries of the Indo-European world must be touched, and points of contact between East and West probed, certainly with regard to mythology, language, music, and art.

We know that the ancient Irish monastic schools, which were successful in maintaining the thin thread of Christianity in Europe during the Dark Ages, were modelled on similar establishments in the East. In terms of art, it is clear from Liam De Paor's researches that some of the forms, motifs and techniques of Celtic art derived from the East, while the artistic construction of the medieval illuminated books may be compared to the calligraphy of the Far East. The connections between the Celtic and Indian worlds exist, not only in terms of particulars, in historical and mythological cross-references, but also in terms of essentials: the belief that a correspondence exists between the cosmos and the individual soul; that pairs of opposites can be reconciled and the soul led to transcendence, to the "rapture" of a state of consciousness that defies intellectual definition; and, more importantly, in the way in which both Celtic and Indian mythology emphasize the inward, the mystical, and read the symbolism of the world in an esoteric way. Brendan's voyage, for example, could be historically interpreted, "as a legend inspired in part by actual Celtic voyages to America" p. 10),[2] but the Christian Celts chose to present *The Voyage of Brendan* in a very different way from a recent book on the subject by Mr. Tim Severin: science, we may say, merely corroborates what the imagination intuits. In the ancient Celtic as well as in the Indian world, human and historical events are interpreted mythologically, are read as correspondences to powers operating in the human being rather than as chronicles of "actual or imagined historical events" (p. 11). In viewing the world in this way, the Celts, as well as their eastern counterparts, released themselves from the chain of historical and social necessity, making possible a spiritual rebirth. The agent of this rebirth, he who discovers the way by which man is brought beyond the biological energies of the body, is the hero, who is central not only to Celtic and Indian mythology, but also to modern Celtic literature.

With regard to the connections between Celtic and Indian music, the modern Irish composer, Sean O'Riada, claimed that what is known as traditional Celtic music, and which is now so popular in Europe and North America, had its origins in the Himalayas, and travelled to the Celtic world via Northern Africa and Spain. Scholars are quick to point out that there is little evidence to substantiate this claim, but in seeking for 'evidence' one is perhaps seeking the impossible. Music, by its very nature, is an evanescent art as compared to the visual or literary arts. What evidence, other than the remains of living tradition, can one discover? With traditional music, too, there is no written score and no historical record of great performances. It is unlikely that the artistically-gifted people who produced the oldest vernacular literature north of the Alps, the richest mythology, and the most elaborate traditions in sculpture and illumination, should have left no musical remains, when the world in which they lived was, and still is, so conducive to the oral transmission of music. It is inconceivable, one writer states, that "all vestiges of the music that sustained our people for ... two thousand years could have vanished without trace" (p. 333). It is far more plausible to assume that the Celtic music that survives today represents the remains of an ancient tradition, and musicologists note similarities in vocal styles between the Indian raga, Celtic sean-nos singing, and to some extent the Arabic Maqam-iqa.

In language too, as Heinrich Wagner has so brilliantly shown, the Celtic languages provide a striking link between the languages of Western Europe, Northern Africa, and those of the Middle East. What is particularly interesting is that the Celtic languages, which exhibit particularly archaic features within the Indo-European family of languages, were imposed on people who spoke languages of non-Indo-European origins. As a consequence, subtleties and variations not found in the Indo-European model, periphrastic verbal constructions for example, were introduced, and the language enriched and made more expressive. The English language spoken in Celtic areas was in turn influenced by the Celtic languages, with, for instance, the incidence of periphrastic forms of verbal construction being much higher in 'Anglo-Irish' speech than in standard English. 'Anglo-Irish' speech becomes the medium of expression for the greatest literary movement in the twentieth century, and when one remembers the extensive literature in Old Irish, one cannot help reflecting how extraordinarily persistent habits of language are, and a language which shows a capability at one point may exhibit the same capability at another.

When one is confronted with the seeming linguistic lawlessness of James Joyce's *Finnegans Wake*, created by an artist for whom not only every syllable but the context of every syllable mattered, polymorphic and polyglottal, an aural counterpart perhaps of the intricate visual beauty and astrological iconography of The Book of Kells, one is startled by the following analysis which is being made, not of *Finnegans Wake*, but of the grammatical structure of the Celtic languages:

> a word pronounced in isolation and a word pronounced in a sentence context may show quite different pronunciations, because in the latter case neighbouring words influence each other in their pronunciation ... As far as the Celtic languages are concerned, the division of a sentence into words, shown in print by spacing, is a mere conventional device which facilitates semantic and grammatical analysis, but which is not justified phonetically. ... [W]e may say that the word in Celtic is like a chameleon which changes its appearance according to its surroundings. Or, putting it in a more extreme way: the word by itself is in Celtic very loose, almost amorphous, and its shape can only be defined by analysing the sentence as a whole. ... Among the modern Celtic languages, it is precisely Irish that shows these properties to their greatest extent. ... [T]he word in Celtic is not a solid, strictly definable unit, but on the contrary something that changes its form constantly under all sorts of influences: phonetic, morphological, and syntactical. This also gives the sentence as a whole an unstable, almost fluid appearance. (pp. 71-5)

III

The roots of language and mythology lie in a prehistoric past, the evidence of which comes to us most directly from the science of archaeology. The evidence systematically accumulated from archaeological investigations (beginning with the major discoveries at Hallstatt and La Tène in the nineteenth century) have led us to appreciate the extent of the Celtic settlement of the continent of Europe and the distinguishing features of their artistic creations and way of life: their changing living styles and their constant religious beliefs; their art, sculpture, and architecture; funereal rites and social customs, with the various class distinctions that these customs indicate; their expansion through Europe, and their interaction with other cultures, chiefly the Etruscan, Greek, Roman, and German. Recently, too, the findings of the Celtic archaeologist have been supplemented by a unique experiment, the Butser Ancient Farm Research Project, which reconstructs a farm as it would have operated at about 300 B.C. (with reconstructed houses, authentic agricultural implements, wheats, sheep, cattle, and fowl) in order to test empirically the evidence provided from traditional excavation and to test too the validity of the hypotheses of the archaeologist. In more general terms, we can say that within the past twenty years Celtic archaeology has emerged as the most exciting branch of archaeological investigation in Europe. It is now recognized as providing the indispensable counter to the culture of the Mediterranean and as supplying the stages in the development of a people from a Neolithic farming community to an aggressive Indo-European aristocracy. This development was in some ways made possible by the advanced technology of the Iron Age, and indeed, "the surviving material remains of Celtic culture show that society was endowed with technology and the craft skills unsurpassed in Europe until the eighteenth century A.D."[3]

With the help of archaeological research, the oldest continuum in Europe has been established, a living Celtic continuum existing for almost three thousand years. In countries such as Ireland, which were beyond the pale of Roman conquest or Germanic invasion, the easy transition from paganism to Christianity can be perceived in the surviving art:

> the varied curvilinear forms of Iron Age times gave way to a fashion for elegant spinning patterns of 'trumpet spirals' winding in and out of one another with increasingly colourful touches of enamel. Interlacings, biting animals, polychrome frets and keys were rapidly added to the patterns in bronzework — soon metamorphosed into enamel-like painted manuscript pages — in an eclectic style that, far from being swamped by the new borrowings, contributed to retain both the spirit and the basic organisation of prehistoric Celtic art. . . . The order comes from within: this is the key to what is 'Celtic' in Irish art of the early Christian period. . . . The Book of Kells is rightly famous as a supreme product of the final phase of this art. As difficult, and in some ways as alienating to the modern consciousness, as *Finnegans Wake*, it repels and fascinates because its order, barely controlling an explosive anarchy, allows us to glimpse the chaos at the heart of the universe which our own Romanised culture is at pains to conceal. (p. 126)[4]

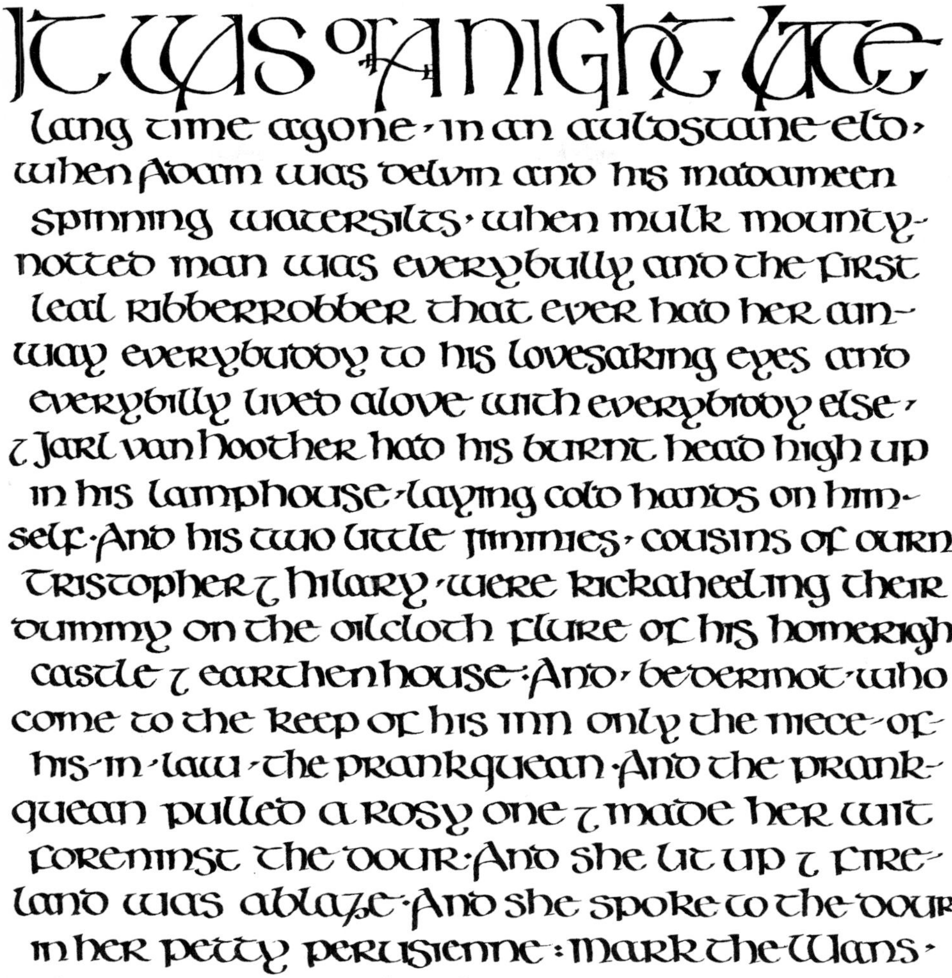

IT WAS OF A NIGHT LATE lang time agone, in an auldstane eld, when Adam was delvin and his madameen spinning watersilts· when mulk mountynotted man was everybully and the first leal ribberrobber that ever had her ainway everybuddy to his lovesaking eyes and everybilly lived alove with everybroody else, ⁊ Jarl van Hoother had his burnt head high up in his lamphouse, laying cold hands on himself. And his two little jimmies, cousins of ourn Tristopher ⁊ Hilary· were kickaheeling their dummy on the oilcloth flure of his homerigh, castle ⁊ earthenhouse. And· bedermot· who come to the keep of his inn only the niece-of his-in-law, the prankquean. And the prankquean pulled a rosy one ⁊ made her wit foreninst the dour. And she lit up ⁊ fireland was ablaze. And she spoke to the dour in her petty perusienne: Mark the Wans· why do I am alook alike a poss of porter pease? And that was how the SKIRMISHES began

Plate 1: *Finnegans Wake* (page 21) in a Celtic Script, by Timothy O'Neill, F.R.S.

In literature, as opposed to art, the problem is more complicated. In the sixth century the Latin alphabet was adapted for the writing of Irish, and within a remarkably short time was being used to record native pagan traditions. Perhaps mythology is committed to writing, or literature is created from mythology, precisely when the divergence between the myths and the life to which they were meant to relate is at its most obvious. Early Christian Ireland provides a rare opportunity to study not merely this transition from pagan to Christian but one of the great transitions in the development of a people: the transition from an oral to a written culture, a transition which is doubly interesting in that Celtic culture continues to be transmitted both in an oral and written form down to modern times. The problems for the scholar, as Proinsias MacCana points out, are extensive: the determination, first of all, of the relationship between the written literature and the oral tradition from which it derives; second, the degree to which the monastic redactor deliberately suppresses material that seems at variance with the Christian ethic; and third, the extent to which the monastic imagination, working in another medium, assimilates the pagan material and changes it involuntarily.

IV

A civilization, however, is not to be judged merely by the literature produced by its educated classes. Recent scholarship in France and Canada has shown the value of investigating a culture not merely in terms of 'high culture' but also in terms of the vernacular idiom and expressiveness of the common people. On the periphery of Western Europe — the very edge of the cauldron — where the Celtic languages continued to be spoken, a harmony developed between the people and the earth, and human habitation became an integral and organic part of the landscape. In these sacred and isolated places where the plough of modern civilization had not cut too deeply, something was preserved that was lost at the centre: a rich store of lore, tradition, song, and poetry, passed on from generation to generation, which embodies the Celtic perception of the world: their belief in the aristocracy of the imagination and the honoured place of the poet; their strong feeling for the supernatural, the interpenetration of natural and supernatural, and a veneration for nature in all its manifestations; their ritualistic expression of grief, their sense of the sacredness of place and of a communion between the living and the dead; and, most of all, their view of themselves as the guardians of a tradition that was older than any that their conquerors could claim.

Through these folk memories a living tradition was preserved. Folklore, therefore, may provide a more intimate link with the past than archaeological remains, historical records, or even sophisticated literature. During the past fifty years, folk traditions in Scotland and Ireland have been recorded with scientific care, and the collections in both countries constitute one of the most extensive folklore collections in the world. This material merits attention not only for its brilliant illumination of the Celtic tradition but because it offers one of the best-documented sources for the study of pre-industrial man. The fact, too, as Estyn Evans points out, that the insular Celts have been settled on their soil longer than any other people in Europe has particular significance for the sociologist and anthropologist, but, as yet, no sustained scholarly use has been made of the millions of pages that have been collected.

V

I was moved to organize the Conference of which this volume is the result in order to demonstrate that the modern literary achievement of the Celtic world, and especially Ireland, is best approached in the context of the tradition of which it is the continuing expression. While some pleasure can be experienced from an isolated reading of this literature, it cannot properly be understood without a knowledge of the background, language, social organization, history, mythology, and aspirations of the Celtic race. To approach it in any other way, as a provincial offshoot of English literature (as is unfortunately the case in most universities today)* is as misguided and as unscholarly as to teach modern Irish history as a branch of British colonial history.

Certainly the significant writers of the modern Celtic world saw themselves

---

*Modern Irish literature in English is cited in most universities throughout the world today as 'Anglo-Irish' literature, and this to my mind is an inaccurate way of referring to it. The term 'Anglo-Irish' has a historical validity when applied to the English-speaking, largely Protestant, class who controlled Ireland from the fall of the Gaelic order at the Battle of Kinsale in 1601 to the emergence of Irish independence during the nineteen-twenties. The term 'Anglo-Irish' may be used to describe some of the writings of this class, those of Maria Edgeworth for example, but the Anglo-Irish as a class have now disappeared, and as a consequence the term has lost its historical usefulness. Certainly it is not an accurate epithet for Irish literature produced in English in this century, for this conveys the impression to the outsider that modern Irish literature in English is some sort of provincial branch of English literature.

The fact that much of this literature has been written in English is not sufficient to merit the appellation 'Anglo-Irish.' The English language as it is used in Ireland is the result of a native manner of thought expressing itself through an acquired language and is very different from standard English, and indeed from English as it is used elsewhere throughout the world. And yet terms such as 'Anglo-Canadian' and 'Anglo-Indian' have been dropped, while 'Anglo-Irish' persists. When one searches for a parallel for the use of the term 'Anglo-Irish', one of the few places where it can be found is behind the Iron Curtain, where the continuing pressure of Soviet dominance is suggested in such terms as 'Soviet-Ukrainian,' 'Soviet-Estonian,' 'Soviet-Latvian,' 'Soviet-Georgian,' etc.

When we turn to the literature in English produced by Irishmen in this century, we find no justification for the use of the term 'Anglo-Irish,' for, as is clear from the extracts quoted in the text of this Introduction, the main writers of the Irish Literary Renaissance explicitly state that they were writing in a tradition that was distinct from the tradition which had produced English literature and the western world. Yeats puts the case clearly in an interview with Radio Eireann during the nineteen-thirties:

> Interviewer: I hope you don't mind my saying what I'm going to say, Mr. Yeats. A lot of people think the Abbey Theatre is only Anglo-Ireland, and that what we want in this country is Gaelic civilization.
>
> Yeats: Of course it is Anglo-Irish. When Chaucer was writing and English literature was being founded, there were people the historians call Anglo-Norman; they became the English people. Anglo-Ireland is already Ireland. ... We have not only English but European thoughts and customs in our heads and in our habits. We could not, if we would, give them up. You may revive the Gaelic language, you cannot revive the Gaelic race. There may be pure Gaels in the Blasket Islands but there are none in the Four Courts, in the College of Surgeons, at the Universities, in the Executive Council, at Mr. Cosgrave's headquarters ... But I hate all hyphenated words. Anglo-Ireland is your word, not mine ... [H]enceforth I shall say the Irish race. The pure Englishman came to Ireland under Cromwell and married into the mixed Irish race. The pure Gael from the Blasket Islands comes to Dublin and goes into the civil service; he will marry into that race in his turn. The Irish people are as much a unity as the German, French, or English people, though many strands have gone to the making of it, and

---

clearly in the context of the continuum we have been tracing. At the very beginning of the Irish Literary Revival, Douglas Hyde declares: behind the expression of Irish nationality

> is the half unconscious feeling that the race which at one time held possession of more than half Europe, which established itself in Greece, and burned infant Rome, is now — almost extirpated and absorbed elsewhere — making its last stand for independence in this island of Ireland; and do what they may the race of today cannot wholly divest itself from the mantle of its own past. Through early Irish literature, for instance, can we best form some conception of what that race really was, which, after overthrowing and trampling on the primitive peoples of half Europe, was itself forced in turn to yield its speech, manners, and independence to the victorious eagles of Rome. We alone of the nations of Western Europe escaped the claws of those birds of prey; we alone developed ourselves naturally upon our own lines outside of and free from all Roman influence; we alone were thus able to produce an early art and literature, *our* antiquities can best throw light upon the pre-Romanised inhabitants of half Europe. . . . The dim consciousness of this is one of those things which are at the back of Irish national sentiment, and our business, whether we be Unionists or Nationalists, should be to make this dim consciousness an active and potent feeling.[5]

Twenty years later Patrick Pearse developed some of these points:

> The rediscovery of this buried [Irish] literature . . . will make it necessary for us to re-write literary history. And it will mean not only a re-writing of literary history, but a general readjustment of literary values, a general raising of literary standards. The world has had a richer dream of beauty than we had dreamed it had. Men here saw certain gracious things more clearly and felt certain mystic things more acutely and heard certain deep music more perfectly than did men in ancient Greece. And it is from Greece that we have received our standards.
>
> How curiously might one speculate if one were to imagine that when the delvers of the fifteenth century unearthed the buried literatures of Greece and Rome they had stumbled instead upon that other buried literature which was to remain in the dust of the libraries for four centuries longer! Then instead of the classic revival we should have had the Celtic revival; or rather the Celtic would have become the classic and the Gael would have given laws to Europe. I do not say positively that literature would have gained, but I am not sure that it would have lost. Something would have been lost: the Greek ideal of perfection in form, the wise calm Greek scrutiny. Yet something it would have gained: a more piercing vision, a nobler, because a more humane, inspiration, above all a deeper spirituality. One other result would have

---

any man who says that we are not talks mischevious nonsense. (National Library of Ireland, Yeats Microfilms, p. 7540)

Neither is the term appropriate for recent Irish writers, and it is anomalous, indeed ludicrous, to categorize such quintessentially Irish writers as Patrick Kavanagh, Brendan Behan, and Flann O'Brien as 'Anglo-Irish.' Surely the time is over-ripe for a practical suggestion: *that the term 'Anglo-Irish' with relation to Irish literature in English be dropped now, and dropped forever.* When the nationality and subject matter of a writer is Irish, then we can only call the literature that is produced 'Irish' also, whether that literature is written in the English or the Irish language.

It is true that until now the term 'Irish literature' has been reserved for literature written in the Irish language, and this has partly been a reluctance to accept that English is as valid a medium for the expression of the Irish consciousness as the Irish language. When we realize, however, that English is now the native language of 98.4% of the Irish people, we realize also that it is time, on the one hand, for scholars and writers in the Irish language to accept their colleagues writing in English as Irish writers, and, on the other hand, for scholars of Irish writing in English to recognize the importance of the Celtic roots of that literature: in the continuum of Irish culture we have one tradition, or maybe even several traditions, being expressed in two languages but from the same common root of experience.

followed: the goodly culture and the fine mysticism of the Middle Ages would not
have so utterly been lost. . . .

Now I claim for Irish literature, at its best, these excellences: a clearer than Greek
vision, a more generous than Greek humanity, a deeper than Greek spirituality. And
I claim that Irish literature has never lost these excellences: that they are of the essence
of Irish nature and are characteristic of modern Irish poetry even as they are of ancient
Irish epic and of medieval Irish hymns.[6]

Yeats, too, saw himself as belonging to an older tradition than that which had
shaped English and much of European literature:

Ireland has in her written Gaelic literature, in her old love tales and battle tales, the
forms in which the imagination of Europe uttered itself before Greece shaped a
tumult of legend into the music of her arts; and she can discover, from the beliefs and
emotions of her common people, the habit of mind that created the religion of the
muses. The legends of other European countries are less numerous, and not so full of
the energies from which the arts and our understanding of their sanctity arose, and
the best of them have already been shaped into plays and poems.[7]

Earlier, in a public lecture in 1903, Yeats had indicated the quintessential
difference between the English and Irish civilizations:

What is this nationality we are trying to preserve, this thing we are fighting English
influence to preserve? It is not merely our pride. It is certainly not any national vanity
that stirs us on to activity. If you examine to the root a contest between two peoples,
two nations, you will always find that it is really a war between two civilizations,
two ideals of life.[8]

At about the same time AE states:

We ask the liberty of shaping the social order in Ireland to reflect our own ideals, and
to embody that national soul which has been slowly incarnating in our race from its
cloudy dawn.[9]

James Joyce explains the motivation behind this impulse:

the Irish nation's insistence on developing its own culture by itself is not so much the
demand of a young nation that wants to make good in the European concert as the
demand of a very old nation to renew under new forms the glories of a past
civilization.[10]

Across the Irish Sea in Wales, David Jones was conscious of his place in a Celtic
continuum and of the difficulties of expressing that heritage in an alien tongue:

It is this break with a whole extremely complex cultural, religious and linguistic
tradition that is the real problem for those of us who, while able only to use English,
have our deepest roots, in some way or other, in the Welsh past. . . .[11]
the poet is a 'rememberer' and . . . it is a part of his business to keep open the lines of
communication. One obvious way of doing this is by handing on such fragmented
bits of our own inheritance as we ourselves received. This is the way I myself
attempt.[12]

For the creators of the Celtic Literary Revival in Ireland, and later of the
movements in Scotland and Wales, the roots of Celtic nationality ran deep,
deeper than the events which have shaped the Western world: the Industrial
Revolution, the Renaissance, Christianity, or the Roman Empire. To study their
work, therefore, in the thin layer of our twentieth-century time space is not only
to distort the work itself but also the tradition of which that work is the
continuing expression.

VI

Like the cauldron of their mythology, the Celts themselves are proving inexhaustible. During the last two hundred years a number of factors have contributed to the accelerating interest in their civilization: the antiquarian and Romantic movement at the end of the eighteenth century; the development, in the nineteenth century, under the direction of German scholars, of the study of the Indo-European languages, of which Old Irish was recognized to be an archaic branch; the linking of cultural with political nationalism and the part it played in the re-establishment of the first Celtic nation in modern times, the Republic of Ireland; and, perhaps most important of all, the development of the modern sciences — archaeology, anthropology, sociology, comparative linguistics, and particularly psychology, with its crucial recognition of the significance of the mythologies of the past in illuminating the internal life of the spirit. More recently, the Celtic consciousness is manifesting itself in the studios of modern artists and is inspiring visionaries with models to counter the materialism of our times.

Celtic society is an "extremely refined and complex society, the dimensions of which we have scarcely begun to understand" (p. 294). This book approaches the subject from the distinctive viewpoint of a number of disciplines and critical approaches: linguistic, archaeological, anthropological, astrological, literary, historical, political, musical, etc. Sometimes the same type of source is used in two different ways. Joseph Campbell, for example, interprets the lives of the saints as translating the language of real or imagined fact into a mythological idiom, while John MacQueen approaches them from the viewpoint of the cultural historian and ethnologist, educing historical evidence to supplement the archaeological in establishing the facts of early Scottish history. In turn, elsewhere in the volume, the evidence of archaeological excavation, at Emain Macha for example, is used to corroborate the picture of the physical cosmos obtained from early Irish saga. Evidence from one discipline can therefore supplement the evidence from another, and indeed, as Anne Ross points out, investigation into the Celtic world "can only be conducted by combining several disciplines" (p. 204).

It is true that Ireland and Scotland provide the main focus of this volume. More cognizance could have been taken of Wales, Brittany, and Cornwall, and this imbalance we plan to rectify in a subsequent volume.

In any case, whatever the focus of any particular exploration, it is lamentable that although the Celtic continuum is the oldest in Europe there is no comprehensive academic programme in any University outside of Ireland and the British Isles, and even what is offered there is sadly fragmented. An academic programme in Celtic Studies, combining the approaches from many disciplines and using primary materials (which are after all the lifeblood of scholarship) will, apart from its own integral interest, correct the fundamental misconception that has for hundreds of years been at the core of our educational system, and this is, as

Claude Levi-Strauss suggests, the mistaken belief that the womb of civilization lies in the Mediterranean. With their advanced farming methods, their technology and trade, with their art and wholly distinctive religious and heroic ethos, the Celts in their relationship to the Germanic and Latin world are as crucial as the Greeks and Romans in the evolution of European civilization.

NOTES

[1] W. B. Yeats, *Collected Poems* (London 1961), pp. 338-9.

[2] The page references in the brackets are to the pages in this book. Some of the points that I make in the Introduction are, of course, derived from the papers that follow.

[3] Barry Cunliffe, *The Celtic World* (London, Sydney, Toronto, 1979), p. 24.

[4] De Paor's comparison between *Finnegans Wake* and The Book of Kells recalls David Jones's words: Joyce "developed an art-form showing an essential Celticity as intricate, complex, flexible, exact and abstract as anything from the visual arts of La Tène or Kells or from the aural intricacies of medieval Welsh metric, an art-form in which the Celtic demands with regard to place, site, identity are a hundredfold fulfilled" (*The Dying Gaul*, London 1978, p. 58).

Although Joyce is, of course, cited frequently in this volume, there is no single paper exploring his work. This lack we plan to remedy in two volumes: the first, *Dream Chamber: Joyce and the Dada Circus* Sorel Etrog and *About Roaratorio* John Cage, edited by Robert O'Driscoll, was published in Toronto for the anniversary of Joyce's 100th birthday on 2 February 1982; the second, *James Joyce and the Celtic Consciousness*, edited by Robert O'Driscoll, will be published on Bloomsday 1982, and will include contributions by the late Marshall McLuhan, John Cage, Joseph Campbell, Hugh Kenner, Leslie Fiedler, Louis le Brocquy, Denis Donoghue, and others.

[5] *The Revival of Irish Literature*, ed. Charles Gavan Duffy (London 1894), pp. 124-6.

[6] "Some Aspects of Irish Literature," *Collected Works: Songs of the Irish Rebels, etc.* (Dublin, Cork, Belfast [1916]), pp. 132-3.

[7] *Ideals in Ireland*, ed. Lady Gregory (London 1901), p. 98.

[8] Unpublished Lecture in the possession of Senator Michael Yeats.

[9] *Ideals in Ireland*, p. 18.

[10] "Ireland, Island of Saints and Sages," *The Critical Writings of James Joyce*, edd. Mason and Ellmann (London 1959), p. 157.

[11] David Jones, *Epoch and Artist* (London 1959), p. 141.

[12] David Jones, *The Dying Gaul*, p. 32.

ACKNOWLEDGEMENTS

Most of the essays contained in this volume were first presented as part of a Symposium, "Canada and the Celtic Consciousness," held at the University of Toronto in February 1978, and attended by over 2,000 participants, some of whom came from as far away as the Near and Far East. The Symposium was arranged by Celtic Arts of Canada as a retrospective celebration of the Sesquicentennial of the University of Toronto and the 125th Anniversary of the founding of St. Michael's College. My first acknowledgement, therefore, is to the Chairman and to the Vice-President of Celtic Arts, Father John Kelly and Catherine Graham, for their good guidance, help, and fellowship during the five years that it took to arrange the Conference and the volume that has emerged from it. I acknowledge the help of the other Directors of the Celtic Arts Board (Christine Bissell, Adrienne Clarkson, Robert Eldridge, Sorel Etrog, Iain MacKay, Leighton McCarthy, the late Marshall McLuhan, Hilary Weston) and our resourceful Manager, Gully Stanford, who with a skeletal staff (Patricia Leeper, Linda L'Aventure, and Elizabeth Cook) dealt ingeniously with the practical aspects of an extraordinarily complex operation. All of us were deeply indebted too to Liam and Jo Miller for their steady hands at the helm during the last turbulent weeks of preparation for the Symposium and play, and for Liam's skill in making the Symposium as visually as it was intellectually exciting. I am deeply grateful, too, to Lorna Reynolds and Anne Dooley for wise counsel in shaping the Symposium and the book.

All that we dreamed and planned, however, would have been impossible without the generous understanding and support of the Ministry of Culture and Recreation of the Government of Ontario, and more particularly the Wintario and Multicultural Development Branches of the Ministry. We were also deeply indebted to the following for financial assistance: the Secretary of State, the Ministry of Multiculturalism and the Ministry of External Affairs of the Government of Canada; Tara Mines, Aer Lingus (Irish International Airlines), George Weston & Co., The Canada Council, The Ontario Arts Council, Air Canada, The McLean Foundation, the Cultural Relations Committee of the Department of Foreign Affairs of the Government of Ireland, the Laidlaw Foundation, Irish Tourist Board, Canadian Pacific Airlines, Northgate Exploration Ltd., Joseph Seagram and Sons, Inland Publishing Company, Corby Distilleries, The City of Toronto, St. Michael's College Students Union, The Globe and Mail, CHUM Radio, Imperial Oil, Simpson's Sears, Jordan Wines, Victoria and Grey Trust, Royal Trust, Canada Life, National Trust, Gulf Oil, Confederation Life, Walter Gordon, The Irish Shop, Jayfran Enterprises, the Consulate General of Japan, William Saab, The O'Neill Foundation, Aerotype Services, Brascan, Canadian Schenley, Genstar, Pigott Construction, General Accident, Sceptre, C. M. Harding, H. Cassels, Walter and Lisa Bowen, Lash Johnston, Daniel Alekiewicz, and of course St. Michael's College and the

University of Toronto which provided a physical centre for the diverse activities that constituted the Symposium. We thank too the Conference Committee of the Canadian Association for Irish Studies which collaborated on some aspects of the Symposium: Anne Dooley (Treasurer), David Bellman, Eugene Benson, Leonard Boyle, John Carey, Maurice Elliott, Finn Gallagher, Brian John, Homer Hogan, Gordon MacLennan, Desmond Maxwell, Ninian Mellamphy, Bruce Mickleburgh, Harry Roe, Robin Skelton, J. J. Sheridan, Douglas Stewart, and Sean Ward.

The shaping of a book is a different experience from the organization of a Symposium, and considerable adjustments have been necessary in achieving the balance and comprehensiveness to which the volume aspires. Apart from the editorial considerations, the team who effected this transformation comprised of the designer, Liam Miller, who has achieved the symphonic blend of illustration and text that is so characteristic of all of his books; our Scottish-Canadian printer, Don Melhuish, whose sure hand and precise calculation made it possible, in extremely pressing circumstances, to meet our Samhain deadline; our Polish-Canadian typesetter, Wanda Kornatowski (with her able assistant, Albert Vilneff) whose deadly accuracy (especially in the setting of Gaelic quotations), patience, and good humour were unfailing on all counts; and Sandra Hellard and Marcia McVea for much dedication in achieving a faithful and beautiful lay-out.

It is impossible to communicate in a book, on the other hand, an impression of certain events of the Symposium: Noirin Mooney's Exhibition of Batiks illustrating the Cuchulain Cycle; Radu Varia 'expressing' Salvador Dali's message at the opening Reception at Toronto City Hall; Sorel Etrog standing on the stage of Convocation Hall and likening Liam Miller's books to a construction of 'black bricks'; Leonard Boyle's skilful on-the-spot editing of Jan Filip's paper to bring it within the compass of a fifty-minute time slot; Anne Yeats's flamboyant opening of the Royal Ontario Museum Exhibition, "The Celtic Heritage"; Treasa O'Driscoll's evocation, with the French-Canadian group Barde, of "Sean O'Riada's Ireland"; the Festival of Canadian Celtic Music with Barde, John Allan Cameron, Laylum, Maple Sugar, and Scottish Pipers and Dancers; and, more importantly, the production of W. B. Yeats's *At the Hawk's Well, On Baile's Strand, The Only Jealousy of Emer,* and *The Death of Cuchulain,* which we presented under the general title, "The Celtic Hero" (see Epilogue, p. 667).

The quotation facing the dedication page is from a lecture that W. B. Yeats gave in New York in January 1904 and I am grateful to Michael and Anne Yeats for permission to quote the extract from the unpublished manuscript.

R. O'D.

The nations of the world are like a great organ. And in that organ there are many pipes. Each pipe is a nation, and each pipe has its own music that is the life of that nation. Now one pipe sounds and now another. A little while ago, a few centuries ago, the great pipe that is the Empire of Spain was sounding and its music was filling the world. And then that pipe fell silent. The Divine Hand moved to another stop on the organ and the pipe that is the Empire of England began to sound and is still sounding. But it may be that it too will fall silent, and it is certain that at last the pipe that is Ireland will awake and that its music will be heard through the whole world!

W. B. Yeats, January 1904

THE CELTIC CONSCIOUSNESS

for

BRIAN BEDELL STANFORD

Bird singing in the night
You linked our spirits
Child of light

FINISTERE

THOMAS KINSELLA

I

One . . .

I smelt the weird Atlantic.
Finistère . . .

        Finisterre . . .

The sea surface darkened. The land behind me,
and all its cells and cysts, dark.
From a bald boulder on the cairn top
I spied out the horizon to the northwest
and sensed that minute imperfection again.
Where the last sunken ray withdrew . . .
A point of light?

A maggot of the possible
wriggled out of the spine
in the brain.

We hesitated before that wider sea
but our heads sang with purpose
and predatory peace.
And whose excited blood was that
fumbling our movements? Whose ghostly hunger
tunneling our thoughts full of passages
smelling of death ash and clay and faint metals
and great stones in the darkness?

At no great distance out in the bay
the swell took us into its mercy,
grey upheaving slopes of liquid
sliding under us and collapsing
and crawling onward, mountainous.
Driven outward a day and a night
we held fast, numbed by the steady
might of the oceanic wind.
We drew close together, as one,
and turned inward, salt chaos
rolling in silence all around us,
and listened to our own mouths
mumbling in the sting of spray:
— Ill wind end well
     mild mother
     on wild water pour peace

who gave us our unrest
whom we meet and unmeet
in whose yearning shadow
we erect our great uprights

and settle fulfilled
and build and are still
unsettled, whose goggle gaze
and holy howl we have scraped
speechless on slabs of stone
poolspirals opening on
closing spiralpools
and dances drilled in the rock
in coil zigzag angle and curl
river ripple earth ramp
suncircle moonloop . . .
in whose outflung service
we nourished our hunger
uprooted and came
in whale hell
                gale gullet
salt hole
          dark nowhere
calm queen
          pour peace

The bad dream ended at last.
In the morning, in a sunny breeze,
bare headlands rose fresh out of the waves.
We entered a deep bay, lying open
to all the currents of the ocean.

We were further than anyone had ever been
and light-headed with exhaustion and relief
— three times we misjudged and were nearly driven
on the same rock.
             (I had felt all this before . . .)
We steered in along a wall of mountain
and entered a quiet hall of rock echoing
to the wave-wash and our low voices.
I stood at the prow. We edged to a slope of stone.
I steadied myself. 'Our Father . . . ', someone said
and there was a little laughter. I stood
searching a moment for the right words.
They fell silent. I chose the old words once more
and stepped out. At the solid shock
a dreamy power loosened at the base of my spine
and uncoiled and slid up through the marrow.
A flow of seawater over the rock fell back
with a she-hiss, plucking at my heel.
My tongue stumbled

Who
     is a breath
that makes the wind
that makes the wave
that makes this voice?

Who
     is the bull with seven scars
the hawk on the cliff
the salmon sunk in his pool
the pool sunk in her soil
the animal's fury
the flower's fibre
a teardrop in the sun?

Who
     is the word that spoken
the spear springs
       and pours out terror
the spark springs
       and burns in the brain?

When men meet on the hill
dumb as stones in the dark
    (the craft knocked behind me)
who is the jack of all light?
Who goes in full into
the moon's interesting conditions?
Who fingers the sun's sink hole?
    (I went forward, reaching out)

SECTION I

PERIPHERIES OF THE INDO-EUROPEAN WORLD

INDIAN REFLECTIONS
IN THE CASTLE OF THE GRAIL

JOSEPH CAMPBELL

As explained earlier, most of the essays published in this book were first presented as part of a Symposium on "Canada and the Celtic Consciousness." Joseph Campbell was the opening speaker, and he integrated the occasion of the Symposium so movingly into the substance of his lecture, which he gave extempore, that for one to remove the rooted references, as is the usual practice when transferring spoken to written lectures, would seem, as it were, to begin the unravelling of a beautiful garment.

Marshall McLuhan, introducing Dr. Campbell, quoted from his Masks of God: "I find the main result for me [in my endeavors] has been the confirmation of a thought that I have long and faithfully entertained: of the unity of the race of man, not only in its biology but also in its spiritual history, which has everywhere unfolded in the manner of a single symphony, with its themes announced, developed, amplified and turned about, distorted, reasserted, and, today, in a grand fortissimo of all sections sounding together, irresistibly advancing to some kind of mighty climax, out of which the next great movement will emerge. And I can see no reason why anyone should suppose that in the future the same motifs already heard will not be sounding still — in new relationships." McLuhan commented: "It is this amazing unity of human consciousness and its symphonic variations in mythology that is the area of Dr. Campbell's mastery." R. O'D.

I

I am greatly honoured in having been appointed the opening speaker of this splendid meeting of Celtic poets, scholars, and artists; and it was an especial pleasure, last evening, at the opening reception, when "The Creature," the Water of Life, was being dispensed to the assembled celebrants (who, I noticed, were zealous to partake of it), to see what a beautiful company this was, to which I was to address myself the next morning. I know that if my grandfather Lynch could see me here initiating what we know is to be a new epoch in the history of the Celtic Consciousness, he would be delighted. For something like three decades, as a leading member of the New York chapters of both The Ancient Order of Hibernians and The Friendly Sons of St. Patrick, he annually rode a horse up Fifth Avenue in the first rank of our spectacular Saint Patrick's Day parades. My grandfather Campbell from County Mayo, and my Scottish grandmother Mac-Fawn, of Dundee: they, too, would be gratified. And with such a galaxy of Celts behind me, I am sure that in a remoter past there must have been more than a few of my forbears who knew St. Patrick; and possibly even one or two, who, centuries ago, arrived in Canada with that great and blessed discoverer of North America, St. Brendan.

The story of the ordeal of that navigator is most remarkable, circulating as he did for no less than forty years among the islands that in those days dotted the Atlantic. He sailed in his coracle eastward, with a company of twelve companions chosen from his monastery of a thousand. And the first island they came to was so rocky that they floated for three days around it before discovering a landing. Ashore, they were greeted by a very comely hound that fell down before the saint and in its own way bade him welcome; then led the company into a noble hall, where a table covered with a cloth of gold was set with a meal of bread and fish. Such magically-provided feasts are common features of Celtic traditional tales, whether of the pagan or of the Christian eras, and in the present medieval example the food provided suggests Christ's miracle of the loaves and fishes, feeding the multitude. And the little scene of Brendan with his twelve at table is in a playful way a reflection of the great scene of the Last Supper: Christ's celebration of the Passover, immediately following which he was to endure the ordeal of Gethsemane and the *Via Crucis*. The original Passover of the Jews had been followed by their crossing of the Red Sea and ordeal of forty years in the wilderness. Brendan, too, with his monks, following their meal on the Island of Rocks, were to be forty years tossing on the briny deep, likewise en route to the Promised Land — though far from Canaan.

Where, then, or what, is that Land? Where is Eden with its two trees — of the Knowledge of Good and Evil, and of Life?

It is one of the prime mistakes of many interpreters of mythological symbols to read them as references, not to mysteries of the human spirit, but to earthly or unearthly scenes and to actual or imagined historical events: the Promised Land as Canaan, for example; Heaven as a quarter of the sky; the Israelites' passage of the Red Sea as an event such as a newspaper reporter might have witnessed. Whereas it is one of the glories, on the other hand, of the Celtic tradition which we have gathered here to celebrate, that in its handling even of religious themes, it retranslates them from the languages of imagined fact into a mythological idiom; so that they may be experienced, not as time-conditioned, but as timeless; telling not of miracles long past, but of miracles potential within ourselves, here, now, and forever. This is an aim that is basic to the Grail tradition, basic to Arthurian Romance; as it was basic, also, to the earlier Celtic way of story-telling, whether of pagan heroes or of Christian knights and saints.

When Brendan's monks had eaten their fill, they found beds prepared for them, and, in the morning, set off to sea again, refreshed. Their second landfall was an island, very green, where they found all about them sheep on every side, the whitest ever seen, every one the size of an ox. And a very well-looking old man approached, who gave welcome and introduction. "This is the Land of Sheep," he told them. "It is never winter here, but a summer everlasting." Then he spoke of the island

Plate 1: The Book of Kells. f124r Matthew XXVII, 38. *Tunc Crucifixerant* page. Trinity College, Dublin.

next to come, the Paradise of Birds, to which his own was but a station on the way.

An extraordinary adventure befell the voyagers half way along, however, which in the memory of this legend is the most famous of its marvels. On what appeared to be an island, level and without trees, they landed and, building a fire, set a cauldron full of fish to boil. However, no sooner was their fire alight than the island began to quake, and when, in terror, they had tumbled back into their boat, they saw the island swim away with their cauldron. It was a whale, a great fish, the biggest of the fishes of the world, and it was ever trying to put its tail into its mouth, but could not do so, because of its great bulk.

One sees in the "Book of Kells" a representation of such a tail-biting monster. It appears on the so-called "*Tunc* page," which is devoted to the Crucifixion. *Tunc crucifixerant cum eo duos latrones,* reads the text: "Then there were crucified with him two thieves." What the tail-biting monster represents is the world-surrounding Cosmic Ocean, a motif known to all of the major mythologies of the world: *Okeanos* of the Greeks, for example, beyond which lie the Hesperides, the blessed islands of the golden apples and immortal life, which correspond precisely to the Avalon ("Apple Land") of the Arthurian legend, and to the mysterious site as well, of the Castle of the Grail.

In Brendan's case, whereas up to this point he had been sailing eastward to the sunrise, he would now, without reversing course, be sailing westward, to the setting sun. He and his shipmates will have passed, that is to say, the point where the pairs-of-opposites come together and are in consciousness transcended: life and death, east and west, good and evil, even being and not-being. And their next adventure, accordingly, was an island full of flowers and trees, the Paradise of Birds, where there was a tall tree beside a well, and on every branch of it so many beautiful white birds happily singing that scarcely a leaf of the tree could be seen. This is a characteristically Irish vision of the mythological Cosmic Tree, the axial tree about which the universe turns, the Tree of Life in the middle of the Garden. And a little bird of the birds flew toward Brendan from that tree, with the flickering of his wings making a merry noise, like a fiddle; and Brendan asked: "If you are a messenger, then tell me why it is you sing so happily." To whom the bird replied: "We were every one of us angels, and when Lucifer fell, we fell with him. But because our offense was but a little one, Our Lord put us here, without pain but in great joy and merriment, to serve what way we can upon this tree."

It is most remarkable! We have just passed beyond the bounding rim of the world of the knowledge of the pairs-of-opposites, good and evil, and so on, and immediately have come to a tree of only somewhat fallen angels, merrily singing. In the version of the Grail legend to which I shall be calling attention shortly, the miraculous vessel itself, which yields to each the meat and drink of his desire, is declared to have been brought from heaven to earth by the "Neutral Angels," who, during the War in Heaven, sided neither with Lucifer nor with God. Between the claims, that is to say, of the ultimate pair-of-opposites they had held steady, and so, in a mystical sense, represent what has been called "The Middle Way" between *all* pairs of opposites, which leads to the realization of transcendence. For any deity named, defined, personified and with qualities — good, not evil; true, not false; merciful and just, not merciless and unjust — is by such definition bounded. God's opposite, Satan, is thus inevitably his fellow. When, however, the Middle Way had been found — as taught, for example, by the Buddha — which is unkown to the Land of Sheep, the merry song of the white birds on the axial tree tells of the rapture of this state of consciousness, transcending definition. This is the order of rapture named in the Sanskrit of the Indian mystics, *nirvikalpa samadhi,* "rapture without qualification," in contrast to the "rapture *with* qualification" of *savikalpa samadhi.* And in the legend of the Grail the sign of such realization is the Grail itself.

Beyond the Paradise of Birds there was but one island more to be passed before the Land of Promise should be gained, and that was not of song but of silence; nor reached before the end of a stormy trial of four months and another forty days: the little craft so hurled between earth and sky that the company were tired of their lives. It was the island of a great abbey of twenty-four monks and their abbot, who for eighty years had kept silence so well that not one of them spoke to the others. One here recognizes something like the holy fellowship of the Grail. Clothed in royal cloaks woven of threads of gold, with a royal crown before them and candles on every side, they were fed miraculously with loaves and drink brought daily by an angel in the form of a strong man, of whom nothing was known. And at prayers in the chapel each evening, Brendan saw an angel that came in by the window and lighted all the candles and went out by the window again, to Heaven; and the saint marveled. "There is a wonder on me," he told the Abbot, "those candles to burn the way they do, and never to waste." He and his monks were at the interface of Eternity and Time — Eternity *in* Time: which is where we all are, actually, if we but knew. For is not the natural world renewing itself all around us continually? It is only in holding on to the idea of ourselves who are to die — that we are blinded to this. Brendan's monks, tired of their lives, had all but died to themselves in their passage of the terrible sea and it was the bliss, now, of an undisturbed meditation on the everlasting mystery of Being itself that held them here in a state of rapture.

Early Christian Ireland was known as the Isle of Saints; and in many parts of the island today, one is shown the little, stone, one-room huts (beautifully built) that are said to have been of the early, sixth to ninth and tenth-century, hermits. For Early Irish Christianity was something very different from the Medieval Roman form of the religion brought in from Norman England at the time of the conquest by Henry II, 1171 A.D. The date of St. Patrick's mission is generally given as A.D. 432. But this, almost certainly, was not the actual date. 432 is a mythological number. For example, in the Puranas, the old Indian epics, it is declared that the number of years in a Mahayuga — a "Great Cycle" of the world creation, flowering, and dissolution — is 4,320,000 years. This is known as a "Day of Brahma," and it is followed by a "Night of Brahma" of the same duration, the sum of the two then being 8,640,000. In one of the verses of the Icelandic Poetic

Edda (Grimnismol 23) we are told that in Valhall, Othin's warrior hall, there are 540 doors, through each of which, at the end of every cycle of time, there go 800 warriors, to give battle to the antigods in a war of mutual annihilation. 540 times 800 is 432,000. And in Chaldean Babylon, from about the sixth century B.C., it was held that between the imagined time of the first city of the world, Kish, and the coming of the mythological deluge of Utu-napishtim (Noah's predecessor and prototype) there were 432,000 years. To my surprise, one day I discovered in a popular book on physical culture entitled *Aerobics,* the following statement: "A conditioned man, who excercises regularly, will have a resting heart rate of about 60 beats per minute or less... Sixty per minute, times 60 minutes equals 3600 beats per hour. Times 24 hours, equals 86,400 beats a day."[1] So then, our little human days and nights are miniatures of the Great Days and Nights of Brahma, the opening and closing of whose eyes bring forth and dissolve, again and again, all the forms of the universe; the beating of our hearts, meanwhile, being in accord with that pulse of creation. There is much more to be told of this number, but one more point will suffice; namely, the notice that actually, astronomically, the number of years in one complete cycle of the precession of the equinoxes is 25,920 (one Great, or Platonic Year), and that this sum, divided by sixty, is 432 — sixty being the basic multiple (the so-called *soss*) of the most ancient Mesopotamian mathematical system.

The dating of Patrick's mission suggests, then, that a world era, the pagan, has ended, and a new, the Christian, begun. However, the very dating itself suggests that something of the old vision of the universe will have been taken over: of a single accord informing not only the great universe of the heavens and earth, but also the little universe of the individual: this accord being the inspiration of the forms of religious art and rite, so that by contemplating and participating in these, one is put in accord with both the order of the universe and the ground of one's own being. There is a good deal of evidence to suggest that many of the earliest Irish monks had been Druids and fili, or bards, before their conversions, and that they carried on in their Christianity something of the momentum of their earlier sense of a common spiritual ground to be recognized, in silent wonder, in themselves and in the natural world, all about.

It was something of this that Brendan experienced during his Silent Brotherhood. And when the time came for departure, the angel of the isle provisioned the coracle, and Brendan with his company of twelve sailed back to the Land of Sheep; then back to the Paradise of Birds, and back again to the Abbey; and so on, round and round, for the length of forty years, annually celebrating Easter on the back of the great fish that now remained still for them, till at last the moment came for them to go sailing in their coracle past the very border of Hell, where the shadow of Judas sat miserably, and past a very blessed island, where a certain Paul the Hermit dwelt alone in piety, on then to the Land of Promise itself — which was the loveliest country anyone could see, of trees full of fruit on every bough and apples ripe all the year.[2]

The mention, especialy of apples, suggests both the classical Hesperides, the western Isles of the Golden Apples, beyond the earth-bounding Ocean, and the Celtic Avalon of King Arthur's enduring repose. It is actually everywhere and nowhere: the Earthly Paradise: that place — or rather, condition of the experienced world — where the transcendent radiance of that which is beyond form is made visible through, and from within, all the forms of all things. This is not a revelation for which one has to wait to the end of time.

In the Gospel According to Mark, 13, where the terrors are described that should occur in the last days — the sun darkened, the moon failing of its light, stars falling from heaven, the Son of Man coming in clouds, and so on: "Truly, I say to you," Jesus is reported to have said, "this generation will not pass away before all these things take place." But actually, that generation did pass away, and many more have passed away, and those things have not taken place. Some theologians speak, therefore, of "the great non-event." Others — the great majority — have reinterpreted the word "generation " of Jesus' prophecy as referring not to Jesus' contemporaries, but to the generation of man: meaning that the generation of mankind and the world will pass away with the coming of all these things. That is to say, taking the mythological symbol of the End of the World concretely and interpreting it as referring to an actual historical event to come, our commentators have postponed it to some undefined future, and we are warned, meanwhile, simply to go to church, receive the sacraments with faith, and await the day.

There is another way, however, an altogether different way, of interpreting the End of the World. Mark 13 has been thought by some to be an interpolated late chapter, misrepresenting whatever words might have been spoken by reading them in the sense of the current Jewish apocalyptic hysteria represented in the texts of the Dead Sea Scrolls. And this view of Mark 13 has been now strongly reinforced by the discovery in 1945 — in a jar found buried in the Egyptian desert, near the village of Nag Hammadi, on the first sharp bend of the Nile (about 26° 1′ N., 32° 2′ E.) — of a Coptic translation from the Greek of the long lost Gospel According to Thomas.[3] Here we read in the last saying (Saying 113) of Jesus, the following:

"His disciples said to Him: When will the Kingdom come? Jesus said: It will not come by expectation; they will not say: "See, here," or "See, there." But the Kingdom of the Father is spread upon the earth and men do not see it."

The function of art, we might say, is to render a sense of this hidden radiance of the Kingdom, right here and now, among us. And all that is required for the vision is a slight but radical shift-in-perspective of the eye to bring us to a realization transcendent of the pairs-of-opposites: I and Thou, right and wrong, this and that. One of the many thoughts that occured to me when listening, last evening, to the welcoming talk of Dr. O'Driscoll at our festival of the Water of Life, was that he, in assembling this Conference, had been serving in the way of many earlier Celtic seers and artists the typically Celtic function of revealing the Hidden Truth: the hidden truth in this case, namely, of our unity here as Celts, and as men of good will capable of recognizing commonality beneath the surface display of difference. And may I point out, by the way, that the French, as well as the Irish, the Welsh, the Scots, and the British, are Celts. Vercingetorix was a Celt. So that, here in Canada, unity is among you even while you confront each other (in true Celtic style) with fighting words.

Brendan's voyage, we may read, if we like, historically interpreted, as a legend inspired in part by actual Celtic voyages to America. For when the Norse arrived in Iceland in the ninth century A.D., they found there a community of Irish Culdees, or mediating anchorites, already long established, who then moved out, no one knows whither, but not impossibly to Greenland and thence to Canada. There was a climate of relative warmth in those northern regions at that time, as in the centuries also of the Norse settlements. In any case, the abbey of the monks of Brendan's Silent Brotherhood must have been inspired by the model of such communities of Irish Culdees in flight from the noise of the world. Years ago, when I was involved in the study of the North American Indian mythologies, I came upon a number of tales of inexhaustible vessels, and it seemed to me that these were particularly numerous among the Algonquin tribes, and especially the Micmac of Nova Scotia.[4] At the time, I recall, this suggested to me the possibility of some kind of influence from the Celts of Scotia proper, namely Ireland; and discovering, then, on the map of Nova Scotia, not only the name Cape Breton Island, but also, off nearby Newfoundland, a peninsula named Avalon, I found myself, as an Arthurian scholar, very much at home. My reason for mentioning the matter here, however, is not to propose a theory of St. Brendan's influence on the Micmacs, or of the Algonquin as possible Celts, but to point out that, like the Europeans of this Canada, the Indians too have in their background a knowledge of the vessel inexhaustible. Hence, they participate in that knowledge of the mystical ground of consciousness that I have been celebrating as characteristic of the Celts.

This mythological theme of the inexhaustible vessel is in Celtic mythology associated with that of the hidden presence of the Earthly Paradise. The Grail is a vessel of this kind, and behind it is the earlier inexhaustible cauldron of the Irish sea-god Manannan.

There is an old old story of the sea voyage of Bran, the son of Ferbal, to the Isle of Joy and the Isle of Women, who, on the way, encountered Manannan. He had heard, one day, in the neighbourhood of his stronghold a lovely music behind him, and as often as he turned around, it was still behind him: the music of the Sidhe, the people of the fairy hills, who are here among us, unseen. For just as the Kingdom of the Father is spread upon the earth and men do not see it, so is the fairy world of the Sidhe. And the music was so sweet that Bran fell asleep, and when he woke he saw beside him a branch of silver with white blossoms, which he carried in his hand to his royal house. And when his company had assembled, a woman in strange raiment appeared who sang in fifty quatrains of the land of apples, without grief, without sorrow, sickness, or any debility. And when Bran with his company of three times nine were sailing to that land, they saw a godlike man coming toward them over the waters in a chariot, and Bran with his company were amazed. The charioteer was Manannan, the Hospitable Host of the Land Under Waves, and he sang to them thirty quatrains. "Bran thinks this a marvelous sea," he sang. "For me it is a flowery plain. Speckled salmon leap from the womb of your sea; they are calves and colored lambs." Again a Celtic counterpart of the image of the Kingdom already here: the interface of the two worlds, of Eternity and Time.[5]

Manannan is especially famous for his palace at the bottom of the sea, where he entertains all that come to him with an inexhaustible meal, serving the flesh of his immortal pigs, which, killed and eaten one day, are alive the next and fit again for use; and along with this, an immortal ale that preserves those who consume it from disease, old age, and death. The cauldron of plenty, the inexhaustible flesh of the pigs, and the ale of immortality, are in the later, Christian context of the Grail translated into the chalice, and the flesh and blood of Christ. And in this we have an intentional recognition of equivalent symbols, themes, and meanings in the earlier, mythological and later theological traditions, the art of recognizing equivalencies of this kind having been a major interest of the old Druidic diviners and bards.

Now the title and topic of my talk today is of Indian reflections in the Castle of the Grail. The fact that the Christianized Celts of the early period tended to place no less emphasis on the inward, mystical, than on the outward historical aspect and implications of the Gospel legend prepared the way for a later recognition of analogies in the mystical tradition of India; and the number of such analogies immediately apparent to anyone familiar with both worlds is amazing. For in India, whether in its Hindu or in its Buddhist teachings, the accent is again on the mystical side: not on the importance of historical events that may or may not have taken place, but on the requirement that something should happen, here and now, in one's mind and will. And this brings me to what is certainly a crucial, if not *the* crucial problem of this whole subject; namely, that of the radical distinction between the esoteric (mystical) and exoteric (historical) ways of reading mythological symbols: as references, on the one hand, to powers operative in the human heart as agents of transformation, or, on the other, to actual or imagined historical events. Take the symbol of the Virgin Birth, for example. This is a motif that occurs in all the mythologies of the world. Consequently, it cannot have referred originally to an extraordinary event that occurred, once and for all, at a certain time and place in Israel. What it refers to in its inward, mystical sense, is the birth in the awakened mind and heart of a realization of the Kingdom of the Father. Man's first birth is biological, as a physical creature motivated by the animal energies of the body. Man's second, properly human birth, is spiritual, of the heart and mind — or, as represented in the Indian symbolic science of the kundalini: of the heart-lotus opening to the radiant sound, OM, of the Lord's creative energy resounding through all things.

Teachers of the ways to such a spiritual realization are commonly, in the myths of the world, represented as themselves born of the awakening, since the meaning of their lives and messages to mankind — or to their various tribes — is of this knowledge; not of the "once-born" biological ends of survival, reproduction and conquest. Demythologizing such a symbol and reading it as referring to a unique, induplicable historical event of the past, impossible to ourselves, deprives it of its psychological force, externalizing its message as institutional of some social establishment, upon which, then, our spiritual life depends. The mythologies of India abound in incarnations, with the implication always that we are to become such beings ourselves. And in the Celtic legends also, whether pagan or Christian — of Bran and Brendan, or of Galahad and Perceval, the heroes of the Grail — the accent of the symbolization is typically on the hero-life as, exceptional indeed, yet paradigmatic of ways to realization that are open to us all.

Galahad entered the fellowship of Arthur's Knights of the Round Table on the feast of Pentecost, wearing red armor symbolic of the presence in him of the grace of the Spirit, to which his life and character were to be witness (*Galaad*, = "heap of witness"). Parzival, too, began his knightly career in an armor of blazing red. So may we all, when we have caught the meaning of Paul's saying: "It is no longer I who live, but Christ who lives in me" (*Gal* 2:20). The reference here is not and cannot be, positivistically, to the corporal person of the historical "incarnation," Jesus of Nazareth, whom Paul never saw nor knew, but, mystically, to the everliving Christ, the knowledge and Knower of the Father, potential within us all, that at that moment awakened within him — and knocked him from his horse. And once this way of reading the symbols, the imagery of vision, and the pictorial script of the religions of mankind has been learned, suddenly all the mythologies of the world become eloquent of the spirit, each in its own way.

Let me, then in this spirit, cite the Buddhist legend of the World Saviour, Gautama, as a clue to the meaning of the Grail Quest.

When the princely youth, Gautama Shakyamuni, had achieved Enlightenment beneath the Bodhi-tree, or "Tree of Awakening" (*bodhi*, "awakening"), which, as the axial tree, at the center of the turning world, is equivalent to that, in the Brendan voyage, of the Paradise of Birds, there came to him from the four quarters of the earth the four guardian kings of those quarters, each with the gift of a begging bowl; and those four bowls, when the kings arrived, became fused into one single bowl of stone, which, like the Celtic Grail, or the cauldron of Manannan, was an inexhaustible vessel. The Buddha had come to his realization only after years of trial and seeking, finally coming to the so-called "Immovable Spot" of the paradisial tree. We are not to seek this place in the world; we are to seek it in our own will. It is the place where the will is moved neither by the quest for life nor by the fear of death; and the Buddha, seated there, had been approached by the Antagonist, the Tempter, as Christ had been, in the desert. The Tempter in his character of the Lord of Desire, Kama, displayed before the seated one his three voluptuous daughters (whose names, by the way, were Desire, Fulfilment, and Regrets); but the prince, who had already left behind the delusions of the senses, was unmoved. The next temptation was of the fear of death, the Tempter now in his character of Mara, the lord Death himself. But again the prince, unattached to

Ego, was unmoved. Then finally, in his character of Dharma, "Duty," lord of the duties of the way of life imposed on one by society, the master of delusion commanded the meditating prince to give up his seat on the Immovable Spot and return to his princely throne. Whereupon, the one there seated only moved his right hand to touch with its fingertips the earth, and the very goddess of the earth, of the cosmic tree, and of the all-enclosing sphere of the sky, with a voice of thunder that resounded from the whole round horizon declared the unmoved and immovable prince to have already so given of himself in compassion to the world that there was in fact no historical person there any more, and he was eligible for that seat. With that, the deluding ruler of the world — the lord Kama, of lust; Mara, of the fear of death; and Dharma, of socially imposed duty — was humbled, his power broken, and the prince, that night, achieved the Enlightenment, which he then, for fifty years of his days, made known as the Middle Way to release from delusion.

II

This tale of the passage of an Oriental prince beyond the claims of lust, fear, and the normal duties of the local social order, was certainly not the model of any of the legends of the Knights of King Arthur's Round Table; yet there is an evident equivalence of essential points, particularly in Wolfram von Eschenbach's version of the Grail legend, Chrêtien de Troyes' *Lancelot* and *Yvain,* and the late Middle English tale of *Sir Gawain and the Green Knight.* The Grail theme — with which I am here concerned — comes down to us through three main lines of tradition. The first is in the style and spirit of a legend of the Celtic fairyland, the people of the Sidhe transformed into the ladies and knights of an enchanted castle, the rules for their disenchantment being known to the knights and ladies themselves, but not to the expected one who should arrive, one day, and release them. There are many early pagan legends of a valorous Celtic prince, who, pursuing some alluring beast of the chase, is led into a fairy hill. There he finds its queen in trouble: in expectation of an attack by the people of another fairy hill, from which he is to save her. And when his work is done, he remains with the fairy queen of the hill in a state of bliss, like Wagner's Tannhaauser in the *Venusberg,* where the centuries pass as years, and there is neither old age, nor sorrow, nor death, nor even boredom. And if by chance he should leave, to return for a brief visit to the historical world, he will have been warned to remain upon his magical horse and not to set foot on the ground, which, in fact, is what he generally does, and immediately he crumbles to dust and disappears. Such was the fate of one of the members of Bran's company who returned from the Isle of Women; such, also, of St. Brendan, when, after a season of only 40 days in the Land of Promise, he returned to Ireland, where he immediately died and, of course, went straight to Heaven.

The earliest surviving version of the Grail legend is the *Conte del Graal* of Chrêtien de Troyes, who declares that he adapted the tale — "the best tale ever told in a royal court" — from a book that had been given to him by the Count Philip of

Flanders. Chrêtien was the court poet of the Countess Marie de Champagne. The date of his writing of his Grail romance was somewhere between 1175 and the departure of Count Philip for the Holy Land in 1190. We do not know why Chrêtien left the tale unfinished; but he did; and we do not know how he would have carried it to conclusion. All the great themes are left in the air. As far as it goes, it is a tale of the type known as "The Great Fool": of a youth, Perceval, of noble heart, brought up in ignorance of the rules of knighthood, who nevertheless sets forth to become a knight, and though in the beginning boorish and clumsy, he becomes in time the very model of a knightly champion; whereupon, by what appears to him to be mere chance, he enters, without knowing, upon the adventure of the enchanted Castle of the Grail. There he is introduced to the Maimed King, "wounded by a javelin through his two thighs," and in the great hall observes a mysterious procession of squires and damsels bearing tokens of unkown import: a sword in its sheath, a white lance bleeding from its point, the golden Grail, set with precious stones, carried by a damsel of great beauty, and a silver carving dish, carried by another very beautiful young woman. He fails, however, to ask a certain expected question "who is served by the Grail" — which would have healed the King and broken the enchantment. And so his quest has failed. And the unfinished poem ends with its hero, Perceval, receiving religious instruction from, and practicing penance with, a hermit.

One cannot but feel that Chrêtien either did not know what his legend was all about and here broke off in frustration, or did know and could not sympathize with its increasingly evident heretical implications. In any case, though gracefully and fluently rendered in delicious verse (one German critic has remarked that Chrêtien could shake couplets from his sleeve like a magician), his legend of the Grail is unfinished and unresolved; the hermit's instruction of Perceval has little or nothing to do either with the sense of the enchantment or with the meaning of Chrêtien's version of the question to be asked; and what the book of Count Philip of Flanders may have made of it all, we neither know nor shall ever know.

The second strain of the Grail tradition is of an ecclesiastical and monastic cast, the Grail being identified explicitly with the cup, bowl, or dish (variously) of the Last Supper, the lance with the Lance of Longinus that pierced the side of the Crucified, and the Grail Hero with Galahad — that saintly, virginal youth, wearing a red armor symbolic of the Holy Spirit, who was introduced to Arthur's dining hall at the feast of Pentecost, the festival of the descent of the Holy Spirit in tongues of flame upon the heads of the assembled apostles. And the principal texts are three: first, *Joseph d'Arimathie*, by a Burgundian poet, Robert de Boron; next, *L'Estoire del Saint Graal*, by a Cistercian monk, unidentified; and finally, *La Queste del Saint Graal*, by another unkown Cistercian, this being the version of the legend translated by Sir Thomas Malory in *Le Morte D'Arthur, Books XIII-XVII*.

There is a prodigious mass of material associated with this version of the legend, containing many inconsistent passages; and the modern literature of the scholarship of the subject is as complex and confused as the medieval texts themselves —

which have been roughly dated to the years between 1199 and 1230, or so. [6] Robert de Boron mentions, without naming, a certain "great book" *(le grand livre),* from which his knowledge of the tale was drawn, and there is evidence that a version of the same may have inspired *L'Estoire* as well. The *Queste,* on the other hand, is apparently original, and from the hand of an inspired master. It is a magnificent work, expressing, as one major critic has observed, "the mystical spirit of the Middle Ages with a power that is hardly equalled elsewhere." [7]

Briefly, the main themes of this tradition of especial relevance to our topic are those touching the history and mystery of the Grail itself. It had been bestowed by the Risen Christ Himself upon Joseph of Arimathea, while the latter was in prison: Joseph having been jailed by the Jews for having offered his own sepulchre as a repository for Christ's body; and the Risen Saviour, bearing the instruments of his passion, had appeared to him in the locked cell, charging him to fare with the relics to Glastonbury (which in the folk memory had become identified with Avalon), there to establish the blessed sanctuary of the Grail.

The great point here, which I very much want to stress, is that the Grail Castle was founded by the *risen* Christ, whereas the Church of Rome, of Peter, which everyone can see and enter, was founded by the historical Jesus, teaching and preaching when anyone in Palestine at the time might have seen, heard, and followed him. Only those spiritually gifted and especially blessed, on the other had, would ever see in vision the risen Christ. Likewise, only those spiritually gifted and blessed in a very special way would ever discover and enter in vision the otherwise invisible church or castle of the Grail.

This legend, then, represents an élite tradition — élite in a mystical sense. And in this sense it represents the challenge of a native Celtic type of alternative mystical Christianity to the historical, and historically oriented, Church of Rome. Indeed, not only was Glastonbury here identified with Avalon, but in de Boron's poem the Grail was passed from Joseph to a younger relative named Bron; and it was this Bron then, who, as its guardian, sailed with the Grail to Britain; just as, in the old pagan legend, Bran had sailed to the everlasting Isle of Women. The name Bron has been identified by the leading modern scholars with Bran, who, when he arrived in that blessed isle, became identified with Manannan, and even served his guests, like that Hospitable Host, from an inexhaustible cauldron — which, in the opinion of most modern scholars of the legend, was the first and foremost model of the vessel of the Grail. Not only in the *Queste del Saint Graal,* but in all versions of the legend, questing heroes may ride back and forth over the very ground of the Castle of the Grail without seeing it: and I am told that in Ireland, one may walk around and right past a fairy hill without seeing it. One seems to be walking a straight line, but actually is curving past an invisible fairy hill of glass, which is right there, but hidden — like the Hidden Truth.

The hero of the third tradition of the Grail Legend is again Perceval (now Parzival), not the saintly, virginal Galahad of the *Queste,* but a married man and father (without benefit of clergy), who for a period of five painful years was even a fervent hater of God. The only text is the *Parzival* of Wolfram von Eschenbach, of a date about 1210.[8] It is a truly magnificent work — in my opinion, the greatest of the Middle Ages. I think of it as a cathedral of love, celebrating the mystery in many aspects. This was the version of the legend, furthermore, that inspired Wagner, though he greatly changed its character and sense by turning Parzival into a Galahad and eliminating the Grail Queen and Grail Maidens. Nor does he open his stage to the great scenes of Oriental crusade that in Wolfram's poem are of the essence. For, whereas the legend in Chrêtien's *Conte del Graal* unfolds in the usual Never-never Land of Arthurian Romance, Wolfram sends his heroes out to participate in the actual historical events of his time. And this was the high period of the crusades. The poet himself was a Bavarian knight — Bavaria, it is worth noting, having been the area from which the Celts originally sprang.

Some time around 1000 B.C., the people of what is known to historians as the Hallstatt Culture began spreading both eastward and westward, out of the lands that are now of Austria and southern Germany. By 500 B.C., those of the westward migration had developed in France and northern Switzerland a new and brilliant culture, known as La Tène. It was these Celts who, in that period, invaded Rome. They entered the British Isles about the second century B.C. with their priests and magicians, the Druids, and they there became assimilated to the earlier Bronze-Age inhabitants, the people of that wonderful cosmic image of the great heartbeat of the universe, which, as I have already shown, was known as well to India as to Europe: its cycles of 432,000 years being a feature of both the Indian *Puranas* and the Icelandic *Grimmismol*.

Wolfram had the gift to recognize in the materials of his legend the numerous analogies with the various Oriental mystical traditions that were becoming known to the crusaders of his day. Indeed, one of the great aims of his thinking was to span the breach of the two worlds. He seems not to have gone on crusade himself; but there were reports enough coming back into Europe, not only from returning crusaders, but also from the Genoese and other returning merchants of the time, whose trade connections extended far into the great East, beyond Palestine, Syria and Egypt, into Iraq, Iran, India, and even Central Asia. We have to remember, furthermore, that the forces of Islam were engaged in serious warfare, throughout that period, not only with the peoples of Europe, in Spain and the Near East, but also with those of Hindu and Buddhist India. Their conquest of India had begun in earnest about the year 1001, and by 1200 they had reached Bengal. Indian and Moslem ideas as well as merchandise were in widespread circulation. Indeed, already in the year 1085, with the conquest of Toledo by Alfonso VI of Castile and León, the gates of Oriental poetry and song, mysticism and learning, had been opened to the courts and monasteries of Europe. And the mystics of Islam, meanwhile, the Shi'ites and the Sufis, had been absorbing influences from India. In southern France the Manichaean, Albigensian heresy was rife, inspired by the teachings of the Persian, third-century prophet Manes, who had combined in one harmonious system Zoroastrian, Buddhist and Christian ideas. It required a full-sized crusade within Europe itself to eradicate that heresy: the infamous Albigenesian Crusade, instituted by Pope Innocent III in the very years of Wolfram's writing of his *Parzival*. And if Innocent was not his model for the malignant, castrated magician of the Waste Land, Clinschur (Wagner's Klingsor), I have missed my guess.

Now, the source to which Wolfram attributes his version of the legend is not Chrêtien, but an otherwise unkown poet, Kyot of Catalan, who, he declares, discovered in Toledo the manuscript of a heathen alchemist and astronomer named Flegetani.[9] It was from this source that he had derived his knowledge of the Grail, not as a vessel of gold set with precious stones, but as a *stone* brought to earth from heaven by the neutral angels, who had sided neither with Lucifer nor with God. Its name was *lapis exilis,* which is one of the terms applied in alchemy to the philosopher's stone: "the uncomely stone, the small or paltry stone." There is in the treasury of the cathedral of S. Lorenzo of Genoa (which was consecrated in 1118) a flat, quadrangular bowl of green glass, which, until broken in Napoleon's time, was thought to have been carved of a single gigantic sapphire. It was taken as booty by the Genoese at the time of their conquest of Caesarea, A.D. 1001-1002, where it was supposed to have been the vessel in which, according to a Byzantine legend, Joseph of Arimathea and Nicodemas had caught and preserved the blood of the Saviour. The late Professor Hermann Goetz of Heidelberg, from whose splendid article on "The Orient of the Crusades in Wolfram's Parzival"[10] I have drawn my information for this part of my paper, has suggested that it may have been this bowl, supposed to be a precious stone, that suggested to Wolfram the idea of the Grail as a vessel of stone.

The legend in this version opens with the life of Parzival's father, Gahmuret, who was a Christian knight in the service of the Caliph of Baghdad, and in the course of this exotic career he arrived, one day, before the city and castle of the black queen, Belkane, of Zazamanc, under seige from two armies simultaneously, a Moslem and a Christian. The situation is standard Celtic-Arthurian, of the beleaguered queen of the fairy hill, to be saved by the blade of an errant knight. As Professor Goetz points out, however, the adventure here is in the actual world. The name of the queen, Belkane, when rendered in its proper form, Balakana, means the wife or widow of Balak: actually, Nur-uddin Balak ben Bahram, who recovered Aleppo from the Crusader-King Baldwin II of Jerusalem, and married there a Seljuk princess. When he was later killed by an arrow, she and her son came under the protection of another Moslem prince, named Timurtash: in Wolfram's work, the black queen-widow Belkane's protector is named Isenhart, which is a translation of the Turkish, Timurtash. Baldwin II of Jerusalem, to recover Aleppo, joined forces with an exiled Seljuk prince, Sultan Shah by name, and thus there were indeed two armies before Aleppo, a Moslem and a Christian at the siege, which soon became famous, of 1122-23. Timurtash (Isenhart) was slain; and defense of the city was undertaken by a Shi'ite leader whose banner displayed a star and crescent on a green field. The flag of Wolfram's Gahmuret displayed an anchor (emblematic of the Christian church), likewise on a green field. The flag of the people of Aleppo displayed a silver hand (the "Hand of Fatima") and a crowned staff on a black field: such was the flag of Belkane also. Thus we have indubitable evidence in this first great section of Wolfram's romance of precise information from the Moslem world having come into the poet's ken; as well as evidence of his intention to represent the Moslem and Christian knightly modes as equivalent.

Well, the black queen Belkane of Zazamanc, having been rescued with her city by the Christian knight Gahmuret, married and conceived by him. She would not allow him to go off adventuring in the good old way, however, and thoroughly bored with her domestic happiness, he one night secretly departed and returned to Wales. The queen subsequently bore a son, whose complexion was piebald, black and white. He was given the name Feirefiz, "son (*fils*) of varied hue," and when he grew to young manhood, he became the Moslem protector of a young Hindu widow and her son. The widow's name was Secondille, a transformation of the Sanskrit Somyagita, which was the name of an actual Indian princess, protected by an actual Moslem warrior-prince, Qutb-ud-din Aibak, who in the years 1206-1210 (the years, precisely, of Wolfram's writing of his romance) became the first Sultan of Delhi and builder of its first mosque, with its famous polished-iron pillar, the Qutb-Minar. This appears in Wolfram's story as Secondille's magical pillar, which reflected on its shining surface events and people far away. Moreover, the name of her Moslem protector, the Sultan of Delhi, Aibak, means "Moon (*ai*) Prince (*beg* or *bei*)," and is a reference to his beauty. But the moon is mottled, as was the complexion of Wolfram's Feirefiz; and so, again we have a playful substitution of the poet's fictional character for a known historical figure of the time.

The story of Somyagita, by the way, is worth retelling. She was the daughter, about twenty years old, of King Jayachandra of Kanauj, and had fallen in love with the young Rajput King, Prithvi Raj III, of Ajmer and Delhi. And perceiving that she was ready for marriage, her father arranged for a *svayamvara*: an occasion, that is to say, once customary in Indian aristocratic circles, when a young princess would herself choose her husband from among a number of assembled candidates by placing a garland around the young man's neck. Well, Somyagita's father, King Jayachandra of Kanauj, had no use for the Rajput Prithvi Raj, who was a youth of about thirty; and so, instead of inviting him to the occasion, he had a statue made of an ugly demon, a *rakshasa*, to be set in the young king's stead. However, Somyagita, when the moment came, placed her garland around the rakshasa's neck, at which instant, with a great clatter of arms, the King Prithvi Raj III himself broke into the hall and carried the maiden away.

There were popular ballads sung in celebration of this brilliant romance. In the year 1192, however, Prithvi Raj was overwhelmed by the Afghan Sultan Mu'zz-ud-din Muhammad; his city of Ajmer was taken, he himself and his bride were made captive; and when his second city, Delhi, had also been destroyed, he was slain. The victorious Sultan went on, then, to conquer the city of Somyagita's father, Kanauj; next, Benares, in 1195; Gwalior, 1197; and Gaur, in Bengal, 1206. Before returning to Iran, he confided the young widow queen with her very little son to the care of Aibak, his viceroy, who, in turn, became the first Sultan of the slain King Prithvi Raj's former capital, Delhi. These were tremendous events, and the noise of them resounded through all of Islam.

But not only the rumors of such great events, accounts also of the *wonders* of the great Orient were coming back into Europe, and of these, four may be named as of immediate relevance to our topic. The first is the polished iron column, already mentioned, of the Qutb-Minar, which Wolfram celebrates and pictures as the magician Clinschur's magical reflecting column, stolen without her knowledge from Secondille, and set standing in a marvelous cupola on the roof of the magician's enchanted Castle of Marvels, where five hundred knights and five hundred ladies were magically imprisoned. The second is the Qasr-at-Taj, the truly fabulous palace of the Abbasside Caliphs on the river Tigris, built by the Chaliph al-Mu'tadid (892-902) and levelled to the ground when the Mongols wiped out Baghdad in the year 1258. In Wolfram's time it was still standing, and many of its known details appear in his description of Clinschur's halls. The third marvel, then, was the great Buddhist stupa built by the Kushana Emperor Kanishka, first century A.D., near Peshawar, which with its tower of steel, nearly nine hundred feet high and bearing twenty-five umbrellas, was at that time the tallest temple in all of India. Wolfram refers to it specifically as "the coffin of Lady Camille" (*froun Camillon sarc*),[11] confusing the title of the Buddha as the "Perfected One" (*al-kamil*) with the name of Virgil's hereoic Amazon Camilla of the *Aeneid* (Books VII and XI). He mentions it in his description, again, of Clinschur's Schastel Marveile. And finally, there was the famous stone begging bowl of the Buddha, preserved in a temple in Gandhara, described by the Chinese pilgrims Fa Hsien and Hsuan Tsang.[12]

This begging bowl, magically amalgamated of the four bowls brought to the Buddha at the moment of his illumination by the four guardian kings of the quarters, had become joined in Wolfram's imagination with the green "stone" relic in the treasury of S. Lorenzo, which once had held the blood of the Christian Saviour. Add the cauldron of Manannan, in his palace of immortal life, under waves; the inheritance of that cauldron by the voyager Bran on the Isle of Women, who appears in the *Queste del Saint Graal* as the Grail King; further, the Philosophers' Stone, *Lapis exilis,* from which spring the Waters of Life, and through which crude matter is turned into spiritual gold; also, perhaps, the Ka'aba, the stone brought down by Gabriel from heaven, now revered as the world center of Islam in the Great Mosque of pilgrimage in Mecca! Mythologically, symbolically, these are all variants of the one great message of a revelation of the world's abundance — in Christian terms, the radiance of the Kingdom of the Father, spread upon the earth and made known to those who have died to themselves and become reborn in the vision of the All in all.

In Wolfram's *Parzival,* as in the legend of the three temptations of the Buddha, the Middle Way, between Heaven and Hell, to this vision is entered through the exercise of three virtues and a fourth: 1. disengagement from the fury of the passions; 2. fearlessness in the face of death; 3. indifference to the opinion of the world; and 4. compassion. Throughout Arthurian Romance, these are the four tests of the heroes, as in the Orient they have been, and remain to this day, the supreme openers to saints of the mystical passage through what in Buddhism is known as the Gateless Gate.

III

So now: when Gahmuret had slipped away from the palace of the black queen of Zazamanc, on whom he had begotten a son, he returned to Britain; and there the white maiden queen Herzeloyde of Wales had proclaimed a sort of Celtic *svayamvara*: a tournament for the winning of her hand and realm. And of course, on her, as well, he begot a son. But then, returning to the service of his lord and friend, the Caliph of Baghdad, he was slain in combat, and six months later, his second widowed queen received the news of his death.

Overwhelmed with grief, Herzeloyde withdrew from the world of courts and battle to a solitary cottage in the woods, where she gave birth to a son, Parzival, whom she thought to keep there in ignorance of knighthood and to herself. But there was at that time a great need in the world for such an authentic hero as her little son was to grow to be, and there is no way a mother can defend her child from the summons of his own nature. This need of the medieval world was in the Grail romances symbolized in the image of the Waste Land: an enchantment of sterility cast over the whole society, which it was to be the task of the hero to undo. T.S. Eliot, in his poem *The Waste Land*, published in 1922, applied the motif to a characterization of our own day and general problem. Many will recognize the memorable lines:

> What are the roots that clutch, what branches grow
> Out of this stone rubbish?

As told in Chrêtien's legend and again in the Cistercian *Queste*, the Grail King had been wounded by a lance thrust through his thighs, and his land, as a result, was laid waste. Modern commentators have recognized in this motif a reflection of the well-known primitive superstition discussed by Frazer in *The Golden Bough*, of the king's health and well-being as the cause and support of the well-being of his realm. It is a primitive, magical idea: but what could it have meant to a modern poet like Eliot, or to such a medieval poet as Wolfram?

The period of the flowering of Arthurian Romance, roughly from 1150 to 1250, was also that of the building of the cathedrals, all the great cathedrals of France. The earliest work in which Arthur's name appears, Geoffrey of Monmouth's *Historia Regum Britanniae*, dates from 1136, and all the great Grail romances, from Chrêtien's *Perceval* to the *Queste* and Wolfram's *Parzival*, appeared between 1180 and 1230. It was a glorious, primary time for Europe, comparable in importance to the Homeric for the Classical world. But there was a grim, negative side to the picture, as well. "Hard by the Cathedral," as Oswald Spengler reminds us, "were the gallows and the wheel."[13] And there was the Albigensian Crusade of Innocent III.

In brief: people were being forced to profess beliefs they did not believe; others, through inheritance and political intrigue, were holding high positions in a politically-oriented Church for which they were not spiritually qualified; marriages were being contracted for social and political ends which a clergy was then blessing and binding in the way of what was called a sacrament: whereas love could enter lives only in the way of a disaster, of a so-called mortal sin, the sin, namely, of adultery, which was punishable by death. And in this connection a passage in Gottfried von Strassburg's *Tristan* is interesting, where the poet (a contemporary of Wolfram) tells of the young couple's drinking of the love potion. It had been an accident, and when the maid Brangaene, who had been responsible, realized what had happened, she came to Tristan, appalled, and she said to him: "That flask and what it contained will be your death." To which he answered: "So then, God's will be done...If Isolt is to be my death this way, I shall gladly court an eternal death."[14] Not only the physical death of the Church and society's punishment for the crime of love, that is to say, but also, even eternal death in the fires of an actual hell! Such spiritual courage in the prospect even of a torture everlasting typifies the heroism of anyone of that period thinking to live a life of his own. It has something to say to us also of the power and courage of a perfect love in any age. The great mystic, Meister Eckhart, a contemporary of Dante, declared in one of his sermons: "Love knows no pain." And William Blake, in that wonderful piece, "The Marriage of Heaven and Hell," remarks: "As I was walking among the fires of hell, delighted with the enjoyments of Genius, which to Angels look like torment and insanity..." The Middle Way, that is to say, is not an easy way, and may require of its traveler indifference to the opinion, not only of the world, but also even of its God; and to this, another word of the mystic Eckhart: "Man's last and highest leavetaking is the leaving of God for God." The God named and supposed to be known, together with his opposite, the Devil, is to be left behind in the passage by the Middle Way to the tree by the well, where the white birds merrily sing.

The Waste Land, then, is the land of people living inauthentic lives, doing what they think they have to do to live, not in the way of the spontaneity of love or of an affirmation of life, but dutifully, obediently, and even grudgingly, because that is the way people are living. That is what T.S. Eliot saw in the Waste Land of the twentieth century; and that is what Wolfram von Eschenbach— Eliot's model — saw in the Waste Land of the thirteenth.

Such a condition is epitomized and personified in Wolfram's figure of the wounded Grail King, whose name there is Anfortas, from the Old French *enfertez*. *enfermetez*, "infirmity". He was a beautiful and gentle youth, but had inherited, not earned, his position and role as guardian of the highest symbol of the spiritual life. And in the way of youth, moved by nature, he had one day ridden forth from the Castle of the Grail with the battle cry, "Amor!" - which for a young knight of the world was fitting, but for the Grail Guardian, inappropriate. Anfortas' spiritual role, that is to say, was formal and external, not consistent with his own will. And as he rode, he saw come charging toward him from a neighboring forest a pagan knight. He couched his lance. The two collided and the pagan challenger was slain; Anfortas, however, wounded sore: the other's lance having unmanned him. Its poisoned head remained in the wound, and on it was inscribed the word, "The Grail."

Thus the sense of the wound in Wolfram's version of the legend was, that in the Europe of his day the spontaneity of nature had been annulled. Nature, represented in the pagan knight emerging from the forest, aspiring to its own spiritual fulfillment as symbolized in the word, "The Grail," inscribed on the head of the pagan lance, had been struck down by the Christian, whose own nature had been thereby undone. For spirit, in the medieval Christian view, was not of nature but against it, since nature had been rendered corrupt by the Fall in the Garden, and the repository of the spirit was the Church, not the heart corrupt. Moreover, at the helm of the ship of the Church, there was a crew of master politicians: their Albigensian Crusade had already been launched in the year 1209, and their Inquisition (established 1233) was already in preparation. Spirit and nature were conceived and taught as contrary to each other: not the spiritual life as the flowering, fulfilment and completion, of the natural. That was the meaning, in Wolfram's work, of the Waste Land: a people's own inherent spirituality cut down by an order of values radically out of accord with the order of nature itself.

In anguish, the destroyed young Grail King returned to his castle, where the presence of the marvelous stone, *lapis exilis*, kept him alive, but of itself could not heal the wound. He remained in such pain, that, as Wolfram states: "He can neither ride nor walk, the king can neither lie nor stand: he leans but cannot sit."[15] Eliot repeats the words:

Here one can neither stand nor lie nor sit.[16]

The people of the hidden castle live on in helpless sorrow, waiting for that one to arrive who will, out of the impulse of his own noble heart, pronounce the words that would break the spell.

It was Parzival who was to play this role.

His mother, the widowed queen, had borne him in the wilderness, on a little farm, far from the company of King Arthur's castle and in ignorance of knighthood. She had taught him, however, of God: "Pray to Him when in trouble; He is faithful and gives help," she had said. And when the lad was about fifteen, out alone in the fields one day, three knights rode by, and thinking they were angels, the farmboy went to his knees. A fourth came along and, seeing Parzival there kneeling, asked if he had seen two knights ride by with an abducted maid. "O God of help!" the youth prayed. "Give me help!" The rider replied kindly, "I am not God; we are four knights." "What is a knight?" Parzival asked, and there he learned about knights. "How can I become a knight?" he asked. "By going to Arthur's court," he was told. So the lad went back to his mother. "Mother, I want to be a knight," he said, and she collapsed.

Herzeloyde, thinking to make her son appear as a fool in the court and so to have him sent back to her, clothed him in a clown's rig of hempen shirt and breeches in one piece, coming halfway down his legs; a monk's hood, and clumsy, untanned boots. And it was in this outfit that he set out for King Arthur's court, riding a farm horse, with a little quiver of javelins that he had made for himself strapped to his shoulder. He galloped off and out of his mother's sight, and she dropped to the earth and died.

As he approached the castle, he saw come riding out of its portal a knight in bright red armor with a golden goblet in his hand. This was a great and famous champion, King Ither of Kukumerlant, who had just seized the cup from Arthur's table in token of his claim to a portion of Arthur's kingdom, and with a challenge to the court to avenge the insult by sending a champion to meet him in the jousting yard. Parzival entered while all were still sitting astounded, and learning of the challenge, before anyone could intervene, rode out to become Arthur's champion. The knight, when he saw what was approaching, not wishing to insult his lance by using it properly, reversed it and with its butt knocked Arthur's champion, horse and all, to the ground. The boy, still on the ground, sent a javelin, with perfect aim through the Red Knight's vizer and into his eye, which killed him, and he dropped from his saddle to the earth. But this was not the proper way to kill a knight, and the court of King Arthur was in deeper disgrace than ever.

A young page who had been sent to recall the fool discovered him dragging the dead Red Knight about, trying to remove his armor. He gave a hand and even helped the youth to put the armor on, over his fool's costume, mount the knight's charger, and ride away. So Parzival was now the Red Knight. He had been able to start the horse, but had no idea how to stop it, and for the rest of the day was galloping, until toward night the magnificent animal pulled up at the little rural castle of a sturdy old knight, Gurnemanz by name, who had lost three sons in jousting tourneys and was now living alone with his daughter. The Red Knight, Ither, had arrived, they thought. But when they relieved their guest of his armor, what they found was this image of a clown, with the physique, however, and the beauty of a noble.

The old knight, Gurnemanz, recognizing the possibility of another son as well as a marriage for his daughter, adopted the youth and taught him the use of arms: taught him, also, the rules of decorum of a knight, of which (unfortunately) one was the directive not to ask unnecessary questions. Parzival took naturally to the training, and when Gurnemanz thought the moment had come, he offered his daughter in marriage. Parzival considered. And here we come to the first critical test of this unintentional saviour-to-be. Throughout the Orient, through all Antiquity, and throughout the Middle Ages, families normally had arranged weddings, and brides had been given to grooms. This young man considered, however, that before receiving a wife and enjoying her love, he should fashion himself into something and gain her through an act of his own will. In the poet's words: "He sensed in noble striving a lofty aim for both this life and beyond."[17] And there follows a gentle, gracious scene, where the old knight bids the magnificent youth adieu, and watches him ride away.

Parzival now lets the reins lie slack on his animal's neck. In the sense of a horse and rider as symbolic respectively of instinctive nature and controlling mind, this suggests a trust, on Parzival's part, in the life-force itself as his adequate guide; and indeed, he was carried to the castle of a young orphan queen, Conduiramurs (*conduire amour*), who, like the fairy queens of the Celtic Sidhe, was in trouble. He was received with interest, relieved of his armor, bathed clean of its rust, and that night, in his bed, awoke to find the young queen kneeling at his side. "Lady," said he, "are you mocking me? One kneels that way only to God." She replied: "If you will promise to be temperate, I shall lie then by your side." And neither he nor she, states the poet, had any notion of joining in love. Parzival lacked, in fact, all knowledge of the art, and she, desperate and ashamed, had come in misery of her life. In tears she told him of her plight. A neighbouring king, Clamide by name, had sent an army under his seneshal Kingrun, to appropriate her land, when he would himself arrive and, in the good old way, make her his wife. "But I am ready," she said, "to kill myself before surrendering my body to Clamide. You have seen the towers of my palace. I would cast myself into the moat." Parzival promised readily to get rid of Kingrun in the morning, and when dawn came, rode as the Red Knight from the castle gate for his first battle. And before another half-hour had passed, Kingrun, whose fame in the world was great, lay on his back, with Parzival's knee on his chest. He was sent to Britain, to Arthur's court, to report himself there, a vassal of the lout that had taken the Red Knight's armor. And the company of the Round Table was amazed.

During the following years, other great victims arrived in King Arthur's court with the same report of submission, until finally the entire fellowship set out to find and recover this prodigy: but that is another large part of the story, not to be considered here.

When her hero returned into her castle from his victory he saw that Conduiramurs had put her hair up in a way of a married matron. She embraced him before all; her citizens paid him homage, and she declared him to be her lord and theirs. That night they were again in bed together, but, as Wolfram says, "he lay with her so decently that not many a lady nowadays would have been satisfied with such a night." Yet she thought of herself as his wife. Two days and two nights more they were together in this way, until, at last, enlacing legs and arms, they found the closeness sweet, and that old custom, ever new, had become theirs. No priest confirmed the marriage. It was confirmed in love and was itself the sacrament of love. And neither lust nor fear, but courage and compassion had been its motivations; indifference to social opinion having been prerequisite to its occurrence at all. What their world would have called good marriages had been by both rejected; and thus Parzival's first great step away from the Waste Land of the way of the world had been accomplished.

The two remained together for fifteen months. Conduiramurs bore a son and was pregnant with a second, when her husband asked permission to leave, to see how things were going with his mother — not knowing that she had died. His wife could not deny him, and it was thus that his next adventure began: of the Castle of the Grail.

In contrast, that is to say, to the version of the Cistercian *Queste*, where the hero is the virgin Galahad, in this romance of Wolfram, the Grail Hero is a married man and father, whose adventure is to be the fulfilment, rather of a life already lived well in the world than of one consecrated to renunciation. Riding therefore with his reins again left loose, he arrived that evening at a lake, where there were two men fishing in a boat, one with peacock feathers in his bonnet, so richly clad that he might have been the king of the world. Parzival called out to know where he might find lodging for the night, and the one richly clad replied that he knew of no habitation but one within thirty miles; to which he then directed the rider. "But have a care," he added. "The roads here lead astray; no one knows where to. If you arrive, I shall be your host."

For this was already Anfortas, the Grail King, known also as the Fisher King and the Maimed King; and Parzival that evening, in a hall that was immense, witnessed the ceremonial of the Grail. There were many knights on couches, all about. Anfortas was borne in on a litter. Processions of maidens, bearing candles and clothed in elaborately symbolic colors, presented the King with various tokens, of which the last was the Grail itself, the Joy of Paradise. It was carried on a deep green cloth of gold-threaded silk by a radiant Grail Queen clothed in Arabian silk, and her name was Repanse de Schoye (*Repense de Joie*). A hundred tables were carried in, to be set before the couches. "And I have been told," states Wolfram, "and I shall pass it on to you, that whatever one reached one's hand to take, it was found there before the Grail."

Parzival remarked all this and the anguish of his host, and was moved by compassion to ask of the King's sorrow. But he considered: "Gurnemanz counseled me not to ask too many questions." And he held his peace.

"For that I pity him" states Wolfram; "and I pity too his sweet host, whom divine displeasure does not spare, when a mere question would have set him free."

The Queen with twenty-four attendant maidens advanced, bowed to Parzival and his host, took up the Grail and returned to their door. The ceremony had ended. The room cleared and, courteously, the guest was conducted by four maidens to his room, where he was seen to bed with wine and fruits of the kind that grow in Paradise. And he slept long, but with threatening, terrible dreams. The quest had failed. For the first time in his life Parzival had suppressed the impulse of his heart in deference to an alien social ideal, his public image as a proper knight. The baleful influence of the motivating principle responsible for the wasting of the Waste Land itself had cut off in him an impulse of his nature. *Dharma*, "duty," the last temptation of the Buddha, the force of social opinion, had turned him from his own noble course, and thereby, the authenticity of his life had been flawed.

Parzival woke to a silent, apparently empty castle, found his horse tethered at the foot of the exit stairs with his lance and shield close by, and mounting, rode away bewildered, not knowing wherein he had failed. But the realization was driven home in due time, to his shame.

The entire fellowship of King Arthur's court, having searched the world for the young prodigy, who, as a fool and clown, had killed King Ither of Kukumerlant, disgracing the Round Table, and then gone on to become the most famous knight of his time (his deeds, most marvelous, were too numerous for retelling here), had at last been found. In celebration, a great circular cloth of oriental silk large e-nough for every knight to be seated by his lady had been ordered spread on a flowery field, and when the whole company was seated, awaiting an adventure (for it was a firm custom of King Arthur that none should eat with him on a day when some adventure failed to visit his court), there appeared an adventure indeed.

A maiden arrived, riding a tall mule, yellow-red with nostrils slit and sides terribly branded. She wore a cape, very blue, tailored in the French style, with a fine hat from London hanging down her back, over which there fell and swung a switch of long black hair, as coarse as the bristles of a pig. She had a great nose, like a dog, two protruding boar's tusks, eyebrows braided to the ribbon of her hair, a hairy face, and in her hand a whip with a ruby grip, but fingernails like lion's claws and hands charming as a monkey's. She was Cundrie, messenger of the Castle of the Grail, and she rode directly to King Arthur. "What you have done today," she said, "in welcoming this one who looks like a knight but is no such thing, has brought shame to you, and destruction to the Round Table." She rode to Parzival. "Cursed be the beauty of your face! I am less a monster than you. Speak up! Tell why, when the sorrowful Fisherman sat here, you did not relieve him of his sighs. May your tongue now become as empty as your heart is empty of right feeling. By Heaven you are condemned to Hell, as you will be by all the noble of this earth when people come to their senses. Your noble brother Fairefiz, son of the Queen of Zazamanc, is black and white, yet in him the manhood of your father never has failed. He has won, through chivalrous service, Queen Secondille of the city of Thabronit, where all earthly desires are fulfilled; yet had the question been asked at Munsalvaesche, the Castle of the Grail, riches far beyond his would here and now have been yours." She wrung her hands, burst into tears, and Parzival rose, cursing God in his heart for having dishonorably betrayed Him when he had thought he was serving Him well. And it was in this perplexed condition of soul that he rode away, to seek the Castle again and thereby heal the unhappy King.

It was to be an ordeal of five lonely years, searching back and forth through the forests. For, like the fairy hills of Ireland, the lake with its two fishermen and the castle of sorrowful knights and ladies lay hidden; though everywhere there was a haunting sense of their presence. The first break in the enchantment came on the fifth Good Friday, when the questing rider chanced upon a hermit's hut. He was bidden welcome, and when the good man learned of his hatred of God, he instructed him in God's love. "Anyone seeing you defy Him with hate," he said, "would take you for insane. For God shares with man His love and His hate. If you wish God only ill, it will be you alone who are lost. So now turn to Him your heart and let Him answer your good will." This hermit was the brother of Parzival's mother, Herzeloyde, and when he realized who his guest was, told him of his mother's death. When he learned of the young knight's quest, he told him to abandon it, since the rules of the enchantment were that no one intentionally seeking the castle would find it; moreover, it could not be visited twice. Parzival's zeal for the healing of the King whom he had failed was so strong upon him, however, that he could not put it aside, and he left with a vow to continue the desperate quest, notwithstanding.

The second break in his own enchantment occurred, when, again by chance (or what seemed to be chance), he was seen riding solitary by Sir Gawain, mistaken for an enemy, and attacked. Gawain, who had been especially kind to him on the calamitous earlier occasion of his welcome to the Round Table, had meanwhile succeeded in dispelling the enchantment that the magician Clinschor had cast upon the knights and ladies in the Castle of Marvels, and he was now about to be married to an exceedingly difficult lady, Orgeleuse de Logroyse, whose consent he had won through invincible patience, incorruptible loyalty, and a season of fabulous deeds — for which wedding, not only the whole of King Arthur's court, but also all the knights and ladies of the released castle, were on hand in high festival mood. And of course, when the two contending knights finally recognized each other and stopped their duelling, Parzival was invited to remain and enjoy the wedding with the rest. However, with many a fair lady tenting by the riverside, love and joy among the pavilions the order of the day, Parzival, amidst all of this, was brooding on Conduiramurs, his own sweet wife and lovely queen, whom he had not even seen these five long years. "If I am to witness here only joy," he though, "where my heart knows only sorrow, then my eyes and heart are ill matched." And he rode away.

The third and final break then came, when, from the edge of a line of forest, there came riding toward him a heathen knight, gorgeously attired. The two clashed and neither was unseated. They wheeled, and the battle continued. Presently, both were afoot. Chips flew from shields as the blows fell, until, coming down hard upon the heathen's helm, Parzival's sword broke in two. The other tossed his own sword away. "I see, brave man," he said in French, "you would now have to fight with no blade, and no fame would I gain from that." They sat together, removed their helmets, and the heathen was piebald, black and white. It was Feirefiz, and the two were brothers.

The rest can be briefly told. Parzival, together with Feirefiz, returned to the wedding scene where the heathen king was immediately an enormous social success. A lawn party was planned for the next day, and again, when all had placed themselves around the circular cloth of oriental silk, the Loathly Damsel, riding on her tall mule, again appeared exactly as before. Hermann Goetz points out in his article, already noticed, that the features of this Grail Messenger, Cundrie, as here described by Wolfram, with her boar's snout and tusks, boar's bristle hair, and riding her tall mule, are exactly those of certain Indian representations of the goddess Kali in her terrible aspect. There is also a Tibetan version of this figure — Lhamo by name — who appears, like Cundrie, riding a tall pink mule for the chastisement of those who reject the gospel of compassion. But as we know from many Irish legends of the goddess of the Celtic Land of Youth below waves, she too may appear with the unappetizing head and face of a pig. When she appeared in this guise, for example, to Finn McCool's son Ossian, with the hint that he should marry her, he boldly kissed her muzzle and she was transformed. And he then spent many a happy year with her, as King in the Land of Youth.[18] Frazer, in *The Golden Bough*, has shown that both Demeter and Persephone were at one time pig-goddesses,[19] and there is evidence enough to suggest that the Irish, Greek, and Indian forms of these goddesses are related variants of a single Neolithic and Bronze Age heritage, where both the wild boar and the domestic pig were associated with a mythology of death and rebirth.

In any case, Cundrie, ugly as ever, has reappeared on her tall mule, but her message, this time, is to be of joy. For, to everyone's amazement, she now invites both Parzival and his heathen brother to the Castle of the Grail. As the hermit, Trevrizent, later remarked when he was told of this surprising conclusion: a miracle had been wrought. For Parzival had forced God by defiance to grant his will. The rules of the enchantment had been changed. Moreover, whereas no ordinary Christian, by virtue alone of his membership in the Christian Church, might be admitted to the Castle of the Grail, here a noble heathen, unbaptized and by virtue alone of his character, was given welcome.

But then it was noticed (and here is an amusing final touch) that when the Grail was carried into the hall, the heathen had no eyes for it. All that he could see were the eyes of the beautiful Queen Repense de Schoye, in whose hands the stone was being carried. Word went round that he would have to be baptized: only then would he see the Grail. An empty baptismal font was brought in by a doddering old priest and tilted slightly toward the Grail, that alchemical *lapis exilis*, whereupon it became filled with the Water of Life. Not a normal baptism, this! And there then appeared on the Grail an inscription: ANY TEMPLAR APPOINTED BY GOD'S HAND TO BE MASTER OVER A FOREIGN FOLK MUST FORBID THE ASKING OF HIS NAME OR RACE AND HELP THEM TO THEIR RIGHTS.[20]

The date of this writing, A.D. 1210, was five years earlier than that of England's Magna Carta. That was to be a document forced from the Norman King John by his barons claiming their own rights, whereas this of Wolfram's Castle of the Grail was a declaration of the rights of others. It was a document entailing a covenant of service, a document of compassion, sprung from the same spiritual ground as the required question of the Grail ceremonial. "*Ocheim, was wirret dier?*" Parzival now asked: "Uncle, what ails thee?" and the King was healed.

Professor Goetz has suggested (I think, rightly) that the vow of absolute anonymity required of Wolfram's Knights of the Castle of the Grail — which was something very different from anything required of a Round Table knight — can have had as model only the vow of the Fidai of the Mohammedan Assassins: an extreme, mystico-revolutionary, fanatical Shi'ite sect of Islam, devoted to the service of the Hidden Imam, who, as the "true" leader of Islam, in secret opposition to the orthodox caliphate, might be thought comparable in import to the hidden Castle of the Grail, in contrast to the visible Church of Rome. The hidden fairy hills of the old Celtic gods: the Hidden Imam of Islam: the Kingdom of the Father, spread upon the earth, unseen: and the Land under Waves, of Eternal Life! In the Indian Katha Upanishad we read:

> Though It is hidden in all things
> That Universal Self does not shine forth,
> Yet is seen by subtle seers
> Of subtle mind and subtle sight.[21]

There is a beautiful essay by Schopenhauer, "The Foundation of Morality," in which he asks the following question. How is it that a human being can so experience the pain and peril of another, that, forgetting his own well-being, he moves spontaneously to that other's rescue? How is it that what we generally take to be the first law of nature, self-preservation, can be thus suddenly suspended, so that even at the risk of death one moves on impulse to another's rescue? And the answer that he gives is this: that such a move is inspired by a metaphysical truth and realization, namely, that we and that other *are* one, our sense and experience of separateness being of a secondary order, a mere effect of the way in which light-world consciousness experiences objects within a conditioning frame of space and time. More deeply, more truly, we are of one consciousness and one life. Compassion, *Mitleid*, co-suffering, unselfconscious love, transcends the divisive experience of opposites: I and thou, good and evil, Christian and heathen, birth and death. And the experience of the Grail, in Wolfram's reading, is of this unity, or identity beyond contrariety. Indeed, the very sense of his hero's name, Parzival, he reads as *perce a val*, "right through the middle" *(rehte enmitten durch)*.[22] And not righteousness, self-righteousness, but compassion alone is the key to the opening of this all-uniting "middle way."

When the brothers, Parzival and Feirefiz, were exchanging mightly blows in combat, "I mourn for this," wrote Wolfram. "One could say that *'they'* were fighting, if one wished to speak of two. They were, however, one. 'My brother and I' is one body."[23] And it was actually through the heathen's act of compassion, when the sword of the Christian had failed, that the two discovered their identity.

NOTES

[1]Major Leonard H. Cooper, *Aerobics* (New York 1968), p. 101.

[2]Following the version of Lady Gregory, *A Book of Saints and Wonders* (London 1920), pp. 185-208.

[3]*The Gospel According to Thomas:* Coptic Text established and translated by A. Guillaumont, H.-Ch. Puech, G. Quispel, W. Till, and Yassah 'abd al Masih (London and New York 1959).

[4]See, for example, Silas T. Rand, *Legends of the Micmacs* (New York 1894), pp. 24, 35, 114; and for other North American examples, the bibliography in Stith Thompson, *Tales of the North American Indians* (Cambridge, Mass., 1929), p. 335, note 210.

[5]Kuno Meyer, *The Voyage of Bran Son of Ferbal to the Land of the Living* (London 1895), I, 2-34.

[6]See Roger S. Loomis, *The Grail, from Celtic Myth to Christian Symbol,* (New York 1927), pp. 3-4, and p. 228.

[7]James Douglas Bruce, *The Evolution of Arthurian Romance from the Beginnings Down to the Year 1300* (Göttingen 1928), I, 423.

[8]Karl Lachmann, *Wolfram von Eschenbach* (Berlin and Leipzig 1926). There is an excellent English translation by Helen M. Mustard and Charles E. Passage, *Wolfram von Eschenbach: Parzival* (New York 1961).

[9]*Parzival* IX. 453:1-454:30.

[10]Hermann Goetz, "Der Orient der Kreuzzüge in Wolfram's Parzival," *Archiv für Culturgeschichte*, II Band, Heft 1 (1967), p. 5; photo facing p. 24.

[11]*Parzival* XIII. 589:8.

[12]*See Goetz, pp. 36-7 and note 59; citing Fattsien, ed. H. Giles (1923), p. 14, and Hsuan-tsang, Records of the Western World, 1, 98ff and 11,278.*

[13]Oswald Spengler, *The Decline of the West*, 2 vols. (New York 1926, 1928), II, 290.

[14]Gottfried von Strassburg, *Tristan*, lines 12463-12502.

[15]*Parzival* IX. 491:1-3.

[16]"The Waste Land," line 240.

[17]*Parzival* III. 177:6-8.

[18]Jeremiah Curtin, *Myths and Folklore of Ireland* (Boston 1890), pp. 327-332.

[19]Sir James George Frazer, *The Golden Bough* (New York 1922), pp. 469-471.

[20]*Parzival* XVI. 818: 25-30.

[21]*Katha Upanishad* 3.12.

[22]*Parzival* III. 140: 16-17.

[23]*Parzival* XV. 740: 26-29.

BEGINNINGS IN THE CELTIC WORLD: ARCHAEOLOGICAL, LINGUISTIC, HISTORIC, AND PREHISTORIC

EARLY HISTORY AND EVOLUTION OF THE CELTS: THE ARCHAEOLOGICAL EVIDENCE

JAN FILIP

During the last millenium before Christ, to the north-west of the Alps, over a territory ranging from France, across southern Germany, as far as Bohemia, a remarkable people was evolving and taking on the form in which they became known to history. Of all the barbarian peoples of Europe (as the "civilized" southern nations called them) they are the classic example. It was they who brought Central Europe and the more sophisticated south into closer contact and brought to a peak the prehistoric civilization of the lands to the north of the Alps. For a long time the world to the south knew nothing about these people, until trade and commerce between them in the sixth century provided at least partial information. The name of the Celts first appeared in the written sources about the middle of the last millenium B.C.; before long they had taken their place on the European stage as a powerful factor and were accounted one of the greatest barbarian peoples of the world as then known, alongside the Scythians and the Persians. At the turn of the fifth to the fourth century, armed bands of Celts attacked Italy and other parts of Europe, shocking the southern world into the realization that somewhere north of the Alps a bold and courageous people had grown up, and had now come to claim their place in European history.

The name Celt is of Greek origin; the Romans called these people Gauls, from which Gaul (Gallia), covering the larger part of what is now France, took its name. Both names cover a number of ethnically-related groups. In the distant past there were many groups and tribes speaking different dialects, and it was a slow and complex development which ultimately formed them into one ethnic whole. In the territory of the ancient Celts, from France to Bohemia, the distinctive La Tène culture evolved from the fifth century onwards, taking its name from the Swiss site La Tène, by Lake Neuchâtel; during the second Early Iron Age it was this culture that revealed to the world the creative talents of the Celts. The La Tène culture, universal in character, represented the historical Celts in Europe from the fifth to the first century B.C., and had a marked influence on the culture of contemporary non-Celtic peoples in northern and south-east Europe.

Interest in the ancient Celtic past can be traced in the literature of classical antiquity and in later traditions; it became particularly strong in the Romantic Age at the turn of the eighteenth and nineteenth centuries, and revived the Celtic tradition not only in western Europe, but in the British Isles as well, the home of many descendants of the Celts. It was only the systematic scientific development of archaeology, however, that led to careful study of Celtic remains, providing new and sound information on the complex structure of the La Tène culture and its origins. Apart from the writings of the Roman general, Julius Caesar (Commentarii de bello Gallico — the Gallic War), with his detailed comments on Gaul of the last century B.C., archaeology alone was able to determine the extent of Celtic settlement in the continent of Europe, and to throw some light on the manner and level of Celtic civilization, suggesting the milieu in which the Celtic peoples evolved. Today almost all the nations of Europe, and many beyond, display a lively interest in the history of the Celts, for they had a direct or at least an indirect influence on our own distant past.

It must be stressed once again that the La Tène culture did not mark the beginning of Celtic history, but was the expression of Celtic ethnic entity from a certain time only, from the fifth century B.C. Archaeological methods have made it possible to trace a continuous line of evolution in the area where the La Tène culture crystallized, a line emerging in the 8th to 7th centuries, in the Hallstatt region. As for the ages before that time, interpretation of archaeological sources allows only the suggestion of working hypotheses which do not exceed the bounds of probability or possibility. This holds, too, for the interpretation of the mysterious megalithic monuments and ritual sites to be found in Brittany and the British Isles, dating from the late Stone Age, and connected by popular tradition (and some authors) with the Celts and their priests, the Druids. From the third century B.C. the La Tène culture radiated from the Continent to the British Isles, but it cannot be assumed that this marked the beginning of Celtic settlement on the islands. Tribal units, ethnically related, assimilated this culture brought to them by smaller groups; it was a higher form of culture, and these contacts meant a closer acquaintance with developments on the Continent. The new culture found very advantageous conditions in Britain and Ireland, where the local environment contributed to a characteristic style and tradition in the art of the Isles. This art continued to develop in the Christian era, when the Celts had already lost their predominant role on the Continent itself. There are signs of whole tribes leaving the Continent for the British Isles as late as the last La Tène period (the Belgae, for instance, who invaded south-east Britain).

The Hallstatt Period (from the eighth to the fifth century, B.C.)

A basic component of the Celtic ethnogenesis on the Continent would appear to be the Bronze Age barrow culture, illustrated by a wealth of finds of barrow graves from north-east France to Bohemia in the east. In the Late Bronze Age these were superseded by urnfield burials, implying cremation of the dead. The succeeding Hallstatt culture (so called from the great burial-ground in Upper Austria, Hallstatt; the Early Iron Age) revived the barrow culture funeral rites. There were already ethnic migrations from the southern German region to the south, across France and on to the Iberian peninsula, and probably to the west as well. These groups on the move no longer played their full part in creating the Early La Tène culture, for they were subjected to local influences in their new environment, as well as to influences from surrounding cultures.

In the Hallstatt period it is already possible to identify the peoples later known from European history: the Scythians in the east, the Illyrians in the south-east, the Germanic tribes in north-west Europe, and of course the Celts. The archaeological sources can even suggest differences in the social and cultural structure of the individual ethnic regions, although common features and period characteristics place them all clearly in the Hallstatt period. The sum of the evidence, as we have already said, justifies the view that the region where the historical Celtic culture crystallized was to the north-west of the Alps, and covered the territory from north-eastern France, across southern Germany, into Bohemia. The Hallstatt period saw social differentiation develop in various parts of the Continent, but in the ancient Celtic regions this evolution had specific characteristics, and resulted in a new social structure. The upper class, apparently hereditary chieftains, were able to hold themselves apart from the rest of the tribe, which remained at a lower standard of living. This can first be seen clearly in the funeral rites of the seventh century B.C. Members of the emergent aristocratic class were buried in barrows, in spacious chamber graves surrounded by rich funeral goods: a four-wheeled chariot (or at least part of it), horse collars with rich bronze ornament, many bronze harness trappings, a sword, a great deal of pottery including vessels with geometrical ornament typical of the Hallstatt culture, symbolic ritual articles and a symbolic funeral feast. It looks as though the funeral itself was conducted with pomp, reflecting the social standing of the deceased. Archaeologists often call these burials 'Wägengraber' or even 'Fürstengräber'; many have been excavated in Bohemia, where they are typical of the Bylany aristocracy, and they have also been found in neighbouring Bavaria and other parts of southern Germany, in Switzerland and in France. Some of these date from the sixth century B.C., and among the funeral furniture we gradually find articles proving growing contacts with the south. Even at this early stage, however, the aristocracy tended to keep itself apart, in well-fortified residences. For the first time in the history of prehistoric Europe, to the north-west and north of the Alps, aristocratic residences of the real castle type began to appear, fortified with walls and gates, the residential quarters and workshops within the fortified walls as well as in the outer bailey (potteries, metal shops, etc.)

The best example of an early Celtic noble residence is that of Heuneberg near Hundersingen, on the Upper Danube, which has been systematically explored for two decades. In the sixth century B.C. a fortified residence was established here, on an area of about three hectares, on high ground; it was still in use in the fifth century B.C. The building materials used were mainly stone, timber and clay. Excavations revealed about ten phases of building, rebuilding and reconstruction, evidence of great activity here during the 6th and 5th centuries B.C. During one of these phases, however, soon after the foundation of the fort, an alien building technique was used which has been found for this period only in the south, e.g. in Sicily. On the south-west the surrounding wall was built of air-dried clay bricks, to a height of at least four metres; the foundation was of stone; on the north-west the fortifications were strengthened by square towers — bastions — also of brick. Numerous Hallstatt finds show that the castle was densely populated during this period, and research has revealed houses and workshops inside the walls. The fort was overcome from without, however, and burned down, together with the buildings in the outer bailey. The new fortifications made no use of bricks but relied on native building techniques, and in the course of time there were several more restorations. Growing contacts with the south are documented by finds of imported pottery, painted Greek pottery, wine amphorae and other goods mainly imported through Massilia, which was founded 600 B.C. in southern France.

It is assumed that in the earliest phase the lords of the castle were laid to rest in the vast barrow of 'Hohmichele' (in the parish of Heiligkreuztal) near the castle; it is 80m. broad and 13m. high. The principal timber-supported chamber, whose walls were lined with gold-threaded textile hangings, had been robbed in antiquity, and all that remained of the funeral furnishings were glass beads and the remains of a chariot. In the second chamber, where a man and woman lay on furs, was a four-wheeled chariot richly ornamented with bronze, harnessings, bronze vessels and necklaces of amber and glass beads. Another seven skeletons and five urn burials, with simpler furniture, were found in the barrow filling; the dead were probably members of the chieftain's entourage.

There are a number of barrows in the vicinity which belong to the time of the castle and its various phases: 'der kleine Hohmichele', about 80 metres from the chief barrow, and the barrows at Giessübel-Talhau, Lehenbühel, Baumburg and others in the neighbourhood of Hundersingen. These large barrows, averaging 70 metres in breadth were not systematically excavated but among the finds preserved are gold necklaces and bracelets, bronze vessels, remnants of chariots, weapons, and so forth.

This type of fortified castle with the large 'princely' barrows in the vicinity became characteristic of the late Hallstatt period. There are other sites besides Heuneburg: Asperg, to the north of Stuttgart, with the fortified residence of Hohenasperg, which cannot be systematically excavated because of a later fortress on the site, but which is surrounded near and far by great 'princely' barrows: Kleinaspergle with its fifth-century burials (the main chamber has been robbed, but the second timbered chamber gave up gold articles, imported bronze vessels, a beaked pitcher, painted Greek pottery etc.); the Grafenbühl barrow, re-excavated in 1964 (the main chamber also partly robbed); the barrow at Bad Canstatt near Stuttgart, with remnants of a four-wheeled chariot, and gold ornaments; and the Ludwigsburg barrow with its four-wheeled chariot. Important late sixth-century finds were discovered in the fortress of Mont-Lassois near Châtillon-sur-Seine, north-east France, including imported Greek pottery, local late-Hallstatt products, etc. A 42 metre wide barrow at the foot of the fortress was excavated in Vix in 1953; in the main chamber a princess of about 35 had been buried with rich furnishings (a four-wheeled chariot, a large bronze vessel — *kratér* — 164 cm.

high, with a bas-relief frieze of warriors and charioteers on two-wheeled chariots around the neck, a rare Greek import; as well as an Etruscan beaked pitcher, a gold diadem weighing 480 grammes, and other jewelry).

All these examples show the position of the ruling class, their opportunities and their standard of living. In graves excavated in the south German region, in Burgundy and in Switzerland, there are remarkably large finds of the goldsmith's craft, the gold having been washed from the sands of the Rhine and its tributaries. The girl buried in a timber barrow chamber at Sirnau (Württemberg) had gold bands on her arms and circles of gold in her hair; a barrow at Kappel in the Rhine valley yielded a neck torque of gold plate (weighing 160 gr.), a gold bracelet and other jewelry; at Gunzwill-Adiswil four necklaces were found, made of gold tubes and rings. Some of the barrows are indeed of imposing dimensions, like that of Villingen (Schwarzwald), 118 m. across, or Buchheim, 120 m. These permanent noble residences on fortified heights became centres of economic and political life, around which culture and even ritual centred. In the ancient Celtic environment, largely agricultural, it was the aristocracy who determined cultural evolution. The 'dynasties' who were buried on their chariots, or nearby, created their own heroic glorification. They were powerful and wealthy enough to maintain trade and cultural contacts with the more sophisticated south. The reliable trade route — Massilia, the Rhône valley, Burgundy — became an important channel for the import of goods from Asia Minor, Rhodes, Greece, and local Provence, and the imports travelled not only to Heuneburg, but on northwards, for example, to Bohemia (painted Greek pottery). In the sixth century the Alpine passes were opened up, and a centre relying on local materials developed to the south-east of the Alps. The importance of the Este Adriatic region of northern Italy grew; Greek trade colonies were set up in the valley of the Po (Spina, Adria), where the Greek traders stored their wares; and in the lake district round Bellinzona the focal points for trans-Alpine trade with Switzerland and the Rhine valley were set up. North of the Alps, in a barrow dating from c.500 B.C. at Hirschlanden in Württemberg, real art statuary, influenced by southern models, has been found (the figure of a warrior, life-size, in sandstone, at the summit of the barrow, discovered in 1962; height as preserved 150 cm.).

Transition from Hallstatt to La Tène (circa 500 B.C.)

The living standards and the opportunities open to the members of ruling class were thus growing, but tension was growing among the people (and, it would seem, between individual noblemen as well). Proof can be seen not only in the repeated attacks on their forts, entailing the need for rebuilding, but also in the emergence of other fortified places elsewhere, the migration of some groups as early as the Hallstatt period, and the low living standard of the masses, rising in numbers, as attested by finds in their burial grounds and settlements. The crisis came to a head at the turn of the fifth to the fourth century. The era of aristocratic fortresses and princely burials ended, and the whole structure of Celtic society seems to have undergone a change. There would seem to have been no alternative open to the leaders but to arm large numbers of the people and organize military raids. The mass of the Celts, now armed, were on the move, seeking loot and a new domain; their leaders guided them towards the flourishing centres of non-Celtic Europe, and particularly to those regions where these social phenomena already existed.

Up to the time of this Celtic expansion, at the turn of the 5th - 4th centuries, we find fortified places throughout the original territory of the Celts, in their immediate vicinity and along the routes of their migrations, but at the beginning of the La Tène era these forts lose their significance. Archaeological research, as yet incomplete, cannot give a reliable answer to the question of their original purpose. Some of the smaller sites, of the late Hallstatt era, may have been aristocratic residences, but some of the larger sites suggest that they served as a refuge for the local people as the Celts moved in, disturbing the stability of life in the old Celtic regions as well as in those they now invaded. This is the situation we read in southern Bohemia, which was part of the original Celtic homeland. In the late Hallstatt era, large fortified sites were established in the mountainous south-west region of Bohemia, at an altitude of 800-900 metres (Sedlo near Sušice, Věnec near Vimperk), and the rocky terrain was further strengthened by stone embankments. These were clearly refuges, for archaeologists have found no traces of permanent settlement, but only of temporary use. It was at this time that the fortified complex of Závist, near Zbraslav to the south of Prague, acquired its importance; it lies 200 m. above the level of the Vltava, and the fortifications for this strategically-chosen site extended over 509 hectares at the end of the Bronze Age (9th-8th centuries). In the early La Tène period (5th-4th century) it once again became an important centre, with a carefully-arranged acropolis with stone walls. The arrangement of the acropolis does not exclude a ritual significance (as in the Greek *temenoi*), especially since no evidence has been found for the existence of a princely residence. In succeeding centuries we have no proof that the centre was of any significance, until in the last century B.C. it became one of the most important Celtic oppida.

It would seem to be a general feature of Central Europe that these fortified sites lost their significance after the Celts began their historic expansion. At the beginning of the La Tène period a belt of fortresses stretching across Germany from the south-west border of Bohemia to Bayreuth, and even (according to German archaeologists) across south-west Germany to the Rhine and Saar valleys, lost their importance, whether they were late Hallstatt forts of the Befort type, or larger refuges. All of this signifies fundamental changes and the emergence of a new social structure, for at the same time the aristocratic residences of formerly non-Celtic regions were also losing their significance, for example Molpir (Smolenice in Slovakia) and the extensive fortified site of Stična now being investigated, about 30 km. to the east of Lubljana in Slovenia, in what was already Illyria.

Trade with Massilia was still flourishing when Etruscan imports of sets of bronze vessels began to assume increased importance; beaked pitchers (beaked jug

— Schnabelkanne) and *stamnoi* were notable in these imports. Closer contacts with the regions of the south brought new impulses for the craftsmen north of the Alps; in the course of the fifth century the Hallstatt style began to lose favour in aristocratic circles, and geometric and schematic designs gave way to new decorative trends employing not only plant motifs but human and animal heads or masks in various forms. Mask-fibulae are one of the phenomena bearing witness to the rise of the Early La Tène style; their construction relates to the Certosa Etruscan fibulae, and each is a unique bronze jewel designed by an artist-craftsman. They have been found over an area stretching from the Rhine across southern Germany to Bohemia, where there have been many finds not only of fibulae, but of mask belt buckles (Gürtelhaken) and horse phalerae ornamented with human masks in the 'fish-bladder' frame. Similar finds, in a milieu of bronze-beaked pitchers and clay imitations, and of stamped pottery, occur in western Austria, especially numerous in Dürrnberg near Hallein, to the south of Salzburg. The La Tène style reached the peak of maturity late in the fifth century and in the early fourth century, when the armed Celtic bands were already on the move. Impulses and ornamental motifs from western Asia and particularly from Greek and Italo-Etruscan sources contributed to form this individual art which was quite independent in content. Combinations of very varied types of mask, palmettes, tendrils, lotus blossoms, droplet motifs resembling the fish bladder, S-shaped and lyre scroll motifs, were used by the craftsmen in complex patterns and compositions which often conceal a symbolism we cannot easily fathom. The spiral and the scroll predominated in Celtic ornament. Perfectly executed articles in gold and bronze were decorated with raised ornament which was sometimes further enriched with engraved lines, coral or enamel.

The finest articles in this mature style, which is also known as the Waldalgesheim style, present Celtic art in its second phase; they have been found particularly on the left bank of the Rhine, in the region of the Nahe and Mosel rivers. It is here that very many wealthy graves dating from the time of Celtic expansion have been found: Waldalgesheim near Hunsrück (the grave of a man and a woman, with gold jewelry, bronze vessels and other objets d'art); a woman's grave at Reinheim near Saarbrücken, with a whole set of gold jewellery and a bronze mirror with an anthropomorphic handle; graves in Rodenbach, Bad Dürkheim (Rheinland-Pfalz) and Weiskirchen (Saarland). In this area a 'princely' milieu still existed in the fourth century, but as yet we have discovered no appropriate permanent settlement nor can we explain where the wealth that made it possible came from. Some scholars believe that the economic basis for such a high standard of living was the growing exploitation of the many local iron ore deposits. It can be assumed that there were some craftsmen working for this wealthy class on the spot, but the unexpected find of a gold treasure in Erstfeld, Switzerland (1962), on the route through the St. Gotthard pass in the Central Alps, suggests that luxury articles may also have been traded over long distances. The four torques (Halsringe) found at Erstfeld, with human and animal figural ornament, and the three bracelets

(Armringe) are masterpieces of the Ancient Celtic goldsmiths' art, equal to any found in the Central Rhine region. They are of exceptionally pure gold (93-94%) and although they show great affinity with the famous Rheinheim treasures, they appear to have originated in a different workshop, in the first third of the fourth century. Isolated finds of similar articles in the mature style have been made in various parts of Europe reached by the Celts in the course of their expansion during the fourth and third century (gold torques, and more rarely beautifully worked helmets). These can be seen in the context of the armour of the men leading the armed bands of Celts into Italy, through Central Europe, and as far as the Balkan peninsula. In some cases they may even have been symbols of rank.

The period of military expansion

From the middle of the fifth century and during the fourth century the territory of the Late Hallstatt princely rulers lost much of its population. The evolution of Celtic society on the continent of Europe took a sharp turn of historic significance; as a consequence the whole structure of society was changed. The fortified residences lost their glory; there were fewer and fewer pompous burials in richly furnished barrows. Instead of barrow burial grounds, some of which were extensive indeed (like that of Haguenau in Alsace), in the fourth century we find simple graves in the ground in flat cemeteries. Throughout Central Europe the various types of fortified site lost their importance. Tension must have grown up in the original Celtic areas as a result of overcrowding and sharp social differences between the ordinary people and their rulers; in all probability there was also tension and a conflict of interests between the different Celtic tribes, who had evolved from proliferating related groups to tribal organization by the time of the 'princely' burials. The ruling class seems to have sought its own solution to the problem by organizing armed incursions into distant regions. Testimony to this is given by the historian Titus Livius (Livy), referring to a Roman tradition that Ambigates the king of the Bituriges sent his nephews Belloves and Sigoves with armed bands, to seek new homes in Central Europe (the Hercynian Forest region) and in Italy, when their homeland became too populated. Armed bands of Celts crossed the Alpine passes to the valley of the Po (Bononia-Bologna, Marzabotto), where their domination meant the end of the Etruscan kingdom; they moved further south, defeating a Roman army in 387 B.C. and threatening Rome; they reached as far as Apulia. The historical sources name many tribes that took part in this invasion: the Insubres, Boii, Senones, Lingones and others. It was not until the following century, and particularly after the Gauls were defeated at Telamon (225), that the Celts were pushed back from Central Italy. In the second century B.C. their rule was restricted to the north Italian region that later became the Roman province of Gallia Cisalpina. In the course of the fourth century the Celts were also spreading through Central Europe, into Bohemia, Moravia, Silesia and Austria, and then on into the Carpathian basin; they set up their rule for a time in Transylvania and Bulgaria, and in 279 attacked the Greek oracle at Delphi. In 335

Alexander the Great received emissaries of the Danube tribes, among whom there were representatives of the Celts. Some streams of Celts on the move found their way into Asia Minor (Galatia), and in the third century we even find Celts serving as mercenaries in the Hellenic armies. At the beginning of the second century they are said to have taken part in the suppression of a revolt in Upper Egypt.

The area settled by Celts in what is now France also grew in size, and we know the names of many tribes especially in Caesar's day: the Aedui, Bituriges, Arverni, Allobroges, and Boii (who gave their name to Bohemia), and in Switzerland the Helvetii, etc. We have definite information about some of these tribes. The Celts also penetrated into Aquitania in south-west Gaul, and moved their settlements south under pressure from the Germanic Belgae in the north. Some groups crossed over to the British Isles from the third century onwards, and before the end of the La Tène period some Belgic tribes also settled there. On the continent, as in the British Isles, the tribes remained scattered. From various sources we also know the names of the tribes settling in Britain: the Dumnonii in Cornwall, the Dobuni in the Thames valley, the Ordovices in Wales, the Cantii in Kent, and elsewhere the Catuvelauni, Atrebates and Durotriges.

The extent of Celtic occupation on the Continent, and especially in Central Europe, can best be judged by the flat cemeteries they left behind from the fourth to the second centuries B.C. These burial grounds cover areas of varying size, with the simple inhumation of uncremated bodies (later cremation was very much used in certain regions), usually without striking grave mounds. The largest cemeteries of this type to be excavated so far (Münsingen in Switzerland, Jenišuv Újezd in Bohemia, Maňa in Slovakia, and others) contain from 100 to 250 graves. Today we know of well over a thousand such burial grounds in Central Europe. A characteristic feature are the graves of warriors in full armour, equipped with a long iron sword, a spear, a shield and sometimes with iron belt chains as well; such warriors' graves often account for 10-20% of the burials in a cemetery, and they have been found even in small cemeteries, where only a few graves have been excavated. The general context suggests that they do not reflect burial customs, but that they are graves of military groups, for some of the skulls show evidence of wounds, healed scars, and some of the skeletons lack part of the upper extremities. In the same social category as these warriors' graves are those of wealthy women; they are often found close to graves furnished with weapons, and reveal a wealth of brooches, bracelets, rings, bronze chain belts sometimes inlaid with enamel, sapropelite rings, and glass bracelets; these contrast profoundly with the meagre or even poor furnishings in other women's graves. Archaeological analysis has enabled us in recent years to distinguish more important graves among those of the warrior class, both by the superior quality of the funeral furnishings and by the special arrangement of the graves themselves, surrounded as they are at times by a rectangular or circular ditch. Other evidence of higher rank is provided by the artistic treatment of the sword scabbards, the existence of short swords with anthropomorphic hilts sometimes inlaid with gold, or by the rare finds of helmets or remnants of armour. During the Celtic expansion, mounted as well as foot warriors were engaged, and two-wheeled chariots were used; four-wheeled chariots are less prominent in the funeral rite. The Celtic warriors were famed for their daring and courage; women also fought in battle. In some regions we find the custom of cutting off the defeated enemy's head as a war trophy. The motif of a warrior holding a severed human head by the hair is found on Celtic coins, and headless skeletons can be found in Celtic cemeteries.

So far archaeologists have not succeeded in finding large fortified settlements in the regions where flat cemeteries abound in Central Europe, centres which could have governed the territory settled by the Celts, or formed the focus of their power. It is probable that there were no such centres in the regions where the Celts settled from the fourth to the second centuries B.C.; it is only from the end of the second century that the late Celtic oppida are found. The Celtic tribes remained fragmented, and the different groups seem to have maintained military domination over the Central European regions without ever combining to form a more permanent organized power. Sections of the same tribes are named as being in different parts of Europe (e.g. the Boii), which is not surprising in view of their ease of movement and the pressures to which they were subjected in both Italy and south-east Europe from the third century onwards. This fits in with the conclusions drawn by archaeologists from their finds of recent years in the south German region, for instance: the Celtic burial grounds are not extensive, a few dozen graves at the most, and in the vicinity there is usually a settlement which has only been lived in for a relatively short time, for two or three generations. Further research will be necessary to determine whether they were not farms (such as are found later in the oppida) which could have been fortified in a simple manner. The task of distinguishing between true Celtic settlements and those of the indigenous population which had lived in Central Europe since the Hallstatt period and now came under Celtic domination, remains for future scholars. Larger centres of Celtic settlement only developed in regions where this settlement was of longer duration and where the Celts came together in greater numbers during their retreat from the south towards some parts of Central Europe or back into Gaul.

La Tène Culture (from the fifth to the second century, B.C.)

The La Tène culture and the art of the Celts of the flat cemetery period can be considered the characteristic feature of the historical Celts, the classical Celtic culture which matured at the time of the armed migrations. It is no longer a culture confined to the aristocratic milieu of princely courts, but has become more accessible to the ordinary people in mentality and even (in the case of certain articles) in fact. The craftsmen drew on the 'mature style' of courtly art, perpetuating certain features as typically Celtic, but evolved in new directions as the migrating bands came into contact with influences both local and from neighbouring cultures. Precious metals, especially gold, were gradually ousted by bronze wrought in an equally masterly fashion; sometimes bronze was replaced by iron, for brooches and bracelets for instance, and here too the craftsman's skill was remarkable. The fact that such brooches and bracelets were produced in large quantities did not mean, however, a mass-produced uniformity; every single object made in the La Tène style was an individual creation. Local workshops grew up in the newly-captured territories, and their products soon began to show local features, although a high level of craftsmanship was maintained. The plastic style now developed, in which three-dimensional relief work took the place of two-dimensional ornament, culminating in bracelets and ankle-rings with a wealth of articulated forms decorated with S-scroll and 'snail-shell' ornament giving an almost baroque effect; torques and brooches were also treated in relief. Delicate bracelets were made with embossed rosette and tendril ornament, and there were attempts to imitate filigree work in bronze-casting. The sword style evolved, with beautiful scabbards decorated with engraved patterns, sometimes treated diagonally, or with animal motifs in beaten metal, on the front; many such finds are known from Switzerland and also from parts of the Carpathian basin. Gold was more rarely used for jewelry; the hoard of small gold jewels with filigree and granulated ornament found at Szarazd-Regöly near Szekszard in Hungary is an exceptional find in a purely Celtic context. The brooch, or fibula, of bronze or iron, and of varying quality, became the ornament of the ordinary people. Subject to changes of fashion, its evolution from the free-pin type to jointed forms, in all its variations, provides a useful chronological basis for dating La Tène finds. In the second half of the fourth century and in the succeeding third century burial grounds in different places already contain free-pin brooches of the Duchcov type (Duxer-Fibel), so called from the rich find of about 2,000 fibulae and bracelets in a bronze cauldron in the Duchcov hot spring in Bohemia, in 1882. This type of brooch evolved still further into many forms. Among the many articles made in Celtic workshops the bronze chain belts are very fine; the links decorated with enamel, they were worn by women. Some objects of a ritual nature are also of great value.

Celtic art in the British Isles can be traced from the middle of the third century onwards; it was then that migrating groups seem to have brought it over from the Continent. Swords with ornamented scabbards testify to links with Europe. Local workshops soon sprang up, combining a high level of skill with an original treatment of design. Today the museums of England and Ireland can boast of remarkable Celtic works of art which reveal the art of the islands as an individual branch of Celtic art. According to some British scholars (Piggott, Fox and others), it is possible to distinguish local styles and 'schools' or workshops. The insular style combined relief ornament with linear engraving, using palmettes, spiral patterns, lyre motifs and tendrils, later terminating in stylised birds' heads. The earlier style was in use mainly in south-east England, from whence it later penetrated to Ireland.

Many of the finds come from rivers or marshes and peat-bogs, and are thought to have been votive offerings. In the last century B.C., when Celtic art on the Continent was rapidly declining in significance, in the British Isles it attained remarkable heights, and went on maturing in the Christian era. Among the well-known finds is a horned helmet found in the Thames near Waterloo Bridge (the ornament is relief work, and enamel inlay), a shield found in the Thames at Wandsworth and another at Battersea, with rich enamel ornament; five hoards of gold jewellery and coins found at Snettisham in Norfolk (Desborough in Northamptonshire, Birdlip in Gloucestershire); late fibulae with relief ornament; discs with beaten relief designs (Ireland) and many other finds which all show characteristic features. It would seem that the Belgae tribes brought craftsmen with them when they crossed to Britain, and that these craftsmen raised the art of the islands to great heights. Hammered metal ornament with animal motifs, human masks and spiral patterns was also used on the bronze fittings of wooden buckets dating from the turn of the millenium (Aylesford, Marlborough).

In architecture and sculpture the southern coast of France must be distinguished from the main Celtic regions of the Continent, for the Celts came relatively late to this original Ligurian area. The coastal region of Provence was strongly influenced by the cultures of the Mediterranean and of Greece (later Gallia Graeca), and spread this influence to the Gallic hinterland. Many specific features are connected with ritual customs. Fortified sites grew up, arranged in terraces, with a pillared propylaeum and an internal plan which was not usual in the Celtic world. The Ligurian-Celtic oppidum of Entremont (Bouches-du-Rhône), the centre and the shrine of the Salluvii in the region of Massilia, dates from as early as the third century B.C.; the path leading to the shrine on the summit was lined by statues of heroes and in the ritual hall human skulls were placed in niches in the stone pillars (the cult of severed heads). The Romans destroyed the shrine in 124 B.C.

In the oppidum of Roquepertuse, in the same region, three stone columns with niches for human skulls formed the façade of the shrine. The remains of statues with traces of paint on them (including one of a hero in the 'seated Buddha' position) prove that local statuary ateliers grew up in the south of France, to meet ritual needs, and that they combined local and Greek influences. The stone monster of Noves rests its forepaws on two human heads. Influences from the Orient and from Greece found their way north through Massilia, founded in 600 B.C., but even before this an urban-type settlement grew up at Saint-Blaise: Mastramele. The oppidum of Ensérune (Hérault), dating from the fifth century, with Cyclopaean fortifications, was said to be able to hold as many as 8,000 people later in the Celtic period. Glanum, on the lower Rhône, still flourishing in Gallo-Roman times, also has a long history; relief carvings on the city gate, which still stands, depict captive Gauls. From the last century B.C., however, the Romanization of southern France brought fundamental changes.

In the interior of Gaul, Celtic sculpture is less common; usually in the form of a stele or column, it became the vehicle for ritual and religious ideas. The limestone figure of a god with a boar carved on his chest and a Celtic torque round his neck, found at Euffigneix in the Marny valley, is only 26 cm. high. The figure of a boar, in bronze or carved in relief on stone, occurs often throughout the Celtic world, reflecting the special importance of the animal in ritual and in military life (where it appears often on standards and emblems). The group of statues excavated at Neuvy-en-Sullias (Loiret), which includes a fairly large figure of a boar and figures of 'dancers', occupies a special place in Celtic sculpture at the beginning of the Gallo-Roman period; some scholars believe that the figures were buried by the druids during the Roman occupation. The obelisk fron Pfalzfeld in the Hunsrück region shows distinctly Celtic elements in the carved ornament. The Celtic figure found at Mšecké Žehrovice in Central Bohemia is so far unique; representing a head with a torque round the neck, carved in marlite, it originally stood in a sacred grove, and was later knocked off its pillar when the shrine was destroyed. This fact testifies to the existence of an independent sculptural art in Central European "Gaul" as well.

The life of the Celts was bound up with innumerable ritual customs based on ancient traditions. Masks played an important part in this life; usually of bronze, they were fixed to wooden pillars in the sacred places. These ritual precincts are an integral element in the Celtic sphere on the Continent and in the British Isles. They were of various types; certain trees (the oak, the beech) were worshipped in the sacred groves, and divine or magic powers attributed to them. A ritual site discovered in Libenice near Kolín in Bohemia in 1959 was 80 metres long and surrounded by a ditch; a series of sacrificial pits and a stone stele were found in the eastern part, and in the centre was the grave of a woman, with La Tène jewellery dating from the late fourth or the third century. In the local Celtic toponyms, the word 'nemeton' recalls sacred sites, usually in the open country. Springs, wells and some stretches of water were also regarded with reverence. Caesar and other writers mention the great votive treasures of gold and silver in the sacred places and waters of the Volci-Tectosages near Tolosa (Toulouse), which were looted by the Romans in 106 B.C. In Anglesey it was the custom to sacrifice arms and other objects by throwing them into the water from a cliff ledge, and similar places of sacrifice have been found in England and Scotland. Ritual cauldrons played an important part in the sacred rites; some of them are of great artistic value. The famous cauldron from Gundestrup, found in a bog as far north as Jutland, gives us a more intimate glimpse of the ritual ideas of the time; its silver plaques are decorated with scenes in relief, and with pictures of gods (Cernunnos and others) and heroes. It came from a Celtic workshop of the second century B.C. The dividing line between gods and heroes is not always clear in Celtic religion. In an involved symbolism some of the many tribal gods acquired a special standing (Taranis, Teutates, Esus and others) and later on were referred to (often in a Roman form) as being worshipped in many different parts of the Celtic world (Epona, the horse goddess). The complicated rites were maintained for a long time in Ireland, in particular, where they later exercised a strong influence on the newly-arrived Christian religion.

The growing volume of production from Celtic workshops and the markedly individual character of Celtic art made it a strong influence on neighbouring non-Celtic peoples as early as the third century B.C. Celtic articles were exported, and they were also imitated by the Germanic tribes to the north as well as by peoples beyond the Carpathians, in what is now the Ukraine, and in the Balkans. The culture of the Germanic tribes pressing southward into Central Europe in the second and last centuries B.C. was strongly celticized; many general La Tène features and types of pottery and metalware had been assimilated. As early as the second century, Celtic settlements with extensive warehouses were formed in many places. The La Tène site itself, in Switzerland, included a number of timber buildings and warehouses on either side of the river Zihl; recent research allows us to consider it a large centre of production and export as early as the second century B.C. A large number of weapons have been found (e.g. 160 swords, some of them stamped and with ornamented scabbards) as well as farm and other implements (sickles, scythes, and waggon parts). The site was occupied up to the middle of the last century B.C. Similar finds of articles and buildings have been made elsewhere in Switzerland, at Port (Nidau) and Cornaux.

With the increase in long-distance trading, the growing volume of production and the importance of permanent marketing centres, it soon became necessary to use a coinage. This was the first to be used in Central Europe, appearing in Gaul in the third century B.C. and in Central Europe no later than the second century; it was based on local deposits of gold and silver. The earliest coins are modelled on the Graeco-Macedonian stater, but subsequently Celtic coins developed their own specific iconography (using e.g. the boar symbol, sunk-panel coins known as Regenbogenschüsselchen, shell-shaped staters, coins bearing the symbol of a coiled dragon or a prancing horse, later coins of the Biatec type, etc.). The coins are known from various hoards of hundreds and even thousands, from graves and from individual finds. Evidence is accumulating that coins were struck in different places and by different tribes. The Celtic coins are of high artistic value, and of original design; they fit well into the context of Celtic art as a whole. Around the middle of the last century B.C. the minting of coins by the Celts came to an end.

At the height of the La Tène culture Celtic craftsmen were masters of practically all the known production techniques, and thus laid a solid foundation for prehistoric Europe to build on after the fall of Celtic power. Specialization increased, trade flourished, and besides the export trade there were imports especially of goods from the Roman territories. The historical situation forced profound economic and social changes on the Celts; military expansion was replaced by commercial and economic expansion. Sometimes techniques were taken over by non-Celtic peoples, so that it is sometimes difficult to distinguish truly Celtic finds.

Late Celtic Oppida and the Fall of the Celts in Central Europe
(last century B.C.)

From the end of the second century the Continental Celts were subject to ever-increasing difficulties. Their domain was threatened by two powerful hostile forces which in the end completely encircled them: from the south there was increasing pressure from the Roman Empire, while from the north the Germanic tribes were pressing down on them. The Romans first penetrated the south of present-day France, setting up the province of Gallia Narbonensis (later to become Provence); before the middle of the last century B.C. they had spread into the other parts of Gaul. The greater part of France then gradually became Romanized and subject to Roman administration. The pressure of Germanic tribes from the north is attested in the literary sources for the year 113 B.C., when the Boii held up the advance of the Cimbri somewhere near Bohemia. They moved on towards the Scordisci in the Lower Danube basin (in the region of Belgrade), defeated the Romans at Noreia, and joined the Teutons to invade Gaul and northern Italy. It was not until 102 B.C. that the Romans finally dealt with this threat. The consequences of this new historical situation can be seen in the archaeological evidence. The Celtic world was entering on a new phase, which after a period of some resistence ended with the fall of the Celts in Central Europe as well.

At the turn of the second to the last century B.C. the period of the flat cemeteries came to an end in Central Europe. The Celts lost their position in Transylvania to the growing power of the Dacians. The situation was changing all round the Lower Danube basin, especially in the mixed territory ruled by the Scordisci, while the Romans were trying to move northwards, towards the Danube. There were population shifts inside the Celtic domain.

Throughout the Celtic domain in Europe, where they remained in power into the last century B.C., extremely well-fortified sites are found; these are the late Celtic oppida. It is a specifically continental phenomenon, found only in those regions where the power of the Celts persisted into the last century B.C. There is a continuous belt of oppida from France across the Rhine and southern Germany to Switzerland, Bavaria, Bohemia and Moravia. In the Carpathian basin Celtic oppida are the exception; even in southern and south-western Slovakia, and north of the Carpathians or in Transylvania they are not archaeologically attested at all. The fortified sites of the Lower Danube basin are of a quite different character, and so are the fortified places of the Dacians.

The archaeological interpretation of the late Celtic oppida now accepted is that they are fortified centres which already have an urban character, with a high concentration of population, large specialized production based on local raw materials, and all the social and economic consequences of this situation. This idea of growing urbanization has become a stereotyped model widely accepted in the literature, although it does not always fully meet the historical facts. There are considerable differences between the function and the significance of individual oppida, according to the milieu in which they existed and the concrete historical situation at that time.

The question of late Celtic oppida as a temporary phenomenon in the last century B.C. does not really arise in Britain and Ireland, where Celtic civilization continued to evolve from its local foundations even in the Christian era, and where development was not violently interrupted. There, too, many fortified sites have been found; they are often circular in shape. Their chronology has not yet been worked out in detail, however, and some of them are thought to have been the seats of local rulers. Only a few have been excavated; Maiden Castle (Dorset) which was mentioned in Caesar's day and later, as the Roman occupation advanced, is surrounded by fortifications of an even older date. The fortifications at Uffington (Berkshire) date from the Early Iron Age and had already been deserted when the famous white horse, about 110 metres long, was cut out on the chalk hillside. There are various hypotheses dating this figure in the last century B.C., in the time of the Belgae, or even later. The Minor Oppida referred to by English writers (of 6 to 30 acres) cannot be compared with the oppida on the Continent. The situation in Ireland was similar. The fortifications at Tara (County Meath), believed to be one of the most important royal residences in Irish tradition, have yielded older and later finds, and the site seems to have been primarily of ritual significance.

In his Commentaries, Julius Caesar has given us an account of the state of the late Celtic oppida in the last century B.C. According to his information, the individual tribes had a number of oppida each (the Helvetii were said to have had twelve), but not many of them were on a large scale. There were at least 200 of them over the territory of France, but only a few of them seem to have been urban in character. Only one is better known to us, from archaeological excavations: the famous oppidum of the Gauls at Bibracte (Mont Beuvray), which Caesar gave as the largest and richest oppidum of the Aedui, and which covered an area of about 135 hectares. It has some features in common with the Bohemian oppidum at Stradonice. During the reign of Augustus the population was moved to a newly-founded town, and only the marketplace and shrine remained in Bibracte. During the reign of Napoleon III, some excavation was carried out both at Avaricum in the territory of the Bituriges, known from Caesar's campaigns, and at Gergovia in the territory of the Arverni, but no systematic investigation was made. The same is true of Alesia, an oppidum of the Mandubii (97 hectares), where Caesar defeated Vercingetorix in 52 B.C., thus completing the conquest of Gaul. The Gallic method of fortification described by Caesar (murus Gallicus) was widely used only in the west, the most easterly example yet found being at Manching on the Upper Danube. The oppida of Central Europe were fortified by a different technique, developed from ancient local tradition.

Most of the many oppida found on German territory have been investigated either by surface methods or by taking soundings; since 1955 Manching, a large oppidum of the Vindelici covering 380 hectares, has been systematically excavated. It had a dense population, and is thought to have fallen in 15 B.C. at the latest, during the Roman advance. The many finds, systematically published in a special series of volumes, prove that the population was numerous and that considerable production of goods was carried on. Partial investigation leads us to conclude that some of the south German oppida were later foundations, dating only from the last century B.C., like Altenburg-Rheinau on the Swiss-German border, or Kelheim west of Regensburg, which is thought to have defended the iron ore deposits and the Danube valley trading route. At present systematic investigation of late Celtic oppida is being carried out in Czechoslovakia, where four sites are being analysed (Závist, Hrazany, Třísov and České Lhotice) to add to the information already collected at the well-known site of Stradonice, where the rich finds are common knowledge. The large fortified complex of Závist to the south of Prague played a unique role in the territory. Excavations continue at Staré Hradisko in Moravia, and have been started at Hostýn. All the Bohemian oppida are in the southern half of the country, and not a single one in the region of the flat cemeteries in north-west Bohemia. It would seem that most of the Celts (Boii) moved south under pressure from the Germanic tribes in the last century B.C., to take refuge in rapidly built oppida in the southern part of the country. In the first half of that century the Bohemian oppida (particularly Stradonice) were still able to trade with the Gauls and with the Roman regions, but in the middle of the century the situation of the Celts on the Continent was already critical. Caesar completed the Roman conquest of Gaul, the Dacian king put an end to the rule of the Boii in Pannonia (where they seem to have moved from Bohemia and Moravia). Times were uncertain, and in the middle years of the century hoards of Celtic coins were buried, minting ceased in the Bohemian oppida, and their fortifications were damaged and had to be repaired in haste. The fall of the oppida at the end of the century meant the end of Celtic rule in Central Europe; to the north of the Danube Germanic tribes ruled, and from the south the Romans were moving into the Danube basin. By the end of the millenium Germanic graves appear all over Bohemia, and the Marcomani and Quadi were taking over the land. This last century B.C. also seems to have brought about a fundamental change in the structure of Celtic society. Although there was considerable concentration of the population in the oppida of Central Europe, we have not yet found any burial grounds. Religious ideas and burial customs also seem to have changed about this time. In the region stretching from France, through southern Germany as far as Bohemia, unusual sites have been found, dating from the time of the oppida; known as Viereckschanzen, they are from 70 to 100 metres long, surrounded by a low earthen mound and ditch. In some of them sacrificial pits have been discovered, and signs of some sort of construction inside; it has therefore been suggested that they may have been late Celtic ritual sites, the forerunners of the later Gallo-Roman temples.

Although the power and political importance of the Celts had declined throughout the Continent by the beginning of the Christian era, their contribution to civilization and art remained of great significance for the evolution of European culture, techniques, art and literature. There is hardly a nation in Europe which has not drawn directly or indirectly on the wealth of this Celtic heritage. The mainspring of Celtic traditions and the Celtic heritage, of course, remained in Britain and Ireland, where Celtic culture developed undisturbed when ancient Gaul was already markedly Romanized. Ireland and Scotland, in particular, where neither the Romans nor the Anglo-Saxons attained a permanent foothold, preserved their Celtic character. From there the ancient Celtic traditions reached back to influence England and the Continent, and came to a new flowering in the early centuries of Christianity and in the minor arts of the Middle Ages. Later the mysterious Celtic world of heroic deeds, legends and tales was a source of inspiration for the greatest minds at the birth of modern European culture. Man today does not always realise how great is the debt of our own age and of the whole of European civilization to that once so courageous people.

NOTE

Professor Filip was unable to attend the Conference; in his absence Father Leonard Boyle of the Pontifical Institute for Medieval Studies read a shortened version of the paper.

NEAR EASTERN AND AFRICAN CONNECTIONS WITH THE CELTIC WORLD[*]

HEINRICH WAGNER

Early in the 19th century it was discovered that Celtic is derived from Indo-European, a reconstructed language which in the third millennium B.C. had its roots in Eastern Europe, probably in the steppes of Southern Russia. Historically this means that some time in the second or early in the first millennium B.C. primitive Celtic was imposed on Western Europe by a powerful warrior aristocracy on various nationalities who originally spoke languages of non-Indo-European origins. The echo of a rather unpleasant social climate created there by the Indo-European Celts and noticed also by Julius Caesar[1] is preserved in the oldest stratum of the ancient Irish Laws. Of the pre-Indo-European languages of Western Europe only Basque survives in the Pyrenees up to the present day. Another pre-Celtic language may have been the language of the Picts in Northern Scotland which was still spoken in the early Middle Ages. The dialect of Indo-European imposed on the aboriginal peoples of Western Europe was in my opinion similar to that spoken by the Thraco-Phrygians, who early in the first millennium B.C. occupied large areas of the Northern Balkans and Asia Minor[2]. Scholars such as M. Dillon, N. Holmer, W. Meid and C. Watkins maintain that primitive Celtic was a particularly archaic Indo-European dialect[3]. Their findings do not, however, rule out automatically, as some of these scholars seem to believe, the recognition of strong non-Indo-European elements in Insular Celtic. As to the Celtic invasions and subsequent occupation of the British Isles little is known. It is likely that they did not involve large numbers of Indo-European-speaking people, a view which has led a number of scholars, including myself, to believe that in the British Isles Indo-European language as imposed by small bands of Celtic invaders from the Continent must have been influenced strongly by the speaking habits of a predominantly non-Celtic population.

In 1899 the Welsh scholar Morris Jones published a paper entitled *Pre-Aryan Syntax in Insular Celtic*[4]. In its introduction he states correctly that "the syntax of Welsh and Irish differs in some important respects from that of the languages belonging to the other branches of the Aryan family". It was the famous John Rhys who had suggested earlier on "that these peculiarities are due to the influence of a pre-Aryan language"[5]. The term Aryan is used by the two Welsh scholars in the sense of the modern terms Indo-European or Indo-Germanic. In his paper Morris Jones shows that most of the non-Aryan features of Insular Celtic syntax, such as its rules for basic word-order, its intriguing system of infixed and suffixed pronouns or the relative forms of the verb are paralleled in Egyptian and Berber, so-called Hamitic languages of Northern Africa. These languages are distantly

[*]Transcription of the words quoted from various languages (especially Egyptian) has been simplified.

51

related to the Semitic languages of the Middle and Near East as well as to the Cushitic languages of Ethiopia and Somalia. It is most likely that the original home of the people who spread the Hamito-Semitic languages was Arabia. Morris Jones concluded that the pre-Celtic language or languages of the British Isles were of a Hamito-Semitic type or origin. From a methodological point of view he remarks: "When one language is supplanted by another — in our case a Hamito-Semitic language by an Indo-European language — the speakers find it comparatively easy to adopt the new vocabulary, but not so easy to abandon the old modes of expression; and thus, whilst the old language dies, its idiom survives in the new"[6]. Morris Jones's work was later developed systematically by Julius Pokorny[7] who extended the field of enquiry to other African languages. Most scholars, however, remained, up to the present day, unprepared to accept any of these findings, although they opened up what must be described as one of the most fascinating subjects in linguistic prehistory. There are several reasons for the predominantly hostile attitudes towards substratum investigations, the most important one being undoubtedly the kind of education comparative linguists receive in universities since the establishment of historical linguistics in the second half of the 19th century. As for myself, the linguistic facts as presented by Morris Jones and Pokorny became evident when in the same academic year I took up Celtic Studies with Pokorny and studied Arabic under the guidance of W. Zimmerli, my old teacher in Hebrew. Orthodox Indo-European philology was established in Germany, almost exactly a hundred years ago, by the so-called Neo-Grammarians. They believed that language development is due mainly to the working of mechanical and psychological laws, the so-called sound laws and the laws of analogy. In their thinking there was no room for the recognition of social history as an important factor in the development of language. Less than ten years after Morris Jones's paper had appeared, Pedersen prepared his comparative Celtic grammar, perhaps the greatest work written in the spirit of the Neo-grammarian school. He was a pupil of Brugmann, one of the principal founders of this school. In the same period Thurneysen wrote his Old Irish Grammar, which was to become the most fundamental work in the teaching of Celtic languages. Following the methods and beliefs of Neo-Grammarianism, both works ignored completely Morris Jones's work. Similarly the English edition of Thurneysen's grammar, which appeared in 1946, ignores Pokorny's work published earlier from 1927-30. Binchy and Bergin, who prepared this undoubtedly most valuable edition, had been trained by German Neo-Grammarians.

Whenever it can be proved by scholars who do not adhere to the teaching of any rigid school that a dying language has influenced considerably the growth and development of the language by which it was superseded, the Neo-Grammarians and their successors use the term substratum theory, as if the recognition of substratum influence were based on theory and not on observation in the field. That we are dealing here with a sociolinguistic fact of the highest historical importance can easily be learned in Ireland. A number of scholars, in particular my friends P. L. Henry and Brendan Adams, have shown scientifically[8] that, although Irish has ceased to be spoken in most parts of the country, the English spoken in Ireland is strongly flavoured, syntactically as well as phonologically, by the old Celtic tongue. As the speech of relatively uneducated people reveals, this flavour would be much stronger had not school education and modern techniques of communication impeded this development in the 20th century. In earlier periods substrata must have worked much more strongly.

Between 1945 and 1955 I was engaged in collecting the material for my *Linguistic Atlas and Survey of Irish Dialects*. Towards the middle of that period news went around among Celtic scholars that on the Isle of Man there were still some very old people left who could be considered as native speakers of the old Gaelic dialect of the island, which had been declared defunct by the Norwegian scholar Carl Marstrander. Subsequently a few specialists, including myself, went to the island and, with the help and assistance of local Gaelic enthusiasts, succeeded in extracting from the old Manx speakers the last oral fragments of this most peculiar Gaelic dialect[9]. One of the features of this idiom which struck me most was its verbal system. Practically every tense-form of every verb was expressed by a periphrastic construction which had become standardised. Examples: *nyim bu:la šu* "I shall strike you", lit. "I shall do striking you"; *ha dyenəm fa:kan u* "I shall not see you", lit. "I shall not do seeing you"; *rin e fo:zlə dorəs* "he opened the door", lit. "he did opening the door"; *ha ridn mi gi:k son e* "I did not pay for it", lit. "I did not do paying for it"; *ti ge:s dorəxə* "it is getting (lit. growing) cold"; *ha nel mi na:gən e* "I have not seen him", lit. "I am not after seeing him"; *dyin gol ta:i* "go home!", lit. "do going home". My distinguished colleague, Myles Dillon, who, for some days in 1949, accompanied me on the island, expressed the view that these sentences must be seen in the light of the moribund and degenerate status in which the language appeared in its last stage of development. Only a few synthetic forms had survived such as *hengk e* "he came" (= Irish *thánaig sé*), *xai e* "he went" (= Irish *chuaidh sé*), *hu:r e: be:s* "he died" (= Irish *fuair sé bás*, lit. "he found death"), *ha gi:l mi* "I did not hear" (= N. Irish *char chuala me*, Scottish Gaelic *cha chuala mi*), *ha nak mi* "I did not see" (= N. Irish *cha n-fhaca me*), *hanik mi* "I saw" (= N. Irish *chonnaic mé*), *du:rt i* "she said" and, of course, forms of the auxiliaries "to do" and "to be" such as *rin* (dialectically *ridn*) "did" or *ta* "is", *va* "was", *ha ro* "was not", *ha nel* "is not", *bidn* "I would be".

Some years before my visit to the Isle of Man I had studied, under the guidance of Ernst Lewy, one of the greatest linguists of all time, the Basque language. Although this language is not related to Celtic, its verbal system as such shows a striking similarity to that of Manx: apart from the auxiliaries and a few much used irregular verbs, practically every tense form of the regular verb is expressed periphrastically in this language cf. *egiten dut* "I do, I am doing it", lit. "doing-in I have it"; *egin dut* "I did it", lit. "done I have it"; *eginen dut* "I shall do it", lit. "done-of I have it".

As in late Manx, in the modern spoken language, apart from the auxiliaries "to have" and "to be", only a few synthetic forms have survived. In the dialect of *Baigorri* (Bas-Navarrais), which I studied in 1976, I noted forms such as *err-o-su* "say it to him!" (-*o*- "to him"; -*su* = ending of the imperative), *d-aki-t* "I (-*t*) know it (*d*-)", *es d-aki-t* "I do not know it", *ba-laki* "if he knew it", *d-oa* "he (*d*-) goes", *doatzen* "those who go" (relative form ending in -*n*), *zauri* "venez!"; *gabiltza* "nous (*g*-) marchons"; *ba-noa* "je (*n*-) vais"; *zoazi* "allez!". As in Manx, imperative forms may have resisted stronger than any other verbal form periphrastic constructions, although these occur quite frequently in the spoken language: cf. Basque *sar* (entered) *zite* (you be) *etchean* "entrez dans la maison!"; Manx *jin gol ta:i* "go home!" (lit. "do going home!"). If one studies older, literary documents of Manx or Basque one can easily detect that, although synthetic forms are much more common in the earlier stages of these languages, the development of almost exclusively periphrastic conjugations is clearly indicated in them. Unfortunately, we know little or nothing about the development of these languages prior to the 16th century. It is also probable that the learned authors and scribes of the 16th and 17th centuries avoided deliberately, and as much as possible, periphrastic forms, which were common in the spoken language. This seems to be the situation with regard to present-day Welsh.

In 1955 I began to study spoken Welsh in a rural area of Anglesey. Anglesey is an island called *Môn* in Welsh. The Welsh name must be basically identical with Gaelic *Manu*, Welsh *Manaw*, the Celtic name of the Isle of Man[10]. Geographically, of all Welsh-speaking areas, Anglesey is nearest to the Isle of Man. I soon learned that in order to communicate in colloquial North Welsh one had to know the conjugation of the auxiliaries, whereas with regard to ordinary verbs a knowledge of the verbal noun was sufficient. My teacher and main source for my study was an old woman whose school education was minimal and who could neither speak nor understand English, a rare situation in twentieth-century Wales. Henry Sweet's study of North Welsh[11] and Fynes-Clinton's well-known dictionary of the Welsh dialect of the Bangor district had made clear to me, prior to the field trip, that spoken Welsh, although riddled with loan-words from Modern English, was in various ways closer to and, therefore, a more genuine descendant of the mediaeval language than standard Modern Welsh, the language of the Church. This view, which in general is not shared by the educated Welsh people themselves, was expressed to me first by my friend D. Greene from whom I learned a good deal in the course of my education in Celtic Studies. Knowing already the situation in Modern Manx and Basque, I was not surprised to find that in Anglesey Welsh every tense form could be expressed periphrastically, although many synthetic forms still do exist. In a book on the verb of the languages of the British Isles including English, I have called this feature "isolation of meaning" from the conjugated verbal complex (*Bedeutungsisolierung* in German)[12]. Examples: *na: i gario* "I shall carry", lit. "I shall do carrying"; *du i am vynd* "I shall go", lit. "I am about (for) going"; *du i yn mynd* "I go, I am going", lit. 'I am in going"; *δary mi vynd* "I went", lit. "finished (or happened) to me going"; *δary o ngweld* "he saw me", lit. "happened he my-seeing"; *du i wedy mynd* "I have gone", lit. "I am after going"; *may o newyδ-vynd* "he has just gone", lit. "is he newly-going". There is, however, no doubt that synthetic forms are still commonly used in this dialect, but it is difficult to work out the difference between, for instance, *δary mi vynd* and *mi eis i*, both meaning "I went", or *neith o vynd* and *mi eith o*, both meaning "he will go". The fact that synthetic forms are still widely used, in particular with much used verbs such as those meaning "to go, to come, to get", fits well into the general picture as derived from the situation in Manx and Basque. *du i am vynd* "I shall go", lit. "I am about going" recalls formally the Basque future tense *joanen niz* of the same meaning, analysed "going-of I am". The genitive suffix *-en* (cf. *aita-r-en* "of the father") added to the verbal adjective *joan* has here the same function as the preposition *am* in the Welsh sentence.

In applying the methods and findings of area linguistics, which I learned from Ernst Lewy and his great pioneer work on the structure of the European languages[13], it became obvious to me that the development of the Manx and, to a certain degree also that of the Scottish Gaelic verb, must be seen in the context of the general development of Brythonic Celtic. In all three languages, but significantly not in Irish or Breton, the form of the Indo-European present tense had become, at an early stage, a future tense, while the original present tense was replaced generally by the periphrastic construction with the verb "to be", of the type W. *ydwyf yn myned*, Sc. G. *tha mi dol* or *tha mi ri dhol*. If one studies the history of Cornish, the defunct Brythonic dialect of the Southwest of Britain, one finds the same pattern of development as in Manx, North Welsh and Basque[14]. Unfortunately, the sources for the historical study of the syntax of this language do not go further back than to the 15th century, and little can be said, therefore, about the syntactical development of Cornish during the early Middle Ages. Had Cornish survived, periphrastic constructions similar to those found in Basque and Manx would probably have ousted almost completely the older synthetic forms which are still common in the earliest texts. The language of the religious Cornish drama, rather like that of the oldest Basque and Manx texts dealing with religious matters, does not perhaps reveal exactly the spoken language of the same period; in spite of this it contains ample examples of the various periphrastic constructions[15]: *ena ef a wra trega* "there he will live", lit. "there (it is) he who will do living"; *my a ra y debry* "I shall eat it", lit. "(it is) me who will do its eating" (Or. 247); *an sarf re ruk ow fholle* "the serpent has deceived me" lit. "(it is) the serpent (which) has done my deceiving" (Or. 286); *thov vî ow môs dho Loundres* "I am going to London". English influence may be seen in the late Cornish future tense of the type *ny a vyn formye an bys* "we will create the world", lit. "(it is) we who wish the forming of the world". Although periphrastic tenses are common in Irish and English, too, in these languages periphrastic constructions have never reached the level of spoken North Welsh, Cornish, Manx or Basque. In this respect Scottish Gaelic takes an intermediate position. The excessive use of the verb "to do" as an auxiliary in the English of Cornwall, as referred to by Franz in his Shakespeare Grammar[16], must be due to the influence of the Cornish substratum.

Periphrastic constructions based upon the verbal noun are common in all Insular Celtic languages and their excessive development in Manx, spoken North Welsh and late Cornish is, therefore, the result of a tendency inherent in the development of Modern Celtic in general. The so-called progressive form of the English type *I am going* is found already in Old Irish as well as in early Welsh, cf. *Wb.* 21c19 *is oc precept soscéli attó*, lit. "it is preaching the Gospel I am". It has been suggested by Morris Jones[17] that the development of this form in English, a feature not common in other Germanic languages, could be due to Celtic influence. All the arguments produced by English scholars against such an explanation seem to me unconvincing. Having started my career as a Germanic scholar, it has since become clear to me that the development of the Modern English tense and aspect system can only be understood in the light of the corresponding Insular Celtic developments.

The central position of the verbal noun in Celtic is revealed also in the morphological development of the Gaelic verb. The bewildering number of irregularly inflected verbs typical of Old Irish has been reduced considerably in the later stages of the language; in many cases the verbal noun of an irregular or strong Old Irish verb is the only form which survives, or forms the basis of a regularly inflected verb in Modern Gaelic. One may compare, for example, Modern Irish *ólaim*, "I drink", *ólfad*"I shall drink", *d'ólas*, "I drank", *ól*, "drinking" with Old Irish *ibiu* "I drink", *-íb* "I shall drink", **ibsiu*[18] "I drank", *oc óul* "(at) drinking". Of Old Irish *-ren* "sells", *-ria* "may sell", *-rir* "he sold", *reic* selling", only *reic* survives in Scottish Gaelic and Manx, but it is regularly inflected (cf. Scottish Gaelic *reicidh mi* "I shall sell")[19]. In Irish I have recorded from Donegal in an idiomatic expression the word *reic* "wasting, throwing out money"[20]; the Modern Irish word for "selling" is *díolaim* "I sell", *díolfad* "I shall sell", *(do) dhíolas* "I sold", which in itself is based upon *díl*, the verbal noun of *do-lá* "he puts away"[21]. If, by any chance, of all the Celtic languages only late Manx and Cornish had survived or left literary documents, Celtic scholars would find it very difficult to reconstruct the early mediaeval verbal system as preserved in Old and Middle Irish as well as in mediaeval Welsh. They would be faced with problems similar to those which puzzle Basque scholars, namely the reconstruction of an original verbal system almost completely superseded by a periphrastic system of secondary origin.

The development of the verb in what must be described as the oldest languages of Western Europe has a close analogy in the development of the Egyptian verb from around 3000 B.C. down to the mediaeval language of the

Christian Copts which not too long ago has ceased to be a spoken language[22]. The similarity between certain periphrastic constructions of Egyptian, already current at a fairly early date, and corresponding Welsh constructions such as *wyf am fynd* "I am for going", i.e. "I shall go", has been noticed, of course, by Morris Jones (p. 625).

The fact, however, that in Coptic the majority of the older synthetic constructions have been replaced by periphrastic constructions based upon the Old Egyptian verbal noun or verbal adjective conjugated by means of auxiliaries, recalls very much the situation found in Manx, late Cornish and Basque. As in Celtic, most of these constructions occur already in the earlier stages of the language, but they possessed, as again in the earlier periods of Insular Celtic, a more limited syntactic range: Coptic *efsótəm* "he hears" is based on a *iw.f-hr-stm* "he is upon hearing", a construction already attested at an early date(cf. *iw.i hr rdit* "I am giving")[23]; Coptic *nefsótəm* "he heard" is based on earlier *wn.f-hr-stm*, lit. "he was upon hearing", and Coptic *efesótəm* "he will hear" upon earlier *iw.f r stm*, lit. "he is to hearing" (cf. Steindorff, p. 145), a construction already well attested in Middle Egyptian to express prospective action (Gardiner, p. 332). As Morris Jones (p. 625) has seen, this construction is identical with the Welsh construction of the type *(yd) wyf am vynd*, a future tense or prospective in spoken North Welsh. The Basque future tense of the type *joan-en niz* "I shall go", lit. "going-of I am", is essentially the same kind of construction (cf. above). In the present and past tense the preposition *hr* "upon, in, at" (Gardiner, p. 582) is frequently omitted in late Hieroglyphic Egyptian;[24] it has disappeared completely in Coptic. This recalls the fact that with regard to the corresponding English progressive form of the type "he is going, he was going" the verbal noun was originally preceded by the preposition *on*, later *a*. In Irish *tá sé ag dul* "he is going", *bhí sé ag dul* "he was going" the preposition *ag* (Old Irish *oc* "at") is practically reduced to zero in the spoken language. In spoken Basque the form *izan-en niz* "I shall be", lit. "being-of I am" one can hear regularly the contracted form *izainiz*[25]. There exists, therefore, in all these languages a tendency to rebuild new synthetic forms from the periphrastic constructions. According to Steindorff (§313,c), Coptic *hafsótəm* "he heard, has heard, had heard" is derived from earlier (Demotic) *wh.f (m, hr) stm* "he has ceased (with, on) hearing"; similarly the North Welsh past tense *δary mi vynd* is based upon a Middle Welsh construction *darfu i mi fyned* which originally meant "has been over, finished to me going"[26]. In Coptic *a-próme sótəm* "the man heard", *a-u sótəm* "they heard" the element *a-* is developed from the old verb *i.ir-* "do, make" followed directly by the noun or the pronominal subject[27]. As in Manx and Cornish, this is the normal procedure in Coptic to express non-durative action in the past, durative action being expressed by the past tense of "to be". Periphrastic constructions with the verb "to do" followed by the verbal noun are already extremely popular in Middle Welsh prose; they occur frequently also in Middle Egyptian (Gardiner, p. 395). In Egyptian as well as in

Insular Celtic the verbal noun becomes direct object of the auxiliary "to do" and the logical object appears as a "genitive" dependent of the verbal noun: cf. Coptic *a-f-hetəv-próme* "he killed the man", analysed "did-he-killing-of man"; this could be translated without any difficulty into Middle Welsh: *ef a wnaeth ladd y dyn* "(it is) he who did killing of the man". Accordingly, if the logical object is a pronoun the possessive pronouns are used, strengthened sometimes by the independent pronouns: cf. North Welsh *δary o i ladd o* "he killed him", lit. "happened he his killing of him"; Coptic *a-f-hotv-əf id.* analysed "did-he-killing-his" (Steindorff, pp. 224f); Cornish *ni wrîgav vi dha welas* "I did not see you", lit. "not did-I, I, your seeing"[28]. In Coptic only a few forms of the original finite verb of Ancient Egyptian have survived such as *pejaf* "he said", *mešak* "you do not know" or *ehnak* "you wish" (Steindorff, pp. 135f.). Thus, the situation in Coptic is comparable with that found in late Manx, Cornish and Basque. If, apart from Coptic, nothing were known about Egyptian, it would be impossible to reconstruct the Old or Middle Egyptian verb. It is, therefore, as we have already said, legitimate to assume that the prehistoric verbal system of Basque was quite different from that of the attested language.

Adolf Ermann, one of the great old Egyptologists, in his grammar of late Hieroglyphic Egyptian (§6), points out that the Egyptian language, in so far as it gradually develops a definite article as well as periphrastic verbal constructions, follows the same lines of general development as our modern languages of civilization. He seems to be unaware of the fact that the strongest and oldest tendencies to develop periphrastic tenses are found in the archaic languages of Western Europe, namely in Basque and Celtic. Considering that there exists a large chronological gap between the Egyptian development and that of the Western European languages, a majority of scholars might be inclined to believe that there is no historical link of any kind between the Egyptian and Basque developments nor between the Egyptian and Celtic developments, whatever one might think of the similarity between the Basque and the Manx and Cornish developments.

My old teacher Ernst Lewy, who was a specialist both in Basque and Finno-Ugrian studies, pointed out that analytic expression or isolation of inflexion ("Flexionsisolierung" as he calls it), is *the* characteristic feature which links French, Iberian Romance, Basque, Insular Celtic and English[13]. The Finno-Ugrian languages of Eastern Europe as well as Russian and Lithuanian do not share this feature and are synthetically inflected languages, while in this respect German takes an intermediate position between East and West.

Pokorny assumed[29], and I have enlarged on this subject recently in Spain (1976), that Lewy's Western European area has an extension in Northern Africa. This would explain the syntactical similarities between the languages of Western Europe and African languages such as Egyptian and Berber. As linguistic areas develop the same grammatical features at different chronological stages and in successive languages, the chronological gap between the periphrastic constructions of Egyptian and those of Western Europe need not surprise us.

Northern Africa, including Egypt, is now populated mainly by Arabic-speaking people. Furthermore, Ethiopian Semitic is closely related to Southern Arabic, from which it branched off some 2000 years ago. The spread of the Arabic language, which in mediaeval times reached Spain, is due to movements of invaders from Arabia and the consequent establishment of Arab empires in the Southern Mediterranean world. It is most likely that the historically attested Arabian invasions were preceded in prehistoric times by analogous invasions from the Arabian and Syrian deserts involving people who spoke archaic forms of primitive Semitic. This explains why Berber, at least from the point of view of its verbal system[30], is the most archaic Hamito-Semitic language. In early historical times this language was spread, probably by the ancient Libyans, all over Northern Africa including the Canary Islands. It is also assumed that the language of the ancient Iberians, spoken on the Mediterranean coast of Spain, was a dialect of Libyan or Berber. Egyptian, which is believed to have been imported into Egypt by people of Arabian or Syrian origins, deviates strangely — in particular from the point of view of its earliest verbal system — from Common Semitic. It has been stated by Alan Gardiner, the famous English Egyptologist, that some of the most important forms of the Old Egyptian verb "find analogies in certain of the most recent off-shoots of the Semitic family, namely the Neo-Syrian dialects".[31]

Verbal forms based on periphrastic constructions as fully developed in late Egyptian and Coptic are not specifically typical of central Semitic languages such as ancient Ugaritic or Classical Arabic, nor of ancient Akkadian in Mesopotamia. They are, however, a characteristic feature which Egyptian shares with the Cushite languages of Ethiopia, Somalia and the Sudan. As Cushite is also of Hamito-Semitic origin, it is probably based upon the language of successive waves of invaders who, like the old Egyptians or Libyans, came from the east at an early prehistoric date. In analysing the Cushitic verb historically it is evident that most of its conjugations are based on periphrastic constructions involving a verbal noun and an auxiliary. In Somali, for instance, only about five verbs survive which preserve synthetic inflexion by means of personal prefixes as inherited from common Hamito-Semitic[32], but strangely absent in Egyptian.

It has been indicated long ago by Leo Reinisch[33], one of the most outstanding pioneers in African linguistics, that the key to Northern African linguistics is to be found in Proto-Hamitic languages such as Nubian spoken in Southern Egypt south of Aswan and in the Sudan, or Kunama, spoken on the old Egyptian/Abyssinian frontier. Complicated as a detailed analysis of the verb of these languages might be, its conjugation seems to be based on similar principles to that of the Cushitic languages, namely upon inflexion by means of suffixed auxiliaries. North-Eastern Africa, including Ethiopia, the Sudan and Somalia, presents itself as a linguistic field where the principles of area linguistics can be studied almost to perfection. In this area, certain grammatical features such as the periphrastic verbal forms found their way into wave after wave of languages presumably imported from the East, the latest one — if we exclude Northern Arabic — being represented by Ethiopian Semitic. The southern varieties of Ethiopian in particular, including Amharic, the official language of the Abyssinian empire, exhibit strong Cushitic features such as inflexion by means of auxiliaries.

In Indo-European, verbs are normally derived from nouns, adjectives or primary verbs by means of formal suffixes. Old Irish *móraid* "magnifies" is derived, for example, from *mór* "great" by the same suffix -*ā*-, which occurs in Latin *nomin-a-re*, derived from *nomen* "noun". In Insular Celtic this procedure seems to have ceased to be productive at a fairly early date. In Brythonic as well as in Goidelic, denominative verbs are derived from nouns by means of a suffix *-sag- Irish -aig-, Welsh-ha-[34]. In origin this suffix is in all probability an independent verb to be identified with Old Irish *saigid*, which has the same meaning as, and is, therefore, etymologically related to English *seek*, German *suchen*. In the meaning "to sue, to claim" *saigid* is an important term of the Ancient Irish Laws. If we take, for instance, the verb *ceannuighim*, it is obvious that this Modern Gaelic term for "to buy" is derived from the word *ceann* "head"; its original meaning must have been "to seek a head (namely of cattle)", an appropriate term in a society like the Irish in which buying and selling of cattle was probably the most significant and most important business transaction up to recent times.[34a] Later, the conjugational type *ceannaighim* extended its field greatly and has become one of the two principal types of conjugation in Modern Gaelic. Gardiner's Grammar (§ 427) explains the Egyptian conjugations characterised by the suffixes -*in*- (*sdm-in-f*), -*hr*-(*sdm-hr-f*) and -*k3*- (*sdm-k3-f*) as a compound of a verbal adjective with auxiliaries of the original meaning "to say" (-*in*-), "to cry" (-*hrw*-) and "to plan" (-*k3i*-) respectively. Derivation of a verb from a nominal or nominalised basis followed by a closely attached auxiliary verb is typical, as we have seen already, not only of Nubian, but also of Cushitic and Ethiopian Semitic. This feature is also found in Hamitic languages of the Lake Chad area, which are related, at least typologically, to Nubian and Cushitic[35]. In all these languages verbs meaning "to say" or the like are frequently used as auxiliaries. Leo Reinisch explains this in the light of the customary law and constitution of the Cushites[36]: in their view "being", in the legal sense of "existing as a true member of society", is synonymous with "speaking up", namely in the assembly of the people. As Old Irish *saigid* "he seeks, he sues, he claims, he proceeds" fits well into the semantic range of the Egyptian and Cushitic auxiliaries discussed above, we have here a remarkable parallel between the formation and consequent conjugation of verbs in Insular Celtic on the one hand and Egyptian, Cushitic and Ethiopian Semitic on the other. The conjugation of verbs by means of suffixing auxiliaries meaning "to say" to a nominalised base is also found in Eastern Caucasian, particularly in Udic[37], a language spoken in the very south-east of the Caucasian linguistic area. Furthermore, it has been noted that in Sumerian texts of a somewhat later period the verb *du* "to speak, to sing" is used in a similar way[38]. In Basque, the verb *etsi* meaning "to consider" occurs in a number of verbs derived from a nominal basis: for example, *onetsi* "to approve" (*on* "good"), *sinetsi* "to believe" (*sin, zin* "true"), *handietsi* "magnify" (*handi* "great")[39].

In linguistic typology, as developed by an old German school independent of the Neo-Grammarians[40], word-order plays a big part in the classification of languages. More recently this subject has been discussed again by J. Greenberg, the well-known American typologist of languages[41]. With regard to the languages of Northern Africa, it is evident that Nubian and Kunama, so-called Proto-Hamitic languages, as well as Cushitic and Ethiopian Semitic represent on the whole Greenberg's type III of basic word-order exhibiting final position of the verb in the sentence; Berber and Egyptian as well as Hebrew and Arabic, in exhibiting initial position of the verb, are exponents of his type I.

In Africa type III is rare and confined to north-eastern languages such as those already mentioned (Nubian, Kunama, Cushitic) as well as to a few more central languages such as Tubu and Kanuri, Hamitic languages of the Lake Chad area. The stronghold of type III is Asia where it dominates most language groups including Caucasian and, of the extinct languages, Sumerian. In this light, it becomes clear that Chad Hamitic, Nubian and Cushitic provide a very old linguistic link between Africa and Asia. Links between Nubian or Chad Hamitic and Sumerian have been assumed by scholars some time ago. Basque, on account of its obvious connections with Caucasian and perhaps also with Sumerian, provides an equally archaic link between Europe and Asia, because it is the only Western European language to show strong traces of the Asiatic type III. Affinities between Nubian and Basque have been suspected long ago by F. Hommel and H. Schuchardt[42].

Finally, Insular Celtic, as a typical representative of Greenberg's type I, provides a striking link between the languages of Western Europe and those of Northern Africa and the Middle East (Berber, Egyptian, Arabic and Hebrew). Interreactions between types I and III are noticeable, as we have seen, not only in Egyptian, but also in Insular Celtic as well as in Basque[43].

One of the most characteristic grammatical categories of Insular Celtic, which Indo-Europeanists claim wrongly as their own exclusive property[44], is the impersonal or autonomous form of the verb of the type Gaelic *rugadh i* (phonetically, depending on the dialect, *rug-əx, -əv, -əg, əγ, -u*), Welsh *ganwyd i* "she was born". In spoken Welsh and Scottish Gaelic this category has become more or less redundant, and is replaced by periphrastic constructions: cf. Welsh *mi gavoδ i ladd* "he was killed", lit. "he took his killing", Scottish Gaelic *chaidh a mharbhadh*, lit. "his killing went". The "autonomous form", *an briathar saor* in Irish, with regard to its functions, is best compared with the French form of the type *on dit* "one says", *man sagt* in German (*deirtear* in Irish).

Fifty years ago R. J. Hayes[45] pointed out that the Irish *Briathar Saor* has a close parallel in Finnish (cf. Finnish *sanotaan* "one says"), where it is due to a development apparently not found in any other Finno-Ugrian language[46]. My own impression was, when studying the spoken language in a rural district of Finland, that the use of the Irish *briathar saor* is indeed similar to that of the so-called impersonal passive of Finnish.

In analysing Irish *rugadh é* "he was born", or *cuireadh é* "he was buried", lit. "he was put", as one might hear in rural Anglo-Irish, it is evident that the logical subject *é* "he", from the Gaelic point of view, must be taken as the grammatical object; the whole construction is to be considered, therefore, as impersonal. A similar situation is found in constructions involving the copula *is*, which in Modern Gaelic does not distinguish person[47]. In the sentence *is fear deas é* "he is a nice man" (analysed "is man nice him"), *é* "he (him)", from the Irish point of view, is the form of the object, the same morpheme, which in proper transitive constructions refers to the direct object; cf. for instance, *mharbh sé é* "he (*sé*) killed him (*é*)". The distinction between an impersonal copula (Irish *is*) and a conjugated verb "to be" (cf. Irish *táim* "I am", *taoi* "you are" etc.), a basic feature of Gaelic grammar, has a close parallel in Berber[48]. We might not be surprised, therefore, to find parallels to the Celtic autonomous form in Africa, too. In Chaha and some other Southern Semitic dialects of Ethiopia, extensive use is made of a morphologically characterised synthetic impersonal form[49]. As in Irish all tenses employ such a form. To this form suffixes denoting the pronominal object can be added: cf. *danag$_w$-i-m* "one hit him", *danag$_w$-ka-m* "one hit you", the active form being *danaga-m* "he hit"[50]. Morphologically, the impersonal form is marked in this case by rounding the final consonant of the verbal stem. The suffixing of the pronominal object markers in Southern Ethiopian dialects recalls the infixing of similar elements in Old Irish. In Old Irish, *ro-m-íccad*, written in the Würzburg Codex as one word, means "I have been healed" (*Wb.* 28a10). From the point of view of Irish grammar, however, this must be interpreted as "one has healed me", because the infix *-m-* is the same morpheme which in active sentences refers normally to a direct, in special cases and frequently in Archaic Old Irish, to an indirect object: cf. *nímcharatsa*, that is, *ní-m-charat-sa* "they do not love me" (*-m-* + emphasising particle *-sa* "me"), *Wb.* 5c6. In one of the most archaic Old Irish legal texts we find the following sentence, again written as one word in the manuscript: *romBororbíth*, analysed *ro-m-Bororbíth*. Here we find infixed between the perfective *ro-* and *-bíth*, the past autonomous form of *ben-* "to strike, to slay", not only the direct object *Boror* but also the indirect object *-m-* "on me". The sentence means, therefore, "one has slain Boror on me", in German "man hat mir den Boror erschlagen" (*Ériu* xiii, p. 20. line 6). It must be admitted, however, that in third person forms the autonomous form of Old Irish could be considered as a true passive[51] and the above sentence translated with equal right as "Boror has been slain on me", German "Boror ist mir erschlagen worden".

Parallels to the impersonal form of Southern Ethiopian are found in Maasai, a so-called Nilo-Hamitic language, and in Nuer, classified as a Nilotic language of the Southern Sudan. The latest and most authoritative Maasai Grammar describes the passive of this language as "a specialised form of the *3rd person active,* in that it takes a «contained object» (Compare French "On vous appelle" for "You are called")"[52]. This definition indicates clearly that the Maasai passive is not a passive but an impersonal form of the Celtic type. The most authoritative grammar of Nuer declares that the so-called middle-sized personal pronouns are used to denote a) the direct or indirect object in active and b) the subject in passive sentences[53], a definition which indicates clearly, too, that the passive of Nuer is an impersonal form. It becomes clear that the category of a morphologically marked impersonal form used in all tenses and moods is a characteristic feature of an Eastern African area which stretches as far south as the border-area between Kenya and Tanzania, where the Masai country lies[54]. In ancient Egyptian the passive characterised by the suffix *-tw-* is also, at least in origin, an impersonal form of the Insular Celtic type; for in reality, as Gardiner's grammar (p.41) says, "*-t(w)-* is an indefinite pronoun like our *one,* French *on*". As a matter of fact "it is sometimes still so used independently, *ex. dd.tw* «one says»" (cf. Irish *deirtear* id.). The typological relationship between the Egyptian and Insular Celtic "Passive" (better "Impersonal") has been recognised clearly by Morris Jones (1899), 622f. The Egyptian morpheme *-tw-* must be identical with Berber *tu-*[55], Bedawie *to-*[56], the prefixes which mark the passive stem of these Hamitic languages. Bedawie is the language of the nomads of the Red Sea Hills from Egypt to Kassala and not only the most Northern but also perhaps the most archaic of all Cushitic languages. It has preserved, for example, the Hamito-Semitic prefix-conjugation[57] better than any other of the related languages in Ethiopia.

Finally, to sum up my conclusions, North-Eastern Africa must have been, in prehistoric as well as in early historical times, a regular target for nomadic invaders from Arabia, Syria and also from further east and north-east. As a result of these invasions, Hamitic and Proto-Hamitic speech was spread — on the evidence of Egyptian from a very early date — not only all over Northern Africa but also, if my reading of the linguistic affinities of Ancient Iberian, Basque and the substratum of Insular Celtic is correct, to Western Europe.

NOTES

[1] Cf. his *De Bello Gallico* vi, 13: *Nam plebes paene servorum habetur loco* "the (ordinary) people are treated almost like slaves". According to Caesar, the only people who counted were the *equites* and the *druides.*

[2] Cf. my *Studies in the Origins of the Celts and of Early Celtic Civilisation* (Belfast-Tübingen 1971), Part One. First printed in *Transactions of the Philological Society 1969,* pp. 203ff.

[3] Cf. in particular Myles Dillon in *The Celtic Realms* (London 1967), Chapter 9, and Watkins's articles in *Celtica* vi (1963) on Archaic Old Irish Syntax and Metre. More moderate is W. Meid in *Die indogermanischen Grundlagen der altirischen absoluten und konjunkten Verbalflexion* (Wiesbaden 1963). Holmer's view on this subject is found in a number of his papers; he has transmitted it to me orally

[4] As an appendix to *The Welsh People*, by J. Rhys and D. Brynmor-Jones.

[5] *Pre-Aryan Syntax in Insular Celtic*, p. 617.

[6] *Ibid.*, p. 617.

[7] *Das nicht-indogermanische Substrat im Irischen, Zeitschrift fur Celtische Philologie*, vols. 16-8 (1927-30). Subsequent references to this journal will be abbreviated to *ZCP*.

[8] For details see *Lochlann* i (Oslo 1958), pp. 49ff; and the bibliography in P. L. Henry, *An Anglo-Irish Dialect of North Roscommon* (Dublin 1957).

[9] For a phonological study of this material cf. K. Jackson, *Contributions to the Study of Manx Phonology* (Edinburgh 1955). F. J. Carmody, who was the first scholar to study spoken Manx after the war, published his material in *ZCP* 24 (1953), 58ff. My own material was published as an appendix to the fourth volume of the Linguistic Atlas.

[10] On this name cf. *ZCP* 33, 4f.

[11] Cf. his *Collected Papers* (Oxford 1913), pp. 499ff.

[12] *Das Verbum in den Sprachen der britischen Inseln* (Tübingen 1959), pp. 98ff.

[13] *Der Bau der europäischen Sprachen* (Dublin 1942). Reprint (1964) by Niemeyer in Tubingen.

[14] Cf. *Das Verbum*, pp. 94ff.

[15] *Ibid.*, pp. 96f.

[16] Second ed., Heidelberg 1909, § 597.

[17] *Pre-Aryan Syntax in Insular Celtic*, p. 626.

[18] Form not attested, but easy to reconstruct.

[19] Due to confusion with *creic* "to buy", which itself is replaced by *ceannacht* in Modern Gaelic, certain Scottish Gaelic dialects use *creic*, 1. sg. fut. *creicidh mi* in the meaning of "to sell" (cf. *LASI* iv, 189).

[20] Cf. Ó hEochaidh, *Sean-Chainnt Theilinn* (Dublin 1955), p. 98.

[21] See *Contributions to a Dictionary of the Irish Language* (Dublin, Royal Irish Academy), under *díl* and *do-lá*.

[22] G. Steindorff, *Lehrbuch der koptischen Grammatik* (Chicago 1951), p. 1.

[23] Alan Gardiner, *Egyptian Grammar* (Oxford 1950), p. 247.

[24] A. Ermann, *Neuägyptische Grammatik* (Hildesheim 1968), § 477.

[25] With stress on the second syllable as noted by myself in the dialect of St. Étienne de Baigorri (Bas-Navarrais).

[26] On the meanings of *darfod* "waste away, perish, happen", cf. Morris Jones, *A Welsh Grammar* (Oxford 1913, impression of 1930), p. 351. His assumption that "two verbs have probably merged" seems unnecessary, cf. L. Fleuriot, *Dictionnaire des gloses en vieux breton* (Paris 1964), p. 129. *dar-* could be equated with the Irish preposition *tar* "over"; in this case the original meaning of *dar-fod* would have been "being (*bod*) over, finished".

[27] Steindorff, pp. 145, 155.

[28] H. Jenner, *A Handbook of the Cornish Language* (London 1904), p. 160.

[29]*Die Sprache* (Vienna) i (1949), p. 245.

[30]Perhaps the most comprehensive study of the "Hamito-Semitic" verb is O. Rössler's article in *Zeitschrift der deutschen morgenländischen Gesellschaft*, vol. 100 (N.F. 25; Wiesbaden 1951-52), pp. 461ff.

[31]*Egyptian Grammar*, p. 3.

[32]Cf. M. M. Moreno, *Il Somalo della Somalia* (Roma 1955), §§ 94ff. The same is the case in Southern Agaw, the substratum of Semitic Amharic, cf. R. Hetzron, *The Verbal System of Southern Agaw* (Berkeley and Los Angeles 1969), pp. 44f.

[33]Cf. his *Die sprachliche Stellung des Nuba* (Vienna 1911), 2ff., as well as Armbruster's discussion in his monumental grammar of *Dongolese Nubian* (Cambridge 1960), §§ 114ff.; in particular §§ 201-8, where he accepts broadly Reinisch's views on the whole subject.

[34]R. Thurneysen, *A Grammar of Old Irish* (Dublin 1946), § 524. Subsequent references to this work will be abbreviated to *GOI*.

[34a]My colleagues Gearoid S. Mac Eoin and David Greene, rightly or wrongly, have rejected my analysis of this verb. For another analysis of the denominative suffix *-sag-* cf. H. Pedersen, *Vergleichende Grammatik der keltischen Sprachen* ii (1913), pp. 23f.: I.E. verbal root *ag-* (Lat. *ago*) added to *s-* stem. Thurneysen (*GOI*, end of § 524) as well as Pedersen (loc. cit.) point out correctly that these denominative verbs "are closely connected with the Irish nouns of agency in *-(a)ige*" which are also reflected in Welsh: cf. *cardotai* "beggar", from *cardod* "alms" (*GOI* § 268). The Welsh agent noun contains a suffix *-sagyo-*, originally meaning "the one who seeks". There exists an O. Ir. word *cennaige* "merchant, trader" attested in the Glosses (cf. *Milan Glosses* 120d 1: *innaní rendae .i. inna cennaige* "of those who sell, i.e. of merchants"). As in Irish society a "trader" was primarily a man who bought and sold cattle in exchange for other goods, I take *cennaige* to mean originally "one who seeks a head (of cattle)". *ceannuighim* "I buy", attested mainly in later sources, may be derived, therefore, from the old agent noun. For an extensive treatment of the Welsh denominatives in *-hau*, which, like their Irish equivalents in *-(a)ig-*, extended their field greatly, cf. J. Lloyd-Jones, *The Welsh denominatives in -hau and -ha*, ZCP 8 (1912), pp. 151ff. The exact relationship between *cennaige* and *cennuighim* on the one hand and the abstract (verbal) noun *cennach* "bargain, transaction, act of buying" on the other remains unclear. The latter must mean literally "the dealing with the heads" and contains a simple suffix *-ako-*.

[35]Cf. J. Lucas, *Die Sprache der Tubu in der zentralen Sahara* (Berlin 1953) § 421, also § 359.

[36]*Die Bedauye-Sprache in Nordost-Afrika* iv (Vienna 1893), p. 17.

[37]A. Dirr, *Einführung in die kaukasischen Sprachen* (Leipzig 1928), p. 338; A. Schiefner, *Die Sprache der Uden* (Mém.Ac.Imp. St.-Petersbourg, viie série, vol. vi, No. 8), § 88. According to Schiefner, Udic *phesun* means "to make" as well as "to say". In my Swiss German dialect *machen* is often used in the meaning of *sagen* "to say".

[38]Cf. Hallo and van Dijk, *The Exaltation of Inanna* (Yale Univ. Press 1968) p. 73, sub *du* "speak, sing".

[39]Cf. P. Lafitte, *Grammaire basque* (Bayonne 1962), § 287.

[40]This school follows in the steps of W. von Humboldt. Its main exponent at the beginning of this century was F. N. Finck, to whom we owe the first scientific description of an Irish dialect (cf. his *Araner Mundart* [Marburg 1899] describing the dialect of the great Aran Island in Co. Galway). Needless to say, he was a thorn in the flesh of the Neo-Grammarians; on Finck's work, which due to his early death ended abruptly in 1910, cf. E. Lewy, *Kleine Schriften* (Berlin 1961), pp. 689 ff.

[41]*Universals of Language* (Cambridge Mass. 1963).

[42]Cf. H. Schuchardt, *Nubisch und Baskisch* (*Revue internationale des Études Basques* vi [1912], 267ff.

[43]For details see my *Common Problems concerning the Early languages of the British Isles and the Iberian Peninsula (Actas del I Coloquio sobre lenguas y culturas prerromanas de la peninsula iberica,* Salamanca 1976), pp. 395ff. (including map featuring the distribution of these types), and my article on *Wortstellung im Keltischen und Indogermanischen* in *"Indogermanisch und Keltisch"* (1977), Wiesbaden, pp. 204ff.

[44]Cf. Vendryes, *Celtica,* iii (1956), 185ff, and Hans Hartmann, *Das Passiv* (Heidelberg 1954). I consider, however, both works as most valuable contributions to the whole subject.

[45]*Comparative Idiom* (Dublin 1927), p. 26.

[46]Cf. L. Hakulinen, *Handbuch der finnischen Sprache* (Wiebaden 1957) I, 173ff.

[47]The impersonal copula of Modern Irish, developed from a conjugated copula in Old Irish and Indo-European (cf. D. Greene, *The conjunct forms of the Copula in Old Irish, Ériu* xix [1962] 73f.), has left many reflexes in the use of the verb "to be" in Anglo-Irish (cf. Henry, part 3, § 22c). A man from an English speaking area in the West of Ireland, who sold us vegetables, used to say when he thought that his potatoes were good: *'them is a great potato'* = Irish *is maith na préatai iad*; in both languages the morpheme of the logical subject *(them, iad)* is an objective form. Compare, too, sentences such as *many's the pub I was in* = Irish *is iomaidh pub a rabh mé ann.*

[48]Cf. *Das Verbum,* pp. 172f.; also p. 171, where I argue that the element -*d*- which appears before class B and C of infixed pronouns in Old Irish (cf. *GOI* § 415) is identical with the element -*d*- of the conjunct copula (*GOI* § 794); cf. now, too, *Festschrift Pokorny, Beiträge zur Indogermanistik und Keltologie,* ed. W. Meid (Innsbruck 1967), pp. 304-307. The fact that it is the -*d*- which, by being either lenited or nasalized, indicates that the verbal form introduces a subordinate or relative clause, clearly reveals that -*d*- is a "verbal morpheme". For the copula as some kind of a verbal prefix, — a common feature in Egyptian, too — cf. my latest article quoted in note 43 (1977). To this I may add that the element -*(h)â*-, which in Berber precedes infixed or suffixed "dative" pronouns, has been identified with the element *(h)a*- which serves as an impersonal (deictic) copula (e.g. *ha-t* "le voici"), cf. Prasse, *Manuel de grammaire touaregue* i-iii (Copenhague 1973), 177; Basset, *La langue berbère* (Oxford 1952), 33. Berber either suffixes or infixes, according to rules which in principal are identical with those governing the Old Irish verb, not only the direct but also the indirect pronominal object. In this respect Berber resembles Basque. With regard to the Insular Celtic verb, direct and indirect pronominal objects, if suffixed or infixed, are not differentiated morphologically. Examples from Berber: *inna-iak* "he said to you (-*iak*)"; *ur-ak-inni* "he did not (*ur*-) say (-*inni*) to you"; *iut-ik* "he struck you"; *a-k-iut* "he will (*a*-) strike (-*iut*) you"; *izenz-as-t* "he (*i*-) sold (-*zenz*-) it (-*t*) to him (-*as*-)"; *ad-ah-ten-ius* "he will give (*ad*- = morpheme of the future tense; *i*- "he"; -*us* "give") them (-*ten*) to us (-*ah*-)"; the examples are taken from E. Laoust, *Cours de berbère marocain* (Paris 1939), 74ff. Another deictic element precedes certain forms of the pronominal infixes and suffixes which denote the direct pronominal object (Prasse, p. 174, sub 6). If Prasse's analysis is correct, we have here another remarkable parallel between the structure of the Old Irish verb and that of Berber. Tuareg is considered to be the most archaic dialect of Berber. The close grammatical relationship between copula and pure deictics is typical not only of Hamito-Semitic (and of African languages in general) but also of Celtic; compare the Modern Irish sentences *is fear deas é* "he is a nice man" and *sin fear deas* "this is a nice man"; in the second sentence *sin,* a pure deictic, replaces the copula.
    De Jubainville's identification of Old Irish -*d*- (before infixed pronouns, classes B and C) with Greek *de* (*Mémoires de la Société de Linguistique,* Paris, vol. 17, p. 349; cf. also Sommer *ZCP* 1, 228, and Watkins, *Celtica* vi, 28) is hardly correct. Is it a mere coincidence that *d* is also the form of the impersonal copula in Berber (cf. *Das Verbum,* 176f.) and *da* the 3. sg. pres. of *izan* "to be" in Basque? (cf. *ZCP* 32, 68).

[49]For a discussion of this category cf. W. Leslau, *The Impersonal in Chaha (To Honour R. Jakobson,* The Hague 1967, ii, 1150ff.); cf. also Leslau, *Ethiopic Documents: Gurage* (New York 1950), p. 30.

[50]Cf. *Ethiopic Documents,* p. 20.

[51]Cf., however, Vendryes, *Celtica* iii, 186f.

[52]Cf. A. N. Tucker and J. Tompo ole Mpaayei, *A Maasai Grammar* (London 1955), 79.

[53]Cf. J. P. Crazzolara, *Outlines of a Nuer Grammar* (Vienna 1933) § 135.

[54]In his book on *Die Sprachen der Hamiten* (Hamburg 1912), Meinhof assumed that early waves of Hamites had penetrated also into Southern Africa. Not only did he consider *Maasai* as a Hamitic language, but also the dialects of the Hottentots. It was, however, J. C. Wallmann, in his *Formenlehre der Namaquasprache* (Berlin 1857), who first drew comparison between Hottentot and Coptic. He recognized that periphrastic conjugation by means of substantive verbs of deictic background was well established in Hottentot. Furthermore, he compared the auxiliary *ra* of Hottentot with the Coptic particles *a-* and *re-* (to denote past tense and subjunctive respectively), which are both derived from Hieroglyphic Egyptian *iri-* "to do" (Steindorff § 313, 2b). The verb of Hottentot is to be compared, however, also with that of the Bushman languages, because if Hottentot is of Hamitic origin Bushman must be its substratum. From the point of view of the gender of the noun the relationship between Hottentot (distinction masc./fem.) and Bushman (no gender) is rather like that between Hamito-Semitic (distinction masc./fem.) and Proto-Hamitic (no gender in Nubian and Kunama).

Finally we must seriously ask the question whether analytic expression of action or state by means of auxiliaries ("be, say, do,etc.,") and closely associated deictics ("here! look! see!") is not the oldest type of verb in Africa as well as in prehistoric Western Europe. Furthermore, an impersonal verbal form, characterised by a suffix *-he*, exists also in Hottentot and is much used as a so-called "Passivum narrativum"; for details cf. Leonhard Schultze-(Jena), *Aus Namaland und Kalahari* (Jena 1907), 392.

[55]E.g. Tuareg *i-tu-ekf* "he was given" (*ekf* "to give"), cf. A. Hanoteau, *Essai de grammaire de la langue tamachek* (Alger 1896), 70f.; cf. also Basset, *La langue berbère* (Oxford 1952), p. 13.

[56]Cf. E. M. Roper, *Tu Bedawie* (Hertford, for the Sudan Government, 1928), 72. (cf. *atomān* "to be shaved", from *min* "shave"); L. Reinisch, *Die Bedauye-Sprache in Nordost-Afrika* iii (Vienna 1894), 48f (*tō-bas* "to be buried", from *bis* "to bury").

[57]The person-markers *y-* (3.sg.masc.), *t-* (3.sg.fem.), *n-* (1.pl.), *t-* (2.sg.), shared by Semitic, Berber and Cushitic, constitute one of the strongest morphological arguments in favour of a genetic Hamito-Semitic relationship. A serious difficulty is presented, however, by Egyptian, where no traces of this kind of conjugation can be found, even in the oldest texts from around 3000 B.C. The question must remain open whether such a conjugation had existed at all in Proto-Egyptian. It is not surprising, therefore, that very different views have been expressed on the historical background of the Egyptian verb; compare in particular T. W. Thacker, *The Relationship of the Semitic and Egyptian Verbal Systems* (Oxford 1954); in this book, however, Berber and Cushitic are strangely ignored.

THE GRAMMATICAL STRUCTURE OF THE CELTIC LANGUAGES*

ELMAR TERNES

The Celtic languages form a separate family of the great Indo-European language-family. They are therefore on the same level as for instance the Germanic, Romance or Slavonic languages, or — to mention at least two examples from outside Europe — the Indic and the Iranian languages. In this huge territory — ranging from India to Western Europe — the Celtic languages occupy the extreme northwest fringe. Linguists know from experience of many languages that a language or dialect, situated at the fringe of a given group of related languages or dialects, generally shows a linguistic development which differs greatly from one at the centre of that language or dialect group. Due to its relative geographical isolation, the border language either preserves certain particularly archaic traits or it develops new features which differentiate it from the centre. In many instances, the preservation of old and the development of new features combine to give the language in question a particularly aberrant appearance. This is what we would expect of the Celtic languages in view of their geographical situation, and this is what has indeed happened to them. The Celtic languages show a number of characteristics which give them a very special appearance. Somebody who has only studied the school languages, English, French, Spanish, German or Latin, cannot imagine to what degree the Celtic languages differ from what we may call the average European type of language. I shall now describe some of the features shared by all Celtic languages, which differentiate them from other languages, not only within Europe, but among the languages of the world.[1]

The first point is the so-called "mutations". This is certainly the most conspicuous peculiarity of the Celtic languages, and every learner becomes aware of them from the very first lesson on. By "mutations" I mean the regular change of word-initial consonants under certain well-defined morphological or syntactical conditions.

For example, the Irish word for "boat" in the nom. sing. with definite article is *an bád* / ən ba:d/. This is the so-called base-form, under which one will find the word in a dictionary. But the gen. sing. of this word is *an bháid* / ən va:d'/, i.e. in the gen., the consonant /b/ of the base-form is replaced by /v/ (spelled *bh*). Another example, again from the Irish: the attributive adjective, which usually follows its noun, takes the base-form after a masculine noun, but changes its initial consonant after a feminine noun. Therefore we have *an fear mór* /mo:r/

*Extract from a paper read at the 12th Annual Conference of the Canadian Association for Irish Studies, Vancouver B.C., May 2-5, 1979. The full version of the paper was published in the Conference Proceedings (The Canadian Journal of Irish Studies, Vol. 6, 1980, pp. 50-73). I wish to express my thanks to Andrew Parkin, Conference Chairman and editor of the Proceedings, for giving me permission to publish this extract separately.

"the tall man" (*mór* "tall"), but *an bhean mhór* /vo:r/ "the tall woman". Whereas the adjective does not change its initial consonant, as we have just seen, after a masculine noun in the sing., it does so when the same noun appears in the plural: *na fir mhóra* /vo:rə/ "the tall men".

This is a rather unusual phenomenon: in more familiar languages, we are accustomed to a stable initial consonant in a word. In English for instance, we could hardly imagine that a word like *dog* might — in certain well-defined cases — become *zog* and in still other cases might become *tog*.

The rules governing the phenomenon are numerous and complex. We may say that in a continuous text of any Celtic language, the initial consonant of roughly every third word is changed in the way described. This is rather awkward in practice, because anyone coming across a word with a changed initial consonant and desiring to look it up in a dictionary will never find it if he does not know the mutation rules. For example, there is no word *mhór* in an Irish dictionary; this word has to be looked up under *mór*. In Welsh and Breton, the orthographic changes are even more drastic than in Irish so that you may have to look up a word beginning with *f* under *p*, or a word beginning with *z* under *d* or *t*, etc.

The examples show us an important characteristic of Celtic inflection which distinguishes it from many other languages. We are used to case distinctions, gender distinctions, formation of plural, etc. being shown at the end of the word. In English we have *father*, genitive *father's*; we have singular *table*, plural *tables*. In Latin we have nominative *amicus* "friend", genitive *amici*, plural again *amici*; the adjective "good" is *bonus* for masculine nouns, *bona* for feminine nouns. In Celtic, however, these grammatical categories are expressed by changes both at the end and at the beginning of the word, or even by a change at the beginning of the word alone. As we have seen, the genitive of Irish *bád* (as of most other masculine nouns) is formed by a change at the end of the word *plus* a change of the initial consonant; the plural of an attributive adjective is formed by the ending *-a* /-ə/ *plus* a change of the initial consonant. The feminine of an attributive adjective is formed by a change of the initial consonant alone. The latter case, with the end of a word remaining stable and the grammatical inflections being shown at the beginning of the word, is to be observed even more typically in Welsh and Breton. We may call this characteristic "initial inflection". Thus the Celtic mutations involve *initial inflection* which is the opposite of the *final inflection* of English, German, Latin and most other European languages.

The description of the mutations, and the conditions under which they take place, are an important part of the grammar of any Celtic language or dialect. We may ask next: How did this rather striking phenomenon come about? It would take much too much space to describe the historical origin of the Celtic mutations in detail. I can give here only a rough outline. The initial consonant changes, as they occur in the above examples, reflect phonetic changes caused by the words immediately next to the word in question. Putting it another way: a

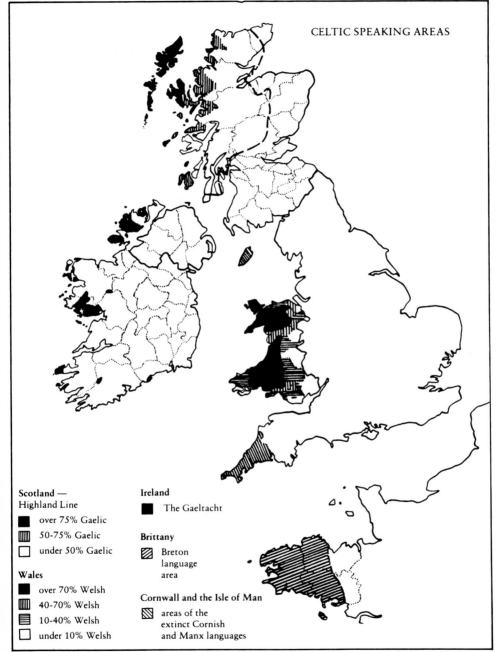

CELTIC SPEAKING AREAS

Scotland —
Highland Line

◼ over 75% Gaelic

▦ 50-75% Gaelic

☐ under 50% Gaelic

Wales

◼ over 70% Welsh

▦ 40-70% Welsh

▤ 10-40% Welsh

☐ under 10% Welsh

Ireland

◼ The Gaeltacht

Brittany

▨ Breton
language
area

Cornwall and the Isle of Man

▨ areas of the
extinct Cornish
and Manx languages

Plate 1: Geographical Distribution of the Modern Celtic Languages. Acknowledgement: Martin
Durrell, *Keltische Sprachatlanten* (1969).

word pronounced in isolation and a word pronounced in a sentence context may show quite different pronunciations, because in the latter case neighbouring words influence each other in their pronunciation. This feature can be observed, to a certain extent, in English. For example, instead of *I need you* /ni:d/ + /ju/, one may hear /ai 'ni:dʒu/. Or instead of *as usual* /æz/ + /ju:ʒuəl/, one may hear /æ'ʒu:ʒuəl/. But these forms are by no means constant.

English, therefore, is not a typical example, neither for the absence nor for the presence of this phenomenon. English lies somewhere in the middle between two extremes. German, on the one hand, is a language that shows few traces of the phenomenon, if at all. In German, the word, in whatever phonetic context it may appear, does not change at all. The word in German retains its individuality as a phonetic unit even in rapid speech (this is, perhaps, one of the reasons why German, to speakers of many other languages, especially to those of Romance languages, sounds somewhat abrupt or chopped). The other extreme is found in Romance languages, especially French. In these languages, the word completely loses its phonetic individuality in a spoken sentence. When one hears a French speaker, one is not able to identify individual words. The whole sentence sounds like one long word. Therefore, especially in French phonetics, one prefers to speak of *rhythm groups* or *breath groups* rather than of words.

The Celtic languages show this characteristic to an even greater extent than the Romance languages. And they have always done so, at least for the last 2000 years, as we may deduce from historical observations and comparisons. There is hardly a language in the world for which the traditional concept of "word" is so doubtful as for the Celtic languages. As far as the Celtic languages are concerned, the division of a sentence into words, shown in print by spacing, is a mere conventional device which facilitates semantic and grammatical analysis, but which is not justified phonetically. Using a metaphorical phrase (which, incidentally, the linguist should not normally allow himself), we may say that the word in Celtic is like a chameleon which changes its appearance according to its surroundings. Or, putting it in a more extreme way: the word by itself is in Celtic very loose, almost amorphous, and its shape can only be defined by analysing the sentence as a whole. There are several other factors, apart from the mutations and the phonetic conditions causing them, that contribute to this impression and reinforce it. Among the modern Celtic languages, it is precisely Irish that shows these properties to their greatest extent.

It is most interesting to note in this connection that the scribes of Old Irish manuscripts used word spacing differently from the practice in Modern Irish. They wrote longer periods, i.e. what appears to us as "groups of words", without spacing. They obviously had a different concept of the word, which probably means also that they understood the nature of Irish better than the grammarians of later centuries. This in turn may be due to the fact that users of Old Irish were still close to the native tradition and had not yet been influenced by foreign (and this means mainly Latin) grammatical concepts.

Another special feature of Celtic in comparison to other languages is found in the verbal system. Anybody who has studied a foreign language speaks of verbal conjugations. Many languages, such as Latin or French, have several verbal conjugations, often numbered from 1 to 3, 4 or 5, as the case requires. Each conjugation is characterized by a verbal paradigm, according to which all verbs belonging to the respective conjugation are inflected. One has to know which conjugation a verb belongs to. Every word belongs to one conjugation. Latin for example has four conjugations, numbered from 1 to 4, or identified also by a characteristic vowel or consonant. So we speak of the first or *a*-conjugation, the second or *e*-conjugation etc. French also has four conjugations, which by and large correspond to the Latin ones. The first are the verbs whose infinitive ends in -*er* (e.g. *fermer*), the second those whose infinitive ends in -*ir* (e.g. *finir*), etc. The conjugation to which a verb belongs is a property of the verb itself which never changes. Linguists say that conjugations of this kind are *lexically conditioned*. This is because all unchangeable grammatical properties of a word should be noted in the lexicon (or dictionary) of a language.

In the Celtic languages, the verb has a potential, irrespective of lexically conditioned conjugations, for additional conjugational differences which are conditioned by altogether different factors. Thus the form of a verb not only depends on whether the word belongs to the first or second conjugation, but also on the type of sentence in which it occurs: whether in an affirmative or negative sentence, or in a statement or question, or in a main or subordinate clause. It may even depend on the type of subordinate clause, whether, for example, it occurs in a relative or temporal clause. We may term conjugational differences of this kind *syntactically conditioned*, as the verbal form depends on the type of sentence in which it occurs, or the position it occupies within the sentence.

I shall illustrate the point with reference to affirmative and negative sentences. In most languages, forming the negative of a verb simply requires the addition of some word or particle meaning "not". For example:

German: *ich sehe* "I see" — *ich sehe nicht* "I don't see"
(*nicht* "not"),
Italian: *vedo* "I see" — *non vedo* "I don't see"
(*non* "not"),
French: *je vois* "I see" — *je ne vois pas* "I don't see"
(*ne . . . pas* "not).

In French we put something before *and* after the verbal form at the same time. But this does not change the fundamental process which says: Negation is formed by adding some negative marker to the positive verb, without change of the verbal form itself.

English does not quite behave in this way. To form the negative of *I see*, we cannot say *I see not* (although this was a correct form in Elizabethan English)[2], but we have to use a different construction, formed with the auxiliary *do: I do not see*. In questions as well, English uses a construction with the auxiliary *do: do you see?* That is to say, English shows a certain disposition to differentiate between syntactically conditioned conjugations. In the Celtic languages, this feature is much more developed. I should like to demonstrate this with examples from Irish:

chím	"I see"
ní fheicim	"I do not see"

The present stem in the affirmative is *chí-*, in the negative *feic-*. The word *ní* "not" incidentally causes a mutation which makes the initial *f* of the stem disappear altogether in pronunciation. In writing, the mutation is shown by an *h* put after the initial *f*, but the group *fh* is not pronounced at all. In the past there are also two entirely different forms for the affirmative and the negative respectively:

chonaic mé	"I saw"
ní fhaca mé	"I did not see"

These two syntactically conditioned conjugations, the first being used (among others) in affirmative sentences, the second (among others) in negative sentences, are known in Celtic grammar as *absolute* and *dependent* conjugation respectively. The use of these two conjugations was even more diversified in Old Irish, to an extent that is truly amazing. It has already been greatly simplified in Modern Irish. The remarkable thing however is: although we may observe a tendency towards simplification of the use of absolute and independent conjugation in the historical development of Irish and the other Celtic languages, new types of syntactically conditioned conjugations have emerged at the same time from quite disparate sources. Since these newly developed conjugational systems are of comparatively recent origin and since they may have come out differently in the various modern Celtic languages, there is no universally accepted terminology for them. But the principle of the existence of syntactically conditioned conjugations persists unchanged. When one system collapses, another will take its place.

I should like to demonstrate this with an example from Breton. Whereas Irish is the most archaic Celtic language, Breton may be called the most progressive one. This means that it has preserved less Old Celtic words or forms than any other Celtic language. At the same time, it has acquired more new words and features than the other languages. But Breton still stands in the "Celtic tradition", as it were. That is, most concepts of Celtic grammar, including the one we are dealing with now, appear in a new guise, but are not changed fundamentally. One type of sentence in Breton has the following form:

(1) subject pronoun + (2) verb + (3) object:

Ex.	*me a gar*	*va c'herent*
	"I love	my parents"

We may now reverse the word-order and place the object at the head of the sentence. But this is not as simple as it seems, because the change of word-order entails the use of a different conjugational form: the personal pronoun *me* disappears, the first person is expressed instead by an ending added to the verb form: -*an*. The sentence then comes out as follows:

>*Va c'herent   a garan*
>"My parents   I love"

These different verbal forms have nothing to do with the old distinction between absolute and dependent conjugation. But they do show the same principle, namely that of the use of different conjugations, conditioned by different syntactical environments.

The use of different forms of the same verb, according to its position in the sentence, reinforces the impression suggested earlier, that the word in Celtic is not a solid, strictly definable unit, but on the contrary something that changes its form constantly under all sorts of influences: phonetic, morphological, and syntactical. This also gives the sentence as a whole an unstable, almost fluid appearance: a slight modification of the syntactical structure of a sentence, such as turning an affirmative statement into a negative one, changing word-order, or turning a main clause into a relative clause, usually entails a whole series of changes which condition each other. As a result, the words may be changed to such a degree that the modified sentence is hardly identifiable with the original one.

I should like to turn next to another grammatical characteristic of the Celtic languages. This time, I shall be concerned with prepositions, words like *in, on, by, for, with,* and many others. In most languages prepositions may combine with either a noun or a personal pronoun, using in either case the same syntactical pattern. In English for example, we may say: *This is for my friend.* We may then replace the object *my friend* by the appropriate personal pronoun, which forms the sentence: *This is for him.*

In the latter case, the Celtic languages follow a different pattern. Instead of forming a phrase, consisting of preposition plus personal pronoun, they use what we might call an inflected form of the preposition. The prepositions themselves are inflected for person, number and gender. That is, they take endings, very much as verbs do, to express these categories. We may therefore set up inflectional paradigms for prepositions, again very much like those for verbs. The preposition ir. *roimh* "before", for example, gives the following paradigm:

Sg. 1. *romham* "before me"   Pl. 1. *romhainn* "before us"
      2. *romhat* "before you"   2. *romhaibh* "before you"
  3.m. *roimhe* "before him"   3. *rompu*   "before them"
      f. *roimpi* "before her"

When learning a Celtic language, seven personally inflected forms have to be memorized for every preposition. Of course, as with the verbal conjugation, the grammatical persons are characterized by certain recurring endings. For example in Irish, as the above paradigm shows, the first person singular by -*m*, the second by -*t*, the first plural by -*nn* etc.

This is rather unusual for an Indo-European language. Celtic grammarians, therefore, did not know how to deal with it in grammars and teaching books. It is not the object of this paper to criticize Irish grammars. But I should like to make one point clear. Especially in Irish (and Scottish Gaelic) grammars, one finds the personally inflected forms of the prepositions in the chapter on personal pronouns. This, of course, is due to the fact that in languages such as English, French, German, Latin, etc., prepositions combine with the appropriate forms of the personal pronouns. Some Irish grammars even take considerable trouble in explaining how, for example, *roimh* "before", plus *iad* "they", combine to give *rompu* "before them". They inevitably fail because this is not the correct way of explaining these forms. We cannot say that the endings, which in the inflected prepositions express person and number, are in any way alternants, or — as it is even sometimes said — distorted forms of the personal pronouns. Such an explanation does not do justice to the structure of these forms. We must simply accept that the Celtic languages have a different way of expressing these relations, namely that the prepositions are used as base-forms and are inflected for person, number, and gender by the addition of personal suffixes. Since this is a property of the preposition, and since the prepositions — not the pronouns — represent the base-forms, these forms have to be dealt with in the chapter about prepositions, not in the one about personal pronouns.

This is one of many examples which indicates how the presentation of grammatical features may often give a false impression of, or even disguise, those language structures that we are delineating as being typically Celtic. If these structures are viewed through the looking-glass of grammatical concepts that have been set up for languages of an altogether different structure — just as traditional grammar is modelled on the structure of Latin — the distinctive Celtic features will inevitably appear distorted or even remain unrecognized.

I should like to mention briefly a few other grammatical traits of Celtic that do not correspond to the grammar that we are familiar with from other languages.

Celtic is what one might call "noun-centered". That is to say, many concepts that we would expect to be expressed by verbs are in fact expressed by nouns. The most obvious example of this is that Celtic languages have no verb for "to have". Instead of "I have a house", one says "There is a house at me" (Ir. *Tá teach agam*). Likewise, there is no verb for "to know". There is a noun which means "knowledge" and thus instead of "I don't know", one says "There is no knowledge at me" (Ir. *Níl a fhios agam*). And, to mention a last example, Irish does not have a verb for "to love". It does have the noun "love" and so, for "I love you" one would say "There is love at me to you" (Ir. *Tá grá agam dhuit*). This might appear an awkward way of expressing oneself, but the seeming awkwardness comes as a consequence of our habit of thinking in terms of the grammatical structures of our own language. To the Irish lover, *Tá grá agam dhuit* ("There is love at me to you") is absolutely normal and it works just as well as "I love you". In summary we may say that except for the non-existence of a verb "to have", which is rather a speciality of its own, it is especially sensations, feelings, mental activities and abilities that the Celtic languages express through the use of nouns rather than verbs.

Another characteristic feature of Celtic is the clear preference for syntactical coordination instead of subordination. Celtic languages generally have very few subordinating conjunctions and they do not even like to make extensive use of those few. No Celtic language has a proper relative pronoun. We do speak of relative clauses, but their structure is again rather special. Some people are inclined to say that lack of subordination is a mark of primitive, crude language and that languages which lack subordination are primitive languages. This is simply not true. Syntactic coordination is in no way inferior intellectually to subordination. It is true that the complicated rules of traditional grammar for subordination, indirect speech, tense concord, etc. do not generally obtain for Celtic. Instead, the Celtic languages resort to syntactical patterns that are rather ingenious and quite complicated in their own way, just in order to avoid subordination.

I shall take two final examples to demonstrate the necessity of freeing ourselves from the concepts of traditional grammar when we deal with the Celtic languages. In syntax, we are used to a subject-verb concord working in such a way that when the subject is a singular noun, the verb has to be in the singular, and when the subject is a plural noun, the verb has to be in the plural as well. This seems quite natural to us. But in all Celtic languages, there is a rule which states explicitly that when the subject is represented by a plural noun, the verb has to be in the singular. The so-called logic of traditional grammar does not work here. Instead, another principle obtains, the logic of which we cannot dispute. It says: when the notion of plurality is shown in the noun, it does not have to be expressed in the verb a second time. We call this principle the *economic* one. Its purpose is to avoid what linguists call *grammatical redundancy.*

The same principle also works in other cases, for example in phrases consisting of a numeral plus a noun. Here, our conception of logic tells us that numerals from *two* on have to be combined with a noun in the plural: *one house*, but *ten houses*. In Breton and Welsh, however, all numerals have to be combined with the noun in the singular. Therefore "one house" in Welsh is *un tŷ*, "ten houses" is *deg tŷ*. The singular *tŷ* "house", does not change. In Irish, the situation is rather more complicated. In certain cases the singular is used, in certain others the plural. This depends both on the numeral and the noun. In any case, we may keep in mind that in many instances in Irish as well numerals combine with a singular noun. The principle of economy here again says that it is sufficient to express the notion of plurality only once, in this case by the numeral itself.

I should like to conclude by repeating that the grammatical rules of the Celtic languages exhibit many features that do not correspond to our traditional concepts of grammatical logic. These traditional concepts, therefore, do not by any means have a universal application, but have to be qualified when confronted with languages that have a different structure.

NOTES

[1]It is worth noting, perhaps, that there is nothing mystical about the grammatical structure of the Celtic languages. They are perfectly accessible to linguistic description. Certain features may be more complex than in other languages, and some of these features may not have been properly worked out yet. But in principle there is nothing that cannot be stated in precise rules.

[2]Cf. in the Authorized Version of the Bible (1611): "They toil not neither do they spin" (Matthew 6, 28).

THE MATERIAL CULTURE OF THE PAGAN CELTIC PERIOD

PETER J. REYNOLDS

The Pagan Celtic period, normally referred to by archaeologists in Britain as the Iron Age, is one of the most exciting periods of our past, exciting because we know so much and yet so tantalizingly little. We have some outstandingly beautiful objects from this time, fine pieces wrought with consummate craftsmanship.[1] An art form, depending essentially upon the open-ended curve, hints at a philosophy of the most sophisticated kind. This art form seems to reach a culminating point of development some time late in the first century B.C. The high degree of sophistication lies in the use of space allied to a brilliant abstraction of form. After the first century B.C. this form deteriorates into the overcomplex and unsure.

Our evidence for understanding the first millenium before the birth of Christ is drawn from two major sources: the writings of the classical authors and excavations of Celtic or Iron Age sites. We understand from the few classical references that Britain in the Iron Age was a 'fairy isle' set beyond the edge of civilisation. A land of mystery and fascination deep in *Oceanus*, the sea which bounded the edge of the world. At the same time these references tell us that grain and leather, hunting dogs and slaves were exported to the continent, a statement which argues social and economic stability, a multilayered society with production and service industries. Indeed it is worth reflecting that today Britain is a net importer of grain. The documentary sources also tell us of the Druids, the scholar-priest class, and of how it was common practice for the Celtic scholars of Europe to come to Britain for the finest training available,[2] a reference whose authority is borne out by the ferocity with which the Romans sought to eradicate the Druid class, culminating in their mass slaughter on the shores of Anglesey in 60 A.D.

The commentaries of the greatest Roman general of all, Julius Caesar, attest to the military skill and expertise of the British during the abortive Roman expeditions of 55 B.C. and 54 B.C.[3] Indeed it is from Caesar's diaries that we know of the first British personality, Cassivellanus, chieftain of the Catuvellauni and commander-in-chief of the British forces. The fact that Caesar was thoroughly out-generaled and out-manoeuvred in his two expeditions to Britain says much for his political acumen and expertise in that he was able to turn these actual reverses into paper triumphs with his own government.

The glimpses into the society of Pagan Celtic Britain afforded by the classical references clearly indicate that it was a most remarkable and important period of our heritage. We are, however, entirely dependent upon the archaeologist for our information about this period. At this point it is worth stressing the unfortunate dichotomy which exists between the work of the archaeologist and that of the linguist. The common element which regularly escapes both disciplines is the recognition that the material culture, as evidenced by excavation or linguistic studies (whether these studies seek to trace an accurate Indo-European antecedent or devote themselves entirely to a specific body of literature), is people. The archaeologist and his associate, the art historian, have an ability to ignore the human factor, the society which was responsible for the artifactual material. Similarly the linguists can totally absorb themselves into the surviving literature and its complexities and fail to recognise that it is an expression of a culture, a people. The emphasis and wonder that is attached to the 'what' must be ameliorated by a clear study of the 'how' and the 'why'.

This paper seeks to present a way by which a greater understanding of the people might be reached by empirical testing of archaeological material. The fundamental data of archaeology comprise post-holes and pits, ditches and banks, sherds of pottery, objects of stone and flint, fragments of bone and carbonised material and the occasional metal object. As archaeology has matured into a science, so other data are being collected, like snails and pollen; other techniques are being employed, like carbon 14 and thermoluminescence dating, aerial photography, model building and re-building. In the final analysis, however, the archaeologist is little more than a highly sophisticated dustman filtering the debris of a society ever more minutely. It is the valid interpretation of this debris which will afford a greater insight into the reality of Pagan Celtic life.

There is little doubt from both documentary evidence and archaeological excavation that the basic economy of the first millenium and probably the first three millenia B.C. was agriculture. To understand that economy, to establish the boundaries of probability, a unique research project in world archaeology has been set up in Southern England. Called the Butser Ancient Farm Research Project, its brief is to reconstruct and operate a farm as it would have operated in about 300 B.C. The date is arbitrary and indicates only a concentration upon the mainstream period of the Iron Age. In reality it is the first open-air scientific research laboratory devoted to prehistoric agriculture and archaeology. The research project is situated on a spur of Butser Hill, some twelve miles north of Portsmouth in the county of Hampshire. The site was actually occupied in the Bronze Age and Iron Age periods. One of the field monuments is an Iron Age house platform. Subsequently it has only been used as rough grazing. For the purpose of the research it is ideally suited.

O. G. S. Crawford once wrote: 'The disciplined use of the imagination is the highest function of the archaeologist'.[4] The philosophy of the research programme has taken this statement a stage further: that it is necessary to test for validity the hypotheses put forward by the archaeologist. The basic data, the excavated material, is the root of the archaeologist's hypothesis; the testing of the hypothesis involves the construction of an experiment, whether a structure or a process. The result of the experiment, conducted under the most rigorous scientific disciplines, once compared with the basic data will allow a judgement to be made as to the validity or invalidity of the original hypothesis. The context of this paper does not permit a full exposition of the philosophy of archaeology by experiment. This has

Plate 1: A General View of the Butser Ancient Farm Research Project. Source of all photographs: Peter J. Reynolds.

been recorded elsewhere.[5] It is important to present here the results of the research programme in so far as they have radically altered our view of the period in question. It is adequate to report that the research programmes necessarily involve a plethora of different sciences ranging from thermodynamics to mycology, from linguistics to model building.

The construction and operation of a farm provides a far greater insight into the realities and practical implications of a way of life than have previously been recognised. The greatest visual impact of the research programme is presented by the farmstead itself (Plate 1).[6] The reconstruction of Celtic houses clearly adds a new dimension to our appreciation of the people. Throughout the United Kingdom and Ireland and along the western sea board of Europe and Spain, the Celtic houses were circular in plan (Plate 2). Depending upon the natural resources available, a variety of building materials and techniques were employed (Plate 3). The houses shown in the plates were developed as individual scientific research programmes, each based upon a specific excavation that had yielded data of the highest quality (Plate 4). Indeed the experiments have successfully demonstrated how the archaeological data can be subdivided into structural and constructional detail. What is immediately clear is that even if the method of construction may be debated, the materials involved and the space they confine is accurate. These are

Plate 2: Reconstruction, built on excavated foundations, of a Celtic Round-House at Monte Santa Tecla, La Guardia, Spain.

hardly the huts of rude savages. The largest of these reconstructions, indeed the largest reconstruction of a prehistoric house ever undertaken, is probably that of an important personage (Plate 5). Perhaps it is best described as a Celtic Manor house. Over 13.0 metres in diameter and nearly 10.0 metres high, it has a capacity well in excess of the majority of modern houses.[7] Caesar in describing southern England refers to *creberrima aedificia* — large numbers of buildings.[8] Evidence from aerial photography suggests dense occupation of the countryside, with settlements every kilometre or less. Archaeology, similarly, is beginning to support this view. House reconstructions like these hint at a three-dimensional view of Celtic life. A very large population, perhaps by the end of the first century B.C. as many as 4 million, occupied Britain. One further implication of this last structure and the large population is the number of trees required in the building. No less than two hundred oak and ash trees were used. Nor were these ordinary trees in the modern sense but trees specifically grown in coppice plantations so that their final form would be ideal for building purposes. The clear implication is that not only was the land thoroughly dominated and exploited by agriculture but also silviculture was an element of the agricultural process.

The arable programme of the Ancient Farm, however, has produced even more dramatic results. Archaeology has provided us with direct evidence of plough, or

Plate 3: The Maiden Castle House, as reconstructed at the Ancient Farm.

Plate 4: The Conderton Round-House, reconstructed from an excavation of a Celtic Settlement on Conderton Hill in Worcestershire.

Plate 5: The Pimperne House, reconstructed on the evidence of an excavation at Pimperne Down, Dorset.

rather ard, types, in this case from Denmark, where wooden ards from the Iron Age have been recovered from peat bogs.[9] Probably deposited there as votive offerings at sowing or harvest time, the tannic acid has preserved their form. Reconstructions of these ard types are used experimentally at the farm where soil attrition of the wooden share is studied in association with soil movement and faunal destruction (Plate 6).[10] Ancient Celtic fields can still be traced in the British landscape by observing the low banks called lynchets which form on the downhill sides of the field areas. (Plate 7). The fields which survive as field monuments are most likely representative of marginal land being brought under the plough in prehistory. Their survival to the present day is due in the main to the change in agricultural practice late in the third century A.D.

Plate 6: Detail of the reconstructed Donnerupland Ard.

Plate 7: Lynchets on the southern slopes of Butser Hill in Hampshire, indicating the contours of a Celtic Farm.

Plate 8: Basic Wheat Cereals of the Iron Age, Emmer and Spelt.

The basic wheat cereals of the Iron Age were Emmer (*Tr. dicoccum*) and Spelt (*Tr. spelta*) wheats (Plate 8). The discovery of carbonised seeds allows for positive identification of cereal types. The object of growing these cereals, which have been consistently cultivated throughout the millenia, is to establish the kinds of yields that may have been achieved in the Iron Age. The basic variable in such a programme is inevitably the climate. The paleobotanists and paleo-ontologists are convinced that the climate in the first millenium B.C. was directly similar to that of Britain today. Tacitus, who described the British weather as *foedum*— 'filthy', provides documentary agreement.[11] The land area of the research project has probably not been cultivated since the prehistoric period and is free from all modern sprays and herbicides. Thus it is ideal for the purpose.

The cultivation of the cereal crop and its assessment is necessarily a scientific process. At no time is there an element of playing at being a prehistoric Celt.

Nonetheless, one in all probability experiences the same emotions as our ancestral farmers in observing the growing crop. Although a mono-crop is both the expectation and the reality of British agriculture today, this was not so even three decades ago. Indeed it is necessary to dismiss the modern chemical agricultural revolution. It is vital to provide the right competition for a growing crop. The weed flora of prehistory as evidenced by carbonised seed recovered from excavations was not dissimilar to that of the 1920's and 1930's. In spring the greatest enemy was the yellow flowered *sinapis arvensis* (charlock). Later *agrostemma githago* (corn cockle), *centaurea cyanus* (cornflower), *bupleurum rotundifolium* (thorow wax or hare's ear) were pernicious weeds. Today they are virtually extinct and the research programme is fulfilling a conservation role as well. At fruition the crops were a blaze of different colours, the red and purple of poppy, the yellows of buttercups as well as the golden grain (Plate 9). The results of these experiments, essentially interim since valid statistics can only be achieved over a long period, give average yield figures in excess of 15cwts per acre. These figures, the first reliable ones to be achieved, make great sense of the documentary sources. They are incidentally better than the national average yield figure of 12½ cwts per acre achieved in Britain in 1910 A.D.

Analysis of these cereals goes far beyond their cultivation. Their food value in terms of protein per gram dry weight is quite remarkable. Modern cereals average at 8-9% while Emmer and Spelt wheat average 19% and 18% respectively. As in modern cereals, the missing component in the amino acid chain is lysine. this deficiency is readily corrected by eating fish. In this context it is relatively simple to suggest the perfect Celtic meal.

Plate 9: Emmer Wheat Growing in one of the Research Fields at the Ancient Farm.

Wheat was not the only crop grown in the Iron Age. A large number of other cereals, barleys and oats as well as flax were also main crops.[12] Undoubtedly, a large number of herbs were cultivated, including caraway referred to as an additive to beer. Other major crops are evidenced by the carbonised seeds recovered from excavations,[13] notably *Vicia faba minor*, the Celtic or tic bean. Probably, since it fixes nitrogen in the soil, it was grown as a rotational crop to benefit the soil. The fruit, in size midway between the pea and the broad bean, has a delicious nutty flavour and like the cereals is highly nutritious. One further potential major crop, a direct result of the research programme, is *Chenopodium album*, fat hen. Today it is regarded as a weed but originally it was a staple vegetable. The precursor to cabbage and spinach, it has a higher food value than either of its successors.

Finally no treatment of prehistoric plants would be complete without *Isatis tinctoria*, woad. Caesar tells us *Brittani se vitro inficiunt*,[14] the British tattooed themselves with woad. The blue dye they used for this purpose is extracted from the leaves of the first year growth of this biennial plant. The magnificent designs of tattooing have been confirmed by the frozen Celtic warriors of the Iron Age excavated in Siberia.[15]

Throughout the experimental programme devoted to crop production attention is always focussed upon the archaeological data. Each phase of the research has direct relevance and implications for the subsequent stage. Archaeological excavations provide the material evidence, and in this context it is noteworthy that the most common feature discovered in excavations of Iron Age sites (which have been conducted on the majority of rock types in England) has been the underground pit. Its high frequency of occurrence — on one site for example over 200 pits were discovered in an area 40 metres by 40 metres[16] — suggests that it is indicative of a particular way of thinking. It is critical that every effort be made to understand the pit since it is fundamental to the overall Celtic economy. Clearly there are many potential functions but the documentary evidence afforded by Pliny,[17] Diodorus Siculus[18] and Tacitus[19] suggest that one of its uses was for the storage of grain. In the research programme devoted to the annual agricultural cycle, exploration of this hypothesis is fundamental.

More than any other experiment, the grain storage in underground pits serve to underline the complexities of what at face value seems straightforward. The assertion that grain was stored in this way is simple to make but takes no account of the number of variables involved in the how and why, nor does it consider the nature of the stored product. The chemistry of grain storage is relatively simple to understand. Grain uses up oxygen in its respiration cycle and gives off carbon dioxide as the waste product. In a sealed container like a pit, the respiration process uses up the available oxygen and produces for itself an anaerobic atmosphere. The carbon dioxide acts as a preservative inhibiting further respiration. The bulk of the grain quickly enters a state of unstable dormancy, the instability being caused by the presence of bacteria and fungi. For successful storage low temperature and lack of moisture penetration are vital.

The significant factors to emerge from this programme can be summarised as follows: grain can be stored in this way but only during the winter period; the grain is most likely to be seed grain rather than ordinary consumption grain; the existence of the pits indicate that the grain was warehoused for a short term. The average Iron Age pit has a capacity in excess of one ton, and the combination of these factors suggest that there was extremely successful arable farming at the time.[20] This implication is supported by the results of the crop experiments described above, and further serves to support the documentary evidence that grain was exported from Britain to the continent. The growing period of both Emmer and Spelt is significantly longer than modern cereals, with harvest normally taking place in September. By the time collection and storage could be effected, the gales of the equinox rendered the English Channel an inhospitable place to be, especially in a sail-powered cargo boat with sixty tons of grain aboard. Bulk storage, therefore, prior to spring transportation is the logical conclusion, and this is supported by both documentary and archaeological evidence. It further enhances the thesis that Celtic society at this time was fundamentally peaceful, highly organised and well able to sustain both production and service industries. Indeed the emergence of the hill town in the late Bronze Age and on through the Iron Age represents urbanisation and the development of a service industry rather than being intended as a bastion to repulse an as yet unidentified enemy. Of all those so far excavated only two provide direct evidence of Celt fighting Celt.

Within the context of building a prehistoric or Celtic farm, the part played by livestock is inescapable. In this area we are both fortunate and unfortunate. The intensive study of sheep bones from Iron Age sites has allowed the zoologist to define the nature and appearance of the animal which formed an integral part of the agricultural economy. In fact the animal exists to this day. It is believed that the Soay sheep are the direct descendants of the Iron Age sheep (Plate 10).[21] By a quirk of fortune the breed has survived intact for the last two thousand years on the St. Kilda islands off the north-west coast of Scotland. Inevitably there have been minor genetic changes in the breed since they have survived in the feral state. Natural selection of colour, for example, may have removed the white-fleeced Soay, though traces of white are sometimes observed on some of the rams. A small flock of these sheep were brought over from Hirta, one of the St. Kilda islands, in the late nineteen-fifties and early nineteen sixties and the sheep kept on the farm are the descendants of this flock. Naturally fawn and dark brown in colour, they give approximately one kilogramme of soft wool per animal per annum. The wool is plucked and not sheared. Our job is to re-domesticate these Soays and study on the one hand how they fit into the organisation of the farm, on the other how the protected environment may alter their bone structure and general characteristics. Their natural athleticism, they can leap nearly two metres for example, suggests they are unlikely to be herded easily. Bearing in mind the intensive agricultural exploitation of the land, some kind of paddock control was probably practised. One final characteristic of the Soay, which goes some way towards countering the

Plate 10: Soay Sheep — part of the research stock at the Ancient Farm.

idyllic picture of Celtic shepherds watching over their flocks, is that they are impervious to dog control. Scottish folk lore suggests that a flock of twenty is adequate to clothe a family of five people per annum.

In the late Iron Age a new artefact makes its appearance, the sheep shears. Not only does it indicate the use of mild spring steel but it also heralds a new breed of sheep. It is believed that the Shetland sheep were that new breed, possibly coming from Scandinavia. Today, like the Soay, the Shetland sheep are rare and their survival is in danger. Their wool is absolutely ideal for hand-spinning and weaving and makes up into splendid garments.

Unfortunately, the small Celtic shorthorn, *bos longifrons*, is extinct. Since cattle were fundamental to the economy we have had to seek out the nearest equivalent. Again it is the archaeological bone evidence which is the source material. The Dexter cattle, bred from Kerry cattle of Ireland, are the most similar breed. Their skeletal form, general appearance and body weight are virtually the same as *bos longifrons*. These have been trained to the yoke and are used in ploughing experiments and provide the general traction on the farm (Plate 11). There is unfortunately no real opportunity here to discuss the place of cattle in Celtic society other than to allude to their overall importance from the practical viewpoint as an indication of wealth. Even today, in many areas of the world, especially in the remote areas of northwest Spain, cattle are still regarded as an

Plate 11: The Dexter Cattle trained for ploughing.

indication of a man's wealth and status in society.

One other breed which qualifies within this context are the cattle of the Highlands. Another unimproved breed, they are basically small, capable of doing well on relatively poor pasture and amenable to training. In many ways they qualify as virtual direct descendants of the Celtic short-horn.

The domestic fowl of the Iron Age are more difficult to isolate simply because their bones are far less durable than those of mammals. In addition one suspects that dogs, including breeds similar to the Irish wolf-hound of today, would have dispatched all traces within a remarkable short space of time. From a few sites, however, we can identify the bones of *gallus gallus* sp., the Indian Red Jungle Fowl, and its immediate successor, the Old English Game Fowl. Probably these were introduced into the Celtic world late in the second millennium B.C. and for the age-old purpose of sport. Cock-fighting was undoubtedly a Celtic pursuit. Bronze spurs for fighting cocks have been recovered from several sites. Caesar also refers to the keeping of animals saying that they, the Celts, thought it wrong to eat chickens and geese but that they kept them *animi causa*. This phrase can be interpreted in a variety of ways but an adequate translation would be 'for the sake of pleasure'. Since cock-fighting as a sport has endured to the present day, there is little doubt that the Celts would have avoided eating the sporting birds; those that failed to qualify, on the other hand, would have taken their proper dietary place.[22]

The geese referred to above were the species *anser anser*, the grey lag. Evidence for their domestication comes from one of the most famous of Iron Age sites at Glastonbury in Somerset.[23]

The livestock, here only cursorily treated, form an integral element within the working of the research project. Indeed the whole programme is exactly similar to a laboratory. Each experiment is an entity and capable of standing as an individual research exercise. In due course the results of all the individual experiments may be taken together to begin to give an overall picture of what a Celtic farm of the prehistoric period may have been.

This paper is an attempt to give a brief exposition of the Butser Ancient Farm Research Project. Inevitably within the space allowed I have been able to refer only to very little of the detailed research that has been carried out and is in the process of being carried out at the present time. Throughout, the emphasis has been placed upon the reality, the people. There is little value in comprehending a people only by their funerary monuments. Our knowledge of prehistory is small and the majority of that knowledge is largely untested.

In conclusion I would like to reiterate the underlying philosophy of the work at the Butser Ancient Farm Research Project. Margenau, in his work *The Nature of Physical Reality: A Philosophy of Modern Physics*, said:[24] "The process of accumulating scientific knowledge involves the formulation of rational, logical, deductive theories, the 'rules of correspondence' between the theories and the real world, and testing whether the observations of the real world confirm or disprove a theory. In the most rigorous sense no theory can be proven true or validated. It can, however, through proper experimentation be invalidated. A theory can be considered valid only after repeated conduct of experiments which by their design appear capable of proving the theory invalid. If such invalidation constantly fails to occur, then the theory may be tentatively accepted as valid."

In short, we are fortunate to know as much as we think we know.

NOTES

[1] See J. Brailsford, *Early Celtic Masterpieces from Britain* (London 1975).

[2] See S. Piggott, *The Druids* (London 1963).

[3] *De Bello Gallico*, Books IV and V.

[4] O. G. S. Crawford, *Archaeology in the Field* (London 1954), 49.

[5] See J. Coles, *Archaeology by Experiment* (London 1973), and my "Experimental Archaeology and the Butser Ancient Farm Research Project" in *The Iron Age in Britain*, ed. J. Collis (Sheffield 1978), 32-40.

[6] See my *Farming in the Iron Age* (Cambridge 1976).

[7] My report on the 'Pimperne' House will be published soon.

[8] *De Bello Gallico*, Book IV.

[9]See G. Lerche, "The Radiocarbon-Dated Danish Ploughing Implements," *Tools and Tillage* 1, I (Copenhagen 1968), 1-20.

[10]See my article, "Experiment in Iron Age Agriculture," *Transactions of the Bristol and Gloucestershire Archaeological Society*, 86 (1967), 60-73.

[11]*Agricola*, XII.3.

[12]H. Helbaek, "Early Crops in Southern England," *Proceedings of the Prehistoric Society*, vol. 18, pt. 2 (1952), 190-233.

[13]See J. M. Renfrew, *Paleaoethnobotany* (London 1973).

[14]*De Bello Gallico*, Book V.

[15]See S. I. Rudenko, *Frozen Tombs of Siberia* (London 1970).

[16]See B. W. Cunliffe, "Danebury, Hampshire. Second Interim Report on the Excavations 1971-5," *Antiquaries Journal*, vol. 56 pt. 2 (1976), 198-216.

[17]*Natural History*, XVIII, 306.

[18]*History*, V. 21.5.

[19]*Germania*, XVI. 4.

[20]See my "Experimental Iron Age Storage Pits — an Interim Report," *Proceedings of the Prehistoric Society*, vol. 40 (1974), 118-31.

[21]See P. A. Jewell et al., *Island Survivors* (London 1974).

[22]See my article, "The Domestic Fowl in Iron Age Britain," *Journal of the World Pheasant Association* (1978).

[23]See A. Bulleid and H. St. G. Gray, *The Lake Villages of Somerset* (Glastonbury Antiquarian Society, 1911).

[24](New York 1950).

Figure 1: Generalized Distribution Map of Passage Tombs.

THE PREHISTORIC FOUNDATIONS OF THE CELTIC WEST:
PASSAGE TOMBS AND EARLY SETTLED LIFE IN WESTERN EUROPE

GEORGE EOGAN

INTRODUCTION

A feature of parts of Europe during the Neolithic period, and the beginning of the Metal Age, was the construction of burial monuments. Sometimes these were rock-cut but more usually they were built above ground; in the construction of the tomb and kerb, massive stones were frequently used, hence the term megalithic (from the Greek words *mega* — great and *lithos* — stone). It does seem that the primary form of megalithic tomb was the passage tomb and it can be defined as a structure that consists of a passage leading into a chamber, the whole being covered by a round mound. Indeed, from the start various forms of passage tombs were constructed; furthermore, some varieties of tombs emerged that are so modified that their line of ancestral development has been lost.

In general, megalithic tombs occur in the western part of the continent, mainly in Ireland and Britain and in the coastal parts, from Iberia to south Scandinavia. Megalithic tombs were also built in some of the Mediterranean islands, notably the Balearics, Sardinia, Sicily and Malta. Certainly the tomb builders were not inland dwellers: tombs, for example, are unknown from central Spain or eastern France. In those regions where megalithic tombs occur there is a tendency to find them on lands that would have been suitable for some aspect of agriculture, although in some areas fishing must have been an important factor in the economy of the builders.

Probably up to 20,000 megalithic tombs were constructed in the relevant parts of Europe. The earliest tombs may have been built during the 4th millennium B.C., even back into the 5th; the latest around 2,000 B.C. As megalithic tomb building covers a large span of time and a wide geographical spread, considerable variation in form is to be expected. In addition the burial rite changes as do the grave goods. However, the passage tombs do show a certain unity of form; therefore, they may reflect cultural cohesion over large parts of Europe. Various views have been put forward as to the place of origin of the passage tombs and their significance. Some authorities[1] have attributed their development and spread to the adaptation of certain religious beliefs by the inhabitants of western Europe, but others tend to consider them as part of a cultural spread. It is at least clear that megalithic tombs were constructed by early farming communities who paid considerable attention to a cult of the dead.

ORIGINS OF FARMING

The development of farming or food production — the domestication of animals and plants and their cultivation — was an event of outstanding importance in the history of mankind. During the immensely long Palaeolithic period and the shorter Mesolithic stage man lived by hunting, collecting and gathering whatever nature could provide; in other words, he was totally dependent upon nature. But man the farmer began to co-operate with nature, and this led to certain beneficial results: the provision of a staple food supply, technological and architectural developments, and, most important of all, a transformation of society. As Gary A. Wright has concisely put it, "food production . . . is the economic foundation upon which the state and modern civilization are built and maintained."[2] In the old world the arts of farming developed in Western Asiatic lands as early as the 8th millennium B.C.[3] In that region one can trace the emergence of farming communities out of hunting-gathering Mesolithic people. Dame Kathleen Kenyon's excavations at Jericho in the Jordan valley of Palestine has enabled archaeologists, so to speak, to see this development taking place under their eyes.[4] From this kernel area farming spread to Europe and it appears that farming was being practised in the west Mediterranean area from around the 6th millennium B.C.[5] These earlier farmers (the so-called Cardium Ware people) sometimes buried their dead in caves.

THE BEGINNINGS OF COLLECTIVE TOMB BURIALS

In the western Mediterranean area an important land is Spain, with Portugal to the west, and it may well have been in this region that new burial practices came into being or were adopted. One of these was the rite of collective burial and the exercise of this rite could have led to the construction of special monuments to contain the remains of the dead. Sometimes the monument consisted of a tomb carved out of the living rock (rock-cut tombs), but more usually an overground structure, a passage tomb, was built. There are several thousand passage tombs in the Iberian peninsula, mainly in the south and west, and these vary considerably in type and in size.[6] Sometimes the tomb consists of a parallel-sided passage often divided into segments by transverse slabs which on occasions have a hole through them ("port-hole"). The chamber can be a well-defined circular structure that on rare occasions can have one or two small side-chambers or recesses opening off it to one side or to either side. In other tombs the distinction between the passage and chamber is not so clear-cut. The passage just widens out and merges into the chamber which tends to be rectangular in shape. In some tombs the passage and the circular chamber are of small dry-stone construction (the tholos tombs), but the majority of examples were constructed with large untrimmed blocks or megaliths. Where the chamber is well defined this is usually roofed in bee-hive shape by corbelling. The covering mound of earth or stones, depending on local geology, is circular, its edge may be defined by larger stones or dry-stone walling.

Some of the mounds and tombs, especially in southern Spain, are very large. Cueva de Menga at Antequera, near Malaga, is over 75 feet long, nearly 20 in maximum width and 9 feet in height. The adjacent tomb, Cueva de Romeral, has a passage about 75 feet long. This leads into a bee-hive shaped chamber nearly 17 feet in diameter and over 12 feet high. At the back of this chamber there is a smaller but similar chamber. The covering mound is up to 280 feet in diameter.

Sometimes tombs were grouped to form a cemetery, Menga and Romeral together with Cueva de Viera being an example of this. But the best known cemetery in Spain is that of Los Millares a dozen miles or so inland from the city of Almeria. There, there are about eighty tombs.[7]

The predominant burial rite is inhumation, and objects, or grave goods, were usually placed with the remains. These include pottery (plain vessels but also decorated ones, some with "oculi" motifs), flint artifacts, polished stone axes, decorated stone objects such as plaques (usually of schist), "crosiers", crescentic objects, "pine cones", and replicas of sandal soles in ivory. Apart from decorated objects in the tombs, on rare occasions decoration is found pecked into the surface of the structural stones.

FRANCE

There are probably 6,000 megalithic tombs in France as well as a small number of rock-cut tombs.[8] There is an important concentration in Languedoc.[9] In the south passage tombs with rectangular chambers are frequent, although tombs with P or Q-shaped chambers are also known. Passage tombs are also known in west-central France; there are also cemeteries in this area, such as that in the Forêt de la Boixe, Charente.[10] But the important area is Brittany.[11] The Breton passage tombs display considerable variety in tomb plan. The chambers may be circular, polygonal, square, cruciform or V-shaped. Most were constructed from large stones, but dry-stone built tombs, tholos-like, are also known. The passage tombs have a distinctive coastal distribution: most occur in Morbihan, indeed the area around the Gulf of Morbihan is one vast cemetery. Cemetery grouping, but on a smaller scale, is known elsewhere, for instance close to Pornic, south of the Loire, and there is also the remarkable site at Barnenez South in north Finistère. This long cairn, 270 feet by 75 to 100 feet broad covers a row of eleven passage tombs. But the covering mounds are normally circular and are often carefully constructed. Internal unifaced walls are a feature of tombs and often a similarly constructed wall formed a kerb. Inhumation was the predominant burial rite and the grave goods consist of pottery, usually round-bottomed bowls either plain or with a slight shoulder. Other objects include stone beads.

The array of decorated objects that were such a feature of the Iberian passage tombs does not occur in Brittany; however, decorated structural stones are more frequent.[12] One of the most highly decorated chambers is in Brittany. This is the tomb of Gavr'inis, situated on an island in the Gulf of Morbihan. The tomb is in a round mound, about 180 feet in diameter, the passage, around 52 feet long, leads

Plate 1: Decorated Orthostat, Gavr'inis, Brittany. Photograph: P. R. Giot.

Plate 2: Decorated Orthostat, Gavr'inis, Brittany. Photograph: P. R. Giot.

Plate 3: Decorated Orthostat, Gavr'inis, Brittany. Photograph: P. R. Giot.

into a smallish rectangular-shaped chamber. Practically every orthostat is decorated and most lavishly at that (Pls. 1-4).

To-day in those parts of Brittany where passage tombs occur the land is poor from the agricultural point of view and even in Neolithic times it may not have been good farming land. In any case, the close proximity of the tombs to the sea suggests that fish was an important economic factor in the lives of the builders. Indeed, they appear to have been seamen as well as land men. If the tomb distribution reflects a settlement pattern it may then be assumed that they were skilled seamen who probably had largish (skin?) boats suitable for use on the open sea and enabling them to follow shoals of migrating fish. It is against this background of land and sea men that we must consider the passage tomb settlement in Ireland.

Plate 4: Decorated Orthostat, Gavr'inis, Brittany. Photograph: P. R. Giot.

IRELAND

This is another key area for passage tombs. Up to three hundred are known and amongst these are the largest and most spectacular tombs that were ever erected (Pls. 5-9).[13] As there is no positive evidence that passage tombs emerged in isolation, it must be assumed that they were introduced into the country from outside. The evidence available, tomb plan and art in particular, strongly suggests that the first passage tomb builders stepped from a boat that had set out from Brittany.

Human occupation commenced in Ireland around 7,000 B.C. but this occupation was very much confined to the north-east, early sites being Toome Bay and Mount Sandel both in the Bann Valley of Co. Derry.[14] There is, however, no evidence that these Mesolithic people developed the arts and crafts of farming or took to the building of burial monuments or other permanent structures. Subsequently, farming and food production were introduced into Ireland and an aspect of the new society that was established were certain religious beliefs, most likely a belief in the after-life; at least an elaborate cult of the dead was practised and this involved the construction of megalithic tombs. The new economy and new burial rite that was introduced appears to have been as an adjunct to the coming of an influx of new people. The passage tomb builders need not be the earliest of these first farmers, but they must have arrived by at least 3,000 B.C., probably even earlier. In view of similarities, close in some cases, between the Irish passage tombs and those of Iberia and Brittany, the background to the Irish series should be sought in those Atlantic lands. But on geographical grounds it may be Brittany, and, as has been previously pointed out, the Breton passage tombs have a marked coastal distribution, indicating that their builders were "sea people" as well as "land people". As the Breton concentration is around the Gulf of Morbihan, it would appear that that was the homeland of the earliest passage tomb builders that arrived in Ireland. Apart from the hazards of the open sea, the distance as the crow flies between Finistère and southern Ireland is no further than between Finistère and the mouth of the River Seine. Indeed, it is possible that Atlantic seaways became active during the 3rd and 4th millennium B.C. It is probable that there were considerable comings and goings; connections, too, between Ireland and Iberia may have been established. But it need not be assumed that connections were solely one way. It does not then seem unreasonable to support the view put forward by Herity that passage tomb builders from Brittany reached Ireland before the end of the 4th millennium B.C.[15] — and perhaps they "discovered" Ireland because they were drawn north-westwards on fishing enterprises.

Distribution. The evidence to hand suggests that, contrary to expectations, the initial settlement of passage tomb builders took place not in the south but well up the east coast in the Meath-north Dublin area. In this connection it may be mentioned that the area from the mouth of the River Delvin at Gormanstown

Plate 5: Knocknarea, County Sligo. Aerial photograph looking northeast. Source: J. K. St. Joseph, Director of Aerial Photography, University of Cambridge.

(Meath) to Bremore (Dublin) contains passage tombs directly on the coast (some have disappeared in recent centuries due to wave action), locations that recall some of the Breton positions. And whatever about deep-sea fishing, certainly coastal gathering of shell fish played its part in the economy, as the shell mound in the covering tumulus of the Knocklea passage tomb shows.[16] From the coastal belt passage tomb builders moved inland. The ridge of Fourknocks is only a few miles inland from the coast up the valley of the Delvin river (Pl.10). There are a number of round mounds in that area and at least two covered passage tombs.[17] But it was a few miles up the valley of the River Boyne, at Brugh-na-Bóinne, that a cemetery of tombs, which includes some of the most spectacular passage tombs ever constructed, was built.[18] Further upstream, at Broad Boyne Bridge between Slane and Navan, a tomb was built on the river bank,[19] while the earliest definite monument known on the famous Hill of Tara is a passage tomb. In the north-west of Co. Meath, tombs occur at Loughcrew (Sliabh na Caillighe) (Pl. 11). There is, indeed, a rich and varied series of tombs in the Meath area and it may have been from that area that passage tomb builders spread to other parts. In the main, passage tombs are distributed to the north of the central plain. There are important concentrations in Sligo, and tombs were constructed in all the Ulster counties with the exception of Cavan and Monaghan. To the south of the central plain the greatest number occur in the hill country of Dublin and Wicklow, but tombs are virtually absent in south Leinster and Munster.

Siting. Passage tombs are generally found on hill-tops. Even in the low-lying Boyne valley the prominent sites are situated on the highest land available. Some occur high up on mountain tops, as in Wicklow, Sliabh Gullion in South Armagh, or on the Bricklieves (Carrowkeel), Co. Sligo.

Grouping is another feature. Tombs may be scattered, as in the Wicklow mountain area, or they may be closely knit into a cemetery. Important cemeteries are those of Brugh-na-Bóinne and Loughcrew (Co. Meath), Carrowkeel and Carrowmore (Co. Sligo), and Kilmonaster (Co. Donegal). Examples of smaller cemeteries are at Fenagh Beg (Co. Leitrim), Sess Kilgreen (Co. Tyrone), and close to the village of Donegore (Co. Antrim).

The Brugh-na-Bóinne cemetery extends over an area of about 3 miles in length: it is a sort of tongue of land that is bounded on three sides by the River Boyne. There are up to thirty sites in this cemetery and amongst these are the three most outstanding passage tombs known: Dowth, Knowth and Newgrange. Each of these mounds cover over an acre, that at Knowth close to an acre and a half: they are therefore the largest passage tomb mounds known. The Dowth mound is 280 feet in diameter and it covers two chambers. The larger of the two has a passage almost 27 feet long. The chamber is cruciform but it is unusual in that there is an extension to the southern recess. The Newgrange mound is pear-shaped and it measures 260 by 280 feet (Pls. 12,13,14). It is about 36 feet in height and is delimited by 97 kerbstones. The passage is 62 feet long and the cruciform-shaped chamber has maximum measurements of 17 feet long and 21 feet, 6 inches wide.[20] The principal mound at Knowth covers two large tombs that were placed back-to-back. The entrance to one tomb faces west; it is about 114 feet long and the chamber tends to be rectangular in shape. The eastern tomb is much more impressive and it is about 130 feet in total length. The straight passage leads into a massive cruciform-shaped chamber.[21] At Knowth there is a cemetery in its own right. To date excavations have uncovered eighteen tombs; more than half of the Brugh-na-Bóinne tombs are concentrated at Knowth.

The Loughcrew cemetery is mainly spread over three summits: it consists of around thirty tombs. Carrowkeel has about a dozen tombs, with a small number at Keshcorran nearby. Carrowmore has the largest cemetery of all. Unfortunately a number of the sites have been destroyed but originally the cemetery may have consisted of between sixty to eighty tombs. A mile or so to the west is the most

Plate 6: Rathcoran, Baltinglass Hill, County Wicklow. Source: University of Cambridge.

dramatically situated passage tomb of all, the great Miosgain Méadhba, situated on the summit of Knocknarea overlooking the broad Atlantic (Pl. 5). There are four small tombs beside it. The Kilmonaster cemetery consisted of about twelve sites but a few have been removed.[22]

Type and Structure. As in other countries, Irish passage tombs display considerable variation in tomb plan and in structure. The mound is, however, circular, but in some sites, Newgrange and Knowth 1, for instance, there is an inward curve of the edge before the entrances. Depending on local geology, stones or earth were the materials used; at Knowth 1 the mound was constructed in an elaborate fashion by laying down layers of different material. It was the practice to delimit the edge by kerb stones set end-to-end. The mounds can vary in size. Some average 15 yards in diameter but Knowth 1 is about 100 yards.

The passage and chamber were constituted from large stones (orthostats) which were set in sockets and secured in position by packing stones. The shape of

Plate 7: Newgrange, County Meath. Aerial photograph. Source: University of Cambridge.

the tomb varies. In the simplest form the passage gradually widens outwards and the chamber is the inner and widest part of the passage but it is usually delimited from the passage proper by a transverse flag set on edge, a sill stone. The passage and chamber could be roofed by laying capstones or lintels across, resting directly on the tops of the orthostats, although in some cases smaller stones were placed on top of the orthostats in order to increase the height.

In the other main variety, the tomb is divided into passage and chamber. The passage is parallel-sided and roofed with lintels. The chamber tends to be rounded. The largest is that of Fourknocks 1; it is nearly 23 feet across. The tomb is pear-shaped (Pl. 10). Side recesses, usually three in number, very often open off the chamber; this gives a cruciform shape. But in some of the Loughcrew and Carrowkeel tombs there is a doubling up of the recesses on the sides. In the roofing of the tombs with a definite chamber, considerable architecture and engineering skills were employed. These roofs were often carried to a great height, 20 feet at Newgrange and Knowth east, and this was achieved by the skilful use of the corbelling technique.

Plate 8: Knowth, County Meath. Aerial photograph. Source: University of Cambridge.

Art. In the Iberian peninsula a number of objects that were placed in the tombs as grave-goods were decorated and it is only rarely that decoration is found on the structural stones of the tombs. Art pocked on to the structural stones becomes more common,[23] and in Brittany there is the remarkably decorated tomb at Gavr'inis (Pls. 1-4). In Ireland, but mainly in the Meath area, decoration is applied in abundance to the stones, both kerb and tomb. Two main techniques were used, incision and pocking. Incision was more sparingly used than pocking. This art of the passage tombs is non-representational: geometric designs such as circles, lozenges and triangles are common. So are zig-zags, spirals and U-shaped designs. Instead of being merely decoration, it is more likely that the designs were part of a symbolism that was associated with a cult of the dead (Pls. 13-17).

Burial rite and grave goods. Cremation was the principal rite. Sometimes the deposit may consist of the remains of an individual but usually the remains of more than one individual are represented. In general, passage tombs were used for communal burial; furthermore there is evidence of successive burials. The burial

Plate 9: Tara, County Meath. Aerial photograph. Source: University of Cambridge.

deposit could have been placed on the ground surface, on a flag, or (more rarely) in a stone basin, a most elaborate example of which occurs in the east tomb at Knowth 1 (Pl. 18). Grave goods are fairly common. Amongst these are pottery vessels, pendants and beads of stone and bone (very likely the remains of necklaces) and antler or bone pins.

Habitation. Very little is known about the living plans of the builders. At Townleyhall, Boyne Valley, the house consisted of a stake structure, hardly used all the year round.[24] Occupational debris, but no evidence for a house, was found under the mounds of passage tombs at Baltinglass, Co. Wicklow, and the "Druid's Stone" at Ballintoy, Co. Antrim[25]

Plate 10: Fourknocks, County Meath. Interior of Chamber of Passage Tomb. Source: Commissioners of Public Works in Ireland.

Plate 11: Loughcrew (Sliabh-na-Caillighe), County Meath. Source: Commissioners of Public Works in Ireland.

Plate 12: Newgrange: Chamber looking out to passage from end recess. Source: Commissioners of Public Works in Ireland.

Plate 13: Newgrange. Entrance Stone. Photograph: M. J. O'Kelly.

Plate 14: Newgrange. Kerbstone, no. 52. Photograph: M. J. O'Kelly.

Plate 15: Fourknocks. Decorated Stone in Chamber. Source: Commissioners of Public Works in Ireland.

Plate 16: Knowth, County Meath. Entrance Stone before Western Tomb. Photograph: George Eogan.

Plate 17: Knowth. Kerbstone to the south of entrance to Eastern Tomb. Photograph: George Eogan.

Plate 18: Knowth. Stone basin in Eastern Tomb. Photograph: Eric Kwint.

BRITAIN

Passage tombs are rare in Britain and they are confined to the western regions. There is a small group of "entrance" passage tombs in the Isles of Scilly and west Cornwall.[26] But these are probably late in date. The greatest concentration of passage tombs occur in Anglesey, about eight tombs.[27] One of these, Barclodiad y Gawres, is a typical cruciform passage tomb with art.[28] In fact there was probably close connection between eastern Ireland (probably the Boyne valley) and Anglesey.

Passage tombs are also known in Scotland.[29] Good examples occur in the Hebrides, such as Barpa Langass in North Uist, and again in the extreme north, at Camster, Caithness, for instance, but more notably in the Orkneys where, at Maes Howe on the main Island, there is a magnificent example. There a 53 feet long passage leads into a 15 foot square chamber. This is formed by a lower course of monoliths with corbelling above. Three side recesses open off the chamber. The circular mound is 115 feet in diameter and 24 feet in height. The Scottish tombs may be related, even derived from, the Irish series but they display evidence of local adaptation.

NORTHERN EUROPE

In particular, Denmark and southern Sweden are exceedingly rich in megalithic tombs, where there are probably as many as 6,000 passage tombs and dolmens.[30] For a considerable time it has been argued that the earliest megalithic tombs were the dolmens which developed in that area. However, the distinction in ground plan between some of the dolmens and passage tombs is not great, so the difference is perhaps exaggerated. The typical Swedish and Danish passage tomb was built from rough blocks of stone. The passage is parallel-sided and the chamber tends to be sub-rectangular. The covering mound is usually circular. Inhumation is the burial rite and at some sites large numbers of pottery vessels were placed as offerings outside the tomb entrance.

THE BREAK WITH ORTHODOXY

What can be considered as considerable changes in the basic tomb plan is especially noticeable in the southern Breton area and southwards to the Gironde.[31] The use of side chambers, or transepts, take on a definite form and the building of long mounds also took place. It appears that sub-groups were emerging and these became vigorous in their own right. It was from that region, or more specifically from around the mouth of the Loire district (there are important transeptal sites at Pornic), that a movement took place to the Bristol Channel area of England and gave rise to the Severn-Cotswold group of tombs with their transeptal chambers and long mounds.[32] These include the great site of West Kennet, Wiltshire. This tomb has two pairs of transepts on each side and an end chamber. The trapizoidal-shaped mound is 330 feet long.[33]

On the chalk areas of England, such as Wiltshire, Dorset, Sussex, Lincolnshire and Yorkshire, there are the "unchambered" long burial mounds.[34] But excavation has shown that a wooden chamber existed; indeed, wood seems to have taken the place of stone in the chalk areas. The chambered and unchambered long barrows of England and Wales seem closely related.

A parallel movement brought another type of megalithic tomb to Ireland. These are the court tombs and they are characterised by having an unroofed ritual court.[35] This may be a full court and it can be centrally placed at the broader end of the cairn. Full court tombs are confined to the north Mayo-south Donegal region and they are usually massive structures. The cairn at Creevykeel, Co. Sligo, is almost 200 feet long. A semi-circular court is more common. This occurs at one end of the cairn but in some examples, notably in mid-Ulster, dual court tombs are known. The chamber, or chambers, lead off the court. These are parallel-sided and they are divided into two or more segments by an arrangement of sill and jamb stones. The long cairn tends to be trapezoidal in shape. It was revetted by stone blocks or dry-stone walling. The burial rite was generally cremation and the grave-goods include plain round-bottomed pottery vessels, flint arrowheads, stone axes and stone beads. Court-tomb builders lived in rectangular wooden houses, a good example is that located at Ballyglass, Co. Mayo. There are about 300 such tombs in Ireland and they are concentrated north of a line from Achill Island in the west to Dundalk in the east. Professor de Valera has cogently argued that the earliest tombs occur in the west. From there they spread across Ulster and later to Scotland.[36]

Out of court tombs developed the portal tomb. These tombs have a small rectangular chamber with a sort of portico at the outer end. They have a huge capstone. The chamber is set at one end of a long cairn. About 150 examples are known, mainly in the northern part of the country. They spread down along the east coast to Munster and also across the sea to Britain, especially to Wales and Cornwall.[37]

REMARKS

While immediately reflecting the religious beliefs of early farming communities of western Europe, the passage tombs demonstrate inter-connections over large areas but above all they throw considerable light on the organisational and constitutional abilities of these early farmers. The construction of a monument, as large as say Menga in Spain or Knowth in Ireland, was a major enterprise. It involved the mobilisation of a large labour force and this suggests that society may have been hierarchial. But it also implies that this society was served by a skilled "professional" class, the equivalents of engineers and architects. None of this could be achieved, however, unless passage tomb societies had developed and secured a sound economic basis and that must have been mixed farming and, no doubt in certain areas, fishing. We can, therefore, picture western Europe during the 4th and 3rd millennia in particular as an area of well-organised, stone-using farmers and fishermen. Already this society was probably stratified and it practised a cult of the dead that involved the construction of what remains some of the greatest architectural wonders of the old world.

NOTES

[1]See V. Gordon Childe, *Prehistoric Communities of the British Isles* (London 1940), p. 45; Euan MacKie, *The Megalith Builders* (Oxford 1977).

[2]"Origins of Food Production in South-Western Asia," *Current Anthropology*, 12 (1971), 447-77.

[3]See James Mellaart, *The Neolithic of the Near East* (London 1975); Purushottam Singh, *Neolithic Cultures of Western Asia* (London and New York 1974).

[4]*Archaeology in the Holy Land* (London 1960), pp. 36-57.

[5]Patricia Phillips, *Early Farmers of West Mediterranean Europe* (London 1975), pp. 44-74.

[6]See Georg and Vera Leisner, *Die Megalithgräber der Iberischen Halbinsel: Der Süden* (Berlin 1943), and *Die Megalithgräber der Iberischen Halbinsel: Der Westen* (Berlin 1956, 1959, 1965).

[7]See Martín Almagro and Antonio Arribas, *El Poblado y La Necrópolis Megalíticos de Los Millares* (Madrid 1963).

[8]See Glyn Daniel, *The Prehistoric Chamber Tombs of France* (London 1960).

[9]For the Hérault Dept. see Jean Arnal, "Les Dolmens du Départment de l'Hérault," *Revue Préhistoire*, 15 (1963), pp. 1-250.

[10]Claude Burnez, *Le Néolithique et le Chalcolithique dans le Centre-Ouest de la France* (Paris 1976), pp. 33-6.

[11]See Jean L'Helgouach, *Les Sépultures mégalithiques en Amorique* (Rennes 1965).

[12]See M. and St. J. Péquart and Zacharie Le Rouzic, *Corpus des Signes Gravés* (Paris 1927).

[13]See Michael Herity, *Irish Passage Graves* (Dublin 1974).

[14]See G. F. Mitchell, "The Mesolithic Site at Toome Bay, Co. Derry," *Ulster Journal of Archaeology*, 18 (1955), 1-16, and Peter Woodman, "Mount Sandel," *Current Archaeology*, 5 (1977), 372-6.

[15]*Irish Passage Graves*, pp. 181-204.

[16]*Ibid*, p. 173.

[17]See P. J. Hartnett, "Excavation of a Passage Grave at Fourknocks, Co. Meath," *Proceedings of the Royal Irish Academy*, 58 C (1957), 197-277, and "The Excavation of Two Tumuli at Fourknocks, Co. Meath," *Proceedings of the Royal Irish Academy*, 71 C (1971), 35-89. Subsequent references to this Journal will be abbreviated to *P.R.I.A.*

[18]See George Coffey, *Newgrange and other incised Tumuli in Ireland* (Dublin 1912), and Séan P. Ó Ríordáin and Glyn Daniel, *Newgrange and the Bend of the Boyne* (London 1964).

[19]See my "A Probable Passage Grave Site near Broadboyne Bridge, Ardmulchan, Co. Meath," *Journal of the Royal Society of Antiquaries of Ireland*, 104 (1974), 146-50.

[20]See Claire O'Kelly, *Illustrated Guide to New Grange* (Cork 1978).

[21]See my "Excavations at Knowth, Co. Meath, 1962-1965," *P.R.I.A.*, 66C (1967-68), 299-400, and "Report on the Excavation of Some Passage Graves ... at Knowth, Co. Meath," *P.R.I.A.*, 74C (1974), 11-112.

[22]See Séan Ó Nualláin, "A Ruined Megalithic Cemetery in Co. Donegal," *Journal of the Royal Society of Antiquaries of Ireland*, 98 (1968), 1-29.

[23]See Péquart and Le Rouzic, *Corpus des Signes Gravés.*

[24]See my "A Neolithic Habitation Site and Megalithic Tomb in Townley Hall Townland, County Louth," *Journal of the Royal Society of Antiquaries of Ireland*, 93 (1963), 37-81.

[25]see P. T. Walshe, "The Excavation of a Burial Cairn on Baltinglass Hill, Co. Wicklow," *P.R.I.A.*, 46C (1940-1), 221-36, and J. M. Mogey, "The 'Druid's Stone', Ballintoy, Co. Antrim," *Ulster Journal of Archaeology*, 4 (1941), 49-55.

[26]Glyn Daniel, *The Prehistoric Chamber Tombs of England and Wales* (Cambridge 1950), pp. 61-4.

[27]Frances Lynch, *Prehistoric Anglesey* (Llangefni 1970), pp. 17-83.

[28]See T. G. E. Powell and Glyn Daniel, *Barclodiad y Gawres* (Liverpool 1956).

[29]See Audrey S. Henshall, *The Prehistoric Chamber Tombs of Scotland*, 2 vols. (Edinburgh 1963 and 1972).

[30]See C. A. Nordmann, *The Megalithic Culture of Northern Europe* (Helsinki 1935), and Ernst Sprockhoff, *Atlas der Megalithgräber Deutschlands*, 3 vols. (Frankfurt 1965 and 1975).

[31]Burnez, *Le Néolithique et le Chalcolithique*, pp. 21-87.

[32]See J. X. W. P. Corcoran, "The Cotswold-Severn Group," in T. G. E. Powell, *Megalithic Enquiries in the West of Britain* (Liverpool 1969), 13-106.

[33]See Stuart Piggott, *The West Kennet Long Barrow* (London 1962).

[34]See Paul Ashbee, *The Earthen Long Barrow in Britain* (London 1970).

[35]See Ruaidhrí De Valera, "The Court Cairns of Ireland," *P.R.I.A.*, 60C (1959-60), 9-140, and "Transeptal Court Cairns," *Journal of the Royal Society of Antiquaries of Ireland* 95 (1965), 5-37.

[36]Michael Herity and George Eogan, *Ireland in Prehistory* (1977), p. 50 (fig. 17).

[37]*Ibid.*, p. 85.

SECTION III
MYTHOLOGY, LITERATURE, RELIGION, AND ART

THE ART OF THE CELTIC PEOPLES

LIAM DE PAOR

For the purposes of this paper I take the 'Celtic peoples' to mean those peoples who, at one time or another in the past, were speakers of languages of the Celtic group. This is a tall order in several respects. For one thing, we have inadequate knowledge of the early history of the Indo-European languages and do not know how to recognise, with reasonable confidence, by archaeology or otherwise, the speakers of original Celtic.[1] Informed guesses on this topic vary widely.[2] Essentially, we depend on early accounts by non-Celtic reporters, such as Herodotus[3], to give us our bearings. Such sources supply the word 'Celtic' itself, a term which has been extended by modern scholars and others to apply to cultures which never heard of Celts, and which had no idea that they might be classified with other cultures in the group now called 'Celtic'.[4]

But even if we define our limits conservatively, we are still left with an enormous range of time and place: from the second millennium B.C. to the present day; from Ireland to Asia Minor. The Celtic peoples today, by a strict definition, consist of some of the people of Brittany, some of the people of Wales, and a handful of people scattered in tiny isolated communities along parts of the west coasts of Ireland and Scotland. Even within this reduced remnant we are dealing with several cultures. Apart from language, what they have in common that we might identify as 'Celtic' is largely artificial and the result of romantic or nationalist revivalism of the past two or three centuries. There is a highly self-conscious Celticism, for example, in the popular music of Alan Stivell and the groups known as Horselips and Lindisfarne which gives them something of a common character, but this is contrived rather than derived from the musical traditions to which they all refer.

One can therefore make few generalisations about 'the art of the Celtic peoples' without employing categories which are observer-imposed. There are, however, certain continuities which give us links from one Celtic culture to another and - in those parts of the ancient Celtic world which escaped the doubly disruptive effects of Roman conquest and Germanic invasion - there are links from the prehistoric to the historic past. To attempt a chronological survey of these would provide an exposition which would necessarily be compressed and would probably be somewhat arid. It seems preferable to examine instead some characteristics of the art of Celtic cultures which may be particularly durable.

The Celts of later prehistory, the people of Central Europe about whom the Greek and Latin writers first inform us, remained on the margins of the expanding world of Mediterranean urban civilisation. Other groups of the Indo-Europeans were drawn into that world - the Hittites, the Greeks, the Iranians, for example - or, like the Aryans, moved into the area of non-Mediterranean urban culture. Some Indo-European groups remained separated at one or two removes from the urban world, for example, the Germanic and Slavic peoples. The Italic and Celtic peoples were ultimately more or less absorbed by Mediterranean culture; but the Celts in particular developed their characteristic institutions, myth, and perception of the cosmos as a high barbarian culture exposed to the great tensions and instability characteristic of systems straddling the divide between the desert and the sown.[5]

It is important to remember, in this respect, that analogies between ancient urban civilisations and modern urban culture cannot usefully be pushed very far. When we compare both with external barbarian cultures we find a vast difference in the technology gradient. Modern empires have imposed themselves on the whole world by a superior rational organisation (including in particular the manipulation of money) combined with greatly superior technology which provided good communications and good weapons. The urban civilisation of the ancient Mediterranean had a social organisation which was much more complex than those of the cultures north of the Alps and which was literate and numerate. But in many respects the barbarians were the superior in technology, in agricultural methods, for example, and in the metallurgy of iron. The old tag, *ex oriente lux*, which thirty years ago could be applied to the diffusion of crafts and knowledge as well as arts and letters from the eastern Mediterranean to prehistoric Europe, has had to be discarded because the coercive evidence of radio-carbon dating has forced us to concede that very often the innovatory and doctoral system was that of the northern or western barbarians. Newgrange and Gav'rinis, both in lands which came to be occupied by Celtic-speaking people, are much older than the pyramids.[6] The German excavations at Numantia, in Spain, where Scipio Africanus, the victor of the Punic Wars, carried out extensive siege operations, recovered large numbers of iron weapons. From these and other finds it seems that the weapons of the Republic, with which Rome was to conquer the Mediterranean world, were largely based on Celtic prototypes.[7] It was neither technology nor innate superiority - for Rome's soldiers came to be drawn from the barbarian world - but organisation that gave the Romans the edge.

Each side of the divide both admired and looked down on the other. The barbarians admired and envied the stability, wealth, order and elegance of the civilisations south of the Alps. But they feared and disliked the organisation which made these civilisations possible. They resented the concept of an order externally imposed upon them, and the speeches which Mediterranean historians put into the mouths of Celtic leaders very frequently touch on the topic of freedom.[8] Freedom, of course, was not for the populace at large, but for the warriors, whose required behaviour was recklessness, vainglory, valour beyond reason: the story of the hero taking his weapons to fight the sea is widespread.[9] The Celts who were met by a general of Alexander the Great somewhere in Dalmatia and asked what they feared most in the world, instead of answering diplomatically that what they feared most was Alexander himself, replied that they feared *nothing* - except that the sky might fall upon them. This may be a reference to the oaths which Celtic people swore by the elements, or by sky, wind or sun, calling on these natural forces to avenge the foresworn oath.[10] Leaders of tribal alliances took megalomaniac titles - Dumnorix, Vercingetorix, etc. An excess characterised them, which was envied, admired, feared and despised by the careful methodical Romans - but also by the earlier Etruscans and Greeks. The relationship between the Roman and the Celt was something like the nineteenth-century relationship between the British colonialist and the Afghan, or the early-twentieth-century relationship between the Englishman and the Arab, with similar overtones of homosexuality, militarism, retarded adolescence, and uneasy comradeship in loyalty or enmity against wily Bengalis, Greeks, Phoenicians or other clever people who lacked the military virtues and were unsound in politics. The Celt was a decent chap, a worthy foe, only occasionally given to regrettable excesses.

The frontier zone, with its military background, is where the acculturation process took place which is the background of the art of the Celtic peoples. Two stereotypes offer us the contrast between the view from the Roman side of the frontier and the view of the Celts themselves. The 'dying Gaul', a favourite Hellenistic theme,[11] shows us the idealised noble savage, caught in the pathos of beauty and nobility inevitably broken and overcome by the majesty of empire. Observation is frozen into a stylised view. A few distinctive points are noted and sketched: the spikiness of limewashed hair, the heavy metal torque, sacred and ornamental, the warrior's nakedness which scorns protective covering but, more aggressively, implies womanliness in the foe, the drooping moustache which both certified the barbarian and distinguished his ethnic species. It is a type, the marble somehow suggesting the blue-eyed blondness which is what the Mediterranean observers perceived in the warrior peoples from north of the Alps (Plate 1).

The head - it might well be of the same warrior - from Mšecké Zehrovice shows the type again, with torque, limed hair and heavy moustache, but quite differently observed. There is no pathos here, of the wild thing tamed by civilisation and death, but rather the deincarnation or apotheosis of the warrior. This is a head: the body is discarded: the Celtic artist's synecdoche, eschewing the mere mechanics of representation, found in the human (or divine) head a sufficient focus for meaning and, in rendering its features, used a notation quite different from that of the classical artist. Psychology, like the body, is omitted. What we have instead is a concentrated expression of meaning, the godhead of warriordom, where the features are stylised, as if the mere accidents of human shape were irrelevant, in favour of an energetic pattern. The large staring ovoid eyes are a durable cipher, and this prehistoric head from Bohemia can be matched more than a thousand years later in metal and stone from Ireland (Plate 2).

The famous coin series - a typology of devolution - in which the Parisii and other Gaulish tribes can be seen imitating and adapting the stater of Philip II of Macedon until both the head of the king on the obverse and the two-horse chariot on the reverse become abstract or geometric patterns, shows us the direction of the process by which Celtic artists adapted classical motifs. They made patterns out of images.

But this particular series is an hypertrophy, for generally the Celt stopped short of the full reduction to abstract pattern and retained in however stylised and distorted a way something of the original natural form. Indeed he regularly complemented the process, finding in abstract patterns suggestion of natural forms, or in foliage the shapes of animals, in animals' limbs and crests the shapes of leaves. A dynamic balance, one form or one mode on the point of passing into another, is characteristic of Celtic design (Plate 3).

For this reason the balanced ambiguity of masks and disguises is especially attractive to the Celtic artist. Men were disguised, or half-disguised, as animals by wearing horned or crested helmets which made them taller, distorted their shapes and suggested tribal totems or divine avatars. Such disguises are, of course, found everywhere, among warrior peoples from the south Pacific to the forests of Africa or the plains of North America, in Greek hoplites and Roman legionaries, and on the Horse-guards' Parade in Whitehall. Celtic artists added a subtlety which is almost a further disguise. Not content with the gross shape of horns or boar-crest which could strike unease into the foe, they added to the warrior's display fine and subtle patterns and techniques which, if they served the same purpose, must have done so in the manner of secret spells written in an arcane language. Beautifully but finely wrought patterns, cast, chased or beaten in sheet bronze, shallowly and subtly engraved, touched with delicate and minute chequers of polychrome enamel, ornament the warrior's equipment. They could not be read across a battlefield, but they must have added greatly to the value of weapons and military harness, and perhaps they conveyed the same message as the warrior's own nakedness: a scorn to bring into the hazard of war anything save what was most fine and valuable: a boast as loud as a warcry. If we look at, for example, British objects like the Waterloo helmet, the Battersea shield or the Stanwick horse-masks, we find in the lavishing of delicate craftsmanship on equipment which must encounter sling-shot, spear-thrust and sword-cut, an extravagance, not merely of material wealth but of spirit, which is echoed in the Irish sagas and in *their* echoes (Plates 4, 5, 6):

> A great man in his pride
> Confronting murderous men
> Casts derision upon
> Supersession of breath;
> He knows death to the bone -
> Man has created death.[12]

This is to say, perhaps, no more than that the world of early Celtic art, the chief patrons of which were warrior aristocrats, was the world of an heroic age. But the extravagance, the scorn for the contingent, endures. The 'white martyrdom' of the Christian monks who stormed the pinnacles of Skellig or Slieve League, or put out on the Atlantic to 'seek a solitude in the pathless sea'[13], found its counterpart in some aspects of the art of the Christian period. The most dedicated and superb craftsmanship in the Tara Brooch is in the ornamentation of the reverse, which would have lain against the wool of the wearer's cloak; the richest metalwork and settings of the Ardagh Chalice are on the underside of the foot: there is a conspicuous absence in this art of bourgeois calculation (Plates 7 and 8).

The prehistoric Celts were a central European people, transmitting to the west impulses from the east, most notably the knowledge and use of iron. Their art initially reflected some of the forms developed by nomads and semi-nomads over the vast reaches of the Eurasian steppe, which extended to the remote east from the Celtic lands. Scythians, Cimmerians, Thracians, Illyrians passed on both skills and motifs, and the Eurasian animal style found its way into central Europe. Bird and animal protoms abound in early Celtic metalwork, and birds and animals figure largely in the religious cults and religious art of the early Celts. Other impulses came from the south: the wine trade, which came to be of great importance, brought Greek and Etruscan vessels and equipment north of the Alps, as we see for example in the rich grave-goods from the Mediterranean buried with a Celtic princess at Vix, in France. The elaborately decorated wine-vessels - great *kraters*, bronze jugs, and other equipment - exercised such an influence on the recipients that one scholar has written forthrightly that Celtic art is a product of Celtic thirst.[14] We can see the absorption of classical motifs beginning in such objects as the wine-jug (oinochoe) of Celtic manufacture from Basse-Jutz on the Moselle. Acanthus and vine scrolls and similar foliate forms gave rise in course of time to the subtle and extraordinarily dynamic curvilinear patterns of developed La Tène art. This sometimes has a baroque richness, as in the Waldalgesheim style, named from exquisitely wrought gold personal ornaments found at a place so called in Germany; sometimes, as in the engraved ornament of the Lisnacrogher sword-scabbards from north-eastern Ireland, or the Birdlip bronze mirror from south-western England, the curves flow into over-all linear patterns - almost wholly abstract in their feeling - with contrasting textures of hatched and unhatched bronze. But whether in chunky repoussé or in chased line-patterns, we find a continuing and very widespread preference for sinuous and coiling forms, for near-abstraction, and for a tense balance which always avoids exact symmetry.

Over much of Europe the originality and liveliness of mature La Tène art gives way to the deadening effects of mass production and uniformity associated with the Roman conquests. A late Celtic industry in small ornamental bronzes catered, under Roman rule, for the military frontiers from Hadrian's Wall to the mouths of the Danube, and beyond, producing a multitude of cast openwork pieces and small polychrome enamels; but these lack life compared with earlier work.[15] Some of the finest productions in the late La Tène style had come from workshops on or near the Irish Sea - they include superb chased and relief bronzes like the piece from Torrs, as well as fine work in lathe-spun bronze - and after the Roman conquests of most of the Celtic lands of the west, the La Tène tradition lived on beyond the frontiers, in Scotland and Ireland.

These countries, however, came under powerful Roman influence. It seems that, from the third century A.D. (if not even earlier) the Irish chieftains began to imitate Roman, or at least Mediterranean, costume and personal ornaments.

Cranked pins and penannular pins came into fashion, and the Germanicised styles of the late imperial frontier - belt-buckles and strap-tags, kerbschnitt brooches, and, finally, animal patterns, began to be adapted in Britain and Ireland. The period of the Völkerwanderung, of the abandonment of Britain by the legions and of the migration into the western provinces of many different groups of barbarians, provided a remarkable variety of stimulus for changes of style. In the old Celtic heartland, there was now a Germanic overlay on the Roman conquest, and this extended to parts of Britain. Beyond, in northern and western Britain and in Ireland, Roman, Germanic and traditional Celtic motifs competed for the fancy of the artists and craftsmen. The steady spread of the Romanising Christian faith added to the complexity of the process. In Pictish Scotland, whirls of prehistoric serpents competed and mingled with strange symbols derived from Roman icons or from native traditions of animal ornament. In Ireland, the varied curvilinear forms of Iron Age times gave way to a fashion for elegant spinning patterns of 'trumpet spirals' winding in and out of one another with increasingly colourful touches of enamel. Interlacings, biting animals, polychrome frets and keys were rapidly added to the patterns in bronzework - soon metamorphosed into enamel-like painted manuscript pages - in an eclectic style that, far from being swamped by the new borrowings, contrived to retain both the spirit and the basic organisation of prehistoric Celtic art. Iron Age society absorbed Roman Christianity without Roman conquest, and the culture remained both firmly integrated and remarkably self-confident. The carapace of imperial order in which Christianity reached the far West was dissolved, to be replaced by an order that was neither rigid nor wholly organic: the obsessive reiterations that are characterised by the serpentine writhings and coiling of Celtic visual forms.

The order comes from within: this is the key to what is 'Celtic' in Irish art of the early Christian period. It cannot be imposed by T-square and set-square, or marked off by numbers like the lay-out of a Roman camp, nor even guided by a development of harmonic modules like a Greek entablature: it spirals out from the heart of the design; it expresses neither essence nor being but constant becoming, and the artist must have been as fully engaged in every veering of a line as in the planning of his overall design. A fair comparison is the calligraphy of the Far East. The master calligrapher can charge and poise his brush, stare at and absorb the blank page, and then swiftly place the right shape in the right balance in the right place. This the early Irish artist could do - with the Chi-Rho Monogram of Christ, for example, on an unsquared slab of stone, as in the Inis Cealtra grave-marker (Plate 15). This is why modern imitations of 'Celtic' (i.e. early Irish) manuscript pages, which depend on elaborate, imposed, setting-out patterns of squares, rectangles, triangles and compass-drawn curves, are as dead as doornails.

The Book of Kells is rightly famous as a supreme product of the final phase of this art. As difficult, and in some ways as alienating to the modern consciousness, as *Finnegans Wake*, it repels and fascinates because its order, barely controlling an explosive anarchy, allows us to glimpse the chaos at the heart of the universe which our own Romanised culture is at pains to conceal.

From the ninth century onwards the Celtic spirit, in so far as it survived from prehistory, was in retreat before the advance of Romanesque Europe. It becomes increasingly difficult to trace continuities, at least in the visual arts. Literature, oral or written, is a different matter. There is some evidence for the transmission of a conspiratorial culture, like that of the European Jews or that of the Japanese Christians, by which some tenuous threads link the distant Celtic past to communities in modern Scotland, Wales or Ireland; the occasional oath or spell, or reference to a forgotten saga:

> in rustic speech a phrase,
> As in wild earth a Grecian vase.[16]

NOTES

[1] The topic has been much discussed. See in particular Barry Cunliffe, *The Celtic World* (London 1979) and H. Hencken, *Indo-European Languages and Archaeology* (Amer. Anthrop. Ass. Memoir 84, 1955).

[2] For Ireland, for example, the range of date offered for the arrival of Celtic speakers is from before 2000 B.C. to round about 350 B.C.

[3] See the discussion in J.J. Tierney, 'The Celtic Ethnography of Posidonius', *Proc. Royal Irish Acad.*, 60 (C)(1960), 189-275.

[4] There is, so far as I know, no evidence that the early Irish ever thought of themselves as belonging to any such grouping.

[5] The Celts themselves, of course, were agriculturalists. See S. Piggott, *Ancient Europe* (Edinburgh 1965), Chapter 6, for a succinct account of these relationships.

[6] See Claire O'Kelly, *Illustrated Guide to Newgrange and the other Boyne Monuments* (Cork 1978), p. 69.

[7] A. Schulten, *Numantia*, vols. 1-4 (Munich 1914-31).

[8] E.g. the speech of Critognatus at the siege of Alesia, Caesar, *De Belo Gallico*, VII,5.

[9] Long accounts of the reputed recklessness of the Celts are given by Diodorus Siculus (V 29-32) and Strabo (IV, IV 2).

[10] See D. A Binchy, "Secular Institutions", in M. Dillon ed., *Early Irish Society* (Dublin 1954), pp. 52-65.

[11] The type is probably derived from the sculptures erected at Pergamon in the late third century B.C. by Attalus I to celebrate victories over the Galatians.

[12] W.B. Yeats, 'Death', *Collected Poems* (London 1950), p. 264.

[13] Adomnan, *Vita Columbae*, ed. A.O. and M.O. Anderson (Edinburgh 1961), pp. 246-51.

[14] J.M. de Navarro, 'Massilia and Early Celtic Culture,' *Antiquity*, 2 (1928), 435.

[15] F. Riegl, *Spätrömische Kunstindustrie* (Vienna 1927).

[16] Padraic Colum, *Collected Poems* (New York 1953), p. 120.

Plate 1: The Dying Gaul. Source: Museo Capitolino, Rome.
Roman copy in marble of a Pergamene bronze original. This famous representation is from a group of figures at Pergamon which celebrated the defeat of the Galatians who invaded Asia Minor in the third century B.C. The sculpture combines observation of the appearance and equipment of the Gaul with a particular perception of the nature of the barbarian. The warrior has fallen on his oval shield; a war-trumpet lies under his left leg, and his sword and its baldric have fallen to the ground; he sinks down on them, bleeding from a mortal wound in the right side of his chest. He is naked except for the metal torque round his neck, and his limewashed hair is stiff and spiky. With all the barbaric detail, the figure is idealised — the type of the beautiful, tall, blond, blue-eyed northerner described by the Greek writers. Naked valour is insufficient against superior organisation; yet it is admired. This is the 'noble savage'.

Plate 2: Head of a Celtic warrior from Mšecké Žehrovice, Bohemia. La Tène period. Source: National Museum, Prague.

Plate 3: Gold coin of the Parisii, a Celtic tribe who inhabited the region of modern Paris. The stylised head derives from a Hellenistic prototype. Early first century. Source: Bibliothèque Nationale, Cabinet des Medailles, Paris.

Plate 4: Horse-mask mounting from Stanwick, Yorkshire. Source: The British Museum.
The latest, or ultimate, La Tène art styles, are expressed most commonly in flowing repoussé curves, swelling and attenuating, swinging with a perpetual uncertainty as to which change of direction will come next, tending always towards the forms of winding and unwinding trumpet-spirals. The uncertainty was used to produce abstract designs of great restlessness, which never quite departed from naturalistic forms, or forms derived from nature which tended towards a restless abstraction — as may be seen in this bronze mounting from the Brigantian territory of northern England, dating from the time of the Roman conquest. It is a stylised horse-mask which is also a composition of repoussé curves.

Plate 5: Waterloo helmet. Source: The British Museum.
It was not the Vikings, but the Celts, who wore horned helmets. Sometimes actual ox-horns were fitted to the helmet; sometimes the horns, as in this example from the Thames at Waterloo, were artifacts. It can be seen that this is a composite object, of sheet bronze, the separate pieces being riveted together, as in the construction of vessels such as cauldrons. The headpiece is enriched with studs and low-relief ornaments of subtle and sophisticated design in curvilinear forms. Compare this battlefield equipment with, on the one hand, the effective but crude blazons of Norman knights; on the other, the intimate, domestic ashtrays and lamps of fin-de-siècle art nouveau: a paradox.

Plate 6: The Battersea Shield. Source: The British Museum. From the Thames at Battersea.
The Celts, if they went unclad to war, carried large shields which could be as extravagant an assertion of barbarian aristocratic contempt for the hazards of battle as the nakedness itself. This example, which dates from the first century B.C., the period immediately before the Roman conquest of Britain, is a remarkable achievement of the bronzeworker's skill. The design is composed around the central boss (found on virtually all shields) and the smaller upper and lower bosses appropriate to this long shape. From these, which are picked out, emphasized and made gaudy with enamels, the metalworker has developed an ornamental scheme of restless, indeed uneasy, stylish complexity in abstraction.

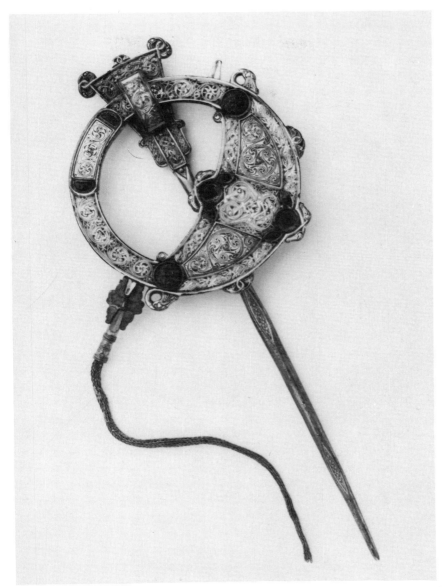

Plate 7: The Tara Brooch. From Bettystown, Co. Meath. Source: National Museum of Ireland.
This little silver cloak-pin, embellished with gold and studded with amber, displays a peculiarly Irish extravagance and excess characteristic of the last phase of La Tène tradition. It was made about A.D. 700. The view shows the reverse of the brooch, that face which would rest against the fabric in use and so would not be visible. The patterns on this side are both more minute and more traditional, relying largely on the old Celtic trumpet-spirals. The spandrels of the crescent plate have splendidly elaborate trumpet-spirals in openwork, cut from silver foil and set against a copper sheet which shows the spinning and whirling designs in relief against the silver. The brooch was probably one of a pair, since there is attached to it by a hinged clasp a trichinopoly chord which was presumably linked to a counterpart brooch on the other shoulder.

Plate 8: The Ardagh Chalice: inner ring of base. Source: National Museum of Ireland.
The splendid silver chalice found at Ardagh, Co. Limerick, in a hoard with a smaller, plain chalice and some brooches, was made probably in the early eighth century A.D. It is in the Hiberno-Saxon style which show the powerful influence of Roman and Germanic techniques and motifs as well as the native tradition. Perhaps the Celtic, or at least the insular, tradition is best illustrated by the extravagance of ornament concentrated on the concave underside of the foot, immediately under the stem of the chalice, where a large crystal is set and is ringed with elaborate kerbschnitt reliefs. These include, as well as newly borrowed animal and interlaced designs (probably, like the kerbschnitt relief technique itself, of Germano-Roman origin) a middle ring of flowing trumpet-spirals punctuated by glass studs with inlays.

Plate 9: The Derrynaflan Paten. Source: National Museum of Ireland.

The hoard, comprising of a silver chalice, silver paten, silver paten-stand, silver strainer and bronze bowl, found at Derrynaflan, Co. Tipperary, in 1980, demonstrates that the Celtic metalworking tradition, heavily Romanised, was flourishing in Ireland about the beginning of the eighth century A.D. The hoard at the time of going to press was being conserved in the laboratories of the British Museum and being studied by the staff of the National Museum of Ireland. Preliminary releases of information indicate that some of the pieces, such as this paten, are of the same superb quality of workmanship as is known from the Tara Brooch and the Ardagh Chalice.

Plate 10: Wine-flagon from Basse-Jutz. Source: The British Museum.
A pair of these was found: they probably came from a grave. The vessel is of bronze and in its general shape and design closely resembles the Mediterranean prototypes. But there are significant and interesting differences. The Celtic craftsman of the early fourth century B.C. who made these objects (found on the Moselle) has made subtle modifications in the form, has adapted the animal forms — e.g., of the handle — to early Celtic taste, and has employed on the other ornaments techniques which by this date had become familiar to the Celts, notably the inlaying of coral, whose colour is heightened by touches of red enamel. Wine was an extremely expensive import from the south, the luxury of aristocrats: the art is the product of aristocratic patronage.

Plates 11 and 12: Gold bracelet and detail of gold torque from Waldalgesheim. Source: Rheinisches Landesmuseum, Bonn.

In a chariot-grave at Waldalgesheim in Germany, dating from about 300 B.C., was found a group of rich objects, including a decorated bucket, a wine-flagon, and these and other personal ornaments in gold. The full flowering of La Tène art, exemplified in this chieftain's equipment, drew heavily on the inspiration of such motifs as the Greek stylised acanthus, but stylised them still further, producing flowing designs in which the natural forms are all but lost, and tending towards a baroque exuberance of surface and feeling.

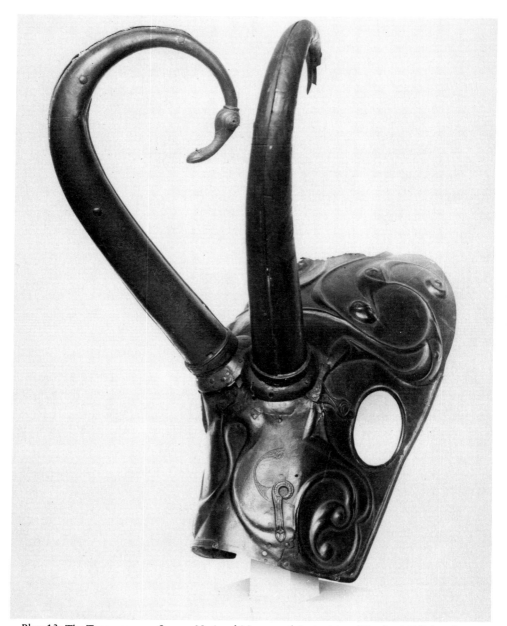

Plate 13: The Torrs ponycap. Source: National Museum of Antiquities of Scotland, Edinburgh. This remarkable animal-ornament, into which two horns have been mounted, comes from Kirkudbrightshire. It displays the features which were to give a distinctive character to the late La Tène metalworking of both sides of the Irish Sea, including the flowing forms, distantly related to foliage, in relief, and the extraordinarily dynamic alternation between plastic and graphic qualities, as between abstraction and a kind of abstract naturalism.

Plate 14: A horned god? Source: Armagh Cathedral.
This stone carving is one of several gathered into Armagh Cathedral which are thought to represent pagan Celtic deities. Its date is uncertain, and may be quite late. It shows a different side of Celtic art from that of the ornamental metalworkers: the attempts made often, as here, by rustic craftsmen, to portray the powers of the otherworld.

Plate 15: Grave marker, Inis Cealtra, Co. Clare. Source: National Museum of Ireland.
Christianity, the most powerful of the Romanising influences which affected the Celtic cultures of the far west of Europe, eventually transformed the art tradition. But this was strong enough to have a powerful influence on the rendering even of motifs imported from the Roman or sub-Roman world. In this little sandstone grave-marker, of the early seventh century, the Chi-Rho Monogram of Christ — a very widespread Christian symbol from the early fourth century onward — has been wholly absorbed into the native tradition, and everything about the way it is handled — including the trumpet-spiral serif of the Rho — is in the spirit of Celtic art.

Plate 16: Durham MS A II 10. Source: Durham Cathedral Library.
The Hiberno-Saxon style of the seventh and eighth centuries A.D. found its fullest expression in Gospel manuscripts, in which Latin letters and Mediterranean motifs were absorbed into an already established tradition of ornament and were transformed by the distinctive Celtic imagination. This fragment of a Gospel book shows an early stage of the process, in the first half of the seventh century.

Plate 17: **Dunfallandy sculptured stone.** Source: National Museum of Antiquities of Scotland, Edinburgh.

The Picts of northern Scotland lived at the remote edge of the Celtic world. They had a distinctive culture which under Roman influence produced an art in which symbols, of uncertain significance, recur, in standard forms. Converted to Christianity by the Britons and the Irish, the Picts left a long-enduring mark on the emergent hybrid culture of early medieval Scotland. Its most striking monuments are the great cross-slabs and sculptured stones on which the old symbols are associated with narrative figured scenes and with fantastic animal forms.

MYTHOLOGY IN EARLY IRISH LITERATURE

PROINSIAS MacCANA

It is in the nature of things that myths and mythologies sooner or later lose their 'truth', their living relevance, when the world to which they relate has fallen apart or been superseded; when this happens they become a mere pastime, a source of entertainment and — especially with the coming of writing — the stuff of literature. The kind of culture change which reduces old myths and creates new ones in their place may be a matter of evolutionary change over a long passage of time or, as in modern colonized territories, it may come about rapidly through political conquest, the introduction of a new language and social values or the establishment and propagation of a new religion. Ireland experienced one such period of rapid change during the fifth and sixth centuries when Christianity achieved the status of a quasi-official religion, bringing with it its Latin culture, its morality and canon law, and the use of writing. The literature which survives in Irish from the following centuries is more or less profoundly marked by the effect of this altered environment, and one of the basic problems for the student of literary tradition is precisely to assess the extent of this influence, in other words to decide how substantially the characteristic conservatism of Irish tradition has been modified by the externally derived innovations of Christianity and its accompanying culture. What I had proposed to do in the present paper was to examine this problem from a specifically literary point of view and to try to show how the authors of the extant written literature handled the mythology they had received from oral tradition, but very soon I realized what I should have known from the outset: that this subject is too vast and too complex to be adequately summarized in a single paper. Instead, therefore, I shall content myself with something much more modest. I shall take a couple of specific texts and seek to show from them how, in recording native mythology, some specially gifted and imaginative authors were able to transcend the role of mere scribe or redactor and consciously to adapt the received material to the artistic sensibilities of their own time and their own relatively sophisticated circle.

But first it is necessary to provide some brief introduction by way of setting the literature in its historical context; and what I mean by literature in its historical context is, of course, that part of Irish literature that is anchored in time by the very fact of its being written.

Sometime in the sixth century one or more monastic scholars adapted the Latin alphabet for the writing of Irish and thereby set in motion a cultural revolution the consequences of which they themselves could not possibly have foreseen. Whatever their initial motivation may have been — and most likely it was proselytistic, as with most pioneers of literacy — the orthographical system they had devised was soon used to record purely secular tradition, first legal and other didactic matter but later comprising a wide range of literary genres. As a result, Ireland can claim to have, apart from the Classics, the earliest written vernacular literature in Europe.

Now it need hardly be said that traditional literatures undergo change when committed to writing, not only because of the transfer to a new medium, but also because of the cultural values and associations that are bound up with the new medium and which tend to be introduced together with it. In Ireland writing was the child of Christianity and continued to be associated mainly with the monasteries up to the cultural and political watershed of the Church reform and the Norman invasion in the eleventh and twelfth centuries; — the remarkable thing is that its use was extended so quickly to include so much of native pagan tradition, a fact which is generally regarded — no doubt correctly — as testimony to the liberalism, or cultural loyalty, of the Irish monastic *literati*. But this should not be taken to mean, as it generally has been, that their recording of native tradition is free of conscious bias or distortion. They preserved a remarkable wealth of pagan story, usage and belief, much of it extremely archaic and a good deal that might seem amoral and scabrous to modern eyes, but, as I have argued elsewhere, they were for all that selective in what they preserved, and there are certain crucial areas of pre-Christian belief and practice which are almost wholly undocumented and yet which we know must have existed because the general contextual pattern suggests so and because the suppression of evidence has not been wholly effective.

Needless to say, the ideologically motivated distortion and recasting of tradition did not begin with Christianity — orthodox 'historical' oral literature will always tend to reflect, explain and justify existing political situations and the actual distribution of political power; but there are several important reasons why the changes that followed the introduction of Christianity were of a very special kind: First, the establishment of Christianity coincided more or less with the rise of great Irish dynasties whose interests alone required that genealogies be reconstructed and mythic narratives re-stated. Secondly, while Christianity came unsupported by military might, it was armed nonetheless with a formidable cultural prestige which no doubt accounts in very great degree for the ease with which it was accepted by some of the Irish nobility. And thirdly there is the fact that the ideological changes introduced by Christianity were compounded with the stylistic and thematic changes that followed from the use of writing. The general effect was that native tradition (which is something wider than what we normally understand by literature, though it includes it) was considerably transformed from the fifth and sixth centuries onwards. Exactly how far-reaching this transformation was we will never know, since only the written, eclectic text survives and only through the exercise of the most delicate and cautious extrapolation can something of the content and extent of the integral oral tradition be inferred from it, but nonetheless, so abundant and so varied is the written text that it carries within itself the clear evidence of manifold alterations and adaptations.

As I have already indicated, a good part of this change springs from the desire of monastic scholars to suppress or to soften traditions of native myth and ritual which clashed too blatantly with the central doctrines of Christianity (a topic which I am not directly concerned with in this paper.) This apart, there are two other (not unrelated) problems concerning early Irish literature which are for me as fascinating as they are intractable: first the relationship between the written literature and the oral tradition from which in the main it derives, and secondly the attitude of the monastic redactors to vernacular mythology and the use they made of it in their texts.

The first of these questions I have touched upon frequently elsewhere and I do not propose to discuss it in any detail here. But one point is worth stressing, if only because it is sometimes forgotten even by scholars working in the field: oral literature did not cease with the coming of writing; on the contrary, it continued as abundant as ever, independent of the written literature though not necessarily unaffected by it. In the nature of things, however, we can know it only in so far as it is reflected in the written text. As regards the form, we can be reasonably confident that the relatively full, extended style, often lapsing into rhetorical prolixity, which we find in Middle Irish texts, is closer to the style of oral narrative than is the prose of the Old Irish period, or classical Old Irish prose as it is sometimes called. Essentially this older prose is distinguished by its terse, direct diction, and I have argued elsewhere that its immediate origins are to be sought in the early attempts at composing written synopses of oral narratives. This partly accidental product was then cultivated as a consciously literary instrument.

But the frame of reference of this written literature was still the multifarious oral tradition which, unlike its written offshoot, was at the disposal of all and enjoyed free passage from province to province and from class to class. Consequently the monastic redactor could shape the phrasing of his narrative in the sure knowledge that his readers (or auditors) would be sensitive to the vast and flexible range of connotation which existed in its full vitality and variety only within the oral tradition. Familiar as they were with the wide reaches of native myth and legend and customary law and ritual, they would have had little difficulty in fleshing out in their imagination what was said laconically or only half-said in the written text. In particular they would have responded instinctively to the dimension of the supernatural, the otherworldly, which is never absent from Irish narrative. Modern anthropologists have commented on the deep and continual concern of people in Irish rural communities of, say, thirty or forty years ago with the inter-relationship between the two worlds, and there can be no doubt that this is one of the underlying continuities from primitive to modern Irish society: certainly it is clear that the monastic *literati* were constantly fascinated by all the possible implications of the interplay of the natural and supernatural orders.

A good example of the literary use of incidental allusion and implicit reference is the tale known as *Noinden Ulad*, 'The Debility of the Ulstermen'.[1] It is one of two aetiological tales intended to account for the strange weakness which afflicted all the adult Ulstermen except Cú Chulainn during the course of *Táin Bó Cuailnge* 'The Cattle-raid of Cuailnge':

Crunnchu mac Agnomain was a wealthy commoner and a widower. One day he saw
a strange and beautiful woman coming to the house. She entered and went round the
room in the ritually propitious manner, *deisel*, 'clockwise', before going into the
kitchen. No word was exchanged, but she immediately began to occupy herself with
the household duties. When the remainder of the household retired for the night, she
remained to smoor the fire — a ritual expression of her assumption of the role of
materfamilies — and then, turning righthandwise again, she went into Crunnchu's
bed. She became pregnant by him and as a result of their union his household
prospered.

When the time of the provincial assembly of the Ulstermen approached and
Crunnchu prepared to go there, the woman sought to dissuade him from going and
then warned him not to mention her name there (this interdiction being a familiar
feature of the 'Melusine' theme which underlies our tale: in this case the woman is
never mentioned in the text, though we know from contextual testimony that she is
the goddess Macha and that the story is taken to be an explanation of *Emain Macha*,
lit. 'The Twins of Macha', the name of the Ulster capital). But when he saw the two
horses of the king racing and heard them praised as being without peer, he forgot
himself and boasted openly that his wife could outrun them (thus echoing other
traditions of goddesses outracing the fleetest horses). His challenge was taken up and
the woman sent for. She begged a respite since her time was at hand, but the king was
obdurate: she must run or see her husband killed. The race was run and she crossed the
line before the horses. Immediately she screamed aloud and bore a boy and a girl at
one birth, and she foretold that for nine generations the Ulstermen would suffer the
same pain and weakness as she in their times of greatest difficulty. And so it
transpired.[2]

For me this is one of the more remarkable pieces of early Irish prose composition,
all the more so for its being so unpretentious. I find myself instinctively pairing it
with the early version of the Deirdre story because both are tales of marriage (of a
sort), both have a supernatural dimension, and both display the same easy, assured
and almost classic sense of style and craftsmanship. Yet in other respects it stands in
sharp contrast to the Deirdre story, and it is this discrepancy that accounts for the
fact that the one tale has been acclaimed by modern men of literature and can boast
a prolific offspring while the other remains little known. They differ even in
structure: while 'The Exile of the Sons of Uisliu' breaks the line of the narrative
with passages of lyric verse in the familiar Celtic fashion, *Noinden Ulad* is straight
prose, and this structural disparity between the texts reflects and accentuates the
disparity of theme and temper. The 'Exile' has for its theme the perennial triangle
of the woman, the old man who possesses her and the young man who takes her —
except that in the characteristic Irish fashion of looking at these things it is the
woman who forces the pace. Deirdre, the beautiful, passionate and wilful heroine
— surely one of the greatest heroines of all literature — compels the youthful,
handsome — and compliant — hero Noisiu to carry her off from the clutches of
Conchobor, king of Ulster, and the greater part of the tale is taken up with their
journeying from place to place in Ireland and into Scotland fleeing from
Conchobor's vengeance, while the main emphasis throughout is on the beauty and
the joys and the tensions of their peripheral existence and on the final tragedy
which (as is the case in so many Irish tales) is foreshadowed from the very
beginning.

How very different to this is *Noinden Ulad* in its setting and atmosphere and in its characters. It is almost as if a single author sought to demonstrate his ability to compose in two contrasting keys. The 'Exile' describes at considerable length at the outset the dramatic circumstances in which Deirdre acquired her name; Macha's name is never mentioned. Noisiu, Deirdre's lover, is a young and noble warrior (who with his two brothers is the literary reflex of a triune deity); Crunnchu is a wealthy farmer and commoner, and a widower to boot. In the 'Exile' the protagonists are continually on the move far from their homeland, pitching their camp beyond the borders of settled society in the natural wilderness untouched by human cultivation, and always ready to lift and go at the first hint of danger; by contrast, *Noinden Ulad* is the epitome of settled rural society, calm, secure and leisurely, with no shadow of violence until Crunnchu ventures abroad into the precincts of king and warrior (or as Dumézil might phrase it, until the *vaisya* falls foul of the *ksatriya*). Deirdre, impetuous, passionate, destined for tragedy from her birth, is the personification of the romantic, mystical, reckless love that flouts convention and social order and imperils the wellbeing of the community. Macha, on the other hand, radiates an air of peace and quiet contentment. She is the guardian of the hearth, and as such she is the patron and protector of domesticity and social stability. The sacred symbolism of the hearth and the fire operates on many levels in Irish tradition — in insular Celtic legal usage the kindling of a domestic fire was an essential part of the ritual for asserting one's claim to possession or land, and in modern times it has been the custom, at least in some parts of Ireland, that the bride's mother-in-law 'handed her new daughter-in-law the tongs and invited her to adjust the fire on the open hearth'.[3] Macha has also in this instance the unmistakeable attributes of the goddess associated with the land and its fertility: she mates with a farmer, assumes control of his domestic affairs, and brings increase upon his holding; she is fruitful in her person and brings forth twins; and like the Celtic goddess Epona and the Welsh Rhiannon 'the Divine Queen' she has an affinity with fast-moving horses. She has two namesakes in other legends, one a seer, the other a female warrior; all three present distinct aspects of the goddess and together they constitute perhaps the most convincing example adduced by Georges Dumézil of his Indo-European tri-functional system operating within the ideology of the Celts. The Macha of *Noinden Ulad* would thus represent the third function, that connected with the land, fertility and wealth, while the others stand for the first and second functions (magico-religious/juridical faculties and physical prowess respectively). Deirdre, on the other hand, cannot be accommodated easily within any of the three functions, for essentially she belongs outside the system that structures and maintains society, and in so far as she acts within it she does so as an agent of anarchy which must in the end be suppressed.

At first glance this little tale is prosaic and simple, but it is a deceptive simplicity. Despite its straightforward economical diction (it runs to only sixty odd lines of text), it somehow manages to create a strange sense of ordinary everyday reality, a sense of real events unfolding dramatically before our eyes, and at the same time (like good poetry) to evoke images and sensations which are not overtly expressed in the text. It is able to do so firstly because it is from beginning to end — even in its very theme — a multiple refrence to the living thesaurus of oral myth and legend, and once the underlying association has been established the creative imagination of the reader or auditor continues to function even in the absence of overt or oblique allusion, drawing instead on a kind of subliminal suggestion generated by the total narrative.

Admittedly I am now speaking as one who has the considerable advantage of approaching such texts with a fairly extensive knowledge of native tradition, but somehow I feel that any thoughtful and reasonably well-informed reader would sense that *Noinden Ulad* has meaning far beyond its literal statement and that it presupposes an underlying ideological complex which is not elaborated, nor even clearly signposted in the actual narrative. Dumézil has pointed out that the tale preserves part of the druidic formulation of the Indo-European tri-functional system in the context of the Ulaid and of their capital Emain Macha, and one suspects — not entirely without evidence — that in the druidic schools of the pre-Christian period such narratives would have been accompanied by a body of exegetical commentary, but that this was later suppressed by monastic redactors by the simple expedient of not recording it.

However, on the synchronic level our text is an accomplished piece of writing by an author who, while immersed in native tradition, is also able to exploit it for his own literary ends, so that in the finished composition mythological concept and literary artifice combine and fuse in an indissoluble unity. This is not to suggest for one moment that oral myth is not literature, with its own characteristic literary features — that would be an extreme of naiveté — but after all our author was a monastic *literatus* and had probably acquired at least some familiarity with ecclesiastically mediated Latin culture and literature, which by comparison with Irish tradition were external, literate, and relatively sophisticated (for instance in their development of abstract thought and of the capacity of language to express it). Moreover he composed his tale in terms of the written text and it seems to me that he consciously shaped his narrative not merely to adjust to the restraints imposed by his manuscript medium, but actually to take advantage of them — to such good effect that his telling of the tale has a peculiar tautness and resonance that a fuller and more explicit narrative could scarcely have achieved.

Which is not to say that our author can be likened to a modern Yeats consciously exploiting native myth to lend depth and symbolism to his own compositions and later relinquishing it when his genius has outgrown it. For the ninth-century (?) redactor the myth was the story, not an embellishment of it, and it would be rash — and probably wrong — to assume that he did not believe it in one sense or another (which he would no doubt have found every bit as difficult to define as we do) — even though in the present instance he makes a brief genuflection to orthodoxy by having Macha invoke the Christian deity in her moment of travail.

Even within intact homogeneous cultures — I use the phrase in a relative sense, naturally — there are always individuals of imagination or intellectual independence who can momentarily stand apart and observe objectively if not dispassionately the workings of the system of ritual and belief that regulates their lives within their society (not to mention those more unruly or more radical individuals who, as the anthropologist Claude Kluckhohn puts it, actually 'buck the system'). In the period with which we are concerned here Irish culture, particularly in matters of belief, was far from being homogeneous. The long drawn-out struggle between Christianity and druidism seems to have come to an end in the seventh century when the druids *qua* druids were finally displaced. Paganism outlived the druids, but not as a system, and the early Church seems on the whole to have taken the pragmatic view that people were free to believe what they liked so long as they accepted the ultimate authority of the Church. Thus from this time on there was a workable *modus vivendi* which guaranteed the formal, as it were 'constitutional' primacy of the Church without compelling people to choose between Christian teaching on the one hand and the vast body of inherited pagan tradition on the other. It would have been as foolish to ask the seventh or eighth-century scribe/redactor whether (or how, or why) he believed in the gods and heroes of paganism as to have asked the Irish countryman of a hundred years ago whether he believed in the fairies. Once organized paganism had been disestablished and dismantled and druidic teaching on fundamental topics like cosmogony and eschatology emasculated, the two systems were able to coexist without undue strain: they became complementary rather than competing, and there is some evidence that they remained so for as long as the Gaelic order endured.

But while normally the monastic scholars would not have been required to make a moral or intellectual choice between the two ideologies, the very fact that they lived with both must surely have caused them, as vocational or professional Christians, to look with a fresh eye at native tradition and to reflect consciously on the possible implications of the coexistence, or even symbiosis, of the two systems. They were — at least some of them were — conscious that they were introducing something new into Irish literature apart from the fact that they used writing. As well as their technical innovations, most obvious in their metrics, they brought with them a certain change of outlook on traditional material, a shifting of values which led, amongst other things, to the enhancement of the status of lyric literature — lyric literature no doubt had always existed, but such evidence as we have suggests that it was cultivated at a more popular level and not among the *filid*, the learned poets who had power and social prestige; but now the various genres of lyric literature were taken up enthusiastically by monastic scholars who were the peers of the *filid* in learning (of one kind or another) and in social standing. This was a revolution of a sort and the monastic writers knew it: after all one of the titles they gave themselves was *nua-litridi* 'the new *literati*'.

One of the things which most preoccupied them, as I have said, was the relationship between the natural and the supernatural, between this and the other world, together with the ambiguities and the relativities of time and space which were implicit in their interaction. The Irish had not developed the faculty of abstract thought beyond a fairly primary level and they tended to present their speculations in concrete, dramatic terms; and nowhere does this emerge more clearly than in their treatment of the several possible artistic and metaphysical refractions of the otherworld theme. 'O wad some Power the giftie gie us/To see oursels as ithers see us!' might have been the thought behind the little story inserted in the Annals of Ulster *s.a.* 749 which tells how the congregation of Clonmacnoise saw a ship anchored above them in mid-air. The anchor got caught in the doorway of the church and a member of the crew swam down to free it and was detained for a time by the people below, but the bishop ordered him to be released, for, he explained, he would die if he were held under water. He then returned as he had come, the rope was cut and the ship sailed away out of sight of those watching. This lyric flight of fancy is the obverse of the common Celtic motif of the sea-voyager who dives to free his anchor and finds himself in a world of fields and flowers and people, and it exemplifies how the monastic *literati* were experimenting imaginatively with the inversions of reality implicit in the whole concept of the Otherworld.

There is a good instance of how they approached the Otherworld theme in the eighth-century (?) *Immram Brain*, 'The Voyage of Bran', a text comprising two series of lyric stanzas with short contextual prose passages providing the narrative. This account of Bran's journey to the Otherworld with its colourful description of Manannan's kingdom, the sea, as it appears to his supernatural eye, tacitly accepts the assimilation of the pagan Happy Otherworld to the Christian concept of the *terra repromissionis* and it underscores this equation of pre-Christian and Christian by drawing a very conscious and clear analogy between the Incarnation and the birth of Mongán, Manannan's semi-divine son by a human mother. As I have remarked elsewhere, the poet's object, or at least his achievement, was to harness the evocative power and resonance of the Celtic Otherworld to the Christian ideal and this he carried off with a benign ecumenism that is totally unclouded by propaganda or polemic (*Ériu* xxvii (1976), 95). The overseas voyage to the Otherworld subsequently became a favourite vehicle for the increasing association of the two ideologies until finally, in one branch of the written tradition, that culminating in the *Voyage of Brendan*, it was wholly transformed into a Christian *peregrinatio*.

But the reconciliation of the two traditions was not always effected so smoothly, as I have already indicated, and such sensitive writers as these were obviously aware of the conflicts and tensions involved. One of them in the eighth or ninth century took for his subject the *Caillech Bhérri*, 'The Hag of Beare', a mythical character still renowned in folk tradition throughout the Gaelic world, who was noted for her longevity, had passed through seven periods of youth and age, and whose descendants were numbered in peoples and races. Perhaps because of their immersion in the mythological tradition, Irish poets and storytellers, like the creators of Celtic art, were very much alive to the evocative power of ambiguity, and this particular one picked on the twofold meaning of the word *caillech* 'nun, hag' and invented the fiction that the Hag of Bérre had taken to the religious life in the end of her days. Now in her old age, crabbed and decrepit, she looks back on the days when she was young and beautiful and richly arrayed and held glorious kings in those arms which are now shrivelled and bony.

'The greatest of Irish poems', Frank O'Connor said of this composition, and whether or not it is the greatest it is certainly not easy to think of a better one. It has the direct, concrete turn of language characteristic of Irish lyric verse, and it is this combined with its multivalent reference and connotation that gives the poem its extrordinary power to suggest ranges of meaning far transcending its explicit statement. It has of course on the human plane the great elegiac theme of nostalgia for lost youth and love and and beauty, but it has also a rich interweave of reference which brings the hag into close association with the land of Munster in its seasonal transformations and pictures her as the one-time consort of kings and princes:

> My body seeks to make its way
> to the house of judgement;
> when the son of God thinks it time,
> let him come to claim his loan.
>
> My arms when they are seen
> are bony and thin;
> dear was the craft they practised,
> they would be around glorious kings.
>
> My arms when they are seen
> are bony and thin;
> they are not, I swear, worth raising
> around handsome youths. . . .
>
> I speak no honied words,
> no wethers are killed for my wedding;
> my hair is scant and grey,
> it is no loss to have a miserable veil over it.
>
> Little do I care
> that there is a white veil on my head;
> I had covering of every good colour on my head
> as we drank good ale.
>
> I envy nothing that is old
> except the Plain of Femhen;
> though I have donned the thatch of age,
> Femhen's crown is still yellow.
>
> The Stone of the Kings in Fehmen,
> Ronan's Fort in Breghon,
> it is long since storms first reached them,
> but their cheeks are not old and withered. . . .

> I have had my day with kings,
> drinking mead and wine;
> today I drink whey and water
> among shrivelled old hags. . . .
>
> The flood-wave
> and the swift ebb;
> what the flood brings you
> the ebb carries from your hand. . . .
>
> Happy is the island of the great sea,
> for the flood comes to it after the ebb;
> as for me, I do not expect
> flood after ebb to come to me.[4]

The poet invokes all the endless variations of what was probably the dominant theme throughout Irish tradition: the goddess, whether as ugly hag or beautiful young girl, who personifies the land of Ireland or of its several kingdoms and who by mating with its rulers legitimizes their sovereignty. This mythic universal concern carries like a subtle counterpoint through the series of stanzas which also express more overtly the deep poignancy of an individual human situation, thus creating a miraculous union of incompatibles analogous to those liminal areas, like the time of Samhain 'Hallowe'en,' or the precincts of sacred festivals, where the natural and the supernatural worlds are temporarily merged. Our poet sustains this literary *coincidentia oppositorum* from beginning to end, intertwining the sacred and the profane, the universal and the individual, the enduring and the transient, and finally, in the most daring *rapprochment* of all, he takes this great goddess-figure who embodied all that is most indigenous and perennial and pagan in Irish life and tradition and reduces her to the level of an aged nun, a wretched old convert to Christianity repenting the high life of her more affluent past. But the underlying irony is that while she repents her sins, she regrets even more the loss of the circumstances which occasioned them. It is not the only Irish poem in which a monastic poet mingles his reverence for the good life with nostalgia for a past life that was even better.

Perhaps no text in Irish literature achieves such a rich and dramatic expression of the interplay of the human and the divine, of the temporal and the eternal, as does the song of the Caillech Bérri. Indeed, I would suggest that what gives it more than anything else its power and inner meaning — and accounts for the impression one has in reading it of a surface simplicity masking a deep ideological complexity — is the fact that it epitomizes so acutely the tensions and ambivalences which were a crucial and probably inescapable part of a society in which formal Christianity was often only a veneer over an ethos which was still essentially pagan and within which individuals of sensibility must often have found themselves nagged by the dilemma of conflicting cultures and moralities. In the poem of the Caillech Bérri, the conflict between native myth and Christian ethic is personalized in the individual predicament of the once beautiful consort of kings who struggles to resign herself to her actual condition as an aged and impoverished nun. At the same time, though on another level, the introverted heroine is the great and immortal goddess of sovereignty who not merely shaped the destiny of kings but also by her inexhaustible chthonic power helped to shape, in other words to create, the very landscape of Ireland. Yet in accepting Christianity she has become subject to age and death, as Oisin, son of Fionn, succumbed to physical decay when he returned from the ageless Otherworld and set foot once more on the finite soil of Ireland.

But if I am correct in suggesting that the whole point of our poem (or perhaps I should say almost the whole point, for so subtle a composition can hardly be pigeon-holed so facilely) is that it symbolizes the clash of ideologies and the disproportion between the human and the divine condition, then it is in some sense a special case and cannot be taken to represent the use of mythology in the written literature in general. For that matter, the same might even be said of the Macha tale, for, despite the fact that this is wholly in prose, it has much in common with the Caillech Bérri poem and with the Deirdre tale, both of which belong to a broad segment of early Irish literature which may be very loosely termed lyric-romantic in contrast to the much more extensive range of heroic-historic prose and verse. All three texts are small in compass and economic in phrasing, all are carefully and skilfully wrought and with that addition of imagination which narrows the gap between prose and poetry, and neither of the prose tales has the glaring discontinuities of style and the unrefined features of oral storytelling which characterize the general run of Irish mythic-heroic narrative. They are all in some sense special cases and cannot adequately reflect the many and varied modalities by which native mythology was adapted to the written medium by generations of monastic redactors. To cover these in reasonable detail would be virtually to write a history of Irish literature from a particular view-point and would entail a fresh examination of a number of categories in Irish and insular Celtic literature as well as of certain basic problems and relativities which affect the form in which these categories have survived: the discrepancy between the two heroic cycles for example, the Fionn and Ulster cycles, in their temper and status; the feminine element in Irish mythology, particularly with regard to its origins and its impact on the written literature;[5] the social and ethnic affiliations of different segments or strata in the mythology and in the literature which derives from it; the insular well-springs of Arthurian romance, and so on. These and a host of other important topics invite close scrutiny in the light of the immense extension of our knowledge of human experience brought about within our lifetime by the (more or less) modern sciences of anthropology, mythology, and comparative religion allied to comparative linguistics (for it must be admitted that Celtic scholars as a whole are a fairly conservative bunch of people — rather like the classicists on whom they unconsciously modelled themselves — and it is only in recent years that they have relaxed their self-imposed bonds and begun to apply effectively to Celtic tradition the findings and methodologies of these more recently developed sciences).

Granted, therefore, that our two (or three) short texts cannot claim to provide a comprehensive over-view of mythology in the literature, they nonetheless exemplify better than most the conscious manipulation of mythological lore for literary ends by men who were steeped in native tradition as well as being educated in the Latin resources of the monastic schools and who were therefore admirably equipped by instinct and training to approach the oral transmitted mythology with a combination of sympathy and sophistication. By a singular good fortune they were also in many cases men of talent and even genius, gifted with imagination, a natural sense of colour and style, and — perhaps most important of all — an artistic feeling for the eloquence of reticence.

NOTES

[1] Vernam Hull, ed., *Celtica* viii (1968) 1ff.

[2] My own paraphrase.

[3] C. Ó Danachair, *Béaloideas* 42-44 (1974-1976), 151.

[4] G. Murphy, trans. *Early Irish Lyrics* (Oxford 1952).

[5] Claude Lévi-Strauss touches upon this topic, perhaps inadvertently, in his autobiographical *Tristes Tropiques*:

> 'If the West traces its internal tensions back to their source, it will be seem that Islam, by coming between Buddhism and Christianity, Islamized us at the time when the West, by taking part in the crusades, was involved in opposing it and therefore came to resemble it, instead of undergoing — had Islam never come into being — a slow process of osmosis with Buddhism, which would have Christianized us still further, and would have made us all the more Christian in that we would have gone back beyond Christianity itself. It was then that the West lost the opportunity of remaining female' (Penguin Books, 1976).

THE HEROIC WORD:
THE READING OF EARLY IRISH SAGAS

ANN DOOLEY

This paper is concerned with early Irish sagas as a subject for literary analysis. Traditionally, Celtic scholars have preferred to see these texts as occasions for a purely textual and philological scrutiny. I should like to state the problem of literary analysis in fairly simple, quasi-structuralist terms because I believe these terms can best express my present concern. That is, what happens when a modern reader attempts to break through the barriers of textual difficulty, of faulty manuscript transmission and of cultural distance in order to arrive at the point where he is actually reading the text itself as it has survived? In short, what ideas about the dynamic of these narratives does this act of reading involve?

We may perhaps begin this exercise in reading with a simple example of an early Irish narrative where the text is short, seems complete, and has a relatively uncomplicated textual history, the story of Deirdriu, *Longes mac n-Uislenn*. The text is of interest to us here, in view of my title, because it would seem that all the elements of the story, character and plot, are bound by the prominence of the various workings of "words" of all kinds. Characters act, accepting the binding power of various verbal projections. Deirdriu kills herself because she has given her word not to be possessed by two men at the same time; Naoise is persuaded to defy the prophecy because, on the advice of his brothers, he ought properly to fear the public ritual words of ridicule spoken by the woman, words which would deny his male warrior autonomy and efficacy; the death of the brothers is brought about because, between the sureties' word and their honouring it, there is inserted another binding word — the constraint to accept hospitality. Action can then be seen as a horizontal linking series of mutually exclusive "words". But the main structuring "word" of the story is, of course, the prophecy with which the story begins and this involves problems of discourse of a different kind. Let us review this incident briefly as it is narrated. At the feast for the Ulster warriors the unborn child cries out in her mother's womb and terrifies the company. A dramatic verse interlude ensues which ends in the druid's prophetic reading of the omen. The solemnity of the prophetic occasion is emphasised by its being marked off as a qualitatively different level of narrative, by being cast in the archaic alliterative long-line which indicates vatic discourse in the early Irish literary tradition. Through a quasi-medical ritual examination of the pregnant woman, the druid insists on the veracity of his reading and furthermore names the child:

> Do-rat iar suidiu in Cathbath a láim fora broinn inna mna coro-derdrestar in lelap foa láim.
> "Fir," ar se, "ingen fil and occus bid Derdriu a hainm ocus biaid olc impe."
> Then the druid Cathbath put his hand on the belly of the woman and the child made a sound under his hand. "True," he said, "it is a girl and her name will be Deirdriu and there will be evil concerning her."

Such is the opening incident, such is the drama of prophecy, and it is marked by two strong contrasts which will continue to operate throughout the narrative. The paradox of prophecy is that it involves an audacious conjunction of over-determination and under-determination of sign. Prophecy moves between two extremes; it is word from nowhere, hence the most arbitrary word of all, but it presumes to be totally omniscient word and normally it is to this latter aspect of prophecy that most narratives pay attention. Narratives which begin with prophecy are under a great structural strain; the idea of word operating within narrative as a totally deterministic force is intolerable. Paradoxically the only human way to respond to such strain is as the Ulster warriors do: *"Marbthar ind ingen!" ol ind oic* ("Let the girl be killed!" said the warriors). The essential dynamic of the present story, however, is that the arbitrary nature of the signifying act is insisted upon. The raw material of this prophecy is the raw material of word itself, the sound from the womb — raw undifferentiated human sound below the level of articulation. This end of the range of word is then itself integrated to another level of narrative by the act of naming the child. When the druid feels the child resonate under his hand (the verb is *derdrithir*) this suggests the name "Derdriu", and this association is re-inforced by reference to the first line of the poetry segment, *"Cia deilm dremun derdrathar?* (What is the violent noise that resounds?). Her identity, partaking of the identity of word, is thus set by this indeterminate quality "resound". So the prophecy involves a double set of expectations. On the one hand, the ensuing narrative is bound by prophecy; the suspense resides merely in the method of its ratification. On the other hand, narrative is free; there is the drama of voice not yet born; the child screams from the womb and we still must wait for what she will say.

This child who screams from the prison of the womb and disturbs the feast becomes the woman who disturbs society by creating her own autonomous language of free desire. Deirdriu, brought up almost in total isolation, is a true *enfant sauvage* and for the crime of secluding her, the king pays a heavy retribution. Her language is learnt apart from society and it is no accident that it is to the individuals who stand so beautifully on the borders of nature and civilization that she unerringly deviates. In the triple refraction of a single personality, the brothers allow a regression of self which signifies a benign availability of the individual to the rhythms of the natural world; and their language, their particular and mysterious *andord* — again human discourse below the level of word — is in perfect accord with this. The sequence where Deirdriu comes to the use of language, where she learns to mate, to exchange herself, is marvellously rendered in the text. In her society women function primarily as signs not as users of signs. They are themselves transactable items, are part of a system of male-dominated exchange, and are, in this system of exchange on a par with the livestock, hence the appropriateness of the language of the herds in the mating riddle game. Naoise reads herds as property: *"Atá tarb in chóicid lat," or-se-sseom ".i. ri Ulad"* ("You have the bull of the province with you" he said, "that is, the king of Ulster"). Deirdriu reads herds as the right to desire; she refuses to thwart the level of nature in the interests of the level of civilization.

We may read then the subsequent account of the exile as the attempt to live by the language of the woman. The narrative of Scotland has three successive stages marked as a downward gradation, and all three work out various positions on the issue of exchange and communication. The first is of short duration, a hunter existence in nature on the mountain which is asocietal and where there is the minimum of manipulation in the supply and demand relationship. The second is an enforced societal warrior existence down to which the brothers are forced because of the exhaustion of the hunter-nature relationship and the subsequent unacceptibility of hunters preying on domestic animals. On this level of culturally manipulated supply, the woman again becomes a transactable item, and so the brothers must revert to nature on the island, this time to a barren nature with no base supply and, as an island, no possibility of survival through social contact.

At this point we might say that the attempt to live through Deirdriu's language has failed, and it is solely on the male initiative of their warrior peers in Ulster that a transition can be effected to the next narrative sequence.

Following the death of the brothers, we can once again attend closely to the word rules that constitute Deirdriu's especial tragedy. For a time she can effectively counter the reality of Ulster by operating only on a linguistic level, the level of retrospective lyricism, recreating in discourse as a static and abiding fact the freedom of the natural world, a world which, in her elegies, is invested with an equilibrium it never had in reality. The narrative appropriately ends with her loss of language. The way in which she loses language is a parody of the way in which she had gained it. As she had once seen what she loved most, named it and mated with it in the language of the herds, so now she is forced in speech through a corresponding ritual of hate:

> "What do you see that you hate most?" said Conchobor.
> "You, to be sure," she said, "and Eogan mac Durthacht!"
> "You shall be, indeed a year with Eogan," said Conchobor.
> "Well, O Deirdriu," said Conchobor, "it is a sheep's eye between two rams that you make between me and Eogan."[2]

To take over Deirdriu's language and to prostitute her are equivalent. And to take over her language and decreate it in this way is to bring her down to an intolerable level of sign, to destroy her. Her only response can be self-destruction, to refuse to make the transition from creating to being created or rather parodied. Deirdriu's life is coterminous with her language.

It has been said that narrative itself is the fundamental theme of all narrative and there is one final aspect of the prophecy which encodes a total sense of narrative. So far we have been looking at the codes which analyse, which parse the narrative. We have seen how the prophecy of Deirdriu constitutes a double way of looking at narrative — narrative as the translation of ideological causality, and narrative as the translation of phenomenological causality; that is, meaning as imposed versus meaning as discovered. Both forms are coterminous with the narrative itself. But the prophecy contained one other element which establishes a definition, a consciousness of what we might call "the narrative as artifact", released from its commitment to mimesis. The second prophecy of the druid ends:

> Biaid do lechtán inach dú;
> Bid scél n-airdairc, a Dheirdriu
> (Your stone will be everywhere;
> It will be a famous story, O Deirdriu)

Now it is mimetically impossible that Deirdriu's stone of death should be everywhere and the prophecy explains this. Deirdriu will be everywhere because her death, the completion of her story as "life", is her release into art. The statement is all the more moving when we remember the terrible pervasiveness of the images of confinement in her story. Celticists like to think of the Deirdriu story as an analogue for the Tristan and Isolde story. It is interesting that both Gottfried von Strassburg and the Irish story-teller should have picked up on this paradox of the translation of life into art. When Gottfried speaks of the lovers' deaths as the reader's life, their lives as the reader's food, he is making essentially the same point.

My second reading example is the *Táin Bó Cuailnge* itself and here I shall stay with one version, the early *LU* text.[3] Here, as the LU text sets up the story, we are dealing with the same problem as with *Loinges mac n-Uislenn*: the sort of pressure that the convention of beginning a story with a prophecy places on a narrative. But here I should like to pay more attention to the context of the prophecy itself. The moment of setting out is a solemn one and is delayed by the druids until a suitable sign is forthcoming. Even Medb, not normally characterised by her sensitivity, can feel the solemnity of the occasion. In the encounter with Fedelm and the enactment of the *imbas for-osnae* divinatory rite, we assist, so to speak, at the birth of a prophecy. The first level on which the three-fold attempt to utter the prophecy is read is as a recreation of the rite itself. The onlookers assist the delivery of the prophecy with the promptings of the questions as it issues in the repeated, hesitant stammering single line with a single unspecified visionary detail, the colour red, around which the message will assemble. But against this straight and reverent reception of the communication of sacred word, we have the contrary reading of the questions, set as Medb's interruptions. Against the evidence of prophetic sign, she peremptorily sets up the status of rival secular methods of information communication, the word of the spies and the enumeration of her own army. We experience the shock of prophecy being denied. We are met twice by Medb's point blank *'Ní fír son'* ("That is not true"), and the third time by a denial which is even more damaging to the status of prophecy; such a statement as *"Atchiu forderg atchiu ruad"* ("I see crimson, I see red") is of no use whatsoever, Medb says, it is merely a useless autography, a mere statement of what happens. We move from a denial of content to a denial of the method itself, of the way in which the seer builds up the layers of specificity, beginning from the single detail. It is a further irony of textual history that we may suspect interpolator H to be of the devil's party on this occasion, for he has substituted for the original poem of prophecy a poem of different length, and quite possibly a smarter more metrically up-to-date prophecy, in rhymed syllabic verse.

It has been said that epic in the Indo-European tradition is transposed myth. We can agree that this has been what has happened to our tradition, but the occasion of transposition itself, the drama of it, remains elusive. It would be audacious to see such an enactment of transposition from the sacred to the secular, to see the birth of a genre, here. Indeed once we set the question we can see how misleading it is to speak in major literary-historical terms at all. Professor MacCana's observations on the purely stylistic features of poetic prophecy are relevant here.

> It is important to remember that the particular *cachet* which [these] types of verse had acquired by the 8th or the 9th century would not have been theirs two or three centuries earlier. In the later period they provided an alternative and a contrast to the normal rhymed, syllabically regular verse-system; in the earlier period they themselves constituted the norm ... [and] their dramatic impact must have been less striking than it became in later centuries, when the very appearance of the form, apart altogether from its content, was sufficient to evoke an impression of archaism and to convey an oblique reference to the remote reaches of native tradition.[4]

The passage of time makes literature possible if we define art as the institution of the impure. The major pleasure in reading the opening of the *Táin* is the modest one of savouring the audacity of literature. As the prophecy poem unfolds we relax, we accept it as a simple method of revealing the hero. But we cannot forget the initial occasion of unease when we viewed the spectacle of the sacred as vulnerable, as sent into the arena to fend for itself. Its message is blocked; it is ignored before it asserts its power unchallenged. The *Táin* then is a text which responds well to a Barthes-type analysis of reading. For Barthes it is the enigmas, the gaps and shifts that become *loci* of pleasure and value. "Neither culture nor its destruction is erotic," he says, "but only the gap between them, the space where their edges rub."[5]

NOTES

[1] All quotations from this legend are taken from Vernam Hull's edition (New York 1971).

[2] The translation is by Thomas Kinsella in *The Tain* (Oxford 1970).

[3] Edited by J. Strachan and J. J. O'Keefe (Dublin 1912).

[4] "On the use of the term *Retoiric*," *Celtica*, 7 (1966), pp. 65-90.

[5] *Le plaisir du texte* (Paris 1973), p. 15; trans. Jonathan Culler in *Structuralist Poetics* (London 1975), p. 262.

THE HEROIC VIEW OF LIFE
IN EARLY WELSH VERSE

A. O. H. JARMAN

The earliest reference to verse composed in the Welsh language is found in the *De Excidio et Conquestu Britanniae* of Gildas, written not later than *c.* 547 A.D. This work contains an uncompromising denunciation of the evil way of life of five British kings of the period, the most notable of whom, in the extent both of his power and of his wickedness, was Maelgwn Gwynedd, king of north-west Wales. In particular Gildas reproves Maelgwn for his readiness to accept the praises addressed to him by the bards of the royal court, twenty-four in number according to later saga, who are described as a 'rascally-crew yelling forth, like Bacchanalian revellers, full of lies and foaming phlegm, so as to besmear everyone near them'.[1] These bards were, no doubt, continuing an ancient and traditional custom but Gildas condemns them for rendering to an earthly monarch praise which should be reserved for God alone. Neither their names nor a single line of their verse have survived. There can, however, be no doubt that the language in which they composed was Welsh, albeit in a very early form. It is clear that the theme of their verse was panegyric and this continued to dominate the Welsh poetic tradition for over a thousand years. Many centuries were to elapse before panegyric again attracted to itself censure in terms similar to those used by Gildas, and in the Middle Ages it was established practice for Welsh princes and nobles to receive the praise of their bards both for their prowess on the field of battle and for their worthiness as pillars of a stable society. In due course the scope of the poets' eulogies was extended so as to include bishops, abbots and other functionaries of the Church, and by the end of the medieval period the praise in verse of the established order was given a sanction expressed in moral, theological and philosophic terms.

Poets composing in Welsh are first mentioned by name in the *Historia Brittonum* of Nennius, a collection of historico-legendary material put together during the first half of the ninth century but using earlier sources. It includes a list of five early poets, of whom two, Taliesin and Aneirin, were considered in the Middle Ages to be the authors of the poems contained in two thirteenth-century manuscripts, known as the 'Books' of Taliesin and Aneirin. The Nennian list also mentions Talhaearn, 'Father of the Muse', and there can be no doubt that in the ninth century he was regarded as the earliest Welsh poet. He may perhaps have flourished during the third quarter of the sixth century but no poems ascribed to him have been preserved. In later Welsh tradition he was displaced by Taliesin, who came to be known invariably as the 'Chief of Poets'. Taliesin was in all probability slightly earlier than Aneirin but both must nevertheless have been comtemporaries who sang towards the end of the sixth century. In considering the poems attibuted to them it must always be remembered that the geographical context of their work is to be found, not in Wales, but in northern Britain, more particularly in southern Scotland and northern England. During the two centuries following the end of the Roman occupation there were large areas of Welsh-speaking territory throughout western and northern Britain, and in the North, in particular, three separate kingdoms maintained a vigorous independence, two until the seventh century, and the third for very much longer. These were Rheged, Gododdin and Strathclyde, with their capitals respectively at Carlisle, Edinburgh and Dumbarton. It was within this region that the medieval Welsh bardic tradition had its fountain-head. Taliesin was the poet of Rheged and Aneirin of Gododdin. After these two kingdoms had been absorbed by the advancing Anglo-Saxon power their cultural traditions were transferred to Wales, possibly *via* Strathclyde, at a date difficult to determine. Taliesin is principally remembered as the poet of Urien, king of Rheged, but one poem ascribed to him is a eulogy of Cynan Garwyn, king of Powys in north-east Wales. If the ascription is correct Taliesin could have commenced his career in Wales and then migrated northwards to become the court poet of Rheged. This would give the poem to Cynan a dating of *c.* 580, making it the earliest existing poem in the Welsh language. On the other hand the poem entitled *Y Gododdin*, attributed to Aneirin, deals with an entirely northern situation and there is no evidence to suggest that its reputed author ever set foot in Wales.[2]

In 1932, in the first volume of their comprehensive work *The Growth of Literature*, H. M. and N. K. Chadwick included a full discussion of the poems ascribed to Taliesin and Aneirin in the chapter on 'Heroic Poetry'. In the same year H. M. Bowra in his *Heroic Poetry* chose to ignore the poems on the ground that 'heroic poetry is essentially narrative'. It is true that only a few brief passages of narrative occur in early Welsh verse. This is largely celebration poetry consisting of eulogy and elegy, and much of it is lyrical in tone. As early as 1912, however, in his pioneer volume *The Heroic Age*, H. M. Chadwick had published a short note on 'The Heroic Poetry of the Celtic People' in which he anticipated many of his later conclusions in this field. Here he claimed that the early Welsh poems 'plainly show all the marks of Stage I' of the scheme which he had constructed to illustrate the development of heroic poetry. This stage he described as that of 'the court-poems of the Heroic Age itself'. In Stage II he placed 'epic and narrative poems based on these'. A consideration of the subject-matter of these Welsh poems led him to conclude either that they must be accepted as genuine products of the period to which they refer, or that they are 'exceedingly clever imitations of such works, composed at a time when the latter were still in existence'. This was a bold claim for Chadwick to make at a time when the prevailing view among Welsh philologists was that in the sixth century Welsh had not evolved out of the parent Brittonic and that to suggest a date of *c.* 600 for the poems attributed to Taliesin and Aneirin was absurd. The researches of later Welsh scholars have pushed the evolution of the essential features of Welsh back to the early sixth or the fifth century, thereby buttressing Chadwick's argument.[3] The controversy, however, continues. The problem, indeed, is not only to what extent the poems, in the form in which they have been preserved, reflect the stage of development reached by the Welsh language in the late sixth century, but also how much textual alteration and corruption has occurred during the lengthy periods of both oral and scribal transmission. We must also ask whether the poems could have been composed by later poets who were able to reproduce and describe in their work the historical background and *milieu*, the atmosphere, and to a considerable extent the language of the sixth century. This seems improbable, whether considered from the standpoint either of feasibility or of motivation. In my opinion the view of the Chadwicks that the early Welsh texts, however much alteration they may have undergone, both contain and reflect an essential nucleus of early poetic composition cannot lightly be dismissed. It is in this poetry that we find the full expression of the ideals and concepts of what is usually regarded as the Welsh or 'British' heroic age. These concepts are its prevailing mode of thought and for the literary historian their expression in verse constitutes one of the main interests of the literature of the period.

Two distinct concepts of the hero are found in Welsh literature. Firstly there is the hero of saga based on myth or folk-tale. He is normally the son of an other-world father and an earthly mother. In his early years he is a wonder-child, as when Pryderi in the *Mabinogi*, at the age of four, bargains with the grooms to let him take the horses to water. As a grown man, too, he usually displays superhuman powers. An early poem says that when Cai son of Cynyr struck his adversary no physician might heal the wound; in battle his death was unattainable 'unless God should accomplish it'. His Irish counterpart was Cú Chulainn, whose powers were even more remarkable. This was the quintessential hero of Celtic saga who, in terms of heroic combat, was invincible. As Marie-Louise Sjoestedt has observed, Cú Chulainn was finally overthrown by the use of a non-heroic force, consisting of magic and sorcery. One may compare the fate of Achilles, struck from behind, and Roland, betrayed by Ganelon.[4] Similarly in the *Mabinogi* Pryderi was slain not only 'by dint of strength and valour' but also by 'magic and enchantment'. In contrast with these heroes of saga, there are the very different heroes celebrated in early Welsh verse. They are not invincible on the battle-field, they wield no superhuman powers, and they belong to a fully-attested historical setting. They nevertheless represent a concept of the hero which, even in the sixth century, was rooted in ancient tradition.

References by classical authors to early Celtic peoples, including assessments of their temperament and descriptions of their martial habits, achieve a basic unanimity of view. In the fourth century B.C. Aristotle mentioned the reckless bravery of Celtic warriors in battle but attributed much of this to ignorance or madness, or simply to high-spiritedness, 'as when the Celts take up arms to attack the waves'. Later writers such as Athenaeus, Diodorus Siculus and Strabo, whose descriptions of the Celts depended on a lost chapter of the *History* of Posidonius

(135-51 B.C.), are agreed about their love of war, their quarrelsomeness, their readiness to boast of their own valour and that of their ancestors, their predilection for single combat and their custom of preserving the severed heads of their vanquished enemies as trophies. Athenaeus in particular quotes a passage which refers to the presence of bards at the assemblies of the Celts. They are described as 'poets who deliver eulogies in song' and their function is further defined as the pronouncement of 'praises before the whole assembly and before each of the chieftains in turn as they listen'.[5]

We do not have evidence of this sort for the British Celts in pre-Christian or Roman times, but the denunciation by Gildas in the sixth century of Maelgwn Gwynedd for his willingness to listen to the praises of his bards shows that at that time the tradition of eulogy was well established in Wales. For Gildas these praises were merely vain flattery. The poem addressed by Taliesin to Cynan Garwyn would no doubt have differed little, if at all, in the sentiments it contained from the bardic effusions so roundly condemned by Gildas, or indeed from the 'eulogies in song' which are first referred to by Posidonius. Its content is fawning adulation of a warrior-king expressed in the simplest terms. The king of Powys is extolled for his victorious campaigns against his fellow-countrymen in Gwent, Anglesey, Dyfed and Brycheiniog. Dire threats are uttered against Cornwall and the 'wretched rulers' of other territories are commanded to 'tremble before Cynan'. The king is also praised for the gifts he has given to the poet, namely horses, mantles, bracelets, brooches and a yellow-hilted sword. Thus the dual character of Welsh panegyric verse for many centuries is well illustrated in this very early poem. The king's prowess in the field of battle is matched by his generosity to those who attend his court. The same two themes are dominant in the eleven other poems which scholars now ascribe to Taliesin. Most of these are eulogies of Urien Rheged, who fell as the result of treachery while besieging the English at Lindisfarne. Taliesin testifies that in his court Urien was as bountiful as Cynan. His bravery and fierceness as a warrior are also singled out for mention. On hill and in dale he smites and subdues his foes, and one poem contains a graphic description of bloodstained men, the defeated enemy, with hands crossed and pallid cheeks laying down their arms before him at the ford, while the reddened waves of the river Eden wash the tails of the warriors' horses. 'Lone weary men', presumably Urien's champion fighters, watch the proceedings. The poem ends with the assertion that 'battle will be the lot of him who is Urien's man'.

Here we have the true *milieu* of heroic poetry. The portrayal is stark and unromanticized. The Urien poems differ from the poem to Cynan Garwyn in one important respect. Cynan is depicted as an aggressor whose sole interest is personal aggrandizement. Urien could, no doubt, be as aggressive as Cynan but the purpose of his actions is primarily defensive. On all sides his kingdom is surrounded by enemies. When he attacks them he does so to protect his people so that they may dwell undisturbed on their homesteads. The poems refer to him as his subjects' 'far-flung refuge', his 'land's anchor', and as a magnanimous dispenser of wealth.

He thus accepts responsibility, not only for leading his people in war, but also for their well-being when victory has secured the peace. Taliesin's poems to Urien stress his courage, his fierceness, his dominating personality. They do not however contain a statement of the heroic ideal in its pure, undiluted and unadulterated form. For this we must turn to the *Gododdin* of Aneirin.

The name *Gododdin* carries three meanings: (1) the tribe or people so called; (2) the territory inhabited by them; and (3) the poem which celebrated their heroes. Containing 1257 lines arranged in 103 rhymed stanzas, the *Gododdin* is formally an elegy. It laments the fall at the battle of Catraeth, or Catterick in Yorkshire, of the war-band of the Gododdin, three hundred strong, which the tribal chieftain Mynyddog Mwynfawr had sent to attack the advancing Angles of Deira and Bernicia. Historical sources tell us nothing of the battle. It could have been one of many unrecorded skirmishes which must have occurred in the conflict between Angle and Briton and may probably be dated *c.* 600 A.D. We gather from the *Gododdin* that for a year Mynyddog had maintained, and no doubt trained, a picked troup of mail-clad horsemen before sending them forth on a hazardous expedition which he must have deemed to be of supreme strategic importance and the success of which he may have regarded as vital for the survival of his kingdom. In the event it was a disaster. The warriors of the Gododdin were annihilated by a numerically superior enemy; only one escaped. The poem, however, does not treat the battle in strategic or political terms. Nothing could be further from the minds of the warriors than calculated planning. Their values are purely heroic. The period of preparation at Mynyddog's court is described as a 'mead-feast' or a 'wine-feast', participation in which bound the warriors in a relationship of absolute fidelity to their chieftain. When, at his command, they have gone forth to battle and fought without flinching until struck down by the foe, they are said to have 'paid their mead'. Their readiness to do this was for each of them a matter of personal honour, and it was the determination never in any circumstances to deviate from honour's stern demands that constituted the essence of the heroic ideal. At some moment during their expedition, the war-band must have realized that their campaign could only end in defeat. Flight, however, was unthinkable. Even if worldly wisdom and common sense counselled it, the charge of cowardice which would ensue would have been unbearable. The war-band fought on until the end. By so doing they achieved the immortal fame to which their steadfastness entitled them. In the words of the *Gododdin*:

> Although they were slain, they slew,
> And until the end of the world they shall be praised.

In this matter, the poet was deemed to be the final arbiter. Another of Aneirin's stanzas closes with the line:

> The poets of the world shall be the judges of the man of stout heart.

Much of the poem is, of course, pure elegy. The youthfulness of the warriors, their short lives and their kinsmen's sorrow after them are continually emphasized. The poet declares that 'their ardour shortened their lives' and that 'before their hair turned grey death came to them'. There is also panegyric in the conventional or Taliesinic sense. One gathers that, like the heroes of the Iliad, each member of the war-band was a minor chieftain in his own right, and the munificence and even opulence of their courts are praised. They dispense mead to their guests, gifts to the minstrels, and the liberality of one is compared to the flowing sea. In battle, however, their ferocity knew no bounds. With expected hyperbole the poem states that before one warrior 'armies groaned' and that 'five fifties fell before the blades' of another. About eighty of the warriors are named and eulogized individually in this way. The poet also took especial pride in the war-band as a whole. For him it was a splendid sight to see them setting forth for Catraeth, riding 'on rough-haired steeds, swan-coloured horses, tightly harnessed':

> A host of horsemen in brown armour, with shields,
> Spear-shafts held aloft with sharp points,
> And shining mail-shirts and swords.

The exultation in these lines does not, however, express the prevailing tone of the poem. Unlike the armies of Urien, Mynyddog's war-band did not go forth to battle with a fair prospect of victory in sight. As a body it was doomed to destruction. The poet was fully aware of this as he composed each line of his poem. It is an indication of his quality as a poet that he was so often able to set this awareness aside momentarily in order to give expression to his admiration for the achievements, the high morale and the resplendent appearance of the war-band. In one line, however, he declares that at Mynyddog's hall the warriors 'drank yellow, sweet, ensnaring mead'. It ensnared them because it was the symbol of a bond which led to ineluctable disaster. This was a bond of the warriors' own choosing. For them renown, achieved at whatever cost, was the supreme good. It was for this, rather than for any tribal, national or political gain, that they fought. Nai son of Nwython 'slew a great host in order to win reputation', and Cydywal son of Sywno 'sold his life for the mention of honour'. Heedless of their own survival, they pledged their personal allegiance to Mynyddog and 'paid for their mead-feast with their lives'. For this the poet promises them 'praise without limit, without end'.

Such is the concept of ideal heroic behaviour as formulated and expressed by the poet of the *Gododdin*. Whether the men of the war-band really felt and acted in this way, we cannot tell. Situations like that at Catraeth have occurred time and again in the history of human conflict. Men have often been required to chose between the demands of discretion and of valour, and have usually done so with less single-mindedness than the warriors of the Gododdin. It is therefore noteworthy that early Welsh literature contains a counter-statement to the *Gododdin*'s assertion of the validity of the heroic ideal. This is found in the verse-cycle associated with the name of Llywarch Hen.[6] Llywarch was possibly a northern sixth-century figure, a cousin of Urien Rheged, who seems to have become the central character in a saga which depicts him as having migrated to Powys in Wales, where he was faced with the task of defending his borders against the English enemy. The scene is set in the late sixth century, but the earliest acceptable date for the composition of the poems is the ninth. Moreover, their unknown author manifests a profound interest in various problems posed by the heroic ideal. He not only probes such questions as the reluctance of some men to go to war and the motivation of cowardice, but he also asks the more fundamental question: what is the justification for the pursuit of renown?

Llywarch is portrayed as an uncompromising upholder of the martial values. He has brought up all twenty-four of his sons as trained warriors, and twenty-three of them have fallen in battle. The sole survivor, Gwên, has been living a life of ease at Urien's court while his father, alone, continued to resist the enemy. Hearing of Llywarch's plight, however, Gwên returns to Powys. In a dialogue between father and son, Llywarch urges Gwên 'not to lose the honour of a man', and Gwên replies that he is ready to endure the hardship of battle and promises that, wherever he chances to be, 'spears will be shattered'. He qualifies these assurances, however, with references to the possibility of retreat if the pressure of battle becomes too great, and in one line he utters the words: 'I do not say that I shall not flee'. This leads to a charge of cowardice and the dialogue ends on a bitter note, with Llywarch boasting of his early prowess while Gwên points out that though he has survived his witness is dead. This poem is followed by Llywarch's elegy to his son. In the sequel Gwên had not fled but had stood his ground fighting until he fell. Now Llywarch claims for himself the credit for his son's bravery. 'Because he was my son', he says, 'he did not flee'.

Parallels to this dialogue are found in other poems of the Llywarch Hen cycle. One of these deals specifically with the theme of cowardice. Cynddilig, another son of Llywarch, cites the frozen lake, the falling snow, the strong biting wind and the short day as excuses for not going to war. Llywarch replies with an outright attack on cowardice but nevertheless resigns himself to an acceptance of his son's failing, telling him that he will not be called upon to serve in the hour of need although he is neither a cleric nor an old man. He then adds the exclamation: 'Alas, Cynddilig, that thou wert not born a woman!' Had that been the case, Llywarch would have been spared the shame of avowing kinship with a self-acknowledged coward.

Thus, in a cycle of verse which retains much of the heroic ethos, we find a poet examining problems which would not even have occurred to his precursor who composed the *Gododdin*. The severe standards of the heroic age are being replaced by a much more complex view of life. This is very clearly shown in a poem entitled 'The Old Man's Lament', in which Llywarch is depicted as a forlorn wanderer, rejected by all, bereft of family and kingdom. Of his twenty-four sons he says: 'Through my tongue they have been slain'. He has now concluded that it was his own immoderate boasting, his incessant exhortations to his sons to emulate his martial exploits, that have led to their destruction. He then adds the general statement that 'too much renown is evil', although 'a little (renown) is good'. Admittedly, he has not been favoured by fortune. Unlike Urien, he has no sons to sustain him. Unlike the warriors of the Gododdin, he has survived his battles. But his final verdict on the heroic ideal is that it is compounded of presumption and arrogance. Its essence is pride and its end is ruin.

NOTES

[1] For the text see H. Williams, *Gildas*, Cymmrodorion Record Series, No. 3 (London 1899), pp. 80-1.

[2] For the text of the Taliesin poems see Ifor Williams, *Canu Taliesin*, (Cardiff 1960); available in an English version by J. E. Caerwyn Williams, *The Poems of Taliesin* (Dublin 1968). For Y *Gododdin* see Ifor Williams, *Canu Aneirin* (Cardiff 1938, reprinted 1977). The poem has been translated metrically in J. P. Clancy, *The Earliest Welsh Poetry* (London 1970), and into literal prose, with discussion and commentary, by K. H. Jackson, *The Gododdin, The Oldest Scottish Poem*, (Edinburgh 1969). A strongly poetic version was published recently by Desmond O'Grady, *The Gododdin* (Dublin 1977), with illustrations by Louis le Brocquy.

[3] See K. H. Jackson, *Language and History in Early Britain* (Edinburgh 1953).

[4] Cf. Marie-Louise Sjoestedt, *Gods and Heroes of the Celts*, trans. Myles Dillon (London 1949), p. 77.

[5] For references by classical authors to the Celts see J. J. Tierney, 'The Celtic Ethnography of Posidonius', *Proceedings of the Royal Irish Academy*, Volume 60, Section C, No. 5 (Dublin 1969), 189-275. A close analysis of the references to bards, etc., has now been published by J. E. Caerwyn Williams, 'Posidonius's Celtic Parasites', *Studia Celtica*, Vol. XIV/XV (Cardiff 1979/1980), 313-43.
  Strictly, the last sixteen words quoted above refer to a class of chieftans' companions described as *parasitoi.*

[6] For the Llywarch Hen cycle of poems see Ifor Williams, *Canu Llywarch Hen* (Cardiff 1935, reprinted 1977); Patrick Ford, *The Poetry of Llywarch Hen, Introduction, Text and Translation* (California 1974).

THE HERITAGE OF CELTIC CHRISTIANITY:
ECOLOGY AND HOLINESS[1]

CHRISTOPHER BAMFORD

> The Maker of all things
> The Lord God worship we:
> Heaven white with angels' wings,
> Earth and the white waved sea.[2]

This much the lettered men, scribes and exegetes find writ in sacral membrana, the historia of our kings, sayings of our prophets, and Τὰ Χροτικά and we that be unlettered, hear what is handed down in tellings told by baldheads to their beardless kin.

But be that as it may, if that vast oak had not the bright-berried growth intwined upon it, which flowering, so I've heard tell, the *filid, vates* or druidae (a kind of Levitic priesthood among the Galatic people) do cut with a golden sickle at certain sacred times in their year of Luna months.

That great lignum arbor una nobilis within the inmost nemeton of this wild Ephraim holt, had for Golden Bough the pierced & hanging son of the Lord of Salem.[3]

Christians of all persuasions have always loved the Saints of the Celtic Church and the traditions of sanctity, learning and stewardship for which they stood; and the Celtic or, as it is also called, the British Church has always represented an ideal for those who have known of it, and not simply as a Golden Age of innocence and purity which, in the words of Nora Chadwick, has "never been surpassed and perhaps been equalled only by the ascetics of the eastern deserts,"[4] but also, and more importantly, as an alternative seed, "a light from the west," perhaps obscure and even alien, but nevertheless powerful and true with the kind of reality we seem to need today. "If the British Church had survived," wrote H. J. Massingham, "it is possible that the fissure between Christianity and nature, widening through the centuries, would not have cracked the unity of western man's attitude to the universe."[5]

This combination of saintliness and ecology is but one aspect of the heritage. The other is made up of the sacred and secular traditions of learning, science, poetry and art, which were seen as the essential concomitants, the frame and the vehicle, whereby God's purpose for the cosmos, its transfiguration, might be aided and fulfilled.

The difficulty, of course, is that the heritage sought for is that of a beginning — which, as a beginning, is shrouded in mystery, continuing in mystery and ending in mystery. One gets the sense, indeed, trying to unravel the different strands of scholarship, legend and archaeology, of entering into relation with a moment of history in which the spiritual is so closely and clearly involved with the phenomenal that all one's usual means of understanding are wanting. "The loom may be of this world," J. W. Taylor wrote, "but the tapestry, the colours and the inscription on it are only partly of this world. They belong essentially to the spiritual and the heavenly."⁶ The point is, I think, that all beginnings, all seeds, are thus mysterious, and so constitute insoluble *aporia* for the merely empirical scholar.

In this instance, it is the coming of Christianity to, and the Christianity of, Ireland and England that is the great question. In the sixth century, Taliesin, the great Welsh bard claimed: "Christ the Word from the beginning was from the beginning our Teacher, and we never lost his Teaching. Christianity was in Asia a new thing, but there was never a time when the Druids of Britain held not its doctrines."⁷ There, perfectly posed, is the first quandary. We do not know when or how Christianity first arrived at those westernmost reaches. It seems always to have been there. Legend tells, for instance, that Irish sages attended the events on Golgotha "in the spirit" and felt, by what means we cannot tell, "the groans and travails of creation cease." Yeats notes a similar story, in which on the day of the Crucifixion King Concubar and Bucrach, the Leinster Druid, are sitting together. Conchubar notices "the unusual changes of creation and the eclipse of the sun and the moon at its full;" he asks Bucrach the cause of these signs and Bucrach replies that "Jesus Christ the Son of God is even now being crucified . . ."⁸

Another legend is that associated with Saint Bridget or Bríd. It tells how Bríd, a child so young she could neither walk nor talk, was cast adrift in a coracle and came to land at Iona, where she began to walk and talk, singing:

> I am but a little child
> Yet my mantle shall be laid
> Upon the Lord of the World,
> The King of the elements Himself
> Shall rest upon my heart
> And I will give Him peace.⁹

The legend goes on to tell how Druids brought her up, until one day she was led by a white dove, through a grove of rowans, to a parched, desert land. There, in a stable, she assisted as 'aid-woman' or midwife at the birth of a Holy Child upon whose brow she placed three drops of holy water to unite him with the earth. Then, because the cows in that desert land had no milk on account of the drought, Bríd sang 'runes of Paradise' to them so that milk flowed freely, and the Holy Child could drink of earthly produce — wrapped in Bríd's blue mantle, close to her heart. Thus, Bríd was called: aid-woman of Mary, Fostermother of Christ, Godmother of the Son of God.

Now Bríd is, in this, a part mythological figure, assimilable to Artemis, aid-woman to Leto in the birth of Apollo, and to the northern Goddess Brigantia, and the Celtic Brigid, Goddess of knowledge and life, mother of poets. But before jumping to rather obvious conclusions, two further aspects of the legend must be borne in mind. First, there is a future Bríd, or rather, perhaps, Bríd is "once and future" and her task is not yet complete. Namely, it is said that another Bríd will come to bind His hair and wash His feet, and perhaps even to be the Bride of Christ Himself. This Bríd is Sophia, surely, the Virgin Wisdom of the World.

But there is yet another Bríd, this time solidly historical, who ranks with Saints Patrick and Columba in Ireland's great Triad of Saints.[10]

I quote these stories to suggest that Celtic tradition experienced a continuity in creation, one that extended from its inception, the Word in the beginning, to its conclusion, Deification. For the Celt, therefore, Christianity and the act of Christ was never an end in itself, but rather was always experienced as a divine means to the true end, God's purpose from which He never deviated though humanity and creation fell, namely, that He should be "all in all." Christ's death and resurrection was thus seen as a healing mediation, a balm, that made possible once again the original dream of paradise, the reconciliation of humanity and nature in God. It is in this sense that Christianity, as the true end for which creation was intended, was always in Ireland and that to seek its historical beginnings there is vain. Another legend bears this out. It is said that when Lucifer tempted our forebears in Paradise, the earth was already in existence, awaiting, as it were, the exile. But in this earth, the legend goes on, Ireland was already different: it was not just another part of the earth, but rather that part of the earth that Paradise, before the Fall, had made its own. Paradise, that is, created an image for itself on earth before Lucifer ever entered into it; and that image was Ireland. No wonder then that Paradise, or First Nature, was said to be more easily discerned there.

The question of Christianity in England is equally unsettled. Gildas, in the sixth century, wrote: "these islands received the beams of light . . . in the latter part of the reign of Tiberius Caesar, in whose time this religion was propagated without impediment or death."[11] The point about this is that Tiberius died in 37 A.D. Nor does Eusebius contradict this date, though scholars of course have difficulty explaining it. Nevertheless, by 199 A.D., Tertullian, listing the many peoples to whom the religion of Christ has come, can include "the places of the Britons, which are inaccessible to the Romans." That is, if Christianity was in England by then it was not necessarily the Romans who brought it. The Gauls already had a Bishop, Irenaeus of Lyons, of the line of St. John, and one may assume much interchange between Gaul and Britain. There is, further, some evidence of a King Lucius at this time "bestowing the freedom of country and nation with privilege of judgment and surety on all those who might be of the faith of Christ."[12] It is also claimed for Lucius that he built the first Church — around 200 A.D. And certainly one hundred years later, during the Diocletian persecutions, there were English martyrs — St. Alban for instance; while in 314, at the Council of Arles, there were three British signatories, Bishops, which already indicates a sizable flock but tells us nothing of origins.

The fundamental story here returns us to the pre-37 A.D. date given by Gildas, or close to it: in other words to the murky waters of St. Joseph of Arimathea and Glastonbury. Joseph's name occurs in traditions in different places. We can track him, as it were, through Provence, Aquitaine, Brittany and into Cornwall. At none of these, however, is he recorded as having stopped: he passes through them.

His only stopping place, the conclusion of his journey, according to legend, is Glastonbury. Here, on the Isle of Avalon, St. Joseph with twelve companions and bearing the Holy Grail, the sacred vessel containing the blood and sweat of Christ, settled and built a round church of mud and wattles. Now, the route he seems to have taken, up from Marseilles, along the Rhone to Limoges, and on to Brittany and Cornwall, is precisely that of the tin trade. And legend, indeed, had made of Joseph of Arimathea a tin merchant, even going so far as to say that during the 'lost' years of Christ, Jesus came as a boy with Joseph to Cornwall and that Jesus taught Joseph how to extract the tin and to purge it of its wolfram. This is the story invoked by Blake in his poem, *Milton*:

> And did those feet in ancient time
> Walk upon England's mountains green?
> And was the Holy Lamb of God
> On England's pleasant pastures seen?[13]

Whatever the truth of these stories, Glastonbury is a plausible first site — scholars see it as constituting an early trading centre, conveniently situated, of easy access to the Bristol Channel and sufficiently inland to deter sea-raiders. Poetry and science thus do not contradict each other.

The next 'problem' to be considered in this attempt to understand the roots of Celtic faith and practice is that of St. Patrick. Patrick was born in Britain — either Wales or Scotland — in about 387 A.D. His was a Christian family, in a period when Christianity was already in decline. His father was a deacon, his grandfather a priest, but Patrick himself seems to have received little formal religious instruction, though Christian ideas must have already formed the unconscious foundations of his thinking. When he was about 16, Patrick was snatched from his father's farmstead by Irish raiders and carried off into Ireland as a slave. Here he remained six years, spending his captivity as a shepherd, a lonely occupation which, building upon his unformed faith, empowered his vision and his way: "But after I came to Ireland —" he wrote in his *Confession*, "and so tended sheep every day, and often prayed in the daytime — the love of God and the fear of Him came to me more and more, and faith increased, and my spirit was stirred, so that in one day [I used to say] up to a hundred prayers and at night nearly as many, and I stayed in the forests and on the mountain, and before daylight I used to be roused to prayer in snow and frost and rain, and felt no harm, nor was there any inclination to take things easily in me, because, as I see it now, the spirit seethed in me. And there without a doubt on a certain night I heard in my sleep a voice saying to me: You are fasting well, and are very soon going to your fatherland. And again, very soon afterwards I heard the response saying to me: Look, your ship is ready! And it was not nearby but about two hundred thousand paces away, and I had never been there nor did I know anyone among the people; and soon afterwards I turned away from that place in flight, and left the man with whom I had been six years, and came in the strength of God, Who set me on the straight road for my benefit; and I was afraid of nothing until I reached that ship."[14]

Where the ship landed is a moot point. It was either Britain, or Gaul. If it was Gaul, then a history is reconstructable for Patrick which is attractive because it puts him into contact with the various streams of Christian life in Europe at that time — particularly the beginnings of monasticism. St. Martin had established Ligugé in 360; Cassian St. Victor around 400; and St. Honoratus Lérins, where in fact Patrick is supposed to have gone, at about the same time. These latter, and one could also add St. Ninian, at Candida Casa in Scotland, brought the Egyptian ideal, "the light from the east," to the west. And since the Celtic Church in so many ways reflects and echoes Egypt and Palestine, it is tempting to see St. Patrick at Lérins, that "earthly paradise," perched like so many Irish monasteries on a small island in the sea. To get a sense of the purpose of these — for such earthly paradises will finally be the bases of the Celtic heritage, of the life of prayer, work and fasting established there — the words of Faustus of Riez, himself a Briton or an Irishman and a semi-Pelagian, are evocative: "It is not for quiet and security," he told the brothers, "that we have formed a community in the monastery, but for a struggle and a conflict. We have met here for a contest, we have embarked upon a war against our sins ... The struggle upon which we are engaged is full of hardships, full of dangers, for it is the struggle of man against himself ... For this purpose we have gathered together in this tranquil retreat, this spiritual camp, that we may day after day wage an unwearying war against our passions ..."[15]

In 432 — which is a traditional cosmological number and synchronizes with the Council of Ephesus that declared Mary *Theotokos*, Mother of God — Patrick was sent as Bishop into Ireland. Now, he was the second Bishop to be so sent — the first was Palladius — and both were sent, firstly, because the Christians in Ireland must have needed, or even requested, a Bishop; and secondly, because there was a fear abroad concerning the Pelagian heresy. Ireland would probably have come up immediately in this connection. Pelagius, after all, was Morgan, a Welshman; he was the first English Christian to write a book, his *Commentary on Romans*; and the Irish always provided, as did the Orthodox east, something of a refuge for Pelagianism in its semi-Pelagian form. This is not to say that the Irish were Pelagians; they were in many ways Augustinian. Nevertheless, they would have agreed with Pelagius that, "since perfection is possible for man, it is obligatory." But they would not have agreed that human free will could accomplish perfection unaided, or that there was no such thing as original, inherited sin. As with the Eastern Church, the Irish believed in a healthy interdependence of nature and grace.

Ireland, we must never forget, was rural, in an almost absolute sense. There were no villages even. Ireland was still a country of isolated holdings, organized in a tribal, familial culture — kinship binding these holdings together. Most importantly, and implicit in the above, Irish society was aristocratic, a hierarchical system of individual, autonomous units. There was no state, or nation, or king over all. There were, however, kings, tribal chieftains; and under them, warriors and, as their equals, "men of special gifts," the *aes dána* — druids, bards, doctors, historians (for the most part in one) — and finally there were ordinary freemen. We must understand exactly what all this means. It means among other things that no single nation or state confronted Patrick. In the world of early Ireland, enormous prestige was enjoyed by the *aes dána*. From this we may infer that, though the society was an oral one, it nevertheless by any standards embodied a "high" culture.[16] There were schools, and a great body of traditional knowledge and lore. As Ludwig Bieler commented: "Ireland is unique in the medieval western world in having not only a native literature but also a native tradition of professional learning."[17] Thus, once having acquired a written script, the Irish were culturally well prepared to preserve not only their own traditions, but those of classical Greek and Latin literature also. This they did, thereby ensuring the continuity of European culture.

Patrick's main work, of course, was that of conversion, establishing bishops, churches and the seeds of monasticism. His success in this seems to have been due to his willingness to accept the indigenous traditions and to adapt his teaching to them. This respect for native tradition seems to have been reciprocated. Two pointers may be given. The first is the legendary story of the conversation in Connaught of the daughters of the High King of Tara. When these questioned him as to who the New God was, and where he dwelt, Patrick replied: "Our God is the God of all men, the God of Heaven and Earth, of sea and river, of sun and moon, and stars, of the lofty mountain and the lowly valley, the God above Heaven, the God in Heaven, the God under Heaven; He has His dwelling round Heaven and Earth and sea and all that in them is. He inspires all, He quickens all, He dominates all, He sustains all. He lights the light of the sun; He furnishes the light of the light; He has put springs in the dry land and....stars to minister to the greater lights."[18]

In these words of St. Patrick has been seen an epitome of the Celtic monk's holy embrace of nature, his sense of "ecology." In them we may catch, as H. J. Massingham has said, "a gleam of the new philosophy of heaven and earth in interdependence and interaction, formulated by a culture in vital contact with the ancient nature-worship. . . ."[19] And it is true: everywhere in Celtic Ireland we will find a holy intimacy of human, natural and divine. In hermitages and monasteries, on rocky promontories and lonely hillsides, we find everywhere a tremendous proximity of the human and divine in nature, an abandonment to spiritual work and simultaneously a cultivation of the earth. There is at once a unique passion for the wild and elemental "as though to break through the crust of artificial convention to the very roots of sheer being," coupled with a gentle human love for all creation.

The other piece traditionally ascribed to Patrick that is indicative is his Hymn, the *Deer's Cry*, the *Breastplate*: "a corselet for the protection of body and soul." St. Patrick invokes "The Trinity, Three in One, the Creator of the Universe" and binds to himself its virtues: those of the Incarnation, Death, Resurrection and Second Coming; of Cherubim, Angels, Archangels; prayers, predictions, preachings, faiths, deeds; the brightness of snow, the splendor of fire, the speed of lightning, swiftness of wind, depth of sea, stability of earth, compactness of rock. Relying on God, all in all, might, wisdom, ear, word, hand, way, shield, host, Patrick comes finally to Christ — with him, before him, behind him, within him, at his right, at his left, in his lying, in his sitting, in his rising. What is indicative here is the sense of the Trinity as all in all, that the fundamental fact of existence is Unity in Trinity, Trinity in Unity, in Christ. As an old Irish poem puts it:

> O King of Kings!
> O Sheltering wings! O Guardian Tree!
> All, all of me,
> Thou Virgin's Nurseling,
> Rests in Thee.[20]

In any event, Patrick seems to have established a church in perfect conformity with the spirituality of the place. The Druids, Bards, being converted, learnt Latin and incorporated their own traditions into the existing Christian ones. They had always cultivated the "lore of places," *dindshenchas*. Like all aristocratic societies they had set great store on memory, learning, genealogy. Thus the bards, the *fili*, now became *fir coimgne*, synchronizers. Just as Eusebius had composed his Chronicle showing how the great world kingdoms of Assyria, Egypt, Palestine and Greece had prepared for Christ, now the *fir coimgne* prepared their column, showing how all Irish history, from the creation, fitted the same pattern. Indeed, by the seventh century, as Robin Flower notes, "the monks accepted the pagan tradition and put it on one level with the historical material which came to them under the sanction of the Church."[21]

This work of compilation and spiritual investigation was carried out in the monasteries whose primary purpose, of course — and with this the more "scholarly" activity was not seen to conflict — was contemplation and the practice of the presence of God. "Live in Christ, that Christ may live in you," Columbanus told his students: "Taste and see, how lovely, how pleasant is the Lord." Continuous prayer was thus the ideal, to "pray in every position." "What is prayer without ceasing?" asks a gloss, and it replies: "The answer is not difficult. Some say it is celebrating the canonical hours, but that is not the true meaning. It is when all the members of the body are inclined to good deeds and evil deeds are put away from them. . . ."[22]

Though ascetic, then, the Irish monks were hostile to neither learning nor nature and practiced greatly the contemplation of both of these. Indeed, these two — Scripture and Nature — were according to Eriugena the two shoes of Christ, whose latchet John the Baptist was not yet ready to undo.[23]

As for nature, a gloss says: "Not less does the disposition of the elements set forth concerning God and manifest Him than though it were a teacher who set forth and preached it with his lips." Another proclaims: "The elements sound and show forth the knowledge of God through the work that they do and the alteration that is on them."[24] This is a sacramental universe, birds, beasts and natural phenomena being the signs of a supernatural grace. Indeed, as one reads the monks' stories and poems, birds, beasts and angels blend in a continuous polyphony of revelation. Two short poems may be quoted in illustration:

> Learned in music sings the lark,
> I leave my cell to listen;
> His open beak spills music, hark!
> Where heaven's bright cloudlets glisten.
>
> And so I'll sing my morning psalm
> That God bright heaven may give me,
> And keep me in eternal calm
> And from all sin relieve me.[25]

And again:

> Over my head the woodland wall
> Rises; the ousel sings to me;
> Above my booklet lined for words
> The woodland birds shake out their glee.
>
> That's the blithe cuckoo chanting clear
> In mantle grey from bough to bough
> God keep me still! For here I write
> A scripture bright in great woods now.[26]

As Robin Flower says, "It was not only that these scribes and anchorites lived by the destiny of their dedication in an environment of wood and sea; it was because they brought into that environment an eye washed miraculously clear by continuous spiritual exercise that they, first in Europe, had that strange vision of natural things in an almost unnatural purity."[27]

Prayer, then, was the natural accompaniment of the cultivation of earth and mind. The monasteries were estates, small farms, with livestock and fields. They were publishing houses, with scriptoria; and finally they were schools. Here the Seven Liberal Arts were practiced while the rest of Europe was still in the "dark ages" of transition: the Trivium of grammar, rhetoric and logic (which in practice meant Latin and Greek) and the Quadrivium of Arithmetic, Geometry, Astronomy and Music. These, however, were not ends in themselves, but were merely the preliminaries and prerequisites for the study of scripture and theology. "What is the best in the world?" asked Columbanus, author of the most severe and ascetical Rule, and he answered, "To do the will of its maker. What is this will? That we should do what he has ordered, that is, that we should live in righteousness and seek devotedly what is eternal. How do we arrive at this? By study. We must therefore study devotedly and righteously. What is our best help in maintaining this study? The Intellect, which probes everything and, finding none of the world's goods in which it can permanently rest, is converted by reason into the one good which is eternal."[28]

Appropriate here is the famous poem about *Pangur Ban*:

> I and Pangur Ban my cat,
> 'Tis a like task we are at:
> Hunting mice is his delight,
> Hunting words I sit all night.
>
> Better far than praise of men
> 'Tis to sit with book and pen;
> Pangur bears me no ill will
> He too plies his simple skill. . . .
>
> So in our peace our tasks we ply
> Pangur Ban, my cat, and I
> In our arts we find our bliss,
> I have mine and he has his.
>
> Practice every day has made
> Pangur perfect in his trade;
> I get wisdom day and night
> Turning darkness into light.[29]

Thus the monasteries assimilated and superseded the ancient bardic and druidic foundations: Bangor, Clonfert, Lismore — such are the names to conjure with. Generally speaking, the theology accepted and practiced was that of the Christian Church — with an unusual emphasis on scripture (so that any work could only really be a commentary thereon) and asceticism. The doctrine of God was fully Trinitarian and apophatic. Creation was *ex nihilo*, by fiat, through Christ: a theophany with a purpose — that the character of God might be revealed, contemplated, enjoyed, fulfilled, embodied. But with human disobedience, creation had fallen apart from God; and not until Christ's material blood was shed was the original purpose possible again. Now, however, if obedient, creation could become immortal once more. For this, the body was the vehicle. As Secundinus wrote in his Hymn to Patrick: "Flesh he hath prepared as a temple for the Holy Spirit; by whom, in all activities, it is continually possessed, and he doth offer it to God as a living and acceptable sacrifice."[30]

But there were differences, of course, between the Roman and the Celtic Churches. There was the question of Easter. The Celtic Church, claiming the authority of St. John, used a form of calculation based upon the Jewish lunar calendar which allowed Easter to fall, as did the Passover, in the month of Nisan (March-April). The first Easter had been on the 14th Nisan. Using their calculation, the Celts celebrated it on the Sunday falling between the 14th and 20th days after the first full moon following the Spring Equinox. They would do this even if Easter, so calculated, fell on the same day as the Passover, and used an 84 year cycle probably inherited from the Council of Arles in 314. The Roman Church made sure Easter never fell on the same day as the Passover, used a solar calendar and had arrived at a different form of cyclical calculation. The Irish were therefore the odd men out, as they were also in the matter of tonsure. The Romans had adopted the tonsure of St. Peter, which left a circle, symbolic of the crown of thorns, around the top of the head. The Irish, however, used what they called the tonsure of St. John, from ear to ear, which their opponents called the tonsure of Simon Magus, perhaps because it was associated with the Druids who were, in Latin, called Magi. Then there were differences in baptismal and rites of episcopal confirmation, but all these, though of symbolic importance, were not what really counted. The overall ethos, which was reflected in organizational habits arising from the tribal background, was the true bone of contention. These made the Celtic Church independent and threatened the growing organizational power of the Romans. In Ireland the spiritual adviser or soul friend (*anamchara*) was primary, rather than the ecclesiastical authority of the Bishops. The episcopal structure was threatened further by the fact that, though the Bishops still held all ecclesiastical jurisdiction, the real power lay with the Abbots. The Abbot, in fact, tended to be of the family of the tribal chief, and the tribal structure meant furthermore that the lineage of a monastery would be passed down along kinship lines, in the family which had made the initial grant. Connected to this, Irish monasteries had a large lay, and non-celibate family attached to them and, to begin with at least, a monastic female population. Most important, however, was the fact that these habits gave extreme autonomy and individuality to each foundation: they were more like Zen monasteries, one-church Papacies. Rites, customs and so forth differed locally, and there was no central organization. And, of course, when it came down to it, it was precisely this lack of organization that cost the Celtic Church its power.

The mere century or so following the arrival of St. Patrick constitutes the Golden Age of Celtic Spirituality. This is the period of the great schools and saints in Ireland, and the beginning of the 'pilgrimages for Christ' which were to sow the seeds of the culture of the Middle Ages in Europe. As Jonas tells us in his Life of Columbanus: "After Columbanus had passed many years in Bangor, the desire to go into exile began to grow in him, for he remembered the words of God to Abraham: 'Go forth out of thy country and from thy kindred, and out of thy father's house, and come into the land which I shall show thee.'"[31] This was 'white martyrdom' when a man for God's sake parted from everything he loved, and suffered and fasted thereby. Thus came about the *consuetudo peregrinandi*. Many were the monasteries and schools these wanderers founded, the kings they influenced, the souls they saved, the beasts and birds they befriended, the poems they wrote. And the greatest of these — or at least the best loved of these — is Saint Columba or Columcille.

Columba was born in 521, in Donegal, probably on December 7th, a Thursday, for tradition holds Thursday to be the day of Columba. His father was the local chieftain, his grandmother the daughter of King Erc, his mother a daughter of the ruling house of Leinster. Columba was thus of royal blood and it is always said that he could have been King of Ireland. But he was great in other ways also; Patrick had prophesied his coming while baptizing a chieftain of his tribe:

> A man child shall be born of his family,
> He will be a sage, a prophet, a poet,
> A loveable lamp, pure, clear,
> Who will not utter falsehood.
>
> He will be a sage, he will be pious,
> He will be King of the royal graces,
> He will be lasting and will be ever good,
> He will be in the eternal kingdom for his consolation.[32]

Just before he was born, his mother was visited by an angel bearing a beautiful colored mantle; she took it from him, but the angel took it back, and it seemed to expand until it crossed and covered valleys, mountains and even seas. Columba's mother was sad at losing such a gift, but the angel comforted her, saying she would have a son who would "blossom for heaven and lead innumerable souls into heaven's own country."

After studying with a local teacher — reading and writing — Columba went to Finian, at Moville, one of the masters of scripture and the saintly life at that time; thence he went to Gemman, a bard of Leinster, master of the ancient ways. Indeed, in his youth, Columba was as much poet as monk. But then he travelled to Clonard on the Boyne. Here he was ordained and he straightway returned to Donegal, consumed by one idea, to found a monastery. This he did, in 545, at Derry: prayer, fasting, charity, agriculture were the order of the day. But Columba realized that the times required something more. He began to travel, preaching, healing, teaching, and founding churches — in all, about 300 are ascribed to him. In this way he continued until his fortieth year took him across the sea to Scotland.

Why exactly he went is unknown. One tradition is as follows: Columba was a great scribe and lover of sacred writing. Finian of Moville, returning from Italy, brought with him a rare and beautiful book — perhaps a manuscript of Jerome — and kept it to himself. However, finally Columba managed to obtain permission to read it — but not only did he read it, but surreptitiously made a copy. When Finian found out about this, he demanded the copy as his by right. But Columba refused to comply. Thereupon, Diarmit, King of Meath, ruled: "To every cow her calf, to every book its copy." But Columba still would not return the copy he had made and war broke out. The men of Ulster slew 3,000 men of Meath at the Battle of Cooldrevny. Columba was heart-struck, repented and in penance swore never to set foot on Irish soil again.

This story is to be doubted. Columba was everywhere revered. Adamnán simply says: "Being desirous to make a journey for Christ from Ireland into Britain, he sailed forth."[33] *Peregrinari pro Christo*. It was the highest to which a man could aspire.

So Columba came to Iona, "the mecca of the Gael in spiritual geography," as Fiona McLeod says, adding: "To tell the story of Iona is to go back to God and to end in God."[34] Iona is a small, soft, green island — about three and a half miles long — with a hill, some cliffs and a pebbly beach, off the island of Mull on the northwest coast of Scotland. Though small in fact, it is in legend one of the largest of places. "Behold Iona, a blessing on each eye that sees it," says Columba.

Columba arrived on Iona on the eve of Whitsun in 563 with twelve companions. His first act on landing was to climb to high ground to make sure that Ireland was no longer visible. Seeing that it was not, the monks then dug a deep tomb and buried their coracle. Geologically, it is one of the most ancient pieces of rock in the world. Upon this rock Columba and the twelve built their monastery, church and guesthouse, and set about cultivating the ground. The fame of the place grew, and soon Columba's family contained upwards of 150 souls. These were of three ranks: the seniors, who transcribed, chiefly, and studied; the working brethren, who tilled the fields and took care of the animals; and the juniors who were still on probation. There was no personal property, and humility and compassion was continuously exercised in both human and natural companionship. From here, the brothers set out on mission and on retreat; from here Columba himself effected the conversion of the Picts and had his famous contest with the Druids, returning only once to Ireland to defend the poets, his brothers in spirit.[35]

Adamnán's *Life of Columba* — one of the greatest of hagiographical works — is written in three sections: prophecies, miracles and visions. The first shows Columba as a person of knowledge; the second as a person of power; the third, epitomizing the first two, as a person of God. Here Columba is shown living in the Spirit of God, in close communion with angels, radiating a divine, immaterial light. Often the other monks would surprise Columba alone at his prayers and discover to their fear and awe the whole structure of the Church filled with a celestial light, "descending from the utmost height of heaven, filling all space." Angels were often seen hovering about him, whispering in his ear. And a column of light was sometimes noticed to rise flaming from his head. These are things that would seem strange to us today, but they certainly would not have seemed so to saints of other times and places — St. Symeon the New Theologian, for instance, or St. Seraphim of Sarov. Nor in Celtic tradition is Columba unique in this. It is related of Fintan for instance that "A certain brother one night hearing that the holy father Fintan was keeping vigil in prayer desired to know in what place he so prayed. And seeking him on this side and on that, he came into the burial place of the holy one. It was a night of darkness; and the brother gazing at him face to face saw about him an exceeding light spreading far, so that his eyes were almost blinded, but God by the grace of the Holy Fintan preserved him."[36]

The most perfect story of Columba, however, is the story of his death. Columba knew he was to die, and he knew when. On the day that he was to die, he told the brothers he was about to leave them, and then went out onto the road to return to the monastery, stopping to rest about halfway back: "And while the Saint, feeble with age, as I said before, sat down for a little while and rested in that place, behold! there comes up to him the white horse, that faithful servant, mark you, that used to carry the milk-pails between the cow-pasture (or byre?) and the monastery. This creature then coming up to the Saint, wonderful to say, putting its head in his bosom, as I believe under the inspiration of God, in Whose sight every animal is endowed with a sense of things, because the Creator Himself hath so ordered it; knowing that his master would soon depart from him, and that he would see his face no more, began to utter plaintive moans, and, as if a man, to shed tears in abundance into the Saint's lap, and so to weep, frothing greatly. Which when the attendant saw, he began to drive away that weeping mourner; but the Saint forbad him, saying, "Let him alone! As he loves me so, let him alone; that into this my bosom he may pour out the tears of his most bitter lamentation. Behold! thou, even seeing that thou art a man, and hast a rational soul, couldest in no way know anything about my departure, except what I myself have lately shown to thee; but to this brute animal, destitute of reason, in what way soever the Maker Himself hath willed, He hath revealed that his master is about to go away from him." And, so saying, he blessed his sorrowing servant the horse, then turning about to go away from him."[37]

Columba then went and blessed the Island; went and blessed the granary; blessed the animals, blessed the monks and passed away, by the altar: "Then, in the next place, in the middle of the night, at the sound of the ringing of the bell, he rises in haste and goes to the church; and, running more quickly than the rest, he enters alone, and on bended knees falls down in prayer beside the altar. Diormit, his attendant, following more slowly, at the same moment sees from a distance that the whole church is filled within, in the direction of the Saint, with angelic light. But when he approaches the door, the same light that he had seen, which was also seen by a few other of the brethren, as they were standing at a distance, quickly disappeared. So Diormit, entering the church, keeps on asking, in a lamentable voice, "Where art thou, father?" And, feeling his way through the darkness, the lights of the brethren not yet being brought in, he finds the Saint prostrate before the altar; and, lifting him up a little and sitting beside him, he placed the holy head in his bosom. And meanwhile, the congregation of monks running up with the lights, and seeing their father dying, began to weep. And, as we have learnt from some who were there present, the Saint, his soul not yet departing, with his eyes opened upward, looked about on either hand with a wonderful cheerfulness and joy of countenance; doubtless seeing the holy angels coming to meet him. Then Diormit lifts up the holy right hand of the Saint that he may bless the choir of monks. But also the venerable man himself, so far as he could, at the same time moved his hand, so that, mark you, he might still be seen, while passing away, to bless the brethren by the motion of his hand, though he was not able to do so with his voice. And, after his holy benediction thus expressed, he immediately breathed out his spirit. Which having left the tabernacle of the body, his face remained ruddy, and wonderfully gladdened by an angelic vision; so that it appeared not to be that of one dead, but of one living and sleeping. Meanwhile, the whole church resounded with mournful lamentations."[38]

By this time, however, the story was already into its next chapter and the Celtic seed had moved closer towards its European germination. For by the kind offices of Saint and King Oswald of Northumbria, Aidan was already about to depart to establish Celtic Christianity in England, at Lindisfarne in Northumbria. There is a slight time lag, in fact, but not much. In the years immediately following Columba's death, Oswald of Northumbria, exiled from his Kingdom, sought refuge on Iona. When he was finally able to return to Northumbria, therefore, his first act was to send to Iona for a Bishop. Corman came first, but he was too hard; so Aidan went, a gentle, beautiful figure, who knew how to feed beginners on the milk of doctrine. Aidan in a way is the last pure Celt: his successors were already part of the Roman/European venture.[39]

Aidan died in 651; and on the day of his death a young boy herding sheep on a lovely hillside had a vision of a great stream of light breaking through the sky, and a choir of angels descending and gathering up a soul of exquisite brightness. The boy was Cuthbert. Cuthbert, in fact, was the first Roman Bishop of Lindisfarne, presiding over the monastery in the period of adjustment following the Synod of Whitby. Though he took little part in ecclesiastical disputes, his position seems to have been that unity of the Church was primary.

Cuthbert, then, in many ways was a transitional figure, but in his love of solitude and nature he was Celtic. Once at Coldringham, having preached to the nuns there, he retired to the beach to pray. A curious monk followed him to see what he did. He saw Cuthbert, his arms uplifted, walk into the icy water until the waves broke under his armpits. In this way he spent the night in prayer and meditation; then, at dawn he emerged from the water and fell upon his knees on the sand. Two small sea otters tumbled and played around his legs. His prayers finished, Cuthbert joyfully blessed the otters, who scurried back into the water again.[40]

Thus, as a sensible, historical unit, the Celtic Church was not long in existence. St. Augustine, the missionary from Rome, landed the year Columba died, 597 A.D. By 664 and the Synod of Whitby, the Celtic Church as a visible entity was over. But this is not to say that its work was done. In a sense it was only just beginning. Heiric of Auxerre exclaimed in 870: "Almost all Ireland, despising the sea, is migrating to our shores with a herd of philosophers." Decade after decade the stream of learned immigrants flowed, bringing with them "divine and human wisdom." The kings and lords of Europe loved these *peregrini*; they were as welcome at court as at church or in the monastery. Their habits of thought in science, music, literature, as well as theology, were to have far-reaching and profound effects. Alcuin and John Scotus Eriugena are only the brightest of these lights and the lesser lights were probably equally effective in the immediate transformation of European culture. "If anyone desires wisdom, we have it to sell," announced two *peregrini* arriving at the court of Charlemagne, who called them into his presence and inquired into the price of their wisdom. The answer was "suitable places and ready students, and food and clothing without which our peregrination cannot continue." These two are described as "incomparably erudite both in secular matters and in Holy Scripture."[41] In both of these, indeed, the Celtic heritage formed the Golden Age of Europe — monasteries, cathedrals, universities — upon whose riches we all still feed.

NOTES

[1] Given as a talk for the Lindisfarne Association on St. Cuthbert's Day, 1981, at the Cathedral of St. John the Divine in New York City. Another version to be published in Lindisfarne Letter 13 (Christmas 1981) available from the Lindisfarne Press, R. D. 2, West Stockbridge, MA 01266, U.S.A.

[2] Quoted in Robin Flower, *The Irish Tradition* (Oxford 1947), p. 48.

[3] David Jones, *The Kensington Mass* (London 1975), p. 16.

[4] Nora Chadwick, *The Age of the Saints in the Celtic Church* (Oxford 1961), p. 2.

[5] H. J. Massingham, *The Tree of Life* (London 1943), p. 40.

[6] J. W. Taylor, *The Coming of the Saints* (London 1906).

[7] Cf. Eleanor Merry, *The Flaming Door* (East Grimstead, 1962).

[8] W. B. Yeats, *Collected Poems* (London 1961), pp. 527-8.

[9] Quoted in Merry, *The Flaming Door*, p. 248.

[10] Alice Curtayne, *St. Brigid of Ireland* (New York 1954).

[11] Taylor, *The Coming of the Saints, p. 76.*

[12] *Ibid.*, p. 201.

[13] *Ibid.*, pp. 173-233.

[14] A. Marsh, *St. Patrick and his Writings* (Dublin 1966), p. 27.

[15] Cf. John Ryan, *Irish Monasticism: Origins and Development* (1972), Section III, Chapter 1.

[16] Myles Dillon ed., *Early Irish Society* (Cork 1954).

[17] Ludwig Bieler, "The Island of Scholars," *Revue du Moyen Age Latin*, Vol. 8, no 3 (1952), p 213.

[18] Quoted in Massingham, *The Tree of Life* p 37.

[19] *Ibid.*

[20] Quoted in Flower, *The Irish Tradition*, p 48.

[21] *Ibid.* p 5.

[22] Leslie Hardinge, *The Celtic Church in Britain* (London 1972), p 67.

[23] John Scotus Eriugena, *Homily on the Prologue to the Gospel of Saint John, translation and commentary*, Lindisfarne Press, West Stockbridge (forthcoming).

[24] Hardinge, *The Celtic Church*, pp. 59-60.

[25] Flower, *The Irish Tradition*, p 54.

[26] *Ibid.*, p 42.

[27] *Ibid.*

[28] Ryan, *Irish Monasticism.*

[29] Quoted in Flower, *The Irish Tradition.* p 24.

[30] Martin Harney, *The Legacy of St. Patrick* (Boston 1972), p 136.

[31] J. Wilson, *Life of Columban* (Dublin 1954), p 15.

[32] L. Menzies, *St. Columba of Iona* (London 1920), p 1.

[33] Adamnan, *Prophecies, Miracles and Visions of St. Columba* (Oxford 1895), p 4.

[34] Fiona McLeod, *The Divine Adventure, Iona, Studies in Spiritual History* (New York 1910), p 94.

[35] Menzies, *St. Columba.*

[36] Flower, *The Irish Tradition,* p 56.

[37] Adamnan, *St. Columba,* p 133.

[38] *Ibid.,* p 135.

[39] The Venerable Bede, *Ecclesiastical History of the English People* (Oxford 1969).

[40] C. J. Stranks, *The Life and Death of St. Cuthbert* (London 1964), p 13.

[41] J. T. MacNeill, *The Celtic Churches* (Chicago 1974), p 180.

ROMAN AND CELT IN SOUTHERN SCOTLAND

JOHN MacQUEEN

The intellectual and cultural history of Scotland has to a considerable extent been governed by its position to the north and west of the British Isles and Europe. Most cultural movements are from the centre to the periphery, and the usual post-glacial experience in Scotland has been adaptation to changes emanating from outside. And while Scotland as a geographical unit has tended to exist on the European cultural frontier, the geological structure of the country has ensured that internally a number of lesser cultural frontiers have also developed. The most obvious is the fault-line dividing Lowland and Highland, but on occasion others have been of substantial importance. In early historical times, the major frontier would seem to have been, not the Highland Line, but the Clyde-Forth isthmus, where the construction by the Romans of Grim's Dyke, the Antonine Wall, was a factor of lasting importance. To the south, in the region between Grim's Dyke and Hadrian's Wall from Tyne to Solway, the Celtic-speaking peoples had been subjected to considerable Roman influence; northward that influence was much weaker. Nor was Roman influence confined to the period between the establishment in 81 A.D. of Agricola's line of forts and the abandonment of the wall, perhaps about a century later; if anything, it increased after the withdrawal of Roman forces to the more southerly frontier. This may well have resulted from the establishment of several client states in the area between the two walls[1]; one, for instance, which formed the nucleus of the future kingdom of Strathclyde; another which developed into Lothian; still others, possibly, in the Tweed valley, Ayrshire and Galloway. The Celtic language of these states eventually developed into Cumbric, closely related to Welsh[2], but in some ways the people, or at least their rulers, seem to have been more Roman than the Romans. Their kings bore names like Caelius, Marcianus, Urbigenus, Eugenius and Constantinus[3], and seem to have regarded themselves and their people as *cives*[4] — citizens, that is to say, of the Roman Empire, and thus to be sharply distinguished from the barbarian Picts and Scots to the north and west; later also from the Angles to the south and east. Their bards developed a vernacular panegyric poetry which has distant affinities with the panegyrical verse and prose of the rhetorical schools of the later Western Empire, with the work, let us say, of Sidonius Apollinaris and Claudius Claudianus[5]. Grim's Dyke marked the northern frontier of this civilization, and the importance of the wall is indicated by the later place-names which have preserved references to the rampart. Duntocher, Kirkintilloch and Kinneil[6] are the most important. Equally for the people of the north, the wall remained a symbol of oppression and hostility. In the long run, it was the northern tradition which prevailed, and it is significant that Grim's Dyke, the name of the wall in vernacular Scots, was believed to contain a reference not to the builder of the wall, but to Grim, the legendary northerner who destroyed it, and who was ultimately, if inaccurately,

185

identified as the founder of the Anglo-Norman Graham family[7]. As late as the sixteenth century, the ruins at Inchtuthil in Perthshire, well north of Grim's Dyke, were regarded not as the remains of a Roman legionary fortress, but as the traces of a Pictish town abandoned and destroyed by its inhabitants when they adopted a scorched-earth policy in the face of the advancing army of Agricola[8]. The chief distinction between the Britons, who lived south of Grim's Dyke, and the Picts, who lived north of it, was, I suggest, the presence or absence of a conscious degree of political Romanization.

So far, the situation is relatively straight-forward. It is complicated by a further development — the fact that in the fourth century the terms Roman and Christian became virtually synonymous. In southern Scotland, as might have been expected, the results were not long in showing. The oldest known Christian establishment in Scotland, Candida Casa at Whithorn in Wigtownshire, was founded before 450 A.D., and is situated in the south-western part of the British territory between the walls. Developments further north were almost as swift. A reasonably well-documented tradition links the founder of Candida Casa, Nynia or Ninian, with a successful missionary journey to the Picts beyond Grim's Dyke[9]. The names of other missionaries from the south, in particular Servanus[10] and Kentigern[11], are also associated with this area, and it seems fairly certain that although southern Pictland had decisively rejected Roman military and civil imperialism, it rapidly accepted Romano-Judaic Christianity, almost certainly well before Columba's missionary expedition from Ireland to the northern Picts, which began in 563.

Some of the evidence for this is archaeological; much, however, is derived from sources usually regarded as suspect, the *Lives* of the saints mentioned. None of these, certainly, is a contemporary account of the life of the saint in question; their value, rather, is as documents in cultural history, and the features which upset most historians — the ubiquity of the miraculous, the improbabilities and impossibilities, even where miracles are not involved, the apparently random repetition and transference of material from one *Life* to another — these, paradoxically enough, are the very features which render the *Lives* important for the cultural historian and the ethnologist. We find in them a late, traditional record of the effect these saints, with their alien cultural ideals, had on societies which they influenced, an effect which inevitably, because these were the features most affected, to a considerable extent became expressed in terms of pre-Christian, and indeed pre-Roman, ideals and assumptions, in terms, if you like, of the folk-lore and folk-belief, the religion and traditions which were superseded by the work of the individual saints. Equally inevitably, the form taken by the *Lives* differed significantly in the more or less Romanised areas under consideration, in Cumbric, that is to say, and in Pictish territory.

In what follows, I shall take the leading features of Christian Roman society for granted. Irish and Welsh sagas and poetry have preserved a reasonably full version of late Iron-Age Celtic society and its beliefs[12], and only the briefest outline is possible here. It was organised round an elaborate system of kingships, with tribal and provincial kings of predominating influence. Kingship depended on ultimate descent from a divine being. Certain powerful individuals and their followers operated outside the tribal system, and had a particularly close relationship with the supernatural Otherworld. The Otherworld, in turn, was not so much a different world, as a different face, the supernatural aspect of *this* world, and the two came into joint view at certain seasons of the year — Hallowe'en and Mayday especially — and in certain places or in relation to certain objects; trees, springs, mounds, to name no others. Otherworld beings exercised their powers in terms of the natural world. Marriage or fruitful sexual union between people of the two worlds was an accepted part of general belief, an exceptionally gifted mortal being often regarded as the offspring of such a union. Insular Celtic beliefs, it is clear, were very different from most current in the later Roman Empire and from Christian doctrine, but on the periphery of the Roman world they survived (as medieval Welsh saga illustrates) to a surprising degree, and beyond the Roman frontier, in Ireland and (one presumes) Pictland, they retained much of their pristine vigour. Christianity everywhere in the Roman Empire entailed a very considerable "cultural shock"; in Britain the evidence seems to suggest that the shock was at its mildest during the pre-monastic fourth century, and in proximity to the secular organisation of the Empire; with increasing distance, the passage of time, and the triumph of monasticism, the effect was magnified. Everywhere it was necessary for the old beliefs and assumptions to reach some kind of cultural accommodation with the new faith. The extent of the shock and disturbance is a measure of the power of the new ideas.

Elsewhere[13] I have written on the significance of the documents which deal with the earliest saint of southern Scotland, the *Lives* of Nynia or Ninian. Here only a few points need be added. Nynia is the most Roman, and in some ways the most secular, of these saints, and operated in what was by local standards a highly Romanized context. It seems possible that his mission belonged to the actual time of the Empire in Britain — the very late fourth and early fifth century — and that Candida Casa was chosen as the centre of his operations at least partly because of its position north and west of Hadrian's Wall, but within relatively easy distance of Roman Carlisle (*Luguvallium*), a town which retained its importance even after the end of the Western Empire[14]. To judge by the miracle stories, the cultural achievement of Nynia included the establishment of a working relationship between the tribal or provincial king and a church based on moderate monastic ideals, the acceptance of monastic ideals as a new way to power over nature, and so to power over human society, and the establishment of new and more secure methods of pasture and agriculture, with a corresponding decrease in the number of cattle-raids which form so striking a part of early Celtic story-telling, and so presumably of early Celtic society. The saint's bull, which in the *Lives* kills the leader of the raiding party, is a less colourful version of the Brown of Cuailnge, the great Ulster bull which dominates the Irish epic *Cattle Raid of Cuailnge*[15], but whereas in the Irish the bull is guarded by an invincible hero, Cú Chulainn, in the

Lives the saint merely draws a line round the herd with the point of his crozier. No other protection is necessary. Once the raiders have entered the charmed circle from which they are unable to escape, the bull itself deals with them. The initial stage of the replacement of physical strength by abstract legal and moral sanctions could scarcely be more aptly symbolised.

The crozier, the symbol of the bishop's authority, soon became regarded as an instrument of supernatural power[16], even when separated from the bishop. The saga of Nynia contains the story of a truant boy pupil, who stole the crozier. By its power he was enabled to escape across the sea to Ireland in a coracle frame which had not yet been equipped with its outer leather cover. This remarkable fact filled him with so much veneration that, when he reached Ireland, he planted the crozier, which at once became a wonder-working tree with a healing spring welling up from its roots. Tree and spring both belong to the older stratum of belief, but they have been Christianised and Romanised, or rather the Christian ideals of the late Empire have been made acceptable by the process of acculturation, in terms of which Nynia's exotic crozier has been credited with the virtues once believed to inhere in tree and spring — or rather the virtues inherent in tree and spring have become simple consequences of the power inherent in Nynia's exotic crozier. The process closely parallels that seen in the episode of the cattle-raid.

These are processes within society, and for the most part the traditions connected with Nynia are concerned with such activities. He is associated, however, with the eremetical figure of St. Martin of Tours[17], and the most obvious departure from the social norm previously accepted is the emphasis laid on celibacy as a religious ideal, an emphasis which in Britain as elsewhere in the Roman Empire was sometimes felt to threaten the very existence of society. The conflict between Nynia and the local king Tudwal may represent not so much a conflict of Christian and pre-Christian beliefs and attitudes as a conflict between pre-monastic and monastic Christianity in a society which under Roman influence had already moved some distance from Celtic paganism. The miracle of the newly-born child speaking to clear a celibate priest accused of paternity points in the same direction. In Celtic lands, generally, monastic celibacy came to be fully accepted only with the recognition of the saint as head of a monastic body which existed apart from secular society, and which on occasion might altogether withdraw in a way roughly parallel to that of the dedicated hero outside society, the secular Finn and the Fenians or possibly Arthur and his warrior companions. For part of the time at least the home of the saint was the wilderness, and it is as a consequence of this fact that the characteristically early Irish poetry of wild nature is normally either monastic or Fenian. The monasticism of the Egyptian and Syrian deserts had already given a precise form to the religious impulse away from society; this was adapted to more northerly conditions, and the word *desertum* is not uncommon among place-names of early ecclesiastical origin[18]; in Scotland, the best-known example is Dysart in Fife, where the most striking feature is the cave inhabited for a time by St. Servanus[19]. The word *Desert* has not survived in connection with

Nynia, but his cave in Glasserton parish on the coast of Luce Bay contains signs of early ecclesiastical occupation, and is mentioned in the oldest extant form of the saint's *Life*.

Another saint, in late records associated with Nynia, is Medana, the patroness of the two Kirkmaidens in Wigtownshire; she too has her cave on the west side of Luce Bay, more or less directly opposite that of St. Nynia. Her legend, incidentally, illustrates[20] another method of acculturation; it is a variant of the international folk-tale type A.T. 706 "The Maiden Without Hands", classified as A.T. 706B "Present to the Lover", and summarised by Stith Thompson[21] in these words: "Maiden sends to her lecherous lover (brother) her eyes (hands, breasts) which he has admired." Stories of this kind, we must assume, were already familiar in secular versions, and could easily be adapted to express the new ideals which, by this very fact, themselves became the more acceptable.

The *Life* of Nynia is the quietest, the least sensational of all the early Scottish legends and this, I suggest, results from the proximity in time and space of Nynia's Candida Casa to the civic actualities of the Christian Roman Empire. The legend of Medana stands in marked contrast, and it is worth noting that although her church-sites are in the neighbourhood of Candida Casa, the saint herself is presented as a refugee from unRomanised Ireland, forced into exile as a result of her adherence to monastic ideals. The element of wonder-story is still more increased when we turn from these southern *Lives* to that of the more northerly saint; Servanus. The difference, I suggest, is to be explained by the greater distance from the Roman cultural centre of the society affected by the labours of Servanus. He is a saint of the area round the Forth estuary, which in early Christian times fell into three main territorial divisions. To the north, entirely outside the Roman frontier, lay Fife, later one of the seven provinces of the kingdom of the Picts, and itself originally perhaps a separate Pictish provincial or local kingdom. To the west lay Manaw[22], consisting of the modern county of Clackmannan and the eastern part of the modern Stirlingshire, with the Stirlingshire parish of Slamannan possibly marking the southern boundary. Manaw lay partly inside, but mainly beyond the Roman wall. South of the estuary and east of the river Avon lay Lothian, represented by the modern counties of East, Mid and West Lothian. This area was entirely Romanised, and included such important centres of Roman activity as Cramond and Inveresk, each the site of a Roman fort, commemorated in the first element, *caer*, of the place-name Cramond[23]. In terms of his legend, the missionary activities of Servanus are almost confined to the western and northern areas of this region — to Manaw, that is to say, and Fife. He is a saint of the un-Romanised Picts rather than of the Britons, and although his historical period is not known with any precision, he is certainly a later figure than Nynia.

His *Life* falls into two main sections, both of which it is interesting to compare with parallel episodes in the various *Lives* of Nynia. The latter, for instance, is described as a native Briton, whose first-hand knowledge of Rome was gained during a single, comparatively brief, visit. Southern audiences, it is clear, had sufficient confidence in their own status as *cives* to require no more than a minimum token of imperial recognition for their saint. On and beyond the frontier, in Manaw and Pictland generally, additional reassurance was required — clear proof that the credentials of the local saint were not themselves merely local, but derived from the cultural centre. Very few Pictish saints are said to have been Picts. The most notable incomer, of course, is the apostle Andrew[24], who later became patron saint of Scotland, with his seat at St. Andrews in Fife. Regulus, who brought the relics of the apostle to St. Andrews, is described[25] as a Greek from Constantinople or the great monastery of Patras. Boethius, the patron of Kirkbuddo in Angus, was an Irishman who had spent long years in Italy[26]. Adrian, who suffered martyrdom on the Isle of May, was a Pannonian, a Hungarian[27]. Apart from Andrew and Servanus, Bonifatius, who founded Restennet near Forfar in Angus, has the most impressive dossier[28]. He is described as an Israelite, descended from the sister of the apostles Peter and Andrew, who had been Pope before he set out to evangelise Pictland. On his journey from Rome, he was accompanied by six other bishops (one presumably for each Pictish province), among who was Servandus, perhaps the same as Servanus, and if so, presumably the patron-designate of Fife, or at least Manaw.

A quite different story is told in the first part of the *Life* of Servanus, which gives the story of the saint's life from conception to his sixty-seventh year. He was born by a miraculous conception, the elder twin son of the king and queen of Canaan. He was educated and made his monastic profession at Alexandria in Egypt, after which he spent twenty years as bishop of Canaan and seven as patriarch of Jerusalem. During the latter period, an angel made him a crozier with wood cut from the tree which had provided material for the True Cross, while he himself carved three other staffs from the wood of the same tree. Thereafter he spent three years in Constantinople, and seven years as Pope in Rome, after which he made the journey to Britain, finally arriving at the island of Inchkeith in the Firth of Forth. Everything and every place that might redound to the ecclesiastical credit of Servanus is included in this part of the narrative. At the same time, the narrator exhibits an essential geographical vagueness — he does not, for instance, know the position of Canaan, which he seems to confuse with Libya; he invents an island of the Savior somewhere between Constantinople and Rome, while between Rome and the English Channel he places a Hill of Tears and a Valley of Beasts, in the latter of which Servanus routs a company of diabolical animals. The landscape is more that of the Otherworld than of the Christian Roman Empire. The aim of the narrator is obviously to awe and inspire the simple inhabitants of a remote territory.

This however is not his sole aim; he wishes also to persuade his hearers or readers that Servanus was intimately associated with them, with their immediate surroundings, their daily lives and needs. Rome, Constantinople, Jerusalem, Alexandria, Canaan — these are names which lend *numen* to the narrative. Flesh and blood is provided by names more local and familiar such as Kinneil, Culross,

Loch Leven, Dysart, Tullibody, Tillicoultry, Alva, Aithrie and Dunning. Of these nine, Kinneil is in West Lothian at the eastern extremity of Grim's Dyke; all the others are in Pictish territory, Fife, Perthshire or Manaw. By contrast with miracles in the earlier narrative, many of the later ones are homely, even humble, concerned with matters likely to interest a community of hill farmers and their dependents. At Tullibody, Servanus cured a man afflicted with an insatiable hunger. At Tillicoultry he restored life to the still-born twin sons of a poor little woman. In Alva one evening a peasant farmer sacrificed his only pig to provide a meal for the saint, but found it alive on his domestic altar the next morning. Servanus had a pet ram which was stolen and eaten by a thief who attempted to deny his crime. The ram however gave him away by bleating from his stomach. The subject-matter of these miracles stands at a long remove from the wood of the tree of the True Cross, or the monsters in the Valley of Beasts, but equally it comes very close to the business and bosoms of people in Dark Age Manaw. The figure of Servanus unites in itself the numinous authority and domestic immediacy necessary for the adaptation of Pictish society into the Romano-Christian cultural community of western Europe.

The second part of the legend contains no geographical uncertainty; the author knows the exact location of each place mentioned, and on occasion — sometimes in a slightly disguised fashion — provides additional individualising touches. In Culross, for instance, which he obviously knew well, he singles out two features. One is the actual meaning of the name, "holly-point"[29]. This is present in the text, but is concealed beneath the remark that Servanus came to Culross "and cleared away all the thorns and thickets which abounded in the place." At some point in transmission, one presumes, an additional remark such as "and that is why the place was called Culenros" has dropped out. The second local feature emphasised is the presence at Culross of a remarkable apple-tree "which among the moderns is called Morglas" ("Sea-green"?). This apple-tree grew from a staff which Servanus threw across the Forth estuary from Kinneil in West Lothian, a more than Olympic distance of some 2½ miles. One is at once reminded of the miracle of Nynia's staff, and the importance of trees in pre-Christian Celtic belief. Kinneil stands at the end of Grim's Dyke, and the name itself means "Wallsend"[30]. Servanus threw his staff from Romanised into non-Roman territory, where it took root and became a tree, in the vicinity of which Servanus, as he was told by an angel, was destined to be buried. The importance of the move from known Roman into unknown non-Roman territory could scarcely be symbolised better. The narrative does not actually say so, but it is tempting to identify the staff with one of those hewn by Servanus from the tree of the True Cross.

It is more certain that the crozier with which Servanus effortlessly slew the hitherto invincible dragon of Dunning in Perthshire is to be identified with the one cut for him by the angel. In the *Lives* of Nynia and Servanus alike, the image of the crozier, the sign of episcopal authority, seems above all to come into its own when the influence of the bishop is extended into new territory beyond the frontier; in the case of Nynia, Ireland; in that of Servanus, Manaw and Pictland generally. The effect is symbolised by the transformation of crozier into living tree, or by its successful use as a weapon against the monstrous powers of evil.

On the evidence of the miracle stories, the mission of Servanus was essentially to the community of Manaw. Fife, Kinross and Perthshire seem to be regarded as circumjacent desert regions, ideally suited for spiritual retreat or solitary encounters with the powers of evil. St. Serf's Isle in Loch Leven, Kinross, is a typically Celtic island sanctuary; it was in a cave at Dysart in Fife that Servanus had his celebrated theological encounter with the Devil, and at Dunning in Perthshire that he fought the dragon. But the narrative centres on Manaw, its Pictish inhabitants and their spiritual and physical needs.

NOTES

[1]See particularly H. M. Chadwick, "The British Kingdoms", *Early Scotland* (Cambridge 1949), pp. 137-158. Chadwick suggested a fairly late re-extension of Roman power north of Hadrian's Wall. "The evidence seems ... to point to the same transaction on the part of a later *Dux Brittaniarum*, whereby he handed over to native princes what was left of the northern frontier army, with its equipment and stores. That might be Maximus, or the officer whom he left in charge. Or it may be that native princes had succeeded to the command, and transformed the army into dynastic forces." For a more recent view, see S. Frere, *Britannia* (London 1967), p. 165: "Under Commodus a new phase opened in which Roman influence was accepted in the Lowlands in return for local autonomy, and the tribes could accordingly be used as a buffer between Hadrian's Wall and the North." And later in the book (p. 352) is the passage: "Much greater reliance came" (i.e. after 369 A.D.) "to be placed upon the federate tribes of the Lowlands; there were now no Roman forces north of the Wall. This change probably marks the inception of a new arrangement under which the Votadini were granted more complete independence with client or federate status, and the assumption of responsibility for frontier protection under their own leaders. ... A similar arrangement may possibly have been made with the dynasty of Strathclyde." It is now commonly held that the new province of Valentia, established in 369, was northern and centred on Carlisle in Cumberland. The first hint of this was provided in J. C. Mann, "The Administration of Roman Britain", *Antiquity* xxxv (1961), 316-320. If the location is accepted, it is likely to be important in any consideration of the career of Nynia. See below, p. 000.

[2]K. H. Jackson, *Language and History in Early Britain* (Edinburgh 1953) pp. 9-10.

[3]The genealogical lists are most conveniently consulted in A. W. Wade-Evans, *Nennius's "History of the Britons"* (London 1938), pp. 101-114. Cf. E. Phillimore, *Y Cymmrodor* ix (1888), pp. 141 ff.

[4]See, *e.g.* St. Patrick's *Epistola ad Milites Corotici* 2, in A. Marsh, *Saint Patrick's Writings*, (Dundalk 1961), p. 23: *non dico civibus meis neque civibus sanctorum Romanorum sed civibus daemoniorum:* Nennius, *Historia Brittonum* 63, in F. Lot, *Nennius et l'Historia Brittonum*, 2 vols. (Paris 1934), I, 202. *Deodric contra illum Urbgen cum filiis dimicabat fortiter — in illo autem tempore aliquando hostes, nunc cives vincebantur.*

[5]N. K. Chadwick, "Intellectual Contacts between Britain and Gaul in the Fifth Century", *Studies in Early British History* (Cambridge 1954), pp. 189-253: *Poetry and Letters in Early Christian Gaul* (London 1955).

[6]Duntocher is Gaelic, and means "Fort on the Causeway", i.e. Grim's Dyke itself or perhaps more probably the Military Way which ran immediately to the south. See W. J. Watson, *History of the Celtic Place-Names of Scotland* (Edinburgh and London 1926) p. 486. The fort itself is now called Golden Hill; see Anne S. Robertson, *The Antonine Wall*, revised ed. (Glasgow 1973), pp. 85-88. Kirkintilloch is a hybrid Cumbric-Gaelic name meaning "Fort at the top of the hill" (Watson, p. 348). Kinneil is another hybrid

Cumbric-Gaelic or Pictish-Gaelic name (Watson, pp. 346-348), and means "End of wall", corresponding precisely to Wallsend in Northumberland at the eastern extremity of Hadrian's Wall.

[7]John of Fordun, *Chronica Gentis Scotorum*, ed. W. F. Skene, 2 vols. (Edinburgh 1871, 1872), III.v; H. Boece, *The Chronicles of Scotland, translated into Scots by John Bellenden 1531*, ed. R. W. Chambers and E. C. Batho, 2 vols. (Edinburgh and London 1938, 1941), vii, 9 (I.p.292).

[8]Boece, iv 13 (I.pp.165-166).

[9]J. MacQueen, *St. Nynia* (Edinburgh and London 1961), pp. 20-28.

[10]"Life of Saint Servanus" in W. F. Skene, *Chronicles of the Picts, Chronicles of the Scots, and other Early Memorials of Scottish History* (Edinburgh 1867), pp. 412-420.

[11]A. P. Forbes, *Lives of S. Ninian and S. Kentigern* (Edinburgh 1874).

[12]See especially M. L. Sjoestedt, *Gods and Heroes of the Celts*, translated by Myles Dillon (London 1949).

[13]"History and Miracle Stories in the Biography of Nynia', *Innes Review*, XIII (1962), 115-129.

[14]C. Thomas, *Britain and Ireland in Early Christian Times AD 400-800* (London 1971), pp. 78-80. The suggestion in the *Lives* that the area round Whithorn was already Christian before Nynia became bishop is supported by the fact that "it was unknown in the ancient church for a bishop to be sent to a place where there was no flock for him to minister to." (R. P. C. Hanson, *Saint Patrick, His Origins and Career*, Oxford 1968, p. 54. Cf. E. A. Thompson, *The Visigoths in the Time of Ulfilas*, Oxford 1966, p. xvii). As late as 685, Cuthbert on a visit to Carlisle was taken by his hosts to see the Roman walls and the Roman fountain. "There is no positive ground for thinking that the continuity of its occupation was broken between Romano-British and Anglo-Saxon times." (P. Hunter Blair, *An Introduction to Anglo-Saxon England*, Cambridge 1956, p. 280).

[15]*Táin Bó Cúalnge from the Book of Leinster*, ed. C. O'Rahilly (Dublin 1970).

[16]In terms of the Stith Thompson *Motif-Index of Folk-Literature* 6 vols. (Bloomington and Helsinki, 1932 ff.), Magic crozier is motif D1277.1 (T. Peete Cross, *Motif-Index of Early Irish Literature*, Bloomington, N.D.). Other motifs in the miracle stories mentioned include: (*Lives* of Nynia): — B.182.3, Magic bull: *D1272, Magic circle: D1294, Magic footprint: D1567.5, Saint's crozier produces fountain: D1673, Magic staff blossoms: D1841.4, Man proof against wet from rain: F952, Blindness miraculously cured: *F971.1, Dry rod blossoms: F971.7, Sowing and reaping same day: Q466, Embarkation in leaky boat: Q451.7, Blindness as punishment: Q552.3, Failure of crops during reign of wicked king: T585.2, Child speaks at birth: (*Life* of Medana): — D1524.3, Magic stone serves as boat: (*Life* of Servanus): — A2711.2, Tree blessed that made the cross: *D954, Magic branch: D1318.7.1, Flesh of animals reveals guilt: D1524.1.2.1, Saint casts staff to distant island: D1817.0.1, Magic detection of theft: D1817.2*, Saints magically detect crime: E32, Resuscitated eaten animal: E168, Cooked animal comes to life: M416.1, Curse; appetite of twelve men: Q572, Sickness as punishment remitted: T540.1, Supernatural birth of saint: V224.2, Food (animals) eaten by saint miraculously replaced.

[17]Bede, *Historia Ecclesiastica*, III.iv, is the earliest authority for this connection, which may have more substance than I was inclined to allow in *St. Nynia*.

[18]P. W. Joyce, *Irish Names of Places*, 2nd. edition (Dublin 1870), pp. 312-314: J. M. Mackinlay, *Influence of the Pre-Reformation Church on Scottish Place-Names* (Edinburgh and London 1904), pp. 35-44: W. J. Watson, pp. 256-257.

[19]See above, footnote 10.

[20]*Breviarii Aberdonensis Pars Estivalis*, ff. 158v-159r, most conveniently consulted in the Maitland Club facsimile, 2 vols. (London 1852, 1854). Her feast day is 19th November.

[21]A. Aarne and S. Thompson, *The Types of the Folktale*, Second Revision (Helsinki 1961), p. 242.

[22]Manaw is not the same as the territory of the Gododdin or Votadini, as seems to be assumed, for example, by S. Frere (op. cit., p. 381). See rather K. H. Jackson, *The Gododdin. The Oldest Scottish Poem* (Edinburgh 1969), pp. 70-75. The phrase "Manaw of the Gododdin" is on record once only, in Nennius, *Historia Brittonum*, 62 (F. Lot, I, p. 202, where Lot falls into the same error as Frere). Professor Jackson suggests that it is called "of the Gododdin" to distinguish it from Manaw, the Isle of Man in the Irish Sea. If the position of Manaw in relation to Grim's Dyke is significant, the name may in effect mean rather "that part of Manaw south of Grim's Dyke and so subject to the Gododdin", as opposed to the more northerly portion which was not so subject. It is also worth noting that the only place-names in Scotland commemorating the powerful tribe of the Maeatae, Dumyat and Myothill, both occur in the Stirlingshire area of Manaw north of Grim's Dyke (Watson, pp. 56-59.). It is usually assumed (as by Watson, *idem.*, and Frere, p. 164), that when the early third-century historian Dio Cassius, as abbreviated in the 11th century by Xiphilinus, refers to the Maeatae as living "close to the Wall which divides the island into two parts" (lxxvii, 12), he is referring to Hadrian's Wall, reconditioned by the emperor Severus in or about the year 205, some twenty years, perhaps, after the final abandonment of Grim's Dyke. The place-name evidence strongly suggests that this is erroneous, that Manaw was the original tribal territory of the Maeatae, even possibly that Servanus was their first bishop. The *oppidum* may have been Stirling, the *urbs Giudi* of Bede, *Historia Ecclesiastica*, I.xii (A. Graham, "Giudi", *Antiquity* xxxiii, 1959, pp. 63 ff.) Glasgow, the Strathclyde episcopal centre, is situated at much the same distance from the *oppidum*, Dumbarton, as Culross is from Stirling.

[23]It seems improbable that the first element is another place-name, Carriden in West Lothian, is *caer*. See Watson, p. 370, A. Macdonald, *The Place-Names of West Lothian* (Edinburgh and London 1941), pp. 25-26, K. H. Jackson, *The Gododdin*, pp. 75-78. The Roman fort at Carriden is three-quarters of a mile from the east end of Grim's Dyke; see Robertson, pp. 42-43. Cramond means "Fort on the river Almond" (Watson, p. 369). Compare such names of Roman sites in Wales as Caernarvon, Carmarthen and Caerleon (also Kirkintilloch; footnote 6 above).

[24]Skene, *Picts and Scots*, pp. 138-140, 183-193, 375-377.

[25]Skene, *Picts and Scots*, p. 140 (Constantinople); p. 183 and p. 375. (Patras).

[26]Skene, *Picts and Scots*, pp. 410-411. For the name Kirkbuddo, Carbuddo, see Watson, pp. 313-314. A Roman marching camp of the first century date is situated nearby.

[27]Skene, *Picts and Scots*, pp. 424-425.

[28]Skene, *Picts and Scots*, pp. 421-423.

[29]Watson, p. 497. Watson understood the name to be Gaelic; it may however have been Gaelicised from a Pictish or Cumbric original, compounded from elements cognate (as is the Gaelic) with Welsh *celyn*, "holly" and *rhos*, "moor". There is no obvious "point" at Culross.

[30]See above, footnote 6.

SECTION IV

THE CELTIC CONTINUUM: FOLK LORE, LITERATURE, MUSIC, AND ART

MATERIAL CULTURE, MYTH AND FOLK MEMORY

ANNE ROSS

Every year, all over the British Isles, people gather together on the dates of the ancient Celtic festivals to celebrate archaic ritual and observe, in no matter how modified a manner, the rites once performed in honour of the powerful pagan deities. In most cases they are unlikely today to understand the significance of their activities. They are simply carrying on age-old tradition as taught to them by their immediate forbears. The summer and winter solstices are noted by the lighting of great bonfires. The feast of the pan-Celtic god Lugos has persisted under various guises on August 1st to mark the beginning of harvest. Singing, dancing, feasting, the racing of horses, often across water, persisted and have survived in some areas into this century. Old myths were re-enacted, telling of the conflict of the powers of bloom and blight, fruition or failure, over one of man's most important staple products — grain. There can be no doubt that this great feast was in honour of the popular young Celtic god — Lugos in Gaul, Lugh in Ireland, Lleu in Wales — a kind of Celtic Mercury. In her brilliant study of the Lughnasa festivities, Máire MacNeill concludes:

> In Irish legend the booty [i.e., the sustaining food] was won by the young god, but the power to produce it was the older god's. The purpose of the festival, in fact, was to win the harvest, and to extort from the old god such an assurance as the aged Mac Creiche gave: 'I leave corn and milk in your land, and mast in your woods and increase in your soil.' The chief god makes the wealth of the earth — only he can. At the right and destined time the young god is to take it and give it to the people. The tensions of longing, need and readiness snap into drama. The chief god appears temporarily hostile because he is about to lose his treasure. The sickles have been sharpened for the cutting of the corn, an act of violence. Hope and expectation mount. Dread must be overcome. Men look for the arrival of the magnetic and free-handed champion. This is the myth of Lughnasa, the festival of the beginning of harvest.[1]

Second perhaps in importance down the ages is the observance of Samhain, Hallow E'en, the beginning of winter when the powers of darkness are threatening to obliterate for ever the life-giving rays of the fertilising sun. As, in old Celtic tradition, the gods were particularly hostile and dangerous at this time, playing cruel tricks on their worshippers, propitiated by sacrifice — human in pagan times — so in the surviving practices the festival is marked once more by fire, violence, the demand on the part of the young men for gifts from those at whose homes they clamour for entry and the subsequent vandalism which ensued when hospitality was refused. Again, as in ancient times, hints of sexual licence and temporary release from the normal conventions are commonplace. As the ancient gods walked amongst mankind on this night, so in the more modern version of the archaic rite the spirits of the dead and the evil supernatural forces are abroad.

February 1st continued into this century to be widely celebrated as the feast day

Plate 1: Garland Day Ceremony, 29 May, Castleton, Derbyshire.
Source: BBC TV.

of the gentle goddess Bride or Bridget, in origin daughter of the Irish god, the Dagda, goddess in triple form with a special interest in the spheres of metallurgical skills, the arts generally, and the flocks in particular. She was taken over into Christianity as St. Bridget of Kildare and her cult spread widely. The feast was known as Imbolc, and on this day the ewes were alleged to begin to lactate. Adorned images of the goddess, known in Catholic tradition as the midwife of the Virgin, were created and elaborate associated ritual was carried out well within living memory.

Bealtaine, May 1st, the feast of the ancient pan-Celtic god Belenos, when the beasts were purified by fire, and the fields and homesteads were protected by men running around them bearing branches of blazing foliage, likewise survives down to the present day as a folk festival.

One of the most amazing survivals is the memory of the power of the horned god who, in his antlered form, had, as one of his names, Cernunnos, 'The Horned One'. Venerable, benign, god of commercial prosperity, lord of the woods and wild life, his cult goes back in Europe for millennia, and in spite of the efforts of the Church to destroy this most potent and deeply-venerated god, he survives vestigially to the present day.[2] It is an extraordinary sight to visit a village in Staffordshire, England, on a certain day in September, and witness three pairs of antlers being taken from their place of honour in the local church — for a wise Church accepted the ancient customs and so rendered them harmless and satisfied the people — and being carried on the shoulders of six local men accompanied by singing and dancing round all the miles of the village boundaries, in spite of their great weight.[3] An even more primitive version of this ritual takes place in Powys, Wales, in April, where the dancers not only have antlers on their heads but also are clad in animal skins. Such survivals could be elaborated indefinitely. Sufficient has been said to demonstrate that we do not learn about the past from a study of the past alone. The truth of our observation of the material evidence and our studies of the manuscripts, classical and vernacular alike, can be strikingly substantiated by careful research into traces of our past in the present. And Canada is the guardian of many remnants of a rich heritage which in Europe has shrunk to the periphery of the western world.[4]

My chosen field of research, that of the Celts, in every aspect of their mundane and spiritual life, is one full of complexities and pitfalls which increase as new information constantly comes to light. I have long been aware of the necessity for Celtic scholars to receive some training in material culture, and for archaeologists to acquire some familiarity with the nature of the Celtic world. Other disciplines are being steadily explored and utilised in order to assist us with the very real problems that confront anyone daring to broach this thicket of thorns, more prickly and more treacherous than any we may chance upon in the rich motifs that Celtic folklore delights in.

Strangely enough, and perhaps because they were men of deep sensibility but outside of the immediate Celtic world, it is two scholars — one a literary writer and the other an archaeologist — who, in their day, have made some of the most perspicacious comments on the Celtic individuality that I, personally, have ever read. The first is the great novelist D. H. Lawrence, who, in a brief trip to the Scottish Hebrides wrote, in an unpublished letter to his sister-in-law:

> There is still something of an Odyssey up there, in among the islands, and the silent lochs — like the twilight morning of the world, the herons fishing undisturbed by the water and the sea running far in, for miles. The cottages are low and almost invisible, built into the earth. It is still out of the world, and very like the beginning of Europe.

How right Lawrence was; and his vivid observations are echoed by the remarks of the brilliant scholar, O. G. S. Crawford, the first Archaeology Officer in the Ordnance Survey in Britain, whose home was at Nursling, Hampshire, from whence the renowned St. Boniface sailed away to convert the heathen of Northern Germany only to find that the Irish missionaries had already done it for him. O. G. S. Crawford had several links with the Celtic world. He did field work in the Outer Hebrides, and had much to say in his autobiography, 'Said and Done', about these strange, remote islands where an Iron-Age way of life lingered on — beyond the disasters of the 1745-46 campaign of Prince Charles Edward Stuart and Billy the Butcher Boy as his antagonists called the Duke of Cumberland — right down into the present century. Like Lawrence, Crawford appreciated the remarkable fact that here, in our own country, an archaic society still existed, speaking an ancient language and possessing a way of life which has the power to recreate for us the beginnings of our own civilisation in a way that any comparison with modern

Plate 2: Sucellos, 'The Good Striker,' Arc-sur-Tille, Côte d'Or: his mallet and *patera* attributes link him with the great Irish God, The Dagda, 'The Good God,' with his club and cauldron.
Source: National Museum of France, St. Germain-en-laye, Paris.

Plate 3: Head of Celtic Horse, La Bussière-Etable, Haute-Vienne. National Museum of France.

Plate 4: Bronze Gallo-Roman Horse.
Source: National Museum of France.

primitive cultures can never attempt to do. Crawford found the people shy and unforthcoming; this is because he did not speak their language and this, of course, formed a great barrier. A knowledge of the Gaelic language imparts an understanding of the subtle, tortuous Gaelic thought-processes; jokes can be exchanged, stories told, situations appreciated. The watchful look of people who have suffered so much in the way of battles and evictions, at the hands of the English and the Lowland Scots, soon goes when the stranger communicates with them in their own tongue. Crawford goes on to describe his Hebridean trip:

> In May and June I visited the Outer Hebrides, bicycling from south to north through South and North Uist, Harris and Lewis, ending up at Stornoway. It was a mistake to do the trip in this direction, for at that time of year the prevalent wind is from the north, as I found to my cost; though my *official* excuse was the ancient remains, I found the modern types of habitation far more interesting, particularly the 'black houses'... there were still a few cottages built entirely of peat, often in lonely and isolated places by the sea shore, and inhabited by almost self-sufficient families of fishermen who grew a little corn. At that time of year the air is marvelously clear, and the treeless landscape has a quality that must be like that of the Arctic lands. The houses are most primitive in structure.[5]

Compare Crawford's statement with that of Lawrence: "The cottages are low and almost invisible, built into the earth." We could do worse than to bear these objective comments in mind while considering the anomalous structures in northeastern America and southeastern Canada which are at present the cause of so much controversy.[6]

Some of the most characteristic qualities of the early — as of the modern — Celts are their love of pattern — pattern in art, pattern in words, pattern in song; a deep feeling for nature, at a time when nature was widely regarded as a force to be attacked and overcome rather than something of mystic beauty and spiritual fulfilment. The insular texts pulsate with this sentiment for wild things. In early Gaul the same sensitivity for creative life is found everywhere. The poet-rhetorician Ausonius from Bordeaux, whose life spanned almost the whole of the calm fourth century A.D. and whose doctor-father could never master the Latin tongue, beautifully exemplifies this in his writings. In the *Technopaegnion* he says, in a piece entitled 'On the beginning of Spring',

> When the year at its uprising unlocks flower-bearing Spring, all things flourish: green is every grove, gay the gold-tressed field, and, soon to spread shade, up from its root shoots the sprout. No longer in thick shower streams to earth the billowing snow.[7]

Those lines could well have been written by an Early Irish scholar quietly observing Nature from his humble cell or hermit's dwelling. The Celts, as we well know, have always venerated hills and streams, springs and trees, and Gildas in his

Plate 5: *Terra cotta* Horse, Banassac, Lozère.
Source: National Museum of France.

Plate 6: Celtic Mercury, Ile-Barbe, Rhône.
Source: National Museum of France

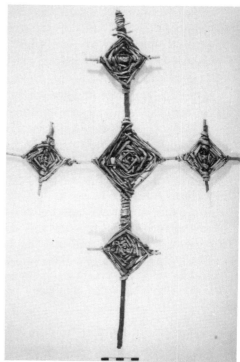

Plate 7: Two St. Bridget's Crosses made in 1977 in Co. Cavan, Ireland. Many different designs for such crosses are fashioned throughout Ireland to honour the Saint's feastday, February 1. Source: Anne Ross.

famous denunciation of his fellow-countrymen, abhors this continuing practice in the sub-Roman period.[8] It must have been one of the most potent elements in Britain, and on the continent of Europe, as Celtic place-names, amongst other things, indicate.

One of the peculiarities of Celtic culture, then, is the unusually early love that it shows for Nature in all its manifestations. It is this close observation of, and delight in Nature for Nature's sake, that makes Celtic writings, even by those whose training was essentially in the Latin schools, so distinctive. For example, Ausonius again reveals his Celtic origins clearly in his famous poem, *The Moselle*. He describes in minute and loving detail every kind of fish to be found in the river Moselle, and compares with deep feeling the vineyards and estates overlooking the water, with his own rich domains in Bordeaux and Cognac.[9] Rivers, then, were sacred to the Celts, places peopled with supernatural beings of every kind. According to belief, even the fish personified divine power. Ausonius was a Christian when the pagan revival was at its height. In his *Daily Round* he begins with prayers and makes an interesting comment: "Grant me, oh Father, the effluence of everlasting light for which I yearn if I swear not by gods of stone."[10] The worship of 'gods of stone', however, continued long after Ausonius' time.

There are many strange practices involving the worship of and actual sacrifice of animals to idols right down to the present day — not only in countries which were *once* Celtic in the full sense of the word, but in the surviving Celtic-speaking areas; and these have nothing to do with black witchcraft.[11]

To understand a people, one must know about their culture. One of the meanings of culture is worship; and this definition of Celtic culture brings us very near to the fundamental nature of the psyche of these people. A capacity for worship, religion, a passionate feeling for the supernatural, for the gods, or, later, God, is, I believe, the truest and most binding cultural element throughout the entire Celtic world — geographically, and down the long ages. The Celts themselves have always been certain that their languages were the languages of Heaven — and the speech used in the Garden of Eden; and there are still people in the Western Isles of Scotland who really believe that unless you have the Gaelic, as they say, your chances of making yourself understood by Saint Peter at the Gate are pretty slender.

William Shakespeare who, as we all well know, had a profound knowledge of the history and folklore of his fellow-coutrymen, used many Celtic themes and characters in his works. In his play *Henry IV*, he brilliantly evokes the Celtic character in the person of Owen Glendower. His lines bring to life all the vanity and superstitious feelings of the Celtic world — the love of power; the respect for aristocratic status; trust in divine portents and belief in the power to command the

Plate 8: Three-headed Grotesque, Bayeux Cathedral, Calvados; the cathedral was constructed over a temple dedicated to the Celtic god Belenos.
Source: J. Roberts, 85 Glenfield Avenue, Bitterne, Southampton.

very elements — characteristics which can be traced back far beyond Shakespeare's time and are attested to in the distant, pagan past. Shakespeare's British chieftain says:

> The front of heaven at *my* birth was full of fiery shapes;
> The goats ran from the mountains, and the herds
> Were strangely clamorous in the frighted fields;
> These signs have marked me *extraordinary*;
> And all the courses of my life do show
> I am not in the role of common man . . .

and:

> I can call spirits from the vasty deep.

Centuries before Shakespeare wrote these words, "I am not in the role of common man", Diodorus the Sicilian had made much the same observations on the Celtic character. He wrote:

> They frequently exaggerate with the aim of extolling themselves and diminishing the status of others. They are boasters and threateners and given to bombastic self-dramatisation; and yet they are quick of mind and with good natural ability for learning.[12]

Of their passion for the supernatural, Julius Caesar says: "The whole Gallic people is exceedingly given to religious superstition."[13] Here he is talking about the Continental Celts. But Tacitus makes it quite clear that the Britons differed little from their Continental fellows in religion and culture; and all the evidence supports this — bearing in mind, of course, the essential modification that insularity must impose upon any culture. And down the ages, the record is the same; the comments on the Celtic world have an astonishing consistency. The Celts have been, unwittingly, the victims of many misconceptions. Even today, the true nature of their culture and influence on Europe has yet to be properly appreciated. This is partly due to the fact that investigation into the Celtic world, pagan and Christian, ancient and modern, can only be conducted by combining several disciplines; by collating the results of these various studies we can achieve, if not a complete picture of the Celtic world, at least a reasonable balance of inferences — and, after all, the stuff of archaeology and linguistics, as well as history, is, at best, inferential.[14]

The main disciplines involved in the study of the Celts are those of archaeology, history, linguistics and folklore. The application of new sciences is, as I have said, gradually helping us in our understanding of this widespread and once deeply-influential people. For too long we have been taught that the history of Britain began with the coming of the Romans who brought with them a novel series of blessings to tribes of blue-painted savages, as wild as any Captain Cook may have encountered. Roman Britain has been depicted as a country populated, not by Britons, but by Romans, with a few gangs of British slaves for their convenience. These were, we were told, then wiped out or pushed into the mountainous periphery of our island by the coming of the Anglo-Saxons. We now know that all these pictures are false. Pliny (XXII, 2) comments that the British women painted

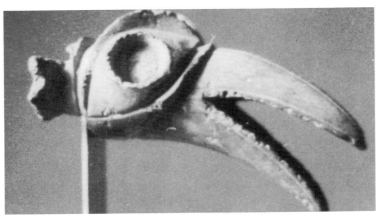

Plate 9: Bronze Raven Head, Hod Hill, Dorset, eye inlay missing.
Source: B. Picard, 164 The Albany, Manor Road, Bournemouth.

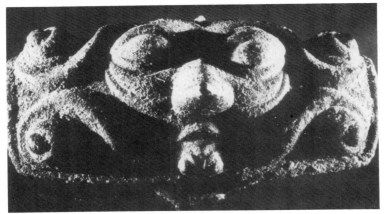

Plate 10: Bronze and Iron Lynch Pin, (?Paris), France.
Source: National Museum of France.

Plate 11: Bronze mount, Malomerice, Czechoslovakia.
Source: Moravske Muz., Brno, Czechoslovakia.

Plate 12: Carved stone pillar, Turoe,
Co. Galway, Ireland.
Source: C.M. Dixon, 21 Ashley Road,
London N19 3AG.

their bodies with *glastum* (woad) for *ritual* purposes, and went naked in this guise
to the funerary rites. We know that professional mourning women (*bean-tuirim*)
were an essential part of Irish and Scottish Gaelic society down to the end of the last
century; and we can infer that this is the implication of Pliny's remarks. The dying
of the body with woad before encountering the enemy may thus have been, like
nakedness, a religious act connected with magic and the gods. We are, then, aware
that the Celtic story is by no means as simple and as obvious as had been thought;
that the Celtic world had its origins far beyond the reaches of the pen of the
historian — the spade of the prehistorian can best define its lower limits. And it
survives, and is still with us, to add its own testimony to that of its commentators
down through the centuries.

We have considered Shakespeare's assessment of his fellow-countrymen. But
how did the Celts envisage their own characteristics and culture? One could quote
indefinitely the passages elucidating this. My own favourite example is taken from
the Irish "Book of Invasions", the *Lebor Gabala*, which I believe sums up
succinctly the entire attitude of the Celtic world to itself.[15] Traditions of the gods,

the *Tuatha Dé Danaan*, were still very active in the Scottish Highlands in the sixteenth century. In 1567 Bishop Carsewell lamented the love of the Highlanders for "vain, hurtful, lying, earthy stories about the *Tuatha Dé Danaan*."[16] When the Gaels were contending with the *Tuatha Dé Danaan*, the 'People of the goddess Danu', the divine race of Ireland, for possession of the land, their poet-sorcerer Amergin placed his right foot on the shore and chanted the following incantation:

> I am a wind on the sea,
> I am a wave of the ocean,
> I am the roar of the sea,
> I am a powerful ox,
> I am a hawk on a cliff,
> I am a dewdrop in the sunshine,
> I am a boar for valour,
> I am a salmon in the pools,
> I am a lake in a plain,
> I am the strength of art,
> I am a spear with spoils that wages battle,
> I am a man that shapes fire for a head.
>
> Who clears the stone-place of the mountain?
> What the place in which the setting of the sun lies?
> Who has sought peace without fear seven times?
> Who names the waterfalls?
> Who brings his cattle from the house of Tethra?
> What person, what *god*,
> Forms weapons in a fort?
> In a fort that nourishes satirists,
> Chants a petition, divides the Ogham letters,
> Separates a fleet, has sung praises?
> A wise satirist.[17]

Plate 13: Opium Poppy *(papaver somniferum)*, widely grown in prehistoric and later times. Source: Peter J. Reynolds.

Plate 14: Water nymphs, High Rochester, Northumberland (Northumbria); such nymphs were believed by the Celts to be present in springs and river sources.
Source: C. M. Dixon.

In these enigmatic lines, translated from Irish, one finds many elements that are absolutely fundamental to Celtic ritual and belief about which we are learning more almost daily: sensitivity to the elements; passion for waves and waters; veneration of the mighty, potent bull; love of birds and a deep appreciation of nature for nature's sake; the magic, prophetic salmon of wisdom; the power of sorcery; the demon-possessed weapon; the power of the severed head. The deep curiosity about the powers behind the functioning of the universe — who clears the stone-place of the mountains? Where *does* the sun set? Who names the waterfalls? Who brings his cattle from the house of Tethra? — no one, because Tethra was a god of death, and his house possibly one of the grim passage-graves, shrines and sepulchres, the dwelling-places of the gods. What *god* forms weapons in a fort? Archaeological evidence is constantly stressing the ritual associations of hill-forts with ever-increasing confidence. They were not only hill-towns, centres of chiefdoms, sites for assemblies. They were also the dark precincts of the gods who must be propitiated with care, and appositely. The satirist was the most feared person in Celtic society. To receive praise from the poet was the highest honour; to incite his satire was believed to cause woe, even unto death. The poets chanted petitions to the king; they knew the secrets of the cryptic Ogham script; they wielded a power second to the Druids themselves.[18]

I have entitled this paper "Material Culture, Myth and Folk Memory." One example of this — one of many that are rapidly coming to light by the skilful work of archaeologists all over Europe — are the excavations at Emain Macha,

Plate 15: Tricephalos, Condat, Dordogne.
Source: Bordeaux Museum.

Navan hill-fort, situated about one and a half miles from Armagh town in northern Ireland. The brilliant excavations conducted in recent years by Dudley Waterman have provided remarkable testimony to the veracity of the early Irish vernacular tradition. Briefly, the written material claims the following: that the site was the seat of the king, Conchobor Mac Nessa. It is alleged to have received its name from a cult legend which told how a horse goddess, Macha, gave birth to twins there after racing against the swift horses of the king and leaving them far behind her. The king's house was known as the House of the Red Branch, or Tree (*Craobh Ruadh*). His warriors were known as the Knights of the Red Branch. The site was closely associated with the great semi-divine hero, Cú Chulainn, Culand's dog or hound. In short, the text connects the site with a goddess, horses, a king, a royal house, a sanctuary, a hero, a red tree or branch, and a dog. Now, let us consider what the excavations there have revealed. There was a large circular house on the hill-top in its own enclosure, clearly a structure of considerable importance. This house was rebuilt several times over a period of some four hundred years. But, by about 250 B.C., this presumptive royal residence was replaced by a sanctuary. Several rings of post-holes occupy the enclosure with a huge post in the centre — all the posts being of oak. After some twenty-five years the whole of the sanctuary was buried with stones and the tops of the posts protruded through this. Here, then, we have the replacing of a royal residence by a sanctuary; the leaving of it open for a given space of time, and then the roofing in of the structure. One wonders whether the great central post was, in fact, the

16

19

17

20

18

21

Craobh Ruadh, the Red Branch itself, for *ruadh* also means red, bloody and turbulent. The Knights of the Red Branch could then have been the initiates of whatever dark rites were practiced here in pagan times. We have the association of the site with the Irish horse-goddess Macha, equivalent to Epona in Gaul and Britain and Rhiannon in Wales. Finally, in the sanctuary the head of a dog was found. Apart from Cú Chulainn's intimate connection with the site, the dog was a revered and sacrificial animal in the Celtic world, especially in the British Isles. Many Celtic names are based on the word for dog — *cú* — and numerous legends have the dog as an important element in the tale. Ritual pits all over Britain contain the remains of dogs which have clearly been placed there as sacrificial offerings. Sometimes the head alone is buried. The excavations at Emain Macha[19] and their substantiation of one of the major Irish legends encourage us to study the huge corpus of Irish and Welsh literary material with a greater confidence in the probable truth of many of the motifs with which it is studded.

This must conclude our brief glance at the nature of the Celtic past and its survival. Severed sacred heads, venerated and sacrificial animals, the cult of heroes and the worship of the dead, reverence for nature in all her moods, gods and goddesses of every kind with their chancy, touchy powers over mankind, all these are to be found in wild, chaotic profusion in this magic make-believe world of our common past. Archaeology and related disciplines are combining with the native documentary evidence to suggest that perhaps, after all, the lost gods of Britain and the wider Celtic world and their related mythology are not irrevocably lost, but only hiding and awaiting rediscovery. And one day, with patience and with true co-operation, we may be able to demonstrate that the gods and goddesses, birds and animals, and the cult legends and folk tales which surround them, add up to a powerful religion which will make the pale cults of the classical world fade into insignificance before its subtle and magic vitality.

Plate 16: Stone figure, Euffignieux, Haute-Marne; as if cut from a dressed tree-trunk, the god wears the sacred torc, has the relief of a boar on the front and a large eye at the side.
Source: National Museum of France.

Plate 17: Bronze figure of squatting stag-god, Bouray, Seine-et-Marne; hooved but not antlered.
Source: National Museum of France.

Plate 18: Relief of priapic bull-horned god bearing shield and spear, from site of Roman fort Alavna, Maryport, Cumberland (Cumbria).
Source: C. M. Dixon.

Plate 19: Hunter God, Touget, Gers; holding hare, naked except for a cloak.
Source: National Museum of France.

Plate 20: Esus-Mercury, great stone figure from Lezoux, Puy-de-Dôme.
Source: National Museum of France.

Plate 21: Mythical three-horned bronze bull.
Source: National Museum of France.

Plate 22: Aristocratic male bronze head, eye inlay lost, Garancières-en-Beauce, Eure-et-Loir.
Source: Chartres Museum.

Plate 23: Two goat heads, La Bussière-Etable, Haute-Vienne.
Source: National Museum of France.

Plate 24: Growing Woad.
Source: Peter J. Reynolds.

Plate 25: Bronze figurine, male dancer, Neuvy-en-Sullias, Loiret.
Source: Musée Historique d'Orléanais, Orléans.

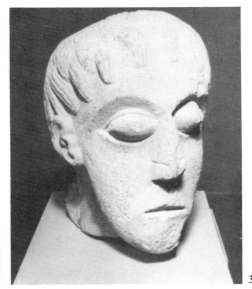

Plate 26: Bronze mythical three-horned bull.
Source: National Museum of France.

Plate 27: Bronze cockerel.
Source: National Museum of France.

Plate 28: Bronze figurine, Arduina on a boar, Jura.
Source: National Museum of France.

Plate 29: Bronze (?chariot) mount, deity with raised arms, Waldalgesheim, Germany.
Source: Rhein. Landesmus, Bonn.

Plate 30: Oolite head, originally painted red, found when preparing the site for the 'Bon Marche' in Gloucester.
Source: Gloucester Museum.

Plate 31: Standing Stones, Clochane, Co. Kerry, Ireland.   Source: Proinsias MacCana.

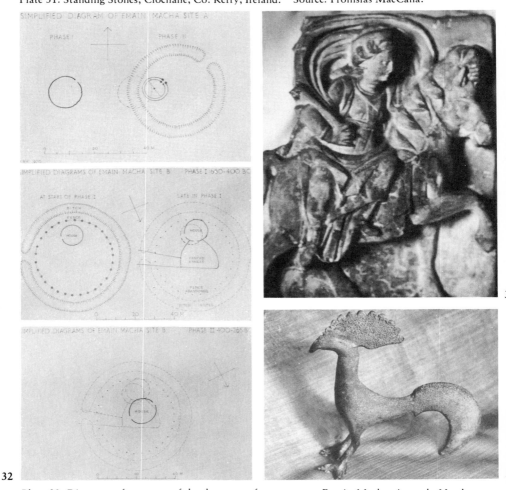

Plate 32: Diagrams of sequence of development of structures at Emain Macha, Armagh, Northern Ireland.
Source: R. W. Feachem, 6 Rose Road, Southampton.

Plate 33: Stone relief, Epona mounted, Gannat, Allier.
Source: National Museum of France.

Plate 34: Bronze figurine of cockerel.
Source: National Museum of France.

35

36

38

37

39

Plate 35: Bronze belt plate, Zelkovice, Czechoslovakia.
Source: Narodni Muz., Prague.

Plate 36: Spring goddess Coventina in triple form, BROCOLITIA, Northumberland.
Source: C. M. Dixon.

Plate 37: Heads separated by the beak of a raptor, Celtic temple at Roquepertuse, Bouches-du-Rhône.
Source: Musée Borely, Marseille.

Plate 38: Phallic stone decorated with head and snakes on one side, a collared serpent on the other, Alavna,
Maryport, Cumberland (Cumbria). Source: C.M. Dixon.

Plate 39: Bronze mount for wooden flagon, Durnberg, Austria. Source: Stadtmus, Hallein, Austria.

NOTES

[1]*The Festival of Lughnasa* (Oxford 1962), p. 429. For discussion of the other calendar festivals see my *Folklore of the Scottish Highlands* (Batsford, London 1976), especially the Bibliography, and my articles in *Folklore, Myths and Legends of Britain* (Reader's Digest Association, 1973): "The Old Gods," pp. 100-3; "The Faraway Hills, pp. 432-53; "The Water-Guardians, pp. 30-3; "Angels and Images," pp. 64-7, as well as other contributions in the book.

[2]See my *Pagan Celtic Britain* (London and New York 1967).

[3]See M. D. Anderson, *History and Imagery in British Churches* (London 1971), pp. 16ff. and notes.

[4]See Charles W. Dunn, *Highland Settler* (Toronto 1953).

[5]O. G. S. Crawford, *Said and Done* (London 1955), p. 227.

[6]For the basis of this controversy, see Barry Fell, *America B.C. Ancient Settlers in the New World* (New York 1976), A. Ross and P. Reynolds, 'Ancient Vermont', *Antiquity*, LII (1978) 100-107.

[7]H. G. Evelyn White (ed.), *Ausonius*, 2 vols. (London 1968), p. 301.

[8]See H. Williams, *De Excidio Brittanniae* (London 1899). See also my *Pagan Celtic Britain*, Chapter 1.

[9]White, *Ausonius*, 1, 225. For sacred fish see *Pagan Celtic Britain*, beginning with the index under fish, trout, salmon, and dolphins.

[10]White, *Ausonius*, 1, 13ff.

[11]For the survival of ancient Celtic customs see the following books already cited: *Folklore of the Scottish Highlands, Folklore, Myths, and Legends of Britain*, and *The Feast of Lughnasa*. See also the Bibliographies in these books.

[12]J. J. Tierney, "The Celtic Ethnography of Posidonius," *Proceedings of the Royal Irish Academy*, 60 (1960), 251.

[13]*Ibid.*, p. 272.

[14]For a general study of the Celtic background and daily life see my *Everyday Life of the Pagan Celts* (Batsford, London 1970).

[15]See T. P. Cross and C. H. Slover, *Ancient Irish Tales*, Revised by C. W. Dunn (Dublin 1969), pp. 2ff.

[16]J. MacKechnie, ed. *The Dewar Manuscripts* (Glasgow 1964), p. 20.

[17]Cross and Slover, p. 21.

[18]For more information on the Ogham script see K. H. Jackson, *Language and History in Early Britain* (Edinburgh 1953), pp. 137ff, and on the Druids see T. D. Kendrick, *The Druids* (London 1927), and S. Piggott, *The Druids* (London 1968).

[19]For a discussion of the excavations see E. E. Evans, *Prehistoric and Early Christian Ireland* (London 1966). A report on the excavations is now pending. For the story of Macha, see Cross and Slover, pp. 208ff; for references to the Red Branch, pp. 153ff; for the naming of Cú Chulainn, pp. 140ff; for Epona and Rhiannon, see *Pagan Celtic Britain*, Index.

IRISH FOLK TRADITION AND
THE CELTIC CALENDAR

KEVIN DANAHER

There has survived in Ireland from the remote into the recent past, and in many instances into the living present, a body of custom, usage and belief, pertaining to the observance of certain times, dates and festivals, which is so extensive and so cohesive as to constitute a folk calendar.

As regards the active survival into the present of the various elements and motifs of this folk calendar, we must remember that in a society which is subject to rapid economic and social change, we cannot always postulate the continued practice of older usages even though we ourselves may have observed them in the recent past. It is, therefore, possible that some of the beliefs and customs which I shall mention are obsolescent or even extinct.

We must, however, also bear in mind that the investigation and recording of folk tradition has been pursued actively in Ireland for almost half a century,[1] that calendar custom has received much attention in that investigation and recording, and that each element of calendar belief and custom to which I shall refer has been queried, in the course of field work and local enquiry, or by means of question-naires, in at least four hundred different locations distributed all over Ireland. Indeed in many instances of more widespread belief or custom we have more than one thousand positive reports of their occurrence within the living memory of the informants. Of course this repetitious multiplicity is what constitutes folk tradition — the body of knowledge which is held in common by large groups of people, and the extent of which can only be ascertained by widely repeated questioning and observation.

As a result of such widely repeated questioning and observation, we have established that the calendar customs and beliefs which I shall discuss were very generally and very deeply held by the ordinary people in Ireland up to, say, the beginning of this century, and in great part up to the present, that indeed they were part and parcel of the everyday life of the community, and not merely the vague memory or the idiosyncratic notion of some individual; that, as Chesterton puts it, they were held by the hundred people in the village who were sane, not by the one self-appointed historian who was mad.[2]

In the Irish folk calendar, there occur four important festival days which are the first days of the four seasons.[3]

The first of these, Lá 'le Bríde, 1st February, known in ancient times as Imbolc, was the first day of spring. Good weather suitable for ploughing was expected, and spring work, tilling the soil, was begun. Fishermen overhauled boats and gear and prepared to put out to sea again. There were prayers and ceremonies, principally the making and putting up in house, byre and stable of St. Brighid's crosses, to seek protection and blessing on house and farmyard, on land and livestock. Fishermen, too, had their protective ceremonies. Fairs were held; servants and work people were hired; tillage land was rented. Divination was practised to foretell the weather and the degree of prosperity of the household during the coming year. The housewife checked her store of food and the farmer his reserve of hay and other animal fodder; at least half of these should still be unconsumed. On the Eve of the festival there was a festive supper of rustic delicacies for the members of the household. Groups of young people, in disguise or fancy dress, went masking from house to house. The good Saint Brighid, patroness of farm work and cattle, and protector of the household from fire and calamity, was said to be abroad, and steps were taken to bid her welcome and obtain her protection. Usually the masking groups represented the saint, or carried her effigy or symbols, and called down her blessing on the houses visited.

The second of these festivals, Bealtaine, 1st May, was taken as the first day of summer. Good weather and ensuing good health for man and beast were confidently expected. Cattle and sheep were put to summer pasture. The main dairy season began, with an abundance of milk, butter and cheese, and the blessing and protection of the cows, the byre and the dairy were invoked with prayers and ceremonies. Rents were paid and grazing land contracts made. Many fairs were held which were festive occasions for family outings as well as venues for buying and selling of livestock and other produce and goods. Weather and marriage divination were practised. On May Eve, bonfires were lit, and in some districts the cattle were driven over or between fires to protect them from harm. Summer was welcomed by strewing of flowers, by setting up green or flowering branches or decorated May bushes. Bands of young people, bearing bushes, garlands and other emblems of May and singing songs to welcome the summer, went from house to house, receiving small gifts from the householders.

The unseen world was particularly active on May Eve. The Good People of the Hills were at their revels and humans had to be careful not to disturb or offend them; by watchfulness, ceremony, prayer and charm, all care was taken to safeguard against their machinations, and against the evil magic of human ill-wishers.

The third of these festivals is Lúnasa, 1st August, the first day of autumn and of the harvest.[4] The good farmer and the provident housewife still had something left of the store of last harvest, but the new corn, potatoes, fruit and other crops were very welcome and a festive meal of these was the supper in the farmer household on the eve of the festival. Weather divination was practised and the serious work of harvest began, while fishermen made ready for autumn fish shoals. There were prayers and ceremonies to bring blessing on the harvest. Fairs were held, among them the great three-day Fair of the Puck at Killorglin and the Old Lammas Fair of Ballycastle, and harvest workers hired. Processions or excursions to hills, woods or lakes formed a main feature of the celebration; groups of people, young and old, went to woods or lake shores, or, most often, to hill tops and spent the day in the open, enjoying the air and scenery, eating food which they had brought with them, together with the first of the wild fruits of autumn, singing, dancing, gathering flowers to strew at certain set places or weaving them into garlands to be worn by the girls. In some places bonfires were lit. A few of these outings were religious occasions; chief among these the ascent of Cruach Pádraic, still one of Europe's greatest penitential pilgrimages, in which as many as fifty thousand people, many in bare feet, climb the rugged eight hundred metre peak.

Supernatural beings, both helpful and harmful, were abroad, and there were ceremonies and prayers to ask their help or obtain protection against them.

The fourth of these festivals is Samhain, 1st November, which was the first day of winter. Bad weather, with rain and cold, could be expected, and all the provision of food, fodder and fuel should be stored away. Cattle were put in the byres and sheep were folded. No more fruits, domestic or wild, were picked. Fishermen drew up their boats and repaired and stored their gear. Many fairs were held, especially for the buying and selling of livestock but also of foodstuffs and fodder. These, too, were occasions for general family outings for a day's enjoyment in the local market town. Rents and debts were paid and servants and workmen received their wages. In some areas great bonfires were lit. Every household had a festive supper at which young and old feasted on rustic goodies and took part in marriage divination games. Groups of young people in disguise or fancy dress went about collecting minor tribute from the householders and often playing tricks upon the ungenerous.

So active were the otherworld beings, that, however much frightened, nobody was really surprised at any apparition or supernatural manifestation. The Good People of the Hills held open revel and even invited humans to join in their dancing and games. The souls of dead members of the household returned to the old homestead and were met with tokens of welcome — the open doors, the fire burning on the hearth, and the table set for a meal. Special prayers for the repose of the souls of the dead were added to those for protection against danger and evil.

These four season days were the outstanding festivals of the Irish folk calendar, and no others approached them in diversity of custom with the exception of the Easter cycle, which is of entirely Christian origin and introduction, completely unknown in pre-Christian Ireland, Christmas which is an inextricable tangle of the Christian celebration and old midwinter custom, all overlaid with more recent additions, and Midsummer which was mainly marked by bonfires and their associated prayers and ceremonies.

Let us now consider the four major festivals in relation to each other. They are separated from each other by regular intervals, to be precise, by intervals of ninety-two, ninety-two, ninety-two and eighty-nine days by our modern calendar reckoning; thus they divide the year into four even quarters which are recognised in popular tradition as the four seasons of the year: —

"Ráthaí fírinneacha na bliana;
Ráth ó Lá Fhéile Bríde go Bealtaine,
Ráth ó Bhealtaine go Lúnasa,

Ráth ó Lúnasa go Samhain
Agus ráth ó Shamhain go Lá Fhéile Bríde."

Their positive relation to each other is very clearly marked in the observances which characterise them as being of one general pattern. There is a very remarkable series of belief and custom common to all of them:

1. Each is a calendar landmark, the first day of a season.
2. Each is regarded as bringing a change in climatic and weather conditions.
3. Each marks an important change in the work of farmers and fishermen.
4. All have ceremonies and invocations to ensure protection and blessing during the coming season.
5. Each was a time for fairs, assemblies, terms of employment, payment of rent and all manner of rural contracts.
6. Divination of the future was practised.
7. Bonfires were lit (except on 1st February).
8. Festive ceremonies, with food, fruit, flowers and symbols appropriate to the season were observed.
9. Groups of young people took part in masks and processions.
10. Supernatural forces and beings were active.

It is, I think, obvious that this concordance of usage is not merely fortuitous and haphazard, but clearly shows that these four days are deliberately identified in the folk mind as a coherent series of occasions which mark and celebrate the beginning and ending of four quarters of the year, which are held in tradition to be Spring, Summer, Autumn and Winter.

As to the antiquity of these Season days as great festivals, evidence from Irish historical and literary sources between the eighth and sixteenth centuries tends not merely to confirm their former importance but also their relation to one another. Three of them, Bealtaine, Lúnasa and Samhain, are still known by their ancient names, and while the change of the fourth, Imbolc to Lá Fhéile Bríde, represents a partial Christianisation, the older name remains in the early literature. An Old-Irish poem celebrates them as the four quarter days and tells of feasting at Imbolc, feasting and fires at Bealtaine, fresh fruits at Lúnasa, and feasting and fires at Samhain.[5]

The great assemblies were held periodically on these days, that of Uisneach at Bealtaine,[6] those of Carman[7] and Tailtean[8] at Lúnasa and those of Tara[9] and Tlachta[10] at Samhain.

The great assembly at Carman is vividly described in a long poem which tells, among the fair's activities, of law giving, the making of treaties and covenants and religious ceremonies as well as trading and merrymaking.[11]

Cattle were driven between fires at Bealtaine to guard them against sickness and the unseen powers.[12] Tribute was paid at Bealtaine and Samhain,[13] on which latter day divination concerning grave matters was practised[14] and supernatural beings were active.[15] Many other references in the old literature leave no doubt as to the supreme importance of these four festival days in the lives of the Irish people.[16] It is significant that none of the many customs and observances associated with these days is enjoined by or directly derived from Christian practice, although some of them have been partly Christianised. It seems reasonable, therefore, to assume that these festivals and their associated observances are pre-Christian survivals; that is to say that they have been observed in Ireland for more than fifteen hundred years.

It is also significant in this regard that there are in the Irish language no native names for the months of the year, and that several of the months take their names from the seasons or the season days. May is *Mí na Bealtaine*, August *Mí na Lúnasa*, November *Mí na Samhna*, and February was popularly *Mí na Féile Bhríde*.

On a similar analogy, December is *Mí na Nollag*, (Nolliag= Natalica, the day of the Nativity). Then we have June *Meitheamh an tSamhraidh*[17] (middle month of Summer), September *Meitheamh an Fhomhair* or *Mean Fhomhair*, middle month of Harvest or middle of Harvest. March was called *Meitheamh an Earraigh* or *Lár an Earraigh*, and December *Meitheamh an Gheimhridh*. The forms *Mí Deire an Earraigh*, *Mí Deire an tSamhraidh*, *Mí Deire an Fhomhair*, (Month of the end of Spring, of Summer and of Autumn, respectively) were often used. The other or alternative month names are Latin borrowings: *Eanair, Feabhra, Márta, Aibreán, Iúl*.

The naming of the months from the seasons or the season days clearly points to the conclusion that the season and not the month was the primary subdivision of the year and makes it probable that reckoning in months was a later introduction, possibly, like the celebration of Easter and the seven-day week, an innovation associated with early Christianity.

Taking all of this into account, the evidence of folk tradition, the non-Christian character of custom and belief, the testimony of the ancient literary record and the subordinate character of the months, we may conclude that the older Irish system of time reckoning was based upon a year divided into four equal quarters or seasons, each conforming to the practical needs of a people whose livelihood was based upon corn-growing and cattle-raising, and each heralded and celebrated by a great festival.

There is no reason to doubt the supposition that this calendar reckoning was determined and corrected, year by year, by observation of the heavenly bodies, sidereal or, more probably solar. It is probable that the duty of determining the dates of festivals was in the hands of some skilled or learned group or class of people, and it is not beyond the bounds of possibility that the association of bonfires with these festivals is a survival of a system of signal fires to announce to all the coming of the season day which was of such vital import not merely as a festival but also as an indication to farmers that the time had come to begin some essential agricultural operation.

On this assumption, the first day of spring would occur 45 or 46 days after the winter solstice, the first day of Autumn 45 or 46 days after the summer solstice, and so on throughout the year. Direct observation made annually or more frequently was, of course, self-correcting. An observation which was faulty, or which because of cloud conditions, was impossible, was automatically corrected by the next observation. Cumulative error in calculation of dates came in only when a set calendar based upon the counting of days was adopted, and the cumulative error would begin at the time of the adoption of the new system. Calculation has shown that this occurred in Ireland during the period A.D. 690 - 820.[18] This clearly came about under the influence of increasing contact with Continental Europe, and it invites comparison with other tendencies, changes and reforms of the same period.

The question now arises as to whether this calendar may be of Celtic origin.

We know very little of the time-reckoning or the calendar organisation of the Continental Celts. There is, of course, the Calendar of Coligny, which has been studied by Seymour de Ricci,[19] R. Thurneysen,[20] John Rhys,[21] Eoin Mac Neill,[22] Paul-Marie Duval,[23] and others. All of these authorities recognise it as a lunar calendar. The few classical references which we have to Celtic time reckoning[24] indicate a lunar system. The old Irish four-season year comes entirely from solar reckoning, without any lunar influence whatever. It has a precisely divided solar year, not a year formed by the setting together of a number of lunar months and requiring frequent correction and intercalation.

One may add that in Irish folk tradition, there is no time reckoning by the moon, indeed there is very little moon lore of any kind. And although scholars may differ on the matter of sun-worship as a major part of pre-Christian religion, all are agreed on the important place of the sun in early legend and myth, while there is little reference of any kind to the moon.[25]

The old Irish four-season year is derived from or adapted to the husbandry of an agricultural population whose livelihood depended upon corn-growing, stock-raising and dairy produce, with ploughing in the early spring, calving and abundance of milk in the early summer, harvest in early Autumn and storage in early Winter: that was their annual cycle of work. Climatic and weather conditions which produce such a four-season year, which, for instance, require ploughing in February, are to be found only in very limited areas of the world. In the European region which concerns us, they are to be found only in a very restricted area of the North West, in parts of North Western France and North Western Spain, in Western Britain, and very markedly in Ireland. We should look for the origin of this calendar within that limited North Western European region. It certainly will not be found in the Celtic homeland of south Germany, Bohemia, Austria and Hungary, where, even allowing for climate fluctuations over the centuries, the pattern is one of long hot summers and long severe winters, giving rise to a twofold division of the year, as is also normal, for instance, in Germanic time reckoning.[26]

It appears reasonable to conclude that the Irish four-season calendar is not of Celtic origin. It remains to be asked, if not Celtic, then what is it? Again it seems reasonable to conclude that it is pre-Celtic and that it survived into the Celtic and later periods, even up to the present day.

It is a farmer's calendar. There is a growing body of archaeological evidence to prove the existence of extensive farming in Ireland in the Neolithic period, by the end of which, about 3,000 to 2,500 B.C. a populous, prosperous society — or societies — with a high degree of social and economic organisation, flourished in Ireland. This is the period of the building of our greatest megalithic monuments, the three great tumuli of Knowth, New Grange and Dowth in the Boyne valley, for instance. When we consider that each of these tumuli contains up to 250,000 tons of material, each representing about one million small cart loads or at least five million man-loads, an impression is gained of the size of the operation, and of the organisation required to direct and maintain the necessary work force.

These great tombs are splendid examples of sophisticated architecture and engineering, and as an indication of the skill of their designers in solar observation we turn to New Grange which, in the words of Professor M. J. O'Kelly, is "so orientated to sunrise on 21st December, that the first rays of the rising sun on that day pass through the deliberately contrived slit in the roof and illuminate the tomb-chamber for seventeen minutes."[27] 21st December, is, of course, the Winter solstice, one of the days on which solar time reckoning is most readily determined.

There is abundant evidence of the continuance, all through the Bronze Age, of populous and prosperous communities in Ireland. They had, for instance, a high degree of craftsmanship in working metals, producing tools, weapons and ornaments in bronze and gold which exhibit very considerable technical and artistic virtuosity, and finds of which, over a wide area of western Europe, betoken a wide and vigorous export trade.

To accept that an active, prosperous, cultured people had a system of time reckoning and a series of popular festivals, as is the case in analogous cultures all over the world, is mere common sense. To assume that their calendar accorded with their environment and their way of life is merely to recognise a normal pattern of cultural development.

Thus we may conclude that the four-season calendar of modern Irish tradition is of very high antiquity, even of late neolithic or megalithic origin, and that its beginnings predate the early Celts in Ireland by at least as great a depth of time as that which separates those early Celts from us.

Authorities are in general agreement that the first significant incursions of Celtic people into Ireland occurred about the fourth century before Christ.

There is much evidence that they never were more than a minority, possibly a small minority, in the population, who had reached a dominant position through the possession of superior military skill and equipment — iron spears and swords and war chariots — a situation quite analogous to that of the Normans in Britain or the British in India. We know that their contribution to Irish culture was large — it included, for instance, the imposition of a Celtic language as well as La Tène art, iron-working, legal forms and much else. However, in the amalgam of Celt and Pre-Celt, of Celtic and Pre-Celtic which ensued, how much is Celtic and how much Pre-Celtic?

It is, I think, significant that the vigorous Irish Bronze Age trade with Europe comes to an end about the time of the Celtic inroads.[28] Is this an indication of unsettled conditions and of a lessening prosperity and influence? Is it also significant that the next upsurge of Irish cultural activity comes some centuries later, in the Early Christian period when Celt and pre-Celt had become mutually absorbed?

Here we have a wide field of investigation into early culture-contacts and trends of acculturation.

The evidence is not abundant, but it is there to be found, and I suggest that much of it may be found in our folk tradition. One lesson which we might learn from this is that we cannot necessarily assume that because something is early Irish it is therefore Celtic. There is at least an even chance that it may be pre-Celtic. Indeed we should hesitate to regard anything early Irish as Celtic unless we can identify the same feature in a Celtic context outside of Ireland — and even then we can never be absolutely certain that both have not come from some wider pre-Celtic culture.

We might even go further, and ask if we are not straining the bounds of scientific credibility by claiming that the Irish are a Celtic people? Would it not be more in keeping with fact if we recognise the Celtic element as an important one, but only one of many ingredients and, to paraphrase Professor David Greene's dictum[29] on the Irish language, whatever elements went into its making, Irish culture was evolved on Irish soil and is neither Indo-European nor Celtic, Pictish or Hamatic, but simply the cultural expression of the Irish people.

II

The small selection of illustrations which follows is largely personal, largely idiosyncratic, and is designed to show an ancient tradition surviving adversity and still able to influence life in our own time. How ancient that tradition may be, we can only begin to guess. Much of it, no doubt, is of Celtic origin, but equally much or even more is still more ancient, reaching back and back into the time of the first human occupation of Ireland. Much of it is of later introduction, an inheritance from Viking, Norman, Flemish, Welsh, English, Scots, Huguenots, Palatines and even more recent comers into our midst, German clockmakers, Italian restauranteurs and so on up to the present day. Thus traditions are established and a vigorous tradition can readily accept contributions from others while retaining its own character.*

*Plates 2, 3, 4, 5, 6, 8, 9, 12, 13, 22, and 23 are supplied from my own files. I am indebted to the following for supplying material for the other plates: Bórd Fáilte Éireann (Plate 1); Office of Public Works, National Parks and Monuments Branch (Plate 7); T. W. Mason (Plates 10 and 21); Donal Ó Cearbhaill (Plate 11); Dept. of Irish Folklore, University College Dublin (Plates 14, 15, 16, 18); *Illustrated London News*, 1852 (Plates 17 and 19); Liam Ó Danachair (Plate 20).

Plate 1: Irish landscape.
The typical Irish landscape is the *bocage* of the north western fringe of Europe — a landscape of fields demarcated and divided by stout fences crowned with hedges and trees. Its roots lie in the distant past; archaeological excavation has revealed its traits as early as the Neolithic period.

Plate 2: Megalithic monument.
Hundreds of megalithic monuments can be found in Ireland, such as this dolmen at Páirc na Binne in County Clare. Their builders have bequeathed to us not only these mighty examples of their skill in architecture, engineering and astronomy, but also much of the less tangible elements of our folk tradition.

Plate 3: A Christian symbol on a pagan pillar stone.
The intrusion of Christianity was gentle. The new doctrine and the old culture accepted each other freely, and many pre-Christian features were blessed with the Cross of the new faith. Here we see the Christian symbol carved upon an older ogham-inscribed pillar stone which stands near Waterville, County Kerry.

Plate 4: Farmhouse.
The snug dwelling house of the "strong farmer" tells of frugal comfort derived from good husbandry and hard work. Farmhouses of the type shown here were typical of the south and east of Ireland, but in recent years have largely been replaced by more modern houses.

Plate 5: Another farmhouse.
The smaller farmhouses of the north and west are disappearing even more rapidly under the pressure of new ideas, materials and methods.

Plate 6: Hill farmstead.
Population pressure in the late 18th and early 19th century drove many people to settle on poor mountainous land. Here a dying hill farmstead looks enviously down on the fertile lands of the Golden Vale.

Plate 7: Tower house.
Hundreds of tower houses, such as this at Clara, Co. Kilkenny, still dot the landscape. Most of them were built between 1400 and 1550 when the English pressure on Ireland was interrupted by foreign and civil wars. This permitted a remarkable Irish revival shown not least in great numbers of fine buildings, both secular and ecclesiastical, among which are the tower houses, the fortified dwellings of minor gentry and rich commoners.

Plate 8: Tillage ridges.
Thousands of hectares of Irish land are marked by the traces of old tillage ridges. These were formed more by spade digging than by ploughing and their use may be traced back in Ireland from recent times to the first remains of Neolithic agriculture.

Plate 9: Antiquated farm implements.
Work on the land was carried on mainly by hand implements until well into the nineteenth century, when agriculture was still labour-intensive. Nowadays, with the coming of new methods and developed machinery, the spade, the scythe and the flail have all but vanished from the rural scene.

Plate 10: The old-fashioned horse cart.
Another quiet revolution may be seen in rural transport. The old fashioned horse cart has been driven off the roads and the fields by the motor car, the lorry and the tractor, and nowadays is seldom to be seen.

Plate 11: The craft of the wheelwright.
Ancient crafts die out as their products become obsolete. It is probable that the craft of the wheelwright came into Ireland with the Celtic invaders a few centuries before the Christian era, and we must feel some regret as its last practitioners die out one by one.

Plate 12: Ancient skills in boat building.
Ireland was an island long before the coming of man. Thus even its first settlers must have had knowledge and skill in building and handling boats. On some of our coasts, as here in the Dingle Peninsula, ancient types and methods still survive.

Plate 13: An example of folk art.
A rich source of folk art is to be found in memorials to the dead. This early 19th century slab at Termonfeichin, County Louth, with its charming Nativity motif, well illustrates the expertise of local stone cutters.

Plate 14: Evictions after the Act of Union.
The Union of Ireland and Britain under one parliament in 1801 brought about a collapse of Irish industry and agriculture, with growing poverty and depression. This was accentuated by the numerous evictions from their homes of people unable to pay the rents demanded.

Plate 15: Mass in the open air.
Prohibitions against the free practice of religions other than that established by the State gradually fell into disuse or were repealed in the late 18th and early 19th century. In a few places, however, bigoted landlords or magistrates continued to harry Catholics, as here in a remote part of County Donegal where the landlord refused permission to build a church, and Mass had to be celebrated under a rude shelter in the open air.

Plate 16: Visit to a holy well in Penal times.
Even at the worst periods of Penal Laws there were among the Ascendency many people of local influence who held liberal views and did not believe in unnecessary persecution. Hence, many religious customs, although forbidden by law, such as the visit to a holy well (still popular in Ireland), continued to be practised.

Illustrated London News, 1852

Plate 17: The Hedge School.
Education, too, fell under the ban of the Penal Laws, and for most people the only access to learning was through the illegal "hedge schools" in which ragged masters taught ragged pupils in the open air or in rude shelters, with varying success from the brilliant to the ludicrous. Thanks mainly to such schools, about half the population was literate.

Plate 18: The blind fiddler.
People had a passion for music, and no visitor was more welcome or more generously received than the travelling musician. If a blind child showed any talent, a profitable and happy life was ensured by musical training; thus the blind harper, piper or fiddler, was a familiar figure.

Illustrated London News 1852

Plate 19: The dancing school.
Dancing was a much loved social grace. The dancing masters also taught deportment and were quick to reprove gauche or rude behaviour. To be expelled from a dancing class was the ultimate disgrace.

Plate 20: Open-air Irish language class in the days of the Revival.
Over the past century an enthusiasm for the ways of the past has been characteristic of Irish society. The open-air Irish language class in the early days of the "Irish Revival" was symptomatic of this.

Plate 21: Robin Flower and Tomás Ó Criomthain.
Scholars and authors sought the company of the tradition bearers. Here we have Tomás Ó Criomhthain, the Blasket fisherman and *seanchaí* and Dr. Robin Flower from the British Museum, whose cooperation gave us *The Islandman* (original title *An tOileánach*) and other works.

Plate 22: Peig Sayers.
Among the many outstanding tradition bearers and storytellers, a foremost place must be given to Peig Sayers.

Plate 23: The shanachie and his audience.
Not an unusual sight on a Gaeltacht strand in summer. A storyteller holds an audience of people of all ages.

NOTES

[1]The Folklore of Ireland Society was founded in 1927 and the Irish Folklore Commission was established in 1935. The latter has now been abolished (since 1971) and its collections were inherited by the Department of Irish Folklore, University College, Dublin, which, as well as its academic research and its undergraduate and post-graduate teaching, is also engaged in field work and the collection and recording of all kinds of folk tradition. For some indication of the range of this tradition, see Sean Ó Suilleabhain, *A Handbook of Irish Folklore* (Dublin 1942).

[2]Gilbert Keith Chesterton: 'Ethics of Elfland', *Sories, Essays and Poems* (London, various editions), Everyman's Library, 913.

[3]See C. Ó Danachair, 'The Quarter Days in Irish Tradition' in *Estudios e Ensaios em Homenagem a Renato Almeida* (Rio de Janeiro 1960), pp. 299-307, reprinted in *Arv*, 15 (1959, Uppsala) 47-55.

[4]For an exhaustive study of this festival, see Maire Mac Néill, *The Festival of Lughnasa* (Oxford 1962).

[5]Translated by Kuno Meyer in *Hibernica Minora* (Oxford 1894), appendix p. 49.

[6]E.g. *Forus Feasa ar Éirinn*, Irish Texts Society, Vol. 8, (London 1908), pp. 246, 248; and *Irische Texte*, Dritte Serie, ed. W. H. Stokes and E. Windisch, (Leipzig 1891), p. 198.

[7]See note 11 below.

[8]Mac Neill, *The Festival of Lughnasa*, pp. 311-3.

[9]E.g. Whitley Stokes, *Lives of the Saints from the Book of Lismore* (Oxford 1890), introduction p. xxxiii.

[10]P. W. Joyce, *A Social History of Ancient Ireland* (London 1903) 2, pp. 438 and 440.

[11]Text and translation in E. Gwynn, *The Metrical Dindshenchas*, Todd Lecture Series, Royal Irish Academy (Dublin 1913), pp. 2-25. For a summary, see P. W. Joyce, *op. cit.*, 2, p. 441-447; see also Maire Mac Neill, *op. cit.*, 339-349.

[12]*Cormac's Glossary*, ed. Whitley Stokes (Calcutta 1868), p. 19 and see *Forus Feasa ar Éireann*, Irish Texts Society, Vol. 8, (London 1908), p. 246.

[13]*Leabhar na gCeart*, ed. John O'Donovan, (Dublin 1847), pp. xvii, 55, 241.

[14]Eugene O'Curry, *Lectures on the Manuscript Materials of Ancient Irish History* (Dublin 1873), pp. 284-285.

[15]See, for instance: Kuno Meyer, 'Macgnimartha Find', *Revue Celtique 5* (Paris 1881-1883), p. 202; Kuno Meyer, 'Eachtra Nerai', *Revue Celtique 10* (Paris 1889), pp. 214-228.

[16]They were clearly recognised as the first days of the four seasons, see for instance *Leabhar na gCeart*, ed. J. O'Donovan (Dublin 1847), pp. xlviii ff.

[17]*Meitheamh* derives from a root meaning *cut* or *reap*. *Meitheamh an tSamhraidh* was, probably, the hay-cutting period and *Meitheamh an Fhomhair*, the corn-cutting. However, the use of *Meitheamh an Gheimhridh* and *Meitheamh an Earraigh* indicate an equation with the middle month in popular tradition.

[18]Information kindly provided by Professor Patrick Wayman, School of Cosmic Physics, Dublin Institute for Advanced Studies.

[19]Seymour de Ricci, 'Le Calendrier Gaulois de Coligny', *Revue Celtique*, 19 (Paris 1898), pp. 213-223.

[20]R. Thurneysen, 'Der Kalender von Coligny', *Zeitschrift für Celtische Philologie*, 2 (Halle 1899), pp. 523-544.

[21]John Rhys, 'Celtae and Galli', *Proceedings of the British Academy* 2 (London 1905), pp. 71-134; do. 4 (London 1910), pp. 207-318.

[22]Eoin Mac Neill, 'The Calendar of Coligny', *Ériu*, 10 (Dublin 1926-28), pp. 1-43.

[23]Paul Marie Duval, 'Observations sur le Calendrier de Coligny', *Etudes Celtiques*, 10 (Paris 1962-63), 18-42, 374-411, 11 (do., 1964-67), pp. 7-45, 267-313.

[24]As, for instance, Pliny's remark in his *Natural History*: 'Sexta luna, quae principia mensum annorumque his facit et saeculi post tricesimum annum'.

[25]See T. F. O'Rahilly, *Early Irish History and Mythology* (Dublin 1946), Chapter 15, and P. Mac Cana, *Celtic Mythology* (London 1970), 32.

[26]See M. P. Nilsson, *Primitive Time Reckoning* (Lund 1920) Chapter 11. There are some references to a two-season year in early Irish literature, see, for instance *Zeitschrift für Celtische Philologie*, 3 (Halle 1901) p. 245; *Leabhar na gCeart* (Dublin 1847), introduction p. 53. This two-season division may derive from Celtic legal usage; cf. the division of the year into a seven-month "hot" season and a five-month "cold" season for the purpose of assessing cattle trespass damages, *Ancient Laws of Ireland*, Vol. 4 (Dublin 1879), pp. 78-9, 89-90.

[27]In a letter to the writer of this paper. Professor O'Kelly draws attention to the fact that the radiocarbon dating of charcoal put in by the builders as part of the main chamber and passage of New Grange, gives, when calibrated, a date for its building of around 3,200 B.C., which is several centuries earlier than had been hitherto supposed.

[28]See, for instance, M. Herity and G. Eogan, *Ireland in Prehistory* (London 1977), chapters 9 and 10. A corresponding decline in agriculture is shown by G. F. Mitchell in "Littleton Bog, Tipperary", *Journal of the Royal Society of Antiquaries of Ireland*, 95 (Dublin 1965), pp. 127-9, and by the same author in *The Irish Landscape* (London 1976).

[29]D. Greene, *The Irish Language* (Cork 1972), pp. 58-59.

THE ROLE OF THE POET IN GAELIC SOCIETY[1]

MÁIRE CRUISE O'BRIEN

A hundred years ago, all along the Western seaboard of Ireland, distributed in fairly large pockets, an interested traveller might have found a self-sufficient, self-reliant, spiritually satisfying culture, the roots of which went back uninterruptedly to the Europe of the Middle Ages and perhaps, in some respects, to Europe before the beginnings of recorded time. I am referring, of course, to the culture of the Irish-speaking districts of Ireland.

Fifty years ago the threats to these communities from our monolithic contemporary consumer civilization would have become obvious to the professional observer — had such there been — though masked by the circumstances of the great depression. To a child growing up there, however, these societies would have seemed as stable and as timeless as ever; even the nationalism of the French Revolution had passed them by.

No such child today, no matter how sympathetically conditioned towards the preservation of the values embodied in these cultures, could fail to realise that they and their days are numbered.

A landscape where human habitation seemed an organic growth, so adapted was it to the environment, is covered now with a rash of tourist bungalows, designed in accordance with varying tastes, but having this much in common, that they stand empty for the greater part of the year — and stand out, if I may say, like sore thumbs: so has been disfigured some of the most beautiful countryside in the world.

Cars carrying the registrations of a dozen different countries throng and curse the narrow winding roads. Tourists, dressed in every variety of present-day international fashion, jostle in the bars and on the beaches — at least during the various, sedulously promoted, 'seasons'. The native inhabitants, drab in their factory-made reach-me-downs, living in their barrack-like local authority houses, reduced to the level of providers of lodging and entertainment, know, in spite of all assurances to the contrary, that their ancestral way of life is an anachronism. Those who can adapt to the new, adapt — many with startling success, some with deep traumatic lesions — those who cannot adapt, die — of the want of the will to live. This is literally true; easily two-thirds of my schoolmates and near contemporaries in one such district are dead — all in their forties and fifties.

I have deliberately tried to realise my *Gaeltacht* for my readers in the most sombre colours possible. I am anxious to emphasise the gloomy viewpoint: first, because it is the one least often adopted in general reflections about Irish language and culture; and, second, because the *view* from this *point* coincides in large measure with the truth. It is not a palatable or welcome truth, particularly to those of us who, for several generations now, have exploited the Irish-speaking way of life as an aesthetic luxury. But it is a truth which makes a useful, and sobering, point of departure for this study.

In just such a dying community, decimated by the incursions of film companies and the closing of neighbourhood schools, there lived until recently a man who, in his personal life, might be held to epitomise all that was dreary and negative in my picture. Mícheál Ó Gaoithín was an old bachelor, living alone in primitive conditions after the death of his mother, his house and person displaying the essential charmlessness of poverty; to the world, the very exemplar of frustration and failure. Not indeed that such exemplars are confined to Irish-speaking districts in Ireland; they are numerous throughout all areas, urban and rural, and have their counterparts at all levels of our society, as readers of modern Irish literature in English will be only too well aware. Entirely true, but — in this particular case — not the whole truth, for Mícheál Ó Gaoithín, his compulsive self-neglect notwithstanding, was not a failure: he had status, he was a poet. He was, in fact, *the* poet, *an File*. He had inherited the rôle which I have made the subject of this exposition, and we know him to have been very conscious of this. In one of his poems he leaves us an account of what we might describe as a scientific experiment which he carried out in order to confirm to himself the authenticity of his calling. It is to be found in a slim collection of pieces, published as a conscience-offering to him from a group of exploiting *literati*.[2] It is unusual among his work, as in that of all his fellow Gaelic poets, in that it recounts his personal experience. Perhaps the most striking characteristic of Gaelic verse is an astringent, objective *pudeur*, a convention of impersonality which allows voice only to the socially-sanctioned emotions and concepts. It is the absolute antithesis of the *confessional*, so that even when the poet employs the first person, it is almost always as a character in a dramatic context. I think that this general proposition will be found to hold true — with only very marginal exceptions — for the entire corpus of literature in Irish up to, but not entirely including, the writers of my own generation. Ó Gaoithín's poem is titled *Na Francaigh (The Rats)*, and I shall quote some stanzas in Irish before going on to give a brief précis of the whole and a fairly literal rendering of the lines which drive home my point:

> Maidean aoibhinn shamhraidh
>   Is mé i ngleann so na dtor,
> Ag féachaint ar na francaigh
>   Ag damhas as a gcorp,
> Do samhlaíodh dom gan amhras,
>   Go rabhadar d'aontoil,
> Is gurbh fhearr teitheadh maith in am as,
>   An fhaid a bheadh spanla ann dem chorp.
>
> Is maith an rud dea-mheabhraíocht,
>   Is cabhair é gan locht,
> Is mór an luach gach am é,
>   Nuair a bhíonn an gantar go docht;
> Ní bréithre binn do labhras,
>   Mar d-órdaigh Maois sa tseanreacht,

Ach cantaireacht na nAltach
   Nár fhoghlamaíos ar scoil.

Ar thógaint mo chinn ón leabhar dom,
   Bhí an dream úd ina sost,
   Nuair a chualadar mise ag labhairt leo,
   An damhsa gur stop!
Pé *power* a bhí sa rann so,
   A bhí chomh seanda leis an gcloich
Do chonac iad ag rith le scanradh,
   Fé chabhaite na gcloch!

The poet walks out on a summer morning in a bushy glen and comes upon a tribe of rats cavorting in the sun. It is borne in upon him that, as in some loathly science-fiction, they are about to round on him and attack. What follows is translated:

Resourcefulness is admirable
   and a faultless help,
It is of great worth at all times
   of severe emergency . . .
They were no melodious words I spoke
   As ordered by Moses under the Old Law —
But the psalmody of sorcery
   which I did not learn at school —

When I lifted my head from the book
   The rout fell silent
When they heard me speak to them
   The dancing stopped —
Whatever power was in that quatrain
   Which was as ancient as the rock
I saw them flee in terror
   Under the overhang of the stones.

The Munster word for sorcerer here calls for comment: it means Ulsterman. Shamanism, it seems, is always to the North.

We are now in the full main-stream of Gaelic, Celtic, and indeed of Indo-European poetry — a stream of which one of the most interesting meanders is represented by the Pied Piper of Hamelin! Rats have always been closely associated with Irish poetry; we have Shakespeare's word for it, and Yeats's, and now this testimony from an actual practitioner of the Gaelic ritual. The words to which Mícheál Ó Gaoithín alludes in his poem are those of a rat charm: *Artha na bhFrancach*. This charm, if recited in the proper manner by a properly qualified person, has the effect of banishing all rodents from the immediate vicinity. There is a catch in it however: if the charm is spoken by an illegitimate operator, by a pirate poet as it were, not only will it not work, but the rats will turn upon their would-be exterminator and tear him limb from limb! This poem is its author's witty and unpretentious way of letting us know that, although he may look a down-and-out layabout, he has the "power", to use his own expression. He is a thaumaturge, a true votary of the Goddess! His recourse is expressly to pre-Christian, even to pre-Judaeo-Christian, lore, not to that learned at school, and I think we may take it that the "book" referred to is a manuscript one, a short step only from strictly oral transmission.

The other poems in Ó Gaoithín's book, by any literary standards which we are capable of applying, are undistinguished, merely competent. It does not matter, their author does not have to prove — his gift to us; he *has* it; he is *the* poet. Cross him at your peril! He can bring you out in blisters or, more ambiguously, put horns on you, and, unless you treat him with munificence and consideration, your cattle will sicken, and your crops rot in the ground. But, if he is favourably disposed towards you, your memory and that of your people will live for ever — admittedly only in the archives of the Folklore Commission, but still . . .

In the Gaelic society of a hundred years ago, of which I wrote at the beginning, the local poet like Mícheál Ó Gaoithín played a conspicuous part. The following passage is taken from a contemporary account of those times, written in remarkable circumstances — space must prevent my elaborating here though I have elsewhere — by a subsistence farmer and fisherman, Thomas Crohan, who was part and parcel of just such a society on the island of the Great Blasket to the west of the Dingle Peninsula, the nearest human habitation in our Irish territorial seas to North America. The piece is, I think, self-explanatory:

"One day I wanted to go and cut some turf, for it was a very fine day, and we hadn't much of the old turf left to hand at that time. I went off through the door with a first-rate turf spade all ready and sharp . . . till I came to a place where, thought I, there was good turf, and enough of it round me to do my business . . .

But I had little chance to turn my keenness for work to profit that day. I hadn't long begun on the job, working hard, when the poet Dunlevy came up with a spade under his oxter, to cut a bit of turf for himself. I fancy that no poet has ever been much good at carrying through any job that had any work in it except only poetry, and that was the way with Dunlevy, too . . .

"Well, says the poet," throwing himself down on a tussock, "isn't it a pity for you to be cutting turf on such a hot day. Sit down a bit, the day is long and it'll be cool in the afternoon."

I didn't care much for what he had to say, but I was rather shy of refusing to sit down with him. Besides, I knew that if the poet had anything against me, he would make a satire on me that would be very unpleasant, especially as I was just about coming out in the world (i.e. marriagable). So I sat down beside him.

"Now," says the poet, "Perhaps you haven't got the first poem ever I made. 'The Black-faced Sheep,' that was my first, and I had good reason for making it as far as provocation goes."

Would you believe it — he started to recite every word of it, lying there stretched out on the flat of his back! There was a hummock of soft heather under him, and the scorching heat of the sun was flaming down from the cloudless, deep blue sky over our heads, toasting the side of the poet that was uppermost.

I praised the poem to the skies, though it was vexing me sorely from another point of view.

"The poem will be lost," says he, "if somebody doesn't pick it up. Have you anything in your pocket that you could write it down with?". . .

It wasn't to oblige the poet that I fished out my pencil and some paper I had in my pocket, but for fear he would turn the rough side of his tongue to me. I set about scribbling down the words as they came out of his mouth . . . I scribbled away at the words as best I could after a fashion that kept the poem more or less in my memory, and, besides, if a word should drop out here and there, the guide wasn't far from me, ready and willing to waste a bit of his life explaining it to me, even if the plough-team were waiting for him in the furrow.

When the pair of us had done with one another, the sun was sinking over the hill, ... and my dinner was utterly ruined: a horse couldn't have champed the hunk of yellow bread, and my milk had turned to stone in the bottle!'"[3]

If one reads *The Islandman*, (*An tOileánach*), from which this passage is taken, one may feel that as my picture of what is happening to these people today seems too impartially black, so this presentation of their way of life a hundred years ago seems too idealised. I can only cite sophisticated observers of the time: Synge; Robin Flower, medievalist and one-time keeper of the manuscripts in the British museum; Father Paddy Browne, linguist, mathematician and Catholic priest; George Thompson, classicist and Marxist. We may see them now as as disparate a group of starry-eyed escapists as the ghastliness of the Edwardian era could produce. Perhaps: the reader must draw his own conclusions and in any case value judgements are not relevant as regards the function of the poet in the culture for better or worse. The evidence for the influential place of the poet in Gaelic society is fairly conclusive. I should add that unlike poor Mícheál Ó Gaoithín, God rest him, Dunlevy was a superb versifier by any standards, who displayed to a very high degree that technical virtuosity which characterises the best Irish folk poetry, and which consists essentially in preserving a tightrope tension between the demands of metrical pattern and those of natural speech rhythm, as also a powerful economy in the use of words, and a reliance on a concision of syntax rather than on analytical elements. All these are characteristic, stylistically, to my mind, of all good Gaelic literary production from the point where it becomes recognisable as such.

What manner of being emerges then and now takes the centre of the stage, wearing his poet's mantle, his *tuíon*, his cloak of feathers, his "singing robes"? He is a magician, a sorcerer, a self-conscious and dedicated artist, and a professional. If he is not paid in cash — and a cash economy is a fairly recent growth in Ireland — then he most certainly is in kind, and, at a further remove, in influence, if not in material terms. He is not necessarily a *he*: Daniel O'Connell's grandmother, Máire Ní Dhuibh, who may well have been illiterate in three if not more languages, was just such a poet, to blast or to bless; or, to put it more simply, as Daniel's enemies used to do in his lifetime, just such a witch. There is a very strong tradition in the Munster Gaeltacht that, when the poetic gift, which tends to be hereditary, and was for centuries formally and explicitly so in Ireland, certainly from the time of the introduction of Christianity to the final destruction of the Gaelic hegemony during the Williamite wars — when this gift is inherited by a female, it dries up and does not go any further. Until very recently the O'Connell family was believed to provide the outstanding example in rebuttal of this brief. Máire Ní Dhuibh was herself an O'Donoghue of the Glens, sprung from a turbulent, aristocratic family who practiced poetry on the side. Her daughter, Dark Ellen O'Connell, was credited with producing one of the most splendid compositions in modern Irish in the *Lament* for her husband Arthur O'Leary and thereby was held to disprove this anti-feminist superstition. It is now to my mind virtually certain, however, thanks to painstaking work by Seán Ó Tuama, that the *Lament*, a splendid rhapsodic production, was not her composition at all, but was put together and elaborated by successive relays of professional keening women at O'Leary's wake and funeral. It was subsequently — because of its intrinsic literary merit — polished and perfected by practiced oral romancers and storytellers, in the interests of entertainment, at winter firesides, or on long summer evenings. "Poor Nelly!" — as her family called her — she has been demoted; she is no longer a poet, only a poem. The late Seán Ó Ríordáin, the first Gaelic poet of any standing to attempt a break — only partially successful — with this vestigial, insular, in-tradition we are exploring, has summed up her dilemma rather splendidly in one of his recently published, alas posthumous, pieces.

> Odd that a woman should be a poet!
> Surely it is the stallion's trade?[4]

Dr. Johnson felt the same way, you will recall, about a dog walking on its hind legs, "You do not wonder at its being done well; you wonder that it is done at all!" According to this view the keening women themselves would figure not as makers, but as vehicles; and anyone who has heard the keen will feel the force of this contention: the keener is as one possessed. The tribe speaks through her, resenting, striving to undo "the vile subtraction", ultimately accepting it and falling back on propitiation of the departed.

We know that to lament the dead was among the primary functions of the Gaelic poet in our earliest records of him. What else may we surmise?

For a start the ancients knew him — from as early as 200 B.C., though admittedly from then onwards almost all of them took their knowledge from the same source: the now lost History of Posidonius, written in the first century B.C. This is true even of Julius Caesar who must have known the poet more intimately in Gaul. For the Irish "file" or poet, is, in one of his functions, Caesar's Celtic 'druid', and, in another, Posidonius's 'bard'. We should not be too ready to blame our early authorities for sticking so close to their one original, however, for — so intensely conservative was Celtic society — Posidonius's account remained accurate in its essentials at least up to the middle of the seventeenth century; and perhaps, if the earlier part of this paper is a true account, it has remained in some respects accurate even to the present day. Etymologically, of course, *file* corresponds exactly to *seer*, but in Ireland in recorded times the functions of poet, priest and prophet seem to have coalesced very early, perhaps under the pressures of having to establish and maintain a *modus vivendi* with Christianity. Posidonius separates them, as is clear in the following passages from his History, which has been transmitted to us by another, later historian, Diodorus Siculus:

> They have also lyric poets whom they call Bards. They sing to the acompaniment of instruments resembling lyres, sometimes a eulogy and sometimes a satire. They have also certain philosophers and theologians who are treated with special honour,

whom they call Druids. They further make use of seers, thinking them worthy of praise. These latter by their augural observances and by the sacrifice of sacrificial animals can foretell the future and they hold all the people subject to them. In particular, when enquiring into matters of great import they have a strange and incredible custom; they devote to death a human being and stab him with a dagger in the region above the diaphragm, and when he has fallen they foretell the future in his fall and from the convulsions of his limbs and, moreover, from the spurting of the blood, placing their trust in some ancient and long continued observation of these practices. Their custom is that no one should offer sacrifice without a philosopher; for they say that thanks should be offered to the gods by those skilled in the divine nature, as though they were people who can speak their language, and through them also they hold that benefits should be asked. And it is not only in the needs of peace but in war also that they carefully obey these men and their song-loving poets, and this is true not only of their friends but also of their enemies. For oftentimes as armies approach each other in line of battle with their swords drawn and their spears raised for the charge, these men come forth between them and stop the conflict, as though they had spellbound some kind of wild animals. Thus, even among the most savage barbarians anger yields to wisdom and Ares does homage to the Muses.[5]

In this passage one can note the passive function of the poet as a conduit between his people and the gods. It is not too fanciful, I think, to equate the "language of the gods" here to the *Berla na bhFiled* of Irish tradition, the recondite, hermetic, professional dialect of the poet, which though sometimes made fun of — as when an unfortunate king, whom we may imagine scratching his head, says, "That is a very good poem, for the man who could understand it!" — must also be treated with respect; for to misunderstand could lead to death, as another story tells us. No wonder the children of Irish mediaeval lords, Norman as well as Gael, were taught the standard language in which, the *Berla* having bested even the bards by then, the poetry of praise or censure was written for over three hundred years. As for the nastier, sacrificial aspect, it must be seen against the background of the more blood-thirsty Irish sagas. Traces of it crop up in accounts of divination and of royal inaugurations, in the ritual slaughter of bulls and horses, well into modern times. Even today the *Cingcíseach*, the child born at Whitsuntide, and fated either to kill or be killed, will be given a little bird to strangle, at the bidding of a wise woman, so as to cheat his destiny. We cannot afford to distance ourselves too censoriously from such goings on.

For purposes of comparison, I now skip about 1500 years and cite an Elizabethan account of our "gentleman subject". The passage is similar in substance to the classical one, although the tone is somewhat less sympathetic:

The third sort is called the Aosdan, which is to say in English, the bards, or the riming septs; and these people be very hurtful to the commonweal, for they chiefly maintain the rebels; and further they do cause them that would be true to be rebellious thieves, extortioners, murderers, raveners, yea and worse if it were possible. Their first practice is, if they see any young man descended from the septs of O's and Mac's, who has half a dozen men about him, they will make him a rime wherein they will commend his fathers and ancestors, numbering how many heads they have cut off, how many towns they have burned, and how many virgins they have deflowered, how many notable murders they have done, and in the end they will compare him to Hannibal or Scipio or Hercules, or some other famous person; wherewithal the poor fool runs mad and thinks indeed it is so. . . .

Then will he gather a rabble of rakehells to him and he must also get a prophet, who shall tell him how he shall speed, as he thinks. Then will he get him lurking to a side of a wood and there he keepeth himself close until morning; and when it is daylight they will go to the poor villages ... burning the houses and corn and ransacking of the poor cottages. They will drive all the kine and plough horses, with all other cattle and drive them away ... and when he is in a safe place they will fall to the division of the spoil, according to the discretion of the captain. ...

Now comes the rimer that made the rime, with his rakry. The rakry is he that shall utter the rime; and the rimer himself sits by with the captain very proudly. He brings with him also his harper, who plays all the while that the rakry sings the rime. Also he hath his bard, which is a kind of foolish fellow, who must also have a horse given him; the harper must have a new saffron shirt and a mantle and a hackney; and the rakry must have twenty or thirty kine and the rimer himself horse and harness, with a nag to ride on, a silver goblet, a pair of beads of coral, with buttons of silver — and this, with more, they look for to have, for destruction of the commonwealth and to the blasphemy of God; and this is the best thing that the rimers cause them to do. ... Fillis, which is to say in English, a Poet. These men have a great store of cattle and use all the trades of the others, with an addition of prophecies. These are great maintainers of witches and other vile matters; to the great blasphemy of God and to great impoverishing of the Commonwealth.[6]

The only function which seems to have disappeared since ancient times is the peace-keeping one, and when one studies Classical Modern Irish poetry one finds that this passage, although hostile, is a very good description indeed of the technique and professional practice of the bardic poet. It leaves out, however, one very important factor in his make-up. We know from Aristotle that the Celts esteemed homosexuality; so also, it would appear, did the Gaels — at least for ritual purposes. The Irish chief was wed to the sovereignty, to the Goddess under one of her many names — *Éire, Banba, Fodhla*; perhaps Bridget or *Íte*; almost certainly *Macha, Emer, Medb* and *Gormfhlaith*. My old professor, Osborn Bergin, used to say to his women students "Medb means 'intoxication' and Emer means 'granite'. I can't see what you want calling yourselves after them for." But people did call their daughters after them — and here surely is the explanation of those much-married, dynastic ladies who puzzle students of the Irish records. Gormfhlaith, for example, which can be translated "cerulean sovereignty", can be at one and the same time the name of the goddess who endures and of successive heiresses. The Hag of Beare speaks words put in her mouth by a votary who sees, with the conquest by Christianity, his occupation gone. The ageless divinity, the lover and spouse of Kings, is made mortal as Oisin is, or the Children of Lir are, on contact with the new religion; she is widowed, old, unlovely and sees before her only dreary conversion, virtue and death. She experiences this not only allegorically, but in the actual person of her priest, almost certainly a man. For the Irish poet never abandoned his supernatural role. When his verse legitimised the ruler he *was* the goddess — in word at least. We know that part of the ritual of a King's inauguration was a ceremonial marriage with the Goddess in her incarnation as the totem of the tribe, as, for example, a white mare. In the bardic poetry this practice is refined to a convention of romantic attachment between the ruler and the poet, in which the poet plays the role of the woman. To this convention we owe one of the most splendid dramatic apologues to be found in any language, that where *Eochaidh Ó hEoghusa*, the late 16th century author of, among other works, "O'Hussey's Ode to Maguire", speaks to his patron in the character of a wife torn between loyalty to an absent husband and the passionate demands of a present lover. What he actually means is that if his present patron does not reward him adequately he will find another who will. In spite of this ulterior motive, or because of it, the poem is a superb and exquisitely expressed insight into the female mind and emotions. There are two tempting speculations to account for O'Hussey's explicitness in handling this convention — and it is found not only here, but throughout his work — one, that he was in fact an actual homosexual and two — which I think the more probable — that he was a genuine poet and a modern, a man of his time, exploiting a once sacred device for kicks. Perhaps indeed both. It may be interesting to consider Shakespeare's homosexual sonnets in this context.

Earlier, in the fourteenth century, there was a gifted amateur, the poet-Earl of Desmond, Gearóid Iarla, a Fitzgerald, a Hiberno-Norman, who wrote first-rate Irish verse. He did something similar. His temperament is such that he cannot treat any subject even, perhaps especially, under the stress of deep and real emotion, without sending it up. For example, when the excesses of his wife made him the prototype of the cuckold in his time, he took it in his stride. He embodied in all his subsequent poems an extra *envoi* in which he casts himself in the person of Fionn MacCumhail, the perennial exemplar of the ageing magnate deceived by his young bride! The following is a little quatrain they wrote about him in his day:

Horseman, by ridicule pursued,
Earl Gerard's story hear;
Or did your countess jilt you too
With a midget for a year?

Historically, as opposed to traditionally, the poor countess appears to have been a normally virtuous lady, but we know that the Earl's father made several disappointed bids for the High-Kingship. These would naturally be known to be present in his son's mind also. Could the fickle Countess of the folk-memory be again the omnipresent Goddess, the sovereignty constantly eluding the Geraldine pretender? The situation displays all the creative ambiguity the Irish genius thrives on.

At all events, we find the Earl dedicating his verse to the friend of his youth, and probable foster-brother, to Dermot MacCarthy, in the character of a court poet addressing his lord. We can be reasonably sure that his love for Diarmuid was an orthodox friendship, *une flamme ordinaire* as Racine has it, but also that he was fully aware of the scandalous connotations of his practice. Whatever else he felt about Irish poets — and a very famous poet indeed is said to have been his tutor — Gofraidh Fionn Ó Dálaigh — he was not afraid of them. Gofraidh Fionn, by the way, was an opportunist's opportunist even among poets. He praised Gael and Norman indiscriminately, glorying in it.

We may take it that it was through men of dual culture like the Earl that the

theme of courtly love was introduced into Irish classical verse — you will find
personal poems in the strict metres earlier, but I suspect they will fall into one of the
recognised categories we have been dealing with: narrative, dialogue, laments,
satires or appeals to a patron, essays also on religious themes. I speak subject to
correction, but I don't think the early professional poets of this school have left us
any love poetry *per se*. The point made by Seán Ó Tuama in his essay in this volume
is relevant here. When an early classical poet wants to write about a woman with
affection he has to lament a dead wife. A living love-poem would debase the
medium. So when mediaeval artists needed to paint a woman with no clothes on
they chose mother Eve. I suspect the same to be true of older Irish — many of the
love lyrics of pagan times are laments.

I should now like to hazard my concluding theory. Irish — that is Gaelic — verse
is so intensely conservative that at all times it has taken a major cataclysm to cause
it to change. The coming of Christianity is such a jolt. Before that you can say
broadly speaking that verse is incantatory or narrative — the sagas may have been
originally in verse. Nature is threatening in the paganism of the Old Irish world
and must be regulated by magic. Birds in particular are sinister. One of the most
chilling lines I know in saga literature is where a doomed king — son of a bird-God
— is addressed by his father in warning as "Bird" and as "Son". In Yeats's
Cuchulainn Comforted, you will find this mood echoed:

> "They sang, but had not human tune nor words,
> Though all was done in common as before,
> They had changed their throats and had the throats of birds!"[7]

The Christian monastic poet on the other hand opened his heart to all creation.
The following translation of a tiny lyric about a bird points to the contrast and
exemplifies a whole school of luminous personal nature poetry.

i. Little Bird,	ii. Trill it free,
Whistle heard,	Across Lough Lee,
Shrill bill —	Curve-perched —
Yellow!	Yellow![8]

I know that Professor Carney — to whom I am so much in debt for the basic
material of this essay — has argued brilliantly that one of the early seasonal songs
— which are pagan and intended to control the progression of the seasons — is a
personal lyric about a pagan enjoying a summer's day and going to the races.[9] I have
the temerity to think he is wrong and that the races referred to are sacred ones, part
of the ceremonies of the Aonach — the summer festival.

The next crisis in the development of Irish poetry is the Norman conquest and
the reform of the Gaelic Church. Hitherto, as we have seen, poet and priest seem to
have established fairly quickly a harmonious relationship — both are recognised as
belonging to the privileged learned classes and the persons of both are sacred. This
last fact may explain the bloodless conversion of Ireland. Saint Patrick vehemently
sought martyrdom, but his status as a new kind of druid saved him, like it or not. It
is to the gentle antiquarianism of the monks that we owe the preservation of our
early literature. We have a letter from one ecclesiastic to another at the time of

Diarmuid Mac Murrough, the quisling of Irish historiology, making an appointment to study *a duanaire* or poem book, where the basically oral compositions of the poets are written down for safe-keeping.

The reformers paradoxically thrust literature back into the hands of the lay caste and ensured the survival of its pagan elements. Incidentally — incredible as it may seem — the indifference of the reformers to the old ways is reflected in a popular couplet which exists to the present day:

> "Sagairt is bráithre
> Is d'imigh an bhairdne eatorthu —"
> Priests and friars and the bardic art
> disappeared between them.

Lastly, we have a final break-down of the Gaelic order after the Treaty of Limerick and the old rythmical metres of the earliest verse re-emerge to develop into the splendid free-flowing line of O'Rahilly and O'Bruadair on the one hand and the extraordinary artistry of the whole body of anonymous, folk, love poetry on the other.

We are taught that these actual metres subsisted underground for centuries side by side with the procrustean syllable count of the Bards and I am sure this is so. The watchword of Irish poetry could be Claudel's *Du nouveau mais qu'il soit exactement semblable à l'ancien.*

Today it is possible that yet another crisis, this time the death-throes of a language, is producing another last flowering. Some very good verse indeed has been and is being written in Gaelic in present day Ireland, verse comparable, say, to that of Berryman in English. Prose on the whole is, as it has always been, much sparser. Prose is normally of minor importance in Gaelic tradition — exception is made for the saga material. Verse is highly developed and is the normal medium not only for the themes we have discussed but also for history, geography, religious instruction, medicine and the law. The Poet in Gaelic society had his hands full. It is not altogether surprising therefore that *Cré na Cille*, our one outstanding contemporary prose work, should treat of a typical Gaelic mythopaeic theme: the entire narrative is recounted through the conversations of a community of corpses buried under the church-yard clay. Typically, Irish country people conceive of death at three levels: one orthodox Christian, one rational, and one primaeval; in this last the dead are present, resentful and vindictive beneath the actual sod. All three co-exist without conflict in the folk mind and this is the stuff of our one entirely mature contemporary piece of prose. We seem to take more naturally to verse!

NOTES

[1]Although the interpretations presented in this paper are, of course, my own, I am deeply indebted to the work of many scholars. Many of them are my old masters and colleagues of my student years, and I should like to make a general acknowledgement to them here rather than to footnote every particular. I should like to mention especially J. E. Caerwen Williams's Rhys Memorial Lecture on *The Court Poet in Medieval Ireland* (1971); James Carney's "Three Old Irish Accentual Poems", *Eriu*, Vol. 22 and his "Society and the Bardic Poet," *Studies*, LVII (Dublin 1973), pp. 233-50. We do have four first-rate anthologies, with text and translations: Gerald Murphy's, James Carney's, Greene's and O'Connor's, and Kuno Meyer's.

[2]*Coinnle Corra* (Dublin 1968).

[3]Tomás Ó Crohan, *The Islandman*, trans. Robin Flower (London 1934), pp. 114-7.

[4]Séan Ó Ríordáin, "Banfhile," *Scríobh*, 3 (Dublin 1978), 27.

[5]Quoted in J. J. Tierney "The Celts and the Classical Authors", in *The Celts*, ed. Joseph Raftery (Cork 1964), p. 33.

[6]Quoted in *Seven Centuries of Irish Learning 1000-1700*, ed. Brian Ó Cuív (Dublin 1961), pp. 45-50.

[7]*Variorum Poems* (New York 1957), p. 634.

[8]Gerald Murphy, *Early Irish Lyrics* (Oxford 1962), pp. 6-7.

[9]"Three Old Irish Accentual Poems" *Eriu* 22 (1970).

THE WOMEN OF THE GLEN:
SOME THOUGHTS ON HIGHLAND HISTORY

HAMISH HENDERSON

Historians who write about the Highland Clearances — the infamous mass evictions in which (as Karl Marx stated in *Kapital*) areas as big as German principalities were systematically and brutally cleared of their inhabitants — invariably refer to the extraordinary lack of resistance on the part of the victims during this cataclysmic period of capitalist "social engineering"; yet none (as far as I know) has ever ventured anything like a convincing answer to the really baffling question which must surely occur to anyone reading the history on record: why was it the women, rather than the men, who offered such resistance as there was?

In his book on *The Highland Clearances*, John Prebble describes one such scene:

> Four miles down the glen, as they came through a wood by the march of Greenyard, their road was blocked by sixty or seventy women, with a dozen or less men standing behind them. The women had drawn their red shawls over their heads, and were waiting silently.
> Taylor, the Fiscal, and Stewart got down from the carriage and walked to the head of the police. Taylor shouted to the women in Gaelic and told them that they must clear the way for the Law, and when they did not move he took out the Riot Act and began to read it . . .
> The constables went forward with their truncheons lifted, and, according to the *Inverness Courier* (which got the information from Taylor), the Strathcarron men immediately ran for the hills, leaving their women alone. Although some men must have remained, for two were injured and one was later charged, the absence of all the others is hard to condone, as it was at Culrain, Gruids, and elsewhere. The assault of the police was short, brutal, and bloody. The *Courier*, again reporting Taylor perhaps, said that there were three hundred women there, and that they were armed with sticks and stones. If they were, they were remarkably inefficient in the use of them, for no policeman suffered more than a bruise or a dented hat . . . (p. 244).

These events took place in 1854. No wonder the Highlanders were disinclined to turn out to fight the Russians. During the war against the French Revolution and Napoleon, the Isle of Skye had furnished thousands of men for the forces. By 1937 Skye had contributed to the British Army 21 Lieutenant-Generals and Major-Generals, 48 Lieutenant-Colonels, 600 Majors, Captains and Subalterns, 120 Pipers, and 10,000 N.C.O.s and men.

The Sutherlanders had fought under Gustavus Adolphus, and became the fame of the armies of Europe. When one remembers the accounts of their martial spirit on the battlefields of Germany, Spain, and the Low Countries, one asks oneself with incredulity why they did not defend their own homesteads. Your guess is as good as mine, and the following tentative explanation is offered with the utmost diffidence. I do not think it is the whole truth, but it is part of the truth.

First of all, one must get the Jacobite period into perspective. It is often said that the ancient clan society was destroyed at Culloden, and in a sense this is true, although the process of disintegration had begun long before. However, it is easier to apply surgical methods to the body politic than to subvert the folkways of a millennium. Passing an Act to abolish the heritable jurisdictions does not mean that you get rid, automatically, of the mental attitudes involved, either on the victim's side, or on the side of the judges. Reading the accounts of some of the clearances, one gets an impression of the ritual of "pit and gallows" still in operation, and the luckless clansman waiting to be topped by the chief's *crochadair* (executioner).

There was, of course, occasional resistance, when the people were goaded to utter desperation, or when a resolute leader was thrown up. In 1849, at Sollas, North Uist, there were wild riots, and here and there one finds reports of men like Archibald Dubh Macdonell, who — threatened with eviction — "called up his seven stalwart sons, armed himself with a broadsword his grandfather had carried at Culloden, and defied both the law and his Chief" (Prebble, p. 150).

But the general picture is one of almost masochistic apathy and defeatism. In 1832, evicted Chisholms living in Canada sent their chief an address of loyalty, although he had just finished throwing half his remaining clansmen out of Strathglass. It was not till the 1880's, with the "Battle of the Braes" in Skye, and the sending of warships to the Minch, that resistance assumed proportions serious enough to force Government action, and, ultimately, to secure the passing of the Crofters' Act of 1886.

Incidentally, the record of the evictions at Knoydart, Strathglass, and Glengarry makes it clear that there is no truth in the statement one occasionally encounters that there was more resistance in Catholic areas than in Protestant.

So why — you well may ask — were things so different in Ireland? To that the short answer must surely be that in Ireland the landlords were felt to be (as indeed in many cases they often were) foreigners: whereas in Scotland the expropriators and savagers were in the main the old ancestral clan chiefs themselves. In spite of their galloping anglicization, and the inner erosion of their patriarchal status, the chiefs were still felt to be the clan fathers — *Mac Gille Chaluim* or *Mac Sheumais Chataich*, or whatever — to whom obedience and allegiance were owed.

It is when we examine the role of the women in resisting the evictors that the folklorist begins to feel he might be able to offer the historians some revealing evidence. One of the most noticeable and most easily documentable characteristics of Celtic tribal society, from the early Irish heroic sagas onwards, is the place in it of tough, strong-minded women.

This is the hidden world of matriarchy, exercising power indirectly, which existed over against the masculine authority of the chief. (Curiously enough, it was when dealing with a subject from Celtic tribal history that Shakespeare drew the archetypal portrait of a hero who is outwardly all panache, pride and swagger, but who depends almost abjectly on his mettlesome wife at moments of crisis.

Infirm of purpose! Give me the daggers!)[1]

At this point we need to recapitulate what is known of the status of women, and of their military prowess, in early Celtic society. Polybius, writing in the second century BC, states that in time of war the women of the Celts accompanied the men to battle, following them in waggons.[2] The bellicose reputation of Gaulish women is attested by Ammianus Marcellinus in an often quoted passage:

> Nearly all the Gauls are of a lofty stature, fair, and of ruddy complexion; terrible from the sternness of their eyes, very quarrelsome, and of great pride and insolence. A whole troop of foreigners would not be able to withstand a single Gaul if he called his wife to his assistance, who is usually very strong, and with blue eyes; especially when, swelling her neck, gnashing her teeth, and brandishing her sallow arms of enormous size, she begins to strike blows mingled with kicks, as if they were so many missiles sent from the string of a catapult.[3]

The most formidable single opponent encountered by the Romans in Britain — with the possible exception of the Caledonian chief Calgacus, who commanded the northern tribes against Agricola at Mons Graupius — was the 'warrior queen' Boudicca (Boadicea), who is thus described by Dio Cassius:

> She was huge of frame, terrifying of aspect, and with a harsh voice. A great mass of bright red hair fell to her knees: she wore a great twisted golden necklace, and a tunic of many colours, over which was a thick mantle, fastened by a brooch. Now she grasped a long spear to strike fear into all those who watched her . . .[4]

In *The Celtic Realms*, an excellent comprehensive survey by Myles Dillon and Nora Chadwick, the high status of women in the Celtic world is continually emphasised:

> History and tradition alike echo the high prestige of women in Celtic mythology . . . In the Heroic Age of Ireland Medb, Queen of Connacht, is the reigning sovereign. Ailill, her husband, is never more than her consort, and Medb is the greatest personality of any royal line of the Heroic Age.
> In Irish and Welsh stories of Celtic Britain the great heroes are taught not only wisdom but also feats of arms by women. In the Irish saga known as 'The Wooing of Emer' Cuchulainn is trained in all warrior feats by two warlike queens — Scathach, who is also a *fáith*, i.e. a prophetess, an expert in supernatural wisdom — and Aife . . . Among the ancient Picts matrilinear succession was the rule till the ninth century. Bede tells us that even in his own day whenever the royal succession among the Picts came in question their ruler was chosen by succession from the female line (pp. 194-5).

The most famous allusion to Celtic fighting women occurs in Tacitus' description of the Roman assault on the island of Angelsey in AD 61. Women and Druids were among the British warriors drawn up to withstand the assault, and to protect the island's sacred groves. After the battle these groves were destroyed — an act untypical of Roman policy, and suggesting a real fear of the Druids as inspirers of opposition.[5] (As Julius Caesar had put it a hundred years previously, *natio est omnis Gallorum admodum dedita religionibus*, "The whole Celtic people is greatly addicted to religion".)[6]

The "man's world" of the Celts was also, of course, a warrior world, and the descriptions of it given by several classical authors tie in remarkably well with the information contained in the Gaelic heroic sagas. Like many warrior societies, in which the young men are isolated from the women for long periods, trained from their earliest years in the use of arms, and brought up to vie with each other in battle and in the hunt, it was a society in which homosexuality seems to have been very widespread. The references of Greek and Latin historians to this subject are quite explicit, and have a remarkable consistency. They are not as well known as might be expected, for the whole idea seems to have embarrassed Celtic scholars, much as the speech of Alcibiades in *The Banquet* about his relations with Socrates is said to have embarrassed and troubled poor Jowett.

Diodorus Siculus, writing in the first century BC, has this to say:

> The Celtic women are not only as tall as the men, but are just as courageous . . . But although they are attractive, the men are much keener on their own sex; they lie around on animal skins and enjoy themselves, with a lover on each side. The extraordinary thing is that they haven't the smallest regard for their own personal dignity or self-respect; they offer themselves to other men without the least compunction. Furthermore, this isn't looked down on, or regarded as in any way disgraceful; on the contrary, if one of them is rejected by another to whom he has offered himself, he takes offence.[7]

This information came to Diodorus from Posidonius, an historian who travelled through Southern Gaul, and observed Celtic folkways on the spot. Strabo, who died about 26 AD, writes laconically that "the young men in Gaul are shamelessly generous with their boyish charms", and Athenaeus, two centuries later, repeats the statement of Diodorus about the Celt's male bed-partners.[8] This evidence of homo-erotic practices in an enclosed warrior society is, of course, in no way surprising. It is confirmed in the most striking manner by several passages in the great Irish heroic saga, Táin Bó Cuailnge (The Cattle-Raid of Cooley).[9] In the versions contained in the Yellow Book of Lecan and (more completely) in the Book of Leinster the tale is told of the fight between Cuchullain and his "ardent and adored foster-brother" Ferdia, who face each other in heroic single-combat at the ford. Ferdia does not want to fight Cuchullain who has been his comrade-in-arms at the battle-school of Scathach in Alba (Scotland), but Medb, the queen of Connacht, sends "poets and bards and satirists to bring the blushes to his cheek with mockery and insult and ridicule, so there would be nowhere in the world for him to lay his head in peace." When Cuchullain learns that Ferdia is on the way to fight him, he says: "I swear I don't want a meeting. Not because I fear him, but because I love him so much", and before their first encounter he reminds him:

> Fast friends, forest-companions
> We made one bed and slept one sleep
> In foreign lands after the fray.
> Scathach's pupils, two together,
> We'd set forth to comb the forest.

In this verse, written down in Ireland more than a thousand years after Diodorus wrote the passage quoted above, we have an unmistakable echo in poetry of the rather ironic down-to-earth description of 'heroic love' in the Greek historian's prose.

The combat of Ferdia and Cuchullain has been compared (by Aodh de Blacam) to the duel between Hector and Achilles, and Cuchullain's lament over the body of his lover to David's lament for Saul and Jonathan. ("The beauty of Israel is slain upon thy high places"). — On another level (more in tune, perhaps, with the native temperament) one feels like repeating of the two champions what Henry de

Montherlant once wittily remarked of the heroes of the Satyricon, that they may be *bougres*, but at any rate they are not *de mauvais bougres*.

In view of the enormous time-gap to which we just alluded, it is maybe advisable, at this point, to recall Gordon Childe's remark in *Scotland before the Scots* that human history comes not so much in 'Ages' as in 'Stages'. It should always be remembered that because of Ireland's relative isolation, aboriginal Celtic folkways continued to flourish there right up until the early Middle Ages. Rudolf Pörtner puts it succinctly when he compares the 'protected' survivals in Ireland, the Off-Off Island, to life in a *Naturschutzpark* or nature reserve [10]

The same general situation undoubtedly prevailed in many parts of the Scottish Highlands and Islands until even later, as voluminous folklore records testify. Ancestral memories of Celtic head-hunting are still to be encountered in parts of the Outer Hebrides — as are hang-overs of some of the other phenomena we have been discussing. The plot of a folk-tale *MacNeil of Barra, the Widow's Son and the Shetland Buck*, which was recorded from "the Coddy" (the late John Mac Pherson, postmaster of Northbay) by John Lorne Campbell, contains some curious motifs. MacNeil (the chief) takes a fancy to the Mingulay widow's son, and carries him off to Barra, in spite of his mother's pleas. All goes well until the boy is big and strong enough to beat the chief in wrestling matches; the latter then attempts to murder him by ordering the crew of the *birlinn* to put to sea in a hurricane.[11]

Much fascinating information about the sexual mores of medieval Celtic society is to be found in Kenneth Nicholls' *Gaelic and Gaelicized Ireland in the Middle Ages*. The rights enjoyed by women under Brehon law — which continued to be operative in most parts of Ireland until the seventeenth century, although 'officially' terminated by the Statutes of Kilkenny in 1366 — would be the envy of women's libbers in many parts of the world in 1980. Women had the right of independent property ownership, could divorce and remarry with ease, and could be practitioners of the arts and sciences if they so desired. "There was no such thing as an illegitimate child; a mother had simply to 'name' the child and if it was a son, he would inherit part of his father's property. Marriage was one of the keys to Irish women's independence, based as it was upon a complex series of property relationships which did not automatically involve property transfer from women to men."[12] Nicholls tells us that "down to the end of the old order in 1603, what could be called Celtic secular marriage remained the norm in Ireland . . . Christian matrimony was no more than the rare exception grafted on to this system" (p. 73).

According to Peter Trewhela, "If a couple chose to part, all they had to do was to stand back to back on the hill of Tailteann near Tara, and walk away from each other. Trial marriages were very common . . ."[13]

Myles Dillon, in *The Celtic Realms*, confirms the statements of the writers already quoted:

> The law of marriage in early Ireland is of special interest, as it shows in great measure the persistence of ancient customs in spite of Christian teaching. Divorce is freely

> allowed. Indeed there is a trace of annual marriage. A marriage may always be ended by common consent ... The practice of placing one's children in the care of foster-parents was a normal feature of Irish society, and it was not confined to the noble class ... The time of fosterage ended for boys at seventeen, for girls at fourteen, and they returned home. Those who had been fostered together were bound in close relationship. This relationship with one's *comaltae* is a recurring motif in the sagas. (pp. 132-3)

Dr. John MacInnes informs me that until the forfeiture of the Lordship of the Isles at the end of the fifteenth century, a very similar judicial system must have prevailed over much of the Highlands. We know of a family of hereditary law-givers — the Morrisons of Ness in Lewis — who, after the Irish pattern, acted as jurists for the Lordship. There can be no doubt that these *breitheamhan* were the far-off heirs of the learned men reported among the Celts of Gaul by Julius Caesar and Posidonius.

That the women of Celtic Scotland were as combative as those of Ireland is attested by Hector Boece:

> The wemen war of litil les vassalage and strenth than was the men; for al rank madinnis and wiffis, gif they war nocht with child, yeid als weill to battall as the men.[14]

In his splendid, erudite book, *A Midsummer Eve's Dream*, which is a discursive commentary on William Dunbar's poem "The Tretis of the Tua Mariit Wemen and the Wedo," Professor A. D. Hope provides much information on the position of women in Scottish society at various periods in our history. He quotes the statement of Thomas Morer (who was chaplain to a Scottish regiment about 1689, and who wrote *A Short Account of Scotland*) that "the women of Scotland are capable of estates and honours, and inherit both as well as the males and therefore after marriage may retain their maiden name," and adds:

> The way in which women retained their own names and often their own property in Scotland impressed many travellers. It was perhaps the last afterglow of an age in which the real power had been theirs to exercise and enjoy.

What light — if any — does all of this throw on the recurrent pattern of women's resistance to the clearers which is so amply documented. If I am on the right track — and I emphasize again that this is a theory, advanced tentatively — then there is more to the presence of the women in the front line than the obvious considerations that they were less likely to be clubbed by police and military; were in themselves (as wives and mothers) the most direct human reproach to the callousness and inhumanity of the evictors; and (to put it at its lowest) were less likely to be proceeded against than the men. All these are valid points, but they are not enough to explain this very perceptible pattern. Surely it is only completely explicable as another hang-over from the mental world of the shattered tribal system. It was the "women's world", which stood in, with all its spirit, courage, and resilience, when the "man's world" faltered.[15]

The swashbuckling "man's world" of chief, gillie-wetfoot, and arms-toting *duine uasal* had come unstuck — finally unstuck — on Drummossie Moor; not long after, it was to be taken over, lock, stock and powder-horn, by the British army. The hidden "matriarchal" women's world, of whose splendid vigour we have so much evidence in Gaelic song-poetry, had remained intact, and when the men took to the brae in ignominious *sauve qui peut* on the appearance of the "baton brigade", it provided a fragile last line of resistance before the fire-raisers moved in. It was as if they meant to show that if the men were not prepared to defend hearth and home, they were.

The male who does appear in baleful prepotent pride on the scene of the Clearances is, alas, on the oppressor's side. Haranguing his cowed subjects from a high wooden throne, and threatening them with hell-fire if they disobey those set in authority over them, he is the Calvinist minister. This sinister character can well and truly be regarded as the devil of the piece; while lambasting the people for their sins, and openly suggesting that they are being made to suffer because of them, he is quite capable at the same time of angling for an extension to his glebe. Donald Mac Leod informs us in *Gloomy Memories* that during the famine of 1836 the Rev. Hugh MacKenzie, moderator of the Presbytery of Tongue, exchanged part of his glebe for more extensive property. "But in consenting to the change he made an express condition that the present occupiers, amounting to eight families, should be removed, and accordingly they were driven out in a body".[16]

And so it was the women who — in accordance with aboriginal Celtic tradition — defied the invaders of their world: the venal Calvinist ministers, and the crowbar-wielding minions of "the gentry with no pity". However, their appearance in the front line raises a number of questions to which one would be glad to have the answer. Where were the children and babies during such scenes as that at Strathcarron? Who was looking after them?

In this connection one must also take into consideration several reports — factual news reports, as well as "folk narratives" — that men dressed as women took part in episodes of resistance. One hesitates to believe that the heroes of Badajoz or Waterloo, or their relatives, would dress themselves in women's attire because they lacked "civil courage". In Ireland the 'Molly Maguires' were the most belligerent of transvestites. Was this an example of military camouflage, the better to do down the aggressor?

Be that as it may, one could wish — reading the accounts of some of the clearances, and their pitiful consequences — that the seven battalions of the Fingalians had been deployed in battle array against the rapacious chieftain-landlords, and their factors and minions, rather than this "petticoat brigade". Donald Ross, a Glasgow lawyer, went to Skye after the Boreraig and Suisinish evictions of 1853, carrying with him large quantities of food and clothing for the people. His account of his experiences was published in a pamphlet *Real Scottish Grievances* the following year: —

"He saw seven children, all under the age of eleven, lying in a shed on a collection of rubbish, fern, meadow-hay, straw, pieces of old blanket, and rags of clothing. Rain and snow fell upon them. They were so thin, and so light, he said, that he could have carried them all in his arms for a quarter of a mile without feeling their weight".[17]

And what were the sanctimonious Calvinist mullahs doing when all these dreadful things were taking place on their manse doorsteps? The discreditable truth (with very few exceptions) is — nothing, or practically nothing. The record of the Free Kirk is better than that of the Established Church in this context.

One cannot avoid the conclusion, from much of the evidence available, that the "judgment of the Lord" fulminations of the ministers tended to induce a hopeless apathetic subjection in the minds of their flocks, and sapped their will to resist their oppressors.

The moral is that no-one surveying this whole subject can afford to leave out of the picture the peculiar psychology of Scots Calvinism — how it can both energize and hypnotize, and — at worst — make thoroughly apathetic. G. K. Chesterton gave gnomic expression to the inner truth of the matter when he wrote (in *The Honour of Israel Gow*): "Scotland has a double dose of the poison called heredity; the sense of blood in the aristocrat, and the sense of doom in the Calvinist."

When the people of Glencalvie were evicted (May 1845), they sought refuge in Croick Kirkyard, and they scratched a few messages for posterity on the window panes. The most pathetic, and in many ways the most revealing of these, reads as follows: *Glencalvie people the wicked generation.*[18]

It seems clear that there were a lot of hidden — and open — persuaders who wanted the people to believe that what had hit them was a sort of divine scourge, and that resistance offered to the landlords was tantamount to resistance offered to the Lord. I suspect that women were less susceptible to the powers of this sinister hoodoo than were their menfolk; the women, as we have seen, were the bearers of very old traditions of custom and belief that were deeply antagonistic to the puritanical (and essentially "father-figure") Church.

It was a woman — Mary MacPherson, *Mairi Mhor nan Oran* — who wrote the most poignant lament for the older Scotland shattered by the Clearances. However, in our own day a male poet, T. S. Law, has written in English a poem on the same subject which strikes a quite individual note of lyric elegy, and of truly Swiftian *saeva indignatio*. I conclude by quoting it in full:

The Clearances

Hear how the names sing,
      Macdonald, Clanranald,
Hear how the names sing,
      Argyll and Lochiel.
Hear them, hear them,
      MacLeod and Glengarry,
hear them,
      Baillie, MacDonnell and Ross.
These are the names that ennobled their line,
these are the owercome in auld lang syne.

These are the names of the traitors and tinkers,
these are the merciless, murdering swine,
these the destroyers, the deaths heads, blood-drinkers,
these are the owercome in auld lang syne,
these are the names that ennobled their line.

Listen to
        Drummond, Breadalbane, and Atholl,
listen to
        Hamilton, Balfour, and Innes,
listen and hear,
        Sutherland, Fraser,
listen,
        Matheson, Seaforth, Robertson.
These are the names that ennobled their line,
these are the owercome in auld lang syne.

These are the cannibals, heart-cruel, savagers,
their Highlanders' bodies and souls meat and wine,
these the procurers of gentleness, ravishers.
These are the owercome in auld lang syne,
these are the names that ennobled their line.

NOTES

[1]*Macbeth*, Act II, Scene 2.

[2]Polybius, *Histories*, V, 78.

[3]XV, xii. (Charles D. Yonge's translation).

[4]*Roman Histories*, Epitome of Book LXII, 3-4.

[5]Tacitus, *Annals*, XIV, xxx.

[6]*De Bello Gallico*, VI.

[7]Diodorus Siculus, *Bibliotheke Historike*, Book V. Diodorus is as frank about the drinking habits of the Celts: "They take such inordinate pleasure in wine that when it is imported by merchants they drink it straight; and when they're intoxicated with excess of drink, they either go to sleep, or go crazy altogether." (The Greeks customarily diluted their wine in one way or another.)

[8]Strabo and Athenaeus, quoted in Gerhard Herm, *Die Kelten* (Düsseldorf 1975), p. 96.

[9]The quotations from the *Táin* are taken from Thomas Kinsella's translation (Dublin 1969).

[10]*Bevor die Römer Kamen*, p. 325.

[11]See *Tales from Barra. Told by the Coddy*, ed. J. L. Campbell (Edinburgh 1960).

[12]Tom Woodhouse, "Lost Freedoms," *Gay Left*, no. 8.

[13]"How Celtic Women fell from Power," in *Celtic Theology*, an SCM pamphlet.

[14]*Chronicles of Scotland*, Bellenden translation, I, 20.

[15]Professor Kenneth Little tells me that the same sort of thing has happened in Africa, when a male warrior caste is broken by defeat, and the women for that reason "have the edge" on the men. While the latter sit around, play cards and get drunk on cheap liquor, the women conduct public and commercial business, and are the purposeful representatives of the group *vis à vis* the outside world.

[16]Donald MacLeod, *Gloomy Memories* (Glasgow 1888), p. 37.

[17]Prebble, p. 292. Ross's account of the treatment meted out to a 96-year-widow is reprinted in full in Alexander Mackenzie's *Highland Clearances* (pp. 239-44).

[18]P. A. MacNab, "The Church at Croick," *The Scots Magazine* (May 1963). MacNab's article epitomizes so well the whole tragic history we have been recounting that I quote it here practically *in toto*:

Croick Church was built in 1827. It is one of about a dozen churches built in Scotland by Thomas Telford, the famous road-maker. It was then the centre of worship attended by a weekly congregation of 200 from the little communities which won a living from the soil and grazings round about. Now they are gone. Nothing remains but old tracks radiating through the heather to green oases on the hillsides, and an occasional rickle of stones which mark where the houses of a thriving people once stood, mute evidence of the Clearances and subsequent depopulation. Every year on the last Sunday in July a Communion Service is conducted in the Church by the Minister of Kincardine Parish, whose consolidated charges and wide district point to the once large population for whom all those churches were established.

. . . Everything is plain and well preserved inside the church. The centre of interest lies, of course, in the east window where a few words and names scratched on the diamond panes remind us of the whole sad story behind the depopulation, the outcome of one of the later clearances or "Improvements" of the last century. The incidents which centred on Croick Church are as reprehensible as any of the more widely publicised Clearances, although, in justice to the landlord, Major Charles Robertson of Kindeace, it should be said that they took place on the initiative of his factor, James Gillanders, who lived in Tain. The object of his policy of Improvement was Glen Calvie, which lies quite near Croick, which itself had suffered in the same manner a few years earlier.

In 1843 the people of Glen Calvie, reduced in numbers to no more than ninety by earlier evictions, were described as a happy, self-contained community. Although the glen was poor and rocky it was rented at £55.10, considered an exhorbitant figure; yet the people paid it. Furthermore, they were free from debt, law-abiding and had sent many soldiers to the wars; they raised sheep and black cattle and grew potatoes and barley. They could trace their tenancies back for 500 years. The events which followed came to the notice of the London *Times* who sent a special correspondent to the scene. He summarised the general position in the north, with special reference to Glen Calvie: "through the actions of the factors in the lonely glens, hundreds of peaceable and generally industrious peasants have been driven from their means of support to become wanderers and starving beggars — a brave, valuable population lost."

In 1843 Gillanders began his scheme to turn the glen into one large sheep farm at an even higher rent. The first step was to serve summonses of removal on the tenants. Anticipating this, however, and on watch just outside the boundary across the river, the women of the glen intercepted the constables and, seizing the wrists of the man holding the writs, they applied live coals to the papers until they were destroyed, seeking to prove they had neither been seen or handled in the glen. Next year, not to be outdone, the crafty Gillanders invited the chief tenants to Tain for a "friendly discussion". Instead he placed the formal notices to quit in their hands. Decree for removal followed, and the law took its course. Stunned and bewildered, the people began to hunt feverishly for alternate holdings; but only six families could find a place, and poor ones at that. The others were at last evicted by force, and for a time, while their menfolk were continuing the hopeless search, they were allowed to shelter in Croick churchyard, exposed to the elements — wishing, as it is recorded, that death would come to allow them to join their forefathers beneath the sward. They were helped only by the minister, who did all in his power to ease their conditions. As the people passed the weary days among the tombs, someone among them, scratching idly on the diamond-shaped panes of the east window, left a short, pathetic message for posterity. In the unhurried copperplate writing of the last century, we can still decipher some of the names: "C. Chalmers", "John Ross, Shepherd, Parish of Ardgay", and others, and, bowing meekly to what was accepted by a God-fearing people as Divine chastisement — "Glencalvie people, the wicked generation." "Glen Calvie people was in the Churchyard here May 24th, 1845". The words "Church Officer" also appear under the name "Ann McAlister" but it is probable that the designation refers to an illegible name scratched below. It is highly unlikely that a woman would be acceptable as Church Officer in the middle of the last century, in a community such as this was. Why were they not allowed to shelter inside the Church? I suggest the answer is simple. In those days it would have been regarded as desecration of a holy place and even under such necessity, and if invited by the Minister, they would probably have refused.

THE SUNNY FOLD/
A' BHUAILE GHREINE

SORLEY MacLEAN

To my eyes you were Deirdre
beautiful in the sunny cattle-fold
you were MacBride's wife
in her shining beauty.
You were the yellow-haired girl of Cornaig
and the Handsome Fool's Margaret,
Strong Thomas's Una,
Cuchulainn's Eimhir, and Grainne.
You were the one of the thousand ships,
desire of poets and death of heroes,
you were she who took the rest
and the peace from the heart of William Ross,
the Audiart who plagued De Born,
and Maeve of the drinking horns.

A' BHUAILE GHREINE

Do m' shùilean-sa bu tu Deirdre
's i bòidheach 's a' bhuaile ghréine:
bu tu bean Mhic Ghille Bhrìghde
ann an àilleachd a lìthe.
Bu ti nighean bhuidhe Chòrnaig
is Mairearad an Amadain Bhòidhich,
an Una aig Tòmas Làidir,
Eimhir Chù Chulainn agus Gràinne,
but tu té nam mìle long,
ùidh nam bàrd is bàs nan sonn,
's bu tu an té a thug an fhois
's an t-sìth bho chridhe Uilleim Rois,
an Audiart a bhuair De Born
agus Maoibhe nan còrn.

265

And if it is true that any one
of them reached your beauty,
it must have been with a gracious spirit
shaped in a beautiful face.
And therefore I ought
to fashion for you the Dàn Dìreach
that would catch every beauty
that has kindled the imagination of Europe.
There ought to appear in its course
the vehemence of Spain complete,
the acuteness of France and Greece,
the music of Scotland and of Ireland.
I ought to put every effect
that Norway and Ireland
and old Scotland gave to my people
together in mellowness
and to offer them to the wonder
that is fair and shapely in your face.

Agus ma 's eadh is fìor gun d' ràinig
aon té dhiubh-san t' àilleachd,
tha fhios gum b' ann le spiorad gràsmhor
air a dhealbh an aghaidh àlainn.
Agus uime sin bu chòir dhomh
'n Dàn Dìreach a chur air dòigh dhut
a ghlacadh gach uile bhòidhchead
a las mac-meanmna na h-Eòrpa.
Bu chòir nochdadh 'na iomchar
dianas na Spàinne gu h-iomlan,
geur aigne na Frainge is na Gréige,
ceòl na h-Albann 's na h-Eireann.
Bha còir agam gach uile éifeachd
a thug Lochlann is Eire
is Alba àrsaidh do mo dhaoine
a chur cuideachd an caoine
agus an ìobairt do 'n ìoghnadh
tha geal dealbhte an clàr t' aodainn.

And since I am not one of them —
MacBride or Naoise,
Thomas Costello or MacDonald,
Bertrans or the Handsome Fool,
Cuchulainn or great Fionn or Diarmad —
it is my dilemma to seize
in tormented verses the longing
that takes the spirits of sad poets,
to raise and keep as I would like,
direct and well-formed in the poem for you,
old and new and full,
the form and spirit of every beauty:
together in the image of joy,
paean-like, deep, jewel-like,
the acuteness of France and Greece,
the music of Ireland and of Scotland.

Agus a chionn nach mise aon diubh —
Mac Ghille Bhrìghde no Naoise,
Tòmas Ua Custuil no Mac Dhòmhnaill,
Bertrans no 'n t-Amadan Bòidheach,
Cù Chulainn no Fionn mór no Diarmad —
's e mo chàs-sa an iargain
a ghabhas spiorad nam bàrd cianail
a ghlacadh anns na ranna pianta,
a thogail 's chumail mar a b' àill leam
dìreach, cuimir anns an dàn dhut,
sean agus ùr is lànmhor,
cumadh is meanmna gach àilleachd;
còmhla an ìomhaigh an éibhneis,
luathghaireach, domhain, leugach,
geur-aigne na Frainge 's na Gréige,
ceòl na h-Albann is na h-Eireann.

THE GAELIC CONTINUUM IN SCOTLAND

JOHN MacINNES

O wad some Power the giftie gie us
To see oursels as ithers see us!

So far as the Gaels of Scotland are concerned Robert Burns's prayer has in large measure now been answered. For practically two centuries most of the social institutions that normally preserve a people's sense of identity have worked together to ensure that the native Gael views himself and his world through alien eyes. The processes of ethnocide work of course at many levels and in many guises, but they are most conspicuous in the domain of formal education. Particularly since 1872, when compulsory education (in English only) was introduced and the Presbyterian Gaelic schools abolished, English and Education became synonymous. Some years ago certain concessions were made in the direction of bilingual education. Even if this may be, as some argue, too little and too late, it has already had an effect. But for the most part English remains the language of authority, in school as elsewhere. Gaelic has of course no official status as one of the languages of the United Kingdom. I am not concerned here with the motives that underlie administrative policy: only with the facts. In a sense, it is as if an English-speaking child derived his education wholly from French text-books and was encouraged to interpret the history of England from a French point of view. Yet even this analogy is in certain respects quite misleading. No effort of imagination will allow us to cast a dominant culture in the role of the weak and dispossessed. We might even be tempted to argue in general for the benefits of an antidote to parochialism and insularity. But we can hardly speak of the salutary corrective of an alternative point of view in a culture if the forces of cultural imperialism have left virtually nothing to correct.

Gaelic society is now, as everyone admits, in a parlous condition. None the less it would be wrong to imagine that the situation is one of straightforward decline or that we can predict the future with confident pessimism. There is certainly evidence of continuing decline in the number of native speakers. At the same time the astonishing growth of interest in the language throughout Scotland has produced thousands of learners, many of whom are completely fluent in Gaelic and some of whom are indistinguishable from native Gaels. This is almost entirely a phenomenon of the last twenty years. The twentieth-century renaissance of Gaelic poetry is well known; it is not so often realised that Gaelic prose, too, has its major writers and that some of these have not yet reached the height of their creative powers. The literary quarterly *Gairm*, founded thirty years ago, largely to make the publication of new work possible, continues to flourish and new authors continue to appear. It is worth observing also that some of the most interesting of our contemporary writers are not native Gaels.

But the core of Gaelic society is of course the native community. Within that community in Scotland there is still a vast reservoir of Gaelic: immense resources of vocabulary and idiom; repertoires of traditional songs and stories; the poetry of the present day as well as that which has been handed down by the oral tradition of many centuries. Between the shennachies of the Gaidhealtachd and the 'non-traditional' modern writers there are several overlapping cultural areas. One of these is dominated by the folksong revival. Folksong groups either draw on the body of traditional song or write their own material, lyrics and melodies alike. One very successful professional rock-group, 'Run-rig,' has a large following in the Scottish Lowlands. In another case, a modern group and a traditional bard have collaborated with enormous success. Murchadh MacPhàrlain from the island of Lewis began, in his seventies, to compose melodies, as well as words, for *Na h-Oganaich*.

The bards of the Gaidhealtachd, who have always been spokesmen for their society, still comment, seriously or in humorous and satirical modes, both on the events of village life and the events of the greater world which the media bring to their notice. More and more, these bards are literate in Gaelic and by that token some of them are coming to occupy an intermediate position between the contemporary 'literary' poets and the pop-song composers.

Gaelic drama has its own following. Although the one professional theatre company, *Fir-Chlis*, is temporarily in eclipse, this is due to the effect of current government policy on regional authority subsidies, not to lack of audiences. At an amateur level, drama is relatively buoyant.

In 1973 a Lewis crofter published his autobiography *A' Suathadh ri Iomadh Rubha* ('Rubbing against many a Headland'). It is the first genuine autobiography to be published in Gaelic and as such would naturally attract attention. But it is also, on grounds of quality alone, one of the great landmarks of Gaelic literature, Scottish or Irish.

What then is the background of this community and how do its traditions retain such vigour in the face of adversity?

The history of the Gaelic people and their language covers over six centuries of expansion and development, followed by a somewhat longer period of slow decline. Gaelic was established in what is now Scotland about 500 AD by colonists from Ireland, the older Scotia. By the middle of the ninth century the name of Scotia came to be used for most of the country north of the Forth and Clyde. This Scoto-Pictish kingdom was now under a Gaelic King. By the early part of the eleventh century King Duncan — the gentle Duncan of Shakespeare's *Macbeth* — had become ruler of the mainland of modern Scotland. The authority of these early Gaelic Kings over a large portion of their realm was merely nominal: the Hebrides, for instance, and sizable tracts of the North and West were under Norse domination. Nevertheless, the existence of a Gaelic speaking court, with its attendant patronage, was of great importance to Gaelic literature, the exponents of which were organised in what practically amounted to a caste system. When the court became Anglicised under the sons of Malcolm Canmore and Queen Margaret, towards the end of the eleventh century, the setback was profound and permanent. No longer the *sermo regius* of Scotland, Gaelic was now fated never to fulfil what had seemed to be its destiny: to become the language of cultured society throughout the kingdom and the medium of expression in its leading institutions. Instead there began the process which ultimately banished it to the remote and inaccessible parts of the land and although development did not by any means cease, Gaelic literature became largely cut off from the influence of the great innovating movements of post-mediaeval Europe.

Meanwhile in the lowlands of Scotland, the northern English dialect was being developed as the national language. This, and the evolution of a distinctive Scots literature, meant that Scotland became a country of two literary cultures. Down to the sixteenth century, the term 'Scots' was used to describe Gaelic, and what we now call Scots was then called Inglis. Later, Gaelic was frequently referred to as Irish or Erse — different forms of the same word. This change in nomenclature serves to illustrate the shift in cultural orientation which the development of the Lowland tongue produced in Gaelic society. Ireland now reassumes a dominant role; in relation to it Scotland becomes something of a cultural periphery. In that redefined situation, the principal focus of Gaelic political and cultural organisation was the confederation known as the Lordship of the Isles, whose ruler was known in Gaelic as 'King of the Isles of the Norsemen and Coastland of the Gael'. This semi-independent state, which exercised influence, if not always authority, over a considerable part of the north-west mainland, was not finally destroyed until the mid-sixteenth century and some of its cultural resonances linger in Gaelic tradition to the present day. Partly because of these facts of history we normally associate Gaelic with the north-west and tend to forget that it was spoken in Galloway, in the extreme south-west, until well on in the seventeenth century, and possibly later; or that on the east, Aberdeenshire Gaelic is still spoken by one very elderly individual; or, indeed, that some fifty miles from Edinburgh it is still spoken in Perthshire.

The special relationship with Ireland remained intact until the seventeenth century. In spite of differences, political or religious, Ireland and Gaelic Scotland continued to be one cultural area. As the vernacular dialects of the two countries began to diverge, the mandarin class who cultivated the arts standardised a common language, a flexible, classical form of Gaelic. These learned men moved freely throughout the lands of 'the sea-divided Gael,' enjoying a kind of diplomatic immunity. Inevitably they promoted a sense of cultural solidarity, within Scotland as well as between Scotland and Ireland.

In this way Scots Gaelic participates in one of the great literatures of mediaeval Europe. It is essentially an aristocratic tradition, developed from an ancient native stock under the influence of mediaeval European rhetoric. In the earlier Middle Ages, poets of the highest caste specialised in historical and mythological lore. Such a poem is the 'Scottish Lay'[1] composed in the reign of Malcolm Canmore and addressed to the poet's peers, the aristocracy of birth as well as the aristocracy of learning: "O all ye learned ones of Alba, o stately yellow-haired company". Later reorganisations, perhaps due to the Anglo-Norman invasions of Ireland and Scotland, modified their role to that of panegyrists who wrote to celebrate great men, wherever patrons who were willing to pay for a poem could be found. They remained a professional intelligentsia, justifying a highly stratified society, advising and exhorting their patrons freely, but also on occasion expressing adverse criticism.

But they did not confine themselves to praise-poetry, nor was all poetry written by professionals. Among the aristocracy, there were men and women who were sufficiently conversant with classical Gaelic and skilled enough in the conventions of its court poetry to write subtle, elegant and passionate poems, even if they did not observe the purists' rules of consonantal and vowel rhyme, or all the other ornaments demanded by the poetic schools. Thus we find Isobel, first Countess of Argyll, composing a charming little love-poem in the fifteenth century:

> There is a youth comes wooing me; oh King of Kings, may he succeed! would he were stretched upon my breast, with his body against my skin.
> If everything were as I wish it, never should we be far divided, though it is all too little to declare, since he does not see how the case is.
> It cannot be, till his ship comes home, a thing most pitiful for us both; he in the east and I in the west, so that our desires are not fulfilled.[2]

In the same manuscript there is an elegy by the widow of the chief of the MacNeills. She addresses the rosary, remembering the hand that had held it until that night. The poem draws upon the conventional images of praise, but it is nonetheless poignant and tender.

> Rosary that has roused my tear, dear the finger that was wont to be upon you; dear the heart, hospitable and generous, that owned you ever until tonight . . .
> A mouth whose winning speech would wile the hearts of all in every land; lion of white-walled Mull, hawk of Islay of smooth plains . . .
> Mary Mother, who did nurse the King, may she guard me on every path, and her Son who created each creature, rosary that has roused my tear.[3]

When the tradition is nearing its end in the eighteenth century, we find Niall Mór MacMhuirich in South Uist writing as elegantly as any of his predecessors. His 'Message of the Eyes' is in the same convention as the Countess of Argyll's poem. The great scholar Robin Flower described that succinctly: "The subject is love, and not the direct passion of the folk-singers or the high vision of the great poets, but the learned and fantastic love of European tradition, the *amour courtois*, which was first shaped into art for modern Europe in Provence, and found a home in all the languages of Christendom wherever a refined society and the practice of poetry met together. In Irish, too, it is clearly the poetry of society. To prove this, we need only point to the names of some of the authors, in Scotland . . . the Earl and Countess of Argyle and Duncan Campbell of Glenorquhy, 'the good knight', who died at Flodden."[4]

A long farewell to yesternight! soon or late though it passed away. Though I were doomed to be hanged for it, would that it were this coming night!
There are two in this house tonight from whom the eye does not hide their secret; though they are not lip to lip, keen, keen is the glancing of their eyes.
Silence gives meaning to the swift glancing of the eyes; what avails the silence of the mouth when the eye makes a story of its secret?
Och, the hypocrites won't allow a word to cross my lips, O slow eye!
Learn then what my eye declares, you in the corner over there:—
"Keep this night for us tonight; alas that we are not like this for ever! Do not let the morning in, get up and put the day outside."
Ah, Mary, graceful mother, Thou who art chief over all poets, help me, take my hand
— a long farewell to yesternight![5]

As a contrast to these, we can quote verses from a panegyric composed by a member of the same family, Cathal MacMhuirich, in the previous century. They are from an elegy for four chiefs of Clanranald who all died in 1636.

Our rivers are without abundance of fishing, there is no hunting in the devious glens, there is little crop in every tilth, the wave has gnawed to the very base of the peaks. For their sake the fury of the ocean never ceases, every sea lacks jetsam on its shore; drinking wine at the time of carousal, the warriors grieve more than the women . . .
Their survivors are gloomy and wrathful; the song of the cuckoos is not heard, the wind has taken on a senseless violence, the stream washes away its banks over the heather. Because the men of Clanranald have gone from us we poets cannot pursue our studies; it is time for the chief bard to depart after them, now that presents to poets will be abolished . . .[6]

The hyperbole of this and similar elegies is rooted in the ancient and universal belief that connects the life of a ruler with the fertility of his land. Earlier still, in the last quarter of the fifteenth century, when the Lordship of the Isles, from which Clanranald sprang, was under attack, we find the anxiety expressed that if Clan Donald, 'the brilliant pillars of green Alba', are destroyed, learning will be destroyed also.

It is no joy without Clan Donald; it is no strength to be without them; the best race in the round world; to them belongs every goodly man . . .
In the van of Clan Donald learning was commanded, and in their rear were service and honour and self-respect . . .[7]

The importance of Clan Donald in the history of Gaelic civilisation in Scotland cannot be over-estimated. Neither can the effects of the destruction of the Lordship of which they became the leaders. In the twelfth century the 'Kingdom of the Isles of the Norsemen and Coastland of the Gael' had created a new centre of Gaelic culture and loyalty. In terms of political and military organisation, no less than cultural patronage and diversity, it is as if Gaelic Alba had been reaffirmed and recreated within narrower territorial limits. The cultural inheritance of this Gaelic province was a rich blend which on the one hand drew on ancient traditions reaching back to the foundation of the Scoto-Pictish Kingdom; and on the other took up some of the attitudes of the *Gallghaidheil* — the Gaelicised Norsemen of the Kingdom of Man and the Isles. It was, indeed, an early 'Nova Scotia'.

Originally the great Campbell clan were members of this confederation. As is well known, the Campbells, especially from the time of Robert the Bruce, whose cause they supported in the Wars of Independence and who in turn rewarded them handsomely — largely at the expense of the pro-Balliol MacDougalls, the senior line among the leading families of the Lordship — pursued a pretty consistent policy of collaboration with the Court and Parliament of Scotland, throughout the centuries filling some of the highest offices of State. As the Lordship of the Isles came increasingly under attack from Crown and Parliament, so did Campbell power increase until they were in a position to make a bid for the leadership hitherto vested in Clan Donald. This status finds symbolic expression in the Gaelic phrase *Ceannas nan Gàidheal*, the 'headship', leadership and supremacy, of the Gaelic nation. The MacDonald claim, in fact, goes back far beyond the eponymous Donald, to Colla Uais, the mythical fourth-century ancestor to whose descendants properly belongs the 'headship of Ireland and Scotland.' The Campbells' bid for power included an attempt, expressed through their poets, to wrest from Clan Donald and arrogate to themselves this proud, ancient title. And it is a curious irony, in view of the Campbell reputation for double-dealing, that their notoriety was built up in Gaelic tradition not so much perhaps by collaboration with the central authorities as, at the diplomatic level of bardic exchanges, by the plain speaking of the Campbells' poets with regard to the Headship of the Gael. However that may be, such explicit claims would have been sufficient to raise the struggle above the level of any other vendetta in Gaelic history. The fact of the matter is that, from time to time, collaboration with Scottish Government policies informed the actions of all the clans, the MacDonalds included: if only, for some of them, to gain a brief respite or a limited tactical advantage. But if we care, we can also see the long hostility between the Campbells and MacDonalds as an ideological struggle in which the ideologies enshrine the options that presented themselves to the Scots Gael after the Scottish dynasty had became Anglicised: resistance or collaboration. Through their genealogists the Campbells claimed descent from Arthur of the Britons, King Arthur of the Round Table. A British ancestry, connecting the Campbells with the Britons of Strathclyde, is not apparently mere propaganda. But the development of this, involving descent from Brutus the Trojan, grandson of Aeneas and eponymous hero of Britain, had psychological as well as political advantages, connecting them with the matter of Britain and the great cosmopolitan world of Arthurian romance and pseudo-history which enjoyed such a prodigious vogue in Western Christendom throughout the Middle Ages. Interestingly enough, in the eighteenth century, the MacDonalds would over-trump this Campbell ace by deriving all the Gaels not directly from Ireland but from the Caledonians and beyond them from the Celts of the continent, from whose "bosom have issued the conquerors of Rome, the invaders of Gaul, Britain, Ireland ... once great and flourishing in Asia ..."[8] Into such a scheme could be fitted the 'British History', Arthurian descent, and the whole panoply of Campbell pretentions! These speculations and fabrications usually served an immediate political purpose but they are also to be seen as attempts by Gaelic men of learning to break free of the constraints of parochial history. Modern scholarship very properly seeks to demythologise the accounts of a Campbell-MacDonald 'feud'. But even in genuine Gaelic tradition, not to speak of Scottish folklore in general, the Campbells are the villains of Gaelic history. In other words, the view of Clan Donald has prevailed, which in itself is an index of their importance. Against that view, if we so desire, we may celebrate the Campbells as the true and loyal *Scottish* Gaels, involving themselves as they did in the affairs of the entire nation to whose kings all Gaels professed allegiance. We are dealing here with two opposing currents in the tide of our history. Looking at it from either way we shall find a profound divide — a dialectical opposition — in the historical experience of the Gael in Scotland. Our traditions have only symbolised that opposition in the roles allotted to two great clans. If the Campbells had not existed we should have to invent them.

The anxiety that the MacDonald poet expressed in the fifteenth century about the fate of the Gaelic world if Clan Donald should fall was well founded, as history was to prove. Yet a remnant of the learned orders, writing in Classical Gaelic, survived in Scotland into the middle of the eighteenth century.[9] And in spite of wholesale destruction of manuscripts, enough has survived of their work, not only in poetry and history and romance, but also in law, medicine, astronomy — not to mention other more arcane pursuits — to show what a rich and varied world existed behind the clouds of political and military turbulence that for most people represents the 'history' of Gaelic Scotland.

Before that world came to an end, however, the poets who composed in vernacular Gaelic had inherited its basic social and political attitudes and were able to draw freely on the resources of imagery developed by their classical brethren. In the late sixteenth and early seventeenth centuries the upper social reaches of vernacular poetry are inhabited by professional bards and members of leading clan families alike. Its range is quite unrestricted and eventually represents all grades of society, who expressed themselves in a wide variety of stanzaic and metrical patterns. Even the Latin-derived, syllable-counting measures of the classical poets are used with sublety and ease as early as the sixteenth century: the Ossianic ballads upon which James MacPherson based his 'Ossian' belong formally to this sector and they too carry on a classical Gaelic inheritance into oral tradition, where they are now on the verge of extinction. But hundreds of thousands of lines, in both classical and colloquial Gaelic, have been preserved.

The classical inheritance thus gives modern Gaelic poetry metrical resources, in the subtle blend of stressed and syllabic verse, comparable to that produced by the fusion of French and Anglo-Saxon measures in English poetry. A demotic syllable-counting verse, with its quiet, tentative movement, is often used for religious and elegiac poetry. The emphasis, however, ought not to be laid so much on choice of subject associated with a particular metrical form as on the relationship between form and its associated rhetorical technique. Some have a rhythmic exuberance, some are exploratory and unhurried, others are abrupt and declamatory. Almost all of this poetry is sung; and in that connection it is relevant to recall the dictum: 'The difference is in the tune, and it is a difference of thought as well.'

Especially declamatory are the ancient rhythmical metres which antedate the introduction of Christianity and Latin learning and which survived in a modified form, though still patently native. The primary function of these particular forms lies in clan panegyric, where the stress is on survival of the group of aristocratic warrior-hunters at the top of society. The diction is codified in sets of conventional images, most densely concentrated in the heroic elegy composed at the point of crisis brought about by the death of a leader — in other words, when it is most necessary to reaffirm the traditional values of the community. One of the stock conventions of this praise-poetry is to rehearse the allies — real or ideal — of a clan. This is developed to its fullest possible extent in poems associated with the eighteenth century Jacobite Risings. For instance, a poem of 1715 opens by referring to a prophecy (attributed to Thomas the Rhymer) that the Gaels will come into their own again in Scotland: this messianic hope of the disinherited is here firmly pinned on the Jacobite cause, and the poet draws up a formidable list of clans, including those who could not possibly be expected to support Jacobitism. But it is appropriate to note that the bards of Hanoverian clans were pro-Jacobite, clearly unaffected by the political and religious motives that put their chiefs on the Government side. And in view of the popular identification made between Jacobitism and Roman Catholicism, it is worth pointing out that it is a Protestant poet who puts forward the strongest arguments on behalf of the '45.

The attempts on the part of poets to preserve at least a conceptual Gaelic unity, a sense of nationhood, were successful up to a point, but at a price. The conventions of panegyric become a pervasive style. The style in turn reflects an attitude towards the world, which is regarded intellectually in terms of praise versus dispraise. Through genealogy it works into love poetry; it extends also to nature poetry, evoking a sense of friendly or unfriendly territory: in short, it bears the Gaelic sense of social psychology, of history, of geography. Although 'panegyric' in this context is only a framework, which allows the imagination a great deal of freedom, it seeks to institutionalise the creative mind and in the end becomes a straitjacket.[10]

Through clan poems, the social and political values of Gaelic society find expression. This strand is the Apollonian poetry of Gaelic, discoursing in a highly deliberate and intellectually controlled manner on issues that affect the clan or the nation: an example is the poem against the Union of the Parliaments in 1707.

At the other end of the poetic spectrum we find the Dionysian poetry that has survived largely in songs used to accompany various forms of communal labour. The majority were composed by women and transmitted in a predominantly female environment: more than one strain in the tradition seems to derive from an exclusively female sub-culture not necessarily connected with work — accompaniment to dance is a possibility. Indeed, their strong, almost hypnotic rhythms give the impression of belonging to an ecstatic ceremony. Their poetry unfolds, not in a smooth linear movement, but unevenly, with quite unpredictable changes in focus. But however disconcerting this may at times be, it is precisely these abrupt transitions from image to image, governed only by the nature of the situation expressed in the poem, that release the creative energy. These songs use language according to a principle which is at the farthest extreme from that of the logical, ordered sequences of prose. Out of this kaleidoscope of images, fusing and separating in oral transmission, certain more permanent forms were from time to time created — for example, the great anonymous poem by a girl to her dead lover Seathan. It ends thus:

> But Seathan is tonight in the upper homestead
> Neither gold nor tears will win him
> Neither drink nor music will tempt him
> Neither slaughter nor violence will bring him from his doom ...
> Dear Seathan, dear Seathan,
> I would not give you to law or king
> I would not give you to mild Mary
> I would not give you to the Holy Rood
> I would not give you to Jesus Christ
> For fear I would not get you myself.
> O Seathan, my brightness of the sun!
> Alas! despite me death has seized you,
> And that has left me sad and tearful,
> Lamenting bitterly that you are gone;
> And if all the clerics say is true,
> And there is a Hell and a Heaven,
> My share of Heaven — it is my welcome to death —
> For a night with my darling
> With my companion, brown-haired Seathan.[11]

These tender, intensely passionate songs with their elemental themes provide the main lyrical impulse of Gaelic poetry. They have sometimes been compared with the Scots ballads, for the Ballad starkness is there, often enough. But they lack the supernatural element of the ballads: they are very much poems of this world, and their measure is the measure of a man.

The seventeenth century, to which most of the vernacular poetry we have touched on belongs, is exceedingly rich in various traditional forms. When we come to the eighteenth century, we enter an age of innovation and individual achievement. Alexander MacDonald, the great poet of the '45, was the first person to have a volume of secular poetry published, in 1751. MacDonald was a university man, aware of the wider political and literary issues of the mid-eighteenth century, and he deliberately extended the scope of Gaelic poetry. This he achieved partly by structural means, partly by borrowing from James Thomson and Allan Ramsay and allowing the grafts to take up the vitality of an old Gaelic stock; for instance, in nature poetry. But it is his own native intellectual power and exuberance that gives his genius its force. Of no other Scottish poet can it be said with greater truth that he was possessed by *perfervidum ingenium Scottorum*. His influence was immense. His innovations were rapidly assimilated by contemporaries and successors, some of them illiterate; but so sophisticated is their art that MacDonald's formal learning gives him no advantage over non-literate poets like Duncan Bàn Macintyre in Argyll or Rob Donn in Sutherland. Rob Donn is on the northern boundary of the Gaelic world, psychologically as well as geographically removed from the influence of the Lordship of the Isles and from the panegyric tradition. For that and other reasons, among them the influence of Alexander Pope in Gaelic translation, his poetry of censure is not in the tradition of splendid invective but has the true, and very rare, satirical humour. Duncan Macintyre, doubtless following MacDonald's example, had his poetry written down for him and published in book form. His masterpiece, 'The Praise of Ben Dorain', is a poem of extraordinary sophistication and sensibility, realising physical nature with a bold sweep of perception but also with a minute, precise, sensual delicateness: the lines of the landscape, the movement of deer, the qualities of the vegetation of the moor. It is a visual documentary, invented before the camera. Duncan Bàn is buried in Greyfriars Churchyard in Edinburgh, but he is still remembered in Gaelic oral tradition: an invariably genial, easy-going man. Tradition also preserves, perhaps as a counter-weight, the memory of William Ross as the poet who became so anguished and obsessed with a love affair that he wasted away physically to the dimensions of a child. He did in fact die at 28, apparently from tuberculosis, and his love poems are among the finest in all Gaelic. Finally, in the eighteenth century, Dugald Buchanan of Perthshire is regarded as the most powerful religious poet. His poetry has a terrible austerity: the flame of his compassion barely perceptible in the blinding light of the justice of God. He was a Presbyterian but his 'Day of Judgement' is in the great European tradition of the *Dies Irae*. These poems are early documents of the Evangelical Revival that was soon to sweep through the entire Highlands and Islands.

Religious poets of the eighteenth century were the first to protest forcefuly against the tyranny of landlords. The next century was the bitter century of the Clearances, when the chaos that the break-up of any traditional society produces was intensified beyond endurance in the bewilderment of a people attacked by their own natural leaders. This broken community eagerly accepted the demands of a passionate and uncompromising faith. It was a new dialectic, powerful enough to replace the deep loyalties of the traditional order, in which not religion but genealogy had been the opiate of the people. Predictably, the Evangelical Revival is bound up with social protest, but since the religion was other-worldly, essentially reclusive although practised in open society, it could scarcely yield an adequate strategy to cope with the full range of human experience. And so Gaelic poetry in the nineteenth and early twentieth centuries is a strange amalgam: the unsettled complex of a transitional age. Partly for that very reason, it is much less dull and trivial than it has often been represented as being. It is sometimes nostalgic and anachronistic, still limited by the stereotype of panegyric. It goes off in. false directions that could lead to nothing but sentimentality, as when it borrows from English or Scots and reproduces weak and prettified aspects of Romanticism. Yet it is still instinct with the old, splendid craftsmanship and there is a palpable widening and deepening of human sympathy. There are contrasts and oppositions almost at every turn, and these serve to remind us that we are dealing not with one simple strand but with what is still the art of a nation, no matter how attenuated. One vivid contrast, one that might almost be made a symbol of that age, is provided by the poetry of two MacLeod brothers from Skye: Neil, the reputable author of a highly popular book of poems, a fine, if limited, craftsman whose work almost always tended toward the pretty and sentimental; John, composer of songs in an oral tradition, a sailor and wanderer all his life, a poet of strong, realistic, compassionate poetry, the polarities of which are rooted in the life of Skye and the brutality of life in the sailing ships. John MacLeod was a bohemian trickster, who apparently had strong hypnotic powers; Neil MacLeod was a respectable gentleman and an honoured member of his community.

Contrasts of a different kind emerge in the poetry of Mary MacPherson, the poetess of the radical Land League agitation. In a dialogue poem composed after the floodtide of the Evangelical Revival had reached Skye and all the pleasures of this world had become vanity, she makes a friend say:

> The people have become so strange
> That sorrow to them is wheat
> And if you will not go into a whelk-shell for them
> You will not be able to stay alive.

Her own reply comes abruptly:

> We will not go into a whelk-shell for them
> And we will be able to stay alive:
> Although we will not wear long faces
> Nor cause our appearance to change . . .[12]

She thanks her friend for her good advice and adds: "Since vanity is a plant that satisfies the flesh, it sticks to me as closely as the thong does to the shoe" (she is probably referring to the old, home-made shoe in which the thong was part of the upper). In that climate she could not escape conscience searching. But she had come to terms with herself and had elected to remain robustly of this world, albeit with a strong religious sense of ultimate justice. Her introspection borrows from religion but never turns morbid. She had undergone a harrowing experience of unjust conviction and imprisonment for theft; it was this "that brought my poetry into being", and the anguish of it remained ardent in her until the end of her life. She had, too, an intense affection for her native community. All these elements combine in her work, resolved and integrated and given a major dimension by being set in the context of nineteenth century Radicalism. She had indeed a perverse strain of panegyric (for instance, a 'Song for the Duke of

Sutherland'!) which a fuller criticism would take into account. Yet her best work gives the sharp feel of immediate experience while at the same time conveying the pressure of contemporary events. And when she exults that "We have seen the horizon breaking, the clouds of serfdom dispelled" she is inaugurating a new vision of Gaelic society.

The background sketched here has dwelt more on literature, particularly on poetry, than on political actions and events. Even in literature much has to be left out that is important in shaping the contemporary Gaelic world. Like any other revolution the twentieth-century renaissance drew its strengths and inspiration from different points of this continuum. But within the century itself the First World War can be taken as a time of perceptible new stirrings. John Munro, who was killed in that War, was a university graduate: his poetry inaugurates the modern movement. Donald MacDonald, a bard from North Uist, was an oral poet whose songs composed in the trenches of Flanders introduce a new note of protest. In one of them the Army command *March at ease!* makes a sad, ironic refrain as it clashes with the Gaelic of the original text of *Oran Arras.*

> Lads, *March at ease!*
> The King of Peace be with us
> as we go into battle
> as we go to the churchyard at Arras.
> Lads, *March at ease!*
>
> Tonight is Monday night:
> time to go on watch
> time to go to the grave
> where not a bootlace will be unfastened.
> Lads, *March at ease!*
>
> Off to defend our land —
> to defend greybeard and babe:
> like men who have gone mad
> we shall draw the knife.
> Lads, *March at ease!*[13]

The influence of the Church in the development of Gaelic has been crucial throughout history. Over the last two centuries, the contribution made by individuals from all branches and denominations is almost beyond reckoning. Over and above these individual contributions, we have in the Church the only major social institution in which Gaelic is used publicly. In minor institutions Gaelic is used as dialect is used elsewhere. The Church uses Gaelic as a language. Moreover, the dignified classical language of the mediaeval and later literati provided colloquial Gaelic with a new dimension when its resources were drawn upon in translations of works of devotion and in the Gaelic Bible. In the denominations which set the sermon at the centre of public worship, extempore preaching and extempore prayers familiarised successive generations with a great range of vocabulary of a learned nature. In church and at family worship, generations of Gaels achieved in their native language the literacy which formal education denied them. Much criticism has been levelled at the Church, especially at the asceticism of the Evangelical denominations. Some of this is superficial, some perfectly justified. But it was pointed out some years ago by Dr. D. J. MacLeod of Glasgow University how significant it is that all the leading contemporary writers are from this background. It is equally significant, however, that all these writers have in different degrees reacted against their ascetic inheritance. But in any case the intense, austere faith which we usually associate with the Gaidhealtachd was at no time practised by all the members of a community. And it is also worth recalling that the Evangelical Revival itself produced anti-authority and anti-ecclesiastical poetry at various levels. This non-conformist protest has probably never been given the emphasis it deserves as a component of the modern Gaelic experience.

Derick Thomson gives one view in *The Scarecrow*.

> That night
> the scarecrow came into the céilidh-house:
> a tall, thin black-haired man
> wearing black clothes.
> He sat on the bench
> and the cards fell from our hands.
> One man
> was telling a folktale about Conall Gulban
> and the words froze on his lips.
> A woman was sitting on a stool,
> singing songs, and he took the goodness out of the music.
> But he did not leave us empty-handed:
> he gave us a new song,
> and tales from the Middle East,
> and fragments of the philosophy of Geneva,
> and he swept the fire from the centre of the floor
> and set a searing bonfire in our breasts.[14]

Whatever the future may hold, it seems appropriate, reviewing the culture of Gaelic Scotland over fifteen hundred years, to assert: *Nec tamen consumebatur.*

NOTES

[1] See K. H. Jackson 'The Duan Albanach' in *Scottish Historical Review*, Vol. 36, pp. 125 ff.

[2] K. H. Jackson *A Celtic Miscellany* (London 1951) p. 116.

[3] See W. J. Watson, *Scottish Verse from the Book of the Dean of Lismore*, pp. 60 ff.

[4] Robin Flower *The Irish Tradition* (Oxford 1947), p. 142.

[5] Jackson, *A Celtic Miscellany*, p. 117.

[6] *Ibid.*, pp. 262-3.

[7] Watson, *Scottish Verse*, pp. 90-5.

[8] From the Introduction (in English) to Alexander MacDonald's *Poems* (1751). For discussion of this background, see J. MacInnes, "Gaelic Poetry and Historical Tradition" in L. Maclean (ed.) *The Middle Ages in the Highlands*.

[9] See D. S. Thomson "Gaelic Learned Orders and Literati in Medieval Scotland" in *Scottish Studies* Vol. 12, pp. 57-78.

[10] See J. MacInnes "The Panegyric Code in Gaelic Poetry and its Historical Background" in *Trans. of the Gaelic Soc. of Inverness* Vol. 50, pp. 435-98.

[11] A. Carmichael *Carmina Gadelica* Vol. 5, pp. 66-83; see esp. pp. 77-9.

[12] Original Gaelic in *Dain agus Orain le Mairi Nic-a'-Phearsoin*, p. 10 ff.

[13] Original Gaelic in *Domhnall Ruadh Choruna; Orain is Dain le Domhnall Domhnallach*, p. 22.

[14] Derick Thomson *The Far Road*, p. 20. Original Gaelic in Ruaraidh Mac Thomais, *An Rathad Cian.*

Plate 1: Tomb of Alexander MacLeod, St. Clement's Church, Rodil, Inverness-shire.
Acknowledgement: Royal Commission on the Ancient and Historical Monuments of Scotland.

Plate 2: Detail from the Tomb of Alexander MacLeod.
Acknowledgement: Royal Commission on Ancient Monuments.

Plate 3: Detail from Tomb of Alexander MacLeod, "Hunters and Deer."
Acknowledgement: Royal Commission on Ancient Monuments.

Plate 4: Looking south over part of byres to deserted cottage, Smearisary, Moidart, Inverness-shire.
Acknowledgement: Eric G. Meadows and the School of Scottish Studies, University of Edinburgh.

Plate 5: Steading, Letterfearn, Ross-shire. Late nineteenth-century photograph. Note wattle construction walls on outbuildings.
Acknowledgement: G. W. Wilson and the School of Scottish Studies.

Plate 6: Croft, Eriskay, Outer Hebrides. Photo: August 1911.
Acknowledgement: School of Scottish Studies.
The croft was the universal dwelling of the farming and sea-faring highlanders; stone-walled, steep-roofed with thatch or slate, a hearth and chimney at one end — home to the "crofter" and his family.

Plate 7: The Interior of a Blackhouse.
Crown Copyright: reproduced by permission of the Scottish Development Department, Edinburgh.
A blackhouse was a Hebridean double-walled (with turf, peat, ash between the two walls) stone house, without windows, with thatched roof and no chimney; an open central fire that escaped through a hole in the thatch; built with the roof set on the inner wall to withstand the relentless winter winds of the islands and to escape the higher taxes levied on buildings with windows.

Plate 8: Parliament, St. Kilda. Photo: August 1927.
Acknowledgement: School of Scottish Studies, Edinburgh.
This refers to the annual communal meeting of the islanders with the MacLeod taxman to deliberate on their problems and needs and to barter island produce (they used no money) of cattle, seabird oils, feathers, etc. in exchange for tea, rent-tax, and other necessities.

Plate 9: Women with 'Fire Balls', Stonehaven, Scotland.
A New Year custom in Stonehaven. Acknowledgement: School of Scottish Studies, Edinburgh.

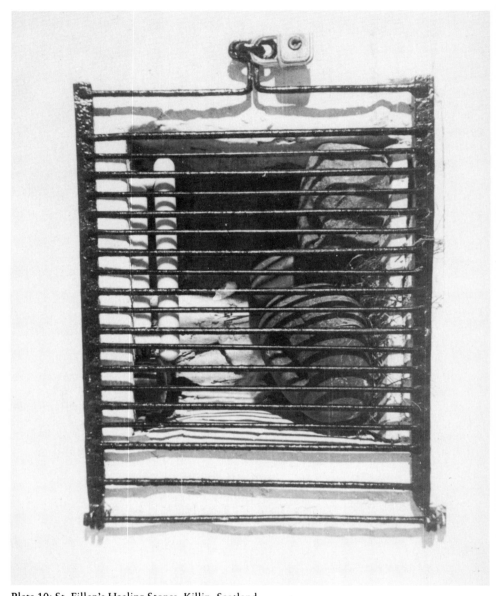

Plate 10: St. Fillan's Healing Stones, Killin, Scotland.
Acknowledgement: School of Scottish Studies.
These holy stones were taken from the hill above the abbey which the leper-saint founded.

THE LINEAGE OF GAELIC LOVE-POETRY
FROM THE EARLIEST TIMES

SEÁN Ó TUAMA

There is no goddess of love in Celtic mythology. There are, however, Celtic goddesses — Medb, the Morrigan — who represent love *and* war, war *and* fertility; etc.[1] One is tempted to speculate that the Celtic peoples found it difficult to conceive of love unaccompanied by blood, produce and tears.

This kind of speculation, being capable of neither proof nor disproof, is, of course, a trifle self-indulgent; but it does serve to highlight immediately a main element in much of the Irish poetry I shall be discussing here: the tendency not to see human love as an absolute, an ideal vision abstracted out of life (as in medieval European poetry), but as a troublesome gift or overwhelming moment of desire at the centre of the mundane routines of life. And, in dealing with it, our poets found it necessary quite often to use a certain amount of irony or hardheadedness to temper any mystic excesses. Robin Flower, in his brilliant essay on the late medieval corpus of Irish love-poetry, has this to say: 'There has always been in the Irish nature a sharp and astringent irony, a tendency to react against sentiment and mysticism, an occasional bias to regard life under a clear and humorous light. . . . We miss the point of much in the literature if we forget this'.[2]

Old and Middle Irish literature (c. 600-1200), perhaps the most distinguished literature in early medieval Europe, contains only very meagre fragments indeed of love-poetry. Yet the qualities of conflict and irony which I have been mentioning are already unmistakeably present in them. Most of these fragments are attributed to women — mythological figures often such as Déirdre, Gráinne, Créd — and in most cases more than likely originally embedded in prose-sagas. In that part of the saga-literature which tells of Wooings (*Tochmarca*) and Elopements (*Aitheda*), the woman is generally the aggressor, the initiator of the love-contest. This, for instance, is the manner in which Déirdre encountered and conquered Naoisi in the prose-saga:

> Once when Naoisi was outside alone Déirdre slipped out to him as if she was going past him and he did not recognize her.
> "That's a nice heifer that's going by me", he said.
> "Heifers ought to be big", she said, "wherever there are no bulls".
> "You have the bull of the province," he said, meaning the King of Ulster . . .
> She made a rush at him and grabbed his two ears.
> "Then two ears of shame and mockery on you," she said, "unless you take me with you."
> "Go on, woman!" he said.
> "You'll have it," she said. . . .[3]

Naoisi and his brothers inevitably became the gory victims of this rather rough bout of love-aggression.

There are other instances in which the lady's love-urge is described in sweeter tones, as in this exquisite lone stanza which tells of the girl who fed some blackberries, and a few seductive strawberries, to the son of the King of the river Muad:

> Mac rig Muaide, mid samraid,
> fuair i fid uaine ingin,
> tuc do mess ndub a draignib,
> tuc airgib sub ar sibnib.

'The son of the King of the river Muad in midsummer found a maiden in a green wood. She gave him blackberries from the bushes, and, as a love token strawberries on a rush-tip'.[4]

Perhaps the one really complete love-poem from this period, the golden era of Irish literature, is that of *Liadan and Cuirithir*, an astonishingly moving and sophisticated lyric from a prose-and-verse story of the 9th century. 'Liadan and Cuirithir were lovers, but Liadan resolved to enter a convent, and Cuirithir then became a monk. She visited him in his cloister, and he had to sail away from Ireland to avoid her. . . . This is her lament.'[5]

> Gain without gladness
>   Is in the bargain I have struck;
> One that I loved is wrought to madness.
>
> Mad beyond measure
>   But for God's fear that numbed her heart
> She that would not do his pleasure.
>
> Was it so great
>   My treason? Was I not always kind?
> Why should it turn his love to hate?
>
> Liadain,
>   That is my name, and Curithir
> The man I loved; you know my sin.
>
> Alas too fleet!
>   Too brief my pleasure at his side;
> With him the passionate hours were sweet.
>
> Woods woke
>   About us for a lullaby,
> And the blue waves in music spoke.
>
> And now too late
>   More than for all my sins I grieve
> That I turned his love to hate.
>
> Why should I hide
>   That he is still my heart's desire
> More than all the world beside?
>
> A furnace blast
>   Of love has melted down my heart,
> Without his love it cannot last.[6]
>
>   (Trans. Frank O'Connor)

The one or two verse fragments on love attributed to men in this period have a much more astringent tone:

> All are keen
> To know who'll sleep with blond Aideen,
> All Aideen herself will own
> Is that she will not sleep alone.[7]

On the other hand, the prose-sagas are full of the most rapturous idyllic praises of women's beauty as perceived by men. One of the most famous of these is the long passage in *The Destruction of Da Derga's Hostel* describing Etain's beauty. Here is a short extract from it:

> A kirtle she wore, long, hooded, hard-smooth, of green silk, with red embroidery of gold. . . . The sun kept shining on her, so that the glistening of the gold against the sun from the green silk was manifest to the men. On her head were two golden-yellow tresses, in each of which was a plait of four strands, with a bead of gold at the point of each strand. The hue of that hair seemed to the king and his companions like the flower of the iris in summer, or like red gold after the burnishing thereof.
>
> There she was, undoing her hair to wash it, with her arms out through the sleeve-holes of her smock. White as the snow of one night were the two clear beautiful cheeks. Dark as the back of a stag-beetle the two eyebrows. . . . Red as rowan-berries the lips. . . . It seemed to king Eochaid and his followers that she was from the fairy-mounds. Of her it was said: 'Shapely are all till compared with Etain; dear are all till compared with Etain.'[8]

Descriptions such as this suggest a near-troubadour type of adoration of the ideal woman. (Of course the woman here, being mythological, was absolutely ideal!). This idealization apart, the prose sagas in common with some of the verse-fragments, contain themes we have come to associate in particular with 12th/13th century troubadour love-lyrics; love hinders sleep, love is a magic sickness, love wounds the heart, love can come in a vision or dream, love can be experienced for some one not seen. And so on.

There is, however, no evidence for the man's love-lyric, as conventionally understood, in Old and Middle Irish literature. The woman's love-lyric, as in the Romance languages, must have been the norm at this period. The man's lyric was to make its appearance in the later medieval period under the influence of the great continental *amour courtois* movement of the 12th-15th century. It is evident, however, that much of the feeling and thematic material I have been noticing in the older Irish literature could quite naturally be transposed into the later medieval type of man's love-lyric. This is all the more probable when one considers that quite often the woman described in Old Irish sagas is not only a mythological woman but a mythological woman who is to be identified with the Sovereignty of Ireland.[7] The later medieval Irish poet who made formal — though sometimes reluctant — obeisance to the beauty of a flesh-and-blood woman might then be seen as merely exchanging one female sovereign for another. . . .

Despite the sophistication in matters of love displayed in our older Irish literature, it is indubitably true that later Irish love-poetry, both learned and folk, bears overwhelming evidence not of Old Irish influence but of medieval continental influence. Even where it can be established that certain love-themes existed already in Old Irish literature, when one encounters them again in post-Norman times, they seem to have been fitted out anew in French or English dress. For instance when one comes on the theme of 'love as disease' the symptoms are generally not of the Irish kind, but of the typical European kind as described in the French and Provençal *Leys d'Amor*. The lover can neither sleep nor wake, eat nor drink, distinguish heat from cold, wine from water. He spends his time sighing or crying (two activities which would be quite anathema to Cuchulainn in his hero-ardour); but if he could manage 'one kiss' — again a puny desire for a hero of ancient times — his cure would be complete. Similarly, many of the medieval European clichés to describe a woman's beauty — the 'lily and rose' description, for instance — tend to supplant in our later love-lyrics the very lovely native metaphors and images, as found in tales such as *The Destruction of Da Derga's Hostel*.

The European love-movement seems to have made its impact on Ireland in the wake of the Anglo-Norman invasion and conquest. One cannot say with any certainty that the external influence always made itself felt through the Norman-French language. English — and even Latin — sources must also be reckoned with. But the probability is that Norman-French influence is the major one. French was the second major language — the prestige language — in Ireland for at least one hundred and fifty years after the Norman invasion (and indeed continued to be the judicial language in Ireland down to the 16th century). As Norman chiefs, their poets and entertainers, became Irish-speaking they carried with them into Irish the matter of France. (This direct language-change from French to Irish happened most often, one surmises, in rural areas.) We know for instance of one poet, the Earl of Desmond, who composed verses in French, while his son, Gerald, composed much finer verse in Irish. This Gerald was the same man who, as Lord Chief Justice and upholder of the Anglo-Norman law in Ireland, was entrusted with the task of applying the Statutes of Kilkenny (1367), which themselves were enacted in French. The objective of the Statutes was to enforce apartheid between the two nations in Ireland — in fact to prevent the Normans being assimilated by Irish culture in general, and in particular by that same language which the Lord Chief Justice himself was most eloquently writing in!

One facet of the international literary love-movement for which there is solid documentary evidence in Ireland is that of the *carole*.[9] The *carole* in France was primarily a light love-song with refrain to be danced to, in the form of a round. There is much reason to believe that the Normans were much more taken with this form of love-song than with many of the more formal manifestations of *amour courtois*. Not having been long established in France themselves before they began their forays throughout Europe, their own literary traditions were thinly-rooted. Consequently, wherever they went they seemed to have particularly cultivated the more popular levels of love-song and dance. Of course, as many scholars have warned, distinctions between 'popular' and 'learned' as applied to medieval literature can be quite misleading. It has been claimed, for instance, that 'popular' French refrains of the 12th and 13th centuries express the basic notions of *amour courtois* as completely as the most elaborate learned lyrics of the period.[10] Such refrains, in association with the requisite *carole* dances, were engaged in by aristocrats and common-folk alike. Carole-dancing and singing spread like a raging fever through all levels of Western European society in these centuries. In Ireland, the great Norman Lord, Guillaume le Marèchal, who ruled the province of Leinster, was known as both expert composer and exponent of the *carole*; then again women and children helping to build the town of New Ross danced and sang their *caroles* on the way to work, after work, and during their lunch-breaks. Priests — Franciscans in particular — were great disseminators of the fashion. Clerics were reported as singing *caroles* in the streets of Kilkenny in the middle of the 14th century (It is noteworthy that their songs were in English as well as in French: English had begun to make a large impact on towns on the east coast of Ireland, just at the time when English began to replace French as the literary language of England.) And somewhere from the second half of the thirteenth century comes a report of an Irish priest who visited London and spent so much time a-carolling in the church precincts on Saturday night, that when he turned around on the altar on Sunday morning, instead of the necessary and liturgical 'dominus vobiscum', blurted out a dance-refrain sung on the previous night: 'swete leman þin ore' ('loved one have mercy on me'). The bishop had him smartly removed from the diocese. . . .

Such snippets of information may be a little recherché, but they do help us to imagine a little more deeply the medieval scene. They help us, for instance, to guess at the real life drama which may underly the lovely medieval *carole* adapted by Yeats:

> Ich am of Irlaunde
> ant of the holy londe
> of Irlande.
>
> Gode sire, pray ich þe
> for of saynte charite,
> come ant daunce wyt me
> in irlaunde.

There is abundant evidence that these Anglo-Norman entertainments were assimilated into Irish-Gaelic culture. It is even probable that all Irish dancing of the square or round type ultimately derive from the *carole*. The two extant words for dancing in Irish derive from either English or Norman-French, while in metrical and musical structure — and sometimes in thematic substance — many Irish folksongs of the verse and refrain type clearly derive from the medieval *carole*.

It is useful to have dealt for a moment in the *carole* phenomenon as it gives some indication of one aspect of the deep Anglo-Norman penetration of Gaelic civilization. It should be remembered, of course, that not alone did the Anglo-Normans leave their own indelible mark on the tone and substance of our love-literature, but, more importantly, that they opened up the channels of literary communication on all levels between Ireland, England and France (including, one thinks, Provençe). Consequently some of the most solemn French or Provençal conventions of the love-lyric manifest themselves most astonishingly, not alone in our medieval poems, but even in our folksong literature as collected in the 19th and 20th centuries. The Irish folk-memory is known to be particularly tenacious, so that the words of a well-known folklore-scholar, Alexander Krappe, are specially relevant to Irish folksong studies. He says: "It is equally clear that a considerable number of songs considered now old folk-songs have in all probability a literary origin. ... In periods of intense literary activity, literary products will sink from the classes for which they were intended in the first place, to lower levels of the common people. When the songs of the medieval troubadours had charmed the knights and ladies, and even after they had ceased to charm them, they still appealed to the peasants."[11] One cannot imagine, however, that either Irish nobles or peasants would have taken so successfully to the new European love-literature had they not been keenly conditioned previouly by their own literary traditions to accept it and adapt it to their own genius.

II

It is generally accepted, as I have said, that one of the large areas of Irish literature extensively influenced by the *amour courtois* movement was that of the Irish medieval literary love-lyric (1350?-1650?). Well over a hundred love poems of that period survive in manuscripts, but this is quite likely only a small fraction of the number composed. The poets generally are anonymous, but quite a few of them were clearly highly-trained bards, both Irish and Scottish. Others were gentlemen poets such as Manus O'Donnell, Earl of Tyrconnell, or Donough McCarthy, Earl of Clancarty. The aristocratic tone of much of what they wrote, the learned frame of reference, the sophisticated emotional antennae, the skilled handling of most intricate syllabic metres, all point to an extremely refined and complex society, the dimensions of which we have yet scarcely begun to understand.

The great bulk of these learned love-lyrics has been collected in one remarkable anthology, *Dánta Grádha*.[12] These poems seem to mirror various types of the medieval European love-lyric; but over half of them, I would say, emanate from a serious, if not solemn, tradition of courtly adoration of the lady. This and other traditions represented seem to me, in the main, to be late medieval; mostly 15th century. The French scholar, Jean Frappier, in a scathing review of an American symposium *The Meaning of Courtly Love*, points out that there were, at various periods, different traditions of courtly love, including that of *'l'amant martyrisé'* from the late 14th and early 15th centuries.[13] This is the era of Chaucer, Deschamps, Lydgate, Christine de Pisan, Alain Chartier and of the scores of their followers who wrote innumerable love-ballads and rondels, in which *les amants martyrisés* have a field-day. So do they also in our Irish love-lyrics: the lover keeps on telling us with delightful casuistry of the death he is suffering; he, also, in 15th century manner, tells us of his love-dreams, his love-epistles, the catalogue of his lady's beauties, his farewells, and so on. The slightly puzzling aspect of all this is that our learned poets should have been so heavily influenced by European models just at the point (1400-1500) when English and French were rapidly receding again as spoken languages in Ireland.

The *Dánta Grádha*, as might be expected, frequently lack the directness and spontaneity of the best lyric poetry. But so does most formal *amour courtois* type of verse everywhere. One finds a certain amount of trite conventional posturing, with no passion apparent — in fact, quite often, with no specific lady apparent. '*Suirghe an cheard do chleachtamar*', 'wooing was the trade we practised', says one of the poets (echoing a similar phrase by Charles D'Orléans). Indeed one is persuaded that most of these poets understood absolutely, as did their counterparts abroad, that love was a game to be played, an elaborate code to be adhered to in verse — whatever of life. There is some acquaintance with the classic feudal and philosophic vocabulary of medieval European love. Rough equivalents of the ideas of *service, homage, humility, mercy, grace* do appear; but these are much less meaningful than even in English courtly love poems of the 15th century. The major concern is possibly with the idea of love as death, or as wasting disease. This, of course, is quite in line not alone with 15th century European feeling, but with one of the oldest love-themes in Irish literature.

What does distinguish medieval Irish love-poets — even the dullest and most fatuous of them — from the main body of French or English love-poets of the same period, is their fine feeling for style. This stylistic flair had stemmed from one of the oldest and most refined literary traditions in Western Europe, and had been cultivated meticulously by the Bards throughout the entire medieval period. So one rarely encounters the solemn aureate tone so familiar in English or continental love-poetry of the 15th century; rather the finely-edged epigrammatic, dramatic, or metaphysical voice, which in the midst of triteness may quite nonchalantly proclaim: 'alas that I have not a charter on her cool skin'; or, 'speak in that speech beyond reproach/the body's speech'. Syllabic verse, as developed by the Bards, was a stylistic instrument of great delicacy and potentiality.

This potentiality comes to its full flowering in a significant number of our love-lyrics, which are amongst the most elegant in late medieval literature. These lyrics quite often take just one element of the conventional material and completely transform it. Here for instance the typical troubadour theme of love for a married woman is posed in a starkly simple and dramatic way:

> Keep your kiss to yourself,
> young miss with the white teeth.
> I can get no taste from it.
> Keep your mouth away from me.
>
> I got a kiss more sweet than honey
> from a man's wife, for love,
> and I'll get no taste from any kiss
> till doomsday, after that.

Until I see that same woman
(grant it gracious Son of God)
I'll love no woman young or old,
because her kiss is . . . what it is [13a]

(Trans. Thomas Kinsella)

Our best love-lyrics are dramatic lyrics such as this. The lady is often spoken to directly, a situation is imagined, a change of mood is reflected situationally, one feels the presence of an audience listening. A theme which occurs, for instance, in 15th or 16th century semi-popular verse is that of the poet who cannot manage, because of the presence of other people, to speak to his loved one. This theme appears in a few of our *Dánta Grádha*, imagined situationally. One of the best of these poems is by the Scottish poet Niall Mór Mac Muireadhaigh, and it includes a sudden flash-back to a night of love enjoyed by the lovers, where the *aubade* theme of 'keeping out the sun' is used to great effect:

Farewell last night; 'tis bitter pain
to see it now receding;
if I were to hang for it —
I would it were again commencing.

There are two within this house to-night
whose looks of love betray their secret;
tho' lips may neither speak nor kiss
eyes — pinpointed — are fiercely meeting. . . .

Alas, across this jealous throng
no phrase or word of mine can reach you:
but listen to what my eyes are saying
to you, apart, in silence seated:

'Keep for me this night again,
would that it might ever last,
oh go put out the sun, my love,
let not daylight in so fast:

Mary, nurse and mother mild!
Queen of poets and minstrelsy,
hear me now and take my part —
farewell last night, most enviously.

(Trans. S. Ó Tuama)

The last verse, one notices, invokes the help of the Virgin Mary to aid the lovers in their adultery. This occurs in several poems, mirroring on one hand the Irish bardic tradition of appending a final verse in honour of the lady of the house (and in religious poems to the mediatrix, the Virgin), and on the other hand the *chanson d'amour* tradition of the poet's appealing to Christ or God to bring his love to its proper fruition. It is doubtful if a better single example could be adduced for the fusing in our lyrics of Irish and continental features.

The lovers' farewells veer towards the dramatic as well. Here for instance is a simple and moving farewell, very reminiscent of Drayton's *Since there's no help come let us kiss and part*, but more than likely written before Drayton's time:

Now, since of this alone, I'm sure,
 That you were false to me,
Do you endure and I'll endure
 That we should strangers be.

So if you chance to hear my name
 In cottage or in hall,
Speak neither praise of me nor blame,
 Nor talk of me at all.

And if we meet, as we may do,
 At church or on the plain,
You'll pass me by as I will you,
 Nor turn your head again.

We'll ne'er admit that it was I
 That did you so adore,
And both of us will soon deny
 We ever met before.[14]

     (Trans. Earl of Longford)

One cannot help feeling that the structure of this poem, couched, as it is, in terms of the withdrawal of the senses (hearing, speaking, seeing) has some relationship with the Provençal love-doctrine of *quinque linae amoris*: 'Looking, addressing, touching, kissing, then love'.[15] Here, however, with the gradual withdrawal of the senses, love disintegrates: 'and both of us will soon deny/we ever met before'.

A slight echo of the same feeling may be present in the poem *O woman full of wile*, by the 17th century priest-poet, Geoffrey Keating. This is more a refusal of carnal love than a love-poem, and probably reflects not alone the medieval *memento mori* theme, but also a traditional situation in Irish literature where the priest or saint refuses a woman (as did the Abbot of Lismore according to a famous 9th century poem). Keating's poem, though a poem of renegation, is imagined in the most sensual love terms:

O woman full of wile,
Keep from me thy hand:
I am not a man of the flesh,
Tho' thou be sick for my love.

See how my hair is grey!
See how my body is powerless!
See how my blood hath ebbed!
For what is thy desire?

Do not think me besotted:
Bend not again thy head,
Let our love be without act
Forever, O slender witch.

Take thy mouth from my mouth
Graver the matter so;
Let us not be skin to skin;
From heat cometh will.

'Tis thy curling ringleted hair,
Thy grey eye bright as dew,
Thy lovely round white breast,
That draw the desire of eyes.

Every deed but the deed of the flesh,
And to lie in thy bed of sleep
Would I do for thy love,
O woman full of wile.[16]

(Trans. P. H. Pearse)

The spontaneous lyric voice is rarely present in our learned love-poems. One of the poems in which it is best heard may in fact be an elegy by the Earl of Tyrconnell on the death of his wife. (It is noteworthy that some of the most uninhibited lyric statements of love in Irish literature are contained in elegies for dead spouses). In general the dramatic or ironic modes — both of which modes often overlap — carry the day. One poet says he shall not die for love:

O woman shapely as the swan
In a cunning house hard-reared was I:
O bosom white, o well-shaped palm,
I shall not die!

(Trans. P. Colum)

Too much has been made, perhaps, of the ironic Irish manner of treating love. Certainly our poets enjoyed love-irony, and developed it enormously in line with their own literary traditions. But there is abundant evidence that ironic or humorous love-poetry of a similar kind was written abroad from the time of the earliest troubadours down to the end of the middle ages. If an Irish poet did say sometimes, for instance, that he waxed fat and slept soundly despite being in love, so did poets in other countries; and if one particular Irish poet declared (as he did) that he was not too much concerned with the shape or age or beauty of his loved one, so did the English poet Hoccleve declare of his lady: 'hir comly body/shape as a fot-bal/and she syngith/ful lyk a papejay'.

The jealous husband was a target for the poet's wit everywhere. Irish poets, however, seemed to have a special flair for this theme:

You're jealous of your wife?
A curious plight you're in.
Take my advice:
forget your melancholy.

A shapeless surly wife
has rarely wrecked a home;
strange as it may seem —
your wife is still your own!

There you stand on guard
in secret misery
shielding your wife's charms:
a fence without a field.

Not one in many thousands
lives as safe a life
from sharp and wagging tongues
a-scandalling his wife.

So if all the world should come
to swear she's been untrue,
no need to flee the land —
she knows no bed but yours.

(Trans. S. Ó Tuama)

The tone is earthy, bourgeois; but even in our more aristocratic bardic style love-poems, one finds a more trenchant, homely approach than is common in similar poems in the French or English traditions. There is a complete fusion in these poems of the old national rural-based and the new international court-centred traditions. Metaphors and images emanate equally from both traditions. Gráinne, Déirdre or Naoise are as central to the frame of reference as Venus, Narcissus or Absalom.

Consequently, even in our most formal or conventional literary poems the relationship between poet and lady is unique, Irish, different. This is, of course, symptomatic of what happens when an international movement makes an impact on a specific national culture. The merging of two literary traditions is finally a reflection of the merging of two different sets of cultural values, attitudes, social structures. And given what we know of these in medieval Ireland it is difficult to conceive of the Provençal ideal of the adorable but unattainable lady being treated with unmodified solemnity. First of all the poet himself was one of the few absolutely privileged people in his society. He was feared and respected. Legally he ranked as high as a petty king — whose bed he seems to have often shared. One cannot imagine him a suppliant in the sense his continental counterpart was. . . .

Then again the Christian ideal of monogamous marriage had made very little impact on our aristocratic society right down to the 17th century. A modern historian says: 'In no field of life was Ireland's apartness from the mainstream of Christian European society so marked as in that of marriage. Throughout the medieval period, and down to the end of the old order in 1603, what could be called Celtic secular marriage remained the norm in Ireland, and Christian matrimony was no more than the rare exception grafted on to this system'.[17] Celtic secular law recognized some ten different kinds of marriage; and, while safeguarding to some extent the rights of wives, permitted divorce and remarriage for a variety of reasons. Consequently most Irish aristocrats were much married men. Polygamy, incest and what Christian society called illegitimacy were acceptable features of everyday life. In fact the British Parliament had to pass an act as late as 1634 forbidding polygamy amongst the Irish.

I am aware, of course, that in Europe in general during the same period monogamy amongst the privileged was honoured more in the breach than in the observance. Even so, monogamy was the ethical and legal ideal, whereas in medieval Ireland it was not. Love poems emanating from societies so differently structured will of necessity have different tonalities: different distances at which one plays the game of love. At any rate the Irish 'lady of the manor' — whether she be the first wife of a McCarthy in Blarney Castle or the fifth wife of an O'Donnell in Lifford Castle — could not be thought of as being as inaccessible to the poet as the wife of a feudal lord in France or Provençe. So despite the spasmodic efforts of the medieval Irish poets to become the tearful one, the submissive one *à l'amour courtois*, his tone of voice often belies him, speaks to us of another tradition, another civilization.

III

After the overthrow of the Irish aristocratic order in the early 17th century, the practice of love-poetry receded rapidly amongst our learned poets. The best of the later professional poets in the 17th and 18th centuries, such as Ó Bruadair and O'Rahilly, wrote no love-poetry to speak of. On the other hand it was precisely at this period that Irish popular love-poetry began to surface. The models on which it was based seem to owe their origins as much to Anglo-Norman influence as do the models of our medieval love-poems; indeed all the available evidence would indicate that the principal types of our popular poetry took root in Ireland in the 13th/14th centuries, a century or two before our learned poets began to devote themselves to the courtly craft of love.

When one comes to examine in detail the large corpus of popular Irish love-song as we have it today, the most significant fact is possibly that it consists in the main of the man's love song. In this our folksong differs considerably from that of, say, England or France. While one finds an abundance of women's love-lyrics in English or French folksong, one finds only the rarest examples of lyrics attributed to men. In Irish folksong there are literally hundreds of men's love-lyrics, most of them wedded to elaborately-structured music. The love-concepts expressed in them — as distinct from those expressed in our learned medieval poems — are uniformly of the idealised courtly kind; on the other hand the tone of the best of them can be quite spontaneous, quite noncourtly. Here, for instance, is a fragment — probably of a *carole* — where the feeling of love created is that of a summer's day; not Shakespeare's early May-time mood of *Shall I compare thee to a Summer's day* — rather that of late summer fruitfulness:

> She is the white flower of the blackberry,
> she is the sweet flower of the raspberry,
> the noblest of growing things
> that eyes have looked on.
>
> She is my treasure, my true one,
> the fragrant flower of the apple tree,
> she is summer in the cold time
> from Chrismas through Lent.
>
> (Trans. S. Ó Tuama)

Lyric utterances such as this are generally not maintained with any consistency throughout the typical man's love song; they tend to appear at random in a sudden astonishing verse:

> When my lady moves towards me on her path,
> The moon awakens and the sun shines forth,
> A honey mist spreads by night or day
> On each side of the road as she makes her way.
>
> (Trans. S. Ó Tuama)

or

> When my loved one goes out
> The sun loses its heat,
> And the moon bows low in adoration.
>
> (Trans. S. Ó Tuama)

or

> My own dark head, (my own, my own),
> your soft pale arm place here about me.
> Honey-mouth that smells of thyme
> he would have no heart who denied you love.
>
> (Trans. T. Kinsella)

The thematic material of these songs, when taken together, can be seen to correspond most amazingly to that of French and Provençal *chansons d'amour*, both literary and semi-popular, of the 13th and 14th centuries. The themes, of course, have sometimes suffered a sea-change: the Irish background to these songs and the native literary traditions will have left their marks. The images will often stem from a non-courtly, non-philosophic rural environment, while such elements of traditional Irish prose and verse as the extravagant praising of the woman's hair will take up an inordinate place in the typical continental catalogue of the lady's beauties. But taking these lyrics all in all they are as near *amour courtois* as one can expect folksong to be. As in the typical *chanson d'amour*, there is everywhere in them absolute adoration of the lady: she, his secret love, is the most gifted of all human beings, a saint from paradise radiating happiness, the mirror and flower of all perfection. Happy is the ground she walks on; she is, for beauty, the rose and lily commingled; she illuminates the darkness — even the sun loses its brightness in her presence. As in the troubadour and trouvère poetry of the earliest period, nature everywhere reflects the love-mood. One poet takes up a theme made famous by the troubadour Bernard de Ventadour:

> How happy the little birds
> That rise up on high
> And make music together
> On a single bough!
> Not so with me
> And my hundred thousand loves:
> Far apart on us
> Rises every day.

Whiter she than the lily,
Than beauty more fair,
Sweeter voiced that the violin,
More lightsome than the sun;
Yet beyond all that
Her nobleness, her mind —
And O God who art in Heaven
Relieve my pain.[18]

(Trans. P. H. Pearse)

The loved one is more often than one would have expected in folk-poetry a married lady (as is the case generally in the more formal *amour courtois* lyrics). She has afflicted him with the wasting disease of love, causing him to spend his time crying and sighing. Only she can be his doctor, cure him from certain death (with 'one kiss'). To sleep with her would be no sin: the joy she gives is greater than the joy of paradise. He prefers her to the wealth of kings, or to God himself.

Here, perhaps, we have the kernel of the magnificent heresy of *amour courtois*: that without woman's love God is in vain; only through her can God be experienced. The philosopher Avicenna, writing in Arabic, had proposed this thesis;[19] and it is more than likely that it was through the influence of a variety of Arabian poets and philosophers that this feeling became strongly established in medieval Provençal and French love-poetry. It is equally strongly established in Irish folk-poetry, as lines such as these attest:

I would prefer to sleep with you here below
than be in the presence of God . . . .
I would prefer to be in bed ever kissing you
than be in the mansion of the Blessed Trinity.   (Trans. S. Ó Tuama)

J. M. Synge in turn made eloquent use of these lines in his *Playboy of the Western World*.

Along with the man's love lyric, some half a dozen other medieval French or Provençal literary song-types are also abundantly extant in our folksong today. These include various manifestations of the *Carole*, the *Pastourelle* — the aristocratic progenitor of the 'As I roved out' type of song — and the *Chanson de la Malmariée*, which was brought to its ultimate bawdy climax in Brian Merriman's 18th century *Midnight Court*. Irish popular song still preserves the original literary prototypes of some of these continental medieval models to an extraordinary degree, including the most minute variations on their ribald themes.

The greatest achievement of Irish folksong, however, — as it is of most Western European folksong — is the young woman's love-lyric (*chanson de jeune fille*), in particular the abandoned woman's love-lament. As I have already noted, this type of song must have flourished, in Ireland and abroad, long before the medieval *amour courtois* movement. Despite its having been long-established in the old Irish period, however, it appears from a thematic analysis that the French or Norman-French version of it must have had an overwhelming influence on this type of lyric as we have it today. At the same time there is in the best of our young woman's love-songs a dramatic tone, and a tendency to develop the poem from one situation to another, which is perfectly in accord with our oldest traditions of the dramatic lyric or monologue. These songs in general are more intense, nearer to life as lived, more assured in style, more finely structured than our other folk-lyrics. They are also full of that 'natural magic' which Matthew Arnold attributed to ancient Celtic nature poetry.

Douglas Hyde published some remarkable examples of the young woman's song in his *Love-Songs of Connaught*, a collection which was to have a profound influence on Yeats, Synge and other writers associated with the Irish literary renaissance. In this simplest of songs, which Hyde says he took down from an old woman in a bog in Roscommon, one feels a naïve and gradual diminution of the vast ocean-space between girl and lover as she names known territories and tells despairingly (I think) of a dream she had where they embraced 'shoulder to shoulder/and mouth to mouth':

> My grief on the ocean
> it is surely wide
> stretched between me
> and my dearest love.
>
> I am left behind
> to make lament
> — not expected for ever
> beyond the sea.
>
> My sorrow I'm not
> with my fond fair man
> in the province of Leinster
> or County Clare.
>
> My grief I am not
> with my dearest love
> on board of a ship
> for America bound.
>
> On a bed of rushes
> I lay last night,
> and I shook it out
> in the heat of the day.
>
> My love came near
> up to my side
> shoulder to shoulder
> and mouth to mouth.
>
> (Trans. T. Kinsella)

One cannot but quote also Hyde's own translation of another poem, where the distance between idealised love and mundane reality is equally well created:

> Ringleted youth of my love,
> With thy locks bound loosely behind thee,
> You passed by the road above,
> But you never came in to find me;

303

Where were the harm for you
If you came for a little to see me;
Your kiss is a wakening dew
Were I ever so ill or so dreamy.

I thought, o my love you were so —
As the moon is, or sun on a fountain,
And I thought after that you were snow,
The cold snow on top of the mountain;
And I thought after that, you were more,
Like God's lamp shining to find me,
Or the bright star of knowledge before,
And the star of knowledge behind me.

You promised me high-heel shoes,
And satin and silk, my storeen,
And to follow me, never to lose
Though the ocean were round us roaring;
Like a bush in a gap in a wall
I am now left lonely without thee,
And this house, I grow dead of, is all
That I see around or about me.[20]

And lastly a few verses from the majestic *Donal Óg*, a song known all over Ireland, and in Gaelic Scotland as well:

And late last night the watchdog spoke of you,
The snipe declared you in the deepest bogland,
And you, like lonely wildgoose, gone through the woodlands —
And be lonely always until you marry me. . . .

You made a promise, a thing unlikely,
That you would give me fine gloves of fishskin,
That you would give me fine shoes of birdskin,
And a suit of silk the dearest in Erin. . . .

That was the Sunday I gave my love to you,
The very Sunday before Easter Sunday,
I was reading the Passion on my knees devoutly
While still my two eyes were sending my love to you. . . .

My heart is black as a sloe inside me,
Or the blackest coal that's in the forge there,
Or a dark footprint in the gleaming hallways,
And 'twas you who turned my life so black and bitter.

You've taken East from me and you've taken West from me,
And what's before me and what's behind me,
You've taken sun from me and you've taken moon from me,
And my fear is terrible you've taken God from me.[21]

(Trans. S. Lucy)

The sense of moral anxiety revealed in the last line of *Donal Óg* is quite unusual. In general there is no equation between love-making and sin in our folk lyrics. They emanate ultimately, of course, as did our literary lyrics, from the aristocratic medieval period when the prevailing ethic in matters of love and marriage was non-Christian. Indeed even after the downfall of the aristocratic order in the 17th century, the strictures and regulations associated with modern Post-Tridentene Catholic teaching on love and marriage only very slowly took root. 'Country marriage', a marriage-pact engaged in privately without benefit of clergy, was quite valid and possible in Ireland down to the end of the 18th century. So called traditional Irish Catholic attitudes to love and marriage are largely an invention of the 19th century, and are closely connected with the linguistic change over from Irish to English.

While the basic models for our folksongs may ultimately date back to the 13th and 14th centuries, most of those sung today, or in our archives, were, more than likely, composed between the 16th and 18th centuries. The composers of the best of them, one feels, must have been professional poets; poet-harpists, perhaps, of slightly less rank than the learned bards. In our Irish-speaking communities today those who sing or listen to these love-songs reckon a large number of them to be 'the great songs' ('na hamhráin mhóra'), the high artistic point of their literary and musical culture.

It is not easy to relate our love-songs to the lives of those who sang them in poor rural communities, where a rigid system of arranged marriage was the norm (even though one should remark, in passing, that the system was probably never as rigid as it appears, especially in Pre-Famine days before the introduction of new customs relating to land inheritance). Peig Sayers, a traditional storyteller and reciter of songs, who even in extreme old age looked a remarkably beautiful woman, recounts how love and marriage came to herself on the wild west coast of Kerry: "One night three men came in . . . . I couldn't make out which of them was trying to make a match with me, because I didn't recognize any of them . . . . My father came over to me . . . . 'Will you go to the island? . . . 'I'll go wherever you want me to' [I said]. 'Good girl,' he said."[22] [Trans. S. Ó Tuama]

It appears from another version of this story that Peig Sayers did indeed recognize the young man she was to marry, had in fact been attracted to him for some time previously. Whatever of that, one must admit that her first version expresses the expected attitude of a young Irishwoman of her time. At the same time, one suspects that the concept of love she and her young husband inherited in their songs was, despite some ambivalence at the edges, quite acceptable to them, but practically impossible to imagine having a central part to play in their own lives.

Irish society today, in Irish speaking as in English speaking communities, seems to me to be rapidly shedding both Victorian and medieval romantic notions about love; and a half-dozen poets since Yeats, in Irish and in English, are exploring our new emerging love-sensibilities. This latest phase of Irish love-poetry merits a comprehensive analysis of its own.

See Anne Ross, *Pagan Celtic Britain* (London 1974), p. 265 & p. 281.

[2]*The Irish Tradition* (Oxford 1947), p. 142.

[3]See Frank O'Connor, *A Book of Ireland* (London 1959), p. 257.

[4]Sean Lucy (ed.), *Love-Poems of the Irish* (Cork 1967), p. 32.

[5]James Carney (ed.), *Early Irish Poetry* (Cork 1965), p. 19.

[6]See Lucy, *Love-Poems of the Irish*, p. 26.

[7]See Frank O'Connor, *Kings, Lords and Commons* (London 1962), p. 53.

[8]Cross and Slover, *Ancient Irish Tales* pp. 93-4.

[9]The history of the *carole* in Ireland, as well as that of other folksong *genres*, is discussed in my book *An Grá in Amhráin na nDaoine* (Dublin 1960).

[10]P. Dronke, *Medieval Latin and the Rise of the European Love-Lyric* (London 1968), I, 33.

[11]*The Science of Folklore* (London 1930), pp. 154-5.

[12]Ed. T. F. O'Rahilly (Cork 1926).

[13]*Romania*, 1972(Paris), p. 188.

[13a]See Seán Ó Tuama and Thomas Kinsella, *An Duanaire 1600-1900, Poems of the Dispossessed* (Dublin 1981). Other translations by Thomas Kinsella quoted in this essay are from the same book.

[14]Earl of Longford (ed.), *Poems of the Irish* (Dublin 1944), p. 47.

[15]See Dronke, II, 488.

[16]*Songs of Irish Rebels* (Dublin 1918), p. 59.

[17]See K. Nickolls, *Gaelic and Gaelicised Ireland in the Middle Ages* (Dublin 1972), p. 73.

[18]Lucy, *Love-Poems of the Irish*, p. 73.

[19]See A. J. Denomy, *The Heresy of Courtly Love* (New York 1947), p. 30.

[20]See Lucy, *Love-Poems of the Irish*, p. 69.

[21]Ibid., p. 71.

[22]See also *Peig*, trans. B. McMahon (Dublin 1974).

A NOTE ON THE NATURE OF IRISH MUSIC

MICHAEL BOWLES

The art of music, as now understood, saw its most extensive advances in Europe between the early seventeenth and late nineteenth centuries. This period saw the refinement of skills in making instruments, in tuning them with precision, and in playing on them. It saw the enlargement and refinement of perceptions of the structure of chords, the relationships of tones, and other elements of the material of music. It saw the evolution of large-scale art forms and the music institutions to realise them.

The art of music exists through its institutions. This point tends to be overlooked by musicologists and theorists as they concentrate attention on the lives and works of composers and the prowess of performers. It tends to be overlooked that Palestrina or J. S. Bach or Johannes Brahms or any of the great men of music could scarcely have come to full stature without their institutional background: monasteries with the daily sung Office, church choirs, town bands, court orchestras, enlightened patronage, interested listeners. For this there must be a reliable minimum of social and political stability.

In spite of the wars with which Europe has been plagued during the last few centuries, the hierarchies and structures of European society have somehow stayed intact, or at least intact enough to sustain the institutions essential to the art of music. During the early years of the French Revolution Cherubini was brought from Italy to be the first director of the Paris Conservatoire, for example.

There was no such stability in Ireland. The seventeenth century began with the Flight of the Earls. The second half of the nineteenth century saw the massive emigrations after a succesion of famines and other vicissitudes. Throughout the intervening period, the social and political structures of the Irish people were disintegrating. Irish life sank steadily to a condition of bare subsistence, impulsively enlivened from time to time by abortive rebellions. There were no church choirs; no opera houses; no family leadership with the financial resources to support music institutions, with the leisure and the educated appetite for the art of music. Ireland remained on the outside while Europe was developing the art and practice of music.

There was, however, some European musical influence in Ireland during this period, mostly in Dublin during the eighteenth century. There was the Viceroy's orchestra directed by Mr. Dubourg; there were the choirs from St. Patrick's and Christchurch cathedrals that sang in the first performance of Handel's *Messiah*; but these and similar activities were part of life within the Ascendancy commun-ity, that minority that had replaced the indigenous aristocracy as rulers but not as cultural leaders. In any case, this source of music development began to fade after the Act of Union in 1800, when the focus of Anglo-Irish society was transferred from Dublin to London, and when, later and increasingly, the native Irish began to think of this type of music and song as a further invasive element.

Since the time of Edward Bunting and Thomas Moore, there have been plenty of eloquent and admiring appraisals of the native Irish melodies, their 'unique and haunting beauty' and so on. One question which may occur to many of us has not been satisfactorily answered so far. What quality makes a melody sound 'Irish,' not only in our ears but also in the ear of other nationals? And when a musical contriver says to himself, 'I must give this composition a bit of a twist and make it sound "Irish",' how does he set about achieving his objective?

Most of the attempted explanations deal with accidentals; with surface markings, as it were. The substantial explanation may possibly be found in the historical circumstances already mentioned.

The middle of the seventeenth century saw the firm emergence of a new scale system based on Equal Temperament. This was a division of the octave into 12 arithmetically equal half-tones, needed to solve certain problems in tuning keyboard instruments. Although the problems, connected with key relationships, were not pressing in other means of music-making, choral and instrumental, the Equal Temperament scales became the basis of all new music theory and the foundation of all new composition. The system modified the modal system, and the 'natural' tuning of a scale. Inevitably, it modified the style of melody based on it.

This difference is difficult to define precisely without using technical jargon incomprehensible to the average layman, but it is easy enough to recognise. To make the point clear, we might recall that, from the seventeenth century onwards, when European artists began to think exclusively in terms of Equal Temperament, Irish musicians who survived their disabilities were still using the modal system, the 'natural' scales. The similarity in style and idiom between Irish melody and the traditional music of the Church's liturgy need therefore cause no surprise.

A definition of 'Irish melody' might be useful before going any farther. For the purposes of these paragraphs, 'Irish melody' is the music that comes to us from the eighteenth century, before most of what we see in the printed collections of Petrie and Joyce and Captain 'Chicago' O'Neill and others. The tradition has been muddied, especially in recent years, with the fashion of using banjos and guitars and melodeons, instruments with pre-fixed tuning in Equal Temperament. If we wish to analyse and identify what really makes a melody 'Irish,' perhaps we ought to refer to the modal system of scales on which they are based. If we want to contrive an 'Irish' melody, perhaps we can do it simply by adhering to these modal scales, together with the melodic procedures outlined by theorists during the Polyphonic Period (to about the 1650's).

In passing, we might come to think of the quality described as 'Irish' as not peculiarly Irish but rather as universal, in the sense that the modal scale system with its 'natural' tuning is valid throughout the world at large.

Ireland, which stood outside the developments in Europe, continued to produce music at folk-style level for longer than in other countries. This is why the corpus of traditional modal melodies that form our heritage is so very large, larger even than the traditional liturgy of the Church. It is also why Irish modal melody brings out a new view on modal music in general. We are accustomed to relate modal music to the measured pace of plainchant and the reticent style of polyphony, even in secular canzonets and madrigals and so on. With their simple melodic constructions, our forebears expressed the secular areas of human interest. The same style of melody associated with the liturgy is used for lively and amusing dance tunes, for love songs of every shade and intensity, for uproarious and, as may be, bawdy drinking songs.

Any compromise implies a limitation in scope. The device of Equal Temperament was a compromise. This may account for the dissatisfaction that emerged at the end of the last century with music theory based on Equal Temperament. There has been much floundering in experimentation, from tone-row systems to electronic music and aleatoric music, experiments which are successively fading as acceptable substitutes for what is being rejected. Perhaps the solution of problems arising from the modal system may be the real direction to follow. Those problems, after all, were not solved but merely shelved by the adoption of Equal Temperament. And what seemed insoluble then might now be resolved, with our accumulation of technical expertise since the seventeenth century.

It may be that in Ireland, with its large heritage of music in the modal tradition, a solution may be found. The solution of an Irish problem could be a contribution to the whole art of music. The current notion of a separation in aesthetics between 'Irish' music and Music is altogether misconceived. The art of music is one.

IRISH VOCAL MUSIC OF LAMENT
AND SYLLABIC VERSE

BREANDÁN Ó MADAGÁIN

Vocal music of lament is probably the oldest Irish music to have survived. If it can be established how the different kinds of poetic laments were performed musically, which is the first object of this paper,[1] then given the conservatism of Irish tradition — most of all with regard to the rites attending something as elemental as death — the great likelihood is that the music will be found to be as old as the verse compositions themselves, and an integral part of the age-old tradition to which these belong. Furthermore, we shall see that some lament-music bears a close affinity, at the least, with the music used for the chanting of heroic ballads and of other syllabic verse from the bardic period.

Irish tradition possesses various kinds of poetic lament for the dead: first, the keen (*caoineadh*) performed in the presence of the corpse, usually by the *bean chaointe* or keening woman, *Caoineadh Airt Uí Laoghaire* (1773) being the outstanding example surviving; second, the learned bardic *marbhna*[2] or elegy composed in syllabic metres by the court poets down to the seventeenth century; third, the learned or semi-learned *marbhna* in stressed metre composed from the seventeenth century onwards by poets such as Dáibhí Ó Bruadair and Aodhagán Ó Rathaille, striving to maintain the traditions of the bardic poets; and fourth, the death-song, such as *Anach Cuain* (1828), which usually recalled some dramatic tragedy, such as a drowning, but was not a direct part of the obsequies.

Each of these kinds of lament was performed to music: neither the keen of the common folk nor the learned elegy was given mere recitation. As well as this, there were instrumental laments, played on the harp and later on the pipes, without words. An abundance of descriptions has survived giving first-hand impressions of the laments and what they sounded like,[3] but, apart from the death-songs and the instrumental laments, what we have of the music itself is meagre indeed. Nor has it ever been recorded — except for a few fragments — even though the keening tradition persisted well into the age of the recording-machine and even of the tape-recorder. This is not to be wondered at: unlike the death-song, the keen was not generally a matter for entertainment, but rather an integral part of the ritual of wake and funeral, to be regarded with cautious deference or perhaps superstition outside of its proper context. I have heard Dr. Seán Ó Súilleabháin, formerly Archivist of the Irish Folklore Commission, say that although he had recorded an abundance of folklore material from people in the Gaeltacht, many of whom — friends of his — he knew to be able to keen, not one of them had ever been willing to do so for recording.[4] Occasionally, up until the present day in the Gaeltacht areas, some old person may be heard keening at the wake or funeral of a deceased contemporary, and at least one tape-recording has been made of such.[5] While these are of great human interest, none of those that I have heard can be regarded as providing any more than a faint echo of a tradition recalled by individuals long after it had ceased to have that continual community usage which alone would maintain its vigour and fulness, either musically or linguistically. Such examples serve, however, to demonstrate how the keen could be a genuine instrument for the heightened expression of personal emotion, notwithstanding professionalism and other abuses.

The task, then, of reconstructing how the keen or the elegies were performed is very much a matter of piecing together fragments of description and music, and attempting to trace the pattern.

KEENING
In manuscript 12 Q 13 (p. 10) in the Royal Irish Academy, Frank Keane from Co. Clare has left us this account (1814):

> The Mourner . . . commences by some deep murmuring, repeating over and over the name of the deceased, such as "A Thomáis, a Thomáis, mo chumha is mo dhíth thú". Then follows the Caoine or Irish Cry, in which, at intervals, and in peculiar strains, the deceased is extolled . . .

And in the slim volume of music — collected from Irish-speaking Co. Limerick for the most part — published (in Dublin) by P. W. Joyce in 1873, *Ancient Irish Music*, there is a piece entitled *Caoine* (No. 59), introduced as follows:

> There are usually in a neighbourhood, two or three women, who are skilled beyond others in keening, and who make a practice of attending at wakes and funerals. These often pour forth over the dead person, a lament in Irish — partly extempore, partly prepared — delivered in a kind of plaintive recitative; and at the conclusion of each verse, they lead a choral cry, in which the others who are present join, repeating throughout, 'Och-ochone!' or some such words.

Piecing together these two accounts, we see that there were three parts to a round of keening. First, the salutation: "The mourner . . . commences by some deep murmuring, repeating over and over the name of the deceased, such as 'A Thomais, a Thomáis, mo chumha is mo dhíth thú' ['O Thomas, Thomas, my sorrow and my loss!']" (Keane). Each section in *Caoineadh Airt Uí Laoghaire*[6] commences with a salutation of this kind which is by way of prelude, and bears little or no relation to what follows: "Mo ghrá go daingean tú!", "A mharcaigh na mbán-ghlac!", "Mo chara is mo stór tú!", etc. According to Keane the salutation was murmured,[7] not sung, but in an example to be discussed shortly we have it complete with music: presumably it could be spoken or sung.

Second part: the verse or dirge, "in which at intervals, and in peculiar strains, the deceased is extolled" (Keane); "a lament in Irish — partly extempore, partly prepared — delivered in a kind of plaintive recitative" (Joyce). The four hundred or so lines that have survived of *Caoineadh Airt Uí Laoghaire* are made up of such verses, of irregular length, sung by various people (though principally his widow Eibhlín Dubh) "at intervals" of minutes, hours, days, even months (if only because of Art's re-burial). In his *Ancient Music of Ireland* (Dublin 1840, p. 88), Bunting gives an example of the music to which the verse was sung, adding the note, "sung by a single voice in praise of the deceased."

Third part, the 'Cry': "at the conclusion of each verse, they (the keening women) lead a choral cry, in which the others who are present join, repeating throughout, 'Och-ochone!' or some such words" (Joyce). This is the communal performance romantically described by the Halls in their *Ireland* (1841):

> in the open air, winding round some mountain pass, when a priest, or person greatly beloved and respected, is carried to the grave, and the keen, swelled by a thousand voices, is borne upon the mountain echoes — it is then absolutely magnificent.[8]

In pathetic contrast, to be keened by *gol mná aonair* ("the cry of a lone woman") is still remembered in the Gaeltacht as a great indignity to the deceased.[9] No doubt this choral cry is the part to which the Irish terms *gol* and *gáir* properly refer,[10] as also the word used by the English 'the Irish cry'. All three terms, however, came to be loosely applied to the entire *caoineadh*.[11]

MUSIC OF SALUTATION AND DIRGE

Liam de Noraidh published two fragments of *Caoineadh Airt Uí Laoghaire*, both words and music, in his *Ceol ón Mumhain* (1965, p. 28). The first fragment he wrote down[12] in 1941 from the singing of Máire Bean Uí Chonaill in Baile Bhuirne, Co. Cork. It consists of the reply made by Eibhlín Dubh to the accusation by Art's sister that she, Eibhlín, had gone to bed on the night of his wake. It seems that Bean Uí Chonaill knew only the reply. Eibhlín Dubh, however, would almost certainly have answered in the same tune as had been used by her sister-in-law for her barbed reproach (just as the poets of that age, as we know from their manuscripts, were accustomed to answering each other's songs using the same tunes). And if we take it that the sister-in-law spoke rather than sang the salutation, *"Mo chara is mo stór tú!"* (cf. Keane's account), her lines[13] fit the music perfectly. Here then, in sequence, is reproach and answer (figure 1), the reproach as I conjecture it would have been sung, and Eibhlín Dubh's answer as sung by Bean Uí Chonaill:

Art's Sister: Figure 1

Mo chara is mo stór tú!

313

ma- cha mór bó dhuit   Agus   do-rn buí-óir   duit

Ná raghadh a chodladh 'na seo-ma-ra   Oí-che do thór-raimh.

Eibhlín Dubh:

Without measure ♩ = 104   ♩ = 80

Mo cha-ra croí is   uan   tú   'S ná   creid-se 'n   ♩ = 104

du- ain   sin   Ná 'n   co- gar   a   fu- air- is   Gur a

chod-ladh chu-as- sa   Ní hea   ' u-ain- igh,   Ach ag   ♩ = 66

cur   do   leinibh   chun su-ai- nis   Do bhí   ró-bhu-ar-tha.

Musically this is very different from the ordinary song-tunes of Irish tradition: indeed it can only be described as a chant, and that of a simple unornamented kind, strongly reminiscent of Latin plainsong. There is no musical metre, complete freedom being given to the language with several syllables and sometimes whole phrases being sung to the same note. Joyce's "plaintive recitative" would be a fairly apt description of it.[14] The verse is of primary significance, but is given an added dimension, a further heightening in dramatic and artistic expression, by being chanted rather than merely spoken. The lively speed at which it was sung (quaver = 208) may seem surprising for a dirge, but the other extant examples are equally fast,[15] and we are reminded of Bunting's emphatic remarks[16] on the "animation" characteristic of all kinds of Irish music as played by the harpers. It is to be noted that, contrary to Keane's account, Bean Uí Chonaill sang the salutation as an integral part of the whole.

The second fragment from *Caoineadh Airt Uí Laoghaire* was written down by Liam de Noraidh in 1940 from the singing of the well-known seanchaí Labhrás Ó Cadhlaigh, An Rinn, Co. Waterford. It consists of the lines sung by Eibhlín Dubh calling on the procession of mourning women to halt (at the last tavern on the route) while Art would show his bounteousness by calling for drink, before they went on to the monastery of Cill Chré for Art's re-burial. The music of this piece (Figure 2) is in regular common time, but otherwise it has the same simple chant-like characteristics as the first piece:

Figure 2

A mh-ná na súi- le bog Sta-dai-gí 'n bhúr ngol, Go

bhfaigh' mo lao gheal deoch Roimh é dhul isteach sa scoil, 'Sní

'foghlaim léinn ná port ach ag iompar cré 'gus cloch.

I am indebted to Mícheál Ó Domhnaill, Principal of Coláiste na Rinne, for a tape-recording of Labhrás Ó Cadhlaigh which includes his singing of two laments. One is a fragment of the *caoineadh* sung by Máire Ní Dhonnagáin for her blacksmith brother: *Caoineadh don Ghabha cois Bríde*.[17] It is clearly an *ex tempore* composition and the fragment includes her acid reply (in verse) to the priest who, in accord with the official ecclesiastical disapproval of the pagan *caoineadh*,[18] had rudely told her to shut up.[19] What is of importance for our purposes here is that it will be seen at once from the following transcription of the first stanza (Figure 3) that it is exactly the same music as that to which he sang the fragment of *Caoineadh Airt Uí Laoghaire*, with only the variations needed to accommodate lines of a different metre, and more of them.

Figure 3

A mhic a' gha- bha ó bhun na Brí- de !

Nach fa-da ó bhai- le thái- nío- sa 'd chaoi- neadh !

Tú 'bua- l'an uird ar thaobh na gaoi- the;

315

'Bua- l'an uird ar thaobh na gaoi- the A-gus

Co-lainn gan chi- neáil ag fri- theáil do bhia ort.

The other *caoineadh* sung by Labhrás Ó Cadhlaigh on the tape-recording was one, which he had learned from his mother, for a girl named Bríd Ní Mhuiríosa of Ceapach. Even though, again, it is not in the *rosc* metre usually associated with keening, it is in very loose simple verse which could well have been extemporised on the night of the wake, drawing on the themes and expressions of the vigorous tradition — "partly extempore, partly prepared," as Joyce put it. Liam de Noraidh edited this *caoineadh* from his own notation of it from the singing of Labhrás Ó Cadhlaigh and published it as a single piece entitled *Caoineadh ó sna Déisibh*.[20] The first stanza is reproduced below (Figure 4) for purposes of comparison. It will be seen that once more the same tune was being used as in the other two from this singer, only that this time there is a more generous use of ornamentation.

Figure 4

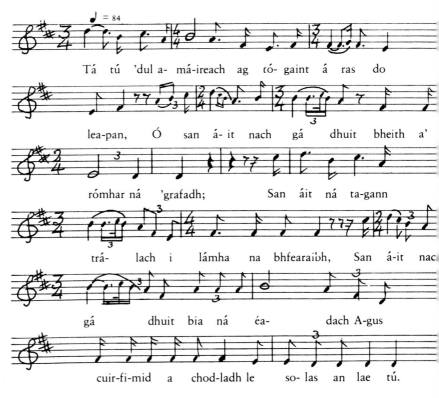

Tá tú 'dul a- má-ireach ag tó- gaint á ras do

lea-pan, Ó san á- it nach gá dhuit bheith a'

rómhar ná 'grafadh; San áit ná ta-gann

trá- lach i lámha na bhfearaibh, San á-it nac

gá dhuit bia ná éa- dach A-gus

cuir-fi-mid a chod-ladh le so- las an lae tú.

Labhrás Ó Cadhlaigh, then, is using the same tune again and again for different laments. It is very remarkable that this chant-like tune is closely related to that of the well-known Donegal song 'Doimnic Ó Domhnaill' (alias 'An Sagart Ó Domhnaill', Fill, fill a rúin ó) in which his mother bewails the fact that her priest son has turned Protestant minister, and implores him to return (fill). Doimnic Ó Domhnaill died in 1793, as we are told on his gravestone in the Protestant cemetery at Carrigart, Co. Donegal, and Énrí Ó Muirgheasa editing the verses gives the probable date of their composition as 1740-50.[21] It would seem that the mother is keening her son and using a keening-tune to do so. In Finland, where the practice of the sung lament has survived down to the present time[22] it is customary to lament not only at times of bereavement but also on other occasions of parting. There is some evidence of such usage in Ireland also.[23] Ruairí Ó Tuairisc (An Spidéal) has told me that in his district emigrants leaving for America were sometimes keened. At the literary level Seán Ó Tuama, believing his fellow-poet Seán Clárach Mac Domhnaill to have emigrated, about 1739, composed his Beo-chaoineadh Sheáin Chláraigh ('Live Lament for Seán Clárach').[24] And in the scene described in the following passage from Memoirs of Jeremiah Curtin (Madison, 1947, p. 457), it is very probable that the old woman was keening:

> The migration of 1892 had begun . . . At a station near Limerick we witnessed a most pathetic scene. A woman, not less than eighty years old, was clinging to her grandchildren, or perhaps they were her great-grandchildren, a young man and woman, and was wailing as at a funeral. She realised that she was seeing them for the last time.

Another example of a recurring keening tune is that printed by J. C. Walker, Historical Memoirs of the Irish Bards (Dublin 1786) under the title Gol na mna 'san ar ('The cry of the women at the massacre'), "said", Walker notes, "to have been sung by the Irish women, while searching for their slaughtered husbands, after a bloody engagement between the Irish and Cromwell's troops" and associated in folklore with a battle fought at Cnoc na nOs, near Buttevant, Co. Cork. This tune is identical with that collected by Bunting 'from Keeners in the county of Armagh', and published by him in his 1840 volume (reproduced below, Figure 6). Neither Walker nor Bunting provide words.[25]

These examples point to there having been a distinctive kind of music for the verse part of the keen (just as we shall see later that there was a special music for the gol or cry); that melodically it was very simple and chant-like, unlike song-tunes; that the same keening-tune could be used again and again, and might have been in use over a very wide area; and that possibly there was only a very limited repertoire of such tunes. It would appear that a single keener could vary the tune for a succession of stanzas.[26] A change of tune with dramatic effect is referred to in the eye-witness account of a keening-scene given by W. K. Sullivan in his introduction to E. O'Curry, On the Manners and Customs of the Ancient Irish (Vol. 1, Dublin 1873, cccxxiv):

> I once heard in West Muskerry, in the county of Cork, a dirge of this kind, excellent in point of both music and words, improvised over the body of a man who had been

killed by a fall from a horse, by a young man, the brother of the deceased. He first recounted his genealogy, eulogised the spotless honour of his family, described in the tones of a sweet lullaby his childhood and boyhood, then changing the air suddenly, he spoke of his wrestling and hurling, his skill at ploughing, his horsemanship, his prowess at a fight in a fair, his wooing and marriage, and ended by suddenly bursting into a loud piercing, but exquisitely beautiful wail, which was again and again taken up by the bystanders.

Sometimes the panegyric on the deceased was begun by one and continued by another, and so on, as many as three or four taking part in the improvisation.

MUSIC OF GOL

It should be noted that according to Sullivan it was not until the very end of his performance that the keener intoned the *gol* "which was again and again taken up by the bystanders." No doubt this would be an example of the spontaneity and flexibility of the entire proceedings, as the more usual thing would have been as given by Joyce (as well as by Bunting, the Halls etc.) that the *gol* be performed "at the conclusion of each verse". Here (Figure 5) is Joyce's example of the *gol*, reproduced from his *Ancient Irish Music* (1873): "The following melody, which I learned long long ago, by repeatedly hearing it [no doubt in Glenosheen, Co. Limerick, where he grew up], may be considered a very characteristic specimen of these musical burdens":

Figure 5

Although many examples of *gol*-tunes have been preserved in the works of Walker,[27] Bunting, Petrie, etc., no words or syllables are fitted to the music.[28] It is likely, however, that the two pieces of keening on the American Folkways record 'Songs of Aran', are essentially of the gol type, although it would seem that they are confused linguistically and blurred in musical outline, perhaps because of the decline of the tradition.

Although he does not supply the words, Bunting gives us a complete sequence of dirge-music and *gol*-music as noted 'from keeners in the county of Armagh' (*Ancient Music of Ireland*, 1840, No. III and p. 88). There is only one line of music in the solo-voice part (i.e. dirge), repeated three times (Figure 6):

Figure 6

Clearly this line could be repeated as often as the verse needed it. The music of the *gol* is essentially as follows (Figure 7):

Figure 7

Bunting's second version (No. 81, entitled "Irish Cry as sung in Ulster") is essentially the same music, protracted by repetitions and concluding with "Half Chorus of Sighs and Tears" to other music.[29]

In Petrie's *Ancient Music of Ireland* (I, Dublin 1855) he published the music of a *Caoine*, "noted from the playing of Frank Keane, a native of the southern part of the county of Clare, in which secluded district he had learnt it from the singing of the women. Of the words sung to it, however, he has no recollection." As a consequence of Petrie's publication, this is now commonly played as an instrumental piece. It seems to be another complete keening sequence with the two parts, dirge and *gol*, clearly discernible as indicated below (Figure 8):

Figure 8

Additional lines could be accommodated *ad libitum* in the dirge part, as in the example from Bunting cited above.

The dirge and the *gol* were musically independent of each other, repetitions of the same dirge-tune being followed sometimes by different *gol*-tunes (e.g. in Bunting's examples).

KEENING IN SCOTLAND

From Carmichael's disjointed notes in *Carmina Gadelica*, V (Edinburgh 1954), 338 ff., it is clear that a similar tradition of keening was practised in Scotland down to about the middle of the last century. Carmichael distinguishes two kinds of mourning: "The 'séis,' 'séisig' or 'séisig-bhàis,' death-mourning, or death-music, was the mourning in the house after the death. The 'tuiream,' 'tuirim,' lament, was the mourning in the open after the journey to the place of burïal" (p. 339). The Scottish equivalent of the *bean chaointe* was called *bean-tuirim*. In *The Traditional and National Music of Scotland* (London 1966), Francis Collinson comments on Carmichael's remarks: "both the *seisig-bhàis* and the *tuiream* seem to have had their proper traditional tunes." Unfortunately for our purpose the vocalists ceased their mourning function in Scotland earlier than in Ireland, giving way completely to the piper, and there seems to be only a single example of the vocal lament on record: Collinson prints it (pp. 113-4) from the singing of Calum Johnston of Barra. It is a *séisig-bhàis*, and clearly corresponds to the *gol* of Irish keening, the words largely consisting of combinations of the syllables *pill-il-il-iú* (cf. *ulla-lú*; see note 28 above). Surely then, the distinction between *séisig-bhàis* and *tuiream* is the same as that between *gol* and dirge (verse-part) in Irish. This is suggested, indeed, by the literal meaning of the terms themselves (Carmichael renders them as 'death-music' and 'lament'[30] respectively) together with Carmichael's account of what the *tuiream* consists of: "All the virtues of the dead, and a few more, were mentioned and extolled, and the genealogy for many generations praised and lauded" (pp. 344-5). The distinction between indoors and outdoors was secondary. The *tuiream*, Collinson tells us, is the 'coronach' of popular usage. As in Ireland, the clergy forbade its practice.[31]

MUSIC OF *MARBHNA* OR ELEGY

The *marbhna* or learned elegy, composed by the bardic poet or *ollamh* in syllabic metre for his dead chieftain, was sung, as was all the official verse, by a special functionary, the *reacaire* (or *marcach duaine*), accompanied by the *cruitire* ('harper') on the harp. There is no indication what kind of music the acompaniment consisted of, nor have we any direct evidence concerning the music used by the *reacaire*. It may well be, however, that we have valuable indirect evidence in the later elegies in stressed metre, a few of which have fortunately survived with what would seem to be their own characteristic music. With the demise of the court poets as a profession in the seventeenth century, following the destruction of their aristocratic patrons, the part-time poets who succeeded them strove to maintain their learning and traditions with all the conservative devotion of an elite whose ideal world had been shattered. One should expect that nowhere would their backward-looking disposition be more evident than in the composition of elegies, and indeed for a very long time the elegies composed by them showed scarcely any difference from those of the bardic poets, other than the change to stressed metre. One such *marbhna* was that composed by Seán na Ráithíneach on the death in 1739 of Donnchadh Mág Cártha of Ballea Castle, Co. Cork.[32] Not only is it in a highly literary and learned style throughout, but it even closes with a very full *dúnadh*, the bardic device for ending a poem,[33] rarely to be found in poems of stressed metre. P. W. Joyce wrote down the music of this *marbhna* in 1851 from the singing of a farmer in Co. Limerick, Phil Gleeson of Coolfree, and published it in his *Old Irish Folk Music and Songs* (1909); he referred his reader to Hardiman's *Irish Minstrelsy* for the words. Figure 9 presents the first stanza as printed by Joyce, but with the words restored:[34]

Figure 9

Ó! os-na's éacht na hÉi- reann tríd an dtreoir, Ó!

or- chra daor is créim d'fhuil Mhí- leadh mhóir

Tor- char- tha tréith i gcré 'na luí fé'n bhfód, Ó!

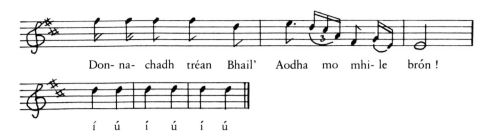

Don- na- chadh tréan Bhail' Aodha mo mhi- le brón !

í ú í ú í ú

It will be seen that this is not an ordinary Irish song-tune; although in regular ¾ time, it has nevertheless marked characteristics of chant and recitative, just as we found in the keening-tunes. As well as this, each stanza was followed by what must have been a kind of chorus, which could well have corresponded to the choral cry which followed each stanza of the keen. Joyce notes:

> As to Phil Gleeson's traditional manner of singing the ode — which he learned of course from older people: To the note D at the end of the air he chanted, in monotone, a sort of *cronaun* consisting simply of the continued repetition of the two vowel sounds, *ee-oo ee-oo ee-oo*, etc., which was prolonged *ad libitum*: the change from *ee* to *oo* being made at intervals of about a crochet. Occasionally he ended the *cronaun* by suddenly sliding his voice up to the third, fifth or octave — a common practice in laments, nurse-tunes, plough whistles, etc.

This terminal jumping of the octave occurs at the end of the example of the *gol* quoted above from Joyce, and also in one of the keening-pieces on the *Songs of Aran* recording (made a century later).

Another later example of the *marbhna*, but much more striking in the chant-like music of the two surviving versions, is the *Marbhna Mhic Fhinghin Duibh* ('Lament for the Son of Fineen Dubh'). On the death of Sylvester O'Sullivan, last bearer of the title Mac Finghin Duibh (used by the head of the O'Sullivans of Derreen, Kenmare, Co. Kerry), who was killed in a fall from his horse in 1809, his sister publicly offered a prize of ten pounds for the best *marbhna*. The example in question here was composed by the Kerry poet Diarmaid na Bolgaighe, one of the five who competed.[35] Two independent musical versions of it were notated early this century. The more complete (again ending, remarkably, with the bardic *dúnadh*) was written down by D. J. O'S[ullivan] in 1919 from the singing of P. J. O'Shea ('Conán Maol') who came from near Derreen; it was published in the *Journal of the Irish Folk Song Society* xviii (1921), 20-23. The first stanza is as follows (Figure 10):

Figure 10

Fairly fast.

Ó! mh'os. .na trí Luim . n .each, Con .nacht is Cléir faoi

chumha, Is go Cor .caigh na loing . eas tar uis . ce dá dtéidhinn an . .

The music is entirely that of chant, with almost complete lines of the verse being sung on a single note. Indeed, there are only two phrases in the music, repeated without change. This is followed, as in the example from Co. Limerick, by the simple chanting of chorus words, *Seo-tho binn, binn, binn*, apparently borrowed from lullaby.[36]

The other version of this *marbhna* was written down in the Ballyvourney district of Co. Cork just before the First World War, from the singing of Peg O'Donoghue, Ballymakeery, by A. M. Freeman, and published by him in his collection of 'Irish Folk Songs' in the *Journal of the Folk Song Society*, Vol. VI (1920-21), 200-03: *Tuireav Vic Inín Duiv*. I reproduce here (Figure 11) the second stanza, in which the musical comparison with the Co. Cork version is clearer than in the first:

Figure 11

The very significant fact here is that although the actual tune is quite different from that of the Co. Cork version the chant-like characteristics are exactly the same (except for the additional one of free time: marked by the collector, 'In free Recitative'). This corroborates the suggestion made above with regard to the keen that the known repertoire of lament-music could be freely drawn upon as required: a lament did not have its own tune.

Freeman also points out that as his version stands the melody of each stanza ends on the (unlikely) seventh, which suggests that there may have been something more to come. And in fact he was told of a man in Ballyvourney, then many years dead, "who used to sing this song with a long wail following the note which appears here as final," and he adds that "Miss O'Donoghue's voice breaks with a sort of upward sob, not musically notable, on the last note." Presumably the "long wail", just as the *seo-tho, binn, binn, binn* of the other version, and the repeated *ee-oo* of the Co. Limerick lament, brought each section to rest on the tonic. Presumably also in each case this represents some kind of vocable chorus in which, in former times, the assembled company would join, just as they did in the *gol* after each stanza of the keen. Commenting on an elegy by the seventeenth-century bard Iain Lom on the death of the hero, Alisdair Dubh of Glengarry, Donald Campbell, in *A Treatise on the Language, Poetry, and Music of the Highland Clans* (Edinburgh 1862, p. 163), writes of the chorus (*fonn*) after each verse:

> The chorus here, as indeed in every song, may be regarded as a solemn amen to the feeling and the sentiment of every verse of the song, bursting spontaneously from the heart of hearts of the audience, who always joined in singing the chorus.

In this particular case, the chorus was in verse, but frequently in Scotland it consisted of vocables only.

This evidence, then, from counties Limerick, Kerry and Cork, seems to point firmly to the conclusion that the *marbhna* in stressed metre was chanted in very much the same manner as the verse part of the keen, and that, again as in the keen, each stanza was followed by some kind of chorus (the chorus, however, in the few examples known to us, is very much simpler in its music than the known examples of the *gol*). It is likely, for the reasons already indicated, that the manner of performing this *marbhna* closely echoed that of the bardic *marbhna* in syllabic metre. If so, it suggests that the bardic *marbhna* had a chorus between the stanzas, which does not appear in the manuscripts at all, presumably because it would have consisted merely of conventional vocables, variable from one performance to another, but which nevertheless added an important dimension to the drama of the occasion. Indeed this raises the further question, beyond the scope of this paper, as to whether some other bardic compositions intended for public performance did not have some kind of chorus, as is suggested by Donald Campbell's remarks. Furthermore, it would imply a close relationship between the music of the keening tradition and that in use by those responsible for the performance of the bardic *marbhna*.[37] This should not be surprising, as the extant examples of the text of the keen bear the clear marks of the heroic tradition, no less than do those of the *marbhna.* Art Ó Laoghaire is the slain hero, nonetheless alive and addressed directly, appeased with the homage of adulation, his lineage and aristocratic relatives recalled, his prowess and his bounteousness, his heroic physique and his splendid attire, nature itself not only mourning him but making obeisance to him. Small wonder if the music used for both kinds should fit the description of that used for heroic poetry in the European tradition. Maurice Bowra in his *Heroic Poetry* (1966, 38-9) gives the following account of it:

> Heroic poetry seems always to be chanted, usually to some simple stringed instrument, like the Greek lyre, the Serbian *gusle*, the Russian *balalaika*, the Tatar *koboz*, or the Albanian *lahuta*. The music to which poems are sung is usually not a real or a regular tune but a monotonous chant in which the bard often keeps whole lines on a single note. Such indeed is said to be the regular practice in Albania, and the heroic Jugoslav chants recorded by Milman Parry are monotonous and lacking in melody. There certainly seems to be no evidence that a special poem has its own tune. Among famous Russian bards the elder Ryabinin knew only two tunes, and "the Bottle" one. This is quite a different art from the melodies which accompany lyric poetry, give pleasure for their own sake, and are as likely to obscure as to illustrate the words. Heroic poetry puts the words first and subordinates the music to them. What it uses is really no more than recitative. To use a regular tune like that of a song would have made the task of heroic poets much more difficult and have interfered with the clear presentation of the tales which they have to tell.

Donald Campbell in his *Treatise* tells us: "The airs of the historical poems were, properly speaking, not melodies, but a musical and pleasing style of reciting poetry."[38]

Such a common relationship is paralleled by the heroic ballads, Ossianic and others, which, although of learned composition in syllabic metres, were chanted or "musically recited" by the common people, down to our own day in Scotland (and even to some extent in Ireland, as in the tape-recordings of two examples — *Laoi na bhFiann* and *Laoi na Mná Móire* — from Teileann and Gleann Colmcille, 1949, in the archive of the Department of Irish Folklore in University College Dublin). A sufficiently large number of Ossianic *duain*[39] complete with chant-like music, has survived in Scotland to enable accurate generalisations to be made about their musical structure and to set down its characteristics. The only two examples recorded from Ireland, referred to above, fit the pattern exactly.[40] What is much more remarkable, however, is the degree to which Irish examples of both the keen (dirge-part) and the *marbhna* exhibit these same characteristics.[41] The most common of these, set out by Francis Collinson in *The Traditional and National Music of Scotland* (p. 44), are: first, a reciting note on a monotone; second, the approach to this by one or more notes from above or below; third, "the use of only part of the scale"; and fourth, the descending cadence at the end. All four features can be noted clearly in the Kerry version of *Marbhna Mhic Fhinghin Duibh*: it is in the Aeolian (Lah) mode but without use of the sixth; the other features — approach note, reciting note and descending cadence — constitute the very structure of the piece.

Approach, reciting note and descending final cadence are again very marked in the Co. Cork version (reciting note C) and also in the Co. Limerick *marbhna*;

although in the latter case the monotone of the reciting note (F sharp) is relieved by ornamentations of the third and passing notes, the pattern remains clear.[42] All .three features characterise also the first fragment from *Caoineadh Airt Uí Laoghaire* quoted above, *Mo chara croí*, while that of the descending cadence is common to almost all the other known examples of the dirge-part of the keen (including, be it noted, *Fill, fill a rúin ó*). The pattern is much more marked, however, in the *marbhna* examples than in those of the keen.

At the very least, then, the vocal music of lament is closely related in kind and structure to that of the heroic ballads: one draws back from the conclusion that the music of the two is identical only because of the paucity of surviving examples of the lament music. This relationship in turn strengthens the likelihood not only that the extant examples of *marbhna* are of the type used for the earlier bardic *marbhna*, but that this was the kind of music used for bardic compositions in general. One further piece of evidence provides yet another link in the chain. It is supplied by O'Curry in his discussion of the music of the Ossianic poems in *Manners and Customs of the Ancient Irish* (Dublin 1873), iii, 392. Having told us that he had heard his own father sing Ossianic poems, and that he could "remember distinctly the air and the manner of their singing," he goes on to say:

> I do not remember having heard any other poem sung to the air of these Ossianic pieces but one, and that is a beautiful ancient hymn to the Blessed Virgin, some seven hundred or more years old. My father sang this hymn, and well too, almost every night, so that the words and the air have been impressed on my memory from the earliest dawn of life ... The air of this hymn is not popular; I have never heard it sung but by my own father. I know it myself very well, and I know several old poems that will sing to it, such as the above poems ascribed to Oisin ...

O'Curry gives the words of the first stanza of the hymn to the Blessed Virgin, beginning *Stiurad me dod mholadh* [i.e. *Stiúraigh mé dod mholadh*]. This is, in fact, a bardic composition, the so-called *Sciathlúireach Mhuire* ('Mary's Breastplate' or 'Prayer for Protection') which has survived in many manuscripts where it is ascribed to Donnchadh Mór Ó Dálaigh, the poet who died in A.D. 1244, well known for his bardic religious poems.[43] It should be noted that in speaking of the music O'Curry uses the word *air* in the singular all through this passage, from which one infers that his father had a single tune to which he sang various Ossianic ballads and also this religious poem. If Eoghan Mór O'Curry (the father) can be taken as representative of the eighteenth-century tradition — and there is every reason to accept this — then that tradition was remembering and handing down the same music for Ossianic ballad and religious bardic verse.

Investigation over a wider spectrum will be necessary before one can discuss the further implications of these relationships — some well attested, some inferential, but cumulatively suggesting homogeneity — between the tunes used for keen, accented *marbhna*, bardic *marbhna*, heroic ballad and other syllabic verse. One external dimension must be adverted to: Collinson, in setting out the characteristics of heroic ballads as enumerated above, was doing so with a view to showing the similarity of their tunes to those of Latin plainsong.[44]

MUSIC OF THE DEATH-SONGS

The only kind of lament which still survives generally in the mouths of the people is that of the "death-song", as Joyce called such songs as *Anach Cuain, Amhrán na Trá Báine,* or *An chéad Mháirt d'Fhómhar.* In a note appended by Joyce to a tune of this kind in one of his manuscripts,[45] he implied a distinction between such songs and the lament performed in the presence of the corpse: "The above is a good specimen of the Caoines still sung by the people — sung only, however, as things of memory, but never as far as I know applied to their original and proper use." In function they are not unlike English ballads, recalling, usually, some tragic happening, but having no part in the obsequies. An examination of the tunes of such songs shows that they are altogether different in kind and structure from the music of the keen and the *marbhna,* and furthermore that they do not differ in any way from the ordinary song-tunes of Irish tradition. In other words, they do not use special lament-music at all: the poet or songwriter seems to have composed his death-song to any known air suitable to his purpose, whether it be that previously used for love-song, political song or whatever. In the Tuam district the same tune was used for Raftery's love-song for Máire Ní Eidhin as for his death-song commemorating the Corrib drowning of the nineteen from Anach Cuain.[46] As the bardic tradition faded, even in memory, the learned or semi-learned poets began to use ordinary song-tunes for the *marbhna.*[47] That composed by Seán Ó Tuama on the death in 1754 of his fellow poet Seán Clárach Mac Domhnaill must have had a special standing, yet it was sung to the air of the love-song *Ar Éirinn ní neosainn cé hí.*[48] Other *marbhnaí* by the Maigue poets are referred, in the manuscripts, to such a variety of song-airs as *Éamonn an Chnoic, Ceo Draíochta, Aonmhac na hÓighe.* One lament, that for Úna Bhán Nic Dhiarmada, has survived in various musical versions, both as death-song and to the music of lament. Indeed there is no better illustration of the great difference, musically, between death-song and lament than a comparison between the version of *Úna Bhán* arranged by Carl Hardebeck,[49] with its elaborate melismatic development, and clearly an Irish art-song in origin, and the version sung by Máire Áine Ní Dhonnchadha (from Cnoc na hAille in Connemara) on her record *Deora Aille* (Claddagh Records, CC 6) which must be the finest traditional illustration we have of the music of lament. One recognises at once in the latter not only the chanting quality of the music but also the structural features discussed above, namely the musically monotonous reciting line (with ornamentations, yet clearly maintained) followed rather dramatically by falling cadence.

INSTRUMENTAL LAMENTS

The harpers and later the pipers had their instrumental laments, the term for that of the harper being, according to Bunting, *cumha.* Such a piece is 'Scott's Lamentation for Purcell, Baron of Loughmoe, who died about A.D. 1599', printed by Bunting in his 1840 volume, exactly, he says, as it was played by Denis

Hempson (who was over 97 years old at the time of the Belfast Harp Festival, 1792). In his notes to this piece he states:

> The caoine was a solemn piece of music intended as a tribute to the deceased, and was looked on as the greatest test of the ability of the harper. It was not intended to be sung.

The complicated instrumental music, then, was very different in character from the vocal music, and a discussion of it is beyond the scope of this article. Mention has already been made of the harper's other function with regard to the lament, namely to play an accompaniment to the chanting of the *marbhna*. If Bunting's terminology can be relied upon literally, it may well be that the harper also accompanied the *caoineadh* at the obsequies of patrons. In his notes on a piece of harp-music called a *Feaghan Gleash* ('Try if it be in tune') or 'prelude' he records that:

> It was with great reluctance that the old harper (Hempson) was prevailed upon to play even the fragment of it here preserved ... He would rather, he asserted, have played any other air, as this awakened recollections of the days of his youth, of friends whom he had outlived, and of times long past, when the harpers were accustomed to play the ancient caoinans or lamentations, with their corresponding preludes.

NOTES

[1] Some of this material has appeared in my article "Ceol an Chaointe" in *Gnéithe den Chaointeoireacht*, ed. B. Ó Madagáin (Dublin 1978); it is reproduced here for the benefit of those who do not read Irish, and for the sake of completeness, with the kind permission of the publishers, An Clóchomhar.

[2] Also called *tuireamh*.

[3] See Diarmaid Ó Muirithe, "An Chaointeoireacht in Éirinn — Tuairiscí na dTaistealaithe," in *Gnéithe den Chaointeoireacht*, pp. 20-29.

[4] Compare the remarks in the notes to the Folkways Record, *Songs of Aran*, on the reluctance of the old Aran woman from whom a fragment of keening was obtained, and on her concern that the neighbours would not hear her. My colleague, Máirtín Ó Briain, told me of a friend of his, now deceased, an old Gaeltacht woman well-known for her singing, who was prevailed upon by a visitor to give a demonstration of keening. It happened that one of her family died some short time afterwards, and nothing would ever dissuade her from the conviction that her performance of the keen out of season had brought the misfortune about.

[5] Broadcast on RTÉ radio, 29/2/1980.

[6] Seán Ó Tuama, *Caoineadh Airt Uí Laoghaire* (Dublin 1961). English translation by Frank O'Connor, *Kings, Lords, & Commons* (London 1962) and elsewhere.

[7] Compare Crofton Croker, *The Keen in the South of Ireland*: "Before she [the keener] began to repeat, she usually mumbled for a short time (probably the commencement of each stanza, to assure herself of the arrangement) with her eyes closed, rocking her body backwards and forward, as if keeping time to the measure of the verse" — quoted by Rachel Bromwich, 'The Keen for Art O'Leary', *Éigse*, V (Dublin 1945-7), 243.

[8] Vol. I (London 1841), 225. In the Halls' account, the performance of the individual keener interrupted the choral cry, which preceded it and was repeated after it; so also the choral cry went up with the arrival of any

newcomers. Regarding the latter, compare [Thomas Campbell], *A Philosophical Survey of the South of Ireland* (London 1777), 206-7: "On this road I met an Irish funeral . . . I met it unexpectedly in turning a corner, and no sooner did the mourners see me, than they set up a yell that frightened my horse not a little . . . As they pass through any town, or meet any remarkable person, they set up their howl."

[9]Mícheál Ó Sé in a program on 'Mná Caointe', Radio na Gaeltachta, 1/3/1977.

[10]Cf. J. C. Walker, *Gair Chonachtnach, Gair Mhuimhneach* etc. in his *Irish Bards* (Dublin 1786), ii, Nos. II-V; Beauford, 'the Gol or Choruses' in his 'Caoinan . . .' paper discussed, my note 11; Bunting, *Ancient Music of Ireland* (Dublin 1840), 81, designates the music of the dirge 'The Goll' and that of the choral cry 'Caoinan', terms which he may have got from Beauford's paper and confused.

[11]The lay-out of the keen, as here proposed, salutation, dirge, choral cry, corresponds basically with that given with great elaboration by William Beauford in the paper which he read to the Royal Irish Academy in 1791, entitled, "Caoinan: or some Account of the Antient Irish Lamentations" (*Transactions* IV, 41 f.). In this paper he purported to give a detailed account (including music and words in the example which he appended) of the part of the *bardic poets* in the ancient funeral rites. He mentioned no sources. I have elsewhere surmised that this account (and especially its music) was more likely to have been drawn from contemporary keening practice. Since then I have found a statement from Beauford that his *Caoinan* "was obtained from an old female keener": in manuscript no. 347 in the National Library of Ireland (my thanks to Nessa Ní Shéaghdha for drawing my attention to this ms. in another connection), there is an essay by Beauford "On the Poetry and Music of the Ancient Irish," dated 1789, where he gives the same *Caoinan* with the above note. He gives no further details of his "old female keener," but he implies that the lines of literary language given with the music were sung "by heart" by her ("without understanding a single word"!). This also one takes to be spurious, as almost all the lines he uses were printed by Edward Lhuyd eighty two years before in his *Archaeologia Britannica* (Oxford 1707), p. 309: Beauford himself even makes a reference on another account to this passage of Lhuyd's, in his published paper (p. 44 footnote). O'Curry was scarcely doing Beauford an injustice, then, when he categorised him with "ignorant unscrupulous fabricators of facts," authors of "audacious forgeries" (*Manners and Customs*, Dublin 1873, iii, 321, referred to by Cathal Ó Háinle in a review of *Gnéithe den Chaointeoireacht* in *Comhar*, Dublin, Jan. 1979, where he also points out Beauford's use of Lhuyd's text). See note 38 below.

[12]B[reandán] B[reathnach] states: "The songs in *Ceol ón Mumhain* were not recorded. They were notated directly from the informants" — *Ceol*, iv No. 3 (Dublin, April 1977), 93.

[13]Ó Tuama, ll. 96-104. We cannot be certain, of course, that the tune noted from Bean Uí Chonaill was that actually used by Eibhlín Dubh 168 years before.

[14]The degree of musicality will, of course, have varied from one keener to another, and from one group to another, and even from one performance to another. Hence the Halls' comment (I, 230): "When the corpse is about to be taken out [of the house] the wail becomes most violent; but as then *nature* is most predominant, it is less *musical*." So too Thomas Campbell, p. 208: "Though the band of criers which I heard, made no very musical dirge of it, it was certainly calculated to inspire melancholy."

[15]With the exception of Beauford's doubtful example discussed below, which is marked *largo*.

[16](1840), chapter 2; printed in greater fulness from his manuscripts by Charlotte Milligan Fox, *Annals of the Irish Harpers* (London 1911), p. 107: "In the year 1792 when the meeting of Harpers took place at Belfast the Editor being selected to note down the tunes was very much surprised to find that all the Melodies played by the harpers, were performed with so much quickness, that they did not bear the least comparison with the manner in which he had been accustomed to hear them played . . . The fact was that the tunes were played with a great degree of animation, . . . a spirited animated and highly lively style . . . It may be well to remark however that . . . let them (our melodies) be played slow or quick they serve the purpose of either grief or most joyous music."

[17]See *Irisleabhar na Gaeilge*, iii (Dublin 1889), 104 f. and iv, 29, for quite a literary elegy on her brother, attributed to her, although she is there said to have been a well-known *bean chaointe*.

[18]See Seán Ó Súilleabháin, *Caitheamh Aimsire ar Thórraimh* (1961), ch. IX; English translation *Irish Wake Amusements* (Cork 1967).

[19]Cathal Ó Háinle, in his review of *Gnéithe den Chaointeoireacht,* (note 11 above), has drawn attention to a similar exchange between priest and keener, in almost identical words, in a story from Adrigole in Co. Cork printed by An Seabhac in *An Seanchaidhe Muimhneach* (Dublin 1932), pp. 278-80.

[20](Dublin 1938).

[21]*Céad dé Cheoltaibh Uladh* (Dublin 1915), p. 33.

[22]Lauri Honko, 'Balto-Finnic Lament Poetry', *Studia Fennica* 17 (Helsinki 1974), 9-61; Séamas Ó Catháin, 'Caointeoireacht an Chine Dhaonna', in *Gnéithe den Chaointeoireacht,* pp. 9-19.

[23]In *Cín Lae Amhlaoibh* (edited Tomás de Bhaldraithe, Dublin 1970), the old woman lamenting her family's eviction (1828) was surely keening, 'agus í ag gol go géar': even as they stand in the prose of Ó Súilleabháin's diary many of her words can be re-written as lines of *rosc*:
> D'fhág sé an bothán gan doras,
> an fhuinneog gan gloine
> an tinteán gan tine
> an deatachán gan deatach . . . (p. 44).

[24]*Beo-chaoineadh Sheáin Chláraigh ar n-a mheas gur imeacht tar sáile do rinne sé tuairim A.D. 1739,* R. Ó Foghludha, *Éigse na Máighe* (Dublin 1952), 94.

[25]The first stanza given by Beauford in the *Caoinan* referred to above is a variant of the same tune, fitted with words apparently concocted by him from Lhuyd's verses. See note 11 above. My thanks to Prof. Seán Ó Cinnéide for drawing my attention to the Cnoc na nOs tradition.

[26]This is done in the *Caoinan* given by Beauford, where he gives, in all, four stanzas, each followed by the *gol*.

[27]See under the titles *Gair Chonachtnach* — 'The Lamentation of Connaught' — *Gair Mhuimhneach* — 'The Lamentation of Munster' — etc.

[28]Beauford's *Caoinan,* for what it is worth, has syllables fitted to the music of the *gol*, consisting of various syllabic combinations of the words *ullalú* and *ochón*.

[29]All of this, one suspects, is influenced by Beauford's *Caoinan*.

[30]*Bean-tuirim* he translates as 'rehearsing or lamenting woman' (339) and goes on to list the themes one such woman 'rehearsed'.

[31]Collinson, p. 114 n.

[32]Torna, *Seán na Ráithíneach* (Dublin 1954), p. 303.

[33]I.e. with an echo or repetition of its opening syllables or words (here *osnadh agus éacht*). See G. Murphy, *Early Irish Metrics* (Dublin 1961), p. 43.

[34]After Donal O'Sullivan, *Songs of the Irish* (Dublin 1960), where however he writes it in the key of B flat major.

[35]See Seán Ó Súilleabháin, *Diarmuid na Bolgaighe* (Dublin 1937), pp. 64-84, pp. 179-186. The prize was awarded to the Limerick poet Séamas Ó Caoindealbháin.

[36]D. J. O'S. notes: "It will be observed that at the end of the air we have a crónán or lullaby in place of the usual caoine. The reason of this is that the poet refuses to believe that Mac Finghin Dubh is dead, and suggests that he has been stolen away by Cliodhna, the Spirit of the Caha Mountains, where he is slumbering."

[37]Beauford, both in his published paper and in the manuscript essay, asserted that the keen was originally composed by the bards and even performed by them, "but on the decline of that order, the Caoinan fell into the hands of women, and became an extemporaneous performance" (R.I.A. Trans. IV, 44). There is no need to give a detailed refutation of this assertion: suffice it to give one or two references. *The Book of Magauran* (edited L. McKenna, Dublin 1947) contains a bardic elegy composed for Fearghal Ruadh Mac Samhradháin, whose death is recorded by the Four Masters A.D. 1322 (when the bardic order was flourishing), where the poet makes a clear distinction between his own *marbhna* and the *caoineadh* already performed by a woman (ll. 671-4):

A-déara mé n-a marbhnaidh
re fleisg an fhuilt fhionnghabhlaigh:
"Agod chaoineadh do bhraith bean,
a fhlaith Taoidhean, ar dteicheadh"

('I will say by way of elegy over the curly-haired prince: "When keening over thee, O Prince of Taoidhe, the woman sensed our banishment" '). And Rachel Bromwich, in 'The Keen for Art O'Leary', *Éigse* V, 236 f., provides ample "evidence, as far back at least as the twelfth century, of the custom of keening by women over the corpses of their near relatives." Nioclás Ó Cearbhalláin has suggested to me that Beauford's account of the keen may have been inspired by Thomas Campbell's *Philisophical Survey* (1777; see note 5 above), where Campbell (pp. 206-9) confused the learned bardic elegy with the keen of his own time, and regarded the latter as a degenerate form of the *marbhna*.

[38]Page 154. He is referring not only to the singing of Ossianic poems but in a general way to "Songs of a narrative or historical character."

[39]Collinson, p. 40n[3], distinguishes between the heroic ballad termed *duan* and that called *laoidh*: "It would seem that musically speaking the *duan* is of a more recitative form than the *laoidh*, which is generally more of a song type of melody than a chant."

[40]This may well be due, of course, to Scottish influence or even origin, in the case of examples from Co. Donegal. For "a composite version of the air" of one of them, "deriving from several stanzas", see transcription by Breandán Breathnach, *Folkmusic and Dances of Ireland*, p. 28, where, as he says, "the chant-like quality and free rhythm style, reminiscent of Latin plainchant, may be observed in the music."

[41]L[ucy] E. B[roadwood] in an editorial note to the Co. Cork version of *Tuireav Vic Inín Duiv* remarked that "It is in type much like West Highland Ossianic narrative airs and laments" (*loc. cit.*).

[42]These ornamentations on the monotone could be a late development, and may not be a feature of the original tune.

[43]It was, however, a common practice to attribute religious poems to him (cf. L. McKenna, *Aithdhioghluim Dána*, Dublin 1939, i, p. xxxii).

I have since discovered that O'Curry's "air" has happily been preserved for us by Petrie: it is to be identified with No. 1205 in his *Complete Collection* [ed. Stanford, London 1903]. I hope very shortly to publish an edition of the hymn-text and music together.

[44]I hope on a future occasion to pursue the relationship between plainsong and the Irish music discussed above. Suffice it here to remark that it is less likely to be a matter of simple borrowing than to be a case of external influence on native Irish musical forms, just as Calvert Watkins suggested for the development of Irish syllabic verse: "In the forms of Classical Old Irish syllabic verse I would suggest, then, that rather than an ultimate importation from Latin metrical forms we have a sort of 'symbiosis' or syncretism of native metrics with certain characteristic features of form and content of Medieval Latin poetry; and that . . . it is in fact the purely native Irish component which predominates." ("Indo-European Metrics and Archaic Irish Verse", in *Celtica*, VI, Dublin 1963.) In addition to some of the features mentioned above, the use of the chorus in Irish lament may be another example of such influence, it being remarkably similar to that in the responsorial psalmody, where the congregation *responded* with *Amen* or *Alleluia* or some such words after each verse had been chanted by a solo voice. The contrary relationship (borrowing from bardic practice into Church usage) was claimed for this feature by Liam O'Looney (1828-1901) in a booklet to which Fr. Diarmaid Ó Laoghaire, S.J., has very kindly drawn my attention since the above went to press. The booklet was entitled *Sciathlúireach Uí Luaighne — O'Looney's Protecting Shield*, Dublin (no date, publisher James Duffy, *imprimatur* Gulielmus [Walsh]). In the 'Introductory Letter' the author discusses the *aidbsi* and says that it was "an accompaniment sung by way of refrain at the termination of each stanza or poetic strain, and

in which the whole class or company united their voices . . ."; he goes on to assert that it was "adopted from the choral panegyric of the ancient bards, as peculiarly adaptable to the solemn strains of the Choral prayer and Church hymns, and from the fact that it was the formula sanctioned by that illustrious saint (Colm Cille) to be used by the bards at his own obsequies, it was universally adopted for the funeral dirge, and has continued in favour in one or other of its varied forms, with the *mná caointe* . . . and with the Tribal Bards, and with all classes of professional mourners in many parts of Ireland even to this day". Whatever about the authenticity of its details (many here omitted), O'Looney's account corroborates the suggestion made above that each stanza of the bardic marbhna (and possibly of other bardic compositions also) was followed by a choral refrain.

[45]National Library of Ireland, Joly MS 25, p. 25.

[46]See Mrs. Costello, *Amhráin Mhuighe Seóla* (Dublin 1923), pp. 102-3.

[47]This is somewhat surprising, as the keening tradition, with its related music, was still strong.

[48]R. Ó Foghludha, *Éigse na Máighe* (Dublin 1952), p. 136.

[49]*Gems of Melody* (Dublin, no date), II, pp. 10-13.

SUGGESTED LINKS BETWEEN EASTERN AND CELTIC MUSIC

FANNY FEEHAN

Speculation as to the Asian origin of Irish music surfaces from time to time: what is often posited depends on the predisposition of the enquirer. Some years ago, however, *Ceol* carried a review, by an anonymous writer, of Breandán Breathnach's *Folk Music and Dances of Ireland*, in which the reviewer argued that while one may speculate about the great age of some of the tunes "it was inconceivable, for instance, that all vestiges of the music that sustained our people for perhaps two thousand years could have vanished without trace".[1] The writer went on to relate how in the early days of broadcasting he had listened to 'moroccan singers' and their "tremulous, plaintive, circular chant to the accompaniment of a type of flute". It seemed to that listener, as it has to me for many years now, that the same combination of embroidery and ornamentation of the melody-line, in addition to the introspective attitude of the performer, might have been experienced in Connemara, Ring or in one of the now ruined cottages in the Comeragh Mountains or Nire Valley.

In 1976 I was invited by Dr. Frank Harrison, then Professor of Ethnomusicology in Amsterdam University, to attend one of the Musicultura Seminars at Queekhoven in Holland. This valuable series of meetings, which Harrison initiated and organised with the help of Ton de Leeuw and Felix van Lamsweerde, brought together the most distinguished of theorists and practitioners. Three seminars were held in all: in 1974, 1975, and 1976. The participants in 1976 included Dr. Sumati Mutatkar from the University of Delhi, Dr. Farhat of Tehran, Ranganayaki Ayangar of Bombay, Thanjavur Viswanathan, Middletown and from the Netherlands Emmy Nijenhuis (whose work on the rāgas of Somanàtha is of immense value), together with practitioners such as Imrat Khan and Mohammed Attiah Omar.

In his introduction to the 1976 Seminar, Ton de Leeuw touched several nerves when he stated: "the myth of progress is only on the surface. New technical devices can be employed by musicians, but the internal impetus is lacking . . . The widespread assumption that music is an insignificant factor in human development underlies this laissez-faire attitude. Everything that earlier thinkers and musicians have stated about music such as the high modal ethics of the Greeks, the Arabs, and the Hindus and those of our mediaeval philosophers becomes empty and meaningless. Music has been reduced to a luxury object."[2] In addition to this, we have never sufficiently probed in the West the role that music can play in the development of personality. If one listens to Maire Áine Ní Dhonnacha singing the Connemara version of *Úna Bhán* or to Jamil Bashir playing *arabesques* on the Ud, it becomes clear that both are inside the music in a way which is different to the manner that a violinist like Yehudi Menuhin will get 'inside' a Bach Partita. The Connemara woman and the Iraqi are personally involved while the composer comes between Menuhin and the music which he interprets.

In India, both North and South, the singer chooses the pitch which is convenient and keeps to it; the high voice is preferred. The Arabian maqam-iqa does allow of a drone, but it is not so frequent or evident as in India; the Arabian singer, on the other hand, uses the high voice which was preferred and even obligatory in sean-nós singing. Like the Indian, the Irish singer uses whatever pitch is convenient. As in some rāgas the great Irish songs revolve around three or four notes which recur again and again. "Marbhna Luimni" was composed, we are told, about 1635, but it is conceivable that the tune which circles like a vulture over a corpse round the notes E flat, F natural, G natural, B flat, G natural, F natural, and E flat could be transformed by changing the rhythm and altering pitch upwards a tone; the result, with a little imagination, could approach rāga style.

The Indian quarter-tone seems more predictable than those heard from a traditional Irish singer in Connemara. This would seem to suggest that rāga is a consciously acquired means of communication whereas the singer of an Irish slow air will, within a short space of time, produce elaborate ornamentation entirely as the spirit moves him or her. A piper or fiddler will act similarly in relation to a *roll* on the pipes or a slide or grace-note on fiddle. The point about all three is that they will rarely act the same way twice, no matter how many times they play or sing a slow air. The rāga singer has if necessary all day to come to his conclusions, and the audience is conscious of the modal function of the rāga as well as the diversification of the singer. In other words the Indian listener seems more sophisticated than the Irish peasant, teacher, musician or pub audience.

Comparisons will inevitably be drawn with the jazz performer who, like the Irish singer, rarely plays any tune exactly the same way twice no matter how well he may play it or know it. The audience simply would not expect it; indeed they would be bored, but like the sophisticated Indian audience they would applaud knowledgeably each small deviation. It is a simplistic exercise to point to negro superiority in the jazz genre and even more simplistic to talk about slaves bringing music from Africa to the United States, but nevertheless it could be reasonable for scholars to raise some questions.

In the area of vocal ornamentation East and West come close. I once played a Claddagh recording of Máire Áine singing "Bárr an tSléibhe" for an Indian Professor of music who refused to believe, until I showed her the sleeve of the record, that it was an Irish song. She claimed, and demonstrated by singing to me, that the song bore a strange resemblance to an Indian (North) rāga about a young girl being lured towards a mountain. The Professor was interested in the mode, the pitching of the voice, and certain notes which were characteristic of both the rāga and "Barr an tSléibhe."

Indian players and singers imbibe for years the music which they play or sing, and it was fascinating to those with whom I spoke at Queekhoven that Irish singers appear to give so little time to a song yet achieve almost similar results. Watching the Indian musicians tune themselves as carefully as a Western musician will tune an instrument, one cannot but reach the conclusion that those born on this side of the world have lost a very great deal. The late Father Henebry has pointed out that sometime prior to 1900 the sean-nós singer was over-run by the instrumentalist. What would he say about performers today with their alien instrumental accompaniment? "The modern educational system," Father Henebry wrote "enforces upon defenceless youngsters whatever fad happens to be uppermost at the time to the exclusion of all others; it has imposed this instrumental tradition everywhere, and, except in Ireland and a few out of the way places like it, has all but completely destroyed the very memory of European human music".[3] Henebry is no longer fashionable in Ireland, but he had a sure grasp of what it was that constituted a well laid-out slow singing air as distinct from an instrumental tune. Anybody who is truly interested in Irish music, should spare the time to read what he has to say because much of it remains extremely relevant. He did well when he spoke of the "grand class of music" in reference to singing airs because no instrument can take the place of a voice in diversity of ornamentation.

Henebry may not have known about the mathematician, Otto Zich, who lived in what is now known as Czechoslovakia and who died in 1909, but he was a collector of folk music as indefatigable as Henebry, Petrie or Bunting. He may not have known of Kodály, Bartók or Smetana, all of whom felt as strongly as Henebry about the memory of European music.

I have only a superficial knowledge of Indian music although that knowledge has been greatly augmented by Dr. E. Te Nijenhuis's magnificent books devoted to the Rāgas of Somanātha, Parts I and II. To attempt to demonstrate the links between the music of North and South India, Persia, North Africa, Spain and Ireland would be a lifetime's work. I have seen and heard enough, however, to be convinced that there are links and even if some of the proof is lacking the suggestions remain tantalising. We know that Irish monks founded the monastery of St. Gall, and we also know that Donat, or someone with a name occasionally spelled Donate, travelled to what is now Israel. Monsignor Patrick Boylan was for many years Professor of Oriental Languages at University College, Dublin, and he told me that he had seen manuscripts in Jerusalem which contained chants remarkably similar to those used in modern Synagogues and similar also to modes used in sean-nós. Egon Wellesz's *Byzantine Music and Hymnography* offers a few thoughts which would find no sympathy from Professor Fleishmann of Cork University: Wellesz refers to the pilgrim routes, and if melodies were brought to the Serbian Church from Syria, and were later introduced to the Balkan Church, by-passing Constantinople, there is no reason why some vestiges of this music did not reach this remote Atlantic island.

Investigations have shown that Arabic melody may have travelled in this way, and similarities found in the melodies follow some of the principles of composition in Oriental music. With the expansion of Christianity over the Mediterranean area, I understand that those competent to analyse Byzantine ecclesiastical music have reached somewhat similar conclusions.

I have also been struck by the remarkable similarity between sean-nós song and the Islamic call to prayer. Spain, of course, was Muslim and Moorish, and its schools in the ninth Century are said to have rivalled those of Baghdad. Alpharabus (Al-Fariba), the greatest thinker of Spanish Islam, had attributed to him the same story familiar to the Irish of the mythical figure who by changing the mode in which he was playing, could also change the mood of the listener from laughter to tears, and even induce sleep. Magical influences were not discounted in tenth-century Spain any more than in nineteenth-century Ireland. Islamic Spain was important not only for its musical achievement, but also for its influence on a large part of Europe, and there appears to be agreement that Arab theory stimulated the study of theoretical accoustics in Europe.

So far I have not discussed the harp, that instrument which has been adopted as a national symbol. The acknowledged authority on the harp in all its ramifications throughout Europe and Latin America is Joan Rimmer. In her book *The Irish Harp*, Miss Rimmer notes that in the earliest manuscript *cruit* is the word for a stringed instrument, and that it continues to be used as the Irish word for harp. She states that *cruit* is a cognate with *crwth, crotta, rote*, and *rota*, and that it is derived from the Indo-European root KER, meaning bent or curved.[4] Miss Rimmer also says, that while evidence is incomplete and fortuitous, there is no record in Europe of oblique lyres, and that those which appear on high crosses in Ireland may have been taken from near-Eastern sources. There were close links between Celtic Christian communities and those of the Near East, particularly Syria and Egypt, and Miss Rimmer suggests that the vertical harps of the Near East, while suited to that dry climate, may have been adapted later to the damp cold climate of Northern Europe.

For those who perceive links between Asia Minor and the West, there is little sympathy to be had from another scholar, Werner Bachman. In his book, *The Origin of Bowing*, he suggests that the only thing we took from the East was the bow itself, but while acknowledging his single-minded pursuit of the bow one could argue that Mr. Bachman does not pay sufficient attention to vocal style or the curious subtle ornamentation common to East and West. One is shaken a little in his judgment by the frequency with which he quotes Grattan-Flood while dismissing Fleishmann's much more authoritative *Music in Ireland*.

Fiddle-players have in the past been as important to dance music in Ireland as pipers. It is not always appreciated that fiddle-playing sounds different now to what it did in the late 'twenties or 'thirties of this century. One reason for this is the use of steel rather than gut strings, but more importantly the incursion into the traditional field of players who use the 'classical' bow grip and technique.

The tone produced in the past is quite different to that reproduced nowadays on modern recordings. As a child in Tipperary I heard many good fiddlers and vividly recall them holding the instrument across the chest, the button resting on the collar-bone while the bow was held in the fist, with only about six or seven inches of it being used. These fiddlers presented the same appearance as the musician sculpted on a stone in St. Finian's Church, Waterville, County Kerry, which is thought to date from the tenth century.

The fiddlers of my childhood produced a sour sound even in a slow air, but changes of bow were inaudible, and even with such a small section of the bow in use they were not inhibited in the number of notes which had to be squeezed in. It was only some years ago when I heard Joep Bor play the Sarangi that it was possible to hear again the type of tone so familiar to me, and which has now vanished. The loose wrist is to blame, in addition to the fact that so many traditional musicians have had some classical training, however slight. Bor spent many years in India studying the Sarangi which has thirty-six strings with a bridge made of bone, and I was interested to observe that it bears a reasonably close resemblance to the instrument held by the fiddler in St. Finian's Church in Waterville, reproduced in Werner Bachman's book *The Origin of Bowing* (Plate 92).

Another matter which deserves some attention is what Egon Wellesz calls 'the accoustic nature of the soul', and to which he devotes so much space in his *Ancient and Oriental Music* and *Byzantine Music and Hymnography*. In Ireland as recently as the 1920's the 'death rattle' was regarded by those who heard it as evidence that the soul had left the body. This, taken with the belief that every human being has his own sound or particular melody, and the custom whereby the personal song, or caoine, may only be sung after the individual has died, point to further similarities between early Irish and Asian belief.[5] In *The Face and Mind of Ireland* Arland Ussher draws attention to the importance of death rituals to the Irish: "in their attitude to bereavement," Ussher writes, "the Irish display richness and splendour of feeling *unequalled in any Christian nation*."[6] Ussher might perhaps have excepted Spain because it was in Spain that the classical Arabian tradition flourished in 713, and it was there also that modal variety was best employed.

Before the Second World War when I was about thirteen, I visited the middle island of Aran, and during my stay I was fortunate to experience at first hand the drama of the caoine. A young islander had died on the mainland in Galway and his body was being brought back to the middle island, Inishmaan, from Inishmore, where it had come by steamer, the Dun Aengus. The coffin was taken into a curragh which was escorted by five or six other curraghs rowed by relatives of the dead man. When the first curragh was sighted, the entire population of the middle island made its way to the quayside: the boats approaching were black against the sea, while the sky was a vivid pink. The women, assembled on the quayside wore their best clothes: red flannel petticoats, black aprons, and many of them had taken out their fawn and white shawls which had been handed down from mother to daughter or mother-in-law to daughter-in-law. The chief mourners, however, wore black shawls. When the boats were about three hundred yards from shore, an elderly woman, whom I was later told was the mother of the dead young man, broke into a thin wail which I at first thought was the cry of a seagull. This was later taken up by the other women, but not before the first woman had insisted that the boy was still alive: to this day I feel a shiver run down my spine when I recall that strange moment. The mother's insistence that he was alive, I was told, was because she personally had not heard the death-rattle nor had she closed his eyes.

So few people have heard of Maud MacCarthy or her links with India that I feel she should certainly be mentioned in this brief exploration of the similarities between Ireland and the music of the East. She was born in Tipperary in 1884 near Fethard. Her parents were affluent flour-millers, and when their daughter showed a good ear and a precocious talent for playing the violin, they were in a position to send her to London to study with the then fashionable teacher, Arbos. She made her debut at the age of nine in London (the Queens Hall has been mentioned, but I have not been able to verify that). Later she played concertos with Nikisch, Henry Wood, Manns and Richter all of whom were at the time conductors of great eminence. Everyone seems to agree that she had unusual talent as a violinist. Developing neuritis at the age of twenty-three, she met Mrs. Annie Besant and went with her to India where she became interested in Indian music and the scales. Later she returned to London and Oxford, having become something of an expert on Indian music, and was invited to lecture to the Folk Society and the Music Association. Most probably when she was in her late twenties or early thirties (I don't have the exact dates), she married the composer-cellist John Foulds, and took him back to India.

Prior to the nineteen-twenties Haba and others in Central Europe and Russia were composing music and inventing pianos capable of playing quarter-tones, while in America Charles Ives looked forward to the day when any schoolboy would whistle in quarter-tones. It may, therefore, have been the avant-garde thing to establish a liaison between Indian music and the micro-tone, but what interests me is that Maud MacCarthy had apparently no difficulty in singing quarter-tones, even when the big bell of Christ Church in Oxford was being tolled. This implies a remarkable ear or a predispositon towards tiny divisions. This capacity in older singers in Tipperary, West Waterford, and Connemara deserves more comment and investigation.

In conclusion, we may say that it is in the interpretation of the melody, and chiefly with regard to ornamentation, that some of the most significant resemblances between Irish and Eastern music can be observed. Melody without ornamentation has been likened to a night on which there is no moon. Depending on the circumstance, a singer uses ornamentation either as an integrated part of the melody or as an added decoration: depth and colour are added to the line. In South India this sophistication developed long before calligraphic documentation, and even today the accomplishment of a performer can be determined by his ingenuity in introducing small differences of ornamentation, or in the way he skilfully links one rāga with another, or rather slips from one to another. Similarly, most of us interested in Irish music will know how exciting, for example, Seamus Ennis can make a seemingly minute change in ornamentation or how Dennis Murphy can slip from one tune to another without altering the mood or key. Indian music affects life in that it has no specific beginning or end, but flows through the fingers uninterrupted. I like to think that some Irish music retains that characteristic.

I close with a warning: modern North American and European composers are turning increasingly for source material to Eastern and to Celtic traditional music with its wide parameters of tonality and capacity for rhythmic invention. This tendency may offer an avenue of escape from the narrow boundaries imposed by classical tradition in the West, but there is real danger that our post-industrial orientation may merely result in the distortion of a musical tradition without our ever having understood it in the first place.

NOTES

[1]*Ceoil*, Vol. IV, No. 2 (Dublin 1973), 65.

[2]Everett Helm ed., "Musicultura," in *The World of Music*, Vol. XX, No. 2 (1978), 20.

[3]*Handbook of Irish Music* (Cork 1928), p. 56

The Irish Harp (Cork 1969), p. 22.

[5]See Egon Wellesz, *Ancient and Oriental Music* , pp. 10-1. Wellesz writes: "Only after its owner's death may a friend or relative venture to sing the dead person's song at the funeral."

[6]*The Face and Mind of Ireland* (London 1950), p. 112. My italics.

SEÁN O RIADA

LOUIS MARCUS

Seán O Riada has been the outstanding artistic figure of post-war Ireland. With his flair and assurance, his sophisticated regard for tradition, his ability to fuse the native and the international in a synthesis that promised real development he typified those qualities of dynamism and national awakening for which Ireland so admired itself in the sixties.

He belonged very much to the short-lived Gaelic renascence that flowered in the sixties after half-a-century of stagnation, only to fade again in the venality and doubts of the seventies. But his achievement seems likely to endure.

In a country that confers popular laureateship only on writers (and only on safe ones at that), he succeeded in creating for himself the post of national composer. His music for George Morrison's Gael-Linn film "Mise Eire" is as fresh and moving now as it was twenty years ago. And while the disenchantment of the seventies has soured much of the enthusiasm for the Gaelic revival, the success of his Ceoltóirí Chualann experiment in the group performance of traditional music continues to spawn endless imitations ranging in style from purist to rock.

Yet for all the homage bestowed on O Riada during his life and in the ten years since his death, much about him remains neglected. Only a small part of his music (even of the most popular kind) is available on disc; only one of his scores has been published. His vibrant personality, perhaps the most brilliant of his time, will go unrecorded, as those who knew him grow forgetful and die. Eventually, O Riada may come to be regarded in a purely regional context as a man who struck a blow for native music.

If this were to happen, it would obscure much of O Riada's real significance. For while his contribution to the development of Irish music was momentous, it was powered by and was part of his broader commitment to music as an international art. O Riada was an artist in the modern sense of someone with an imperative need to interpret himself and his world through a chosen medium. He pursued that aim with a rare intensity. To recognise this is to enhance rather than diminish his contribution to the Irish tradition, and to explain something of its force.

I

In his youth in Cork, John Reidy was already a noted figure as one of the city's most promising violinists. One kept hearing about him — a degree at University College Cork, a stint in the music department of Radio Eireann, some months living in Paris, his return as musical director of the Abbey Theatre. He was said to be writing strange music — atonal or serial or some other of the new styles.

His arrival as a major musical talent, though little noticed at the time, came in

1958 when Seán Mac Réamoinn commissioned him to write the background music of two radio programmes for the opening of Radio Eireann's new Cork studios. In one of these, an evocation of the city by Robert O'Donoghue, John Reidy showed a startlingly mature command of orchestral mood and colour in capturing such diverse elements of Cork as its commercial bustle, historical mystery and romantic sense of *angoisse*.

In the other programme, a study of Gaelic Munster by Aindreas O Gallchóir, Reidy did something unique. He scored *sean nós* and other ancient traditional themes for orchestra in a way that leaped beyond the idiom of Victorian-Celtic to create a fusion of Gaelic and European music that was as revolutionary as it was successful. In particular, his arrangement of "Clár Bog Déil" for French horn over dark tremolando strings produced a genuine *frisson* and was a dress rehearsal for his later treatment of "Róisín Dubh."

By 1960, Seán O Riada had Gaelicised his name and had become a national figure with the release of the film "Mise Eire." He was glowing with the energy, self-confidence and glee of an artist who was enjoying both critical and popular success. He was earning only a pittance playing interval music with a tiny band in the Abbey Theatre, then operating in the Queen's. But his nightly theatre commitment spared him much of the wasteful bonhomie of the Dublin pubs, and in the Abbey you could have long talks with him while the curtain was up. If Ernest Blythe was not on the prowl, you could drink in one of the empty theatre bars. Otherwise you followed O Riada from the Stage Door, through a maze of smelly backstage passages and rickety stairways, to a cramped den lined with paperbacks in many languages.

He was a brilliant companion. His reading ranged from the ancient world to the latest science fiction (he had started Classics at University College Cork before changing to B.Mus.). Apart from Latin and Greek, he read in English, French, German and, increasingly, in Irish. He had strong enthusiasms (he adored Cavafy and that kind of Alexandrian decadence). There was nothing of the academic's considered caution in his response; he read with a greedy passion that fuelled his feelings to a high pitch.

II

He was a most complex person. He could discuss problems of mind and spirit with uncorporeal concern, yet he had the best collection of dirty stories I've ever heard. His theories of music and art were intricately abstract, but he was sensual to the point of being sybaritic. (One day he hauled me out of Peter Hunt's recording studio down to May's Music Shop where, in a listening booth at the back, he played a beautifully erotic new pop-record, "The Girl From Ipanema," with something like orgasmic relish.) He affected the down-to-earth, inverted snobbery of someone who could claim a bit of rural background, yet he luxuriated for a while in the ownership of a second-hand Jaguar, and if a cheque had arrived from a freelance job with Radio Eireann or Gael-Linn he would treat you to a gourmet lunch on his account at the Red Bank.

There were too many of him to be contained in one frame, however wiry. One day he would insist on speaking French, another only Irish. Sometimes he would be a Montenotte Corkman, other times a Viennese academic and yet others a West Cork peasant. But there was more to this than masks and mimicry, for he genuinely contained all of these elements. When the ebullience subsided, however, he was earnest and even anxious. For a time, he was to grow darker still.

Only one thing mattered to O Riada — his music. As a composer he had all the gifts to the point of genius — melodic invention, rhythmic subtlety, a feeling for harmonies that were fresh and true, an orchestral palette that ranged from the sumptuous to the bleak. He had abundant sensitivity and an imperative need to create. He had the drive and self-confidence essential in a world where composers were no longer kept by princes, archbishops or anyone else. He lacked only one thing — a language.

O Riada was born into a country that had missed two centuries of European musical development, and into a time when that development had itself collapsed in confusion. Unlike an artist in a stable framework, O Riada found a world in which there was chaos between the incongruous poles of serialism and Gaelic *sean nós*. I always felt that in his efforts (successful as they turned out) to rehabilitate the eighteenth-century harpist Carolan as a composer there was, along with genuine musical regard, a longing to touch the hand of the last Irishman for whom the Gaelic and European traditions of music were not irreconcilable.

Of course, the problem was not purely a musical one. Art does not exist in a social or historical vacuum. Both serialism and *sean nós* are responses to types of human experience. But these experiences, like their musical counterparts, were also worlds apart, for Ireland had long been isolated by geography, history and an element of choice from the upheavals of Western culture. O Riada was an exception. More than anyone working in the early sixties (perhaps more than any Irish artist since Joyce), the aged mind of Europe and its current *Zeitgeist* were to Seán matters of urgent reality rather than intellectual curiosity. The art and ideas of his time affected him deeply; he was shattered for days by Alain Resnais's film "Hiroshima Mon Amour." The way he littered his concert music with elements of ancient Greece, the Renaissance or German poetry was a necessity and not an affectation.

Had O Riada been satisfied to work in a purely regional context, he might have led a happy and useful life applying his superb taste and craftsmanship to various finite developments of Irish music. Or had he been shallow enough to strike a trendy international pose, he certainly had the equipment, both musical and intellectual, to sustain it. But his integrity would not allow him half-measures, or postures. Like Joyce, he had to integrate all of what he was in an artistically successful pattern. And, like Joyce, he had to create a language in which to do it.

III

So, faced with a gap of centuries in Ireland's musical development, O Riada set about filling it himself. He tried to work his way through the tunnel, and his experiments with Irish music can be seen as a series of stages in this process. But while he accomplished each step with taste and success, he was singularly unsatisfied himself. He seemed to look back on each layer with the indifference of a snake that has shed a redundant skin.

He was dismissive about his arrangements of reels, jigs and hornpipes for the Radio Eireann Light Orchestra, deft and all as they were. He deprecated his beautiful settings of Irish songs for baritone and piano (though he admired Tomás O Súilleabháin's fine recording of them). These had fused Gaelic melodies and the *Lieder* style of Europe with a grace that conquered any possible incongruity; but, once achieved, they left O Riada's thirst unquenched.

He even tired of Ceoltóirí Chualann, the chamber ensemble with which he revolutionised the group playing of traditional music in a development that continues still. While he was excited at first about the textural and rhythmic possibilities of the device, what he was really looking for was a development in musical form or expression. But this eluded him. Within a year of Ceoltóirí Chualann's successful launching, he complained irritably: "I can't take Irish music any farther." Although he continued to work with the group on radio, television and film, and to refine its texture along the way, it had early become yet another cul-de-sac in his restless search for a language.

The one achievement, apart from his concert music, that I never heard him disparage was his score for the film "Mise Eire." I think he realised that here he had done something quite extraordinary. Film music, of necessity, is a repository of established idioms. Vying with visuals, speech and sound-effects, it has to be instantly assimilable to the general ear and must therefore trade in well-worn currencies. The Hollywood romantic climax could never repay what it owes to Tchaikovsky and Rachmaninov.

Ideally, in an Ireland of unbroken musical development, any competent composer could have written a useful score for "Mise Eire" on the residue of our national contribution to the music of nineteenth-century Europe. But we made no such contribution; there was no Irish Smetana or Grieg to echo. O Riada's feat, dress-rehearsed in his Cork radio music of a few years before, was to write a film score in the idiom of an Irish symphonic period that had never happened.

This was true not only in melody, harmony and orchestration, but also in thematic development. If the complete tapes of his "Mise Eire" and other background music were made available along with their written scores (as opposed to the existing commercial discs that contain only the tuneful highlights), people could observe how O Riada developed fragments of themes such as "Róisín Dubh" and "Sliabh na mBan" through the inversions, variations and other personality changes that give European symphonic music its particular unity and fascination.

But even this genre was to lead to despair. When I asked O Riada to write the music for "An Tine Bheo," the 50th anniversary film of the Easter Rising which I was making through Gael-Linn for the official Commemoration Committee, he had already written not only "Mise Eire" and "Saoirse?" but several radio scores on that subject for Radio Eireann and the BBC. He wanted to do something different, to get away from what had become a stock nationalist idiom. But the film was commissioned as an official celebration of an official mythology for an audience that, in 1966, was still blissfully free of the doubts and shadows of the coming decade. It would have to be well-known tunes yet again, treated with the dignified élan which O Riada had so well imparted before to the national struggle.

As the time for the recording approached, with Seán silent in the Co. Cork village of Cúil Aodha to which he had moved from Dublin, I began to fear for our very tight schedule. But he never missed a deadline, even one as formidable as this. The result, within the limits of that particular film, was another miracle of freshness and invention. But it cost him more than anything of the kind ever had.

With the recording date only days away, he wrote from Cúil Aodha:

"Herewith all the music *except* for Music 17, at which my imagination is still boggling. However, I hope to have it to you in the first post tomorrow . . .
This is the hardest job I have ever had to do — to try and bring a fresh mind to this subject — my mind was already overexposed to 1916 before I started. I know now what my hell will be."

IV

He had already experienced at least one other hell that I knew of. It started towards the end of 1961, when he was still living in Dublin, and lasted several months. No doubt there were personal problems involved, and the strain of trying to keep a large family on a few pounds a week didn't help either. But the crisis went much deeper than that. While he maintained something of his public ebullience, in private he was sometimes close to tears and, I feared, to losing his reason.

As usual with Seán, the manifestations were diverse and brilliant. One day in the Oval Bar, with only a pound between the two of us to get drunk on, he was agonising about the limit he seemed to have reached with Irish music. (Only in his later liturgical music was he to make any further real advance.) Suddenly he began to tell me with manic glee his idea for a musical horror film to be called "The Killer Chord."

The hero is a renowned composer who performs secret experiments on the lethal possibilities of music. Starting with the known power of sound to smash a glass, he discovers increasingly ghastly potential for destruction. Finally, he devises a chord which, by its particular combination of pitches, harmonies, tone colour, volume and duration, could kill the listener.

His next work is announced with the startling news that the final chord will not be played in rehearsal and that the orchestral parts for it will be distributed only as the concert begins. Tension mounts as we see the work performed and observe not only the musicians and audience in the concert hall, but also the millions listening at home or on car radios. As the final moment approaches, the composer, who conducts the piece himself, stuffs his ears with impenetrable plugs. Then the fatal chord is played. The orchestra and audience collapse dead, people slump by their firesides all over the country and cars with radios slaughter hundreds as they career out of control. The composer, calmly removing his ear plugs, has survived. I pointed out to Seán that such an event would decimate the cultured section of society and leave the rest virtually unscathed. He didn't seem to mind.

There were blacker moments though. Antonioni's film L'Aventura caused him the anguish that Resnais had a year before. "It's about giving, about not being able to give any more. Either in your work or in your life, you've got to give. But," he added ruefully, "you can't do it in both." For a few days he was obsessed with the idea of going to live in Rome. But that passed. He was very disturbed too by an ancient poem he had come across in Irish about a child, locked in a prison cell, who knocks on the wall but receives no reply. He listened to music a lot at this time, music that seemed to have some urgent meaning for him: Edith Piaf, "She's saying no, but she's saying it affirmatively;" and Mahler's "Das Lied von der Erde," in which the agony on the word "Ewig" always brought tears to his eyes.

At the root of all this anxiety seemed to be his struggles with his new work, the Nomos No. 2. Scored for baritone, choir and orchestra, it was based on verses from the Theban plays of Sophocles that were drenched in the knowing pessimism that so assailed O Riada at that time. But his despair was at least as much artistic as it was emotional. For he could not solve the musical problems of the work. For a time he was elated when he hit upon the rhythmic figure, a dactyl and spondee, that he felt was at the core of European music and on which his ideas for the Nomos blossomed.

But eventually he came up against the ultimate problem of form. With the collapse of European sonata form, the question of how to organise a major work was a daunting one. O Riada revelled in the cyclic form of the Gaelic tradition, which applied layer after layer of ornamentation on the basic frame. He could argue eloquently that this was the characteristic mould of the Celtic creative imagination, citing examples as remote from each other as the Book of Kells and Joyce. But he knew it was not the answer to the Nomos problem. Also, he sensed that the solution to this problem was bound up with questions of underlying meaning and of the artist's ability to overcome some terror involved in facing it.

I didn't have the musical training to follow his reasoning, or perhaps he only needed to expiate verbally some of his inner anxiety, but he explained to me once in despair how Brahms had failed to resolve this joint problem of form and vision in the last movement of his 4th Symphony ("funked it" was O Riada's phrase) and had taken purely technical refuge in a *passacaglia*. Beethoven too had failed in the last movement of the Ninth, though, as Seán put it, "not for a lack of guts."

As it turned out, O Riada's solution was a startling one. As he hummed his way through the completed score for me one day, I could not suppress my disbelief as we came to the first of the quotations with which he peppered the end of the Nomos —

the opening bars of Mozart's 40th Symphony. After some frenzied choral play with sardonic use of the word "happy", there came a quote from the Beethoven 7th. Finally we had the start of Brahms's "St. Anthony Chorale." All of these quotations, incidentally, featured that form of a dactyl and spondee (or its inversion) which meant so much in O Riada's view of European music.

These quotations have been faulted by some critics for introducing an extramusical idea into the work, for using music to make an intellectual statement about the death of the European tradition. This is a valid reservation. But it seems to ignore the resonance that this device has given to so much else in modern art. Some of the best effects in Eliot and Joyce arise from the ironies, paradoxes and poignancies evoked by juxtaposing the emptiness of the present with the glories of the classical past. O Riada was certainly daring in his use of this tool in the Nomos. I am not yet sure that he was wrong.

I have referred more than once to similarities between O Riada and Joyce. Naturally, one could take any such correspondence too far, but in several respects it holds true. Both were possessed by a demonic need to forge an uncreated conscience, their own as much as their country's. Both had the gifts to pastiche their way through to easy success, but neither was venal enough to attempt it. Both spurned the provincial Irish idiom of their time and sought its renewal through the cauldron of Europe. And both found it necessary, at different times in their lives, to flee from the paralysis of Dublin.

Yet this is where their ways parted. Joyce went into exile. O Riada, with his adoption of the Gaelic world and his eventual remove to the Irish-speaking village of Cúil Aodha, went into a state for which there is no word in the English language because it is unknown in English experience. Could one call it "in-ile"? At any rate they both understood keenly and struggled to their utmost with the acute problems of the modern Irish artist who aspires to see the universe in the lineaments of his own land. And in this they shared one other supreme quality — courage. Joyce was bloody-minded about his purpose; O Riada may not have been quite so ruthless. But he gave all that he had, including his health and, eventually, his life.

Plate 1: Sean O'Riada. Photograph, 1960, by Lensman, courtesy of Gael-Linn, Dublin.

O'RIADA'S FAREWELL

JOHN MONTAGUE

Roving, unsatisfied ghost,
old friend, lean closer;
leave us your skills:
lie still in the quiet
of your chosen earth.

Woodtown Manor, Again

I

We vigil by the dying fire,
talk stilled for once,
foil clash of rivalry,
fierce Samurai pretence.

Outside a rustle of bramble,
jack fox around the framing
elegance of a friend's house
we both choose to love:

two natives warming ourselves
at the revived fire
in a high ceiling room
worthy of Carolan —

clatter of harpsichord
the music leaping
like a long candle flame
to light ancestral faces

pride of music
pride of race

II

Abruptly, closer to self-revelation
than I have ever seen, you speak;
bubbles of unhappiness breaking
the bright surface of *Till Eulenspiegel.*

I am in great danger, you whisper,
as much to the failing fire
as to your friend & listener;
though, *you have great luck.*

Our roles reversed, myself cast
as the light-fingered master,
the lucky dancer on thin ice,
rope walker on the precipice.

III

Magisterial, ruddy moustached,
smiling, I sense the strain
behind your jay's laugh,
your sharp player's mask.

Instinct wrung and run
awry all day, powers idled
to self-defeat, the vacuum
behind the catalyst's gift.

Beyond the flourish
of personality, peacock
pride of music or language:
a constant, piercing torment!

Signs earlier, a stranger
made to stumble at a bar door,
fatal confusion of the powers
of the upper and lower air.

A playing with fire, leading
you, finally, tempting you
to the unforgiveable, the
calling of death for another.

IV

A door opens,
and she steps into the room,
smothered in a black gown,
harsh black hair falling to her knees,
a pale tearstained face.

How pretty you look,
Miss Death!

V

Samhain

Sing a song
for the mistress
of the bones

the player
on the black keys
the darker harmonies

light jig
of shoe buckles
on a coffin lid

*

pale glint
of the wrecker's lantern
on a jagged cliff

across the ceaseless
glitter of the spume:
a seagull's creak.

the damp haired
seaweed stained sorceress
marshlight of defeat

*

chill of winter
a slowly failing fire
faltering desire

Darkness of Darkness
we meet on our way
in loneliness

Blind Carolan
Blind Raftery
Blind Tadgh

VI

Hell Fire Club

Around the house all night
dark music of the underworld,
hyena howl of the unsatisfied,
latch creak, shutter sigh,
the groan and clash of trees,
a cloud upon the moon.

Released demons moan.
A monstrous black tom
crouches on the roofbeam.
The widowed peacock screams
knowing the fox's tooth:
a cry, like rending silk

& a smell of carrion where
baulked of their prey,
from pane to tall window
pane, they flit, howling
to where he lies, who has
called them from defeat.

Now, their luckless meat,
turning a white pillowed room,
smooth as a bridal suite
into a hospital bed where
a lucid beast fights against
a blithely summoned doom.

At the eye of the storm
a central calm, where
tearstained, a girl child
sleeps cradled in my arms
till the morning points
and you are gone.

VII

The Two Gifts

And a nation mourns:
The blind horseman with his harp-carrying servant,
Hurrying through darkness to a great house
Where a lordly welcome waits, as here:
Fingernail spikes in candlelight recall
A ripple & rush of upland streams,
The slant of rain on void eye sockets,
The shrill of snipe over mountains
Where a few stragglers nest in bracken —
After Kinsale, after Limerick, after Aughrim,
After another defeat, to be redeemed
By the curlew sorrow of an aisling.

    The little Black Rose
    (To be sprinkled with tears)
    The Silk of the Kine
    (To be shipped as dead meat)

    'They tore out my tongue
    So I grew another one',
    I heard a severed head
    Sing down a bloody stream.

But a lonelier lady mourns,
the muse of a man's particular gift,
Mozart's impossible marriage of fire & ice,
skull sweetness of the last quartets,
Mahler's horn wakening the autumn forest,
the harsh blood pulse of Stravinsky,
the hammer of Boulez
               which you will never lift.

Never to be named with your peers,
I am in great danger, he said;
firecastles of flame,
a name extinguished.

VIII

Lament

With no family
& no country

a voice rises
out of the threatened beat
of the heart & the brain cells

(not for the broken people
nor for the blood soaked earth)

a voice
like an animal howling
to itself on a hillside
in the empty church of the world

a scream
an imprecation
a yelp
a cry

a lament so total
it mourns no one
but the globe itself
turning in endless halls

of space, populated
with passionless stars

and that always raised voice

CELTIC CALLIGRAPHY:
FROM PENSTROKE TO PRINT

LIAM MILLER *and* PAT MUSICK

I

Over twelve hundred years ago Irish scribes developed a book hand which has never been excelled and seldom equalled as a vehicle for the visual expression of words. To this scribal hand the Western world owes the form of the so-called Roman lowercase or small letters in which the greater part of Western writing is presented today. These letterforms, combined with Roman capitals and Arabic numerals, make up our complete equipment for the visual presentation of language. In the native letterforms of Ireland, then, we have an important link in the social and aesthetic development of Western culture.

II

According to legend, the earliest known writing system in Ireland, called Ogham, originated with seven strokes made by the Celtic God Lugh on a birch branch. Archaeologists conjecture that it developed in the third to the fifth centuries. It consists of up to five straight lines on either side of, or intersecting — at right angles or diagonally — a central line. It was used primarily for memorial inscriptions on standing stones but it appears in some Irish medieval manuscripts. From Ireland the system spread to Wales, Devon, Cornwall, the Isle of Man, and Scotland.

During the fifth century the introduction of Christianity into Ireland led to the establishment of a great monastic tradition, and in a comparatively short time Ireland became a centre of learning and Irish scribes developed from the Roman alphabet a cursive script of great beauty and clarity and of a highly practical form for the recording of texts. The inscriptional capitals of the Roman Empire could, in turn, trace their descent through the Greek and Hellenic letters back to the Phoenician. From their incised inscriptional letters the Romans developed written forms. A cursive, stylus-written version of Rustic was early Roman Cursive; both these scripts date from before 100 A.D. By the fourth century Late Roman Cursive (still written with a pointed pen, giving a letter line like that produced with a stylus) was the common business hand, while uncial and half-uncial scripts had been developed as bookhands. Both of the latter were written with an edged pen at a constant, fairly flat angle. Elements of all these styles appear in the earliest example of Irish writing in the Roman alphabet. The wedge-shaped serif, unique to insular scripts, was probably stylized from the 'blobs' formed by the edged pen when making the loops found in the stylus-written cursive. The Irish style of writing developed from the fourth and fifth-century Roman quarter-uncial styles which were brought to early Christian Ireland. Formal and informal scripts developed and reached their greatest power of beauty and expression in Latin manuscripts from the seventh to the ninth centuries.

The formal, round script is generally known as insular majuscule; the more cursive, less formal one as miniscule. The informal script was used as the normal style for practical writing, including less elaborate religious and classical works, and the recording of deeds, annals and stories in the Irish language. In the calligraphy of the Western traditions, from classical Greece and Rome to Judaism, Islam and Christianity, variations in line thickness were formed by an edged pen generally held with constant pressure at a constant angle. Direction of the stroke — horizontal, vertical, diagonal — determined the stroke width, and the width of the pen nib served as a unit of proportion in the letters. Formal scripts tended to be written with a fairly flat pen angle, producing thick vertical and thin horizontal strokes. A steeper pen angle was maintained for producing less formal, cursive strokes. Texts in the Irish language are generally found in such semi-formal hands,

Plate 1: Springmount Bog Tablet, late sixth century.

often as interlinear glosses in the manuscripts between the lines of formal uncial, and many of the manuscripts which record the Irish historical and cultural traditions, such as the *Liber Hymnorum* in Trinity College Dublin, are written in this style.

The earliest example of Irish writing in the Roman alphabet is a fragment of the

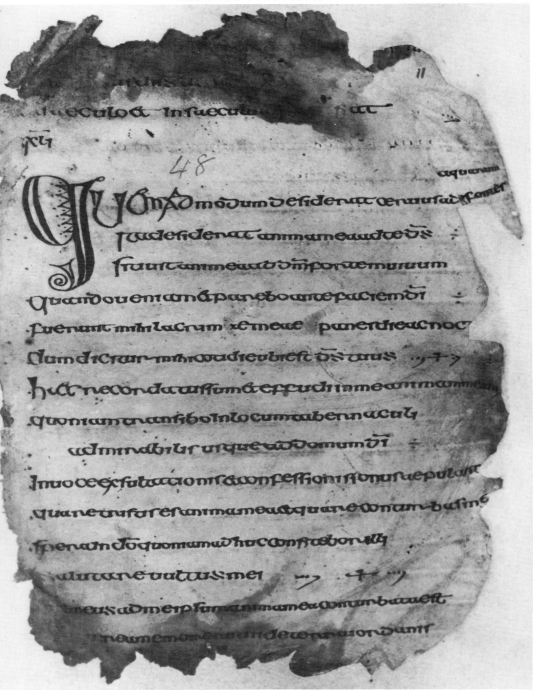

Plate 2: The Cathach, 560 A.D.

psalms written with a stylus on wax-coated yew-wood tablets found in Spring-mount Bog, County Antrim, and dated to the late sixth century (it is now in the National Museum of Ireland). The writing is a version of the Italian quarter uncial script (a further distinction between uncial and half-uncial), which appears written with an edged pen in Codex Usserianus I (Trinity College Dublin). Most of the letter forms and the loops on ascender strokes prefigure characteristic features of the majuscule script later developed in Ireland and Northumbria.

The first example of Irish majuscule writing is the calligraphy of the Cathach in the Royal Irish Academy, dated at 560 A.D. by Dr. Gunther Haseloff, Wurzburg. The loops of the cursive script have become stylized wedge-shaped serifs; the letters are wide in proportion to their height, and letters following a decorated initial gradually decrease in size until they are the same as the rest of the text, characteristics found in later insular majuscule manuscripts.

These decorated initials are the forerunners of one of the most elaborate aspects of Irish manuscript art. If the act of writing developed into an art, the decoration of initial letters flowered as never before or since. Whole pages were painted in asymmetric, colourful, and highly detailed compositions, sometimes so complex that the fact that the design was based on lettering was almost obscured. Initial letters in the text displayed a similar inventiveness, formed as twisted animals or as near-abstract geometric designs.

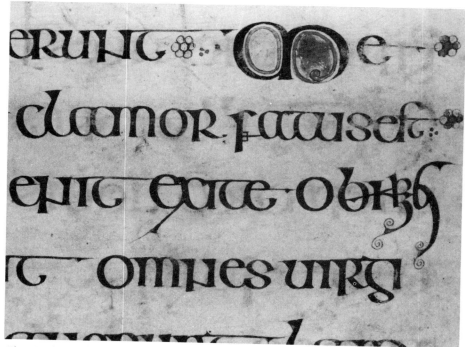

Plate 3: The Book of Kells.

With use in more and more elegant manuscripts, the script became increasingly refined. Features like the serifs, the curvature and proportions of letters, finishing touches at the end of pen strokes, and ingenious treatment of the letters themselves became characteristic of the style. Unusual treatment of letters generally was for the purposes of adjusting spacing and it included decorative elongation of letters or parts of letters, abbreviated forms of letters, letters turned sideways, written inside, above, below, or between other letters, and letters intricably joined as monograms or ligatures.

This scribal ebullience is at its peak in the Book of Kells, early ninth century (Trinity College Dublin). The letterforms themselves are more subtle and graceful than in most insular majuscule, though judging by the appearance of the ink, the pen moved with a steady rhythm, not with painstaking hesitation.

The calligraphy in the Lichfield Gospels (Lichfield Cathedral Library) is very similar to that in Kells, though more highly retouched by the scribe. The decoration in Lichfield recalls that of the Lindisfarne Gospels, a Northumbrian manuscript of the late seventh or early eighth century. Its calligraphy is extremely regular and exhibits the inventive space-saving device of stacking letters above and below one another, sometimes guided by an extended ascender or descender. The Gospels of MacRegol (Bodleian Library) are written in a heavy, bold and rather careless hand full of character. Numerous other insular majuscule manuscripts dating from the seventh to the ninth centuries are in collections in Ireland, Britain, the Continent and America.

In the early period the scribes wrote on vellum — calfskin — with pens cut from the quills of large birds such as goose, swan, or possibly raven. Ink was generally made from tannic acid derived from oak galls (although one poem mentions 'ink of the green-skinned holly'); a thicker blacker ink was made from lampblack, the soot or carbon obtained from burning pitch, resin, or some other substance. Later scribes wrote on paper rather than skins.

III

Although the period of lavishly ornamented gospel books came to an end, the importance of scribes and of manuscipts continued, not only in religious centres, but also in the secular schools of law, poetry, and so forth, until the seventeenth century. Scribes were accorded distinction in the Annals, and according to the Brehon Laws whoever shed the blood of a scribe was liable to crucifixion or a fine of seven slave girls. An entry in the Book of Ballymote records that it was sold by the MacDonaghs to Aed Dubh O'Donnell for 140 milch cows. An entry in the Lebor na hUidre records how it and the Lebor Gerr (Short Book) were forcibly recovered by Hugh Roe O'Neill from the men of Connaught, after having been given as a ransom for two prisoners more than a century before. The seventh-century Book of Durrow, valued as a holy relic, was used in medieval times as a cure for sick cows, by dipping it in water and giving the water to the cows to drink.

The scribes seem constantly to have been jotting in their margins various comments on the text, complaints about their materials or the cold, bits of verse, remarks about the purpose for which they were copying:

...'let me not be blamed for the script, for the ink is bad, and the vellum defective, and the day is dark.'

'Here ends the book of Walter on the doses of medicines. Cormac MacDonlevy turned the substance of it into Gaelic for Dermot O'Lyne and may it be profitable for him and his children (1459).'

'Uch a lam/Ar scribis do memrum ban!/Béra in memrum fa buaidh/Is bethair si ad benn lom cuail cnam. ('Alas, O hand, how much white vellum hast thou written! Thou wilt make famous the vellum, while thou thyself will be the bare top of a faggot of bones!').

'The poor simple friar Michael O'Clery ... whose inheritance it is from my ancestors to be a chronicler ... I wrote this as I found it, but I confess that a great deal of it is disgusting and false, and in much of it utter nonsense; but I make my excuse that it was enjoined on me to follow the track of the old books.'

[Brother Michael] ' ... sought and serached every part of Erin in which he had heard there was a good or even a bad book [Gaelic *mss.*], so that he spent four full years in transcribing and procuring the matters that related to the saints of Erin. However, though great his labour and his hardships, he was able to find but a few out of the many of them, because strangers had carried off the principal books of Erin into remote and unknown foreign countries and nations, so that they have left her but an insignificant part of her books.' (M. O'Clery, 1630).

Plate 4: Autograph signature of Michael O'Clery, seventeenth century.

Professional hereditary scribes continued to be employed until the nineteenth century. The copy made by Joseph O'Longan in the 1870's of the old manuscript, Lebor na hUidre (Book of the Dun Cow) is so exact that he even squeezed and bent his writing on paper to simulate the slight distortions of letters around a tear in the original vellum that had widened over the years.

The Irish manuscript tradition continues today. *Leabhar na hAiseirghe* (the Book of the Resurrection) was begun in 1921 and commemorates 'those who died for the Irish republic since 1916'. It consists of some twenty-six pages of complex twentieth-century Celtic illumination and lettering by Art O Murnaghan. The book is preserved in the National Museum in Dublin.

The Roscrea Missal is a manuscript altar Missal written in a script inspired by twelfth century Irish hands, using various edged pens, Japanese stick ink, and egg tempera on handmade paper. The approximately 150 pages were written in "a month of nights and a couple of days." The scribe, Timothy O'Neill, is virtually self-taught and in the last few years he has experimented with scripts based on various historic Irish styles.

IV

In *Writing, Illuminating and Lettering* (1906), Edward Johnston writes of the Irish scribes and the great illuminated Irish manuscripts: "As a beautiful writing they attained in the seventh century a degree of perfection since unequalled." In the centuries after the fall of the Roman Empire Irish monastic influence spread throughout Western Europe, and manuscripts in that tradition were produced in the scriptoria of many monasteries, playing a vital part in the preservation of traditions of learning which would otherwise have been lost during the Dark Ages. The Carolingian hand associated with Charlemagne's empire is a close derivative of the scripts used in the Irish monastic settlements in Europe which provided the teachers and scribes for Charlemagne's court. The Carolingian hand was, in turn,

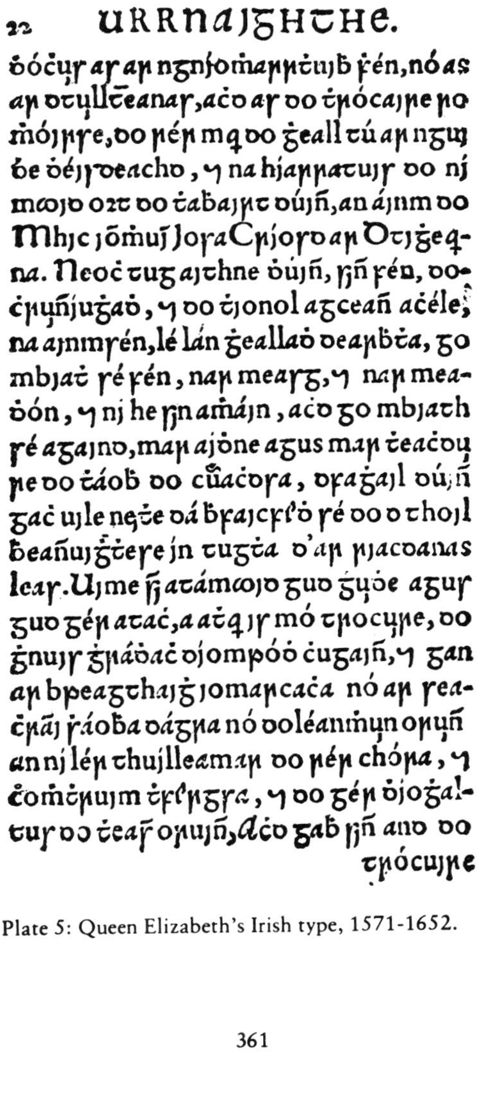

22 URRNAJŜHƆHE.

óócuſ aſ aſ ngnſomaſſcuꞁꞃ ſén, nó as
aſ ocuꞁꞇeanaſ, acó aſ oo cſócaꞁꞃe ſo
móꞁſſe, oo ſéſ mq oo ŝeall cú aſ nŝuꞁ
be óéꞁſoeacho, ꞇ na hꞁaſſacuꞁſ oo nꞁ
moꞁo oꞇ oo ċabaꞁſc óúꞁñ, an áꞁnm oo
Mhꞁc ꞁómuꞁ Joꞃa Cſꞁoſo aſ Oꞇꞁŝeq-
na. Neoꞇ cuŝ aꞁchne óúꞁñ, ꞁꞁñ ſén, oo-
ċſuñꞁuŝaó, ꞇ oo ꞇꞁonol aŝceañ aꞇéleꞁ
na aꞁnmſén, lé lán ŝeallaó oeaſbꞇa, ŝo
mbꞁaꞇ ſé ſén, naſ meaſŝ, ꞇ naſ mea-
óón, ꞇ nꞁ he ſñ amáꞁn, acó ŝo mbꞁach
ſé aŝaꞁno, maſ aꞁóne aŝus maſ ꞇeaꞇoꞁ
ſe oo ꞇáob oo cúaꞇoſa, oſaŝaꞁl óúꞁñ
ŝaꞇ uꞁle neꞇe oá bſaꞁcſſó ſé oo o choꞁl
beañuꞁŝꞇeſe ꞁn cuŝꞇa o'aſ ꞁꞁacoaꞁus
leaſ. Uꞁme ſſ acámoꞁo ŝuo ŝuóe aŝuſ
ŝuo ŝéſ acaꞇ, a aꞇq ꞁſ mó cſocuſe, oo
ŝnuꞁſ ŝſáóaꞇ óꞁompóó cuŝaꞁñ, ꞇ ŝan
aſ bſeaŝchaꞁŝ ꞁomaſcaꞇa nó aſ ſea-
ċſáꞁ ſáoba oáŝſa nó ooléanmuſ oſuñ
an nꞁ léſ chuꞁlleamaſ oo ſéſ chóſa, ꞇ
ꞇomꞇſuꞁm ꞇſſſŝſa, ꞇ oo ŝéſ óꞁoŝaꞁ-
cuſ oo ꞇeaſ oſuꞁñ, acó ŝab ſſñ ano oo
cſócuꞁſe

Plate 5: Queen Elizabeth's Irish type, 1571-1652.

the model for the humanistic script which had developed and was perfected in Northern Italy by the fifteenth century and on which the first Roman lowercase printing types were based. Roman lowercase printing types are thus more nearly derived from Irish forms than from any other model.

The first Irish printing house was established in Dublin about 1550 by order of the Privy Council in England, and the first types for printing in the Irish language were made in 1571 for the express purpose of printing Protestant texts. The fount was adapted from an existing Anglo-Saxon type by cutting the necessary extra characters and by 'borrowing' from an available Roman fount. This first type, generally known as 'Queen Elizabeth's type,' cannot really be regarded as an Irish typeface. The type remained in use in Dublin until 1652 after which date it apparently was not used, nor were any further types made after this model.

The appearance of 'Queen Elizabeth's type' prompted a retaliation by the Catholics and in 1611 the Irish Franciscans, exiled at Louvain, had a type cut to print devotional and historical texts in Irish. Probably cut at Antwerp by a local craftsman, the type was based on a semi-formal contemporary hand. As a type design the result was disastrous; the punch cutter, unfamiliar with either the Irish

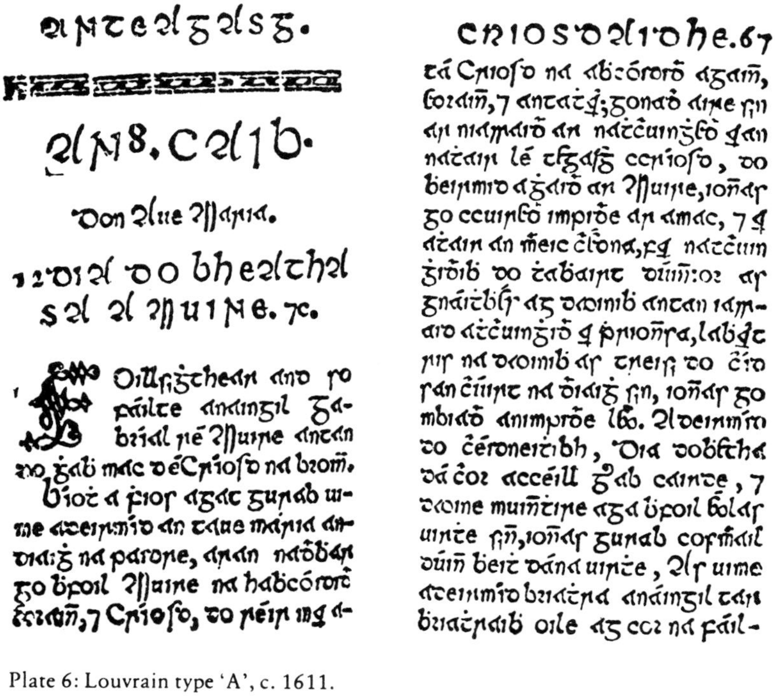

Plate 6: Louvrain type 'A', c. 1611.

language or Irish calligraphy, produced an exotic type that intensified the peculiarities in his model, resulting in a spiky, ill-fitting and uneven design of poor legibility.

The next Irish type cut in London for Protestant use, that cut by Edward Moxon in 1680, was modelled on the Louvain fount which thus became the prototype both for the Catholic founts cut at Louvain, Rome and Paris and for the 'Bible' founts cut in London during the succeeding one hundred and fifty years. One of the

loChR2ᴎᴎ ᴎ2l

ʒcꞃejˑomheᴈch.]

Ⱶ1oʒaᴅ ꝺ1oʒlomċa , aꞃ ᴅa pꞃ1oṁuʒꝺaꞃv1ɓ lʒ ꞇꞃaċꝺaꞃᴏ lejʒeaṅ ᴅa ɓſꞇa1ꝺh , ꞃaṅꞇa a ꞇꞃ1 ccoꝺċꞃɓ; a ꞇſʒaſʒ ċꞃ1oꞅ· oꞃꝺe , á m1ᴅ1ᴅʒaꝺ ᴅa ᴅajꞃꞇſʒal , ꞃa mb1 lꞃꝼ a1ᴅbꝼ1ꞃ ꝺeaꞃba1ꝺ á ꞇꞃʒſ1oᴅa , aʒ ꞇabċaṅ ᴅa ccꞃejˑomheach; 7 á ccomh- ꞃaꝺ ʒeaꝃ ꞃjmpl1ꝺe , lʒ cclao1ꝺꞇſ1 ʒaċ ꞃoꞃꞇ ejꞇꞃ1ce ʒo huꞃaꞅca , 7 lʒ ᴅꝺa1ᴅʒ̄n1- ꞇſ1 ᴅa caꞇo1l1c1 ʒo lejꞃ v̇le ꞃaᴅ ccꞃe1ˑoſ̄m ċo1ꞃ . 2lꞃ ᴅa chꞃꞃ a cclo ꞃaᴅ Ꞃomh , ma1lle ꞃe vʒhˑoaꞃaꞃ San Ꝺhꞃoꞃa- ʒaᴅꝺa , le bꞃaꞇꝭ boꝼ ꝺoꞃꝺ S. Ꞅꞃojᴅſ1aꞅ . Ꞅꞃojᴅſ1aꞅ ó Ꞃꝭolṁua1ꝺ, 1 6 7 6 .

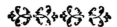

Plate 7: Rome (Propaganda) type, c. 1675.

Rome publications was an Irish Catechism, *Lucerna Fidelium*, published by the Propaganda Press in 1676.

During the early part of the nineteenth century some founts were cut in which mechanical regularity was imposed on the letter forms, but it was not until 1840 that a type was created which was based on the formal manuscript lettering of the early Christian period. In that year the Irish Archaeological Society announced the forthcoming publication of John O'Donovan's edition of *The Annals of the Kingdom of Ireland*, stating that "considerable expense and trouble have been incurred in selecting models for the Irish type, from the best written and most valuable of the early Irish manuscripts." The typeface, designed by George Petrie, was used for a number of publications by the Society, including the *Leabhar Imuinn* (Book of Hymns of the Ancient Church of Ireland), published in 1869. It is an unusual example of actual Irish-character typographic design, not merely the use of an Irish typeface.

χps in nostra. Nimnib lámiban mac echach irre bo pigni hunc çmnum bo brigic. Uel ir piac rleibce bo pigne. Dicunc alii combab Ultan airbbrccean bo gnec. An ire no teclamarcan penca brigce in oén lcbon. Aubice uirginir lauber ire a chorpach. Onb airgicncch rain. Tpé pichim bna bo pigneb. Tri caibcil anb, 7 cechri líni cech caibcil 7 re rillaba béc cech líne. Dicunc alii combab mór incimmunpra, achc ni railec runb achc cechri caibcil bc, .i. in cec caibcil, 7 na cri caibcil bebencha, caura breuicacir.

ps in nostra insola que uocatur hibernia
ostensus est hominibus maximis mirabilibus
que perfecit per felicem celestis uite uirginem
precellentem pro merito magno in mundi circulo

ς mnus iste angelice summeque sancte brigice
fari non ualet omnia uirtutum mirabilia
que nostris nunquam auribus si sint facta audiuimus
nisi per istam uirginem marie sancte similem

Plate 8: Irish Archaeological Society type, Dublin, c. 1840.

'Colmcille,' designed by Colm O Lochlainn and cut by Monotype in 1930, was the first attempt to apply the traditions of Irish letter design to the problems of producing a type suitable for the machines of the day. It provides a full alphabet with accents necessary for Irish printing and alternative forms for some characters. It is the only Irish typeface with an accompanying italic.

Ro bá bruigean ar tír agus bruigean ar
cuinn aige, agur no cappaing ré pig an bomain
agur cri pigce Innre cuile gur an mbruigin no bá
an cuinn aige, fá comain bo cinn bo bain biocra.
Ro bá an fleab bá cabairc amac ar an mbruigin no bá ar cír aige, agur cug ré cuireab

Colmcille (Monotype 121) – see (15)

Plate 9: Colmcille, designed by Colm O Lochlainn, 1930.

The lifetime work of Victor Hammer in studying and designing with uncial letterforms has resulted in the most successful 'round' typefaces now in use. 'Hammer Uncial' and 'American Uncial' are constantly seen both in Ireland and all over the world, from book covers to building signs and in conjunction with every subject from greeting cards to Oriental art. This international popularity demonstrates a real interest in well-designed typefaces derived from 'round' manuscript letterforms.

V

Plate 10: Stone-cut building sign by Michael Biggs, Dublin, c. 1970.

Modern use of the Irish lettering style includes fine work in books and inscriptions, building and street signs, banknotes, and in advertising of Irish products. In the design of the new Irish banknotes some traditional features of banknote design were retained while the design team departed from others. Portraits were retained for their security value. The curlicues and geometric lines of nineteenth-century banknote design were replaced by lettering associated with the figure portrayed: on the £5, from manuscripts contemporary to John Scotus Eriugena; on the £1, from the earliest manuscript in Irish, telling the story of Queen Medb and the Tain. Modern printing technology, such as phototypesetting, escapes many of the constraints of metal type. Modern designers can thus more easily take inspiration from some of the unique calligraphic treatment of letterforms found in the Irish manuscripts of centuries ago.

Plate 11: Lettering on telephone kiosk, Dublin.

LIAM MILLER'S DOLMEN PRESS

SOREL ETROG

In his article on Celtic Calligraphy, Liam Miller did not mention the achievement of his Dolmen Press in producing books that are truly a part of the great Celtic tradition of book creation. During the Symposium, we presented an Exhibition of fifty Dolmen Press books. The Exhibition was opened at Convocation Hall, University of Toronto, by Sorel Etrog.

R. O'D.

I can imagine the wonder and the excitement on the face of a Babylonian 'printer' after he had prepared the text and carefully carved it in reverse on the face of a hard stone cylinder or plaque and finally when he rolled it on a sheet of soft clay and got his first impression: his first 'print'. Liam Miller, in 1978, has the same wonder and excitement on his face when he shows you a page printed at his Dolmen Press in Dublin. For Liam, printing a book, aside from its visual presence, must also be a tactile experience. This obsessive dedication he has shown through his books for almost thirty years since he founded, with his wife Jo, the Dolmen Press.

It was at that time he decided to give up architecture in favour of making printing into an art form. Personally, I wonder if he ever gave up architecture. His books have the experience architecture recalls — a structure of 'black bricks' put together with the same spatial consciousness as a building will occupy in nature.

His love for poetry carried him to the young unknown poets of his time. These limited editions are far from being commercial 'successes' but nevertheless have allowed him to develop his list into a documentation of Irish poets and thinkers. Liam Miller's steady search for graphic material and his commissioning of artists to illustrate his books has made possible a healthy dialogue between the writer and the artist.

A NOTE ON THE
CELTIC CONTRIBUTION TO SCIENCE

LARKIN KERWIN

Nowhere in the endless literature dealing with the Celtic contribution to the Western world does one find mention of one of its important dimensions: the contribution to scientific thought and theory. Scientific thought and theory, of course, demand objectivity, precision, discipline; but also, and more importantly, imagination, simplicity, love of beauty, and a mystical appreciation of the universe and the human spirit. These qualities, which are part of the Celtic make-up, and which have inspired Celtic poets, writers, and musicians, are the same qualities which have enabled Celtic scientists to make major contributions.

The fact is that the pages of scientific history are filled with the names of Celtic scholars who have contributed to the great themes of thought that today dominate and maintain the world. From the endless catalogue one could mention the Scot Robert Brown of fluid dynamics; Francis M'Clintock, the Arctic explorer; Brian and William Higgins of the laws of chemical combination; M'Clure of Wexford who negotiated the first North-West passage; another Scot, MacAdam, whose name is associated with every paved road in the world; George Francis Fitzgerald of the theory of relativity; E. T. S. Walton, the nuclear physics Nobel prize winner; C. T. R. Wilson of cloud chamber fame, or names of further renown such as Wm. Thompson (Lord Kelvin), Sean O'Faolin, A. W. Conway, Robert Boyle, and the Earl of Ross.

Two examples may be considered in particular, the Irishman William Rowan Hamilton (1805-1865) and the Scot James Clark Maxwell (1831-79). The first developed the fundamental basis of theoretical mechanics, the second elaborated the electromagnetic theory. These two developments, without parallel until the later work of Bohr and Einstein, have influenced the entire globe and made possible the emergence of the twentieth century as we know it. That their Celtic temperaments helped shape their work is unquestionable. One is reminded of Arthur O'Shaughnessy's lines:

> We are the music-makers
> And we are the dreamers of dreams . . .
> Yet we are the movers and shakers
> Of the world for ever, it seems.[1]

The tradition continues into contemporary times. We might note J. C. Dooge of hydrological science; M. F. McCarthy, chairman of the stellate photometry section of the IAU; P. Wayman, Asst. Sect. Gen. of the IAU; Lochlainn O'Raiffeartaigh of the Dublin Institute, and of course James McConnell of Maynooth with whom the great Erwin Schroedinger did much of his work in Dublin.

The mention of Maynooth brings to mind the educational approach of the University-Seminary. Although primarily a training institution for priests, the Celtic scientific tradition is so strong that it had its pure science departments two centuries ago, and boasted of such international scientists as Callan, the inventor of the induction coil, and McLoughlin, one of the few contemporaries to record Celtic scientific scholarship. The Celtic tradition was that priests, as the cultural leaders of their communities, should be well versed in all of the arts and sciences and of course the basic sciences were given pride of place.

This tradition was continued in my own country, Canada, and when in the mid-nineteenth century an Irish priest, Edward Horan, found himself on the Council of the expanded Laval University, as well as being a professor of science. One of the first things he did was to equip the University with a most complete and up-to-date laboratory, whose apparatus is today the basis of one of Canada's interesting science museums. For Horan, a Theological Seminary meant an avant-garde scientific establishment.

The Canadian record remains to be documented, but there is much evidence to indicate that both there, and elsewhere, the Celtic consciousness in science is influencing the scientific scene. But the whole subject of the scientific component of the Celtic consciousness has been neglected, and remains one of the challenging new areas in the developing field of Celtic studies.

NOTE

[1]*Penguin Book of Irish Verse* (London 1970), p. 265.

SECTION V

MODERN CELTIC NATIONALISM: LITERARY AND POLITICAL

THE ROOTS OF IRISH NATIONALISM

MARGARET MacCURTAIN

In 1979 one of Ireland's most distinguished historians, Professor F.S.L. Lyons, published a series of essays exploring the resonances of a dominant culture in Irish society, that of the Anglo-Irish tradition. His book, based on the Ford lectures which he delivered in Oxford, he has called *Culture and Anarchy in Ireland 1890-1939*. He described his central pre-occupation as follows: "in these lectures ... which are concerned primarily with conflict between the main cultural traditions in the island, I have sought deliberately to emphasize what divided one tradition from another and have therefore left largely (though not entirely) on one side the variations, regional and otherwise, that undoubtedly existed within each of these traditions,"[1] My point of departure for this paper is the concluding paragraph of *Culture and Anarchy:*

> During the period from the fall of Parnell to the death of Yeats, it was not primarily an anarchy of violence in the streets, of contempt for law and order such as to make the island, or any part of it, permanently ungovernable. It was rather an anarchy in the mind and in the heart, an anarchy which forbade not just unity of territories, but also 'unity of being', an anarchy that sprang from the collision within a small and intimate island of seemingly irreconcilable cultures, unable to live together or to live apart, caught inextricably in the web of their tragic history.
>
> > Out of Ireland have we come;
> > Great hatred, little room,
> > Maimed us at the start.

That collision of seemingly irreconcilable cultures so profoundly analysed by Professor Lyons is, in my opinion, based upon premises to which all of us who study Anglo-Irish relationships have become negatively bound ever since those premises were first posited in the writings of a group of Elizabethan English in Ireland who - like Irish historians of the late twentieth century - were caught up in the investigation of "culture". The premises I refer to are those underlying the sixteenth-century debate on culture in Ireland; such ideas as Edmund Spenser's "civility", Sir Francis Bacon's "nurture versus nature", and Montaigne's "Cannibal" also permeated much of the thinking that went into the Irish plantations of the seventeenth century and into settlement patterns of estate-making in the eighteenth century.

Rather than push back the terms of reference set up by Dr. Lyons in his examination of Mathew Arnold's thoughts on culture, I wish to come upon this topic from a different angle, that of divining the perplexities of a society that never had to question its identity until it was confronted with the challenge of having to articulate the *raison d'être*, not only of its cultural and religious traditions, but of its sytem of law, and way of life. There occurred, at the end of the sixteenth century, a cluster of writings shaped by the Elizabethan conquest of Ireland which provide necessary clues to the origins and nature of Irish nationalism. In selecting the works of Edmund Spenser, William Camden, and Fynes Moryson for particular scrutiny, there is evidence that the Irish literary mind recorded for posterity the received impressions of English writers in areas affecting the nature of Irish culture (from Spenser), the shape and confines of Irish geography (from Camden), and an image of themselves refracted from the first of a long line of travel-writers, Fynes Moryson. The Irish writings of Edmund Spenser, in particular *The Faerie Queene* and *A View of the Present State of Ireland,* Fynes Moryson's *Itinerary,* and William Camden's section on Ireland in his great book, *Britannia Sive ... Angliae, Scotiae, Hiberniae,* demonstrate the ease with which, at an opportune time, facilitators of a flow of culture from one direction could alter and continue to alter the intellectual climate of the inhabitants of a particular territory, and bestow on them the expectations of what they *must* become in order to find acceptance within that particular cultural ambience.

Increasingly, the Elizabethan Irish wars have been interpreted by historians over the last twenty years in the context of two confronting civilizations: the one, a Renaissance state, centralized and superior in terms of technology, articulate, literary, creative; the other, fragmented, backward anachronistically Celtic. The discovery of the New World, with its perplexing variety of cultural forms, presented European man with a challenge to impose order not only on those primitive landscapes he encountered in the New World, but also on the societies that inhabited the outer perimeter of civilized Europe. It was a process that developed throughout the sixteenth century and its refinement in terms of conceptual argument took place in the old world. Those parts of Europe which were geographically remote from the centres of Renaissance civilization began to be considered within the same set of references as those beyond the Atlantic: as an opportunity for the introduction of "civilities" to the rude dwellers.

Edmund Spenser came to Ireland as secretary to Arthur, Lord Grey of Wilton, in 1580. Two months later the Spaniards landed in County Kerry at Smerwick Harbour, taking possession of the fort on the cliff, Dun an Óir. In November Lord Grey, accompanied by his secretary Spenser and a choice group of English officers, of whom Sir Walter Raleigh was the most famous and Sir Richard Grenville the most celebrated, arrived on the Dingle peninsula. Spenser and Raleigh were both twenty-six years of age. Spenser had already written his "Shepherd's Calendar," published in 1579. He was in the process of writing 'The Faerie Queene', and was most likely germinating the work which gave his Irish phase its character, *A View of the Present State of Ireland.*

Lord Grey's stay in Munster was one of ruthless devastation, a scorched earth policy with which Spenser colluded but the consequences of which horrified him, and he parted company from his patron, Lord Grey, when the latter was recalled to England in 1582 for mismanagement and as a result of the private complaints of his officers, principally Sir Walter Raleigh. In 1589 Spenser became a Munster Undertaker, being allotted a modest seigniory at Kilcolman Castle in the lonely outreaches of a territory that stretched into the Duhallow country, an outpost where native met foreigner and exchanged bardic quatrains before revenge was taken. The fact that Spenser's origins were not of the ruling class, like Grenville or Raleigh, may have been the reason for the modest allocation of 4,000 acres at Kilcolman. It was there that he read to Sir Walter Raleigh, then high in the Queen's favour, the first three cantos of *The Faerie Queene* and was persuaded by Raleigh to go across and present them to the Queen.

All of the important things in Spenser's life happened at Kilcolman. There he wrote his "Colin Clout's Come Home Again", and his beautiful marriage-ode, his "Complaints of the World's Vanity", and his four "Hymns to Earthly and Heavenly Love and Beauty". It was at Kilcolman that Spenser's children, Sylvanus, Lawrence, Peregrine, and Catherine were born, and it was there that his small baby, the fifth, possibly a son, perished in the flames when the 1598 Rising broke out. Spenser died four weeks later. He was forty-six years of age.

Edmund Spenser, the poet of Elizabethan expansion in Ireland, wrote in prose, *A View of the Present State of Ireland,* a treatise containing much of value for an understanding of Irish culture against the background of "civility". The book is cast in the fashionable Erasmian form of dialogue, and the plain prose style and illustrations chosen from classical antiquity reflect a mind educated in Renaissance learning. For Spenser, as for Shakespeare, the mutability of things, the shortness of life, the end of human beauty, haunted him as it had haunted Ariosto and Tasso.

There was, however, an underlying realism in Spenser's view. As soldier-secretary, and later as planter in Munster, Spenser realized that the Elizabethan conquest posed new problems for English officials in Ireland, and chiefly the problem of governing an alien people; as a consequence, Spenser's delineation of the origins and history of the Irish could almost be termed an essay in anthropology. Though he participated in the scholarly debate on "nature and nurture" which accompanied colonisation, he was himself a settler and he had taken part in the military conquest of his own territory. His observations came from hard-won experience, and his love of nature in its wild setting was tempered by the fear of retaliation, and the necessity for restraints upon a subject people who were still, from a security aspect, unreliable. Fear breeds repugnance and Spenser's feelings oscillated between distaste for the rebel Irish and a genuine desire to see that beautiful countryside peacefully populated. Spenser, who came from a modest clothmaking family, put a premium on aristocratic behaviour: for him the cultivation of courtly refinement embodied the Elizabethan ideal of "civility", and he recoiled in dismay when confronted with the "lewdness" of Irish manners and customs. "Civility" however represented more than the adoption of sophisticated habits for Spenser whose mind was steeped in Renaissance humanism. It was no less than a total way of life emanating from a particular way of looking at politics and the world.

The lesson of the learned dialogue in *A View* is that of *The Faerie Queene:* society is held together by harmony, an order imposed by Divine decree. The individual must be controlled by temperance, the State upheld by justice. Spenser, surprisingly, does not fully endorse the imposition of Common Law, so enthusiastically advocated by Sir John Davies, Attorney-General for King James in Ireland. Spenser's opposition to the introduction of Common Law into Ireland may have been the result of his partiality towards Antiquity and Roman Law; in any case, he was contemptuous of Brehon Law and castigated the Irish for their lack of temperance. The recurring victory of the disciplined knights in *The Faerie Queene* over the "rascal many" was Tudor in its notion of the stability of order, maintained, not only by divine Decree, but also by Power in the Machiavellian sense.

The desire for stability, for order planned from on high, runs through Elizabethan literature, but Spenser's reliance on Jean Bodin's thought is remarkable. Bodin's concept of "power by conquest" was to become the rationalization behind the theory of "Ireland as a kingdom by conquest" which Sir John Davies developed later. Bodin's terse statement, "according to the opinions of all peoples what is acquired in a just war belongs to the conqueror and the conquered should be slaves to the conqueror," is echoed in Spenser's remarks, "the which sithence they first conquered and by force subdued unto them what needed afterwards to enter into any such idle terms with them to be called their king, when it is in the power of the conqueror to take upon himself what title he will over his dominions conquered."

Bodin's ideas on the polity, its ordering and structure, the place of religion, of tradition, and of antiquity are implicitly the same as Spenser presents in *A View*.[2] The role of Fortune in the history of the individual and the state, which Machiavelli had expounded, was being diminished by Spenser's time as man became more aware of the control which he wielded over his environment. Spenser was influenced by the classical Bodin, and apparently not at all by his contemporary, Montaigne, but all three, and the later Francis Bacon, looked back to Machiavelli; like him they conceived of the State primarily in terms of the science of statecraft drawing most of its data from the records and examples of the past.

Spenser's world in Kilcolman was an Arcadia "that still sought its future in the past and accepted mentally the existence of human monsters."[3] Elizabethan colonists such as Spenser, Robert Payne, possibly Barnaby Rich, and to a certain extent Raleigh, regarded Ireland as a kind of haven of primitive simplicity. For them, Ireland was unspoilt by the competitive sophistication and complexity of life as it was developing in the final Elizabethan decades. Yet the longing for *Arcadia perdita* was in the air of the fifteen-nineties. It provides the background of "Colin Clout's Come Home Again," the charming, primitive landscape, and the barbarous simple people. It provides also the background of *The Faerie Queene:*

> Whylome, when IRELAND florished in fame
> Of wealths and goodnesse, far above the rest
> Of all that beare the *British* Islands name.
> The Gods then us'd (for pleasure and for rest)
> Oft to resort there-to, when seem'd them best:
> But none of all there-in more pleasure found,
> Then Cynthia; that is soueraine Queene profex
> Of woods and forrests, which therein abound,
> Sprinkled with wholsom waters, more then most
> on ground.[4]

Spenser's Irish Arcadia went up in a sheet of flame, if indeed it ever existed. Robert Payne was its ardent propagandist, so also was Derricke in his book, *The Image of Ireland* (1581). The idea was still prevalent in the Advertisements for Ireland in 1623, and in Thomas Blennerhasset's remarks about the rich lands of Fermanagh in the mapping for the Ulster Plantation.

Spenser's treatment of Ireland, although indispensable for an understanding of the cultural presuppositions which infused Elizabethan inquiry into Irish manners, had little sense of a geographical dimension. It was William Camden, who created for his readers a picture of Elizabethan Ireland equivalent to that which Leland had accomplished for England a generation earlier. This was the age of cosmography and of "surveys". When Camden produced his massive *Britannia* (1586ff.), historical geography was masked under antiquities, chorography and topography. Camden benefitted from the scientific curiosity of the antiquarian set in which he moved: Burghley, Cotton, the Goodmans, Hooker, Sir Henry Spelman, and Sir Francis Bacon. Like Spenser he went back to the classical authors, in his case to Polybius, and then advanced to the scenes of action and war-marches which were visualized as the basis of Elizabethan maps. Camden, by his philosophy of organic growth, raised both the critical and artistic level of English cosmography; his arrangement of material contained not only the geographical situation but also descriptions of the government and history of the country he was writing about. Though he never visited the country, his descriptive chorography of Ireland became a kind of model of subsequent geographies of the island. He commences by categorizing the fruits grown in the country and this is followed by a brief discussion of the climatic reasons why grapes do not grow in Ireland. There follows a historical sketch from pre-Christian times and a rather elaborate account of the contemporary government of Ireland, its courts of law, including that of Castle Chamber. Camden then lists the geographical divisions of the country, county by county. In his concluding section he discusses the customs of the inhabitants, quoting Giraldus Cambrensis, and incorporating 'The description of Ireland c. 1566' by the English Jesuit, Fr. Good.

Writing of the Irish, Camden and Spenser were in agreement in one respect: they were, according to Spenser, "wilde fruit, which savage soil hath bred" and to Camden the Irish were "in some places wilde and very uncivil." Camden also incorporates Good's accusations that the Irish were moon worshippers: quoting extensively from Fr. Good, Camden states: "Neither divine service; nor any forms of Chapelle — no alters at all — the Missal or Masse booke all torne — I cannot tell whether the wilder sort of the Irishry yeald divine honour unto the moone for when they see her first after the change, commonly they bow the knee, and say over the Lord's prayer — They have taken unto them wolves to be their Godsibs - the shoulder blade of a sheepe — they use to looke through and thereby foretell of some corse shortly to bee carried out of the house". For Camden the real irritant was to become the one which vexed English administrators down through Jacobean period: "they are so stiffly settled in observing of the old rites of their country, that not only they cannot be withdrawn from them, but they are also able easily to draw the English unto the same (so prone is man's nature to entertain the worst) that one would not believe in how short a time some English among them degenerate and grow out of kinde".[5]

Pre-Tudor observers of Ireland registered their awareness of cultural and moral peculiarities with disapproval, but the Elizabethans in Ireland were self-conscious about their gentility as Gloriana's courtiers. "Civility" for the Elizabethan Englishman or Counter-Reformation Jesuit was as heavily loaded semantically as "primitivism" was for the colonial administrator or Christian missioner in the early twentieth century.[6] The desire to extoll the superiority of the nation-state and its monarchial system of government was pressing. By the fifteen-nineties a political situation had developed in Ireland when rebellions forced statesmen like the Cecils or soldiers like Mountjoy to formulate a new policy for governing a society that, while white and European, was primitive and seemed degraded in comparison to the English. This policy was marked by an extension of English "civilities" to all parts of the country, the Crown ostensibly taking the initiative in establishing a lasting peace by which the natives could effectively be placed in the context of a superior civilization. This policy demonstrated a distinct change from the earlier one of advancing the Pale, a change influenced by complex geographical considerations bearing upon the strategies of administrators and military leaders. By the end of the age of Elizabeth, therefore, geographical understanding of Ireland for the English involved the extension of the administrative area, the establishing of civil colonies and the securing of these colonies by garrisons and forts.

In a war-situation all frontier marauders look murderous. Spenser's green woods assume a sinister and crackling aspect in Canto VI of *The Faerie Queene* where he is describing the woods of Aherlow in County Tipperary. Whether Irish or Iroquois, at home or in North America, the enemy seemed ignorant and savage when one lived on the frontier. Spenser looked back to Bodin and the classical authors, but with the cessation of hostilities after 1603, the English vision of a conquered Ireland took in not only the imposition of English "civilisation" but more significantly the extension of Common Law to replace

Gaelic law and customs. In this we can see the influence of the great French essayist Montaigne, in his celebrated essay "Of the Cannibals". To what, Montaigne asked, was the partition of nations into civil and uncivil to be ascribed?

> These nations, then, seemed to me to be so far barbarous as they have received very little fashioning from human wit, and are still very near to their original simplicity. The laws of Nature govern them still, very little debased with any mixture of ours.[7]

When the Elizabethans thought about Ireland (which was frequently) their dilemma might be summed up in the phrase "nature or nurture." Spenser's longing for a primitive Arcadia cut across the desire for order and the imposition of "civilities" for which he wishes in remote Kilcolman. The position taken up by Sir Francis Bacon and Sir John Davies, who viewed the conquest of Ireland in 1603, was pragmatic: "England, Scotland and Ireland well united in such a trefoil as no prince except yourself (who are the worthiest) weareth in his crown —." Thus Bacon's words to King James I were echoed by Sir John Davies: "heretofore the neglect of the law did make the English degenerate and become Irish and now, on the other side, the execution of the law doth make the Irish grow civil and become English."

For Montaigne barbarism was an absence of those complexities which constitute European civilisation and hence there was something grand about it. For Davies, as for Bacon, the rule of law supplied the text. King James was to exert the power of the crown in the establishment of authority and law in place of the wild rule of the native Irish. Sir John Davies's famous description of the entry of the circuit courts in Ulster conveys the shift in emphasis from settlement to colonization that took place after the conquest.

> They passed into the country of Cahane through the glannes and woods of Glanconkayne where the wild inhabitants wondered as much to see the King's Deputy as the ghosts in Virgil wondered to see Aeneas alive in hell.

Both Davies and Bacon recognized the importance of the natives as distinct from the territory they inhabited: for these Englishmen civilization and the reduction of Ireland to law and obedience went together. Bacon, more than Davies, saw the difficulties inherent in plantation. For him the first task was to extend the legal authority of the crown over Ulster; as for Machiavelli, visible power was more important for Bacon than the viable economics of plantation.

His 'Discourse on the Plantation of Ireland', an eleven-page essay addressed to His Majesty, is a compact, closely-reasoned exposition as to how to set about a plantation that would avoid the mistakes of former ones, and at the same time set a seal of excellence on His Majesty's endeavours. "The wisdom of laws and government given to barbarous people" is the prime justification Bacon cites for the King's personal involvement in the plantations. He also warns King James to let the planning of the countryside come "from the public estate of this Kingdom" (and not from private persons) and he urged that a council of plantation be set up.

Bacon was a man of studies. Sir John Davies was appointed Solicitor-General for Ireland in 1603, later Attorney General, and later still, having with Chichester pushed through the Ulster Plantation, he became speaker of the Irish Parliament which legalized it. Vigorous, active, at times over-optimistic, Davies was far-seeing, and he believed that colonization could yield a profit: "If justice be well and soundly executed for but two or three years the Kingdom will grow rich and happy and in good faith, methinks lawful." This was penned in 1604 when Davies was still euphoric. Eight years later he wrote his book, *A Discoverie of the True Causes why Ireland was never subdued.* Here we have for the first time the idea of the conquered kingdom influencing the ruling class in Ireland, an idea that was to persist down to the period on which Dr. Lyons focuses. Davies typifies the English administrator in Ireland striving to reconcile the irreconcilable, to enforce law and order, and to uphold what had gone before. And, in his treatise, Davies demonstrates that the idea of conquest had progressed beyond the Elizabethan idea of classical settlement. Seventeenth-century colonization was to be based upon conquest: "A barbarous country must first be broken by war before it will be capable of government." A colony, however, need not necessarily be regarded as mere confiscation but as an opportunity for the conquered to achieve uniformity with the conqueror "until the people have perfectly learned the lesson of obedience and the Conquest be established in the hearts of all men. . . ."

Davies's energetic circuit of Ireland provides evidence of yet another level of awareness, a consciousness that goes beyond that of Spenser of Fynes Moryson: it is that of a man intent on wresting from the people of the conquered territory a conformity and docility to the Superior Laws of the realm. Great seems his satisfaction in recording for Salisbury that the common people were flocking to the assizes and courts in order to have their claims heard and to surrender their lands. One area in which Davies departs from the older Elizabethan concept of a colony as a plantation of men or as a region into which men were sent, was his belief in the efficacy of harsh punishment (a belief shared by other Europeans and developed in their concept of slavery as a legitimate state of nature for the less civilized). It was Davies's relentless prosecution of rebels and his delineation of the grounds for treason (Bacon supplied the legal interpretation) that set in motion the processes of law which with time the Irish accepted but never assimilated. A year later, when Davies addressed the Irish Parliament of 1613, he noted that the King's writ ran throughout the land but that the country's allegiance was still problematic. At least one area remained, the area of religion, in which uniformity had not been achieved, and the question of religious conflict introduced a new note into the continuing debate on the idea of order. For the new Jacobean antiquarian circle, as for the later Caroline divines, the tensions between nature and order came to a crisis in the question of church government: nowhere was this issue more critical than in the new Ulster Colony.

King James I believed that the most effective means for ensuring a tranquil Ulster was to plant the Gospel firmly there. The arrival of George Montgomery as commissioner for the plantation of Ulster and as appointed bishop of Derry exposed the raw nerve of insecurity that existed between Chichester's administration, based in Dublin, and the Privy Council in London. Montgomery had been chaplain to King James and he was energetic in advising James on ways of strengthening the Church. James took an active interest in this aspect of the Plantation and the political centrality of the new bishop of Derry was an indication of the growing importance of the church prelates in the settlement. Previously Chichester, the Lord Deputy, had observed in a memorandum to Sir John Davies that the situation in Ulster was similar to that pertaining in America and prophesied that "the natives will settle themselves and their dependancy upon the bishops or the undertakers". King James knew the temper of Ulster better than either his deputy or Sir John Davies and he re-iterated emphatically his conviction that the planting of religion in Ulster "offers the greatest hope of good success in this scheme ... planting the Gospel in the churches for the comfort of the settlers and reducing the natives to God's services".[8]

Ulster became and was to remain a place where religious conviction became woven into the strands of political life and government, and the fate of Ulster at every later turn of Irish history was inextricably bound up with evangelization. Ulster identity suffered set-backs at this period and became unsure of its deepest roots, one aspect of which was its Gaelic past. In any case, the native culture was grappling with the metaphysical problems of its religious and cultural roots at a time when the visible institutions which enshrined its deepest values were passing away. Spenser had sympathy and understanding for Irish cultural institutions but both he and Fynes Moryson recommended that they be destroyed so that they could be replaced with the institutions of a better civilization. This is particularly poignant in the case of ecclesiastical institutions: in seeking to spread the reformed church, English administrators were compelled to examine Gaelic institutions and religious life as embodied in the characteristics of Irish monasticism. Ironically they learned and even came to admire what had been destroyed. Thus, in the sixteen-twenties, antiquarianism became a substitute for remorse.

In the decades between Spenser's arrival in Ireland and the enthusiastic formula of law-enforcement postulated by Sir John Davies for the opening of the Irish parliament in 1614, the spirit of antiquarianism had been dissipated. In England it had been suppressed nervously by King James as being treasonable. In Ireland it persisted as a scholarly inquiry into the deeper meaning of Gaelic society in a manner that would have scandalized Davies, though not Spenser. The gentle Ware, whose father had come to Ireland as secretary to a lord deputy, was a student of Trinity College, Dublin, a friend of Ussher, and of Cotton. From 1626 onwards he wrote or collected material which exemplified the older learning and culture of "Hibernia". In his treatment of Elizabethan writers — Spenser, Hanmer, and Marlborough — Ware showed his sense of historical tradition by assessing the spread of law and order in the sixteen-thirties with what had been lamentably absent fifty years before. Schooled by his father, and by James Ussher, his great model in antiquarian pursuits was William Camden. Like Camden and James Ussher, Ware turned to a native scholar to unlock the mysteries of the manuscripts he wished to consult. Dudley Firbisse, better known to Irish scholars as Dubhaltach MacFirbisigh, had translated the Irish annals for Archbishop James Ussher, perhaps the greatest scholar of this period, a churchman who remained resolutely outside the political power play. Ussher drew Firbisse's worth as the last historian-genealogist of Gaelic Ireland to the attention of Sir James Ware. The contact was beneficial to both and they worked closely over the next decade and a half. In 1650 Firbisse's *Genealogies* appeared: it is of inestimable value to the Gaelic scholar. In 1654 Ware's *De Hibernia et Antiquitatibus Ejus,* clearly showing the influence of Firbisse, was published: it is of inexhaustible value to the archaeologist.[9] Antiquarianism in seventeenth-century Ireland had become the great reconciling angel between the conflicting and divided mentalities, a reconciliation exemplified in the co-operation between Ware and Firbisse.

Spenser, Fynes Moryson and Davies had held Ireland up to the mirror of English "civility," and they defined what they found in negative terms. They were astonished and dismayed at the reluctance of the "Scythians," Spenser's term, or "barbarous natives," Fynes Moryson's dismissive phrase, to abandon their ancient ways. Their failure to examine native sources in the manner advocated by Montaigne circumscribed their understanding of the culture which they were in the process of transforming. Ware's belief in the dignity of that cultural past, and his knowledge of classical literature, gave him the flexibility to discover parallels between what Ussher and Firbisse offered him as evidence of early Irish civilization and what he had studied in classical antiquity.[10]

The apparently harmless pursuit of scholarly gentlemen was capable of arousing hostility and suspicion in a government. Professor Hugh Trevor-Roper has written with intelligent sensitivity of the suppression of antiquarian meetings by King James I as treasonable activities.[11] Though its respectability was restored by King Charles II, antiquarianism in England never again captured the excitement of those early years of the seventeenth century. Far different was the case of Ireland. As Ireland moved into the eighteenth century, antiquarianism became increasingly pre-occupied with the preservation of those aspects of Irish identity most closely associated with the spirit, the language and literature of a submissive population who spoke and sang in another tongue - one that was venerable, rich in linguistic complexity and seemingly inexhaustible as a storehouse for literature and mythology. The strong thrust of eighteenth-century antiquarianism, with its emphasis on collections of Gaelic manuscripts, on archives and on the storing of records, led, by way of Charles O'Connor of Belanagare and his circle, to the founding of the Royal Irish Academy in 1785.

The Royal Irish Academy was to become the most significant learned society investigating Irish history, antiquities and the sciences. Were it not for the tradition for preservation which marks eighteenth-century antiquarianism in Ireland, then the impulses which inspired Samuel Ferguson to make his translations of Irish poems during the eighteen-thirties, or the cultural nationalism of the Young Irelanders a decade later, might not have forged the links that led to the Gaelic revival of the early twentieth century. Similarly, Bunting's collections of Irish music bring the student of Irish music to the threshold of the nineteenth century and to the unlocking of the delights of Irish songs by Tom Moore. Hardiman's work of musical restoration founded a tradition of academic Irish musicianship in Queen's College Cork and in time produced from its Music Department the composer Seán O Riada.

Antiquarianism in nineteenth century Ireland was not harmless. We still await a parallel analysis of what really happened to Irish society during the period of F.S.L. Lyons's *Culture and Anarchy, 1890-1939* which will explain, among other things, the impact of certain forces on the dying language: the academic founding of the study of Old Irish and the re-discovery of *The Táin Bó Cuailgne*, the editing of Irish texts and bardic poetry, the writings of Eoin MacNeill and the founding of the National University of Ireland.

Thus while F.S.L. Lyons can arrive at the conclusion of "an anarchy that sprang from seemingly irreconcilable cultures, unable to live together or to live apart," one can also, on the balance of other issues, arrive at quite different conclusions. That the importance of the geographical identity which Camden bestowed on this island was the beginning of Irish geography and of the ordered landscaping which emerged from the "nurture versus nature" controversy is clear. The fact that the teaching of geography in Irish universities has until very recently remained in the hands of English-trained geographers merely serves to underline the strength and the benign efficacy of this particular strand in the antiquarian tradition. One can appreciate too that Spenser was intellectually striving for the concepts elegantly expressed by Montaigne, whose definition of barbarism was, as we have seen, an absence of European Renaissance civilization. Yet his perspective was such that he was not quite capable of the kind of understanding which Gaelic Ireland merited. If the Elizabethans could have perceived that this dispossessed "uncivil" society might possess a specific and real cultural cohesion, that it might possess both an assured self-awareness of its own resources and permanence, and a concomitant pride in its grandeur, then the sheer tenacity with which that Gaelic society held onto the elements of its identity might have been understood to the benefit of all. Happily for Ireland and England, as F.S.L. Lyons tardily admits, antiquarianism became a bridge not only between the "irreconcilable" cultures but between the divisive elements of religious belief and educational institutions. Antiquarianism was a bridge in more than this, however. On the lines I have suggested, the study of the antiquarian tradition brings one on the certain path backwards to the origins and the reason for Irish nationalism.

NOTES

[1] (Oxford 1979), p.17.

[2] See Edmund Spenser, *A View of the Present State of Ireland*, ed. H. Morley (London 1890), and Jean Bodin, *Oeuvres philosophiques* (Paris 1951), trans. M.J. Tooley, *Bodin's six Books of the Commonwealth* (Oxford 1955).

[3] See P. Cullen, *Spenser, Marvell and Renaissance Pastoral* (Cambridge 1970).

[4] *The Faerie Queene*, ed. J.C. Smith and E. de Selincourt (Oxford 1970), p.398.

[5] W. Camden, "Preface," *Britannia Sive . . . Angliae, Scotiae, Hiberniae*, trans. P. Holland (London 1695).

[6] In a series of illuminating studies, Professor D.B. Quinn has probed the reasons for this cultural misunderstanding between two societies geographically so close to each other. See *The Elizabethan and the Irish* (New York 1966).

[7] "Of Cannibals," *The Essays of Michel De Montaigne*, trans. Jacob Zeitlin (New York 1934), p. 182.

[8] King James to Chichester (8 July 1609), *Calendar of the State Papers of Ireland, 1608-10*, p.245.

[9] See M. Herity, "Rathmullach, Ware and MacFirbisigh," *Ulster Journal of Archaeology*, Vol. 33 (1970), pp. 49-53.

[10] The links between Spenser and Ware were strong, for it was James Ware who published the first edition of *A View of the Present State of Ireland* in Dublin in 1633, using a manuscript copy of the work from the library of James Ussher.

[11] Hugh Trevor-Roper, *Queen Elizabethan's First Historian William Camden and the Beginnings of English 'Civil History'* (London 1971).

THE IRISH LITERARY REVIVAL:
PREPARATION AND PERSONALITIES

LORNA REYNOLDS

There can be little doubt, it seems to me, but that anyone now looking back on the Irish Literary Revival of three-quarters of a century ago must see it in the context of the general national movement of the time, partly conscious, partly a mysterious stirring of the bones, a mysterious hearing of ancestral voices, appearing as unexpected and as compelling as any manifestation in the natural world. I say "appearing", because I do not believe in that lost, hidden Gaelic world of Daniel Corkery: I believe that the traditions of Irish culture wore thin for a short period, but I do not believe that they were ever broken. After all, only twenty-five years intervene between the 1840 collection of Bunting's *Irish Airs* and the birth of W.B. Yeats.

Douglas Hyde invented a phrase for what he wanted done in the Ireland of his time and what he saw as the programme of the Gaelic League; he called it the "de-Anglicization" of Ireland: and this is as good a term as one can find for the literary, linguistic and intellectual aims of the leaders of the movement: Hyde, Yeats, AE, Synge and Lady Gregory, each wanted, though each used different words to express his intention, to de-Anglicize, to de-provincialize Ireland and to make it live again in all its individuality as a Celtic country, different in race, in traditions, in ancestral glories from the neighbouring island that had looked, not only across, but down on it for so long.

I say that in this there was some mysterious stirring of the bones, some mysterious hearing of ancestral voices, because nobody at the time was in possession of the knowledge we now have of the greatness of the ancient Celtic world, of its vast extent and the glory of its stupendous store of artistic treasures. The Celts, we now know, at the height of their power during the third century B.C., dominated Europe, from Finistère on the Atlantic to the Black Sea and from the North Sea to the Mediterranean. They "created Europe's first major industrial revolution, its first common market, its first international court of arbitration."[1]

They were a remarkably talented people, endowed not only with artistic gifts, but also with technological skills, not only imaginative but also practical. It was they — some may be surprised to hear — who introduced soap to the Greeks and Romans, and though they often fought naked, as all of us know from the statue of the dying Gaul in the Capitoline Museum in Rome, it was they who invented chain armour: they were the first moreover to shoe horses and shape handsaws, chisels, files and other tools still in use today. They invented seamless iron rims for their wheels, the iron plough-share, the rotary flour mill, a wheeled harvesting machine; and, sensible to a degree far from common today, regarded women as equal to men. They made nothing of death, and women as well as men were ferocious warriors.

For them life after death was not very different — only happier — from life on earth; they were matter-of-fact in their other-worldliness and thought of the supernatural as penetrating the natural. In addition to all this, their artistic gifts were such that the style of art they created lasted for many hundreds of years.

The Celtic world of Europe, though it put up a good fight, eventually went down before the ruthless efficiency of Julius Caesar and his marching legions. But it so happened that the Romans never crossed the Irish sea, that Ireland never became part of the Roman Empire and no Irish chieftain had to stoop under the Roman yoke. Celtic civilization and Celtic art continued to flourish in Ireland: it was given a new lease of life by Christianity, and indeed reinforced by it, setting off the evangelicisation of the barbaric Europe left behind by the Romans; it was despoiled but not destroyed by the Vikings, invaded but not conquered by the Anglo-Normans of the twelfth century and only brought to its knees by the great Elizabeth of England, herself mainly a Celt, her father a Tudor, and her mother, Anne Boleyn, of a family owning land and residences in Ireland. Ironically, the Elizabethans believed that they were bringing civilization to a barbarian people: the great Hugh O'Neill was to them a rebel kern.

From that time on Celtic Ireland was in retreat, but it was a slow and stubborn retreat and until the end of the eighteenth century many features of the Celtic way of life persisted, especially in the west and north-west of the country. Charlotte Milligan Fox in the *Annals of the Irish Harpers*, which begins with an account of the last gathering of the Harpers of Ireland in 1792, includes the autobiography of Arthur O'Neill. This is mainly the story of his "ramblings", his peregrinations as itinerant harper from one gentleman's seat to another's, from Cavan to Leitrim, Roscommon, Tyrone and Antrim, and of how he spent eighteen successive Christmas days with the O'Reilly of Cavan. Of one of his hosts, Mr. James Irvine of Streamstown in Sligo, he tells us that there was "at one time a meeting in his house of forty-six musicians who played in the following order: —

The three Miss Irvines at the piano	3
Myself at the harp	1
Gentlemen flutes	6
Gent. Violoncellos (*sic*)	2
Common pipers	10
Gent. fiddlers	20
Gent. clarionets	4"[2]

If the occasion had arisen of comparing Mr. James Irvine of Streamstown with any of the petty princelings of Germany who maintained a private orchestra in the eighteenth century, he would not have come badly out of the comparison.

These harpers, many of them blind, had been taught their art through the medium of Irish, and they kept up one Celtic custom — the equality of the sexes — by including women in their ranks. What they played was, of course, Irish music of great anitiquity. In 1796 Bunting, who had been engaged by Dr. James MacDonnell of Belfast to transcribe the airs played at the gathering of 1792, brought out his first collection of some sixty-six Irish airs never before published. It was some of these airs that Tom Moore "stole", Bunting always felt, to write his melodies to: Moore did violence to them, Bunting believed, because he forced the airs to the words, instead of making the words fit the airs. For his second collection, published in 1812, Bunting employed a native speaker of Irish, Patrick Lynch, to travel through Connaught and collect not only airs but the words of the accompanying Irish songs; and in his third collection of 1840 Bunting published a list of Irish technical terms used in the playing of the Irish harp.

According to Charlotte Milligan Fox, Patrick Lynch, in that summer journey of 1802, "collected versions of a great many of the songs that are in Douglas Hyde's *Love Songs of Connaught*," and certainly some of the examples quoted by her come close to the naive tenderness and transparent simplicity of the Hyde renderings. Would anyone, listening to the following, question the information if he were told that it was by Douglas Hyde: —

> There is a quicken tree out in the garden
> That still drops honey when I lay my hand on it,
> Only Son of Mary and King of Graces,
> Who can blame me that my heart is grieved?

> My love is like the blackberry blossom,
> Or like the moss-berry blossoms on a bright day of sun,
> And as the blossoms of the blue-berry on the mountain-side,
> And there has often been a fair body under a black head.[3]

I have myself experienced an instance of the continuity of the Irish musical tradition. A few years ago I heard sung by a young Australian man, to the accompaniment of the guitar, played by another young Australian, the exquisite song of "Ballinderry". The singer had learnt it in Australia from his Irish grandmother. Neither of the young men knew that the air had been published by Bunting nor the words reproduced by Charlotte Milligan Fox: —

> It's pretty to be in Ballinderry
> It's pretty to be in Aghalee;
> But it's prettier to be in little Ram's Island,
> Sitting under an ivy tree.

> Oh, that I was in little Ram's Island,
> Oh, that I was with Phelimy Diamond;
> He would whistle and I would sing
> Till we would make the whole island ring.

> Och on! Ochone!
> Och on! Ochone![4]

This, according to Bunting, is a very old tune and had the unusual accompaniment of a bass chorus.

It had been the idea of Dr. James MacDonnell to call the gathering of Irish Harpers in 1792 and, as I have already mentioned, it was he who engaged Bunting to transcribe the airs. On the publication of Bunting's third collection in 1840, Dr. MacDonnell, then an old man, wrote to Bunting, who had moved to Dublin years before, to make the following comment on the Preface to the book: —

> In the next place you say nothing of the spirit of patriotism and the actual utility in
> a national point of view, of keeping alive all opinions, customs and innocent
> prejudices, which bind mankind to their country whatever that may be, whether it be
> the Deserted Village, or the Mountain that leads to the storm — these when early
> cherished, act like instinctive impulses and carry with them a magic charm, they are
> delightful in prosperity, console us in adversity, they accompany us in the city or the
> wilderness — when old we dote upon them. Now there are no associations or feelings
> of the kind so strong as those connected with music and language.[5]

Though the baggy, impulsive syntax of this is far from the compactness of
Yeats, the sentiments are among those reiterated again and again by him. The
importance of early individual associations, that what a man holds in his memory
and knows in his blood is what he must write about, Yeats preaches in season and
out. The ground was being prepared for him before he was born.

If we return from the traditions of music and language to others no less
important, the visual records of a great past, we find that the Royal Irish
Academy began its famous collection of Irish antiquities about the year 1840.
These were transferred from the Academy to the newly built National Museum
in Kildare Street in 1890. George Coffey, who wrote a guide to the collection in
1909, discussing the croziers, bells and shrines, informs us that the custody of
such sacred objects were hereditary in certain families.[6] For instance, St. Patrick's
bell and shrine was in the hereditary keeping of the O'Mellan family until, in
1441, the O'Mellan of the day committed some misdemeanor which rendered
him unworthy of the privilege. He was deprived of his hereditary right and the
keeping of the bell and shrine passed to the Mulholland family. This family
retained right to the custody until custody had become possession, and in 1758 the
Mulholland of the day bequeathed the treasures to a Mr. Adam McClean of
Belfast; after his death they were bought by the Rev. James Henderson Todd,
D.D. of Trinity College and on his death the Royal Irish Academy purchased
them.[7]

Here is another instance of cultural continuity. St. Patrick's bell is mentioned
in the Annals of Ulster under the year 552 A.D.[8] The shrine was made sometime
between 1091 and 1105, when St. Patrick's successor, Domnall MacAuley, was
Bishop of Armagh,[9] their custody and whereabouts were known until, as I have
said, custody had become possession and they could be bought and sold. After
that, before long they became a national possession, on exhibition to native and
stranger alike.

When we pass to consider the languages of Ireland, we are told by the latest
authority that in 1800 there were six different languages spoken in Ireland:

> ... there were not two, but six distinct speech communities in the country. Apart
> from the two principal languages, Irish and English, the old dialect of Yola [an Old
> English dialect] might be heard in the baronies of Bargy and Forth in County
> Wexford. French and German-speaking communities, some of them established
> over a hundred years, were still to be found: French at Portarlington, Lisburn, Dublin
> and other places; German at Gracehill near Ballymena, and at places in Tipperary
> and Limerick. The sixth speech community was Lallands, or Lowland Scotch, which

was extensive in many parts of the North. It was a very pure dialect of Scottish and
we are told by various observers that it was almost unintelligible to strangers.[10]

English was spoken in the Pale and in the parts of the country planted in Tudor
times, Irish in the West, the North-West and most of the South. But we must not
think of Irish as having disappeared even from the towns: there were two
Irish-speaking communities in Dublin, one on the North quays bounded by
Stonybatter, and the other in the Liberties, in the heart of Swift's Dublin. Galway,
however, was in 1825 almost exclusively Irish-speaking and in Connaught in
general English was practically unknown.

It has often been said that Irish was suppressed. This is not so, according to de
Fréine. The famine had been such a cultural shock that post-famine Irish people
did not want Irish: they wanted to learn English.[11] They wanted to be able to
emigrate without the disadvantage of not knowing the language of the country in
which they would land. There were, of course, parts of Ireland where English had
been spoken for centuries, still at the end of the last century, with an Elizabethan
freedom, with Elizabethan idioms and contractions, and with certain vowels
pronounced in the way that had been correct before the great vowel shift of the
eighteenth century but which was no longer heard in standard English. This
English was also, of course, influenced by Irish and was characterized by the
periphrastic syntax that Professor Wagner discusses elsewhere in this collection.
As a child I heard this kind of English spoken all around me: I still hear it spoken
by the country people in County Galway. Standard English was also to be heard.
We sometimes forget that there was considerable coming and going of English-
born people and that the 'gentry' sent their children to be educated in England. In
my childhood it was not uncommon for people to use either standard English or
Anglo-Irish, depending on the person spoken to.

By the middle of the last century, after the famine, a great many people were
probably shifting from one language to the other, thinking still in Irish, though
speaking in English. By that time too the scientific study of Irish was being
undertaken by German scholars and its importance as an Indo-European
language of great antiquity recognized. In 1853 Zeuss published his *Grammatica
Celtica*. From the early years of the century we find also the beginning of a
literature written in English by Irishmen, though for the most part this was either
provincial, in so far as it was deficient in skill of presentation, or it was
propagandist and had some political end in view. But we also have the beginning
of a true literature, written by an Anglo-Irish author, in the *Castle Rackrent* of
Maria Edgeworth. But this was in a way a false dawn.

What I have been trying to show in this preliminary material is that Irish
cultural traditions, though worn very thin, were never broken. Even the period
between Bunting's third collection and the birth of W.B. Yeats was taken up by
the Young Irelanders, and it is worth remembering that the poems of the original
Spirit of the Nation were published with accompanying Irish airs. The movement

at the end of the last century was not quite the new growth that it can seem if looked at without a glance backwards.

Let me now, however, turn to my subject proper. It seems to me that for a great literature to arise a moment must occur when certain factors combine. An energizing vision of life must coincide with the possession or the discovery of a fluid and malleable language, instinct with the power of embodying sensible and animistic impressions, and the writer must believe himself to be capable of expressing a deeper life than his mere individual one, must feel that the personal, the national and the universal can all be brought together. Such a moment is at hand when, to adapt a sentence of Yeats, "the work of a supreme culture" appears "as much the growth of the common soil as the grass and the rushes."[12]

Such a moment occurred towards the end of the nineteenth century in Ireland. The vision of life came from the re-discovery of the heroic ideal in the mythology of Ireland, and the writer who revealed it was Standish James O'Grady. O'Grady recognized the value of the legacy left by the "ancient shapers of legend." Writing of the bards of Ireland, and of how they had aroused and stimulated, for many centuries before the introduction of Christianity, the intellectual, moral and imaginative powers of the Irish people, he praises them as follows: —

> But perhaps the most valuable work achieved for Ireland by these ancient shapers of legend and heroic tales, is like all that is best done in the world, incapable of being definitely grasped and clearly exhibited. Their best work is probably hidden in the blood and brain of the race to this day. Those antique singing men, with their imagined gods and superhuman heroes, breathed into the land and people the gallantry and chivalrousness, the prevailing ideality, the love of action and freedom, the audicity and elevation of thought which, underneath all rudeness and grotesquerie, characterizes those remnants of their imaginings and which we believe no intervening centuries have been powerful wholly to destroy. Theirs, not the monks, was the *perfervidum ingenium Scotorum.*[13]

In the next paragraph O'Grady continues:

> I would also add when I consider the extraordinary stimulus which the perusal of the literature gives to the imagination even in centuries like these, and its wealth of elevated and intensely *human* characters that as I anticipate with the revival of Irish literary energy and the return of Irish self-esteem the artistic craftsmen of the future will find therein and in unfailing abundance the material of persons and sentiments fit for the highest purposes of epic and dramatic literature, and art, pictorial and sculptural.

This was written in 1881, eight years before the publication of Yeats's *Wanderings of Oisin and Other Poems.* O'Grady did indeed prove himself a literary prophet, but even he did not foresee that the elevated characters would prove so intensely human as to serve as models for the revolutionaries of the next rebellion and that Cuchulain would become the ideal not only of Yeats but of Pearse. Yeats was alive to the importance of O'Grady's work and in 1898 wrote to him as follows:

> There is humour and fantasy as well as miraculous poetry in all our old legends, and one can find in them all kinds of meanings....They are the greatest treasures the past has handed down to us Irish people and the most plentiful treasure of legends in Europe; I have always considered that you yourself have done more than all others to dig away the earth that has so long lain upon their beauty.[14]

O'Grady lifted the 'blazing torch' of his own poetic apprehension and lighted up that wonderful past for all who read him, not least for the poet who would come to identify himself with the greatest hero there depicted and would see in Cuchulain an image of the noblest manhood, inspiration for his life as well as his work.

The other source of inspiration for the writers of the time, folklore, Yeats had access to from childhood. In *Mythologies*, describing the effect of listening to Irish songs sung by the roadside, he tells us that he was so transported that it was as if he had come to one of the four rivers and followed it under the walls of Paradise to the roots of the Trees of Knowledge and of Life. "Folk art", he writes, "is indeed the oldest of the aristocracies of thought . . . it is the soil where all great art is rooted."[15]

The energizing vision of life, therefore, came from the reconstruction of the past through the work of scholars and the discovery of the same past in the living tradition of the people. As for the fresh and vivid language, the moment also provided that. By the end of the nineteenth century English had been assimilated everywhere in Ireland except in the Gaeltacht: in some parts of the country the English spoken was archaic in many respects, as I have already pointed out: in the West, in addition to archaisms, it was characterized by the literal translations of Irish constructions and of many Irish idioms. Moreover, almost everywhere the animistic habits of mind of a people living in close touch with a spiritualized nature persisted and showed themselves in imagery and personification. I suspect that Latin also played a part in the English of Ireland but this is an unexplored subject. Here I shall just mention that classical learning was highly respected and most hedge schoolmasters knew Latin, if not Greek, and taught them in their ramshackle schools. Candidates for the priesthood who left before ordination often set up more formal schools for the teaching of the classics. Such a one was an t-Athair Peadar O'Laoghaire's mother's brother: his mother, before her marriage, taught French and English in her brother's school: Irish, however, was the language of an t-Athair Peadar O'Loaghaire's home. The Anglo-Irish dialect was a creation of the Irish people from their mixed linguistic past.

There is a great deal to be said about that complex man, Douglas Hyde, but from the point of view of this paper his importance lies in the fact that it was he who revealed the possibilities of this Anglo-Irish dialect, this Hibernian English (as it should properly be called, if pedantry did not have to yield to usage) as a literary medium, and his *Love-Songs of Connaught,* published in 1893, must be regarded as an historic document. Here the language of the heart could be heard, without sentimentality, without cliché, a limpid medium for the expression of passionate feeling. The Irish Literary Revival is marked by many ironies, not the least of them being that it should be Douglas Hyde, untiring promoter of the Gaelic language and founder of the Gaelic League, who should have provided the writers in English with an essential tool for their work. No individual writer can create a language: only a people can do this. But it takes great originality to perceive the literary possibilities of a 'new' language.

How far the other writers of the time were directly influenced by Hyde would be difficult to determine. Lady Gregory, for instance, translated several of his one-act plays from Irish into English: *The Workhouse Ward, The Tinker and the Fairy, The Marriage, The Lost Saint, The Twisting of the Rope, The Nativity Play*. But Lady Gregory had been listening to the speech of the people from childhood and, as we all know, she collected folk tales from them. Perhaps Hyde's practice merely confirmed her instinct that she was doing the right thing in reproducing their dialect. Whether or not Yeats was directly influenced by Hyde is another open question. Diarmuid Coffey, in his biography of Hyde, declares in forthright fashion:

> Yeats owes much to Hyde. He has been by him introduced into a realm of literature which has profoundly influenced his writing. Yeats fell under the spell of the movement for the revival of Irish and for some years used to appear on Gaelic platforms. Thus Hyde may, without detracting from Yeats' genius, be said to have left a mark on his writing. Yeats also helped Hyde's work. He has always been a consummate debater and in words and writings has supported the Irish language movement.[16]

But Yeats himself in retrospect tended to look on Hyde's work from the point of view of a patron rather than a colleague:

> The man most important for the future was certainly Dr Douglas Hyde. I had found a publisher while still in London for his *Beside the Fire* and *Love-Songs of Connacht* and it was the first literary use of the English dialect of the Connacht country people that had aroused my imagination for those books.[17]

This was written after the events, but in the letters contemporary with the events Yeats, while showing himself aware of the quality of Hyde's writing, takes care to assert his independence of Hyde and his access to other sources of knowledge. For instance in a letter to O'Leary (probably late May 1887) he encloses a ballad for publication in *The Gael*, the official publication of The Gaelic Athletic Association, describing it as a "ballad on another Sligo story, something like Douglas Hyde, though not suggested by him, for I have long had it in mind."[18] In August of the same year he sends O'Leary a poem made "from a prose version given by Walsh in his introduction to his book of poems."[19] This was Edward Walsh's *Irish Popular Songs*, published in 1847. Yeats's poem was published in *Poems and Ballads of Young Ireland*, but never subsequently reprinted. It shows Yeats experimenting, though not very successfully, with those 'wavering rhythms' he was afterwards to say he wanted to introduce into his poetry. Here the wavering rhythm is produced by rather feeble repetition, and the original is padded out in the English for the sake of the rhyme: the result is diffuse writing. In this same letter he praises the poems of Hyde as "very good indeed", and in the following year in a letter to Katherin Tynan (September 1888) he says of Hyde: "he is the best of all the Irish folklorists. His style is perfect — so little literary."[20] The following month, discussing his Fairy and Folk-tale book, he asks Ernest Rhys to "make plain to the mind of Scott that I have taken much trouble and that there is *original matter of value which no one else could have got*, that is to say

Douglas Hyde's stories — one of them the finest thing in the book."[21]

Putting these scattered bits and pieces together, I suggest that the naturalness and simplicity of Douglas Hyde's style did seem to Yeats an ideal to be aimed at, but that he had access to a similar simplicity in the tales familiar to him from childhood, that he had read widely in the writings of nineteenth-century Irishmen and that dialect, no matter how delicate, would not answer all his purposes. All was grist that came to Yeats's mill and nothing of value was ever discarded, though much might be laid aside until its useful moment had come. He had the rare gift of being able to recognize the worth of his contemporaries as well as of his predecessors, and, as I have said elsewhere of him, he had not only genius but the power of eliciting genius in others. He was a great collaborator and told his publisher on one occasion that he, Lady Gregory and Douglas Hyde wrote *Where there is Nothing* in a fortnight to prevent George Moore from stealing the plot.[22]

In *Autobiographies* Yeats mourns for the loss of Hyde's genius. He saw the loss of the literary genius in the success of the practical man who founded the Gaelic League: —

> He was to create a great movement, far more important in its practical results than any movement I could have made, no matter what my luck, but, being neither quarrelsome nor vain, he will not be angry if I say — for the sake of those who come after us — that I mourn for the greatest folklorist who ever lived, and for the great poet who died in his youth. The Harps and the Pepperpots got him and kept him until he wrote in our common English . . . and took for his model the newspaper upon his breakfast table.[23]

Looking back now, one must agree with Yeats. Hyde, the delicate and sensitive poet, went astray among the emblems of a dead Ireland, was quenched in the stupendous, ultimately doomed attempt to reverse an historical process and return a country to its original Gaelic tongue. But the accidental achievement of Hyde in helping to de-Anglicize Ireland by revealing the uses of a fresh and living form of English, Hibernian English, has not yet been properly assessed. Synge, reviewing *Lady Gregory's Cuchulain of Muirthemne* in the *Speaker*, June, 1902, states:

> The intellectual movement that has been taking place in Ireland for the last twenty years has been chiefly a movement towards a nearer appreciation of the country people, and their language, so that it is not too much to say that the translation of the old MSS into this idiom is the result of an evolution rather than a merely personal idea.[24]

There is some truth in this, but it underestimates Hyde's part in effecting the mutation that began the evolution. The most significant point, however, is that such a language was to hand, "in a true sense a language of Ireland", to use Synge's words once more, or, as he put it for his French readers, "une véritable langue maternelle."[25]

The third — and most important — factor necessary for the rise of a great literature is the appearance of writers who can feel that they are mouthpieces, not merely for their own personalities, but for their people, and who write out of a profound culture, with a naturalness that seems the product of simplicity and not of art, who have learnt in a long apprenticeship the art that conceals art. All the writers of the movement under discussion have these characteristics. Nothing is more remarkable about the young Yeats, as he is revealed in the *Letters*, than his insistence that the writer must deal with what he knows at first hand: "We should make poems on the familiar landscapes we love, not the strange and rare and glittering ones we wonder at,"[26] he writes in 1888 to Katherine Tynan — his unabashed interest in old ballads, Sligo fairies, the magazines and journals that published Irish material, his ability to pick hints out of the air. Indeed a casual reader of these early letters might find them rather boring, full of gossip about side-ways and by-lanes. But Yeats had a purpose in mind, a practical as well as a professional one. "Remember", he writes as early as 1887 to Katherine Tynan, "by being Irish, as you can you will be the more original and true to yourself and in the long run more interesting, even to English readers."[27] By being Irish and by relentlessly insisting on it Yeats was helping himself to overcome the difficulty of every young poet, how to strike an individual note, how, manifestly, to be different from one's predecessors.

But there was more to it than this. Yeats was being true to his deepest instincts when he immersed himself in these old traditional fragments about ghosts, banshees, country tales, translations from the Irish, memories of Young Ireland, and the rest of it, matters that might, on the surface, seem not far removed from the Harps and Pepperpots that 'got' Douglas Hyde. It was the buried world of spirit beneath these surface fragments that interested him, and the people who preserved them were 'his' people. Writing, once again to Katherine Tynan, eight years after these early letters, about the Gore-Booths, he aligns himself with her and 'our own people', as opposed to the Unionists, giving the latter their due, however, and remarking: "These people are much better educated than our own people and have a better instinct for excellence."[28] He consistently aligns himself with what we call nationalist Ireland. In a short letter to the Editor of *United Ireland, a propos* of a review of his *Countess Cathleen* and a misreading of his wish to be accounted "one with Davis, Mangan, Ferguson," all he claims, he asserts, is "community in the treatment of Irish subjects after an Irish fashion".[29]

But Yeats was not being merely national when he urged Irish subjects and Irish landscape on other writers. He saw individual life as related to the national life and through that to the universal life. In a review of Allingham's *Irish Songs and Poems* for the *Providence Sunday Journal*, written in 1888, he has no doubts about this:—

> ... nothing is an isolated artistic moment; there is a unity everywhere; everything fulfills a purpose that it is not its own; the hailstone is a journeyman of God; the grass blade carries the universe upon its point. But this universalism, this seeing of unity everywhere, you can only attain through what is near you, your nation or, if you are no traveller, your village and the cobwebs on your walls. You no more can have the greater poetry without a nation than religion without symbols. One can only reach out to the universe with a gloved hand — that glove is one's nation, th only thing one knows even a little of.[30]

Not merely nationalist, though firmly nationalist, is how Yeats stood. He wanted to educate nationalist Ireland and take it beyond undiscriminating praise of all things Irish, and to interest and impress unionist Ireland and win it from "undiscriminating indifference". "Political passion has made literary opinion in Ireland artificial,", he tells the reader of the Dublin *Daily Press*, in a long letter to the Editor in February 1895.[31] He worked hard, both in England and in Ireland to effect his ends, founding the Irish Literary Society in Ireland, trying to get a series of good Irish books published, sending lists of representative Irish books to editors, endlessly encouraging, critizing, exhorting. His general aim might be summed up in the words of the letter he and Lady Gregory wrote to describe their intentions in founding the Abbey Theatre: "We will show that Ireland is not the home of buffoonery and of easy sentiment, as it has been represented, but the home of an ancient idealism."[32]

That is what Yeats was himself attempting, what he wanted to encourage in others: the expression of that ancient idealism; the recovery of a mythology that by marrying the race to rock and hill would give it unity; the recovery also of the sense prevalent in ancient Ireland of the sacredness of the land, of every spring and stream, mountain and tree, of the indivisibility of all life, past and present, dead and living. One might say that he wanted to be the first great poet to express "the Celtic consciousness in the English language", as an early writer on the movement put it.[33]

Yeats had a fine sense of timing, of knowing when it was practicable to attempt something and when not. "It was the death of Parnell", he writes in "Four Years", that "convinced me that the moment had come for work in Ireland, for I knew that for a time the imagination of young men would turn from politics". In the last pages of "Four Years" he discusses the possibility of a "common design", of "unity" for Ireland.[34] His suggestions are very cautious, very tentative. He had "begun to hope", no, only to "half-hope". Though the words have not been taken as expressing any nationalist ambitions, I see no reason to exclude such a reading. I suspect that Yeats in his wild and great ambitions did hope that a great artistic purpose, accepted by all, Unionist and Nationalist, Catholic and Protestant, would have, as one result, national unity.

Yeats must be considered a great man, apart from being a poet, because he was able to engage so many other people in his visions and aspirations, and because he was able to release powers of creativity in other people, set them flowing where they had been locked up, or merely dribbling in a minor channel. He did this for both Synge and Lady Gregory. They were both prepared for the lifting of the locks, but it was his finger that did the lifting.

In *Memoirs*, Yeats seems to suggest that he considered Lady Gregory an answer to his invocation of the lunar power,[35] an answer, as we lesser mortals might say, to prayer. When he visited her for the first time she asked him to set her to some work for "our intellectual movement". Yeats had no immediate answer for her, but she soon found her way to her own work and from the beginning she was of practical help to him and involved him in her interests. In many poems and in the *Autobiographies* he makes elaborate and generous acknowledgement of all that she meant to him. In *Memoirs* he is more succinct and more open: "I found at last what I had been seeking always, a life of order and labour, where all outward things were the image of an inward life."[36]

All the world knows what came of that historic meeting between Lady Gregory and Yeats: the founding of the Abbey Theatre; the collection of folk-tales, written by Lady Gregory in the dialect of the people, which afterwards she used on the stage, being the first, according to him, so to do;[37] the plays of Yeats and of Lady Gregory herself, of Synge and of many others. The plays of Lady Gregory are out of favour at the moment, perhaps because so many of them are such airy trifles, built on fantasy. In the one-act plays the development of the plots tends to a certain sameness, to a reversal of the situation posited at the beginning: her use of dialect does not always seem to me unerring, but she conveys wonderfully well the irrational working of imaginative but simple and untrained minds and the wild undisciplined instincts of the heart. She also has the gift of being able to visualize the details of an imagined situation, as evidenced by her remark to Bernard Shaw that she would have made the little boy sneeze in the scene in *Joan of Arc* where all are waiting for the wind to change. Above all she can make plays out of delicious and absurd foolery; and she tells us herself that she always tried to see her characters and action in a universal, and not merely a local setting.[38]

Like Yeats there is no doubt about Lady Gregory's aims and ideals. She too wanted to bring upon the stage "the deeper thoughts and emotions of Ireland."[39] She wanted to bring "back dignity to Ireland", she said again and again. She also worked to preserve the old stories of Ireland, with their endless recording of an interchange between this natural world and that other, supernatural world, hidden behind a veil, at times delightful, "the happy Other World", at other times terrifying, but in all its aspects just as real as the natural world to the Celtic Imagination. She worked to bring out a translation, in the language of the people, of the great heroic cycle of the Red Branch stories, in which the ancient idealism of Ireland was embodied and which showed the possibilities of the Anglo-Irish dialect for sustained narrative. She slaved at the practical duties involved in running a theatre. That theatre was the breath of life to her. "The sight of the Abbey audience makes one glad to have been born."[40]

Lady Gregory would in any circumstances have made something of her life, but without Yeats she could not have done the precise work she did. But one can be quite certain that, with or without Yeats, his old friend, AE, George Russell, would have been what he was and done what he did. AE was inspired, as Yeats was, by the revelation of Irish mythology and by love of Ireland in all its physical manifestations. AE's interest in the occult was as intense as Yeats's, his visions of the other world much clearer than any Yeats enjoyed, and of common occurence in his life; as a painter he had the advantage that he could yield visible evidence of the "plumed yet skinny sidhe" that appeared to him. AE went further than Yeats in his reactions to O'Grady's revelations of ancient Ireland. He felt himself a descendent of the old Irish race. The Irish could not be governed by the English, he held, because they were of a different and incompatible race and had shown their refusal of English rule by rising in rebellion in every generation.[41] The 'national being' of each country was different.

AE, however, was not an artist pure and simple. He was distinguished, to use Yeats's phrase, by an 'impassioned versatility'[42], and he was also possessed of the religious temperament; the combination of the two created problems for him as an artist. The impassioned versatility expressed itself in his writing and painting but it also led him into practical life: in 1897 he was invited by Horace Plunkett to help him run the Irish co-operative movement, or the Irish Agricultural Organisation, as it should more properly be called, and in a few months he was being accepted as an expert on pigs and cows and co-operative banks and the like. The Irish Co-operative movement did a great deal to improve rural life in Ireland and was quite remarkably successful. AE could see the irony of his two selves, the contrast between his visions of the past and his efforts to improve the present; on one occasion he wrote of its being a sacrilege to talk about banks in the shadow of Mount Nephin, which was "largely stocked with Gods, immortals and fairies." He felt, nevertheless, that the Gods were fighting a losing battle against the banks.

AE's religious temperament led him to theosophical speculation, occult investigation and experiments in communal living. It caused him to lead a life of great asceticism and benevolence and to become the spiritual leader of a group of people. He was respected by everybody and venerated by many. He is the only one who escapes being made a mock of by George Moore in *Hail and Farewell*, unless it be mockery to be called 'maiutic' AE, the one who helps others to give birth. As an artist, AE was injured by his altruism and versatility. He lacked the egotism necessary to become a great writer or painter; worse, he was not interested in literature for its own sake: — "I simply want to live a natural energetic life and if a poem ever takes me along the way I will welcome it but won't go out of my way to look for one."[43], he wrote to his publisher.

Yeats could be irritated by the egalitarian streak in AE and by his capacity for indiscriminate enthusiasm and lack of intellectual and literary precision. He writes sometime in a very schoolmasterish way to his old friend, for instance in a letter of May 1900 in which he objects to AE's use of the word, 'vague', and to his distinction between the word which gives one's "idea and the more beautiful word". "If you want to give ideas for their own sake, write prose,"[44] he orders. He tells Lady Gregory that AE 'bemoralized' him as long as he could remember. "His moral enthusiasm is with him an active inspiration", he writes, "but it makes him understand ideas and not human nature. One pays a price for everything".[45]

AE served the cause of a new Ireland with unselfish ardour and worked for the reconstruction of Irish life, to help restore it to the dignity and unity which belief in the indivisibility of sense and spirit can create. Like Yeats, he believed that the individual mind and memory is part of *anima mundi*, the universal mind and memory. Rightly understood, the stars will be seen as "villages in God's great depth withdrawn", and the human spirit can clothe "the vast with a familiar face" and reach its right had forth "to greet the starry race". For all his extraordinary gifts, however, AE remains something of a blurred figure, the gifts somewhat dissipated over too large a ground. Like Hyde, he lacked the critical faculty. This makes him appear a rather naïve figure when contrasted with either Yeats or Synge, who both possessed a fine critical discrimination, or with Lady Gregory, who also was a good critic and in addition had the tact of a woman of the world. His was not a concentrated nature.

The very opposite must be said of Synge who came of a family that had constantly thrown up extraordinarily intense and narrow-channelled types of human being, the commonest channel for this intensity finding its way in religion, a very strict form of religion, a pietistic evangelism that saw life in black and white and people as either saved or damned. The Synges married into similar families, and it is quite startling to read of Synge's mother and her mother's determination to keep their children unspoken to and unplayed with by stray Catholic children. John Millington Synge had all the family intensity but with him it took a new channel, the channel of art: Synge knew he was to be an artist before he had found out what his medium was to be. He was forced to be self-absorbed, one might say, because of his upbringing, and to make out of self and the simplest experiences a whole world. If he had not done so, he would have lived in a vacuum. He belonged to the category of writers of whom Coleridge said that their egotism is an expression of genius.

Synge's importance seems to me to be two-fold and to consist in his own achievement and in the effect that he had on Yeats, who was quite aware of the quality of Synge's genius and said of him finer things than has any subsequent critic. "Synge", he writes in the *Death of Synge*, "is that rare, that distinguished, that most noble thing, which of all things still of the world is nearest to being sufficient to itself, the pure artist." He sees Synge as outstandingly important, as being the only Irish writer who, apart from Maria Edgeworth in *Castle Rackrent*, had written in such a way as to change a man's thought about the world or stir his moral nature; the others, he believes,

> but play with pictures, persons and events, that whether ill or well observed, are but an amusement for the mind when it escapes from meditation, a child's show, that makes the fables of his art as significant by contrast as an Egyptian wall: for in these fables, an intelligence on which the tragedy of the world had been thrust in so few years that Life had no time to brew her sleepy drug, has spoken of the moods that are the expression of wisdom. All minds that have a wisdom come of tragic reality seem morbid to those that are accustomed to writers who have not faced reality at all.[46]

I have written elsewhere[47] that Yeats is here suggesting that the facing of tragic reality is wisdom, that the expression of it is the highest art and that Synge is the first Irish tragic artist. We know that Synge spent much of his short life in isolation and study, in wanderings at home and abroad, seeking an understanding of reality and a medium through which he might properly express this. He found the one and the other in the remote country life of Ireland. By living close to the primitive communities of western Ireland and at the same time seeing all with the detached eye of the artist, Synge was able to set these primitive communities on the stage. He was able to write about a period of development once common to all humanity but long vanished from the modern world. His characters represent man living in a pre-industrial world, and Synge was able to give expression to the animistic habits of mind natural to such people. Synge's famous language is among other things the result of this. It, like himself, is pure art; it is artificial in the proper sense of the word, not the result of casual observation but of deliberate invention in which the idioms of Anglo-Irish speech are carefully modulated after the rhythms of the Authorized Version of the Bible.[48]

Such a people and such a language enabled Synge to write with supreme originality. He knew that originality was not enough to make a great writer, that the great writer must also be 'rich' and that no writer will be rich, unless the time and the locality are favourable. It was his good fortune to come into his strength at such a time. Yeats recognized Synge's originality, saw him as a free and strong spirit: "In one thing he and Lady Gregory are the strongest souls I have ever known", and I have wondered if Synge did not embody for Yeats, who was reading Nietzsche at the same time as he was writing about Synge, the Nietzschean concept of the artist's conscience which has become a commonplace of modern thought. Yeats tells us explicitly that Synge affected his whole way of work,[49] and that he felt he must henceforth renounce the deliberate creation of a Holy City in the imagination. Now I doubt if Yeats ever renounced anything. But that he should have felt like this is a measure of Synge's influence on him at the time.

Synge's discovery of old Irish myth and Irish folk-lore was independent of Yeats. He knew Irish and attended Arbois de Jubainville's lectures at the Sorbonne. He published a review of R.I. Best's translation of de Jubainville's *Irish Mythological Cycle and Celtic Mythology*, in which he states: — "Irish Mythology has been found to give, with the oldest mythology that can be gathered from the Homeric poems, the most archaic phase of Indo-European religion".[50] Synge, like Yeats, AE, Hyde, Lady Gregory was a lover of Ireland as a physical entity and knew it better, perhaps, certainly more extensively than any of them.

He realized the literary value of the Anglo-Irish dialect, regarding it, as we have seen, as "une véritable langue matérnelle," a real creation springing from the merging of Irish and English, and he argued fiercely against the Gaelic League's intention of restoring Irish as the vernacular of Ireland. This he saw as a retrogressive step likely to halt the intellectual development of Ireland:[51] he was conscious of living in an intellectual and artistic movement that was revolutionizing Ireland and rejected everything that he feared would put a stop to that. I think

Synge was right in this matter and Hyde wrong. The Anglo-Irish dialect was the spontaneous creation of the people, an expression of Irish mentality through the English language, a miraculous growth without which the Irish Literary Revival could not have taken place.

Yeats once wrote to Fiona MacLeod, whom he did not know at the time to be the same person as William Sharp whose appearance he so disliked: — "I am luckier than you in having a very fierce race to write for." The Irish are indeed fierce, tenacious, intricate, adaptable and indestructible. Because of such qualities the Irish nation rose again from the ashes of conquest and a new literature sprang from the mingling of two languages.

NOTES

[1] Merle Severy, "The Celts", *National Geographic*, Vol. 151, No. 5 (May 1977), 588.

[2] Charlotte Milligan Fox, *Annals of the Irish Harpers* (London 1911), p. 181.

[3] *Ibid.*, pp. 263-4.

[4] *Ibid.*, p. 271.

[5] *Ibid.*, p. 291.

[6] *Royal Irish Collection. Guide to the Celtic Antiquities of the Christian Period. Preserved in the National Museum* (Dublin 1909).

[7] *Ibid.*, p. 49.

[8] *Ibid.*, p. 47.

[9] *Ibid.*, p. 49.

[10] Seán de Fréine, "The Dominance of the English Language in the Nineteenth Century", in *The English Language in Ireland*, ed. Diarmuid Ó Muirthile (Cork 1977), p. 74.

[11] *Ibid.*, 82-7.

[12] W.B. Yeats, "Introduction" to Rabindranath Tagore's *Gitanjali* (London 1913), p. xiv.

[13] *History of Ireland: Critical and Philosophical*, Vol. 1 (London and Dublin 1881), pp. 60-1.

[14] *The Letters of W.B. Yeats*, ed. Allan Wade (London 1954), p. 308.

[15] *Mythologies* pp. 138-9.

[16] Diarmid Coffey, *Douglas Hyde: President of Ireland* (Dublin 1939), p. 134.

[17] W.B. Yeats, *Memoirs*, ed. Denis Donoghue (London 1972), p. 54.

[18] *Letters*, p. 38.

[19] *Ibid.*, p. 47.

[20] *Ibid.*, p. 88.

[21] *Ibid.*, p. 91.

[22]*Ibid.*, p. 503.

[23]*Autobiographies* (London 1966), pp. 218-9.

[24]J.M. Synge, *Collected Works*, Vol. II (Oxford 1966), p. 367.

[25]*Ibid.*, p. 379.

[26]*Letters*, p. 99.

[27]*Ibid.*, p. 51.

[28]*Ibid.*, p. 254.

[29]*Ibid.*, p. 213.

[30]*Letters to the New Island*, ed. Horace Reynolds (Oxford 1970), p. 174.

[31]*Letters*, p. 251.

[32]Lady Gregory, *Our Irish Theatre* (New York 1965), p. 9. First published in 1913.

[33]Lloyd R. Morris, *The Celtic Dawn, 1889—1916* (New York 1970), p. 10. First published in 1917.

[34]*Autobiographies*, pp. 194-5.

[35]*Memoirs*, pp. 100-2.

[36]*Ibid.*, p. 101.

[37]*Autobiographies*, p. 400.

[38]*Collected Plays*, Vol. 1 (Gerrard's Cross 1979), p. 266.

[39]*Our Irish Theatre*, p. 9.

[40]*Lady Gregory's Journals, 1916—1930.* ed. Lennox Robinson (London 1946), p. 63.

[41]*Thoughts for a Convention on the Present State of Ireland* (Dublin 1921).

[42]*Autobiographies*, p.242.

[43]Richard Kain and James O'Brien, *George Russell* (Lewisburg 1976), p. 33.

[44]*Letters*, p. 343.

[45]*Ibid.*, p. 345.

[46]*Essays and Introductions* (London 1961), p. 323.

[47]"Yeats, Synge and Nietzsche", *Essays and Studies of the English Association* (London 1973), p. 94.

[48]See my article, "The Rhythms of Synge's Prose", *Yeats Studies*, No. 2 (Shannon 1972), pp. 52-65.

[49]*Autobiographies*, p. 473.

[50]*Collected Works*, II, 365.

[51]*Ibid.*, pp. 399-400.

THE AESTHETIC AND INTELLECTUAL FOUNDATIONS OF THE CELTIC LITERARY REVIVAL IN IRELAND*

ROBERT O'DRISCOLL

In a little time places may begin to seem the only hieroglyphs that cannot be forgotten, and poets to remember that they will come the nearer the old poets, who had a seat at every hearth, if they mingle their own dream with a story told for centuries.

W. B. Yeats

I

Before the flowering of the Celtic Literary Revival in Ireland at the end of the nineteenth century, there had been much conscious and unconscious preparation for the movement. In those crevices of significant soil that progress and industrialization had passed by and where the Irish language was still spoken, Celtic traditions survived, traditions in music, myth, and folklore that stretched back hundreds, and some of them even thousands of years to pre-Christian and pre-Roman times: successive invasions by the Vikings, Normans, and English had in many ways left the native culture undisturbed. But in the parts of Ireland that had not chosen the weapons of silence and exile for self-preservation, those parts of the country that, through force, necessity or expediency had adopted the tongue of their temporary conquerors, the great Celtic traditions that had been the heritage of their ancestors were, to all intents and purposes, lost. There were, of course, points of contact, but as time progressed the Celtic civilization slipped further and further out of the literary and historical consciousness of the modern world, until in the nineteenth century the civilization had to be dramatically re-discovered: to many it was not a discovery but a revelation.

James Macpherson was in some ways the catalyst for this re-discovery, producing during the 1760's his Ossianic translations which, as every undergraduate knows, were forgeries, in that they puported to be authentic translations of a third-century poet. Nevertheless, Macpherson's work did open up Celtic literature to English and European attention, and caught off guard some scholars and historians who went so far as to deny the existence of any Celtic civilization whatsoever: the Scottish historian, John Pinkerton, for example, writes in 1789:

*I express my gratitude to Bill and Cathy Graham for a log-cabin and a portion of Glenariff Farm, Ontario, where this paper was written. The paper was prepared for the Conference on "Canada and the Celtic Consciousness," but was not delivered because of the scarcity of lecture slots. Instead, it was delivered at the Conference of the International Association for the Study of Anglo-Irish Literature in Galway, and part of it was published in Andrew Carpenter, ed., *Place, Personality and the Irish Writer* (Bucks., 1977), pp. 41-68.

The former [the Irish antiquaries] say, their country was highly civilized, had letters and academies, as the Greeks and Roman. The latter [the European antiquaries] say, the Greeks we know, and the Romans we know, but who are ye? Those Greeks and Romans pronounce you not only barbarous, but utterly savage. Where are your authorities against this? In the name of that degree of rationality which even some beasts have, where are the slightest marks of civilization among you? Where are ruins of cities? Where inscriptions? Where ancient art or science in your whole island? The old inhabitants of your country, the Wild Irish, the true Milesian breed, untainted with Gothic blood, we know to be utter savages at this day. Can a nation, once civilized, ever become savage? Impossible![1]

The nineteenth century witnessed the gradual recovery of the Celtic civilization: it was a century of painstaking research and of imaginative flashes. Early Christian artifacts and treasures of the Bronze Age were discovered; coins and inscriptions were studied and historical records published; pioneering topographical, archaeological, and architectural investigations were conducted; philologists began to study the Irish language in its broader Indo-European context; the ancient Brehon laws were published and traditional Irish music rescued; poems in the Irish language were translated, and their metrical patterns and idioms introduced for the first time in English; Celtic legends were edited and the first expository poems based on Celtic myth were written. There were, as I say, a few flashes: by the Unionist Ferguson, who began his investigation of the literary legacy of his Catholic countrymen as an intellectual curiosity and was led into an imaginative immersion in the past: by Mangan who, in his achievement of self-expression by a passionate identification with past heroes and crucial moments in his country's history, knew instinctively the mythic mode; and by Standish James O'Grady, whose *History of Ireland* presented an imaginative reconstruction of early Celtic life and made the heroic period and mythic characters "once again a portion of the imagination of the country".[2] O'Grady's *History*, Yeats writes, did more "than anything else to create that preoccupation with Irish folklore and legend and epic which is called the Irish literary movement."[3]

II

From the faltering, painstaking, and sometimes intuitive work of the nineteenth-century poets, antiquaries, and historian to the full critical and artistic articulation of the ideals of the Celtic Renaissance was a great imaginative leap. This leap of the imagination was accomplished by the two poets and visionaries who were the spiritual leaders of the Renaissance, W.B. Yeats and George Russell (AE), and in exploring the ideals of the Revival I shall illustrate my arguments now from the one writer, now from the other: indeed, so close are their ideas that it is sometimes difficult to indicate where the first articulation of a particular perception originates.

It is difficult to say at what precise point, and in what circumstances, the being or genius or deity that shapes a national character enters once again the poetic and popular consciousness.[4] What one can say is that almost from the beginning of their creative careers Yeats and AE recognized what they had been chosen to accomplish: they believed themselves to be mediums chosen to express the uncreated consciousness of their race, and the movement they created was not "a self-conscious endeavour to make a literature," but the spontaneous expression of an impulse that had been gathering power for centuries.[5] In the beginning of all important things, Yeats writes, "there is a moment when we understand more perfectly than we understand again until all is finished."[6] Yeats and AE cannot be dismissed as being involved in a kind of provincial primitivism, or of concerning themselves with Celtic lore and legend in order to give their work local colour: what they deliberately set out to accomplish was to lay the spiritual and intellectual foundation of the modern Irish nation, to make what was instinctive, and on the point of being lost, part of conscious art, and, by extension, once again part of the national consciousness.

III

For Yeats and AE, frontiers, boundaries, race, language, religion, or even blood do not define or constitute a nation: the bonds that bind a people into a nation are not physical but 'psychic'. A nation, AE writes, is "a collective imagination held with intensity, an identity of culture or consciousness among millions, which makes them act as a single entity in relation to other human groups."[7] Neither is a nation the creation of practical parliamentarians or politicians: centuries of subjective and brooding thought precede its creation, and the true architects of a nation are artists, the heroes of history, and the figures of mythology:

> A nation exists primarily because of its own imagination of itself. It is a spirit created by the poets, historians, musicians, by the utterances of great men, the artists in life. The mysterious element of beauty, of a peculiar beauty, exists in every nation and is the root cause of the love felt for it by the citizens, just as the existence of spirit, the most mysterious and impalpable thing, is the fountain of the manifold activities of the body.[8]

The figures of mythology, these writers suggest, are not an individual creation, but the communal creation of the people themselves, "through a slow process of modification and adaptation," to express their ideals and their passions, their loves and their hates.[9] For AE the figures of mythology are a gift from heaven: they "come out of the spirit," descending "from the heaven-world of the imagination into the national being."[10] It makes little difference whether these figures had any historical existence, whether they ever lived in a physical sense: the fact is that they have lived in the national consciousness, and to generation after generation, brooding and recounting their fantastic deeds, they are living presences, "as real", AE claims, "as flesh and blood."[11]

The heroes of history also contribute to the national being: when they die their heroic acts pass from earth and become part of the "immortal memory" of the nation, chiefly because of the dramatic or artistic quality of the acts themselves, or because of the way in which the heroes and their heroic acts are mythologized by the artist. Art is, therefore, the agency through which the essence of a nation "filters into [the] national consciousness,"[12] and the artist is an instrument by which the heroes of history and the figures of mythology become living presences in the mind of the people: nothing is more important in the life of a nation "than the images which haunt the minds of its people, for it is by these they are led to act."[13] Imagination, AE writes, whether "spiritual or national, is the most powerful thing in human affairs. Intangible itself, it moves bodies. Invisible itself, it changes visible civilizations."[14] The artist too, when his work is done, enters the national imagination, is consumed into the dance or trance of his own art: "the poetry of Yeats," AE writes, "is the greatest spiritual gift any Irishman has made to his tribe."[15] And elsewhere AE suggests that Yeats and the writers of the Celtic Revival "will act through many men and women, and the birth of their imaginations will be as important in the evolution of Irish character and nationality as the fight in Easter week."[16]

A nation, therefore, is a living entity constituted "of immortal deeds and heroic spirits, influencing the living, a life within their life, moulding their spirits to its likeness."[17] Every heroic deed in the life of a nation is an act of the spirit; every perception of beauty by an artist or visionary brings the divine essence animating the nation closer to the articulated consciousness of the people, until by a sequence of heroic acts and artistic perception the "accumulated beauty" of the ages becomes more compelling than the necessities of daily life: "the dream ... [begins] to enter into the children of our race, and their thoughts turn from earth to that [divine] world in which it had its inception."[18]

IV

For the writers of the Celtic Revival the roots of Irish Nationality ran deep, deeper than the events that have shaped the Western world: the Roman empire, Christianity, the Renaissance, and the Industrial Revolution: "Behind all Irish history," Yeats writes, "hangs a great tapestry, even Christianity had to accept it and be itself pictured there. Nobody looking at its dim folds can say where Christianity begins and Druidism ends."[19] And in his lecture with the arresting title, "The Necessity of De-Anglicizing Ireland," Douglas Hyde writes, rather flamboyantly, that behind the expression of Irish nationality

is the half unconscious feeling that the race which at one time held possession of more than half Europe, which established itself in Greece, and burned infant Rome, is now — almost extirpated and absorbed elsewhere — making its last stand for independence in this island of Ireland; and do what they may the race of to-day cannot wholly divest itself from the mantle of its own past. Through early Irish literature, for instance, can we best form some conception of what that race really was, which, after overthrowing and trampling on the primitive peoples of half Europe, was itself forced in turn to yield its speech, manners, and independence to the victorious eagles of Rome. We alone of the nations of Western Europe escaped the claws of those birds of prey; we alone developed ourselves naturally upon our own lines outside of and free from all Roman influence; we alone were thus able to produce an early art and literature, *our* antiquities can best throw light upon the pre-Romanised inhabitants of half Europe. . . . The dim consciousness of this is one of those things which are at the back of Irish national sentiment, and our business, whether we be Unionists of Nationalists, shoud be to make this dim consciousness an active and potent feeling. . . .[20]

The Celtic civilization, Yeats and Hyde and AE contended, was unique in Europe because it had escaped the yoke of the Roman Empire, the secularization of the Renaissance, and, perhaps more importantly, the material domination of the industrial world. But Ireland, although achieving an advanced civilization when the rest of Europe was plunged in darkness, had, at the end of the nineteenth century, not yet been born as a modern state, as a collective political unit, the reason for this being the cultural, political, and economic oppression the Irish had suffered at the hands of the British. Throughout these centuries of oppression, however, Ireland had never lost the consciousness of herself as an independent entity, and of her essential difference from the English nation.

V

The difference between the two nations was clearly apprehended by the leaders of the Celtic Revival. The English nation, they argued, had been shaped on the principles of imperial domination and material success,[21] and although the incorporated ideals of the Italian Renaissance had brought to England a sense of personality and a new emphasis on the capabilities of man, they had, when subsumed into the Anglo-Saxon mentality, resulted in a scientific approach to the world, imperialism, materialism, industrialization, urbanization, collectivization, and a false sense of progress.[22]

Imperialism, whether it be of the visible physical kind practiced by England from the seventeenth to the twentieth century, or of the subtle, even more effective, invisible variety being successfully pursued by several world powers today, imposes on the individual or nation the model of another people, and insists that all citizens have "their minds poured into the same mould," and that "varieties of gifts" and distinctive cultural traditions be obliterated.[23] This imposition of an imperialist ideal was rejected by the writers of the Celtic Revival long before the political and military leaders created a physical body for the spiritual principles:

> empires do not permit the intensive cultivation of human life: . . . they destroy the richness and variety of existence by the extinction of peculiar and unique gifts, and the substitution therefore of a culture which has its value mainly for the people who created it, but is as alien to our race as the mood of the scientist is to the artist or poet.[24]

Imperialism and materialism are closely linked. Materialism is built on the belief that matter is the sole reality, that only the limited life of the body is real, that there is no essential difference between the natural and spiritual order, and that knowledge can be discovered through observation of the external world and the analysis of impressions derived from the five senses. Materialism contracts man's consciousness by limiting him to personal experience. Because it originates in egotism, in action for the consequences of action and for the acquisition of possessions, materialism must conclude in rigid laws, barbed-wire fences, and conspiracies.

The principles of imperialism and materialism had, Yeats and AE contended, affected the development of English literature. In the first place, English literature had no native mythology. Shakespeare had, of course, used English history as the subject of some of his plays, and had there been no Renaissance and no Italian influence, English history might, Yeats contends, "have become as important to the English imagination as the Greek myths to the Greek imagination."[25] When they attempted to use myth to express their own personalities, English writers looked therefore to Greece, Rome, or the land of the Bible, to myths of foreign lands, and to myths that had grown threadbare with use, until by the time a William Blake emerged, he was, in Yeats's words, "a man crying out for a mythology," and having no national myths, he had to invent his own.[26] England, of course, had over the centuries produced a great literature, but it was a literature of the few that had been shaped almost completely by the printing-press, and during the nineteenth century England succumbed to what Yeats called the "cold, joyless, irreligious" scientific movement.[27] Nineteenth-century English novels and the poetry of Wordsworth, Tennyson, Browning, and even that of Shelley and Swinburne, tried, Yeats claimed, "to absorb into itself the science and politics, the philosophy and morality of its time."[28] Literature, as the nineteenth century advanced, became utilitarian, rhetorical, sentimental, and journalistic: it turned to study and mimesis of the external world, to commentary on the social, humanitarian, and topical interests of the time, to moral judgement and accusation. English literature, in short, turned into a criticism of life, and began to use as its means of expression the weapons of science: observation, explanation, argument, theory, and erudition.

VI

The writers of the Celtic Revival maintained that the development of Irish literature and history and character was distinct and separate from the development of the English, that the Celtic perception of life was different from the English, and that the Irish people constituted a nation with a distinctive cultural and spiritual heritage. Indeed, so deep was the antagonism between Ireland and England that it sprang, AE claims, from "biological and spiritual necessity."[29] This antagonism had expressed itself throughout the centuries in rebellion after rebellion, and the leaders of these rebellions were, AE contends, not merely fighting for a political change, but were the "desparate and despairing champions of a culture which ... was being stifled from infancy."[30] But no amount of physical force or oppression can, AE argues in his seminal pamphlet, *The Inner and The Outer Ireland,* kill the desire to express a national spirit, and so the Irish nation had hung on for centuries, waiting patiently for circumstance to enable them to escape their conquerors, or for the mills of God to grind the British Empire to dust, as other empires had been ground to dust before. This desire to express the national character in literature and in life may seem at times a hopeless cause, but physical death, AE argues in 1901, is preferable to spiritual defeat, or to the denial of the spirit that animates a nation: "God gives no second gift to a nation if it flings away its birthright. We cannot put on the ideals of another people as a garment."[31]

At the root, then, of the antagonism between Ireland and England, of the historical rebellions and the literary revival, was the battle between two traditions, two ways of perceiving the world: "What is this nationality we are trying to preserve," Yeats asks in a public lecture in 1903, "this thing we are fighting English influence to preserve? It is not merely our pride. It is certainly not any national vanity that stirs us on to activity. If you examine to the root a contest between two peoples, two nations, you will always find that it is really a war between two civilizations, two ideals of life."[32] What the writers of the Celtic Revival were demanding was the freedom to express the "spiritual life" of the Irish race, the right to work out the national destiny,[33] and to manifest the national genius in a civilization that was not an echo or an imitation of another: "We ask," AE pleads, "the liberty of shaping the social order in Ireland to reflect our own ideals, and to embody that national soul which has been slowly incarnating in our race from its cloudy dawn."[34] On the outcome of this battle there was more at stake than the destiny of Ireland: the battle was not merely one of Ireland against England, not even one of people against people, but of the individual soul against bureaucracy, of spiritual forces against the forces of empire and state,[35] and a portion of the "everlasting battle" between light and darkness, good and evil, spirit and matter.[36] In the resolution of this battle, AE contends, lies the hope of humanity, the realizations of "universal human hopes," the solution of "eternal problems": the "typical humanity" of the world, AE writes "exists in germ in the spiritual and intellectual outcasts of our time, who can find no place in the present social order."[37]

VII

The Celtic Revival was deliberately created as a counter-movement to the materialism of the post-Darwinian age. Yeats and AE did not believe in evolution or progress: for these poets, change in the history of man was not slow and methodical, but sudden and miraculous, a leap of the imagination: "all life is revelation," Yeats writes, "beginning in miracle and enthusiasm, and dying out as it unfolds itself in what we have mistaken for progress."[38] Neither did they believe that literature was a criticism of visible life, but that it was a revelation of an invisible world. They saw the poet not as the servant of society, nor as a passive commentator on the political or social concerns of the time, but as the medium of immortal emotion, writing out of a deeper life than his own, receiving his inspiration from the Collective Memory of his race, interpreting and remaking the modern world according to the impulses he receives in meditation and vision. "Talk to me of originality and I will turn on you with rage. I am a crowd, I am a lonely man, I am nothing," Yeats writes at the end of his life.[39] With Plato and Plotinus, Yeats and AE believed that individual human life was an ephemeral flower blooming from the perennial rhizone, with death returning to the great ocean of being, withering and descending into the rhizone, to bloom again in another spring, in another incarnation. Mankind is not complete, the initiator of action, but merely the foam upon the deep, merely the momentary blossom of some spiritual impulse. Through man, and more particularly through the poet, the invisible moods of the universe work their will; the great unchanging myths are constantly being enacted and re-enacted. The images that present themselves to the poet, therefore, do not originate in his individual consciousness, but are given to him from the composite mind and living memory of his race. They come, as it were, "out of the ancestral being," and are more easily apprehended in places where the traditional order of life remains unbroken.[40] This visionary communion of the individual personality and the racial memory, of the modern Irish poet and the Celtic past, Yeats and AE considered as an aspect of the Celtic approach to experience, and over and over in their work they probe the nature and significance of vision, meditation, dream, intuition, imagination, and magic.

In the beginning of the world, and in places where the plough of modern civilization had not cut too deep, as in the Celtic world, there was no separation between matter and spirit: when "a man beheld a natural object the spiritual thing it expressed came at once into his mind."[41] All of the material forms of nature were holy and haunted. But as the centuries progressed, mind and matter, the inner spiritual meaning and the outer material form, began to separate, and man turned from the expression of his own mind to the study of the external world for its own sake. Yeats and AE, on the other hand, viewed the world symbolically, seeing the visible material world as the means by which an invisible spiritual essence becomes manifest to mortal eyes, and interpreting all physical and intellectual forms, all art and nature, as the expression or embodiment of the universal mood at the centre of the universe which Yeats calls God.[42] Materialism, according to Yeats, reaches its zenith during the twentieth century, but at this point, suddenly, miraculously, the opposite of all that is characteristic of materialistic thought is born. Man, having become enchanted to the outer form, to possessions and the consequences of action, suddenly becomes sated with science, sensation, and analyses of the external world, and he returns instinctively and dramatically to the spiritual world he has neglected. Yeats links the Celtic Revival to this symbolic apocalypse that was to sweep away the concept of literature as a criticism of life and to usher in "an age of imagination, of emotion, of moods, of revelation."[43] "This revolution," Yeats writes, "may be the opportunity for the Irish Celt, for he has an unexhausted and inexhaustible mythology to give him symbols and personages, and his nature has been profoundly emotional from the beginning."[44]

VIII

Rejecting the earlier traditions of Irish writing in English — the tradition of Congreve, Goldsmith, Sheridan, and their followers, who used England and London as a platform for the expression of Irish wit and anarchical wisdom; the tradition of Edmund Burke and Bernard Shaw who, starting from the premise that Ireland was an integral part of the United Kingdom, went on to posit that the moral purification of England and the Empire could be accomplished by Irishmen; and the tradition of the Young Ireland writers, who created "images for the affections" of the Irish people by using English literary models[45] — rejecting these traditions, the writers of the Celtic Revival turned to poetry in the Irish language, to folklore, and to myth.

Yeats was interested in Gaelic poetry because of the natural energies it celebrated, because it was not a poetry of material security, success, and complacence, but a poetry articulating the beliefs and hopes of the weak and vulnerable, and, like the poetry of the Rhymers' Club, created out of the despair and desolation of defeat. The fact that it was a poetry built on dreams linked it in Yeats's mind to the nature of all great poetry:

> poetry is the utterance of desires that we can only satisfy in dreams, and . . . if all our dreams were satisfied there would be no more poetry. . . . The children of the poor and simple learn from their unbroken religious faith, and from their traditional beliefs, and from the hardness of their lives, that this world is nothing, and that a spiritual world, where all dreams come true, is everything; and therefore the poor and simple are that imperfection whose perfection is genius.[46]

In their collections of folklore and in their work based on folklore, Yeats, Lady Gregory, Douglas Hyde, and John Synge discovered or created an approach to life that contravened the modern materialistic approach. Ireland, they maintained, was one of the last spiritual strongholds in Europe, and the Celt, they held, still retained contact with the mystery and imagination that existed before man fell a slave to the external world. In Celtic folklore, too, Yeats and AE found corroboration for their occult experiments and philosophic reading: evidence of the existence of an invisible world, of the continuance of life after death, and proof of the immortality of the soul.[47]

The Celt, in the stories collected or created by the writers of the Revival, is not concerned with probability or necessity, but only with the expression of emotion. He perceives the correspondence between sensuous form and supersensuous meaning and recognizes instinctively the spirit that gives a voice to the dumb things that surround him. Not distinguishing clearly between the natural and the supernatural, and believing that all nature is full of invisible spirits that can be perceived by those willing to look beyond the cobweb veil of the senses, the Celt sees everything as enchanted. He is filled with reverence for the past and a sense of the sanctity and mystery of everything that surrounds him. The mythical associations of topographical sites are fresh in his mind. To the Celt in these stories the land is still holy and haunted.

The Celt, the writers of the Revival found, did not live in a shrunken over-defined world, but lingered constantly "on the edges of vision," learning to live with the spirits that haunted his solitary world, seeking to capture in imaginative idiom or tale "some high, impalpable mood," attempting to express "a something that lies beyond the range of expression" [48] creating, like the Rhymers, in the deprivation of material life a mask or compensating dream. Like great artists, these visionaries had the power to mythologize places and people, to transform mortal men and women into the immortal images of art, to transform, for example, Mary Hynes and Raftery into "perfect symbols of the sorrow of beauty and of the magnificence and penury of dreams." [49] And like great artists, these Celtic visionaries possessed a living permanent tradition that refused to surrender to the "small arrogant oligarchy" of those who merely happen to be walking around; they possessed traditional images and emotions that carried "their memories backward thousands of years." [50] They communed with the dead generations, receiving from the racial Memory images that come to meditative minds. They were fully cognizant of the tragedy and imperfections of unaccommodated man, realizing the brevity of life, accepting the conditions of life, and summoning courage and dignity when faced with defeat and death.

Alone among European nations, Ireland, Yeats claimed, possessed a wealth of folk stories and legends that had not yet been shaped into modern literature:

> Ireland has in her written Gaelic literature, in her old love tales and battle tales, the forms in which the imagination of Europe uttered itself before Greece shaped a tumult of legend into the music of her arts; and she can discover, from the beliefs and emotions of her common people, the habit of mind that created the religion of the muses. The legends of other European countries are less numerous, and not so full of the energies from which the arts and our understanding of their sanctity arose, and the best of them have already been shaped into plays and poems. [51]

The aim of the leaders of the Celtic Revival was to combine the imagination that is expressed in folklore and legend with the imagination that has produced the wrought sophisticated literature of the world, in other words to bridge the written and unwritten traditions and to establish a modern literary tradition on emotions that come from the heart of the people. The artist, they argued, must realize that he is the spiritual leader of his people, and he must adopt the "method and the fervour of a priesthood." [52] Like the priest, he must root his art in ancient ceremonies and use them to illuminate and interpret the unchanging passions of daily life. The scientific movement had pushed modern literature into one of two directions: into subservience to an external reality or a concern with rarefied essences. One type of literature was concerned with the spiritual element which the other type denied, but neglected the interest in common life with which the other literature was too much concerned.[53] We remember Synge's famous stricture of both types in the Preface to *Playboy of the Western World*, of the literature of Mallarmé on the one hand, and the literature of Ibsen on the other. The Celtic literary Revival aimed at the reconciliation of the past and the present, art and life, the spiritual and the common, the seen and the unseen. The modern Irish poet, these writers maintained, must learn what the common people knew instinctively: sanctity of place, a sense of tradition, love of the unseen, the daring and imaginative impulse that animates folk life and legend.

IX

When we turn from folklore to myth and to the problems in creating a modern literature out of old myths, we find ourselves on a more difficult terrain. The scientific explanation of the phenomenal world, separating as it did the intellect from emotion and the imagination, did not satisfy the whole being: it left the senses cold. We can trace the horror of the poet caught in a scientific age without the resources of myth in two of the characteristic poems produced in England during the nineteenth and twentieth centuries, *In Memoriam* and *The Waste Land*. Myth is created by the imagination acting on the evidence of the senses and is a pre-rational attempt to explain human life and the universe. Since, as Professor Lorna Reynolds argues, the new areas of human experience that Yeats and his fellow-writers were elucidating were part of the subconscious deposit of the pre-rational development of man, they turned instinctively to myth.[54] Myth is sensuous and tactile: it explains and dramatizes events in the external world in terms of the "unconscious drama" of the human psyche:[55] the adventures of mythic heroes, AE explains, may "correspond to adventures of the spirit, conflicts between the bright power and the dark powers in ourselves."[56] Without a traditional mythology, a writer must rely on the inventiveness of his own mind; his creations, consequently, must be arbitrary and original. Through myth, on the other hand, an artist is brought beyond the limitations of his individual being, beyond the accidental forms of the world to the essence that these forms embody and to the imaginative events and characters in which these essences were first expressed in the national consciousness. A modern man living without myth is, Jung writes, "like one uprooted, having no true link either with the past, or with the ancestral life which continues within him, or yet with contemporary human society. He ... lives a life of his own, sunk in a subjective mania of his own devising, which he believes to be the newly discovered truth."[57] Myth provides an extravagant expression of pure emotion — of love, terror, joy, friendship — a means of re-shaping the world according to the impulses and desires of the human psyche working in communion with the collective Memory of the race, and without any regard to prudence, practicality, probability, or necessity.[58] It deals with imaginative events and characters which, having been brooded upon by generations and tested throughout the centuries, are "steeped in emotion;"[59]

characters and events created at a time when "the elemental virtues" were prized[60] and which have been brought to a kind of perfection because they are not the work of one mind but of many minds, the same feature, incidentally, that attracted Yeats to Byzantine mosaics. With myth, therefore, and a literature created from myth, modern man is released from the despair of an industrialized Iron age, and is provided with a link between his own age and the heroic age of the past, between his own individual consciousness and the consciousness of his race.

A race does not change in essentials: only the circumstances of life change. What was embodied in the Celtic mythic heroes may, AE argues, still be natural and innate in the character of the race. Cuchulain, AE goes on to suggest, must be restored to the twentieth-century consciousness at the precise point when the modern Irish nation was beginning to form, because he embodies "all that the bards thought noblest in the spirit of their race.[61] Myth is concerned with the heroic, and in their work the writers of the Celtic Revival consciously created for the popular mind heroic models of human behaviour and encouraged the nation to emulate these models through all the vicissitudes of earthly life.[62] One does not have to search deeply in Yeats's work to discover what he thought characteristic of the heroic approach to life: self-possession, acceptance of the conditions of life, abandonment to impulse and emotion, to whatever impulse is most immediate and pressing, courage when confronted with impossible odds, gaiety in the face of terror and defeat, indifference to death. One should also consider in this context the way in which Yeats contributes to the imaginative entity that we have called a nation by celebrating and mythologizing the heroic acts and character of his contemporaries, the gallery of living presences he creates in his poetry by releasing his contemporaries from cold history and time, capturing each in his most characteristic pose, making out of mortal men and women symbols to be brooded over in the coming times: Maud Gonne, Roger Casement, Patrick Pearse, The O'Rahilly, John Synge, John Butler Yeats, Robert Gregory, MacGregor Mathers, and many others.

Myths are also connected with places that men still inhabit, places sanctified by the passions enacted there in ancient times, and which still retain emotional residues of that passion: "in our land," Yeats writes,

> there is no river or mountain that is not associated in the memory with some event or legend. . . . I would have our writers and craftsmen of many kinds master this history and these legends, and fix upon their memory the appearance of mountains and rivers and make it all visible again in their arts, so that Irishmen, even though they had gone thousands of miles away, would still be in their own country. . . . I would have Ireland re-create the ancient arts, the arts as they were understood . . . in every ancient land; as they were understood when they moved a whole people and not a few people who had grown up in a leisured class and made this understanding their business. . . . I would have . . . [scholars and artists] begin to dig in Ireland the garden of the future, understanding that here in Ireland the spirit of man may be about to wed the soil of the world.[63]

By rooting his art in places with mythic associations, an artist makes his country live in the imagination of his own people and in the imagination of the world. We are familiar with the way in which Yeats mythologizes places in many of his poems, capturing the light and colour of the Irish climate and scenery, restoring to places their mythological associations, and giving them new levels of poetic association,[64] while some of his plays — *The Dreaming of the Bones, The Words Upon the Window-Pane,* and *Purgatory* — derive their dramatic strength from being set in places where human passions played out in ancient times prove more powerful than the presence of the living.

<h1 style="text-align:center">X</h1>

"In a little time," Yeats writes, "places may begin to seem the only hieroglyphs that cannot be forgotten, and poets . . . will come . . . nearer the old poets, who had a seat at every hearth, if they but mingle their own dream with a story told for centuries."[65] What the writers of the Celtic Revival attempted to do was to knead the qualities that animate myth and folk literature into the circumstances of the life of an Irish artist living in the twentieth century, to produce a literature that retained the idealism of country people without "renouncing the complexity of ideas and emotions which is the heritage of cultivated man."[66] We may cite a few examples from Yeats's work to indicate how he used myth to dramatize moments or situations that have become or are becoming part of the twentieth-century approach to experience: the juxtaposition of intense vision and orthodox concerns which forms part of the art of the 1937 *Vision, Ideas of Good and Evil,* and the occult stories he produced during the eighteen-nineties. In *The King's Threshold,* the hunger strike is, I gather, used for the first time in modern life or literature to gain a personal or political objective. Deirdre, Yeats makes symbolic of twentieth-century woman and of woman's liberation from domestic and sexual enslavement, of her right to choose her fate, and having chosen it, to face heroically the consequences of that choice: Deirdre, Yeats writes, "might be some mild housewife but for her prophetic wisdom."[67] *On Baile's Strand,* a play filled with emotion of multitude, is one of the first plays of the absurd, where we have a true juxtaposition of incongruities: of the spiritual and the common, the Golden Age and the Iron Age,[68] the heroic impulse and the material betrayal of that impulse all caught in one moving moment at the end of the play.

In rooting his art in myth, the artist, Yeats suggests, may be responding to impulses which "have been accumulating for centuries,"[69] but once he has chosen his subject he must be concerned with nothing further than the expression of his own personality: he must, in Yeats's words, "think of nothing but giving it [his subject] such an expression as will please himself. . . . He must make his work a part of his own journey towards beauty and truth."[70] Personality is the expression of the energy that is unique to an individual engaged in active life or literature,[71] an expression unmotivated by ulterior advantage, material advancement, or that "last infirmity of Noble mind," what John Milton calls "Fame." Personality is the living personal element that animates action, language, and thought. It is what makes one man's perception of the world different from another, originating in the uniqueness of each individual, and expressing itself in action or in a work of art with an energy that remains after the dictates of logic and necessity have been satisfied.[72] Initially the artist's vision may seem at variance with his countrymen's preconceptions, for he presents his images as he sees them, not as his people expect him to see them.[73] The battle between the artist and his audience, and Yeats's defence of the right of the artist, whether he be a Synge or an O'Casey, to embody his own vision without regard to any utilitarian or obviously nationalistic cause, could be traced in another paper.[74] A national literature, Yeats writes, is created by writers "who are moulded by influences that are moulding their country, and who write out of so deep a life that they are accepted there in the end."[75] And in *Portrait of the Artist as a Young Man* Joyce writes: "This race and this country and this life produced me. . . . I shall express myself as I am."[76] By expressing his own personality an artist inevitably expresses the deeper thoughts and emotions of his race. To be national is to be personal.

XI

In modern Ireland the relation between literature and politics is a profound one. The economist Maynard Keynes writes: "The political fanatic who is hearing voices in the air has distilled his frenzy from the work of some academic scribbler of a few years back."[77] When we are dealing not merely with an "academic scribbler" but with a community of great artists, the voice that stirs the fanatic to political activity may be irresistible. The language that Yeats and AE used to advocate cultural and political separation from Britain was as uncompromising and as calculated to stir the soul of the nation as the language of Patrick Pearse, James Connolly, and their revolutionary associates. In *The National Being*, published in 1916, AE writes:

> when national ideals have been created they assume an immeasurably greater dignity when the citizens organize themselves for the defence of their ideals, and are prepared to yield up life itself as a sacrifice if by this the national being may be preserved. . . . There are occasions when the manhood of a nation must be prepared to yield life rather than submit to oppression, when it must perish in self-contempt or resist by force what wrong would be imposed by force. . . . We are standing on the threshold of nationhood.[78]

Earlier, in 1903, a year after the stirring production of *Cathleen Ni Houlihan* with Maud Gonne playing the lead, Yeats stated in a public lecture which is as yet unpublished:

> When I speak to myself those names that are rated upon the rosary of our national life; when I repeat to myself the name of Parnell, that haughty and austere spirit, or the name of Wolfe Tone, that joyful spirit, who kept his triumph and [triumphant?] air even under the shadow of death; when I think of the Red Man of the O'Donnells and of that Hugh O'Neill, who seemed, even when a lad, to be born to be a prince of men, who was born, the chronicler said, for the great weal or woe of his country; when I think of those men I say to myself that the greatest sin a man can commit against his race and against mankind is to bring the work of the dead to nothing. . . . We all hope that Ireland's battle is drawing to an end, but we must live as though it were to go on endlessly. We must . . . pass on into the future the great moral qualities

that give men the strength to fight .... It may be that it depends upon us to call into life the phantom armies of the future. If we keep that thought always before us, if we never allow ourselves to forget those armies, we need have no fear for the future of Ireland.[79]

Through the power of the imagination of the leaders of the Celtic Revival, Cuchulain, a Bronze Age hero, suddenly re-appears in the twentieth century, and he appears not only in literary works, but he becomes a living image and presence, a model for the expression of the heroic impulse. Cuchulain provides the inspiration for one of the most significant historical events in the twentieth century, the Easter Rising of 1916 which heralded the break-up of the mightiest empire ever forged in the history of the world.

The Rising was itself conceived and enacted as a theatrical event, and the theatrical aspects of the occasion are clear in the time and setting chosen for the event, and in the dress, actions, and theatrical concerns of the major participants. Many of the leaders — Pearse, Plunkett, and MacDonagh — were, as we know, poets and playwrights, and perhaps more importantly, they had directed plays. F.X. Martin directs our attention to the conspicuous theatrical element in their dress and public gestures: MacDonagh with his sword-stick and cloak; Eamonn Ceannt with his kilt and bagpipes; Plunkett with his immense Celtic rings and bracelets and marrying in a midnight ceremony the night before his execution at dawn; the dying Connolly tied to a stretcher to be shot; Countess Markiewicz "concluding her activities in Easter Week at the time of the surrender by ostentatiously kissing her revolver and Sam Browne belt as she handed them over to the British Officer"; and Pearse himself reading the Proclamation of the Irish Republic with the "classical front" of the General Post Office and its "Ionic pillars and portico" serving as a background, and the night before his execution writing the final moving poem to his mother.[80]

The theatrical aspect of the Rising was also apparent in the choice of setting, the seizing of the public buildings in Dublin which, although disastrous choices as military headquarters, meant that the insurrection would cut across the routine life of the city. The time chosen for the event was also theatrical, spring and April being associated with the emergence of new life from the dead of winter, and Easter with the traditional religious associations of the Resurrection.

Viewing the Rising from the inside of the Post Office, Michael Collins said that "it had the air of a Greek tragedy."[81] The rebels in many ways seemed to have conceived of themselves as characters in a tragedy; in casting themselves in their self-appointed roles, in imagining themselves as sacrificial heroes, they were conscious of re-enacting myth, and when the moment of reckoning came, as was inevitable, they refused to shirk the responsibility that was involved in living up to the roles that they had chosen. When facing the might of the British Empire in an insurrection that had no possibility of succeeding in the way that we understand success, the insurgents were conscious of the spirit of Cuchulain when he too faced impossible odds: Pearse and his companions imagined themselves as sacrificial heroes and gave up their lives not only to free their country, but to demonstrate that heroes still could be found in the modern world:

> When Pearse summoned Cuchulain to his side,
> What stalked throught the Post Office? What intellect,
> What calculation, number, measurement, replied?[82]

The Rising was a calculated theatrical gamble and a daring success in that it ignited the political imagination and energy of the country. One of the reasons, perhaps, why Ireland was so easily galvanized into coherent resistance after 1916 may be because the British, by shooting the insurgents, and chiefly the artists, had defiled something far more holy than the human body — the imagination of a people. The survivors of the Rising did not make the military mistakes that the initiators had made, and in their successful achievement of Irish independence they pioneered the techniques of modern guerilla warfare, and opened the way in which many other oppressed small nations secured their independence. It has indeed been suggested that the three greatest experts on guerilla tactics were Tom Barry, Ché Guevara, and Ho Chi Minh, and Tom Barry's *Guerilla Days in Ireland* was Ché Lynch Guevara's bible and source book.

XII

The figures of mythology are created early in the life of a nation and not only continue to live in people's imaginations, but are embodied in each generation.[83] It was the power of the literary interpretations of the figures of myth that led to the creation of the modern Irish state:

> What was in Patrick Pearse's soul when he fought in Easter Week [AE asks] but an imagination, and the chief imagination which inspired him was that of a hero who stood against a host. . . . I who knew how deep was Pearse's love for the Cuchulain whom O'Grady discovered or invented, remembered after Easter Week that he had been solitary against a great host in imagination with Cuchulain, long before circumstance permitted him to stand for his nation with so few companions against so great a power.[84]

In any movement, as William Irwin Thompson demonstrates in his brilliant book *The Imagination of an Insurrection*, the artists come first. They are the antennae of the nation, picking up impulses before they can be perceived by what Coleridge patronizingly call the poor, loveless, ever-anxious crowd. AE states clearly:

> It was our literature more than our political activities which created . . . a true image of our nationality, and brought about the recognition of a spiritual entity which should have a political body to act through.[85]

After the artists come the politicians and parliamentarians who create a physical body for the spiritual and intellectual ideals, then finally the murderous mob who repeat what once was a discovery until it becomes a dead cliché, a hollow and meaningless formula:

> The night can sweat with terror as before
> We pieced our thoughts into philosophy,
> And planned to bring the world under a rule,
> Who are but weasels fighting in a hole.[86]

XIII

What is happening in Northern Ireland in the nineteen seventies and eighties may indeed be the inevitable working out of the Irish system of the ideals that led to the creation of the Irish Literary Renaissance and the Republic of Ireland. That noble ideals should have this end is perhaps the way of the world, but our condemnation of the violence to which ideals sometimes lead should not necessarily entail a condemnation of the ideals themselves: to do so would be to condemn us forever to the *status quo*.

NOTES

[1] John Pinkerton, *Inquiry into the History of Scotland* (London 1799), II, 18-9.

[2] *History of Ireland: Heroic Period*, 1 (London 1878), p. v.

[3] *Uncollected Prose of W.B. Yeats*, ed. John Frayne, 1 (London 1970), p. 368.

[4] AE, "Nationality and Imperialism," in *Ideals of Ireland*, ed. Lady Gregory (London 1901), p. 15.

[5] *Uncollected Prose*, p. 348.

[6] *Essays and Introductions* (London 1961), p. 111. Subsequent references to this volume will be abbreviated to *E & I*.

[7] *The Living Torch*, ed. Monk Gibbon (London 1937), p. 134.

[8] *Ibid.*, p. 183.

[9] *Uncollected Prose*, p. 273.

[10] *The Living Torch*, p.135.

[11] *Idem.*

[12] *Ibid.*, p. 184.

[13] *Ibid.*, p. 259.

[14] *Ibid.*, p. 197.

[15] *Ibid.*, p. 263.

[16] *Ibid.*, p. 135. Elsewhere AE writes: "Yeats has made the name of his country shine in imagination to the rest of the world a hundred times more than any of the political notorieties whose name are on every lip here, but who have rarely uttered a sentence which could be taken up and echoed by people in other lands and made part of their thought. It was by the literary movement of which Yeats was the foremost figure that Ireland for the first time for long centuries came to any high international repute" (*Ibid.*, pp. 256-7).

[17] *The National Being* (Dublin 1916), p. 12.

[18] *Ideals in Ireland*, p. 15.

[19] *E & I*, pp. 513-4.

[20] *The Revival of Irish Literature*, ed. Charles Gavan Duffy (London 1894), pp. 124-6. For a different view of this we can turn to the eighteenth-century historian, David Hume: "The Irish, from the beginning of time, had been buried in the most profound barbarism and ignorance; and as they were never conquered or even invaded by the Romans, from whom all the western world derived its civility, they continued still in the most rude state of society, and were distinguished only by those vices, to which human nature, not tamed by education nor restrained by laws, is for ever subject." (*History of Great Britain*, 1 (London 1767), p. 454).

[21]"It is possible to argue," AE writes, that Shakespeare's imagination of Henry V was "the first imperial mood in English literature and the begetter in millions of men's minds of like moods" (*Living Torch*, p. 135). Yeats, also, comments on the part that Shakespeare's imagination of Henry V played in the shaping of the imperialistic consciousness (see *E & I*, pp. 104-5).

[22]The growth of cities, AE argues, cuts the cord that connects man to Nature, the Great Mother: "life shrivels up, sundered from the source of life. . . . [I]n the cities there is a slow poisoning of life going on day by day. . . . It is only in Nature, and by thoughts on the problems of Nature, that our intellect grows to any real truth and draws near to the Mighty Mind which laid the foundations of the world." (*National Being*, pp. 62-3). Yeats also argues that life in cities "deafens or kills the passive meditative life," and that modern education merely "enlarges the separated, self-moving mind" and makes our souls less sensitive to supernatural influences (*E & I*, p. 41).

[23]AE, *Thoughts for a Convention* (Dublin 1917), p. 10.

[24]*Ibid.*, p. 7. AE wrote these words after the 1916 Rising, but he had made the same point several times earlier in his writings.

The rejection of the imperialist ideal is the recurring theme of an important, often overlooked book, *Ideals in Ireland*, edited by Lady Gregory in 1900, and containing contributions by Yeats, AE, Douglas Hyde, George Moore, Standish O'Grady, and D.P. Moran. AE argues that acceptance of the imperialist ideal threatens the destruction of the Irish national being, and he rejects the desecration of Irish traditions and the sacred earth with a passion and persuasion that any politician would envy:

> A few ignoramuses have it in their power . . . to train the national mind according to British ideas . . . and are trying their utmost to obliterate the mark of God upon a nation. It is not from Shelley or Keats our peasantry derive their mental nourishment, now that they are being cut off from their own past. We see everywhere a moral leprosy, a vulgarity of mind creeping over them. The Police Gazettes, the penny novels, the hideous comic journals, replace the once familiar poems and the beautiful and moving memoirs of classic Ireland. The music that breathed Tir-nan-og and overcame men's hearts with all gentle and soft emotions is heard more faintly, and the songs of the London music halls may be heard in places where the music of fairy enchanted the elder generations. The shout of the Cockney tourist sounds in the cyclopean crypts and mounds once sanctified by druid mysteries, and divine visitations, and passing from the mortal to the immortal. Ireland Limited is being run by English syndicates. It is the descent of a nation into hell, not nobly, not as a sacrifice made for a great end, but ignobly and without hope of resurrection" (pp. 19-20).

George Moore also makes the same point in *Ideals in Ireland*, which was, of course, produced during his phase of enthusiasm for the Revival:

> Those who believe that dreams, beauty, and divine ecstasy are essential must pray that all the empires may perish and the world be given back to the small peasant states, whose seas and forests and mountains shall create national aspirations and new gods. Otherwise the world will fall into gross naturalism, into scientific barbarism more terrible than the torch and the sword of the Hun (p. 50)

Yeats writes of the counter-balancing effect of the Celtic Revival against the influence of England: he refers to the "subtle net of bribery which England has spread . . . by Courts, by Colleges, by Government offices, by a social routine, and they fold and unfold their net before us that they may make us like themselves, and we have answered by discovering an idea, by creating a movement of intellect, whose ever-growing abundance, whose ever-deepening energy, would show their education its sterility, their wealth its raggedness " (p. 106).

[25]*E & I*, p. 109.

[26]*Ibid.*, p. 114. In *Literary Ideals in Ireland* (Dublin 1899), Yeats writes: "Modern poetry grows weary of using over and over again the personages and stories and metaphors that have come to us through Greece and Rome, or from Wales and Brittany through the Middle ages. . . . The Irish legends, in popular tradition and in old Gaelic literature, are . . . numerous, and . . . alone among great European legends have the beauty and wonder of altogether new things (pp. 18-9).

[27]*Explorations*, ed. Mrs. W.B. Yeats (London 1962), p. 205.

[28]*E & I*, p. 190.

[29]*The Inner and The Outer Ireland* (Dublin 1921), p. 5.

[30]*Thoughts for a Convention*, p. 6.

[31]*Ideals in Ireland*, p. 20.

[32]Unpublished Lecture in the possession of Senator Michael Yeats. The lecture is one of four lectures which are to be published by the Cuala Press in 1982.

[33]AE writes: "If the universe has any meaning at all it exists for the purposes of soul, and men or nations denied essential freedom cannot fulfill their destiny, or illuminate earth with light or wisdom from that divinity without them, or mould external circumstance into the image of the Heaven they conceive in their hearts" (*The Inner and The Outer Ireland*, p. 15).

[34]*Ideals in Ireland*, p. 18. In the same collection of essays, D.P. Moran writes: "A literature steeped in the history, traditions, and genius of one nation is at best only an imperfect tutor to the people of another nation" (p. 31).

[35]On this point AE writes: "The battle which is going on in the world has been stated to be a spiritual conflict between those who desire greater freedom for the individual and think that the state exists to preserve that freedom, and those who believe in the predominance of the state and the complete subjection of the individual to it and the moulding of the individual mind in its image" (*Thoughts for a Convention*, p. 27).

[36]AE writes: The "struggle is in reality not against flesh and blood, but is a portion of the everlasting battle against principalities and powers and spiritual wickedness in high places, which underlies every other battle which has been or will be fought by men" (*Ideals in Ireland*, p. 21).

[37]*Ideals in Ireland*, p. 17. See also p. 22.

[38]*E & I*, p. 171.

[39]*Ibid.*, p. 522.

[40]*Ibid.*, p. 36 and p. 42. In his essay on "Magic" Yeats argues that the images which present themselves to the poet from a deeper life than his own bear a "definite relation to dominant moods and moulding events" of his own age. When the poet looks beyond the external and the superficial, however, these images or visions seem "symbolical histories of these moods and events, or rather symbolical shadows of the impulses that have made them" (*E & I*, p. 36).

[41]Yeats and Ellis, *The Works of William Blake*, 3 vols. (London 1893), 1, 291.

[42]*Ibid.*, pp. 241-2. See also my Dolmen monograph, *Symbolism and Some Implications of the Symbolic Approach: W.B. Yeats during the Eighteen-Nineties* (Dublin 1975), pp. 10-19.

[43]*E & I*, p. 197. In his essay, "John Eglinton and Spiritual Art," contributed to *Literary Ideals in Ireland* in 1899, Yeats writes:
> I believe that the renewal of belief, which is the great movement of our time, will more and more liberate the arts from "their age" and from life, and leave them more and more free to lose themselves in beauty, and to busy themselves like all the great poetry of the past and like religions of all times, with "old faiths, myths, dreams," the accumulated beauty of the age. I believe that all men will more and more reject the opinion that poetry is "a criticism of life," and be more and more convinced that it is a revelation of a hidden life.... I believe, too, that, though a Homer or a Dante or a Shakespeare may have used all knowledge, whether of life or of philosophy, or of mythology or of history, he did so, not for the sake of the knowledge, but to shape to a familiar and intelligible body something he had seen or experienced in the exaltation of his senses (pp. 36-7).

[44]*Uncollected Prose*, p. 377.

[45]*Explorations*, p. 313. The poetry of the Young Irelanders, Yeats contends, was shaped at a moment in history when it was "the desire of everybody to be moved by the same emotions as everybody else" (*Ideals in Ireland,* p. 88), and at a moment in Irish history when the whole country was attempting to unite in order to accomplish one thing: freedom from England. Literature to the Young Irelanders was designed, therefore, to express the "common will." As a consequence, their ballads and stories were calculated to excite immediate and universal emotion and were focused on certain simple and recurring subjects: they wrote about "the need of unity against England, about the martyrs who had died at the hand of England, or about the greatness of Ireland before the coming of England" (*Ibid.*, p. 87). Their subjects, although stereotyped, related to the destiny of Ireland, but the metrical models and style in which they chose to express these stirring subjects were the "formal and conventional" rhythms "which would give the most immediate pleasure to ears that had forgotten Gaelic poetry and not learned the subtleties of English poetry;" they turned from native Irish models to English models — Burns, Macaulay, Scott, and Campbell.

Despite the fact, however, that Ireland's popular ballads in the nineteenth century had derived so much in form from an alien literature, Yeats was moved by the emotional intensity of the poetry, by its love of the land, by its celebration of defeat not victory, of "visions of unfulfilled desire" and not "the sordid compromise of success" (*Ibid.*, p. 101). The danger came when the poetry of Young Ireland came to be regarded as the only model for the expression of national feeling. Images and ideas which could make the nation secure during a period of deprivation became with constant repetition separated from the tradition and life they were designed to express. Literary characters were created which were supposed to be typical of the nation but which were interchangeable and stereotyped; generalizations were substituted for individual man and women; abstraction, rhetoric, and sentimentality were born; language became habitual, and bitterness and restlessness were born in the minds of those who condemned all that did not conform to pre-ordained formulas:

> abstract thoughts are raised up between men's minds and Nature, who never does the same thing twice, or makes one man like another, till minds, whose patriotism is perhaps great enough to carry them to the scaffold, cry down natural impulse with the morbid persistence of minds unsettled by some fixed idea ... and at last a generation is like an hysterical woman who will make unmeasured accusations and believe impossible things, because of some logical deduction from a solitary thought which has turned a portion of her mind to stone. (*E & I*, pp. 313-4)

The predictability of thought and argument that emerged, the perpetual apology and defence of pre-ordained virtues, the substitution of casuistry for first-hand passionate experience, and the enchantment of the popular mind to nationalistic images and abstractions, stifled individuality and natural impulse and created a tension between the practical propagandist and the truly national writer. With the Celtic Revival, Yeats contends, the literature that was designed to express the "common will and hope" was replaced by a literature designed to express the personality of the individual writer, and the new writers were intent on moulding, "without any thought of the politics of the hour, sane utterance of the national life" (*Ideals in Ireland*, p. 90).

[46]*Ideals in Ireland*, p. 94.

[47]In *Visions and Beliefs in the West of Ireland*, Lady Gregory writes:

> if by an impossible miracle every trace and memory of Christianity could be swept out of the world, it would not shake or destroy at all the belief of the people in Ireland in the invisible world, the cloud of witnesses, in immortality and the life to come. For them the veil between things seen and unseen has hardly thickened since those early days of the world. . . . Here in Connacht there is no doubt as to the continuance of life after death. (New York Oxford University Press, 1970), p. 190.

[48]*The Celtic Twilight* (1893), pp. 24-5 and p. 20. For the earlier quotation in this sentence, see *E & I*, p. 42.

[49]*Mythologies*, p. 30.

[50]*E & I*, p. 6.

[51]*Ideals in Ireland*, p. 98. Elsewhere Yeats writes:

> 'The Celtic movement', as I understand it, is principally the opening of this fountain, and none can measure of how great importance it may be to coming times, for every new fountain of legends is a new intoxication for the imagination of the world. It comes at a time when the imagination of the world is

as ready as it was at the coming of the tales of Arthur and of the Grail for a new intoxication. The reaction against the rationalism of the eighteenth century has mingled with a reaction against the materialism of the nineteenth century. . . . The arts by brooding upon their own intensity have become religious, and are seeking, as I think Verhaeren has said, to create a sacred book. They must, as religious thought has always done, utter themselves through legends. . . . [T]he Irish legends move among known woods and seas, and have so much of a new beauty that they may well give the opening century its most memorable symbols. (*E & I*, pp.186-7)

[52] *E & I*, p. 203.

[53] In his essays on "The Irish Dramatic Movement," published in *Explorations*, Yeats explores this question at length. The change which had begun in the Renaissance was completed, he argues, by the "newspaper government" and scientific movement of the nineteenth century (p. 149). The external world was no longer seen as an expression of an invisible essence, but as an entity in itself; man no longer believed that the "root of reality" was in the centre, in his own breast, but was somewhere in the "whirling circumference," in the external world (p. 150). With this decline of faith in an unseen reality, literature turned to study and mimesis of the external world. Dramatists strove to present on the stage the "sensation of an external reality" (p. 167), whether of action or character or language: action was crushed into the "narrow limits of possibility" (*E & I*, p. 275); characters were created to resemble as closely as possible average men and women, and were made to speak as people speak in the streets. The change in stage design, from platform to proscenium, with its consequent emphasis on scenery and costumes; the development of the scenery at the expense of the actor, and the attempt of the actor to superimpose meaning on the words through gesture and intonation rather than allowing the emotion to speak through the words themselves; the choice of subjects of contemporary interest, and the presentation on the stage of what an audience would be expected to approve or disapprove — all sprung from a desire of the dramatist to picture an external reality, and all were, Yeats contends, a denial of the true impulses of drama. Situations had become stereotyped; language had become clichéd; literature had become abstracted from what it was designed to express, the deeper life. Science and civilization, the persistent and predictable repetition in art of what once were "real discoveries" (p. 185), the substitution of moderation for excess, and the tendency on the part of artists to copy surface thought and action had destroyed what once was natural, instinctive, and beautiful. The interest of beauty, Yeats concludes, is exhausted by the "logical energies of art" (*E & I*, p. 289):

A civilization is very like a man or a woman, for it comes in but a few years into its beauty, and its strength, and then, while many years go by, it gathers and makes order about it, the strength and beauty going out of it the while, until in the end it lies there with its limbs straightened out and a clean linen cloth folded upon it. (p. 150)

With the concern of modern literature for an external reality, the best writers, Yeats argues, cut themselves off from contemporary life and contemporary literary trends and concerned themselves with states of pure mind and imagination, with intellectual essences and impossible purities. This is how Yeats viewed his own work and the work his contemporaries produced during the eighteen-nineties:

I was interested in nothing but states of mind, lyrical moments, intellectual essences . . . I had not learned what sweetness, what rhythmic movement there is in those who have become the joy that is themselves. Without knowing it, I had come to care for nothing but impersonal beauty. I had set out on life with the thought of putting my very self into the poetry, and had understood this as a representation of my own visions and an attempt to cut away the non-essential, but as I imagined the visions outside myself my imagination became full of decorative landscape and of still life . . . I was always seeking something unchanging and unmixed and always outside myself, a Stone or an Elixir that was always out of reach, and that I myself was the fleeting thing that held out its hand. (*E & I*, p. 271)

This type of literature, Yeats came to recognize, was too subtle, too spiritual, too abstracted from life. The artist was separated from what he presented in his work: "It is life in the mirror, and our desire for it is as the desire of the lost souls for God" (p. 163). Aspiration was separated from a delight in the body and in the things of common life, and art sought to achieve loftiness and "marmorean stillness" by choosing for its scenery "strange and far-away places" (*E & I*, p. 296). This movement culminated in the disdainful cry of Villiers de L'Isle Adam with which Yeats was so enchanted during the eighteen-nineties: "'As for living, our servants will do that for us.'" During the eighteen-nineties Yeats himself was concerned with rarefied essences, but during the first part of the twentieth-century Synge helped him to restore the proper balance between art and life, the spiritual and the common.

[54]"Response to the Assessors," one of the documents which formed part of the *Yeats Studies* Application to the Canada Council (1975-6), as yet unpublished.

[55]*The Basic Writings of C.G. Jung*, ed. Violet Staub De Laszlo (New York 1959), p. 289.

[56]*The Living Torch*, p. 244.

[57]*Basic Writings*, p.5.

[58]Yeats writes:

> Its events, and things, and people are wild, and are like unbroken horses, that are so much more beautiful than horses that have learned to run between shafts. . . . The great virtues, the great joys, the great privations come in the myths, and, as it were, take mankind between their naked arms, and without putting off their divinity. Poets have taken their themes more often from stories that are all, or half, mythological, than from history or stories that give one the sensation of history, understanding, as I think, that the imagination which remembers the proportions of life is but a long wooing, and that it has to forget them before it becomes the torch and the marriage-bed (*Explorations*, p. 10).

Elsewhere Yeats writes:

> There is . . . something in their tumultuous vehemence, in their delight in sheer immensity, in their commingling of the spirit of man with the spirit of the elements, which belongs to the wild Celtic idealism rather than to the careful, practical ways of the Saxon. The heroes of 'The Idylls of the King' are always merely brave and excellent men, calculable and measurable in every way; but the powers of Cuchulain are as incalculable and immeasurable as the powers of nature (*Uncollected Prose*, p. 350).

[59]*E & I*, p. 114.

[60]*The Living Torch*, p. 240. AE writes:

> As that extraordinary bardic literature, so much richer in imagination than the ballad poetry which influenced Scott, becomes more widely known, may we not hope Irish writers of genius will see in its legendary heroes and demigods the noblest symbols of their own emotions? That bardic literature was written at a time when little was prized except the elemental virtues, and the study of it excites the spirit in an age of complex thought, when people are praised for scientific attainment or intellect (*The Living Torch*, pp. 239-40).

[61]*The National Being*, p. 12.

[62]"Our political life in the past," AE writes, "has been sordid and unstable because we were uncultured as a nation. National ideals have been the possession of the few in Ireland, and have not been diffused. That is the cause of our comparative failure as a nation. If we would create an Irish culture, and spread it widely among our people, we would have the same unfathomable sources of inspiration and sacrifice to draw upon in our acts as a nation as the individual has who believes he is immortal, and that his life here is but a temporary foray into time out of eternity" (*The National Being*, p. 136).

[63]*Essays and Introductions*, pp. 205-10. Yeats makes this point several times throughout his work. In *Literary Ideals in Ireland* he writes:

> Our legends are always associated with places, and not merely every mountain and valley, but every strange stone and little coppice has its legend, preserved in written or unwritten tradition. Our Irish Romantic movement has arisen out of this tradition, and should always, even when it makes new legends about traditional people and things, be haunted by places. It should make Ireland, as Ireland and all other lands were in ancient times, a holy land to her own people (pp. 19-20).

Every lake and mountain in the land where a people live must, Yeats writes in *Ideas of Good and Evil*, be made "an excitement of the imagination" (*E & I*, p. 209). And in *The Cutting of An Agate*, Yeats writes:

> Until the discovery of legendary knowledge and the returning belief in miracle, or what we must needs call so, can bring once more a new belief in the sanctity of common ploughland, and new wonders that reward no difficult ecclesiastical routine but the common, wayward, spirited man, we may never see again a Shelley and a Dickens in the one body. . . . I am orthodox and pray for a resurrection of the body, and am certain that a man should find his Holy Land where he first crept upon the floor, and that familiar woods and rivers should fade into symbol with so gradual a change that he may never

discover, no, not even in ecstasy itself, that he is beyond space, and that time alone keeps him from Primum Mobile, Supernal Eden, Yellow Rose over all (*E & I*, pp. 296-7).

64Yeats writes: "I sought some symbolic language reaching far into the past and associated with familiar name and conspicuous hills that I might not be alone amid the obscure impressions of the senses" (*E & I*, p. 349).

65*Ideals in Ireland*, p.100.

66*Ibid.*, p. 91. AE maintains that the Celtic Revival, which was an assertion of the "spiritual personality" of Ireland, produced a literature that was both ancient and modern, ancient because it was rooted in the "almost forgotten fountain of Gaelic culture," and at the same time "intensely modern" in that it had "enough of the universal in it to win recognition from lovers of literature in Europe and America" (*The Living Torch*, p. 247).

67*Explorations*, p. 11.

68With myth, and a literature created from myth, Yeats and AE argue, we have a sense of the Golden Age balancing the Modern age. Yeats writes: "romantic art is ... about to change its manner and become more like the art of the old poets, who saw the golden age and their own age side by side like substance and shadow" (*Ideals in Ireland*, p. 99). AE claims that with myth we "feel ... that we are travelling in the realms of gold ... the Golden Age has never passed away but is always about us, and it is a vision which can be regained by any who will light some of the candles in the many mansions of the spirit" (*The Living Torch*, 240-2).

69*Uncollected Prose*, p. 360.

70*E & I*, pp. 206-7.

71"I have always come to this certainty," Yeats writes in 1906, "what moves natural men in the arts is what moves them in life, and that is, intensity of personal life, intonations that show them, in a book or a play, the strength, the essential moment of a man who would be exciting in the market or at the dispensary door" (*E & I*, p. 265).

72See *E & I*, pp. 253 ff. See also my essay, "Yeats's Conception of Synge," in *Sunshine and the Moon's Delight: A Centenary Tribute to John Millington Synge 1871-1909*, ed. S.B. Bushrui (Gerrards Cross, Bucks 1972), pp. 159-71, and my essay, "Yeats on Personality: Three Unpublished Lectures," in *Yeats and the Theatre*, edd. Robert O'Driscoll and Lorna Reynolds (Toronto 1975), pp. 4-59.

73See the "Introduction" to my *Theatre and Nationalism in Twentieth-Century Ireland* (Toronto and London 1971).

74Yeats's essays on "The Irish Dramatic Movement," published in *Explorations*, focus on this problem: the gulf that inevitably develops between national expectations and the artist who has the courage to express his own vision. Literature, Yeats argues in these essays, needs no "external test" beyond the artist's delight in the beauty he creates (p. 152); truth and beauty need no justification beyond themselves; pure joy can never come from anything "indentured" to a cause (p. 103); a sincere work of art is a "portion of the conscience of mankind" (p. 111), and the morals it presents will undoubtedly contravene the morals with which men to that point have been content. The creative impulse need no political or social justification, and should seek no foundation beyond individual life and the human heart. If an artist puts into his art the life in which he is actively involved, he will inevitably create characters which could not have existed at any other point in history. Life, Yeats claims, never remains static, is never the same at any particular moment in history, is "always taking some new shape, always individualising" (p. 120), and a literature that presents a vivid image of individual life must of necessity be opposed to the generalized personifications presented on the political platform, in the pulpit or the press. Indeed Yeats contends that the struggle of all fine literature is the struggle between what has been accepted and established, the law, and what is not accepted or established, individual life. If a writer's work is dictated by external necessity, or some obviously patriotic intention, if he attempts to express thoughts and emotions which are calculated to appeal to others, he is guilty of insincerity, and it is, Yeats contends, only when literature is sincere and free, when it expresses without regard to compromise or consequence the vision that consumes the artist's heart that it has power to move a nation:

Literature is . . . the great teaching power of the world, the ultimate creator of all values, and it is this, not only in the sacred books whose power everybody acknowledges, but by every movement of imagination in song or story or drama that height of intensity and sincerity has made literature at all. Literature must take the responsibility of its power, and keep all its freedom: it must be like the spirit and like the wind that blows where it listeth; it must claim its right to pierce through every crevice of human nature, and to describe the relation of the soul and the heart to the facts of life and of law, and to describe that relation as it is, not as we would have it be; and in so far as it fails to do this it fails to give us that foundations of understanding and charity for whose lack our moral sense can be but cruelty (p. 117).

Always, therefore, the centre of creative activity must be the artist himself, the life he has experienced, the "symbolism of incident and scene" he has discovered and mastered (p. 160). He may be denounced by the practical propagandists for creating exceptions, characters not "typical" of the nation, but, as Yeats contends, it is only in exceptions, in individuals, in "the few minds where the flame has burnt . . . pure," that one can see the "permanent character of a race" (p. 147). One can only create characters which are typical of one's own way of thinking, and in expressing what is true of oneself one is inevitably expressing what is true of the nation of which one is a part. Truly national writers, therefore, do not satisfy an "expectation," are not made upon the national mould, but are the "moulders of their nation" (p. 158), and a truly national literature is not committed to a cause nor to an approach to life that everybody accepts; it is not created from the surfaces of national activity but is an indifferent explosion of a deeper buried life and is created by writers "who are moulded by influences that are moulding their country, and who write out of so deep a life that they are accepted there in the end" (p. 156). By "deep life" Yeats says he means that men have "put into their writing the emotions and experiences that have been most important to themselves" (p. 157). An artist, therefore, who is true to the vision in his own heart and who has the courage not to allow this vision to be tempered by the political or social exigencies of the time must inevitably overturn the law of his time, and must in the process create a new way of looking at the world.

Because the business of the established order is to preserve and build, and the business of the artist is to shatter forms which have become habitual, controversy becomes inevitable. An original image of individual life instigates the opposition of the established order, and the established order attacked the new literature because it did not conform to its own stereotyped images of Ireland.

[75]*Explorations*, p. 156.

[76](London 1964), pp. 204-5.

[77]Quoted in J.R. Talmon, *Political Messianism: Romantic Phase* (New York 1960), p. 256. I am grateful to William Irwin Thompson for bringing this quotation to my attention.

[78]*The National Being*, pp. 134-40. AE does go on to argue, however, that moral and economic forces are "more powerful than physical" ones (p. 153): the "military and political institutions of a small country are comparatively easy to displace," but it is a task "infinitely more difficult to destroy ideals or to extinguish a national being" (p. 135). He advocates the application of the disciplines one learns from military training, the sacrifice of the individual for the general welfare, to civil life. AE is, indeed, more interested in the creation of "intellectual and spiritual" armies: "some time in the heroic future," he writes, "some nation in a crisis . . . will oppose moral and spiritual forces to material forces. . . . [N]othing will put an end to race conflicts except the equally determined and heroic development of the spiritual, moral, and intellectual forces which disdain to use the force and fury of material powers" (pp. 154-6).

[79]"The Intellectual Revival in Ireland." in the possession of Senator Michael Yeats, pp. 2-17.

[80]See F.X. Martin, "1916 — Myth, Fact, and Mystery," *Studia Hibernica*, No. 7 (Dublin, 1967 [1968]), pp. 10-11.

[81]Rex Taylor, *Michael Collins* (London 1958), p. 77.

[82]Yeats, *Collected Poems*, p. 375. The question that inevitably arises is, of course: why were not Yeats and AE in the Post Office? It is not simply a case of the artist being a contemplative man and the politician being a man of action, but rather a matter of the politician becoming enchanted by the abstraction of his own ideals, while the artist is full of a sense of the complexity and the ever-changing patterns of human life. Yeats

explores this in *Easter 1916*, and in *The Living Torch* AE writes: "The poet always has his heart fixed on life in its fullness, on the complete man, and will not starve life for the sake of the patriotic man, and he is a truer patriot than those who have nothing else but patriotism. Our spiritual, intellectual and economic life, all that is necessary to our humanity and its fullness, has been ravaged by those who have set abstractions above humanity" (p. 167).

[83] "They are immortals," AE writes, "and find bodies from generation to generation" (*The Living Torch*, p. 134).

[84] *The Living Torch*, pp. 134-44.

[85] *Ibid.*, p. 247. Elsewhere AE writes: "The spirit which brought about national independence was a spirit created by the artists in life [i.e. heroes and great men of history], but the poets, the musicians, the architects, and, in some way, those who struggled for freedom were inspired and sustained by thoughts and images created by the artists in life and associated with the national being" (*Ibid.*, p. 184).

[86] Yeats, *Collected Poems*, p. 233.

REVOLUTION AND
THE SHAPING OF MODERN IRELAND

CONOR CRUISE O'BRIEN

As explained earlier, most of the essays published in this volume are reworkings of the actual papers delivered at the Celtic Symposium in Toronto in 1978. Conor Cruise O'Brien spoke from notes, and in his case the transcription of his actual words will best communicate the impact these words had on their hearers. No transcription, nevertheless, can capture the seemingly detached precision with which these passionate words were enunciated, nor the spirited equilibrium in which Dr. O'Brien and his audience were for a moment held. R. O'D.

I rather fear that some of things I have to say this afternoon may grate or jar. I don't intend or wish them to do so, but that sometimes does happen. It can happen particularly in such a context as this, because you have been having, as I understand, a very rich experience in the exploration and illustration of an ancient, beautiful, attractive, unique culture. Some of you may perhaps be drawn to think of what is called the Irish revolution as in some sense the culmination or that culture. That is precisely the point of view against which I would wish to warn you. The so-called Irish revolution, the revolutionary movement in Ireland, is an outgrowth not of that ancient culture, but of the impact of the French Revolution in Europe. It is one manifestation of an international force. My wife in her lecture to you, suggested that in the Irish-speaking areas of Ireland the ancient culture was untouched by the French Revolution and by the Nationalist militant movements growing out of that revolution. So, in my remarks here today I shall try to secure you against a temptation, as, shall we say, the sailors secured Ulysses to the mast to prevent him fatally rushing at the siren call. The siren is, of course, Kathleen Ni Hoolihan; the lady looks attractive at a distance, rather less so close up. I don't want her to gobble any of you up.

I have been speaking so far of a *concept* of revolution. What of the *fact*, if any. That is to say: what revolution? Was there an Irish revolution? And if so, when did it take place? There were, obviously, a number of unsuccessful rebellions. One of these was in 1916. 1916, obviously, was not a revolution, but an insurrection, militarily unsuccessful, though posthumously glorified. The period 1918-1921 is rather often thought of as constituting a revolution because the sporadic fighting of that period ended in a major political change — or rather, as we sometimes forget, *changes*: the political disintegration both of Ireland and of the United Kingdom of Great Britain *and* Ireland and the establishment of devolved governments in Dublin and in Belfast. Now these were drastic changes which were brought about, or at least were generally thought of as having been brought about, by violence, and drastic social or political change brought about by violence is generally described as revolution. I think that is the *normal* usage of the term. This, then, was the Irish revolution, if you have to find a political revolution in Ireland. The political revolution is that of 1918-1921, to which the finishing touches were put in 1932, 1937, 1949 — the transactions of which momentous years it is needless to identify in any gathering of Celts.

As, however, there may be some Saxons lurking in your midst, I shall proceed to identify them. 1932 was the year in which Eamon de Valera came to power and which began that long and seldom interrupted period of the hegemony of the Fianna Fáil party, the mystic form our freedom has put on, the chosen garment in which Kathleen, the daughter of Hoolihan, has come to dwell among us forever and forever and forever. 1937 was the year in which Mr. de Valera gave us our constitution, wherein it was shown, in at least two languages, that the Island of Ireland is indivisible, and that Irish is the first official language. Ireland remained divided, as before, and people continued as before to speak the second official language which is English. But no matter: the situation had been, as they say, *clarified.* They was once an Irish peer called (some of you will probably remember him: I do with affection) Lord Ashburne. He was a nice man and he wanted to be liked. There was only one way for an Irish peer to be liked and that was to become a patriot. So Lord Ashburne became a patriot. A saffron kilt set off his well-scrubbed knees, he sported the sporran and the sgian dubh. You would all have loved him. Thus attired and accoutred, he set off for Paris. It was at the time of the Versailles Peace Conference where it was hoped that Ireland's case would be heard. Lord Ashburne's mission was supportive. When he came back to Ireland, he had a memorable tale to tell to the members of the Dublin Arts Club of which he was a cherished ornament — and I have the story from my father who was also in his way, a cherished ornament. In fact I'm not quite sure my father didn't make it up, but anyway it runs like this: "As I went down the Champs Elysées", he said, "I met the President of the French Republic. 'Ah, mon cher Lord Ashburne,' said the President, 'comment allez-vous?'. I replied 'Tá mé go maith, M. le Président', and that," said Lord Ashburne, "made everything clear." Or, rather, it made them as clear as the Irish people wanted them to be. No fanatics for clarity: clear like chocolate, as the Russians say.

1937, the year of the constitution, was the year of the ideal and of appearances: 1938 was the year of the pragmatic and the real. In that year Eamon de Valera prevailed on Neville Chamberlain to hand over control to the Dublin government of the Irish ports, thus making possible Irish neutrality in the Second World War, the proof of the genuine sovereignty, once contested by de Valera, of the state that was established in 1921. De Valera then went on to crush, with implacable severity, those who attempted to act on that famous watchword of all Irish republicans: "England's difficulty is Ireland's opportunity." Like so many other states established by revolution, the Irish state was no longer revolutionary, although alas, it clung to revolutionary traditions and slogans, which were among the means of carrying the revolutionary infection, with its attendant death and destruction, to impressionable young people in every generation, including the present.

The fourth and final spasm of the revolution, as far as the State was concerned, occurred in 1949 here in Canada. For that, not de Valera, but John A. Costello and some of his colleagues, including Mr. Seán MacBride, were responsible. John A. Costello was the head of the first of those coalition administrations which from time to time have appeared in Ireland like atolls to break the smooth continuity of permanent Fianna Fáil rule. It has sometimes seemed to some of us that a moderately merciful God provides these in vindication of the principle or law laid down by the poet and unacknowledged legislator, Shelley, when he wrote: "Many a green Isle needs must be/In the deep wide sea of misery/ Or the mariner, worn and wan,/ Never thus could voyage on." In any case, John A. Costello, perhaps to cheer the mariners up a bit, declared his State to be a Republic. The more slap-happy of his followers acclaimed the millennium: the attainment of the Republic for which Pearse and Connolly had died. De Valera, however, who was well known as a mathematician, pointed out to Mr. Costello that as the republic of Pearse and Connolly was intended to consist of thirty-two counties, the Costello republic was six short of the proclaimed ideal. The name of the twenty-six county state had been changed, that was all. And it was, indeed, all.

I have chosen to cover these *sequelae*, or concluding stages — as you will — of the revolution, because they give some idea of the oddity of the State which grew out of that revolution, and which by implication holds up a mirror to the revolution itself. I have discussed these matters as if they were rather funny. And so they are — in the aspect in which it is most bearable to contemplate them. There is another aspect, not so bearable: the establishment of an atmosphere of intellectual dishonesty, solemn lipservice to dead men whose aims have long since been abandoned in practice, but who themselves remain the object of a vague cult on the part of the State. Intellectual dishonesty of this kind pervades Parliament and the media, befuddles the public mind and provides the killers who operate in that sluggish, turgid culture with the justification that legitimizes their deeds, or half-legitimizes them. Everything is done by halves in the half-dark. In some moods — the mood of 3 o'clock in the mornings, for example — I am scared stiff, and not laughing at all, at this clammy green cloud that permeates, clogs and corrodes our Irish discourse and thought processes whenever the phantom shapes of our national aims heave dimly into view. The official national aims, I need hardly remind you, are the restoration of the Irish language and the reunification of the national territory. Most people in the Republic don't give a tinker's curse about either of these aims: if anything they are opposed to both of them. But they do like to elect people who proclaim their dedication to these aims. They elect them on the tacit understanding shared by both electors and elected that the proclaimed dedication reflects no practical purpose at all. It is a kind of 'bleep', a signal of a shared ethnicity, and of a comfortable, if bleary righteousness in terms of the ethnicity. A poet wrote a line that often comes to me in a distorted form. What he wrote was: "Dear God, to feel the fog in my throat." It is a nightmare which in one form or another must have come to anyone in Ireland concerned for the integrity of his or her thought processes, menaced and infiltrated by that bland impalpable cloud of unknowing, taking on as it does, the outward forms of calm and rational discourse. If you doubt that statement, I have a prescribed course of reading for you: the speeches of Mr. Jack Lynch (the Taoiseach), the sermons of Archbishop O'Fiaich, the Catholic Primate, and the editorials in the *Irish Times*. But, to get the full flavour and meaning of these, I'm afraid you would have to go to Ireland and live in the culture out of which these bubbles of marsh gas are emerging. Live in that culture which they are supposed to reflect, and laugh if you can at the reflections in that fairground hall of mirrors.

Now Yeats's Fenian master, old John O'Leary, was in the habit of saying that no man should cry in public even to save his country. This is one of the very few Fenian precepts in which I fully concur. We have no choice then, but to laugh that we may not weep. It is well to do so. Laughter is one of the healthier aspects of our national culture. To say that it keeps us sane would be a considerable exaggeration. But it protects such sanity as we have. It is enjoyable in itself: it is an appropriate response to the pretentiousnesses of our life, and most particularly to the hollow pretenses of our so-called revolutionary tradition.

Having thus, as it were, I hope, prepared the ground, I should like to make an affirmation about revolution in Ireland. That affirmation is that the basic revolution in Ireland was a *social* one which occurred in the nineteenth century and that the so-called *political* revolution of the twentieth century—the *politico-military* revolution — was a mirage or freak, in that its declared aims were and remain, impossible of attainment, while its apparent achievements were attainable without any revolution at all, other than the social one, *which had already occurred*. The twentieth-century revolution, in fact, represented the superfluous in pursuit of the unattainable. The nineteenth-century revolution occurred in two phases: the first was the great famine of 1845 to 1847, directed by the most formidable of all revolutionaries, the God of the Old Testament, and aided, someone will surely say, by John Bull. Not exactly, Sir Robert Peel did as much as any nineteenth-century Premier in any country could have been expected to do at that time, to fight the famine. It is true that his successor, Lord John Russell, stood idly by — something which in our own time an Irish Premier refused to do and then, naturally, did. But before we call on Heaven for vengeance on Britain for its callousness during that calamity we should do well to reflect, perhaps, that famine is at present raging in the world we live in, claiming more victims every *three weeks* than the Irish famine did in all its three years. Do we, as states, governments, individuals, people, show ourselves more compassionate in practice that did that infamous British government of 1846? Perhaps we do — but the difference is hardly so wide as to make it advisable for us to call on Heaven for a vengeance which might after all, just possibly, descend on us. That great famine was, you all know, a revolution indeed. Its consequences include, together with a million dead, a massive reversal of demographic patterns; a falling population, instead of a rising one; late marriages instead of very early ones; social and psychological changes on a scale we still find it hard to apprehend. Add to that the destruction of what was left of the Gaelic way of life and of the Irish language in most of the country; a peasantry turned English-speaking. Add to that again, the tremendous political factor of the creation of a large Irish population in the democracy of the United States, vengefully disposed against Britain, and acting as a powerful magnet in favour of Irish separatism, whatever names and slogans that might assume. In the perspective of these mighty events, the political revolution of the second decade of the twentieth century seems on the whole a fairly tin-pot affair, its gun-play small beer in comparison with a microscopic fungus, Michael Collins as a revolutionary no match for Jehovah.

The second phase of the social revolution was in part a consequence of the first. That second phase began almost exactly one hundred years ago, the movement of the "new departure" headed by Michael Davitt and Charles Stewart Parnell in Ireland and backed by John Devoy in America. That movement led to the destruction of the landlord power in Ireland, the creation of a landowning peasantry, and the establishment of home-rule for Ireland as a cause espoused by one of the two great English parties. After that, English political power in the Catholic part of Ireland hung by a thread, a thread that unravelled and finally snapped in the first half of the twentieth century. Unlike the first phase of the social revolution, the second was of human origin, designed and carried out by human beings. Again, it was on a greater scale than the political revolution of the twentieth century, penetrating far more deeply into human lives. The social structure established by the agrarian revolution carried on through the political revolution without any major change, and formed the social character of the political entity that came into being on 6 December 1921 and has since continued in being under various avatars of nomenclature. Why, I wonder, *why* do we more willingly accord the title of revolution to the political change of the twentieth century than we do to those more momentous changes of the nineteenth century? The famine certainly was an act of God and Irish people are disposed to think of God as a conservative, wherein He has us fooled as in much else. But the revolution of the "new departure" was consciously willed and intelligently carried out and its revolutionary character and consequences were correctly diagnosed and assessed by contemporaries. Why then has it so shrunk in retrospect? Was it because it was a non-violent revolution? Not exactly. the revolution of the "new departure" was accompanied by a fair amount of violence. Some landlords and agents were shot. Many recalcitrant peasants were beaten. Some were tortured by carding and other methods. The threat of violence always lurked behind the boycotting, but this was a violence disavowed and discouraged by the political leaders, a violence devoid of any least tinge of the romantic (the romantic is deeply interconnected with the concept of revolution in Ireland), businesslike violence in its sordid, cruel, undisguised effective reality: no dressing up as soldiers, no military titles, flags, trumpets, words of command, no glory, just a screaming peasant manhandled in front of his screaming family by other peasants in a kitchen. Not nice to think about. Therefore not "Irish history", in the sense that everyone knows what Irish history is.

The romance of that period, the upstairs of the downstairs, was provided by Parnell's love affair with Mrs. Katherine O'Shea. And it was Parnell, that great political calculator and rationalist who, as he fell, deliberately romanticized Irish politics, beginning to set the stage as Yeats saw, for the symbolic blood letting of 1916. Yeats himself, in the wake of Parnell, helped set it too. You remember that as he approached his own deathbed he asked himself "Did that play of mine send out/ Certain men the English shot?" That play was *Kathleen ni Hoolihan* which he wrote for Maud Gonne in 1902 and in which she played the title role; we know from Constance Markiewicz's letters, which she wrote in Ailesbury prison, under sentence of death for having gone out in arms in 1916, that it was *that* play that was in her mind. She wrote rather pathetically "they shall be remembered forever" (the most famous line of the play about the revolutionaries of 1798) "They shall be remembered forever, and even poor me will not be forgotten."

I mentioned earlier that the ancient Irish culture — what was left of it — was not interested in the revolution. But Anglo-Irish culture was to some extent interested in it, mainly through Yeats's long love-affair with Maud Gonne for whom he wrote that play. In the context of my wife's lecture, one could put him in a certain tradition of *fili* supporting rebels — which was what he was doing. Later, after Maud Gonne's marriage and other events, the poet went sour on the nationalist mystique and the violence it bred — and he wrote "We have fed the heart on fantasies,/ The heart's grown brutal from the fare." As we have seen, his own contribution to that diet, that mess of poisoned shadows, came to haunt him at the close of his life. His words, the words of the manic, not the depressive phase, are still at their revolutionary work. The sinister line, "A terrible beauty is born," is likely to be quoted by certain politicians and journalists in breathless tribute to the organizers of explosions in Belfast pubs. "A terrible beauty" — that line just by itself — is enough culture for most of the boys. But there is evidence that at least one IRA man knows at least one other Yeats line and that actually, from another poem, "The Second Coming". There was a very curious quotation by the journalist Mary Holland who quoted recently a leading IRA man whom I assume to be Mr. Daithi O'Connell, as saying "The falcon cannot hear the falconer". He meant that not in the general philosophic sense in which the poet had used the term — but it was clearly part of some cultural connection in his mind. What he meant was that it was difficult for IRA active service units — terrorists — living in Britain, to get the orders from Dublin for specific action such a blowing up pubs, etc. That's what *he* meant by "The falcon cannot hear the falconer". It's an interesting example of the power of our national culture.

As I have said, by the second decade of the twentieth century, English political rule in the Catholic part of Ireland hung by a thread. All that really stood in the way of ending it was the curious, but generally accepted assumption that Ireland had to be dealt with as a unit, combined with the rather obvious fact that the Protestant part of Ulster would not have Home Rule in any shape or form. Home rule minus that part of Ulster *was* obtainable without violence. It was for being willing to accept that version of Home Rule — Home Rule with partition — that Redmond and his party were discredited; and it was for refusing to accept it, as they said, that Sinn Féin rose to prominence. Recourse to violence was justified as the only means of winning freedom for all Ireland, political agitation having been tried and failed. And then: Sinn Féin itself accepted partition, bitterly and reluctantly, that is to say with the same feelings as those with which Redmond had accepted it. One wing of Sinn Féin accepted partition, through the Anglo-Irish treaty of 1921. The other wing, Fianna Fáil, accepted it, as P.S.O'Hegarty pointed out, when they complied with the formalities needful in order to take their seats in the Parliamnet of the partitioned state.

What exactly, then, had been achieved by what are called the four glorious years, the years of revolutionary violence? There are those, and surprisingly there is at least one historian among them, who argue that those years won us our freedom — us, being of course, the Catholic Irish in the Republic. According to this theory, had it not been for the gunnery of those years, Dublin and Cork would still be under British yoke, jack-boot or what-have-you. In the light of the evolution of Canada and the rest of the Commonwealth, this theory seems to me quite untenable. The most that can be said for the four glorious years is, I think, that they may have won a rather wider measure of autonomy for the twenty-six counties more quickly than peaceful political pressure would at that time have done. Was *that* worth all the lives in those years? And was it worth the establishment as an official creed of the cult of heroic political violence — the cult of the freedom-fighter? I for one do not think it was worth while or that it should now be celebrated. I believe that the Republic of Ireland, that is the Catholic state, would be as free as it is today and that the whole of Ireland would be a better and more peaceful place if the Rising of 1916 and the four glorious years had never happened at all. What the revolution appeared to achieve could, I believe, have been as well achieved and better achieved without it. But what that revolution set out to achieve was not achieved, and indeed it is inherently incapable of being achieved. For what that revolution set out to achieve was the fulfilment of the grand ambition of Theobald Wolfe Tone: to break the connection with England, the never-failing source of all our political evils.

It should be noted that this, and nothing less than this, is still the aim of the contemporary IRA. They are not fighting just to liberate the north against the will of the majority of its people. Even if the British were to leave northern Ireland, that would by no means be the end of the matter. The IRA want to liberate the south too, against the will of the majority of its people. As you can see, their idea of liberation is a rather technical one. Their propaganda makes it clear that as long as an Irish State has any ties at all with Britain, even entirely voluntary ties — such as common membership in the EEC for which the people of the Republic voted in enormous majority — then that Irish State is not in their opinion free. If it is not free they have of course Pearse's mandate to go on killing: 'While Ireland holds these graves Ireland unfree shall never be at peace'. And it is for them, in their view, to be the judges of whether Ireland is free or unfree, meaning that they as the IRA can legitimately make war on that State as well as on Britain whenever they decide the moment to be tactically opportune: the choice, they feel, is entirely in their hands.

Now Ireland and Britain being situated as they are geographically, speaking a common language as they do, and modern communications being what they are, this goal of breaking the connection is quite simply insane: a flight out of reality into nightmarish fantasy. To take a local parallel: if Quebec were to say that it wants to break the constitutional link with the rest of Canada, they might be right or wrong, but it's certainly feasible — it can be done. But if Quebec were to say that it insists on breaking the connection with North America, the never-failing source of all its evils, Quebec would be crazy. In Ireland, breaking the connection not only means driving a million Protestants out of the United Kingdom or out of Ireland — both have been mooted. Not long ago the Catholic hierarchy in Northern Ireland said very sensibly that it was crazy to try to bomb a million Protestants into a united Ireland. At that point a member of the Sligo Corporation and of the Fianna Fáil party, now a junior Minister in the present government, said "Well, if they can't be bombed into it, maybe they could be bombed out of it." Breaking the connection with Britain not only means that horrible proposition: in the Republic it means dragging the farmers kicking and screaming out of the EEC where they have been doing very well indeed. It also means dismantling the T.V. cable systems by which all households in Ireland's densely populated east coast voluntarily maintain a valued connection with British television. All of these things, and many others, which are part and parcel of the realitites of Irish life — as distinct from the fantasies — would have to go, and none of them are going to go. But the IRA's objective is still intact, its license to kill still valid in its own eyes. In taking human life in pursuit of an obviously unattainable goal, these people claim that they are treading in the footsteps of Tone and of Pearse. Quite right: they are treading in those honoured footsteps — footsteps that today lead no place at all. These grisly contemporary somnambulists have an eerie kind of authority over us: moral authority, perhaps, because they actually move in a direction in which we have no intention at all of moving, but in which we are in the habit of pretending we want to move. Pretence is our curse. Our shams have proved costly shams, these nine years past and more.

To say these things which I have said is supposed to be anti-Irish. To be pro-Irish you are supposed to hate Britain and beat your head, or someone else's head, against a wall until the blood comes. I think one should say 'no' to all that. And say it loud and clear. To love Ireland should surely not mean to love a mystical abstraction, an idol, a ritualized version of history, an endlessly repeated blood-sacrifice for an unattainable goal. It should surely mean an effort to free oneself and others from these ruinous inheritances, and above all, from the web of pretense and evasion, by means of which they are enabled to exert their unexamined and calamitous power. I believe we should love Ireland by that effort of compassion and of understanding — the two go together, though we often think they don't — and not by that military and patriotic ardour which Jean Giraudoux called "L'Amour des Impuissants" — the love that can only prove itself by killing and by dying.

REVOLUTION AND THE SHAPING OF MODERN IRELAND: A REPLY TO CONOR CRUISE O'BRIEN

JOHN MONTAGUE

I am not a politician, a poet merely, one of those "unacknowledged legislators" whom Dr. O'Brien loves to cite, and usually to blame, especially if it is Yeats. He quotes poets with such relish that one wonders if he has not forgotten that, like M. Jourdain, he writes pure prose only, and should not deploy the words of great poets, his linguistic betters, as Aunt Sallies, smart allusions for public amusement ("Come let us mock at the great").

A poet rarely has any direct political effect, although he may incarnate the conscience of a country, as Neruda did in Allende's Chile, and Yeats sometimes did in Ireland. But he can dream visions, and as I listened to Dr. O'Brien's calculated rhetoric I closed my eyes and found myself, not in Dáil Eireann, but in the British Houses of Parliament, with some righteous English politician declaiming exasperatedly against "the bloody Irish": perhaps, considering his condoning of British behaviour during the Famine, the benevolent Sir Charles Trevelyan who declared that "the great evil with which we have to contend is not the physical evil of the famine but the moral evil of the selfish, perverse, and turbulent character of the people."

To Dr. O'Brien's rhetoric I can only oppose a few simple, even naive facts. Ireland is a geographical unit, though perhaps only a curlew can see it. Our efforts should be to make it an agreed political unity and the first historical obstacle to this has always been England. Seamus Heaney sees us in bed together, with England still 'Imperially male'; I would prefer to see our neighbour as a bulkier relative who keeps banging his older sister or mother on the head, to keep her quiet: John Bull and Cathleen seems more of a Beckett than a Lawrence scenario!

My impression has always been that the Irish actually liked the English, and sometimes *vice versa*, except that the latter have rarely found a way of speaking to us which does not, consciously, or unconsciously imply superiority, the chilling irony deployed with such acclaim by Dr. O'Brien this afternoon. After all, Yeats's wife, his muse, and the woman who gave him his theatre were all English, and perhaps if Dr. O'Brien read our great poet with less *parti pris* he might be able to understand that "Easter 1916" is both a criticism of fanaticism and a recognition of its historical effect; the beauty is terrible because it may not have been necessary. O'Brien's late doubts about it were far better expressed by Yeats, immediately *after* the occasion:

> Was it needless death after all?
> For England may keep faith
> For all that is done and said.

Again, Dr. O'Brien makes great play with the word *revolution*, but its primary meaning is cyclical, as Yeats always knew; a turn of the historical wheel, often back to the same point again (Tsarist and Communist Russia share unhappy traits). I would agree with him that 1916 was an incomplete revolution, an effort towards partial independence, with no consistent social objective. I said as much in *Patriotic Suite*, during the bi-centenary celebrations. Neither 1916 nor 1922 have much to say to someone of my Northern background, except the bitterness of being ignored, and then betrayed.

But Dr. O'Brien knows all this, professionally. When I first met him he was head man in a Government Department, involved in the diffusion of what he would now call 'poisonous rhetoric', that is, explaining the distressing facts of Northern Ireland's public life, the gerrymandering and systematic injustice which have brought us to our present tragic impasse. Unlike the present campaign, there has always seemed to me a direct connection between such propaganda and the Border Raids of the 1950's, when barracks like Derrylin and Roslea were attacked, mainly from the South. Remember "Sean South, of Garryowen"? When Dr. O'Brien lies awake at night does he wonder, like the great poet whose words he loves to misuse, if words of his sent out "certain men the English shot"? I doubt it, because self-righteousness and not self-questioning is the province of the self-appointed prophet; witness the way Dr. Paisley has managed to disassociate himself from the excesses provoked by the propaganda in "The Protestant Telegraph" and its even more inflammatory predecessors.

"Violence", to quote a brilliant South American political analyst, "inevitably begins from the top." The main cause of the Northern Troubles is not ritual republicanism in the Dáil but the continued existence, over sixty years, of a semi-fascist, sectarian statelet in Northern Ireland. Why has this systematic injustice been necessary, to the point of partial genocide; the bleeding away, and ritual debasing of the Catholic part of the Northern population? Because — and here I would cite another simple fact, so often ignored — there is *no* geographical Protestant majority in the North of Ireland, only in the enclosure East of the Bann, the New Pale acknowledged by the creation of the New University of Coleraine and the new city of Craigavon. Despite forced emigration, through lack of employment and housing, my own home counties of Fermanagh and Tyrone have maintained a frail majority for their very different ideals, as well as large areas of Derry and Armagh, including the *breac* Gaeltacht of South

Armagh, where community relations were excellent, until a Paratroop regiment was sent in to destroy them.

It is this impossible situation which has helped to breed the bloody reaction of the Provos, not the political waffling of a Republic they respect as little as Dr. O'Brien apparently does. They are dragon's teeth growing out of the poisoned lands of the North, seeds nurtured by long injustice, genuine monsters from the grassroots. To this day over 90% of the shipyard workers in Belfast are Protestant and the few Catholics go in fear of their lives. So the Catholics of Belfast will not mourn their closing, for they feared the Hammer of the Lord. All the largely Protestant police force are armed, and always have been, and all my Protestant neighbours (many of whom were transformed, like werewolves, by Black Special uniforms at night) were legally armed. Attending Dr. Paisley's church, as I have meekly done, seeking to understand such hatred, I have met the old racialism of the Deep South, where he got his theological doctorate. To hear John Calvin crudely crossed with John Knox is a despairing experience. Is it any wonder that we have spawned Green Panthers?

Dr. Paisley, of course, thrives on the Provos: they stoke his most fiery sermons. In my darker moments I wonder if they do not provide Dr. O'Brien with the same equivalent of inspiration in his journalism. Who else has got as much mileage from the I.R.A.? His banning of them from RTE gave them political status, for if their position is as untenable as he says, it could easily have been demolished, instead of receiving the accolade of censorship, which has graced more distinguished Irishmen. But I believe that he is unaware of the help that he has given them in his more hysterical diatribes, and would prefer, like myself, that they did not exist. But unfortunately they do, created by Protestant reaction, and the blunders of the British Army in ransacking the Catholic ghettos of Belfast, or using a G.A.A. pitch in Crossmaglen as a helicopter pad. As for the internment camps, they are, as they were sixty years ago, recruiting offices and training grounds for the paramilitary of both sides.

I can try to pinpoint the changes. Dr. O'Brien and I might also have marched together during the Sixties, under the banner of Civil Rights, of social justice. The violence that broke it came from the Protestant Right, the cudgels and stones used on the marchers at Burntollet, under the approving gaze of the R.U.C. I knew it was coming because on a train from Derry to Belfast, only a few weeks earlier, two charming young women confided to me that "the Tagues were getting out of hand again, and needed a good lesson to put them back in their place." Probed for my credentials, I was glad of the Norman-French *mons* or *Mont* that hid from them that I also was of the untrustworthy and disloyal tribe of Tagues!

As the Civil Rights movement sagged, the Provos emerged. Again, one can see a turning point, from passive resistance to violence. When more Protestant extremists attacked the Catholics in Belfast in August 1969 there were only a few shots to answer them; the Catholic ghettos of Belfast and Derry were largely unarmed. And we all know how welcome the British troops were, after the attentions of the R.U.C. and the Protestant snipers; almost as if they were the blue helmets of the United Nations.

But before long they had turned against the Catholic ghettos they had come to protect. Again, I may have the advantage over the theoretical Dr. O'Brien because I visited the Falls, Ardoyne and Glen Road during a period when it was being systematically ransacked by the British Army. They found little, but the depredations they caused in those small homes, and the way they mishandled the people, especially the menfolk, made them the best recruiting officers the I.R.A. could ever have had. They may have had their good reasons, but it was noticeable that the Shankill and Sandy Row did not get such intensive treatment.

It is clear to anyone who knows the North that the majority of operations are local. Dr. O'Brien would not have us consort with them to find out their views, but from what little I can glean the present-day I.R.A. are neither anti-Protestant, nor anti-English; they are products of its mass culture, after all, and, thanks to Dr. O'Brien, more likely to see themselves on cross-Channel T.V. screens. They argue despairingly that if there is no change in the basic injustice of the Northern state they will be forced to destroy it. I understand but cannot sympathise: it gives me no pleasure to see the towns of my childhood, like Omagh or Dungannon, blown down. Violence is no answer to violence. I do not especially believe in nationalism, which seems to me a nineteenth-century concept, something to forget once you have achieved it. I regret the attitude of the Catholic hierarchy towards mixed education and mixed marriages, and regard these as sources of bitterness. But to deliberately misread the situation as Dr. O'Brien has done here today, and blame the vaguely tolerant South for the violence inbuilt into the North, is not history, but hysteria. That is what links him in a love-hate relationship with the Provos; his violence about non-violence makes him their most distinguished apologist. If Dr. O'Brien was jilted by the Irish nation, he should accept the fact, and not try, like all jealous men, to transform his Cathleen into a mænad. The Ulster problem is more serious than his emotional need to be a Parnell in reverse.

EASTER AGAIN (1981)

KATHLEEN RAINE

What is any cause
That young men should die for it? Who now cares
Whether Guelf or Ghibellin
Were in a sordid power-struggle right or wrong?
But Dante found in history the human scope
From hell to heaven.
What matter whether Left or Right had won
In the Spanish civil war, violence in vain
But for the poetry pulsed from that wound.
Not argument justifies, but the noble heart
That makes of these
Occasion to proclaim what a man is.
This Easter yet again
Remembering the short life and swift death
Of the world's thorn-crowned king
Whom rulers with good reason had put down
(Better one man should die than a rebellion
With loss of innocent lives) I meditate
On how the cross was exalted by the man
Who on that shameful gibbet died.
And now in the Maze Prison Bobby Sands:
I judge a cause
By the dignity of the act its dream inspires.

DECLARING THE IRISH REPUBLIC:
A REPLY TO CONOR CRUISE O'BRIEN

SEAN MacBRIDE

At the Conference Banquet on 11 February 1978, Sean MacBride (Nobel and Lenin Peace Prize Winner and then Assistant Secretary General of the United Nations), in the course of an address tracing some of the connections and modern diplomatic initiatives between Ireland and Canada, gave a different version of one of the events to which Dr. O'Brien alluded in the course of his speech. R.O'D.

For me it is a tremendous pleasure to have this opportunity of addressing a Canadian audience here in Toronto, in order to be able to express the gratitude of the many Celts who in the course of the last couple of centuries have sought shelter in Canada and who have received hospitality and help and guidance from the people of Canada. I think that probably one of the features of Canada, certainly one of the features which I have appreciated, is the progressive and constructive calibre and friendliness of Canada and of the people of Ontario. Irish immigrants escaping from the Famine and from the results of British rule were always received with understanding and compassion in Canada. So we have this fundamental link between Ireland and this great nation of yours.

Later, when Ireland achieved a measure of self-government in 1922, and when the Irish Free State was set up, it was Canada who extended the hand of friendship to Ireland in the Council of the then British Empire. Many of us may have had different views as to the set-up of the Irish Free State, but we must acknowledge the tremendous role which Canada played in planning for the evolution of the British Commonwealth of Nations into a free association of self-governing states.

A very close relationship developed in the period from 1926 to 1930 between the leaders of the Government of the Irish Free State and the Canadian Government. It was also during this period that a close relationship developed between an eminent Canadian Prime Minister, Mr. Mackenzie King, and Mr. John A. Costello who was later Taoiseach of Ireland, and Mr. MacGilligan and Mr. Desmond Fitz Gerald who were Ministers of External Affairs for Ireland. I think it may well be said that the Statute of Westminster in 1931 was the result of the co-operative effort of the Canadian and Irish statesmen who played an important role in securing the emancipation of the Commonwealth nations at that period.

As I have mentioned Mr. Costello's name, let me try and set the record right as a result of a mis-statement that was made yesterday by an Irish Senator who should have known his history slightly better. It was stated by this rather misguided Senator that Mr. Costello declared the Republic of Ireland in a speech he made here at some dinner in Ottawa. This is a complete misrepresentation of the factual position. Mr. Costello as Taoiseach came to Canada on the invitation of the Canadian Bar Association to deliver a speech. I was then a member of his Cabinet and the speech he made detailed the various reasons why the continuance of Ireland in the membership of the Commonwealth had ceased to be acceptable to the Irish people. He stated this very clearly and definitely in a speech which he prepared and circulated to the Cabinet. This speech was considered and approved by the Cabinet in Dublin at least a week before he came to Canada and the speech represented a statement of the considered policy of the Irish Government. I think in fairness to Mr. Costello who died a couple of years ago, I should state that he was acting in the name of a united Irish Government in expressing what had been the decision of that Government. It would be quite erroneous to create the impression that Mr. Costello was doing this in a casual or off-hand manner. It was the only occasion upon which the Prime Minister had ever circulated a speech to the Cabinet and had it discussed and considered by the Cabinet before he delivered it ...[1]

NOTE

[1]Later, on 7 January 1979, Owen Dudley Edwards wrote to the editor from Scotland: "I have just returned from the P.R.O. in London looking out the newly-released government papers on the External Relations Act and writing them up for the *Irish Times*. To my great amusement I found myself recording what a spendid job Sean MacBride did; the British thought of him as very constructive and moderate; and the documents very much bore out his recollection of events as opposed to the HMG one."

DECLARING THE IRISH REPUBLIC:
ANOTHER VIEW

W. B. STANFORD

During the course of an informal conversation with Senator W. B. Stanford I referred to Mr. MacBride's and Dr. O'Brien's differing views as to the manner in which the Irish Republic was declared. Senator Stanford had further light to throw on the subject. R. O'D.

The debate on the Republic of Ireland Bill began in the Senate on 9 December 1948. The Taoiseach, Mr. Costello, in his opening speech repeated the reasons he had given in the Dáil for its introduction: 'to take the guns out of politics' and to remove uncertainties about Ireland's international status. Early in the debate Professor J. W. Bigger, the senior representative of Dublin University, accused the Fine Gael Party of having deceived pro-Commonwealth electors with a 'confidence trick,' since they had voted for Mr. Costello's party on the basis of its clear promises not to change the existing relationship with the British Commonwealth. Later I, as the junior representative of Dublin University, supported the Bill, but I also appealed to the Taoiseach to give some further explanation for his change of policy and for the suddenness of his announcement in Canada. (Mr. Costello had argued that the Bill did not in fact constitute a change of policy, but critics found his arguments unconvincing.)

Apparently as a result of this appeal, Mr. Costello invited Professor Fearon, the other representative of Dublin University (who had not supported Professor Bigger), and myself to a private interview with him. There, besides repeating his previous reasons for making the announcement in Canada, he spoke with strong feeling about some personal matters. He had not, he said, been treated at official ceremonies as befitted a Head of State. At the dinner given by the Governor-General and Lady Alexander, only the toast of the King was given and not that of the President of Ireland, although the Irish diplomatic representative had made it clear that Mr. Costello would not attend unless it was included. Further, the Taoiseach told us, at the same dinner, part of the table decoration near where he sat consisted of silver replicas of artillery used by the defenders of Derry during the siege by the army of James II, and the Governor-General referred specifically to one of them, 'Roaring Meg', in his speech. Though Mr. Costello tried to make light of this, it clearly had annoyed him strongly. Alexander, a staunch Ulsterman, several years later repudiated any intention to cause annoyance, but at best it was thoroughly tactless to place such a symbol of Ulster resistance in full view of an Irish nationalist.

Next came the 'leak' in an Irish Sunday newspaper, asserting that the Government intended to repeal the External Relations Act (it has never, to my knowledge, been revealed which member of the Cabinet prompted this). Consequently, Mr.

Costello announced his decision to break the last link with the Commonwealth two days later, though (as he admitted to a reporter nineteen years later) Mr. Sean MacBride had sent a telegram advising him to make no comment.

Senator Fearon and I agreed after the interview on three points. We had been given no satisfactory explanation why the leader of the Fine Gael party had originally decided to abandon its pro-Commonwealth policy, though we surmised that the likeliest reason was pressure from Clann na Poblachta (Mr. Costello subsequently denied this). Secondly, that though the decision had been made before the visit to Canada, Mr. Costello had not intended to announce it there. Thirdly, that the sudden and surprising announcement in Canada — two Ministers, Mr. James Dillon and Dr. Noel Browne, have stated that it came as a surprise to them too — was ultimately due to justifiable indignation. If the Canadian authorities had treated Mr. Costello better, the break with the Commonwealth would propably have come much less abruptly.

NOTE

[1]This short piece is based on the following sources: Vol. XXVI of debates in the Senate; interview of Mr. Costello by Michael McInerney in *The Irish Times* (8 September 1967); personal recollections.

IRELAND AND NATIONALISM IN SCOTLAND AND WALES

OWEN DUDLEY EDWARDS

The nationalisms of Scotland and Wales, and indeed the minds of both countries in their totality, are far less historically-conscious than is the case with Ireland. Scottish nationalism in its contemporary political form has been strongly charged with being materialistic; in fact, it is more true to say that it has expressed itself in more materialistic terms than have the nationalisms of either Ireland or Wales. But Irish nationalism always possessed very strong underlying materialistic bases, spoken or unspoken, and Welsh nationalism, while far the most formally cultural in its expression of the three, is forced to show that it has answers to materialistic questions in its efforts to appeal to a majority of Welshmen to whom its cultural preoccupations might seem irrelevant or an object of hostility. But of the three, Ireland employs a historical dimension in a way that neither Wales nor Scotland does. The argument from history in Wales and Scotland tends to operate in terms of specific institutions, cultural in the Welsh case, legal in the Scots. There is a paradox here. Scotland and Wales have in a sense preserved more of their pasts, whether through Scots law or through the Welsh language: but the ancient Celtic mode of justification by citing ancestral custom has a vitality in modern Irish history which is only sparsely present in the other countries.

On any but the purely Dr. Pangloss, or official Fianna Fáil, interpretation, Irish nationalism is an Eden after Man has fallen. There will be argument as to what the nature of that Fall was: but it is hard to see a sensible dispute as to its having happened. Welsh and Scottish nationalism, on the other hand, exist today in forms of innocence. The relationship of Irish nationalism with them, then, is twofold: the evolutions of all three forms of nationalism have points in common, and even certain common origins, notably their debts to and reactions against English nationalism. In character all three differ dramatically from one another at the present time, and these differences are suggestive, but these contrasts are at their most profound on this question of being before or after the Fall.

On one point we may as well be very blunt at the outset. There is little of value in Irish observers taking the view that because nationalism has failed so disastrously in Ireland, it must be doomed in Wales and Scotland as well. The Irish critic must not fall into the trap of the ex-alcoholic who wants to prescribe universal prohibition, or the ex-homosexual who wants gays hounded down and imprisoned, or the ex-Communist who insists that his own experience obliges us all to join the John Birch Society. In many ways the Irish critic of nationalism who automatically opts for an instinctive anti-nationalist stand, reasoning from his Irish experiences, is a greater chauvinist than those he condemns: he assumes that to know Ireland is to know the world, and thereby denies the right of anyone else even to their own identity. It is urgent that the Scots and the Welsh pay far more attention to the Irish experience than they have, if only for lessons in what to avoid: but in fact they do know rather more about Ireland than do the Irish about them. Let us give an obvious illustration of that. The English are today learning to say "England" when they mean "England" and not when they mean "Britain", apart from certain ageing mandarins such as Professor H.R. Trevor-Roper or Mr. A.J.P. Taylor (who — and it is a significant fact — are at one in ruderies about the Scots, or, as they prefer to say, Scotch, widely though they differ on almost everything else). But the Irish, true to the principles of Nancy Mitford, still commonly employ "England" and "Britain" as synonyms. (In the discussion following the original delivery of this paper, Mr. John Montague involuntarily gave direct support to this argument by alluding to "the island of England".) And so do the Americans: the Canadians, I think, would be more circumspect, not only because of the high incidence of Scots in Canadian history but also because the Canadian emphasis on ethnic identity is designed to keep such differences alive in the mind.

One reason for this is that the Irish perception of the Scots and the Welsh, other than at Rugby matches and Celtic Congresses, has been in the last fifty years a very English one, and an old-fashioned English one at that. I will argue in this paper that what drove the nationalisms of the Irish, on the one hand, and the Welsh and Scots, on the other, apart, was the nature of the victory of nationalism in Ireland in 1919-21. *Sinn Féin* — we ourselves — meant just that. The subsequent attempts to create an Irish cultural protectionism — and however ill-fated the official revival of Gaelic might have been, both the Irish Censorship Board and Irish neutrality made for high cultural tariff walls — created something of a time-capsule in Ireland. The Irish Renaissance had offered the exciting possibility of an alternative culture, but the eminently respectable petit-bourgeois heirs of the 1916 leaders had little sympathy for the ideas of the more original minds in the Irish Renaissance. They may have claimed greater kinship. But the Yeats they acknowledged, for instance, was the author of "The Lake Isle of Inisfree" and "The Ballad of Father Gilligan". A glance at the school state-examination syllabus proves the point. Ireland had rationing during World War II, but no commodity was rationed as severely as the Irish Renaissance. The very fact that British history was outlawed in the schools for children under 15 ensured that old attitudes remained frozen and preserved and that Scotland and Wales had roughly the same place in the Irish consciousness that they did in the consciousness of imperial England, if that. Nationalist Ireland, like imperial England, seemed to mention Scots most frequently in the context of military regiments, albeit with a ratio of goodwill in inverse proportion to that of the English — e.g. the King's Own Scottish Borderers being always given their national title in any citation of the Bachelors' Walk massacre of 1914. And nationalism, an official gospel in Ireland, could not allow the admission of any failure; hence comparative study of Wales and Scotland was not wanted. The only comparative yardstick acceptable was that of political independence, on which Wales and Scotland were failures. But Wales did demonstrate linguistic survival under a hostile English-dominated government, whereas under Irish independence the linguistic revival came to a complacent halt. And Scotland possessed the nearest approximation to a representative parliament, the General Assembly of the Church of Scotland: the Church of Scotland was not progressive, but its democratic tradition and open debate offered an embarrassing contrast to the ecclesiastical diplomacy behind closed doors which so distinguished politics in an independent Ireland. Comparisons might elicit questions as to whether the new rulers were good practitioners of nationalism and hence were as welcome as in 1968 comparative study of Czech communism was in the USSR.

One of the oddest factors was that the Irish perception of Scotland and Wales was as English as it was because Ireland itself, in certain important respects, was much more English than were either Scotland or Wales. For instance Irish linguistic nationalism turned on a *hope* of revival, whereas its Welsh counterpart was based on the *existence* of large Welsh-speaking areas. In Scotland the situation was even more curious. The student who, having mastered the elements of Latin, goes on to take his first steps in Greek is confronted by an extra mood, an extra number, and an extra voice: the view of Scotland from eyes hitherto familiar only with Ireland is analagous. I leave it to the literary critics to pursue the symbol most directly and demonstrate how while the Irish are indicative, imperative, subjunctive and above all infinitive, the Scots are also optative; that while the Irish insist on being either singular or plural, the Scots are also prepared to be dual; and while in Ireland our voices are firmly active or passive, in Scotland, the middle voice is also heard. And herein lies our analogy: Scotland has an extra law, an extra language and an extra religion. Contemporary Irish law is a variant of English law, with such modifications as obsolescence and the existence of a written constitution might supply, but the Scottish legal system is vastly different, being much more Roman in character; to the three religions of Ireland, which indeed in the eighteenth century were three castes, modern Scotland in terms of political significance must add a fourth, the "wee frees"; and of course there is the third language, Lallans, which only ceased to be the language of official speech in law and high society in the early nineteenth century.

Most important of all, Scotland is the only country of the three to have retained a separate identity; although Scottish military disasters are numerous, Scotland was never in any permanent sense a conquered country. Ireland was: so was Wales. This meant that a great deal of the nationalism that grew up in both Ireland and Wales had quite alien features, in contrast to the institutionalism of Scottish nationalism. The nationalism of eighteenth-century Irish parliamentarians was the self-interest of privileged colonists, but in order to assert their own legitimacy the more popularly-based nineteenth-century Irish nationalists invoked the rhetoric with which the eighteenth-century élite glorified its crusades in its own self-interest. Twentieth-century Irish nationalism made a point of getting away from the legacy of Grattan, but in fact their own alternatives were often much more alien still: Patrick Pearse commonly cited Wolfe Tone, Thomas Davis, John Mitchel and James Fintan Lalor as the four evangels, but if British radicalism,

French revolution, German romanticism and the popular writings of Scott and Carlyle had been taken away from them, there would have been very few rags left on the four evangels.

In one way, of course, Irish nationalism might thereby claim to be a less parochial animal than the Scottish form, but it also was a much more synthetic one, with an inferiority complex about that artificiality. The very fact that so many Irish nationalist writers were sufficiently alienated in origins or culture from the Irish norm to be unsure of their hold on Irish realities led to a neurotic defensiveness in their definitions of Irish nationalism: we may contrast the hyper-insistence on Irishness by Davis, Mitchel, Pearse and de Valera with the certainty of identity and self-confidence of those shrewd pragmatists and compromisers, Daniel O'Connell and Charles Stewart Parnell, or even Michael Collins. Scotland might seem to the outsider to be absorbed in Britain, but Scotland in institutional terms had an identity Ireland lacked. And while the more romantic contours of Scottish history — religious sectarian conflict, agrarian struggles, Jacobite movements, and occasional left-wing revolutionary prophets — might seem familiar to the Irish observer, some of the basic myths are wholly different. Scottish democracy, the democratic intellect, the Scottish enlightenment are traditions which now supply ideological institutions for Scottish nationalism at least as far as its most interesting contemporary thinkers — notably Stephen Maxwell, Tom Nairn, Isobel Lindsay, Neal Ascherson — are concerned. There is certainly dreadful *kitsch* attached to Burns nights, but they do symbolise a common popular heritage without parallel in Ireland. Burns's counterparts in Ireland wrote in Gaelic, the very parallel figure — in all senses — being Eoghan Ruadh Ó Súilleabháin, and in post-Gaelic Ireland they simply no longer have a popular reference. Ireland can argue today that her Merriman summer school is a much more intellectual business than are the Burns nights, but it is an élitist cult, however valuable a one. Burns's vernacular may no longer be spoken, but it is wholly comprehensible to its audience. Irish attempts to provide national Anglophone counterparts fell between two stools: either they were good and unpopular, or they were bad and popular. If one wants to see precisely how artificial Irish popular nationalistic culture became, one need do no more than study the versification of the national anthem. The sentiments of *Scots Wha Ha'e* may be equally sanguinary, but at least one is not ashamed of the poetry.

But if the complexities of Irish cultural and linguistic history made for extreme — and ultimately most fruitful — controversy and uncertainty about Irish cultural identity, Ireland resembled Scotland in that one does not speak of either country struggling for survival, though on many occasions one has to say it in the fullest economic sense about huge masses of the peoples of both. The case of Wales is wholly different. Welsh nationalism is a consciousness of having lived historically in permanent peril of being blotted out. Irish and Scots bards might denounce the likelihood of the countries being reduced to no more than "West Britain" or "North Britain". Wales established its identity as the major survival of an episode in genocide, the destruction of the ancient Britons by the Angles, Saxons, Jutes, Picts, Scots and Irish. The case of Cornwall is similar; the fate of Cornwall is a reminder of what confronted Wales. Between the fifteenth and eighteenth centuries it was doubtful if Wales would survive as more than a geographical expression, to use Metternich's description of Italy. Ironically, Welsh survival turned on one of the greatest ironies of the lot. Rome and Geneva respectively added distinctive strands to the assertion of Irish and Scottish identity, even if their votaries claimed too much in insisting that Ireland was "a Catholic country", Scotland "a Presbyterian country". Neither Calvin nor the Counter-Reformation, however, could be regarded as the real makers of Scottish and Irish religious identity: Presbyterianism is essentially home-grown in Scotland, the result of a popular revolution, just as Catholicism is home-grown in Ireland, the result of a popular resistance. But Welsh religion really is an import. If one wants to produce a Welsh nationalist pantheon then, to the great names of Llewellyn the Last and Owain Glendower, and Michael D. Jones, and Owen Morgan Edwards, one must add the improbable figure of John Wesley. Methodism, said the historian Élie Halévy, prevented a revolution in England: but it certainly started one in Wales.

Yet the founding father of Plaid Cymru was not, in fact, a Methodist at all, but a Roman Catholic, Saunders Lewis. This raises fresh points of convergence and divergence. Despite all of the Protestants either in the think-tank or the shop-window of Irish nationalism, it was from the nineteenth century onwards clearly destined to benefit and to appeal more to Catholics than to Protestants. Lewis's Catholicism might suggest an Irish infection, given the foundation-date of the *Blaid* as 1925: although a civil war had already afforded evidence for the state of the Irish Eden, the actual *condition* of independence is certainly attractive to Welsh and Scots with nationalist sympathies. George Orwell saw a common link between Irish, Scots and Welsh nationalism and British political Catholicism of the Chesterton-Belloc variety. This was in fact correct: and the interaction of all four is more relevant than any Irish influence on its own. After all, *English* nationalism has been a really important influence — and by no means a wholly negative one — on the other three nationalisms, and it was understandable that a national myth which identified Protestantism and progress, explicitly, and aggrandised the Oxford-Cambridge-London triangle at the expense of the rest of the islands, more implicitly, should lead those rejected by it to question it on more grounds than one. Nineteenth-century English élitists increasingly offered places in Society in much the same terms as did the imperial Romans whom they so greatly admired. Provincial origin, as it was termed, could be overcome, but at the tacit abandonment of the values of those origins. The Oxbridge training was designed to produce sophisticated chameleons, even intellectual janissaries. It was not totally rigid: a little Scotticism, a little Catholicism, might be indulged or winked at here or there among votaries. Nor was it dependent on Oxbridge: John Redmond and his followers were unfairly charged with having become Anglified (they had aged, which is not the same thing), but the real case of a Roman emperor evolving from noisy tribal origins is that of Lloyd George, undoubtedly in his youth one of the greatest precursors of modern Welsh nationalism.

The trouble about the process of assimilating the young lions from the periphery was that the price had to be worth it: disappointed janissaries could revert — and today are reverting — very pointedly. There had always been some cases of attempted assimilation reverting disastrously after promising starts, as two products of English education, James I of Scotland and Hugh O'Neill of Tyrone, remind us. And English prophets of assimilation failed to imitate the Roman example in one important respect. The Romans invited their prospects for compulsory Romanization to add their own tribal deities to the Roman pantheon; the new converts would also worship the Roman gods, especially the deified emperors, the Romans would smilingly acknowledge the presence of the deity from the backwoods as well as their own. But in Victorian England an increasingly Protestant historical triumphalism from the later nineteenth century gave few opportunities to immigrants from the periphery to express a cultural self-respect, and this was followed by the post-1918 xenophobia. So Catholics found it harder to see their identity vindicated in English nationalism. They looked elsewhere, but it was not just what George Orwell has called "transferred nationalism". The Bellocs and Chestertons who praised France, the Martin Humes, Allison Peerses and Trevor Davieses with their love of Spain, the Popular Front enthusiasts for Mother Russia, were negative, but there were also positive sides to them. They loved as well as hated, and in the cases of Belloc, Peers, and Davies they knew a great deal about what they loved.

No greater Anglophobia can be found in really distinguished literary writing than in that of Hugh MacDiarmid, yet his place as a celebrant of the complexity and real identity of Scotland in its own right is secure. Moreover, no more trenchant critic of Scotland's shortcomings could be found. Orwell linked MacDiarmid's Anglophobia with that of Sean O'Casey: in fact O'Casey's denunciations of Britain often collapse into sheer bad temper of a humourless, although not unfunny, kind — MacDiarmid's Anglophobia always has more of a mischievous glint — but O'Casey's famous plays on Ireland between 1916 and the Civil War are notorious, not just for their criticism of Irish nationalism as it expressed itself in those years, but for their outright hostility to it. On the other hand, it could be said that O'Casey's attack on the dishonesty to which Irish nationalism gave rise does not deny him a place in modern Irish nationalism, though not of the type which became official doctrine.

In any event Saunders Lewis will not fit into the category of transferred nationalism at all: if MacDiarmid and O'Casey were far more important in their positive than in their negative, Anglophobe, sides, Lewis is less negative still. Tom Nairn, in his classic analysis *The Break-Up of Britain*, very rightly cites Lewis's famous address to Plaid Cymru summer school of 1926:

> People talk of the betrayal by the Tudors, of the decline of the Welsh nobility; of the disappearance of the bardic profession; of the beginnings of the middle class and

wealthy merchants who saw nothing in Welsh culture; of the wrong done to the Welsh language; of the Anglicizing of education . . . All these are secondary causes. There was a deeper cause: the thing that destroyed the civilization of Wales and ruined Welsh culture, that brought about the dire plight of Wales today, was *nationalism* .

As Tom Nairn says, Lewis was warning the *Blaid* "against the perils of a merely political, power-hungry nationalism — against a development in any way like what he imagined the course of modern English history to have been." This at once poses a strong contrast with Ireland. Where there is, in Ireland, a stress on cultural as opposed to political nationalism, it has often been socially élitist in origin, as it largely was not in Wales. And nationalism in Ireland could not escape from politics. The Irish developed the first mass popular movement in representative politics in the world, with Daniel O'Connell: his genius gave Irish nationalism a universalism, a humanitarianism, a liberalism, an enmity to violence and a joy which too few in later generations honoured, but he also brought in the necessary tactics of the hard bargain, the financial support for the boss, or bargaining agent, the use of pressure-groups, and the insistence that politics is about power. Thomas Davis and others afterwards, who criticised the pragmatism of O'Connell on cultural grounds, simply settled for a more ineffective kind of political nationalism. Since O'Connell's time, Irish Catholic emigration throughout the world has been distinguished by its preoccupation with political skills and the notion of power as primarily linked to socio-economic gains. When a goal of cultural nationalism obtained the support of the political nationalists, such as the Irish language revival movement, it became a means by which to penalise the hold on power of a formerly superior class. If Irish nationalism in its moment of triumph did not try to return to eighteenth-century caste standards, with the social order of the castes reversed, it did use culture to show its votaries were the victors in a psychological status revolution. Old sneers against the Irish language would be repaid by making it compulsory for public servants; old sneers against Gaelic athletics would be repaid by making attendance at non-Gaelic athletics a matter for Gaelic athletic excommunication; the former exclusion of Irish history from the schools would be answered by the exclusion of British history. Cultural nationalism was subordinated to socio-economic vengeance, and to insurance against the old caste surreptitiously gliding back into ascendancy.

It could have been worse, much worse. But the contrast with Wales is important. Because Welsh nationalism put culture as a priority, it was saved — though it was not permanently immune — from the danger of making culture a socio-political stick, to beat the old masters, or a new knife to make different cuts in the economic cake. In one way, Welsh nationalism was a reaction against Welsh success-stories. A Welshman might obtain the throne which had formerly supported the weight of the murderous Edward I; but, despite the joyful prophesies of Thomas Gray's bard, what good did that do Wales? Less remotely, a graduate of Welsh nationalism won the premiership, David Lloyd George, with something of a Welsh *mafia* to protect him: but did they protect Wales? *Plaid Cymru* is in politics: but it cannot be understood without the fact that it regards its identity as much deeper and richer than a political one. It is the ally of the Scottish National Party: but it is privately indignant at the SNP's departure from its cultural preoccupations and somewhat naked stress on political pragmatism for nationalist goals. *Plaid Cymru* will not even speak of "independence": it dislikes so political a term in an interdependent world. It speaks of freedom. And it is primarily concerned with cultural freedom, a term no less real for having been exploited in another context by the CIA.

This is of course the most critical point for the *Blaid*, and one of which it is exceedingly conscious. Is it to be monocultural, and then seek to impose that culture on a predominantly Anglophone Wales? If Wales is to have a meaning at all, it cannot be one which seeks to create a national ethos at the expense of a society most of whose members do not share the ideas of Welsh nationalism. Certainly, Welsh culture can gain converts: the Welsh language has been remarkably capable of making its own converts, with the reluctant assistance of modern technology and its metropolitan masters. But Welsh nationalism, if it is to succeed, must not make the error that Ireland did. If one culture is justly to flourish, it can only do so by not seeking to injure those committed to other cultures. There are in Wales movements of the usual lunatic variety which seek to display their purity by trying to injure and degrade those of another culture as much as possible. *Plaid Cymru* itself is hostile to that thesis. It must remain so. And because of its own enormous cultural strength and sophistication, it cannot hope to make its case for a Wales which is only part of Wales. It must conquer the Wales of the mines. It must prove itself the Wales of Aneurin Bevan as well as the Wales of the young Lloyd George. Nor, indeed, should it be assumed that the Welsh-speaking Wales is totally turning toward the *Blaid*. The Eisteddfod is certainly not the sole preserve of the *Blaid*: indeed the *Blaid* thought itself fortunate in 1977 that one of its three MPs was invited to be one of the five Presidents of the Eisteddfod — the brilliant young MP for Merioneth, Dafydd Elis Thomas, perhaps the most Left-wing person in the British House of Commons. But having heard his speech I can say that if the *Blaid* was fortunate, so was the Eisteddfod.

This problem of seeking to avoid monocultural dictatorship makes the Irish example a very disturbing one to the Welsh. It is significant that several of the party's intellectuals — and *Plaid Cymru* is the most intellectual party in the British Isles — have only a slight command of Welsh: Vice-Chairman Phil Williams; the journalist and political thinker John Osmond; the internationally famous literary critic, Raymond Williams. The insistence of all three of them on the party's maintaining a profound cultural consciousness is, if anything, stronger than those of their colleagues who are Welsh-speakers by birth or adoption. But they know that to insist on a monocultural solution would be wrong and stupid. The Welsh language has been the subject of the most brutal assaults of an oppressive culture. Irish and Scots-Gaelic were not killed, for the most part: they committed suicide. But Welsh was too near the metropolis. Welsh was a victim of attempted murder. As a result there is particular reason to fear a punitive spirit from the resurgent Welsh, who have far more of a grievance in the matter than the Anglophone Irish could have. A struggle for survival glides all too easily into a war of attrition, in cultural as well as in social, economic and political terms. Ireland shows that, too. Well, at least Wales knows it.

Ironically, one of the primary sources of deepest resistance to Welsh and to Scottish nationalism is the huge mass of Irish-descended Welsh and Scots in both countries. *Plaid Cymru* does not receive the support of many Welshmen called Callaghan, although one Welshman called Callaghan drew his strongest support in Scotland from the Irish, most of whom can no longer pronounce his name. As Proinsias MacAonghusa indicates, the Irish as emigrants are profoundly assimilationist. For all the myth of their individuality — a myth perhaps more asserted by their host cultures than by themselves, until they found the myth obligatory — they are natural chameleons. The Fenians invaded Canada to prove what good Americans they were: their great and noble enemy, Thomas D'Arcy McGee, resisted them in the cause of Canada. Indeed it would be tragic to allow this conference to pass without paying a tribute to his work, to his splendid and mature reappraisal of the frothy romantic nonsense of his very Young Ireland, to his excellent analysis of the tragedy of Irish ghetto culture in America, to his insistence to the Canadian that cultural pluralism means British cultural love of French, and French of British, and to his martyrdom in the cause of resistance to Irish militaristic and violent nationalism. If there was one man from whom all Celts and all Canadians have everything to learn today, it is Thomas D'Arcy McGee. But if D'Arcy McGee was a man of originality as well as assimilationism, most Irish migrants — much as most migrants of other countries — are fairly crude in their assimilationism. Specifically in Scotland, many persons of Irish descent have expressed hostility to the Scottish National Party because it is deemed anti-Catholic, while many more persons of different Irish descent have attacked it for being over-Catholic.

SNP has in fact avoided the monocultural trap by recognizing itself to be a national party. Here words are important again. If *Plaid Cymru* refuses to use the word "independence", SNP angrily rejects the name of "Scottish National*ist* Party" which the ignorant foist on it. A nation consists of much more than mere nationalism. Hence SNP deliberately seeks to be truly representative, multi-ethnic, multicultural, multireligional. To adapt a phrase of Henry Grattan's, Scotland hears her mountains protesting against centralization: geographically, the back of the country is so broken that no one region can hope to dominate another. Moreover, recent political history has had the same effect. SNP won its first post-war victory in suburban Hamilton, but the subsequent defeat of that victor at the next general election, that of 1970, forced the party to look north and west. The very last result announced of that election was the only nationalist success: Donald Stewart's victory in the Western Isles. It was to be followed in the election of February 1974 by victories in Argyll, Moray and Nairn, Banff and Aberdeenshire East, as well as by urban success in Dundee East and a smalltown-rural triumph in Clackmannan and East Stirlingshire. It was, then, healthy for SNP that success in the central belt of Scotland has been slow in coming. As to its ethnicity, it is now beginning to draw some Irish support, but it is coming slowly. The Irish in Britain resist the *Blaid* and SNP for the same reason that their ancestors opposed James Connolly's anarcho-syndicalism: they take themselves to be doing well enough with the present cake-cutting process. Having been traditionally concerned with politics as power, they won early and they don't want change. SNP did have Catholic and Protestant origins as the *Blaid* did: Moray MacLaren, Compton Mackenzie, Ruairi Erskine of Marr, and even some mildly dotty neo-Jacobites; SNP MPs from 1974 to 1979 — 11 in all — included two Catholics, one — a convert — the son of the former leader, John MacCormick. It also has *intellectual* origins with Catholic undertones. The "small is beautiful" anti-centralist philosphy which it shares with *Plaid Cymru* is at bottom partly derivative of the distributist philosophy of Belloc and Chesterton, as well as of the milder variety of anarcho-syndicalism. The Irish Catholics have little use for intellectual British Catholics: remember, in this context, the misfortunes of Newman and his university. Their concern with power leads them to prefer power at the centre — witness the migration to Dublin after the Irish settlement of 1921 — rather than diversification. Connolly makes no difference to this: most Irish people think of him as an orthodox pre-Stalinist, rather than the anarcho-syndicalist he was. My argument is this: Irish nationalism is fundamentally Stalinist — without the Marxism, of course — and Scots and Welsh nationalism have much more in common with Bakunin.

In saying this I do not mean to suggest for a moment that this is more than a philosophical basis to SNP, almost more a style than an idea. *Plaid Cymru* would be quite ready to agree with that statement about their common ground with Bakunin: a few SNP intellectuals might — Stephen Maxwell and Isobel Lindsay, former vice-chairmen, probably would — but the party at large would find it distressingly lacking in respectability. If SNP's success in becoming increasingly nationally representative makes it far more certain than *Plaid Cymru* to avoid the Irish tragedy of monoculturalism, it is in considerable danger of another pitfall: that of ending up with no culture at all. Its origins were cultural, as my earlier citation of Compton Mackenzie and Moray MacLaren should remind us (indeed, if we want to find a single event from which modern Scottish nationalism should be dated, it is the publication of Hugh MacDiarmid's *A Drunk Man looks at the Thistle*). But Mackenzie and MacLaren are dead, and as for MacDiarmid, although his son is a prominent figure in the party, he himself — I reveal the sober truth — was literally expelled from the party before it was founded. The first Minute — which I have inspected — states that this party shall be called the Scottish National Party and if Mr. C.M. Grieve attempts to pay his shilling it is to be given back to him. *Plaid Cymru* has an impressive list of publications, including newspapers and magazines in both languages, plus a vast range of supportive literary publication of related interest without specific affiliation: SNP has only one monthly newpaper — of embarassingly Philistine quality — and is not even its owner. Only one magazine with SNP tone (though not total commitment) existed in recent years, and it died in 1977. Yet the Scottish nationalist movement is thriving electorally, considerably beyond the Welsh.

In one respect the Scots and Welsh nationalists present a most forcible contrast to the Irish: in the matter of violence. Irish nationalism has an important heritage of non-violence, and also of anti-violence. In some instances, this was the consequence of earlier experience of violence and even military action. The most famous instances are, of course, Daniel O'Connell — who had the terrific courage to call off the Clontarf meeting of 1843 rather than expose his followers to the risk of governmental gunfire, regardless of the attractions of martyrdom — and Michael Davitt, ex-Fenian, who consistently preached non-violence to the agrarian insurgents whom he inspired in the early 1880's. But there is a further point. Folklore supplies some quite strongly anti-militaristic traditions as well as the usual praises for the triumphs of local heroes: There is a strong mock-heroic tradition, as well as a heroic one. We may remember the Ballad of Mrs. McGrath and her son's lost legs, or "Johnny, I Hardly Knew Ye"; or, for that matter the splendid song of Mickey Free in Charles Lever's *Charles O'Malley*:

> Bad luck to this marching, pipe-claying and starching;
>   How neat one must be to be killed by the French!
> I'm sick of parading, through wet and cowld wading,
>   Or standing all night to be shot in a trench.
> To the tune of a fife, they dispose of your life,
>   You surrender your soul to some illigant lilt,
> Now, I like Garryowen, when I hear it at home,
>   But it's not half so sweet when you're going to be kilt.

The tradition of militarism in Irish nationalism was culturally a spurious one, beginning with the Young Irelanders' imitations of Walter Scott. The cult of the exiled Stuarts evoked vigorous Gaelic poetry in the eighteenth century, but, to put it mildly, the strategic arrangements which the poets promised the returning rulers were pastoral rather than military. It is to the Young Irelanders that we must chiefly ascribe the circulation of the blood. A tradition of remarkably bad verse in praise of violent nationalism continued from there: even politicians hostile to the use of force found it expedient to sing songs about the martyrdom of violent men. As Desmond Ryan says, T.D. Sullivan achieved the distinction of being the enemy of the Fenians in prose and their laureate in verse with his famous account of the Manchester Martyrs in "God Save Ireland".

> High upon the gallows-tree
> Swung the noble-hearted three
> By the vengeful tyrant stricken in their bloom

But they met him face to face
With the courage of their race
And with hearts undaunted they went to their doom, &c.

The word "race" is rather important. More, the importance of war led to extensive Irish enlistment, and thence came the works of such emigré sweet singers as Joseph I.C. Clarke whose "The Fighting Race" asserted firmly that the Irish were distinguished above all other peoples for their enthusiasm for human slaughter. It is a nice point as to whether any more offensive racial insult was ever hurled at an ethnic group in what was intended as an expression of admiration for them. Irish nationalism in its turn increased the cult of violence after the Easter insurgents resorted to it and their heirs made their cult an official state religion.

Of course all of this was merely an embarrassing reflection of the mores of nineteenth-century metropolitan culture and an effort to win a suitable credential by imitating it. Irish nationalism had a great deal to do with a search for status improvement, and hence even at a point when independence is being most strongly asserted, an eye is cocked to see how Mother England is taking it. As I have said earlier, Sinn Féin and its bards simply time-capsuled the imperialist ethos of the day by colouring it green. Of course Scottish nationalism has some mild concomitant of this sort of thing also, by preoccupations with Scottish regiments, and so forth, but the odd thing is that the roots of both the Scottish and Welsh parties are non-violent. The nationalist culture, as opposed to the parties themselves, may include some glorification of violence, although it is important to notice that nobody in Wales or Scotland seem anxious to imitate the dreadful Wagnerian and Baden-Powell overtones of Pearse's Cuchulain cult, outside of the Conservative party at any rate. But SNP outlaws recourse to violence for nationalist ends, and so does the *Blaid*. The Campaign for Nuclear Disarmament supplies a significant origin for the political activism of many members of both parties. Several of the leaders are pacifists, and the *Blaid* is privately very critical of SNP for accepting the position that an independent Scotland would remain in NATO. If Ireland is thought of at all in this connection it is as a dreadful warning. This does not mean that either Scottish or Welsh nationalists are aware of the extent to which the self-delusions of Sinn Féin rhetoric actually conduce to a state of mind which assumes the justice of fulfilling the dictates of a historic doctrine by violence, and which answers questions about the wishes of the various interest-groups capable of self-expression in a peaceful democratic society by appeals to historic destiny dictated by the presumed wishes of the dead and by the assumed desires of generations yet unborn. But the swift instincts of both groups are sure enough. As a reporter at the party annual conference I once asked the then SNP press officer, Douglas Crawford (later MP for Perth and East Perthshire), what the party's policy on Northern Ireland was, to which he replied "Jesus Christ!"

The last time when Irish nationalism really influenced Scottish and Welsh nationalism was, as it happened, when Irish nationalism in the form that found acceptance among the Irish Catholic masses was strongly opposed to recourse to violence. This was, of course, the Parnell era. A few bitter opponents of Parnell's constitutionalism and Davitt's agrarianism perpertrated actions of violence which won bitter condemnation all over Ireland. A few hot-blooded agrarians attempted or succeeded in crimes of violence in defiance of a leadership which insisted on pressure by moral force alone. But the prevailing ethos outlawed violence, and in the latter part of the 1880s the Parnell movement was winning allies and imitators in Scotland, Wales and Cornwall, among crofters and miners. Apart from the formal alliances of prominent individuals, what was most notable about this was the influence of the Irish example. Although the Irish themselves were thick on the ground in Scotland and Wales as well as in England, it was less the influence of the Irish emigrants than of the movement in the country they had left that had its effect. Support movements in favour of the Parnell party and of the Land League kept the issues before Scottish and Welsh eyes, but the Irish emigrants were much more inclined to think primarily of Irish issues than to identify themselves with Scottish and Welsh ones. But the Irish example brought specifically Scottish, Welsh and Cornish responses and their cultural effect was to be considerable for what may be loosely termed the entire Celtic periphery. (The word "Celtic" is in many ways very misleading for Scotland; but it was the Celtic areas of Scotland, highland and island, which had most reason to ponder the example of Ireland with respect to agrarian agitation and the struggle against landlordism.) As for the cultural, economic and political effects, there would be much that would be questionable; if the decades after Parnell would see the Irish Renaissance they would also see the consolidation of the kailyard school of Scottish journalism; and the frontiers of kailyard and renaissance in all of the three countries were much greater than might be thought. The cult of Irishness or Scottishness or Welshness induced its own self-serving coyness as well as its own efforts to liberate its culture and stand up for its own traditions; the vigour of the new Celtic consciousness was consistently strengthened by rage against the Celtic image which other Celts were selling to the English metropolis. But good or bad or mixed, the interaction has to be seen as a totality. That interaction was to be rejected with so much else that was progressive in the Parnell movement when Sinn Féin in its hour of triumph rejected the past in whose name it declared it acted, and rejected with it a sense of common interests with the non-English nationalisms in the larger island.

It is appropriate that a Canadian tribute to the Celtic Consciousness should remember perhaps the most remarkable testimony of all witnesses to what the awakening of the Celt in the Parnell era meant, all the more so because the author was himself a Canadian, of Scottish origin, Grant Allen. Allen is neglected now, but in his day he was a writer of great power, insight and courage, who braved the orthodoxies of his day with a remarkable work in defence of sexual liberation *The Woman Who Did*; whose social purpose in detective fiction produced a splendid attack on capitalist ethics in *An African Millionaire*; and whose circle of friends among the emerging Celtic writers of his day stretched from the Irishman Bernard Shaw to the Scotsman Conan Doyle. At the commencement of 1891 he published in the London *Fortnightly Review* a remarkable essay "The Celt in English Art," and its opening passages were to be transcribed in full by Holbrook Jackson when in 1913 he wrote his chapter "The Discovery of the Celt" in what still remains the classic work on the literature of the decade, *The Eighteen Nineties*. It is noteworthy that in the great litany which Allen produced here he does not mention Yeats, Wilde, Synge, Ernest Rhys, John Davidson, Douglas Hyde, Andrew Lang, Lady Gregory, Tom Ellis, David Lloyd George, Lionel Johnson, William Archer, George Moore, J.M. Barrie, Bram Stoker, Conan Doyle or — remarkably — Parnell. Some were as yet unknown; others were perhaps so obvious that he wished to show he did not need to stress some of the most famous names. But his recital does draw to our attention how deeply nationalism and culture were interacting, and how much the soul of Welsh and Scottish nationalism owes to one kind of Irish nationalism:

> The return wave of Celtic influence over Teutonic or Teutonised England has brought with it many strange things, good, bad, and indifferent ... It has brought with it Home Rule, Land Nationalisation, Socialism, Radicalism, the Reverend Hugh Price Hughes, the Tithes War, the Crofter Question, the Plan of Campaign. It has brought fresh forces into political life — the eloquent young Irishman, the perfervid Highland Scot, the enthusiastic Welshman, the hardheaded Cornish miner: Methodism, Catholicism, the Eisteddfod, the parish priest, New Tipperary, the Hebrides, the Scotland Division of Liverpool; Conybeare, Cunninghame Graham, Michael Davitt, Holyoake; Co-operation, the Dockers, the *Star*, the Fenians. Powers hitherto undreamt of surge up in our parliamentary world in the Sextons, the Healys, the Atherly Joneses, the McDonalds, the O'Briens, the Dillons, the Morgans, the Abrahams; in our wider public life in the William Morrises, the Annie Besants, the Father Humphreys, the Archbishop Crokes, the General Booths, the Alfred Russel Wallaces, the John Stuart Blackies, the Joseph Arches, the Bernard Shaws, the John Burnses; the People's Palace, the Celtic Society of Scotland, the Democratic Federation, the Socialist League. Anybody who looks over any great list of names in any of the leading modern movements in England — from the London County Council to the Lectures at South Place — will see in a moment that the New Radicalism is essentially a Celtic product. The Celt in Britain, like Mr. Burne Jones's enchanted princess, has lain silent for ages in an enforced long sleep; but the spirit of the century, pushing aside the weeds and briars of privilege and caste, has set free the sleeper, at last ...

HUGH MacDIARMID AND THE GAELIC MUSE

ANNE DOOLEY

In 1966, in the second volume of his outrageously idiosyncratic biography, *The Company I've Kept*, Hugh MacDiarmid begins by quoting approvingly David Daiches's comments on his, MacDiarmid's, work for a Scottish Renaissance and a Scottish national identity:

> It was not simply a literary endeavour: it was bound up with questions of Scottish identity which had for the most part been slumbering for nearly two centuries when he came upon the scene. And not only with questions of Scottish identity; for the question of the quality of modern industrial democratic society, which prevails over the whole western world, is also involved.[1]

Daiches's comments are fine and incisive:

> His driving vision of the fulfilled man in the fulfilled society — a vision which is as much responsible for his choice of language, his kind of imagery and the course of his poetic career from lyricist to discursive epic encyclopaedist as it is his ever-shifting syntheses between nationalism and communism — would not leave him alone.[2]

It is with one element of this protean and urgent vision that this paper is concerned, the place of the Celtic, more precisely the Gaelic tradition, in MacDiarmid's work.

MacDiarmid was aware of the Gaelic dimension of the Scottish identity as early as 1922. In the first number of *The Scottish Chapbook*, a principal objective of the publication is given as

> To encourage and publish the work of contemporary Scottish poets and dramatists, whether in English, Gaelic, or Braid Scots.[3]

That he may have been thinking of a literary movement along the lines of the Irish Literary Renaissance is indicated by another stated objective — to support the movement towards a Scottish National Theatre. The ensuing numbers of *The Scottish Chapbook* offer perhaps the best chronological documentation of MacDiarmid's endorsement, possibly under the influence of Ruairi Erskine of Marr, of the Gaelic voice of Scotland. By the late twenties he was beginning to see the renewal of contact with the Gaelic heritage as the most important task of the Scottish Literary Renaissance. In 1931 he published two crucial papers in which he elaborated his theory of the Gaelic Idea. Ireland's reassertion of political independence he could now perceive in the context of the ruination an English ascendancy was enforcing on the civilization, not only of the British Isles, but also on the native traditions of all the Empire peoples. Ireland's recovery of her ancient civilization, he argues, could offer a blueprint for both Scotland and Wales: MacDiarmid recommends especially the work of re-translation and literary history, using the literary models of Corkery, Robin Flower, Douglas Hyde, Eleanor Hull, Osborn Bergin and James Stephens.[4] He espouses with enthusiasm Corkery's rallying cry of "getting back behind the Renaissance", a Renaissance by which Greek international standards stifled the national cultures of Europe. He would like to make the claim, with Corkery, that the Gaelic world — not knowing a Renaissance — was in touch with its own roots in a way denied to other European areas. Corkery's assumptions about the identification of interest between poet and people in eighteenth-century Munster are now somewhat discredited, but for MacDiarmid they were attractive and cogent and could be used, not just as persuasive pamphlet rhetoric, but as insights to be incorporated bodily into his own poetry:

> Our Gaelic forebears possessed their great literature
> As nothing is possessed by peoples today,
> And in Scotland and Ireland and Wales
> There was a popular understanding and delight
> In literary allusions, technical niceties, and dexterities of expression
> In which the English even in Elizabethan times
> Had only the poorest counterpart,
> And have since had none whatever
> And have destroyed it in the Gaelic countries too.[5]

The Gaelic Idea as a creative idea he claims as being vital to the future of Scotland and the world:

> Only in Gaeldom can there be the necessary counter-idea to the Russian idea . . . The dictatorship of the proletariat is confronted by the Gaelic commonwealth with its aristocratic culture — the high place it gave to its poets and scholars.[6]

This espousal of the Gaelic tradition is to be quite specifically distinguished from allegiance either to the Celtic Twilight neo-Romantic school or to the activities of An Comunn Gaidhealach:

> It calls us to a redefinition and extension of our national principle of freedom on the plane of world-affairs, and in an abandonment alike of our monstrous neglect and ignorance of Gaelic and of the barren conservatism and loss of the creative spirit on the part of those proposedly Gaelic and concerned with its maintenance and development.[7]

The Gaelic poetic posits a central role for the poet in society and assigns to him a political as well as an aesthetic voice. For MacDiarmid this concept resolved the antimony he had earlier perceived between the creative and didactic function of poetry.[8] He repeatedly stressed the need for Scottish poets to study the Gaelic bardic heritage in perfecting their craft, and there is something immensely touching about his own patient and humble apprenticeship to the great eighteenth-century Gaelic masters: Duncan Ban Macintyre and Alasdair Mac-Mhaighstir Alasdair.

The first attempts to integrate Gaelic poetry with his own personal style occur in *Circumjack Cencrastus* (1930).[9] "The Irish in Scotland" is a poem in two segments, the first segment in English, the second in Lallans. In the first part the poet uses a jaunty ballad-type narrative to rush his French visitor through the Western Islands, providing at the same time a crash course in bardic poetry. The bardic quotations, it has been noted, all derive from Flower's *Gaelic Literature Surveyed*, but they are blended carefully to provide a cultural and political lesson. Tadhg Óg Ó hUiginn's fifteenth-century opening line for an Ó Neill prince, "From the North comes help," embodies MacDiarmid's belief in a revitalized Gaelic culture which could change the world. His quotation of the fourteenth-century Irish "O messenger who comes from Rome" (assigned by Flower to Giolla Brigde Mac Con Mhidhe) indicates the pride of the Gaelic poet in refusing to exchange his birthright for a Christian internationalism. In this way the Gaelic concept of poetry is singled out as a civilizing means of raising man above the level of mindless subsistence. Giolla Brigde's other poem cited, on the Scottish travels of the Irish harp, provides a metaphor for the ideal of a new cultural unity for Ireland and Scotland.

The second part of the poem returns to MacDiarmid's own Lallans voice and dispenses with the didactic convention of traveller and guide. Instead, we are offered MacDiarmid's own response to the tradition in a visionary experience, a magisterial poetic calling-up of the Celtic poetic pantheon. The vision has both Biblical and bardic overtones. In his visionary joy, the poet invokes the symbol of the Phoenix from a patriotic poem in bardic metre from the seventeenth century (also quoted by Flower). The pantheon is outlined against a Deluvian scenario, probably inspired by Alasdair MacMhaighstir's poem on the Deluge. If this poem can be seen as MacDiarmid's analogue to Yeats's invocation of the Celtic Muse in "The Secret Rose" — and there are many Yeatsian echoes in this poem — then the Scots dissenter reference to "Great poems manifestin' at aince" has even stronger resonance. Scots humour constantly threatens to overwhelm the, as yet frail Gaelic idea and, in an ensuing poem in the volume, "Aodhagan Ó Rahaille Sang This Song," reverence for his Gaelic heritage cannot prevail over a mischievous Lallans perspective. The poem works to devastating effect to puncture the Celtic Twilight reverence for the Celtic Muse: the parody of Yeatsian ballad language, twisted by the slyly lecherous and drunken repetition of "Its oh my dear, and oh my dear," is deadly accurate. It remains something of a jolt to see the *aisling* convention subverted as a Scots joke:

> And favoured here wi' nae King's dochter,
> But juist . . . a minister's rinawa wife . . .

The joke is probably on us, however, as the traditional Irish reverence accorded "Gile na Gile" as an evocation of unearthly beauty makes an Irish audience forget the savage satire with which O Rahaille attacks the goddess. In a much later poem, "The Gaelic Muse," MacDiarmid will discover the full poetic potential of the Gaelic *aisling*, this time as *rosc*, as political rallying cry and will commit the Gaelic Muse to the cause of the proletariat awakening. The Gaelic poet will awaken the sleeping Fenian giants, the larger-than-life, heroic proletarian man.

It is not, however, until the succeeding volume, *Stony Limits and Other Poems* (1934), that MacDiarmid achieves the strong note which characterises his use of Gaelic themes. There is an abandonment of irony and heavy humour and a commitment to an agonistic and passionate stance. What he subsequently was to note in Joyce and Yeats as the hallmark of the Celtic poets' trade, "This single-minded zeal, this fanatic devotion to art" (*In Memoriam James Joyce*, 1955), this, in addition to other qualities in the poems — absolute devotion to native place, to the ethos of heroic integrity, a responsiveness to the political reality, and to the supreme value of the craft itself — all of this MacDiarmid would have found ratified in the picture of the bardic poet as Flower describes it in

Gaelic Literature Surveyed. He would also, in bardic poetry, have found ratified his own evolving ideas of poetic form. For the bardic poet, the poem does not function as an isolated art object with its contemplative potential hermetically sealed inside. It forms rather a segment in a continuum of discourse. With the bardic image of the poem as relevance, as attention to the vital signs of the collectivity, of speech channeled into committed statements of praise or blame, incitement or curse, of speech as real exchange, with the insistence also that poetry's deepest sources lie beyond the reach of man's achieved knowledge, MacDiarmid could be free, as bardic verse is free, from the poetic confinements of lyric form and closure. In his essay on Pound in *The Company I've Kept* MacDiarmid will assert that the long poem — the epic as contrasted with the architectonic symphony — equates with the classless society and that his espousal of the long poem is an expression of his Marxism. But the analogy of music has its source in his earlier understanding of what is central to a Gaelic aesthetic. In a note added to "English Ascendancy in British Literature," he had pointed to the analysis of Scottish pipe music by Francis George Scott. He quotes approvingly:

> The piobaireachds of the Golden Age, like plain song, transcended the time factor in music and became unmeasured music, literally and metaphorically timeless. Later piobaireachd writers, working unsuspectingly against a background of tonality and harmony, had given a "tuney" flavour to their productions, and this was the distinguishing feature of the period of decadence. To such a point had we come today that most people understand music to be tunes and tunes to be music. A similar criterion, applied to poetry, taking lyrics as the standard of measurement, would cancel out Milton, Shakespeare, Dante and all the major names of literature.[10]

The format of the 'great music,' the *ceol-mór* piping, consists of a basic melodic theme explored through the alternation of the movements called *urlár* (ground) and *siubhal* (variation), with a final climactic movement, the *crun-luath*. As in all Gaelic music, the ornamentation is individual to each performer. This structure of classical *ceol mór* may have influenced MacDiarmid's ideas of structure for his larger poetic compositions. Indeed the eighteenth-century Scottish Gaelic poetic tradition which he loved afforded him several well-known examples of a long poem constructed with the *ceol mór* in mind. There is Macintyre's "Moladh Beinn Dobhrain" which MacDiarmid translated and MacMhaighstir's "Moladh Móraig" which shows a specific, albeit bawdy, awareness of the intertextuality of musical and literary form.

> Ah! the chanter with its grace-notes,
> a hard, sharp, clean-cut music,
> sedate now, and now quavering,
> or smooth, controlled, soft, tender;
> a steady, stately march then,
> full of vigour, grace and battle-zest
> a brisk and strutting crunluath.[11]

Gaelic music as a medium which transcends time, and the analogy of the long poem as a freedom from time strictures, provides the essential meditative image for the greatest of the "Gaelic" Poems, "Lament for the Great Music:"

Thou language where language ends; thou time
Standing upright for ever on the path of vanishing hearts;
Thou feeling to whom, O thou change of feeling into what?
Heartspace growing out of us; innermost part of us rising over us,
Surging out in holy farewell! Thou Inner standing round us
As experienced distance, as the other side of air,
Pure, towering, uninhabitable — once inhabited here!

Before examining this poem, however, it would be useful to look at the shorter poem in the same volume "In Memoriam: Liam Mac 'Ille Iosa" in which music, the bardic tradition and time are also integrated. The poem correlates beautifully the loss and consolation movement of a classical elegy, with MacDiarmid sensing his inability to continue to express the Gaelic dimension of his beloved Scotland, now that his friend is lost to him forever. The poem offers more than a classical elegy in the Western tradition. The Gaelic word for elegy, *caoineadh*, defines both a musical and poetic genre. Only in the Gaelic world can words and melody be so closely identified, can the mystery of poetry be offered as transcendence. From the dignified Eliot-like choral invitation to mourn, to recreate the authentic Gaelic communal ritual, the poem moves into a majestic evocation of the land, sky and sea-scape of the Western Islands. It is a landscape which communicates the sense of personal loss but which at the same time is capable of signposting the inner realities of poetic inspiration:

O Liam, Liam, sheer white-top speeding full sail,
Lost world of Gaeldom, further and further away from me,
How can I follow, Albannach, how reachieve
The unsearchable masterpiece?

The poets's response to the call of poetry is with a child-like faith, a commitment to the way rather than proceeding with the certainty of arriving at a total vision.

Meaning as an end of desire is value.
But an end of desire for Scotland?

In this tragedy of personal loss which involves also a loss of contact with the Gaelic world, MacDiarmid faces squarely a basic artistic crisis, the fear of extinction of insight. But a basic stratagem for endurance is also perceived. By holding fast to a Gaelic poetic identity, the sense of loss, both personal and aesthetic, is transcended. The tradition itself stands as a bulwark against the erosion of historical time. It becomes a home for the poet. The earlier arrogant dictates of the young radical poet on the necessity for the new in art and the uncertainties of middle age are tempered and resolved by a new conviction of the permanence and stability embodied in the Gaelic muse. Through the great resonant phrases of the bardic tradition, through the global musical reflections in Gaelic music, MacDiarmid arrives in this period of crisis at a new sense of intellectual and poetic integrity of vision.

I have already noted the attention to Gaelic musical values in "Lament for the Great Music". It remains now to consider the poem in greater detail. The form of the *caoineadh* had already served him well in "In Memoriam: Liam Mac 'Ille Iosa." His beloved Alasdair MacMhaighstir's poems celebrating the Edinburgh harpers' festivals may also have been an inspiring factor. Most of the Gaelic items he quotes, however, belong once again to the period of the break-down of the old Gaelic order at the beginning of the seventeenth century. Again the bardic phrases are not mere catch-words culled from a popular secondary source. They mediate the meaning of the poem, forming their own distinct thread of privileged discourse within the poem. In a phrase such as Sean Ó Neachtain's satiric "buidhe le Dia", where the distorted and mistranslated Irish phrase represents the distortion of the Gaelic tradition at the hands of the English, in the plucking of Liam Dall Ó hIfearnain's phrase "uaill-ghuth an aoibhnis" to sum up the transcendent power of language, in the use of Flower's quotations from seventeenth century philosophical treatises in Irish to represent the critical vulnerability of Scotland, one can see a new Gaelic language of reference in the process of being created.

In addition, there is added a Fenian poetic persona. Both Oisin and Caoilte in the Gaelic tradition are survivors, solitary spokesmen, in an unappreciative Christian era, for the earlier Celtic music. Their intense evocations of the joy of the music of the natural world and their extraordinary sensitivity to landscape form the implicit backdrop to the meditation on the art of the MacCrimmons. Both the MacCrimmons, the Gaelic bardic poets and the Fenian survivors provide fitting analogues for MacDiarmid's personal struggle against the forces that destroy Scotland and destroy true human creativity and joy. Out of a sense of his isolation in these matters from his contemporaries, and even from his friends, MacDiarmid creates, not a poetry of bitterness but a poetry of humility, patience and total dedication:

> It is not lawful to inquire from whence it springs,
> As if it were a thing subject to space and time ...
> So we ought not to pursue it with a view to detecting
> Its secret source, but watch in quiet till it suddenly shines on us.

The poem itself mimes this process. Discourse circles patiently and prosaically until a landscape image, suffused with the language of light or of music, lifts the poem in a movement of transcendence to a place where discourse is transformed and suspended. Scotland itself, from the vantage point of the total universe, is itself a thing of limits, itself to be superseded along with its particular genius, the music of the pipes. But characteristically MacDiarmid brings the poem home at the end:

> I long to hear the great pipers play their great music themselves ...
> And have one glimpse of my beloved Scotland yet.

The poem began on a note of extreme heroic assertion with all the attendant vulnerability of this stance: the vulnerability of Diarmait, the "fold of value of the world west from Greece" who was also the harried outlaw; the vulnerability also of Christ who cried out on the cross for fear of God's desertion. The poem ends by playing through a sequence of naive resolution — the resolution of the Christian minor theme of the poem — in the scene of the Last Judgement. From bardic poetry MacDiarmid had learned the value of the assertive vision as a poetic stratagem: cosmic dissolution need not involve man in any failure of imagination or self-possession. Both the Christian and the Gaelic traditions combine to defeat any sense of individual annihilation and to give the individual a sense of "coming home." The poem resolves its unbearable tensions and responsibilities by creating a world of simple love and childish hero-worship:

> And you playing: "Farewell to Scotland, and the rest of the Earth"
> The only fit music there can be for that day
> — And I will leap then and hide behind one of you . . .

In sequences such as this MacDiarmid's touch is faultless. What he had quoted approvingly from Adolph Mahr as the keynote of Celtic poetry, he also intended to apply to himself:

> That which generally excites the greatest admiration for the "opus hibernicum" is the combination of complication of design and delicacy of execution, though it is not this extrinsic aspect — *but rather some emotional quality which constitutes its innermost essence.*[12]

Other poems work successfully with a Gaelic *substratum* but none, with the possible exception of "Direadh III," aim for the same emotional complexity as the "Lament." Working from present and remembered occasions when he explored the Western Isles with his wife, he realizes in "Direadh III" the depth which human love has added to his understanding of the Gaelic Muse. Through the profound civilizing power of love he achieves a new intimation of the goddess in all her manifestations. Deirdre's loss is more fully understood in the context of his returning to the same landscape with his beloved. His connection with Scotland is perceived in a new way:

> I am with Alba — with Deirdre — now
> As a lover is with his sweetheart . . .

Deirdre's lament for her joy in Scotland is rescued: the joy lives again and Alba emerges at the end of the poem shining in the tenderness of a Celtic Paradisal innocence.

> So does Alba surpass the warriors
> As a graceful ash surpasses a thorn,
> Or the deer who moves sprinkled with the dewfall
> Is far above all other beasts
> — Its horn glittering unto Heaven itself.

The image of the deer reaches back to Duncan Ban Macintyre's beloved deer of Ben Dorain, to the deer hunts of Celtic saga, to Cernunnos, the great antlered god of the northern Celts. It can also serve as a fitting, final image for MacDiarmid's own intellectual and poetic achievement.

NOTES

[1] *The Company I've Kept* (London 1966), p. 28.

[2] *Ibid.*, p. 29.

[3] Quoted in Duncan Glen, *Hugh MacDiarmid and the Scottish Renaissance* (Edinburgh and London 1964), p. 74.

[4]"English Ascendancy in British Literature", *The Criterion* (July 1931); reprinted in *The Uncanny Scot* (London 1968), pp. 131-132.

[5]Quoted in "Round the World for Scotland," *Lucky Poet* (London 1943), p. 373.

[6]"The Caledonian Antisyzygy and the Gaelic Idea" *The Modern Scot* (1931); reprinted in *Selected Essays of Hugh MacDiarmid* (London 1969), p. 67.

[7]*Ibid.*, p. 68.

[8]"Art and the Unknown," *The New Age* (1926); reprinted in *Selected Essays of Hugh MacDiarmid*, p. 45. "Ground covered in any direction ceases to be art for those who have covered it and lapses into education or entertainment for those who haven't."

[9]All quotations are taken from *Collected Poems of Hugh MacDiarmid* (New York and London 1967).

[10]*The Uncanny Scot*, p. 132.

[11]Translation by Derrick Thomson in *An Introduction to Gaelic Poetry* (London 1974), p. 170.

[12]"The Kind of Poetry I Want," *Lucky Poet*, p. 166. (Italics my own).

HUGH MacDIARMID: A PARTING GLOSS

JOHN MONTAGUE

In mid-August 1978 I called on Hugh MacDiarmid for the last time. Although dying, he was still alert, sharing a noggin of malt, signing a book with a clear but shaky hand. His eighty-sixth birthday had gone unnoticed in *The Times*, but he was used to such slights. He did not even seem afraid of death, although he hoped to see his *Complete Poems* published.

The *Complete Poems* finally appeared, two months after his death, ensuring that 1978 will be a landmark in both Scottish and English literary history. For there is no denying the massive achievement on several levels: *Sangsehaw* (1925) and *Penny Wheep* (1926) were the finest lyrics in Scots since Burns. And for added richness, *A Drunk Man Looks at the Thistle* (1926) was the finest long poem since Dunbar. In a few years, MacDiarmid had revived and revolutionised Scottish literature.

But he was never one to rest comfortably on his laurels. During his middle years, MacDiarmid wrestled with a vision which would make him not only a local but an international thistle. *To Circumjack Cencrastus* (1930) is a failure, compared to *A Drunk Man*, but the scope is enormous, an invocation of the snake on the Cosmic Tree, with its double nature, creative and destructive. And moving between the swarming horror of the Glasgow slums and the remoteness of the Scottish moors and islands, collections like *Stony Limits* (1934) are both frightening and magnificent.

For those who are uneasy with greatness there are always the marvellous lyrics: "At My Father's Grave" in *First Hymn to Lenin* (1931), "Of John Davidson" in *Scots Unbound* (1932), "The Skeleton of the Future" or "In the Foggy Twilight" in *Stony Limits* (1934). But longer poems, like "Water of Life," "Depth and the Chthonian Image," and, above all, "On a Raised Beach" have the energy of great poetry, hymns to that mystic materialism which is the centre of his Communism.

> These stones have the silence of supreme creative power,
> The direct and undisturbed way of working
> Which alone leads to greatness.

In such poems he is the nearest equivalent in English to Pablo Neruda (who was also, both personally and poetically, obsessed by stones, like the French Communist poet, Guillevic). It may be galling to some but on the strength of these volumes it is MacDiarmid, and not the modish Auden, who is the major poet of the thirties, the only really Socialist voice. Invalided from one war, a factory hand in the second, the postman's son from Langholm was well equipped to speak for the working class, although, fed as they were on popular newspapers and football results, they were unlikely to hear him:

> This Scotland is not Scotland
> But an outsize football pitch ...

The literary middle class, in Edinburgh as well as London, did not wish to come to terms with such a prickly presence: he is still excluded, even from such sympathetic surveys as Robin Skelton's *Poetry of the Thirties*. It was this lack of understanding, as well as personal problems, which seems to have driven MacDiarmid back upon himself, in a skirl of defiance. The third, or didactic MacDiarmid, the logomaniac who paints his own magnificently immodest portrait in *Lucky Poet* (1943), is the most difficult to judge. Especially as many of the best passages are quotations, not always acknowledged.

> This rag-bag, this Loch Ness monster, this impact
> Of the whole range of Weltliteratur on one man's brain

is how he describes *In Memoriam James Joyce* (1955) which, with *The Kind of Poetry I Want* (1957), best represents this attitude. Both are sustained by a fierce loneliness, the boy who ransacked a village library still present in the isolated poet, determined that the world which had not recognised him should flood into his work. I can testify that the Irish and French at least are reasonably correct, and who else would couple Sequoyah, and his Cherokee alphabet, with Johannes Scotus Eriugena?

Pound might, because he was also an admirer of the Irish philosopher, and their approaches have much in common, although MacDiarmid's reliance on the prose line makes for a heavier music. Having succeeded in two major areas, it would be charitable to emphasise his partial failure to invent a new mode of world poetry, to which English society and literature were inimical. Where then do these amazing volumes place him in English literary history?

A possible answer. Not since Wordsworth has there been a poet who so combined the brilliant and the banal, the poetic and the prosaic. The parallels are many: the flowing waters of childhood's landscape, the stern lack of intimacy in the middle years, the didacticism of the later. Both achieved an early masterpiece but had to abandom more grandiose projects. And more than any poet since, MacDiarmid has tried "to follow the steps of the man of Science," as prescribed in the 1805 Preface. But we must remember that they were both Borderers, aliens to the literary London; from Langholm to the Lake District is but a day's ride!

SCOTIA

In memory of Hugh MacDiarmid

We have come so far North,
farther than we have ever been
to where gales strip everything
and the names ring guttural
syllables of old Norse:
Thurso, Scrabster, Laxdale,
names clang like a battle-ax.

Then further West. There beauty
softens, a darkening estuary,
Farr or Borgie or Skerray where
waist high in shallow waters
silent shadows cast at night
to lasso the lazily feeding trout
to gleam upon our hotel plate.

Still farther, mountains gather,
blue peak lifting beyond blue peak,
Ben Loyal and then Ben Hope,
noble, distant as the Twelve Bens
or Brandon; single-tracks on
endless moors, or threading along
the flanks of melancholy lochs.

Loch Loyal and Loch Naver,
where Alpine flowers blossom,
the wilderness's blessing;
as MacDiarmid will proudly remark
in our last, rambling conversation,
"strange, lovely things grow up there,
ecologically, *vairy* inter-resting."

By such roads, only sheep prosper,
bending to crop the long acre, or
whiten the heather, like bogcotton.
The name of this country, Sutherland,
synonym for burnings, clearance,
the black aura of Castle Dunrobbin,
stone cottages broken, like Auburn.

We are not Thirties aesthetes, leaving
on impulse 'for Cape Wrath tonight'
but fellow Gaels, who have come
as far as the Kyle of Tongue
to see a sister country, Scotland,
or what is left of it, before
Scotia, like Wallia, is plundered.

Along the new motorway, trucks
and trailers strain, an invasion
grinding from England, the Grampians
pushed aside, in search of wealth;
the North Sea's blackening pulse,
the rigs towed from Moray Firth
to prop a fading Imperial strength.

Beyond Tongue, still rises Ben Hope
and that star of mountains, Sulliven,
that beckons to an intent fisherman,
MacCaig, with whom I share a patronym,
His unswerving eye and stylish line
pierce through flesh to dying bone.
May Scotland always have such fishermen

Nourishing a lonely dream of how
this desolate country might have been!
The rightful arrogance of MacDiarmid's
calling together of Clann Albann,
or the surging lamentations of MacLean,
the sound of his echoing Gaelic
a fierce pibroch crying on the wind.

THE DEATH OF AE: IRISH HERO AND MYSTIC

PAMELA TRAVERS

His story is the story of a soul, and therefore cannot be bound by geographical limits or biographical events. I come into it merely as a recorder, a sort of apprentice *file* of his last years, and the days that led up to his dying.

I met him at a time when it was growing late in his life and while it was still early in mine.

I had been brought up by an Irish father and a mother of Scottish extraction in a home in the wilds of Australia where, amid the Antipodean sounds there sounded continually the rhythms of another hemisphere, the place they both called "Home." The Celtic Twilight had cast its long blue light over my childhood but by the time I had crossed the ocean it had practically turned into night. I was fortunate to catch it, as it were, by the tail.

One of the first things I did on arriving in England was to send AE, then editing the *Irish Statesman,* a small poem, tentatively, with no covering letter of explanation, just a stamped addressed envelope for return. And the envelope indeed came back — but with Two Guineas in it! Not only that, but there was, too, a letter from AE saying he felt the poem could not have been written by anybody who was not Irish and a suggestion that if I was ever in Ireland I should come to see him and bring some more poems.

If I was ever in Ireland — and I bent towards it all my thinking life! And anyway, I was about to visit my father's relations and that would make it possible to accept the invitation.

At Merrion Square in Dublin I was welcomed as though I were an expected Avatar. I was overwhelmed to find myself in a painted forest, every wall a woodland; to have the one unchipped cup picked out for me, the poems I had brought at once accepted and an invitation given to come again on my way back to England.

I went off to my relatives in the southern counties in a maze of happiness and wonder. How could it have happened that this world I had dreamed of for so long had, in the person of AE — whose famous initials I seemed always to have known — drawn me into it?

Only a month or two before, I had stood in the Australian bush, listening to the silence — a pursuit I had been about ever since early childhood. Be still long enough, I thought, and the trees would take no notice of me and continue whatever it was they were doing or saying before I happened upon them. For nothing was more certain, to my mind, than that they lived a busy and communicative life which ceased — as at a command given — whenever I appeared. I have never lost it, this sense of the secret life lived by forests that withdraws itself at the sound of a footstep. And the painted woodland of AE's

471

office, all of it from his own hand, had its own particular kind of silence. If one sat with it long enough, would one hear what it was saying? Would I ever get the chance to listen?

But now I was off to the long green hills, of which I had been so often told, and a family that, I soon discovered, had no need for poetry, except in a book; by whom Cathleen ni Houlihan — perhaps because they lived with her, cheek by jowl — was dismissed as an aberration and where twilight was simply twilight, a patch of time between night and day. Moreover, my enthusiasm for these things was cause for family murmurings. Was Robert's streak of Quixotry — going off to Ceylon to plant tea and then to Australia to plant sugar — showing up in his daughter? It was earnestly hoped not.

"I don't approve of you taking up with men who see fairies," said my uncle, shaking a sombre head. "And going to London to be a writer — well, you'll meet such frightful people. There's a terrible great boastful fellow — his family lived in a white-washed cottage, over there, across the fields —" a wave of the hand described the landscape. "If you meet him, be courteous, but do not pursue the acquaintance. He calls himself Bernard Shaw."

"Bring her to me. Let her have the choice," Shaw said, delightedly, when AE later, and with relish, recounted this incident to him.

But all of that was still in front of me and I set out from the home of my family in happy anticipation of my dreadful London life.

I walked through Dublin to Merrion Square and AE and the painted woods. Hadn't I been pressed to return? But I found I could not touch the bell. I was face to face with my diffidence, my inability to believe in my fortune, or to dare to trust my luck.

"It was just politeness, "I told myself. "A great and busy man like that — he'll not want to be intruded upon." And I turned away and went back to London.

Three weeks later, answering a knock at my door, who should I find standing there but AE, and under his arm a great parcel of books.

"You're a very faithless girl," he accused me. "You said you would come on your way back and then you never turned up. I had these waiting for you."

"These" were his collected works, each of the many books inscribed.

So — it was true. I had to believe in my good fortune and not waste any of it in asking a useless "Why?" If there was an answer, it would come in good time. From then on I was as much at home in Dublin as in London and in both cities AE fished up friends for me from his inexhaustible cauldron. For, as well as being his own best friend, he had a talent for friendship, even something more than friendship, for which we have no word. He said once: "We can hardly tell where our own being ends and another begins or if there is any end to our being. We are haunted by unknown comrades in many moods, whose naked souls pass through ours and reveal themselves to us in an unforgettable instant."

And, to his mind, these friendships had antecedents. I was to discover this one day when walking with him in Regent Street. I must have made some remark about the strangeness of our meeting — two people from the ends of the earth! He stopped in mid-stride, his round blue eyes growing rounder still with surprise at my ignorance.

"But surely you don't imagine," he said, "that this is the first time we've met!"

Well, I did imagine it and was thereupon introduced for the first time to the idea of reincarnation as he understood it. That I did not myself have any inkling of having known him before did not disturb him in the least. He could remember for both while I, listening to his reiterated chantings of the *Bhagavad Gita* and snatches from the old Celtic legends, was happy to accept what I was being told without trying, merely with my mind, to verify it.

But other things I could comprehend. "We only love what is our own and what is our own we cannot lose." That needs no verification. Nor did his Law of Spiritual Gravitation. "Your own will come to you" was a constantly repeated axiom and in a letter to me, dated April '32, he wrote:

> Ireland as a nation I have no further interest in. Indeed, I have no interest in nations at all. I feel I belong to a spiritual clan whose members are scattered all over the world and these are my kinsmen. And I would sacrifice any nation, my own quite readily, to promote the interests of that spiritual clan.

As a member of that clan, however humble, I was permitted to see much of the Ireland that he nevertheless loved. I stayed with him often in his beloved Donegal, at Janie's-on-the-Hill above Dunfanaghy — a white-washed cottage where at night one would hear the cows moving about in their stalls below the attic bedroom and in the daytime Janie churning butter or clanging the lid of the iron cauldron that swung on a chain above the peat fire and in which everything was cooked: bread, meat, cake, soup.

Much wisdom was dropped into my ears over mountainy mutton and dark brown bread. Once, talking about poetry, he said: "All artists should take the vow of poverty, that is, the inside vow. It does not mean that if somebody leaves them a hundred thousand dollars, that they refuse it, but that they stand ready at any time to desert prosperity or fame if these conflict with the spirit."

Or again, as he later was to write to the Scottish poet, Hugh MacDiarmid: "We have nothing to write about truly except ourselves. I use the word 'ourselves' to include the conscious personality and that vast ocean of life that envelopes us and in which we find our most intimate understanding of the minds of others." John Eglinton said of him: "His mind was a natural inhabitant of that region of thought in which myths are 'true'." So, there would be tales told from the *Táin*, while the heroes of Ireland strode invisibly through the room. And, once, teasing me from a pensive mood to laughter, he told me the Story of the Three Druids who decided to live together in hermetic silence. At the end of the first year, the first Druid remarked "This was a good decision." At the end of the second year, the second Druid replied "It was." And at the end of the third year, the third Druid said "I must get away from all this chatter."

From Janie's, he would take me with him on his excursions to friends in the neighbourhood or to those parts of woodland or strand that set up in him the strongest vibrations. Was he intentionally educating me, I wondered! No matter: it was being done, with or without intent.

Once, as we were setting out one morning, I saw, looking down at the little stone-fenced fields below us an enormous footprint of flowers among the grass. The shape was unmistakable, as though somebody of great size, coming from Uranus, perhaps, had landed on the earth for a moment, taken a step or two upon it and set off again, leaving his mark.

"Look, AE," I said. "Someone has been here overnight."

He glanced calmly at the footprints. "He has." he said. "It often happens."

So, there was nothing I could show to him and everything he could show to me.

On another occasion, when we had been asked to lunch with his closest of all friends, Mr. and Mrs. Hugh Law, who lived about a mile away, he glanced down at my London footware.

"You can't go in those," he said firmly. "Our way lies through the deep bog. Haven't you anything stronger?"

I hadn't.

"Well, you'll just have to wear a pair of my boots."

His boots! But he was twice my size and I wanted to look my best. A cry of horror broke from me but he was away, up the rickety stairs, to return with several pairs of socks, two huge seven-leagued boots and copies of the London *Observer* and the *Times*.

I found that I was to wear them all: Sock upon sock, then the boots, and the *Observer* round one leg, the *Times* the other, securely fastened by AE with what looked like a cow's halter but which turned out to be merely string.

I knew it was a loving act. Kindly meant. All for my welfare. So I bore it in seething silence and followed him, less like a lamb to the slaughter than some ungainly dinosaur cub, readier to kill than be killed.

We came to the bog. AE, serenely chanting Eastern scriptures, walked ahead of me, almost tripping, his feet sure of every step: even his boots knew the way. The other pair — I could hardly be said to be wearing them — evidently did not. I was stuck fast in the bog, as Brer Fox to Tar Baby, and giving vent to more vitriol than I had known there was in the world, let alone in myself. I *hated* the *Baagavad Gita* and, as for the shining Celtic heroes, let them rot in Hell.

My silent violence must have communicated itself to him as I stood there, unable to move. For he turned, gave one look at me and, to crown all the indignities, burst into peals of laughter.

"I'm a fool!" he declared. "You don't want a philosophy. You want a life. Slip your feet out and come barefoot. I shall enjoy escorting a dryad to lunch."

"But your boots, AE!" I was now contrite.

"Leave them. Let the bog have them."

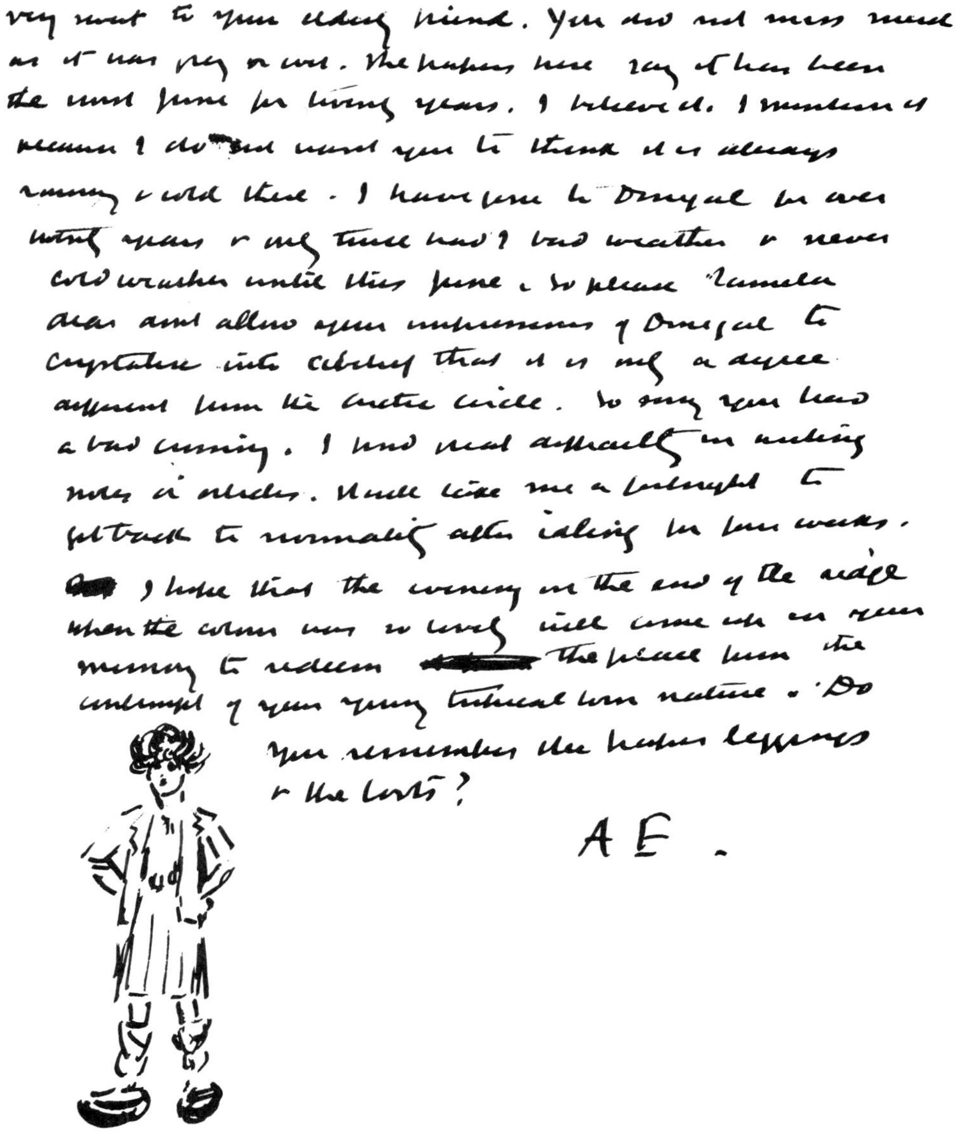

very sweet to your elderly friend. You did not miss much as it was grey or wet. The papers here say it has been the worst June for twenty years. I believe it. I mention it because I don't want you to think it is always raining & cold there. I have gone to Donegal for over twenty years & only twice had I bad weather & never cold weather until this June. So please Pamela dear don't allow your impressions of Donegal to crystallize into belief that it is only a degree different from the Arctic circle. So sorry you had a bad crossing. I find great difficulty in making notes on slides. It will take me a fortnight to get back to normality after idling for four weeks.

I hope that the evening on the end of the ridge when the colour was so lovely will come up in your memory to redeem the place from the contempt of your young tropical born nature. Do you remember the paper leggings & the boots?

AE.

Plate 1: AE drawing, Pamela Travers in paper leggings, at the conclusion of a letter from AE to Pamela Travers (1 July 1927).

And the bog got them — unless he went back and retrieved them later. All I could see was the newspapers, hurriedly sinking into the peat as though ashamed, as I had been, of being so burlesqued.

On another occasion and another year, setting out on a painting excursion with myself at his side — I do not know in which role he saw me, as daughter, acolyte, apprentice, or as all three — he thrust into my hands a paint-box, chalks and sketchbook.

"But I can't paint, AE!"

"Of course you can. Everyone can do it." Later, Augustus John said the same thing to me: "If you have one gift you have them all. One comes to the surface but the others are latent." And it is recorded that when they had both been in the same art school, Yeats said of him that, in spite of being hailed as a budding genius, or rather because of it, AE refused to accept it. He was set, he said, on making his mind strong and vigorous and calm and could not afford the moving emotional life of the artist. "I prepare myself," he declared," for a cycle of activities in some other life. I will make rigid my roots and branches. It is not now my turn to burst into leaves and flowers."

Nevertheless, burst he did, no sooner finishing one picture than starting on another. But one felt that this was less a series of emotional excursions than his way of finding out about the world he lived in.

So, having arrived at his chosen position, a long yellow tongue of sand, laced with a thread of moving water that changed its colour as the sky changed, I sat beside him, making an occasional sweep of a crayon but more intent on watching his way of working than on what was in my sketchbook. Somehow, it seemed to me that he was seeing more than landscape for he kept looking up intently at some thing or person that, as far as I was concerned, was not there.

"Do you see them?" he murmured, half turning to me and then looking raptly up again.

"No," I said, awed and regretful. I felt he would have liked me to see whatever it was that he was seeing, and that in some way, all unripe, I had failed him.

I put aside my sketchbook and climbed up into a nearby tree, watching intently as there crowded, swiftly, into the canvas creatures from some other world: bright, authoritative, beckoning. It was then, as he paused to mix a new colour, that I saw smoke rising from where he sat. Was this part of the process, I wondered? Was he to be wrapt from my mortal eyes? I remained as still as a moth on my branch, watching the course of events.

But the smoke continued to thicken and blacken and the smell of burnt serge rose up like incense.

"AE!" My cry shattered the silence. "AE! Be careful! You're on fire." Hand to my mouth, I waited for what would happen next, cursing myself for having, with my mortal voice, broken into an immortal moment.

Calmly, moving serenely from that world to this, he looked down, beheld the smoke and took his pulsing pipe from his pocket.

"My poor wife!" he said, remorsefully. "She'll have to reline another pocket." "Never mind," he beamed, "I got them down," and spread out before me a canvas alight with starry figures.

"And also this, which I rather like." He turned a page of his sketch-book and there was I upon my branch, not at all part of the scene but in a way witness to it. As if one had stood, unseen, at the portal of Paradise.

Plate 2: AE drawing, "A Witness to the scene,"

All that was his country world. His famous weekly evenings in Dublin were yet another one. Everybody was prodigally made welcome in that room crowded with pictures where, he once told me, Maud Gonne used to sit by the fire, braiding her loose gold-brown hair and keening for the wrongs of Ireland.

Friend met friend there and, as well, enemy met enemy. It was a crossroads. One was reminded of the chapter in *The Candle of Vision* where he speaks of how things and entities draw to themselves their own affinities. No sooner does one become aware of certain stirrings within than he meets others with the same search; or one takes a book from a shelf and finds there what he has already himself thought or envisaged; or one seeks no friends but discovers many. "I need not seek," the passage goes, "for what was my own would come to me. I knew that all that I met was part of myself and that what I could not comprehend was related by affinity to some yet unrealized forces in my being .... There is no personal virtue in me other than this, that I followed a path all may travel but on which few do journey .... None need special gifts or genius. Gifts! There are no gifts. For all that is ours we have paid the price. Genius is not bestowed but won."

Conversation blossomed in that room. People came and went, drinking from his generous chalice and wandering off to give place to others. And always, moving among them, diffidently bringing in tea and cakes, almost invisibly replenishing cups, a fragile, grey-haired feminine figure came and went, speaking little and to few before disappearing into the beyond of the house.

When I learned that she was AE's wife, I followed her one evening, asking to be allowed to help. Gently and shyly, she put me aside. "No, no, you go back in. People come to see George, not me."

But I persisted. And at last, to my delight, she allowed me to help fill the tea-pots and slice up the cake. We became, demurely, friends, sharing the myths and stories like two Old Wives, discovering mutual favourites in her flower garden. For what was he without her? Or, at any rate, from what established contentment did he draw — and bestow upon others — his strength?

After her death, the house in Rathgar lost for him its *genius loci*. Added to this, the demise of his weekly paper, *The Irish Statesman*, gave him the sense that Othello's occupation was gone. It was then that he came to England to live and this, together with his lecture trips to America, gave many people grounds for thinking, even loudly saying, that he had left Dublin for good. But it was not so. He never really withdrew from that root. He constantly assured me of this, as he surveyed the dark walls of his London lodgings. "In a year or so I may return. I shall want to go to Donegal for three or four months of the year."

But his many lives of poet, painter, mystic, prose writer, economist, editor, — for all that there was left to do — were gathering into one. The Prodigal Son had already, at some unnoted moment, turned, and was bent towards his Father. Indeed, the very fact that he sensed himself now bound for Heaven, seemed to make him ever more in love with earth, with the planet itself which he continued to write of as a living being with its own eternal memory that could be tapped in meditation.

It had been his custom, when in Dublin or Donegal, to boast to me that Ireland was full of springs of life — Fountains of Hecate, he called them — that the countryside of England lacked. But when he came to live in England and explored the stretches of moor and woodland where his friends lived, Constance Sitwell's in Northumberland, my own in Sussex and those of others, he had to admit, albeit grudgingly, that Hecate was in England too.

His life in London and in America — where farmers, after he had lectured on economics, kept him for hours reciting poetry — was as overflowing as ever, outwardly with friends, many of whom he had not seen for years, and inwardly with poetry. But he was not well. A doctor friend of many years standing, went over him with a pendulum which did not appear to inform him of anything unduly serious. Nevertheless, each time I saw him, which was often, he seemed a little greyer — greyness of skin rather than of hair, with something of his vividness fading. I begged him to see another doctor. Characteristically, he was unwilling: it would hurt the feelings of the man with the pendulum.

But when I went to meet him after his hurried flight from America — his last trip — all the colour had gone from him. He knew he was ill, told me of his symptoms and now he agreed to see a specialist. And again, nothing drastic was prognosed and he was put on a diet of milky food. We agreed that he would leave London and come down to the country where I could take care of him. A date was fixed and I went hunting for one of those turntable sheds so that he could sit in it all day and write, turning with the sun as it turned.

But on the day when he was expected, there was no AE. Only a post card saying he had been hurriedly sent off to a nursing home in Bournemouth.

I waited for news, day after day expecting to hear, wondering what I should do. And at last, on the telephone, was the voice of the pendulum doctor. "Where the hell are you? Why aren't you at his side? He's asking for you hourly. He hasn't a fortnight to live."

And I realized that again I had let myself be caught — as long ago on that first encounter in Dublin — in that base, timid streak of myself, diffident and self-distrustful, the fear of being in the way, not wanted. I had not rung the bell in Merrion Square, though I had longed to do it, and I had not rushed to Bournemouth. In the first instance, he had brought me his books; in the second he was asking for me. Again I had not trusted my fate!

I was in Bournemouth as quickly as four wheels could take me and the surgeon was waiting for me. He had examined AE as he had not been examined before, found he had cancer and had operated to give him ease for the time that was left to him. He told me that when he had broken the news to his patient, he had been given a long blue look and words of acceptance of such serenity that he had had to leave the room in tears. "I have had a very interesting life, I have done nearly all the things I wanted to do. I have rejoiced in the love of friends. What man could want more?"

In the hall of the nursing home, a small man, reddish as to moustache and looking like some shy hedgerow animal, came to greet me: "You may know of me as John Eglinton." I did know of him and his clear tidal rhythmic prose had made me think of a tall, languid man, exquisite as a lily. But John Eglinton was now Willie McGee, one of AE's oldest friends and his best biographer. "I'm glad you've come. He keeps asking." His voice was gruff with shyness. "And I can't make up to him for you." He turned me towards AE's room.

Confronted with reality — with what inevitably is — one does not falter. It sends one its own courage. I opened the door. Serene as Socrates after the hemlock, his long shape was deep in the bed, his beard newly tinged with gold, a remade image of himself. I was sent at once to the chair beside him and laid my head on his pillow. He put up a slow hand to my cheek. "Kind, sweet girl," he said smiling. He had had no doubt that I would come.

He was prepared. He knew exactly what he wanted done and was setting about the business of his dying as he had set about his life, practical, unflustered. There was his lawyer to be sent for from Dublin to arrange for his burial; close friends to be apprised of what was to happen so that they should not read of it in the newspapers. A pile of letters lay on the table and fresh batches came with every mail. I was to read them to him and take down the answers dictated by a voice firm for all its frailty. From time to time he would take a rest and we kept a communicative silence, his hand resting on the copy of Tennyson John Englinton had brought at his request. His first encounter with poetry had been the Tennyson given him by his father. He was thus completing a circle.

Then he would sleep a little or the nurses would come to do what had to be done. One of them said to me wonderingly as she came out of his room: "There's Somebody in there, isn't there?" as though she were remembering — and yet could not quite remember — a legend she had heard.

"Yes," I agreed, and said no more. I felt that he would have been happy enough with "Somebody" and recalled how he had said to his old friend Charles Weekes who had protested that by editing a small provincial paper he was lost to the world: "I will go back to the stars without any flourish of trumpets. I am not going anywhere I can be seen."

And yet, while life at its highest point was being lived in that room, there was, in a sense, a flourish of trumpets. The summer days were radiant and there was about them an air of festival. People came and stayed at nearby hotels, happy to see him for a moment and then congregate on the nursing home's lawns. He was not unaware of this.

"Have you been swimming today?" he would ask and because I felt that that made him part of the shining days, I went swimming and talked to him about the tides. Then again I would stand beside him, taking down more letters: "I am not curable by medical or surgical means" — he did not spare his friends as he did not spare himself. Sometimes he would hand me a special letter: "I think you would like to keep that."

Only once, to one who wrote asking to see him, did he tell me to say "No." I gently pleaded with him to retract. But he again refused: "he has had his share of me. That is enough." Now, looking back upon those days, I see that he was determined to deny himself any emotional deathbed scene; that he needed all his strength for dying — reconciliation would come later, once he was free and away. He had written in *The Avatars*: "There must be a lordly way out of the body by one of those secret radiant gateways into light. If we do not find this way, I think we must return again and again to the body until we have mastered the secret of death and can take that lordly way out by our own will."

This, clearly, was what he was trying to do. And except for that one refusal, he saw everybody. I telephoned one whom he had called "the nicest nasty person he had known" thinking she might like to come. "Well, but what could I do for him?" she replied. Nothing. There was nothing any of us could do, but much that he could do for us. The mere sight of him, growing more golden every day, was a lesson in living and dying.

There was one friend, however, from whom he urgently wanted to hear. Each day, as I opened the letters, he would ask me "Nothing from Yeats?" And at last, seeing his disappointment and that this was the one thing he wanted, I dashed off a wire to the poet. "AE dying and daily looking for a word from you." It struck home. "Give my old friend my love," wired Yeats. And with that AE seemed content. He had come to the end of his wanting.

That day the nursing home seemed to be the still centre of a shining, turning world. His friends were scattered upon the lawns, laughing — nothing here for tears — waiting in the hope that one or another would be sent for to have a glimpse of him. But I noticed that in the high windowed porch a bird was flying backwards and forwards as though restrained, in spite of the windows, by something only birds know from making its way to freedom. It could have flown out but it did not. And remembering the axiom that if a bird flies into a house it will bring death in its train, I thought to myself "He will die tonight." And in my heart, if not in my mind, I urged him not, for our sakes, to stay a minute longer.

Oliver Gogarty had wired to me — "Is there time for me to see my friend?" And I replied "Come quickly." He came. "Be ever blessed for this," he said, as I led him to the door. And before it closed, I had a glimpse of Dublin's Mocking Bird, its Wag, its Comus, kneeling in tears beside the bed as he kissed the drooping hand.

Gogarty was the last of the visitors. When he had gone AE asked for a drink and was able to move his pillow into an easier position. Why should one not die in comfort? And when a package arrived from Scotland he was able to take a morsel of its contents into his hand and sniff it, saying "Ah, how good!" It was evident that with this moss and peat and heather — part of his beloved planet — he was soon to be one and a nurse took me by the hand and led me away.

I had hoped I would be allowed to stay to the end. But no: "It would be too hard for you," she said. And while I was ready for what was too hard, I felt it was also my part to be ready to do what I was told, and not by any request or protest disturb the harmony.

So, I joined the others — there were about eleven of us — in the big downstairs room that had been put at our disposal. I do not think that one of us was less than happy. He had let his myth sustain him to the last and to me it was a vindication of the Iron Age that such a man could live and die in it. And it was clear to all of us that the Pilgrim, whatever his destination, was content to go towards it. There is a time for tears but this was not it.

So we sat and waited, knowing that upstairs an Event was taking place. At last, about eleven o'clock, the doctor with the pendulum came in quietly and said: "It is all but over — the death rattle has him."

And at that I cried out. I heard myself say "No, no, it will not be like that." That was not the secret way. He had said to John Eglinton that he was not afraid of death; all he objected to was being what he called "Thrust out" of the body instead of leaving it as he chose.

"That is not the way of it. Go back!" I cried. "It is not over."

Clearly assuming that I was unhinged and with the air of one who pacifies an hysteric, he shrugged and turned away.

After twenty-five minutes, he came in again, shaken and surprised. "She was right," he said. "The rattle ceased. He has quietly breathed his life away."

At once, Con Curran, AE's lawyer, stood up and said

> Let us now praise famous men
> and our fathers that begat us.

and we departed.

As I came out, the bird came soaring from the porch. It, too, had found its secret gateway into the light.

And it *was* light — such light as there was, perhaps, on the first day. Never before or since have I seen such a moon. It came up slowly out of the sea, full, golden and enormous, dazzling as the sun.

And I remembered the chapter of the *Bhagavad Gita,* the Eighth, that he had recited to me so often. I have his copy, given to me by his son Diarmuid, and one particular passage is marked and remarked with different inks and crayons.

> I will declare to thee, O best of the Bharatas, at what time yogis, dying, obtain freedom from rebirth. Fire, light, day, the fortnight of the waxing moon, six months of the sun's Northern course — going then and knowing the Supreme spirit, men go to the Supreme. But those who depart, in smoke, at night, during the fortnight of the waning moon, and while the sun is in the path of his Southern journey, proceed for a while to the regions of the moon and again return to mortal birth. These two, light and darkness, are the world's eternal ways; by one man goes not to return, by the other he cometh back upon earth.

Those markings of inks and crayons tell us what he hoped for and worked towards and also that we shall not see his like again. And the great moon, reflecting the sun on its Northern journey, would stand witness for him at whatever tribunal might await him.

The journey back to Dublin was a royal progression. Small gatherings stood at wayside stations to salute him; the High Commissioner for Ireland ceremonially met him at Euston and later he lay in state in the hall of Merrion Square — this man who asked nothing, who was frugal in all things — except in his prodigal giving of himself — lay in state, not in any worldly sense, but merely as a last courtesy to his friends.

With Yeats and de Valera among others in Mount Jerome, Michael O'Donovan, later to be Frank O'Connor, spoke the oration, taking the words from an Eastern scripture:

> He saw the lightning in the East
> And he longed for the East;
> He saw the lightning in the West
> And he longed for the West;
> But I, seeking only the lightning and its glory,
> Care nothing for the quarters of the earth.

So, in the earth and yet gone beyond it, we left him. In his obituary notice, Oliver Gogarty ended with this quotation from the Classics:

> "Now, Apollo was ever with Admetus — until today!"

There could have been no better phrase — the Olympian herdsman, tending the flocks of the mortal man!

These notes are written by one who counts herself fortunate to have spent some time in the fields of Admetus during that notable sojourn.

DAVID JONES

KATHLEEN RAINE

Upon David Jones, a Londoner by birth and upbringing (his father had come from Wales, his mother was Italian by descent), Wales exercised all the power of that native land of the imagination from which he was in fact an exile. The region of Wales was for him an imagined land, laden with all its riches of history, legend and mythology. This is not to say that for him Wales was less real than for a native Welshman — on the contrary, his was a land distilled into its imaginative essence. This invisible region is indeed wedded — and not for David Jones alone — to a natural landscape, to a sea-coast looking towards the sunset, with all its power to draw the imagination after the departing light towards some land-under-wave or St. Brendan's Isle distilled from light and distance; for every artist finds in nature a continuous correspondence to whatever themes the imagination may generate. In David Jones's case, however, it must be understood that imagination sought its equivalences rather than the other way around.

David visited Wales as a child but actually lived there only for a few years when after the first World War he became a member of Eric Gill's Catholic lay community at Capel-y-ffinn. There he found indeed deep confirmation in all that lay before his painter's eye of the Wales he carried always within him; but in fact he was always painting that interior Wales, whether in Brighton or Harrow-on-the Hill or in Northumberland. The loyalty of the exile is no less deep than that of the native — it may well be, on the contrary, a much stronger passion, rooted as it is in a yet deeper exile innate in us all: exile from Paradise. James Joyce (David Jones loved his work) was in a sense his opposite: Ireland was for Joyce all too bitterly real and hampering, and only became imaginatively assimilable when he himself had left it, thus allowing it to become interiorized.

Wales was, for David Jones, above all a palimpsest of memories reaching back through his own childhood and youth in a virtually unbroken retrospect into history and into the past. Not for him Dylan Thomas's robust satire of *Under Milk Wood* — the love-hate flesh and blood intimacy of the native — but rather for him Wales was to become a cultural totality whose "matter" — the Arthurian "matière de Bretagne" — and the older epic Y *Gododdin* and yet older *deposits* (to use his own favourite word) — is enwoven throughout his writings. Beyond that again Wales is holy land, the *mundus imaginalis* itself. For him the last transformation of the "matter of Britain" is not the death of Arthur but the transmutation of the knights of his Round Table into Christian penitents and hermits, while their cavalry horses, grown wild and stunted, were themselves metamorphosed into those Welsh hill ponies he so lovingly depicted in so many of his paintings. This becomes, in his work, a kind of apotheosis, a raising of the natural into the spiritual order, the knights to prayer, the horses resumed into unfallen Eden.

David's love of what he calls the "deposits" of history and pre-history is apparent in every page of his writings, in every painting and lettered inscription. All he did, all he loved, is laden with history fading into romance, romance into mythology, mythology into something immemorial, into Paradise itself. Or perhaps laden is the wrong word, with its implication of weight and erudition — rather in his work we have screens of transparency fading not into darkness but into light which is itself fluid, elusive, a recession never closed but always intensifying into something beyond, which can only be Imagination itself.

Palmer and Calvert and their circle of painters called themselves "The Shoreham Ancients" in order to distinguish themselves from "the moderns" whom they despised because they dismissed the past. In this sense — and at the height of "the modern movement" — when Herbert Read's memorable exhibition of "two thousand years of modern art" set the mood of a generation, David Jones was an "ancient" and Wales was his antiquity. Not, indeed, a Wales separated from European history and Roman Christendom, but, rather, a region within that totality, and, within European Christian culture, custodian of one of its richest treasuries — the "matter of Britain" itself, largely lost in England, but in fact the foundations of the cultural inheritance of the whole island, not of Wales alone.

> To conserve, to develop, to bring together, to make significant for the present what the past holds, without dilution or any deleting, but rather by understanding and transubstantiating the material, this is the function of genuine myth, neither pedantic nor popularizing, not indifferent to scholarship, nor antiquarian, but saying always: 'of those thou hast given me I have lost none.'[1]

Such was David Jones's own self-imposed task, triumphantly realized.

He never invented: all is exact, down to the cordage and tackle of the ship on which Tristan escorts Iseult to Cornwall, and the position of the constellations in the sky: or, in one of his last fragments, *The Narrows*, the "hinged cheek-pieces of tough/resistant work of iron" that

> hide the green-gilled aspect of
> the Optio of Maniple IV
> Or of Legionary '59 Artox, but lately
> posted back to his forward station, from
> his job as furrier's mate at
> Cohort H.Q. horse-lines.[2]

On such details of craftsmanship, military disposition and tactics, the way in which things are made and done, David spent hours of minute care on his works; treasuring pieces of exact information, archaeological, technical, or liturgical, more than any general impressions or personal feelings — these are implicit in the detail. It cannot too clearly be said that the transportation of history into an imaginative world is by no means a subjective undertaking: on the contrary, it is objective exactness that enables the artist to build up a shared universe. Deeply felt, as is everything in his work, all is concrete and exact. Sacramental transformation of the elements of this world — Aristotelian Thomism — not otherworldly subjectivity — was of the essence of his spiritual realization. By such things he weds his world of imagination firmly to a shared world of times and places. His Virgin Mary listens to the angel of the Annunciation in an accurately depicted Welsh wattle enclosure, a foxglove not a lily in her hand; but not because for him the Queen of Heaven is seen as a Welsh country girl at her cottage door — indeed circular wattle enclosures belong to the past not to the present Wales — but because to Her, a Person of humankind's inner world, he dedicates the thrice-distilled essence of all that Wales is to the imagination; not only his own but that of a race, a culture: the quintessential Wales. So in his inscriptions he intertwines Latin liturgical phrases with words from the Welsh language, at once warming cold Latin with native love, and giving the Welsh language its rightful place within the Roman *imperium*, and the Roman *ecclesia*.

And yet as between objectivity and imagination, it is imaginative vision which is always paramount, seeking out and discovering its equivalence in an objective world; as in this passage he is describing his own vision no less than a characteristic he finds in the Welsh genius:

> The folk tradition of the insular Celts seems to present to the mind a half-aquatic world — it is one of its most fascinating characteristics — it introduces a feeling of transparency and interpenetration of one element with another, of transposition and metamorphosis. The hedges of mist vanish or come again under the application of magic, such as Geraint ab Erbin encountered, just as the actual mists over peat-bog and tarn and *traeth* disclose or lose before our eyes drifting stumps and tussocks. It is unstable, the isles float, where was a *caer* or a *llys* now is a glassy expanse. The young herdsman offers his barley cake to the yellow-haired girl, 'a ransom in her comb', who rises from Llyn y Fan Fach; his ecstasy is short-lived, but a second time and a third she appears — there is courtship and marriage — but nevertheless 'the three inadvertent blows' are given and water-bride and all her dower of fairy-kine the waters claim again, just as Arthur's power dissolves with the disappearing, in dark water, of Excalibur.[3]

Perhaps this account of David Jones's Welsh loyalty as essentially of the imagination may seem too extreme in the face of his descriptions of the trench warfare of the first World War in *In Parenthesis*. There indeed the private soldiers of B-company of the London Welsh Fusiliers are real enough in their vulnerable "creaturely" lives and all too bodily deaths. Yet in contrast with all other war books known to me, *In Parenthesis* is a work of the Imagination, a great modern epic poem. In it David Jones has indeed "made significant for the present what the past holds" for it is by integrating the brutal present into the "matter of Britain" — an intent he makes explicit in the very first page — that David Jones has accomplished this. The men in B-company are the same as those celebrated in *Y Gododdin*; it is the same war (all wars are the one war, one of the eternal states of the human condition) and their deaths are the same deaths as in all epic poetry. He raises their obscure deaths into this heroic tradition by placing the present in the context of the cultural heritage of their race.

David himself never wrote an Arthuriad; but he wrote in 1948 (for *The Tablet*) a review of Charles Williams's *Arthurian Torso* in which he confesses to grave doubts about Williams's work as "lacking in one exceptionally difficult to express particular." This is "something wholly to do with time — with 'now-ness'. Somehow, somewhere, between content and form, concept and image, sign and what is signified, a sense of the contemporary escapes."[4] This quality of "now-ness" was to David Jones, traditionalist as he was, all-important; not that subject-matter should necessarily be contemporary but that the imagination that welds the material should be aware of the present, because a sense of history includes a sense of the present — of that ever-moving present that is life itself. Perhaps it is a mark of the Celtic genius that its memory — its present — is so long. I remember the American classical scholar, Edith Hamilton, describing a barbarian as one who has "no past": and if that be so a culture is, precisely, a retrospect of a past. Whether by reason of temperament or of historic circumstance, the Celtic races of Wales, Scotland and Ireland are more retentive of their past culture in this respect than are the modern English. Perhaps for conquered races the past, more than the present, holds their identity; and thus that identity becomes an imaginatively transmuted one, perforce removed from the realism of what David Jones calls the "fact-men". Thus the Celtic genius has in a great measure become the custodian of the past. This is particularly true of Wales, whose Arthurian material is the "matter of Britain" as a whole; "The stories of Arthur are the acts of Albion" as David Jones quotes from Blake (in whom he was not otherwise greatly in sympathy). It is Wales which sustains Albion's retrospect, that guards the burial-site of Albion's *rex quondam rexque futurus*. Of this David was continuously aware, and this is one significant reason why he is a great British writer and not merely a great Welsh writer, the frustration many of his readers must feel at the presence of so many Welsh words in his writings notwithstanding. He has given continuity to the supporting imaginative structure of the whole Island.

Although he painted several Arthurian themes — Trystan ac Essyllt, Guenever, The Three Queens, the Chapel Perilous — his only explicitly Arthurian fragments are *The Hunt* and *The Sleeping Lord*. In the latter, one of his finest pieces of writing, Arthur's unknown "bed" is the whole of the "deposits", geographical, topographical and historical, the land of Wales together with its legend and history, back to

> ... the carboniferous vaultings of Gwyr
>   (where in the sea-slope chamber
> they shovelled aside the shards & breccia
>   the domestic litter and man-squalor
> of gnawed marrowbones and hearth-ash
> with utile shovels fashioned of clavicle-bones
>   of warm-felled great fauna ...[5]

— to disinter human remains, ritually buried, "of a young man of the Paleolithic period, so many, many millenniums prior to Britain becoming an island." He leads us through the great Arthurian boar-hunt, the legend of the Blessed Bran whose head buried in London was the defense of the Island; through Christian burial-rites and legend to the living present of "the folk of the land, the Welsh coal-miners:"

> does Tawe clog for his sorrows
> do the parallel dark-seam drains
>   mingle his anguish-dream
> with the scored valleys' tilted refuse

— and so to the sleeping presence of the King who is the very-life-spirit of the Island of Britain, whose past secures the future:

> Yet he sleeps on
> very deep in his slumber:
> how long has he been the sleeping lord?
> are the clammy ferns
> his rustling valance
> does the buried rowan
> ward him from evil, or
> does he ward the tanglewood
> and the denizens of the wood
> are the stunted oaks his gnarled guard
> or are their knarred limbs
> strong with his sap?
> Do the small black horses
> grass on the hunch of his shoulders?
> are the hills his couch
> or is he the couchant hills?
> Are the slumbering valleys
> him in slumber
> are the still undulations
> the still limbs of him sleeping?
> Is the configuration of the land
> the furrowed body of the lord
> are the scarred ridges
> his dented greaves
> do the trickling gullies
> yet drain his hog-wounds?
> Does the land wait the sleeping lord
> or is the wasted land
> that very lord who sleeps?[6]

NOTES

[1]"The Myth of Arthur," *Epoch and Artist* (London 1959), p. 243.
[2](Interim Press 1981).
[3]*Epoch and Artist*, pp. 238-9.
[4]*Ibid.*, p. 209.
[5]*The Sleeping Lord and other Fragments* (London 1974), p. 71.
[6]*Ibid.*, p. 96.

DAVID JONES: 'CARA WALLIA DERELICTA'

NEIL BARTLETT

Information first: David Jones was born in 1895 and died our contemporary in 1974. His father was Welsh; he served in the First World War with the Royal Welsh Fusiliers; he was a Roman Catholic; he painted and lettered first, and later wrote with equal skill.

It is the Welsh connection that is my starting point. I shall use Jones's own method of accumulating fragments, deducing histories, identifying designs. He himself was not a Welshman. Apart from the times with Eric Gill at Capel-y-ffin, and with the community of Caldy, he lived as a Londoner (the other half of his family history was tied to the Pool, to the Thames, to Rotherhithe) for a large part of his writing life in a closed room in Harrow on the Hill. He got his "Celticity" from Giraldus Cambrensis, from the translated Mabinogion, from Nennius and from George Borrow, from all the fragments in Welsh and of Wales that his magpie reading could heap together; from his sympathies with Hopkins and with Joyce. It was Welshness at second hand, Welshness in exile.

Underwriting all this was the real and felt connection with the Welsh father: he was the figure through whom the loophole entry into the lumber-room of all things Celtic was made actual. The first language of James Jones was English, and David Jones's Welsh, its pieces inserted with such affecting precision into his texts, is the evidence of a painstaking attempt to rescue and revive as much of the recently lost tradition as he could. The footnotes that explain pronunciations and place allusions with such care are a model of his Welshness; they are entirely a labour of love.

The family history is a paradigm; the loss of the privileged and lovely language which Jones could see traced between his grandfather, John Jones, in Treffynnon, and himself in Harrow is a pattern of history which his writings struggle to understand and repair, and within which they strive to place themselves. Two other histories provided the same sequence, and should be remembered here. In association with Eric Gill, Jones was involved in the Catholic revivalism of the nineteen-twenties and thirties; the project was acutely conscious that the moment at which it was concerned to defend its ancient tradition was one at which that tradition, in relation to contemporary capitalist society, was threatened with dilution and potential irrelevance. He also fought in Flanders, and in retrospect (in writing) he experienced the trenches as another point at which a continuity was threatened, with the new technology of warfare seeming to deny everything that the men he fought with signified: the Cockneys and Welshmen who are pictured in the writings as standing at the end of rich and sustained traditions. Along with others of his generation, he experienced the move from tradition as the medium of a culture to "tradition" as the archaic or the deliberately constructed.

Jones's term for this lurch of history was "the Break". He articulated the idea most clearly in terms of the First World War. *In Parenthesis* is about "the Break", is about the experience of a profound dislocation, and is, in the material of the text itself (1927-1937) an attempt to construct a bridge, a connection that, by means of however strained and elaborate stratagems, fills in and somehow redeems the divide which Jones rightly saw the War opening in personal and much larger histories. It attempts the maintenance of tradition, and in so doing it defines the threat presented. The inhumanity of the War was specific for Jones in that it broke the traditional attributes which for him constituted the human. For Jones, the soldier, in his ordered, well-made and wholly dedicated life, is the type of man properly engaged in his activity (he is *homo faber*); his actions are ritual; his tools and his care of them (it is said of a rifle in *In Parenthesis*: "Marry it man! Marry it.") make him an image of the craftsman, the maker; above all he carries into the conflicts of No Man's Land an acute sense of his nationality, his locality, the history which is behind him. He can without affectation claim (especially as he is a Welshman):

> My fathers were with the Black Prinse of Wales[1]

and the poet can talk reasonably of his war as

> the intimate, continuing, domestic life of small contingents of men, within whose structure Roland could find, and, for a reasonable while, enjoy, his Oliver.[2]

This mythology experiences its débacle in the Metz Wood bombardment.

The significance of the War is that it is radically new: it makes today other than yesterday. Since it has no precedent, the ancient descriptions of Y Gododdin and Malory are useless; if there is no history, then the landmarks and quotations which sustain the connections between soldiers past and soldiers present are rendered meaningless; the invocations of continuity become tenuous and desparate. The land is made waste.

The reduction to formlessness was not only in the literal events of Flanders: Jones saw the Break repeated again and again in the cultural transformations of the English twentieth century. The intricate language of identity, memory and allusion became the property of learning; the signs were divided from that which they properly signified. The historically enriched and validated, the intimately connected, was replaced by the derelict or the merely useful. So described, the Break could be understood as (reduced to, perhaps) the especial problem of the artist:

> Normally we should not have far to seek: the flowers for the muse's garland would be gathered from the ancestral burial-ground — always and inevitably fecund ground, yielding perennial and familiar blossoms, watered and, maybe, potted, perhaps 'improved', by ourselves. It becomes more difficult when the bulldozers have all but obliterated the mounds, when all that is left of the potting-sheds are the disused hypocausts, and when where was this site and these foci there is *terra informis*.[3]

We should remember the other argument beneath Jones's passionately sad figure of the artist; it is clear that the Break (in its historical form) may also be a sign of that break (outside history) which makes all humanity, for Jones, not just that in the trenches, 'in parenthesis': it is the Fall. As such the metaphor claims a vital consequence: it predicts another and more crucial event.

If the land after the Break was waste, then it was as a restorer of the landscape that Jones saw himself. His task was — using the litter and timber of what he called the 'mythos', the known and discovered from Lascaux to Coleridge to de Chardin — the building of bridges, the maintenance of walls, the keeping open of lines of communication. The military imagery is his own; the room in which he conducted his writing, surrounded by the debris of information and the weapons of learning, became a trench. The image is of the writer stubbornly sending out messages and allusions, insisting on elaborate systems of annotation and dedication in the face of a bleak opposition. By the effort of a maker 'so late in time'[4] the precarious confusion of the trench is made, made over into another significance. The texts created have all the appearance of archaeological sections through some rich ancestral rubbish dump: they give their precious myths an encrustation, a matrix of accumulated details. As each syllable, each typographic move is placed with exact care, so the seeming-rambling antiquarianism solidifies into providing a locality, a place, for the stories. History is inscibed; it is given the appearance of the concrete, and so a reconstruction appears. The land-marks are re-erected, the calendars observed, the litanies respoken, the *viae* retraced.

In this manner of making, Jones's true mentors are not Eliot and Joyce, but the antiquarians and pseudo-historians; Nennius, Giraldus, Frazer, de la Taille. His manufacture is characterized by its desire not to submit to the denuded order of modern things after the Break; it is concerned to achieve a production "indelibly marked by locale and incidence"[5] rather than that of "our present intense technological phase"[6] — that which has as its aim the satisfaction of merely (con)temporary needs, rather than the achievement of a place in a larger order. To this end, the work is always history, since it must achieve this authenticity by allying itself to *past* traditions of making. It is to the past that it is responsible in its reconstructions, since it is of the past that the work is an effective recalling, an anamnesis. If "the Break" is the space across which Jones's texts stretch themselves, then it is by making themselves part of other histories, other traditions, that they become "some sort of single plank in some sort of bridge".[7]

It was to a Celtic world that Jones built his bridges. The Catholic associations of the *urbs* — the stiff, layered, codifying history of Rome and London — provided one pole of the work, but it was especially the (antithetical) history of the Celts, conceived of as fluid, diverse, generative, that provided the energy with which to oppose the devastation of the Waste Land: instead of *terra informis*, a traditional sense of place; in place of destruction and dispersal, the cherished and the focussed; in place of monochromatic devastation, a landscape to which Hopkins's vocabulary could be reapplied: dappled, plotted, couple-coloured, particular. This world provided him with all the myths, especially the myth of the artist, that he needed to sustain his perverse project. His own sense of potentially radical exile, of the artist as exiled from contemporary society by the conditions of production (by the Break), found its complex alibi in the exile of the Celts; Wales figures as an alternative tradition, that of the marginal, the oppressed, the forgotten, that of values made bright by their distinction from the mainstream. The particular quality of a mysterious "vitality", which the English (central) tradition has always ascribed to the Celtic, and which Jones sought to appropriate to his own attempt at tradition — that brightness of Welsh words and phrases that stiffens and makes resonant the sound and text of *The Sleeping Lord* — resides in the introverted, self-sustaining, *traditional* nature of relict Celtic culture: it can be construed as only paradoxically defeated, subdued. Such is Jones's construction: in his love of Wales, his taking sides with the Fallen, he hopes to be counted among the Resurrected.

Let me take a single figure from Jones's texts, and pursue it as an example of his sense of the "mythos" as obscure and devious but, because Celtic, finally resistant and consistent in its archetypal patterns, a continuity having a profound historical and metaphysical significance.

The Sleeping Lord appears with a retinue of forms in Jones's texts. He is widely travelled; he is allied to all Kings, especially to Lud (and thence to Lugh) and whoever's head it is that maintains the foundations of the White Tower; he includes Cymbeline; he is of course Arthur; his most precious palimpsest is that paean to "tha geong Haeleth" in Caedmon's dream. The variety of his forms is a homage to his source: in all his disguises he is Christ (who as an individual, distinct and speaking, rather than as a spoken-of, mythologised, presence is absent from Jones's texts). As the fallen Prince, he is the point at which power passes into the hands of those who have no intimate connection with the lands they govern; he thus recalls and embodies the whole principle which makes Wales crucial for Jones: that of indigenousness, of connection with the actual and the local. "Historically" he is a Celt: he is most specifically Llewelyn the Last, whose death at the hands of the English in Builth Wells in 1282 makes him a prototype of the Victim in Jones's theology; the death was in the woods, and is therefore an anamnesis of that of Christ on the Tree, and of those in the Metz Wood; it was at the hands of a foreign power, and so recalls the deaths of Hector and again Christ; it was that of a last ruler, the defeated one who lives on to sustain myths of revival; the Bear, Arthur or Christ. In the text *The Sleeping Lord* he is the land of Wales itself, mutilated, enduring and occupied, embalmed in history and awaiting resurrection. He represents the moment when the Sleeping Lord becomes *Cara Wallia Derelicta*, when the archetypal appropriates the local. When history is patterned as myth, when its recurrences are rewritten as inevitabilities, it may incarnate, demonstrate, a continuity.

In the same way the hunting of the Boar Trwyth becomes (in passing) the type of all passionate military exploits: the lost hall of Aberffraw may embody all cities of which Troy is the first; Rhiannon and Brigit can join the women who are understood to be one woman, having their implicit apotheosis in the figure of Mary (in Jones's drawing of the Annunciation, Gabriel brings his message among

cara·Wallia·derelicta
ÐVGWYL·DAMASEVS
BAB·YRVNVED·DYÐAR
ÐEG·OVIS·RAGFYR
DVW·GWENER+
AC·YNA·I·BWRIWYD
HOIL GYMRY
Y'R·ILAWR. VENIT·SVMMA·DIES
ET·INELVCTABILE·TEMPVS
DARDANIÆ.PENN·DRAGON
PENN·DREIC·OED ARNAW
PENN·ILYWELYN·DEG
DYGYN·A·VRAW·BYT·BOT
PAWL·hAEARN·TRWYDAW.
ab·hieme·añ·1282

NYT·OES·NA·XYN GOR·NA·XLO·NAC EGOR.

David Jones: Cara Wallia Derelicta. Acknowledgement: Professor William Blissett and the Tate Galler Publications Department.

Welsh hills). This interlacing of allusions and genealogies is itself a Celtic habit; it models itself on those stories which have been continually retold, keeping their myths but changing their names and actions to fit new histories and geographies: it is a form of shape-changing. It remembers (with regret) the great strength implied by that form: the ability of a culture to sustain itself in the complication and adaptation of traditional materials, which is the opposite of the reductive, technological habit of modernity. In its incantational use of name and appelation, it revives the lost art of the sign as the locus of a mass of specific cultural allusion. The Celtic, for Jones, is that region in which the culture has a particular sense of its own indigenousness, in its simplest form of nationalism, but more significantly in the general association of name and form with specific locality and occasion. His term for this culture is 'contactual'; the word coincides with 'sacramental'. When the name (within the landscape of a close culture) is dedicated to the thing as much as thing is to place (when the names of the Lord are as embedded in history as the Lord himself is embedded in the hills) then the act of naming is genuinely an embodiment: it is sacramental. The practice of artefacture (of naming) then predicts for its spokesman, the poet, a role in which he can properly claim that the nature of the bard touches that of the *sacerdos*. It replaces the poet as the one whose function is to correctly remember and re-present the details of history, of place and name, in order that the continuity of the culture be maintained. The memory of the text and the memory of that especial text, the liturgy, are brought into alliance.

We may perhaps identify Jones's manner of making as 'Celtic' by parallels with other things Celtic. It shares with those artefacts and institutions a defining complexity of reference, an introversion and abstraction which displays an eagerness to acknowledge and glorify the rules of a particular occasion. There is an obvious parallel with Celtic visual art: the testing against a sense of containment, of enclosure; the resolution produced by the acknowledgement of boundaries. In Jones's scripts, each letter marks as individual its own character, but recognises that that character is determined by its place within the script; in the texts, the strangeness of language (which can reach such a furious precision) remembers and retouches a similar intricacy within the rules of a particular craft, that of the Welsh metrical tradition, of the *cynghanedd*. It is the principle of pattern which is the essential Celtic one for Jones; the sense of geography and history as patterned (as myth), and a sense of necessary and particular pattern in word and in visual form.

The connection between Jones and his Celtic theme is not, however, justly revealed by the invocation of such hazy notions as Celtic "tone" and "habit". What is crucial in Jones's elaborate aesthetic/theological theory is the idea of 'patterned' production as being opposed to that of mechanisation (as his painted Word is opposed to the printed word), and of historical "essential Celticity"[8] as antithetical to modern, after the Break, social and cultural forms. It is at this point that we should touch and test his argument.

The (en)closure, locality, of Celtic forms is tied to the historical closure and isolation of Celtic society, its longstanding role as a minority culture. The aristocratic society of Wales, hieratic in organisation and mythological in thinking, to which Jones alludes, was in a sense completed, sealed by its historical isolation (Jones's chosen date is 1282 and all its implications): it was made a text, an artefact which could then be read, mythologised, alluded to, quoted from. This is the root of the desire of Jones's texts to appear as fragments, as if they themselves were, like the Celtic artefacts, remains of a larger and more glorious whole. By appearing relict they claim the status of relics, and imply a religion, a pattern, a history.

The first characteristic of the Celtic, then, is that it is distinct, *dis*continuous with Jones's actual social position as an artist. The society was arrested at a completely pre-Industrial stage, in which the artist (especially the poet, using oral forms essentially tied to tradition and occasion) can be seen with hindsight as having that intimacy with his society so hankered after by later practitioners. Bearing in mind Jones's despair with 'modern' (after-the-Break) form, we may re-read his texts as showing an alternative, sympathetic, (Celtic) tradition being drawn on, touched, to support his own concept of the artist. Later, in the Fifties, the enthusiasm was repeated in the making of new anathemata and the heralding of new artistries. André Breton presented "Le Triomphe de l'Art Gaulois" as one of the dark countries in which the mythologising of surrealism was prefigured; he talked of "the development of artistic movements which have abandoned Latin realism in favour of a more rhythmic concept" (1954). In terms of direct influence, Jones's contemporary tutor in the use, by the withdrawn artist, of Celtic intimacies was Joyce. The argument of Stephen Dedalus, that *quidditas* is the precondition of *claritas*, anticipates Jones's ideas about the especial and essential mode of significance of the local. The complexity of *Ulysses* is a model of the interweaving of allusion within devotion to a particular place; the *Wake* submerges itself in a Jungian version of the Celtic twilight, excavating intricately obscured myths, deepening its craftsman's concern for the word as historically and personally local to the level of pun and syllable. It was a text for which Jones had the deepest admiration. He perceived its manufacture to be as Celtic "as anything from the visual arts of La Tène or Kells."[9]

In his homage to James Joyce in *Epoch and Artist*, Jones makes it clear that he had read Joyce as sharing his own premises, that the microcosmic is a "showing forth of the macrocosmic realities", that the contactual is necessarily the sacramental. It is a *sense of place* which allows Finnegan (the Sleeping Lord) to wake. As Dublin for Joyce, so 'Cara Wallia Derelicta' for Jones; it is the locality in which, through the intervention of the artist, signs regain their ancient and remembered vitality; it is the country in which the artist can properly speak Jones's preface to *In Parenthesis*:

> This writing has to do with some things I saw, felt, was part of.[10]

It is Jones's very use of the Celtic, however, that begs the question as to how we are to take the words of his preface. The use is deliberate (stretched across a discontinuity, not within a continuity) not only in that it is booklearning, acquired with painstaking attention to what is and is not valid, but also in that it is the use of an artist after the Break, striving to place himself within a tradition, an order of signs. It does not itself traditionally inhabit a locality, but constructs it (as Jones was not Welsh, but made himself Welsh) and in a manner far from the obviousness of seeing, feeling and being involved. A tradition, a continuity is being invented, in order that the function of the maker may be maintained. If the poet is to retain the garb of the *sacerdos*, then his 'history', like that of the priest (like that of Joyce) must be converted, transmuted by the invocation of extra-historical continuities, authorities. Jones's making is a conversion of the historic into the mythic, the local into the archetypal: Llewelyn is made Christ. One must then ask in what exact sense may the continuum being posited be spoken of as 'felt'.

One answer has been to dissolve the complexity and "elusive hardness"[11] of Jones's position entirely in the idea of "loving and knowing" his works; to accept his own invitation to view his work as that of the "true" poet; to read his deliberate, motivated practice as that of an artist "so late in time", possessing ancient and essential secrets, crying out in the wilderness of modernism. In this Jones himself is made a Celt, is made the Sleeping Lord: Cara Wallia Derelicta: the repository of the Tradition. This is to assign the vitality of any possible tradition, any continuing practice of making, to its innate, inevitable quality: consequently it is to reduce Jones to the faithfulness (feebleness) of his own statement in *An Aspect of the Art of England*:

> Whether such 'pied beauty' can survive the arid and uninviting sub-cultures of today and tomorrow remains to be seen . . . I expect it will crop up in some form or other, come what may.[12]

It is also to reduce his work to that which is only available to those (academics) who are initiated by their sympathies, and to accept Jones's invitation to ascribe this not to a cultural failure but to a truly Celtic condition of glamorous defeat, precious minority. It consumes the work within a tradition: in its reverence for the supposed continuum it nullifies the real dangers and decisions presented in the text's struggles with the Break. It takes Jones out of his particular place, and removes him to an unlocated 'Celticity': the state of being-an-artist.

> This writing has to do with some things I saw, felt, was part of.

We should recall Jones's 'feeling', supported as it is by the whole idea of a Celtic continuum, into the company of his English predecessors. Instead of allowing him the privileged but vague space of 'Cara Wallia Derelicta' we should replace him. I have already noted the affinity of his texts to those of Joyce. His writings are also close to those of Hopkins: they share an innovative rediscovery of Wales as an alternative, a source of intricate order and of pattern as incarnation; a sense of the artist as frustrated, acutely troubled by his time: both are in hindsight closely linked to Victorian, Ruskinian theories of an anti-modern particularity and colourfulness. Jones's drawings are close to and in love with those of "that very

English phenomenon"[13] the Pre-Raphaelites, Rossetti and especially the Celtic subjects of Burne-Jones. His social theories are heavily influenced by those of Eric Gill, himself deeply within the tradition of Ruskin and Pugin. All the artists share a concern for the intricate, the various, the handmade: all are connected by a historically specific form of melancholy for earlier and lost modes of production; and all were dogged by the increasing retreat, into social isolation, of the artist. Their 'loving' and 'knowing' were contrived, difficult activities.

In this company, we may remember that it was hard for Jones to sustain his ideal of art as contactual without the primary contact of artist and audience. His writing became increasingly fragmentary; the posthumous appearance of the *Kensington Mass* in his own handwriting, irrecoverably removed from the arena of public contact, of *actual* involvement in the 'mythos', is something of a logical conclusion. Another quotation from the preface to *In Parenthesis* locates the problem:

> We are shy when pious men write A.M.D.G. on their notepaper — however, in the Welsh Codes of Court Procedure the Bard of the Household is instructed to sing to the Queen when she goes to her chamber to rest. He is instructed to sing first to her a song in honour of God. He must then sing the song of the Battle of Camlann — the song of treachery and of the undoing of all things; and afterward he must sing any song she may choose to hear. I tried so to make this writing for anyone who would care to play Welsh Queen.[14]

Any sense of the text as an effective recalling of its *materia poetica*, as the medium of a continuity, is made problematic by the simple fact that there exists no audience of Welsh Queens. We cannot place ourselves so easily within a tradition; it is not simply a question of the 'difficulty' of Jones's texts, but that their difficulty, the straining after validity of their signs, rests on a strange and specific idea of continuity in the practice of making: of the (Celtic) 'Tradition' as *inevitable* rather than *cultural*. As readers, we cannot forget that we are not the inhabitants of Cara Wallia: the conditions of seeing, feeling and involvement, after the Break, are radically different.

NOTES

[1] *In Parenthesis* (London 1937), p. 79.
[2] *Ibid.*, p. ix.
[3] *The Anathemata* (London 1952), p. 25.
[4] *Idem.*
[5] *Ibid.*, p. 73.
[6] *The Dying Gaul* (London 1978), p. 17.
[7] *Idem.*
[8] *Ibid.*, p. 58.
[9] *Idem.*
[10] *In Parenthesis*, p. ix.
[11] *Epoch and Artist* (London 1959), p. 198.
[12] *The Dying Gaul*, p. 62.
[13] *Ibid.*, p. 121.
[14] *In Parenthesis*, p. xiii.

SOME GAELIC AND NON-GAELIC INFLUENCES ON MYSELF

SORLEY MACLEAN

From the middle of the sixteenth to the end of the eighteenth century, as far as such things can be dated, Scottish Gaelic had a song poetry that is nothing short of marvellous. Most of this song poetry is by unknown or obscure authors, and it has been handed down and often much modified by an oral tradition which lasted until well into the nineteenth century and in some places even well into this century. Inevitably, the 'originality' of any given one of those song poems is a matter of much argument, but many of them are breath-taking fusions of the music of poetry and the music of what is normally called 'music.' A great deal of this poetry is the high-keyed expression of the tragedy of circumstance or passion, crossed with magical 'objective correlatives' in brief evocations of natural and social environment.

In the eighteenth century, Alexander MacDonald and Duncan Macintyre and others achieved near miracles in the realization of dynamic physical nature, but they had little to say explicitly of the human heart and the human condition. Dugald Buchanan expressed, in intense and powerful poetry, a vision of sin and its consequences, the vision of an ultra-Evangelical and ultra-Fundamentalist Calvinist. Robert MacKay has an unusual and piquant sermo-pedestrian comment on life, and William Ross has now and again the "echoing detonation, the auroral light" of Saintsbury's verdict on the greatest of Shakespeare, Shelley and Wordsworth, what that fine man and fine modern Gaelic and English poet, Iain Crichton Smith, has called the "infinite resonance that is in Wiliam Ross."

Many, including myself, have unjustly depreciated nineteenth-century Scottish Gaelic poetry, which has often a social poignancy that in some ways recalls the solipsist tragedies of the old songs: when this is crossed with the natural joie-de-vivre, pride, anger, and feeling of personal wrong of Mary MacDonald (Mrs. MacPherson), the result is a poetry of strange complexity and power. The Land League of the late nineteenth century brought a mature political consciousness into Gaelic poetry, with the result that it is very different from the political naivety of the poetry produced by such famous English poets as Tennyson.

I have been trying to give an idea of what Scottish Gaelic poetry impinged most on myself before I had reached my late teens. Much as I admired the triumphant realization of external nature in the poetry of MacDonald and Macintyre, it was the organic fusion of words and melodies in the old songs that was to me the greatest creative glory of the Scottish Gael. Perhaps chiefly because of this fascination, I took eagerly to Croce's doctrine of the lyrical nature of all real poetry, that if poetry was not song, it ought somehow to suggest song. Of course, this was what Grierson was telling us about lyric poetry, but Croce was in a way extending it to all poetry, calling the long poem merely a series of flats among lyric peaks. I saw the ideal poem as a song in which the music grew out of the words, coming simultaneously, but since such could come only once in a blue moon, the second best was the Crocean lyric.

During my late teens I had been writing verse in Gaelic and in English. I was not quite eighteen when I went to Edinburgh University and found the seventeenth-century English Metaphysicals, Eliot, Pound, and Hopkins — the writers most admired by the undergraduate literary aspirants whom I met during my first two years in Edinburgh (1929-31). Like others, I was then writing English verse after the fashion of the early Eliot and the Pound of "Hugh Selwyn Mauberley," but about the age of twenty I came to realize that what I did in Gaelic was far more myself. Strangely enough, I did not know the middle and later poetry of Yeats until well on in the Thirties, but from then on it affected me considerably.

It was not until the spring or summer of 1933, when I was twenty-one, that I was introduced to the poetry of Hugh MacDiarmid by two brilliant undergraduates, George E. Davie and James B. Caird. Davie had for his age a phenomenal knowledge of European and Scottish thought, and Caird combined a great knowledge of European, English and Lowland Scottish literature with a sensibility that was as unusual. In the lyrics of "Sangschaw" and "Penny Wheep" I found a poetry that moved me far more than any other modern poetry I knew and almost as much as the greatest of the old Gaelic songs. In them there was to me, and there still is, the most percipient and valid occupation of the frontiers of consciousness that I knew in any modern poetry, and perhaps in any poetry. Besides, MacDiarmid was bearing the burden of the human condition and the particular condition of the Scottish people. He had done the impossible with a long poem, *A Drunk Man Looks at the Thistle*, in which Symbolism had come to peaks of an inevitable organic growth, and in his lyrics there were rhythms that struck one as the natural language of a man reporting from a forward observation post on the frontiers of consciousness.

"Sangschaw," "Penny Wheep," "A Drunk Man Looks at the Thistle," and, to a lesser extent, "To Circumjack Cencrastus" and "Scots Unbound" enraptured me for many a year from the spring or summer of 1933 onwards, but the lyrics themselves were strangely inaccessible. One could feel their strong and captivating radiation but could not transmit it into one's own creativity. In many ways I felt a greater kinship with Yeats than with the MacDiarmid of the lyrics, and was myself probably more influenced in my creativity by Yeats than by MacDiarmid. In 1933 I was not much interested in being a poet, though I had already written poems such as that called in translation "The Heron," before I had read a word of MacDiarmid's. My obsession was the preservation of the Gaelic language so that there would be people left in the world who could hear its great songs as they really were. No poetry could be translated, still less could song poetry, and the great language of Gaelic song made me fanatical about the beauty of the Gaelic language and its astonishing ability to indicate shades and positions of emphasis with natural inversions and the use of particles.

I have always believed that the highest poetry is either that which is a passionate comment on life of "high seriousness" or that which gets near to saying the unsayable. MacDiarmid's lyrics said the unsayable. Some years later, I came to believe that much of Yeats's middle and later poetry was, of the modern poetry I knew, the most consistently and convincingly passionate comment on life, much as I disliked Yeats's élitism and some of his other attitudes. Although MacDiarmid's lyrics were so inaccessible, the medley, *A Drunk Man Looks at the Thistle*, could suggest ways to follow. The drunkenness itself was an artifice of genius liberating the imagination just as the medley form liberated the expression of the variety of moods, juxtaposing the high passions with the pedestrian discursive, the comic and even the cheap.

I was not one who could write poetry if it did not come to me in spite of myself, and if it came, it had to come in Gaelic. Political and personal events between 1935 and 1939, especially the Spanish Civil War, the increasing likelihood that Fascism was to take over Europe, a pressing family obligation, and between 1939 and 1941 a strange and terrible love affair made poetry come to me without any conscious ambition of my own. By this time, the personal and political tensions, which were so big a motif in my poetry, made the non-Gaelic influence on me more Yeats than MacDiarmid, for Yeats had in his poetry, notably in his great political poetry, much of the personal and confessional, a troubled, self-doubting and, to me, implicit confessional that was more akin to my own political reactions than the single-mindedness of the post *Drunk Man* MacDiarmid.

Later, I came to admire and love the finely blooming virtuosity that fused the old Gaelic virtuosity and the new in the poetry of George Campbell Hay, and still later the manifold sensitivities of the Gaelic and English poetry of Iain Crichton Smith, and, of course, the noble integrity of the two men, but I cannot say that I was influenced in any way by any Gaelic poetry after William Ross and Mary MacDonald, one of whom is late eighteenth century and the other late nineteenth century. I am talking of modern Scottish Gaelic poetry, for I do not know Irish well enough to pronounce on modern Irish Gaelic poetry. Of the younger Scottish Gaelic poets whom I have read, I have been struck with the robustness of Angus Nicolson, a robustness that is very Gaelic if one remembers Alexander MacDonald and many others, just as the delicacy and rhythmic sublety of the Montgomery sisters is also Gaelic. Of course, there is in modern Scotland Gaelic verse much that is factitious and much that is contrived, laboured and still-born, but that is inevitable in the verse of any country at any time. The astonishing thing is that there is so much that is new and authentic just as there is in the modern Scottish Gaelic prose of John Murray, Angus and Norman Campbell.

COILLTEAN RATHARSAIR

Gallain a' ghiuthais
    air lùthadh an fhirich;
gorm-chlogadan suaithneis,
muir uaine gun dinneadh;
treun, aotrom, ceann-ghaothail,
neo-shaothrach, gun shireadh,
a' choille mhór ghuanach,
ruadh, uaine, dà fhilleadh.

Urlar frainich is beithe
    air an t-seòmar àrd uaine;
am mullach 's an t-ùrlar
trom dhathte le suaimhneas;
mith-chuachan na sóbhraig,
bileag bhuidhe air uaine;
is cuilbh dhìreach an t-seòmair,
giuthas òirdhearc an luasgain.

Thug thu dhomh clogadan,
    clogadan buadhmhor,
clogadan mireanach,
buidhe is uaine;
clogadan glaganach,
clogadan uallach,
clogadan drithleannach,
clogadan ruadha.

Ghabh mi do bhrataichean
    umam 'gan suaineadh,
ghabh mi do bhrataichean
buidhe is uaine.
Sgeadaich mi aignidhean
beadarra luaineach:
sgeadaich 'nad bhrataichean
buidhe is ruadha.

THE WOODS OF RAASAY

Straight trunks of the pine
    on the flexed hill-slope;
    green, heraldic helmets,
    green unpressed sea;
    strong, light, wind-headed,
    untoiling, unseeking,
    the giddy, great wood,
    russet, green, two plaitings.

Floor of bracken and birch
    in the high green room:
    the roof and the floor
    heavily coloured, serene;
    tiny cups of the primrose,
    yellow petal on green;
    and the straight pillars of the room;
    the noble restless pines.

You gave me helmets,
    victorious helmets,
    ecstatic helmets,
    yellow and green;
    bell-like helmets,
    proud helmets,
    sparkling helmets,
    brown-red helmets.

I took you banners
    and wrapped them round me,
    I took your yellow
    and green banners.
    I clothed pampered
    volatile thoughts:
    I clothed them in your
    yellow and red banners.

Ghabh mi an t-slighe
  troimh fhilleadh an luasgain:
  thug mi an cùrsa
  thar ùr-fhonn a' bhruadair,
  a' siubhal 's a' tilleadh
  's a' sireadh na buaidhe,
  am mire 's an deann-ruith
  is m' annsachd gu h-uallach.

A' choille mhór shiùbhlach
  's i ùrail am meanmna;
  a' choille àrd uaine
  ann an luadh ioma-dhealbhach;
   a' choille 's mo bhuadhan
  ann an luathghair nan gealachas;
  a' choille bàrr-gùcach
  le ùrachadh falbhach.

Coille na gréine
  's i éibhneach is mireagach,
  a' choille ioma-ghaothach,
  an leug fhaodail dhrithleannach;
  coille na sgàile
  's i tàmhach neo-dhribheagach;
  coille a' chrònain
  's òranach luinneagach.

A' choille 'san sgarthanaich
  dùsgadh 'sa chamhanaich:
  a' choille le langanaich
  brùchdadh gu tabhanaich:
  a' choille le dùbhlachadh
  crunluaidh chabhagaich:
  a' choille 's i mùirneach
  ri sùgradh nam marannan.

Bha thu labhar tràth nòine
  le òrain 'nad fhàrdaich
  is fionnar le driùchdan
  a' tùirling gu sàmhach;
  agus bhristeadh tu loinneil
  le doireachan smeòrach;
  's a' dùnadh gu suthain
  bu shruthanach crònan.

I took my way
　　through the restless intricacy:
　　I took the course
　　over the new land of dream,
　　going and returning
　　and seeking the triumph,
　　in delight and in swift running,
　　with my desire proud-spirited.

The great wood in motion,
　　fresh in its spirit;
　　the high green wood
　　in a many-coloured waulking;
　　the wood and my senses
　　in a white-footed rapture;
　　the wood in blossom
　　with a fleeting renewal.

The sunlit wood
　　joyful and sportive,
　　the many-winded wood,
　　the glittering-jewel found by chance;
　　the shady wood,
　　peaceful and unflurried;
　　the humming wood
　　of songs and ditties.

The divided wood
　　wakening at dawn,
　　the wood with deer-belling
　　bursting to baying;
　　the wood with doubling
　　of hurrying crunluadh,
　　the wood delighted
　　with the love-making of the sea.

You were eloquent at evening
　　with songs in your house,
　　and cool with dews
　　silently falling;
　　and you would break out in splendour
　　with dells of thrushes,
　　and be silent always
　　with a humming of streamlets.

Ri d' thosd anns an oidhche
    bhiodh loinn-chruthan òmair
    thar ciaradh nan coilltean
    's fann shoillse na glòmainn,
    ag èaladh gu cuireideach,
    ioma-chruthach seòlta,
    a' falbh 's a' sìor-thighinn
    's 'gam filleadh 'nad chrònan.

Thug thu dhomh clogadan,
    clogadan uaine;
    clogad a' bhioraidh
    is clogad an t-suaimhneis:
    clogadan ùrail
    'gam chiùrradh le buaireadh,
    clogadan àrdain
    'gam mhàbadh le luasgan.

Bhuair aodann sàmhchair choilltean,
    ceilearadh shruthan is suaineadh aibhean,
    ciùine reultan buidhe a' boillsgeadh,
    lainnir a' chuain, coille-bìonain na h-oidhche.

Nuair dhòirt a' ghealach na crùin shoilleir
    air clàr dùghorm na linne doilleir
    agus a dh' iomair mi 'nan coinneamh,
    's ann a dh' fhiach mi ri shloinneadh.

'S e Sgurr nan Gillean a' bheithir
    cholgarra gharbh le cheithir
    binneanan carrach ceann-chaol sreathach;
    ach 's ann tha e bho speur eile.

B' e 'n t-aon-chòrnach Sgurr nan Gillean,
    foistinneach, sgiamhach le ghile,
    le ghile shneachda 'na dhrithleann,
    ciùin agus stòlda 'na shitheadh,

'na shitheadh sleagha air an fhàire
    sgurra foinnidh geal na h-àilleachd,
    sgurra m' iargain 's mo shàth-ghaoil,
    sgurra 's biothbhuan suain thar Clàraich.

In your silence at night
    there would be lovely amber shapes
    over the dimming of the woods
    and the faint light of the gloaming,
    creeping wilily,
    many-formed, subtle,
    going and always coming
    and winding themselves into your croon.

You gave me helmets,
    green helmets,
    the helmet of the poignant
    and the helmet of the serene:
    new helmets
    hurting me with temptation,
    helmets of pride
    maiming me with unrest.

A face troubled the peace of the woodlands,
    the bird-song of rivulets and the winding of burns,
    the mildness of yellow stars shining,
    the glitter of the sea, the phosphorescence of night.

When the moon poured the bright crown pieces
    on the dark blue board of the sea at night
    and I rowed to meet them,
    I then tried to work out its genesis.

Sgurr nan Gillean is the fire-dragon,
    warlike, terrible with its four
    rugged headlong pinnacles in a row;
    but it is of another sky.

Sgurr nan Gillean is the reposeful
    beautiful unicorn in its whiteness,
    in its snow whiteness sparkling,
    calm and steadfast in its thrust,

its spearthrust on the horizon,
    the shapely white peak of beauty,
    peak of my longing and full love,
    the peak that sleeps forever over the Clarach.

Coille uaine taobh bhos na Clàraich,
    coille Ratharsair le ceòl-gàire,
    coille Ratharsair gu ciùin sàmhach,
    coille aoibhneach bhrònach ghràdhach.

Cladh air dà shlios dheas an fhirich,
    dà chladh saoibhir leth mo chinnidh,
    dà chladh sàmhach air bruaich na linne,
    dà chladh fir Ratharsair air tilleadh.

Air tilleadh gu tàmh an fhuinn
    bho latha gréine an speur chruinn,
    cladh fo sgàil bho àile tuinn,
    dà chladh leasraidh an fhuinn.

Coille Ratharsair,
    m' ionam, labharag:
    mo chiall cagarain,
    mo leanabh cadalach.

Anns a' choille thàinig straonadh,
    an coille na h-oidhche braonaich,
    an coille nan duilleagan maotha,
    coille luaineach, coille chaochan.

Dhùisg an nathair 'na lùisreadh,
    'na duilleach ioma-luath caol ùrar,
    'na geugan duilleagach gu ciùrradh,
    gath a' chràdhghal anns an t-sùgradh.

Thàinig an sitheadh bho 'n Chuilithionn,
    bho na beanntan bu duilghe
    dìreadh gu mullach suilbhir:
    lotadh a' mhaothanachd le uilebheist.

Chunnaic mi an triùir gu siùbhlach,
    an triùir bhan-dia chuimir rùiste:
    b' aithne dhomh Actaeon brùite
    le triùir fheargach 'ga sgiùrsadh.

Chunnaic mi an triùir 'sa choille,
    an triùir gheal rùiste loinneil,
    an triùir 'nan aiteal mu m' choinneamh,
    an triùir dho-labhairt an coinneamh.

Green wood on the hither side of the Clarach
    the wood of Raasay with the music of laughter,
    the woods of Raasay, mild and peaceful,
    the joyful, sorrowful, loved wood.

Graveyard on each south slope of the hill-side,
    the two rich graveyard of half my people,
    two still graveyards by the sea sound,
    the two graveyards of the men of Raasay returned,

returned to the repose of the earth
    from the sun's day of the round sky;
    a graveyard shaded from the breath of the sea,
    the two graveyards of the loins of the land.

The wood of Raasay,
    my dear prattler,
    my whispering reason,
    my sleeping child.

There came a startling in the wood,
    in the wood of dewy night,
    in the wood of the tender leaves,
    the restless wood of the rivulets.

The adder awoke in its rich growth,
    in its multi-swift fine foliage,
    among its leafy branches to wound,
    the venom of the cry of pain in the love-making.

The thrust came from the Cuillin,
    from the mountains hardest
    to climb to a pleasant summit:
    the tender softness was stung by a monster.

I saw three in their swift course,
    the three shapely naked goddesses,
    I recognised the bruised Actaeon
    harried by the three angry ones.

I saw the three in the woods
    the three white naked graceful ones
    the three a glimmer before me,
    the three unspeakable in meeting.

Té a liubhair na pògan
    nach do shàsaich an tòrachd
    dhùbailte bha anns an fhògradh,
    am fear ruagte dian 'san tòrachd.

Bu choille Ratharsair an té
    a liubhair pòg mheala réidh,
    a' phòg nach fóghnadh do 'n chré,
    a' phòg chuir luasgan 'sa chléibh.

Chan eil de dheann-ruith 'nan dàn
    a dheanadh dheth an doineann àrd,
    chan eil ann de bheatha làin
    a chuireadh a' choille 'na tàmh.

Coille Ratharsair 'na ciùine
    ri taobh na Clàraich gu mùirneach,
    siubhal uaine an ùrlair
    th' aig a' Chuilithionn ris na sùghan.

Coille Ratharsair an labharag,
    coille bhrìodail, coille chagarain,
    coille aotrom ri taobh nam marannan,
    coille uaine an suain neo-chadalach.

'S e bhith creidsinn le feòil
    le eanchainn 's le cridhe
    gu robh aon nì coimhlionta
    àlainn so-ruighinn:
    nì a sheachnadh allaban
    na colainne 's a' chruaidh-chàis,
    nach millteadh le meapaineadh
    tìme is buairidh.

Dé fàth bhith toirt do nighinn
    gaol mar ghormadh speur
    ag éirigh as a' chamhanaich
    gu lomnochd ri gréin?
    Ged bheirteadh gaol cho coimhlionta
    ri gaisge 'n aghaidh chàs,
    gun athadh, gun teagamh, gun dòchas,
    goirt, crò-dhearg, slàn;
    ged bheirteadh an gaol do-labhairt
    cha bhiodh ann ach mar gun cainte
    nach b' urrainn an càs tachairt
    a chionn gun robh e do-labhairt.

One who gave the kisses
    that did not satisfy the pursuit
    that was double in the flight,
    the pursued man vehement in pursuit.

The wood of Raasay was the one
    that gave the smooth honeyed kiss,
    the kiss that would not suffice the clay,
    the kiss that put unrest in the body.

There is not the speed in their poem
    that would make the high tempest of it;
    ther is not in it the full life
    that would make the wood rest.

The wood of Raasay in its gentleness,
    joyful beside the Clarach,
    the green variation on the pibroch theme
    that the Cuillin makes with the waves.

The wood of Raasay is the talking one,
    the prattling whispering wood,
    the wood light beside the seas,
    the green wood in a sleepless slumber.

To believe with flesh,
    with brain and heart,
    that one thing was complete,
    beautiful, accessible:
    a thing that would avoid the travail
    of the flesh and hardship,
    that would not be spoiled by the bedragglement
    of time and temptation.

What is the meaning of giving a woman
    love like the growing blue of the skies
    rising from the morning twilight
    naked in the sun?
    Though a love were given as perfect
    as heroism against circumstances,
    unhesitant, undoubting, hopeless,
    sore, blood-red, whole;
    though the unspeakable love were given,
    it would be only as if one were to say
    that the thing could not happen
    because it was unspeakable.

Dé fàth bhirt toirt do dhòchas
    gaol steud-chrodhanta crò-dhearg,
    bhith liubhairt do àird a' Chuilithinn
    gaol a ni strì thar gach duilghinn?
    dé fàth aoradh do Nàdur
    a choinn gur h-i choille pàirt dheth?

Chunnacas mùr a' Chuilithinn leagte,
    prann briste, an slochd sgreataidh;
    agus chunnacas an gaol singilt
    do-ruighinn, caillte, neo-mhillte.

'S e gu bheil iad ag éirigh
    as an doimhne thruaigh reubte
    tha cur air beanntan an éire.

Bochd mi-chinnteach am bonn
    tha stéidheachadh Cuilithionn nan sonn
    ionnas mar reubar an conn
    chur àilleachd air dàn is fonn.

Och a' choille, och a' choille,
    dé na tha 'na doimhne dhoilleir!
    Mìltean nathraichean 'na lùisreadh:
    an t-aoibhneas 's e briste brùite
    agus an cràdh bha riamh ciùrrte,
    nach toir bàrr air a' chiùrradh.

Och a' choille, och a' choille!
    Fiamh na bòidhche foinnidh,
    na sùla tha maoth soilleir,
    seud beothanta anns an doille.

Tha eòl air slighe an t-snodhaich
    a' drùdhadh suas gu ghnothach,
    am fìon sìor ùrar beothail
    gun fhios dha fhéin, gun oilean.

Chan eil eòl air an t-slighe
    th' aig fiarachd cham a' chridhe
    's chan eil eòl air a' mhilleadh
    do 'n tàrr gun fhios a cheann-uidhe.

Chan eil eòlas, chan eil eòlas
    air crìch dheireannaich gach tòrachd
    no air seòltachd nan lùban
    leis an caill i a cùrsa.

What is the meaning of giving hope
 a steed-footed blood-red love,
 of offering to the Cuillin's height
 a love that will strive over every difficulty?
 What is the meaning of worshipping Nature
 because the wood is part of it?

One has seen the Cuillin wall knocked down,
 brittle, broken, in a loathsome pit,
 and one has seen the single-minded love
 unattainable, lost, unspoiled.

It is that they rise
 from the miserable torn depths
 that puts their burden on mountains.

Poor, uncertain the base
 on which the heroic Cuillin is based
 just as the reason is torn
 to put beauty on poem or melody.

O the wood, O the wood,
 How much there is in her dark depths!
 Thousands of adders in her rich growth:
 joy broken and bruised,
 and the pain that was ever in anguish,
 that cannot get over its anguish.

O the wood, O the wood!
 the aspect of pleasant beauty,
 of the eye that is soft and bright,
 the lively jewel in blindness.

The way of the sap is known,
 oozing up to its work,
 the wine that is always new and living,
 unconscious, untaught.

There is no knowledge of the course
 of the crooked veering of the heart,
 and there is no knowledge of the damage
 to which its aim unwittingly comes.

There is no knowledge, no knowledge,
 of the final end of each pursuit,
 nor of the subtlety of the bends
 with which it loses its course.

CELTIC VISION IN CONTEMPORARY THOUGHT AND ART

DALI, TRAJAN AND
THE CELTIC CONSCIOUSNESS

Le Message de Salvador Dali

adressé au Celtic Arts - Celtic Consciousness

Profesor Robert O'Driscoll
University of Toronto
81 St. Mary Street Toronto

JE SUIS TRÈS HONORÉ DE VOTRE INVITATION. MAIS L'ÉTUDE PASSIONNÉE
ET URGENTE SUR L'EMPEREUR TRAJAN NE ME LAISSE PAS UNE SEULE JOURNÉE LIBRE.

LA MYSTIQUE CELTE APPARAIT BEAUCOUP PLUS MULTITUDINAIRE QUE CE QU'ON A CRU
JUSQU'A PRÉSENT ET CONSTITUE ENCORE UNE GLOIRE DE LA GARE DE PERPIGNAN.

Salvador Dali

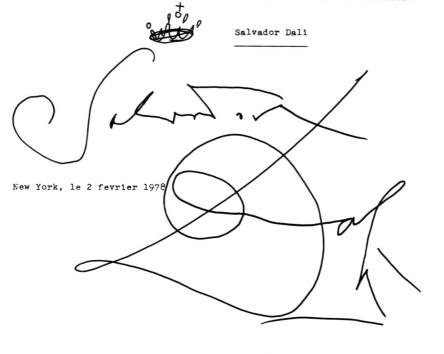

New York, le 2 fevrier 1978

CELTIC VISION IN CONTEMPORARY ART

RICHARD DEMARCO

In this paper I should like, first of all, to write about modern artists who live in Celtic countries, or who use Celtic motifs or who embody in their work qualities once possessed by the Celtic and pre-Celtic peoples. I shall also write about an annual journey, Edinburgh Arts, which I have created as a consequence of my work with modern artists and out of the reawakening interest in Europe's most ancient cultures, particularly that of the Celts. But first I should like to make some general observations about art, aesthetics and the trends of modern civilization.

Some starting premises

I believe with others that art, as we know it, is simply one kind of manifestation of human experience, no more useful than science, and equally as dangerous when left to itself as a means of investigating reality. There was a time when neither art nor science would have been used exclusively to define or express reality. What has bifurcated into art and science to modern perception was in the ancient world two inseparable parts of a single energy, now incomprehensible to us. We experience the true force of art only when art is perfectly conjoined with technical skill and knowledge, producing a force before which we are dumb, at Stonehenge, for example, or at the 4½ mile-long parallel alignments at Carnac, even though both examples convey but a faint impression of their original grandeur. In that ancient world, or later in the stone beehive-shaped cells built by the Celtic monks on Skellig Michael, the Trulli houses and farms of Puglia with their conical roofs, or the spiral-formed Sardinian Nuraghe towers, shapes were produced which were not merely pleasing architectural shapes for habitation; they were often markers or ritual points of energy where human beings felt themselves in harmony with the Earth Spirit. It was this Spirit, that recognises no separation between art and technology or male and female ways of knowing, which once animated the powerful cultural life and energy all over Europe from the Eastern Mediterranean to the West coast promontories and islands of Scotland and Ireland. It was first expressed by the megalithic builders, the mysterious wandering people who established in Western Europe the holy places later revered by the Celts. Like their predecessors, the Celts did not acknowledge the separation of matter and spirit; and because they have survived into the twentieth century they are one of the last European cultures to know how to live with a spiritual dimension in their lives; to them the ever-changing physical realities of sky, land and sea were nothing less than the expression of the divine energy of the Earth Spirit.

At various points in this paper I have used the term 'Celtic' (which is after all an invented term) to incorporate a much wider frame of reference than is contained within the present boundaries of the Celtic world. I see the Celt as the representative of all the peripheral and rejected cultures created out of the European experience and as being the European equivalent of the Hopi, the Apache, and the

Plate 1: Sunhoney, Aberdeenshire. Photo: Chris Jennings.

Aztec. More is known about the Celtic civilization than about the others, and because of this I intend to evoke through the term 'Celtic' the experience of all these other alternative cultures. To our sophisticated modern world, the Celts represent the nebulous in-between states of human experience; twilight as the mid-way point between dark and day, material and spiritual; mist as the poetic creation of water and air; the shore line as the demarcation between solid and liquid matter; dreaming as the state between sleep and waking. Perhaps more than any other European people, the Celts have felt the need to journey. In their literature the journey is the all-important metaphor for the travels of the soul through life on this earth. Celtic art represents 'psyche' the intuitive female principle, as opposed to what Renaissance art has come to represent in the twentieth century, 'techne', the mere mechanical application of outworn rules of proportion, a harsh linear male principle. In a world preoccupied with 'techne' we need the forces of 'psyche' to restore the balance which the twentieth century requires.

At various points in the history of Western man the balance achieved by the Celts and the megalithic builders has been repeated: in the great medieval

Plate 2: Sundial on Northleach Church. Photo: Chris Jennings.

cathedrals, and later during the Renaissance. Chartres and Canterbury, for example, embody a spiritual energy that cannot be defined in terms of art or technology. They are not merely power stations of prayer and religious rituals: they represent a reality defying any purely technological or artistic consideration, something which comes out of art being so intertwined with science that a force is created which is greater than either. The medieval stained glass windows, to take one example, cannot be limited by aesthetic considerations: they serve practical and political functions as well. That they are beautifully made can be taken for granted: their function is to communicate sublime truth, to reveal the light of eternity, and, at the same time, fragile as they are, to stand as a bulwark in defence of a moral order in medieval society. As we view them, and they appeal as much to the contemporary mind as to the medieval, we realize that they were created from a different energy and a different point of view from those who see art only in the form of easel painting or small-scale sculpture.

The same unity of life and art, what David Jones would call the 'utile', was achieved in the Renaissance, in for example the city of Florence. Even now in this jet age of Concorde, which offers the ultimate in the 'non-journey' as something to be experienced for as short a time as possible, the streets of Florence offer us that journey beyond price when each step we take leads us into a man-made environment impregnated by art of a sublime nature. Florence represents for me the ideal national gallery of art, and at the same time a large house for a family representing countless generations. The rituals of everyday courtesy, eating, and good conversation can be incidentally observed and taken for granted within the framework of doorways and windows, stairways and courtyards, fountains and arcades, as well as in every kind of public building including churches, hospitals and even military defense systems within the very walls of the city. Inside and outside spaces flow easily in and out of each other and everywhere the pleasure of supremely beautiful painting and sculpture can be enjoyed.

We, in the modern world, have all but ignored the spirit that unites art and life, or art and science. Not only is this apparent in modern technology, academic learning, and science, but also in the forms of music, theatre, literature and the visual arts that we have created in the wake of a fading Renaissance vitality. Art, like technology, is beginning to look more and more like an excrescence on nature, a malign growth, perhaps even an outright insult to the sacredness of the Earth Spirit. All art should exist as a manifestation of that Spirit, yet we create pollution everywhere in the form of ill-conceived, badly-built houses, in the ill-advised journeys we call tourism and in the egocentric activities we call art. Our world is contaminated with too much art, and modern art cannot remain in one place long enough so as to become acceptable to future generations. There are too many art galleries, too many self-styled artists concerned only with aesthetics and with buying and selling easily transportable artifacts.

Our Western world is becoming full of useless man-made things. In our lives, we have turned away from direct contact with nature, denying the sacred essence embodied in all matter. We have misused our industrial methods of mass production. Everything is less and less well-made, less and less capable of being loved. We seem to be systematically cutting our links with our past and immersing ourselves totally in twentieth-century space. We do not build our dwellings with the desire to create something beyond our lifetimes. We litter our streets with paraphernalia and fill our cities with ugly and functional walls, windows, doorways, corners, corridors and rooftops, all ignoring the cycles of the year, the setting or the rising sun. Digital clocks, neon lights, and metric systems blunt our inbuilt sense of space and time. We can no longer sense the length and breadth of things with our feet and hands. We design furniture to be replaceable and disposable, substituting mass-production for unique, hand-made objects which, possessing characteristics in harmony with a family, can continue to be loved for generations. To the medieval family every object in the living space was precious, not because of its monetary value, or its basic usefulness, but because of its associations with the family habits and traditions. Each chair or table was,

Plate 3: Mason's Mark, Minster Lovell. Photo: Chris Jennings.

therefore, unique with a personal character of its own, acting as a companion to the family on their journey through life.

We have lost our capacity to see the truth in mythology and fairy tale. In this world the Earth is full of innumerable marvels; nothing is wasted; a single leaf falling from a tree, or even a step taken in the wrong direction, has in it some divine significance; human actions are seen as sacred and indestructible. We must return to this way of viewing the world, of seeing a door, for example, as a sacred threshold or a window as an aperture, making us consider the mysterious difference between "outside" and "inside," between spiritual and material.

Our world is full of foreboding. We feel insecure and threatened by bureaucracy, by nuclear power, by the Cold War. Can we know the true nature of the threat we feel? Who can reveal the full extent of the problem facing us and what are the methods of dealing with it? The artist has a role in doing this and he can do it more effectively than the politician or military leader. It is the artist who can reveal the hollowness of the promises of revolutionaries, anarchists, gurus, false prophets, mystagogues, and leaders of cults who offer easy panaceas to our mental and physical malaise. The artist can instinctively signal the danger when man takes such pride in the false glories of his artificial environment that he begins to usurp the role of the Creator. With the religious leader, the artist has the responsibility too of reminding us of the awe with which the handiwork of God is to be contemplated, so that we can perceive the spirituality manifest in the most ordinary human act or object.

The Edinburgh Arts Journey

In modern times the artist has begun to fail in this role, believing on the one hand that he is a useless creature working on the periphery of society, or, on the other hand, allowing himself to be drawn into the false security of the international art world where art is looked upon as a form of leisure activity, a cure for neurosis, or a means of attaining fame or fortune, or even of developing sophisticated forms of entertainment. Nevertheless, I have more faith in art as an instrument of survival than I have in the tools of the politician or the economist or nuclear physicist. For that reason I have initiated a quest or journey, Edinburgh Arts, in which the artist explores the reality of European culture beyond the walls of the art world, whether this reality be expressed in the form of pre-historic sites, medieval or Renaissance cities, villages, houses, work-places, artist's studios, art galleries, universities, or art colleges.

I had evolved my concept of the Journey long before I read David Jones's essay on "The Utile," but drawing on his experience in the Great War trenches, he best expresses what I mean by the artist as explorer:

> The contactual is essential. You have to have been there. Ars is adamant about one thing: she compels you to do an infantryman's job. She insists on the tactile. The artist in man is the infantryman in man, so that unless the central contention of these pages is untrue, all men are aboriginally of this infantry, though not all serve with this infantry. To pursue the analogy, this continued employment 'away from the unit' has made habitual and widespread a 'staff mentality'. Today, most of us are

staff wallahs of one sort or another. That may be why so much that is said concerning the things of Ars reminds one more of what the General's wife said to the Cabinet Minister concerning war aims than of what is factually 'war' for those in the place of contact.

Those actually engaged on what are now called 'the Arts' sometimes give the impression of being more interested in movements, aims, and ideologies than in the nature of Ars herself. . . . As with Mars, so with Ars. But no matter how removed we all may be, by habit of thought and behaviour and the incidence of our technocracy, from an understanding of these matters, we still are of this infantry. We are listed into it at birth. We were born for these trenches and are happiest in them. For they are our earthy *patria*, and it is from this traversed earth that the carried *signa* and marks of cognizance show their true function.

Art should be about risk and danger, not about the shelter of an art centre. It should be a search for the impossible and should certainly take the artist beyond the known, safe orbit which he controls, what I prefer to call the "nest". Our twentieth-century world has encouraged us to move more and more towards those "nests" that we recognize as ultra-safe and without risk, whether in political, economic, educational or artistic terms. We should remember, however, the lesson of that most powerful of Celtic legends, the story of Arthur and his knights. Camelot represents the ultimate image of the "nest" created by an idealistic world, but the Holy Grail was to be found outside the walls of Camelot, and the most noble and valiant knights went forth into the unknown to seek the Grail. The "nest" that is over-protected is most vulnerable to attack: becoming static, it crumbles from within, a victim of complacence and atrophy.

Only in terms of science and technology do we seem capable of taking risks and investing the physical energy required to launch us from the known into the unknown: from the earth to the moon, or to satisfy our demand for oil, from the land to the sea. Too many artists with Western European sensibilities seem to be "holed up" in a defensive position, viewing the world outside the international galleries as alien territory. The art world, unlike the world of science, does not appear to deal with the physical reality of the world we inhabit. Artists are too eager to make art rather than observe the natural world. Yet they feel powerless and insecure when overwhelmed by the complex gadgetry of an over-industrialized world.

For seven consecutive years the Edinburgh Arts Journey has represented an experiment and a risk. The very title "Edinburgh Arts" defines the point of balance it seeks: a point between two sources of energy, one associated with the nest, the other with the movement to and from the nest. "Edinburgh" is a key part of the title because it represents the home of the Richard Demarco Gallery, its place of birth, its point of contact with the earth, its achievement within the art world. "Arts" is the ideal that takes one beyond the walls of the Gallery: ideally it should include many kinds of human activity whether in terms of music, performance, or visual expression, indicating our need to go beyond even philosophy and theology in communing with the ineffable mysteries of the cosmos, what will lie forever beyond our ken, certainly beyond the walls of Edinburgh or indeed any city, no matter how beautiful. The nature of Edinburgh Arts can be indicated by a simple diagram with a list of complementary words to the right or left of an extended point of balance — a vertical line which represents the dynamic unifying the masculine and the feminine, or the fragile ever-moving edge of reconciliation and transformation:

EDINBURGH		ARTS
The Walls of Camelot		The Pathways of the Grail
Left Hemisphere of Human Brain		Right Hemisphere of Human Brain
Nest		Journey
Known		Unknown
Inside		Outside
Logos		Insight
Security		Risk
Past	←—Expanded Present—→	Future
Harbour		Voyage
Male		Female
Terrestrial		Cosmic
Marriage	←—Honeymoon—→	Courtship
Arrival	←—Threshold—→	Departure
Cityscape	←—City Gates—→	Landscape
Robert Burns		Hugh McDiarmid
Motor Power		Sail Power
Science		Art
Phlegm		Passion
The Poet		The Bard
Prose		Poetry
Darwin at University		Darwin on the Beagle
David Jones: Paintings at the Tate		David Jones: Paintings under his bed
Art work		Creative Act
Historic		Prehistoric
Orthodox		Unorthodox
St. Thomas Aquinas — Theologian		St. Thomas Aquinas — Alchemist
Entrance		Exit
Answer	←—Dialogue—→	Question
Matter		Spirit
Centre		Periphery
Linear		Cyclic
Roman	←—Romano-Gallic—→	Celtic
Closed	←Half-Closed Half-Open→	Open
The Parthenon		Chartres Cathedral
Festival Goer		Pilgrim
The Road to London	← Milnathort Crossroads →	The Road to Meikle Seggie

Edinburgh Arts owes its origins to my work and exhibitions of contemporary artists since the foundation of the Demarco Gallery in 1966 and particularly the 'Strategy Get Arts' Exhibition of 1970. This exhibition of 35 artists from Dusseldorf had a profound effect: Nigel Gosling, art critic of *The Observer*, wrote:

> The peculiar vibrations set up by the Dusseldorf-Demarco show in Edinburgh described last week still rumble on in my mind. In particular, they aggravate nagging doubts about the whole gallery set-up today. For two centuries museums and galleries have existed to display and dispose of finished art objects. But suddenly the creative current has changed course and a lot of work is being done (and I expect more to be done in the near future) which has no end product. The act of creation is itself the work.

Michael Shepherd, art critic of the *Sunday Telegraph*, wrote:

> It is the work of the great folk-tales such as the Brothers Grimm collected, a world where every created thing has a presence, watches and can speak and be heard — you stand wondering what to do and the old tree behind you chips in with a sound word of advice.
>
> And the effect of this art can be magical — there is much loose talk about new art rinsing one's eyes, but in the Beuys room someone had left a cake-wrapping and it shone out as the most beautiful treasure. The studio sink, the telephone, the light switches, the puddle outside and, after one had left the exhibition, all the throwaways of life, were invested with this presence and mystery, and all the cliches of Dada and Surrealism, whose battered truth one had begun to doubt, came alive again. The Edinburgh Festival, Dusseldorf, Demarco and contemporary art have gained stature by this show.

The Exhibition altered dramatically the Demarco Gallery which up to this point had been modelled on the concept of a London Bond Street Gallery. Yet important as 'Strategy Get Arts' was considered in the world of contemporary art, I regard it merely as a milestone in the creation of Edinburgh Arts which was set up in 1972 as a form of experimental summer school. From the outset I attempted to link the Celtic spirit with that of the most significant contemporary artists: the physical reality of Scotland was as important as the exhibitions in the Gallery. Gradually all of the lectures and seminars were presented 'on site' as it were, dealing directly with the character of the Scottish landscape and people. In time the journey to the site came to be as important as the activity 'on site'. Because the language of art knows nothing of national boundaries, the experience of Scotland at its deepest inevitably led us deeper than our present age and the origins of history to prehistory and the timelessness of mythology. It brought us beyond the Scottish boundaries to Ireland, Wales, and Brittany, to the Celtic world of Europe, and inevitably to the periphery which all pre-Renaissance cultures represent. By 1975, therefore, Edinburgh Arts has become a pilgrimage or Journey, and each successive Journey attempted to link the periphery of Europe to the centre and again to the periphery. The 1975 and 1976 journeys were entitled "From Hagar Qim to Callanish" and "From Hagar Qim to the Ring of Brodgar" respectively. In the mid-seventies, few scholars or artists, or indeed explorers, would have heard of Hagar Qim. It is probably the oldest prehistoric temple in the Mediterranean, older than Stonehenge, and it stands on the obscure edge of Europe, on Malta's west coast, the point where Europe ends and Africa begins. Both Callanish and the

Ring of Brodgar are northern European equivalents of Hagar Qim. They stretch
our imagination beyond history, yet they represent the highest possible achievements of engineering, and at the same time resemble sculpture in its most advanced
twentieth-century form, those large-scale sculptures which contemporary artists
call "land art." Callanish is on the extreme edge of the west coast of Lewis, facing
the immensity of the Atlantic. The Ring of Brodgar is part of the Orkney Islands

Plate 4: "Snowfall" Performance devised by Howard Hull, 25 February 1979.

where it is difficult to imagine anything further north except the Arctic polar
regions. They mark "the Finistère," the edge of Northern Europe. This was a
Journey far from the restricting space of the contemporary art world. Prehistory
and history were seen to be complementary and representative of that same
timeless spiritual energy which is perceived and acknowledged when we make
rituals.

The 1979 version of the Edinburgh Arts Journey was subtitled "From the
Hebrides to the Cyclades", which deliberately linked Athens, the centre of
Mediterranean culture, with Edinburgh, its northern counterpart, or the centre
with the periphery, the classical with the Romantic. The core of the 1979 Journey
was constituted of a new element, a voyage to the islands and coast-lines of the
Celtic world — Scotland, Wales, Ireland, Cornwall and Brittany — in order to
trace the developments and movements of ancient cultures, and how these are
relevant to artists who are learning to work with the instincts and attitudes of
explorers. The voyage was made by means of one of the most beautiful and poetic
forms of transportation ever devised, completely in harmony with the elemental
forces of fire, air, and water — a square-rigged, ocean-going sailing ship built of
Spanish pine in Spain in 1915. Originally rigged as a brigantine, the sailing vessel,

"Marques", traded around the Mediterranean and East Atlantic with cargoes of wine, nuts, olives, etc. She was purchased in Mallorca in 1972 and brought to Cornwall, where she was given a thorough refit, and was re-rigged as a brigantine. The "Marques" became the best-known sailing ship in the British Isles when she was rigged as a barque and became "H.M.S. Beagle" in the B.B.C.'s extraordinarily successful television series on the voyage of Charles Darwin. For this reason the 1979 Edinburgh Arts Journey became linked with Darwin's voyage, but unlike Darwin's voyage our emphasis was on the search for the poetic and spiritual origins of mankind's presence on this earth, rather than the search for a scientific or rational explanation.

The ship was, of course, the perfect symbol of the artist as explorer. It had three masts, reminding us of the beautiful painting of David Jones in the Tate depicting Tristan and Iseult sailing through "the Narrow Seas" — the English Channel. We followed in the wake of their ship, and their forbidden love symbolized for us the search for the ideal beyond the confines of the world. And yet we learned to look upon the ship at times not as a symbol or metaphor, but as a place of learning

Plate 5: Detail from "Snowfall" performance devised by Howard Hull, 25 February 1979.

and, in an age when make-believe and fantasy are preferred to reality, as an instrument by which a direct relationship can be brought about between the objective world and the human experience of it. From unfurling the sails and caulking the decks, to seminars on artists and writers (such as Yeats, Pound, and David Jones), to the exploration of Celtic and prehistoric sites, all of the participants were called upon to reawaken their powers of imagination through direct physical contact with reality. The voyage became a journey into the miracle of reality, where we learn to see all real and apparently ordinary things as forever beyond our power to imagine them. One of the participants, Howard Hull, evokes in his prose the harmony between man and nature that we achieved:

> Man too, and his body, is built to the size of grain seeds, the height of branches, the roughness of stones, the density of water. Nature without man is not barren because it builds and contains him, it ordains him. Man without nature is barren because he loses the world for which he is shaped; the length of his stride, the strength of his toes, the shape of his face, his thickness of hair, all become meaningless. And his need for wonder goes; his sense of adventure, his intuitions and tolerances of variety go.

> With nature? Well, we sailed with the wind; phosphorescent plankton blessed our hull, the black-tipped gannets' wings, the black sharks' fins, they brought us only blessings.

> Darwin would have said: learn from all nature your own nature, evolve and be evolved. To see Darwin's own ideas take form shaped by the world he perceived and fitted to it, is to see the way in which man, in humility before creation, may in learning and expression, join as an individual in the process of nature and evolution, not bettering nature (which cannot be done) nor destroying her (which is only ever a ruination) but becoming a true part of her, entering the crystal mystery which is to become part of, and be, God.

> It starts with the pull of the rope in our hands, and it goes with the rope pulling in our hands, and it is always and ever the reality of the sap-stain in the grass blade, the flintcut foot, and the tarred rope pulling. The goddess lives and walks in one's wife. If not there, where else could she be?

> The clearest crystal we may not see.

> Such things are part of an evolution. We hope that one day our work may achieve such naturalness of form, and that it may test and work for man.

Edinburgh Arts 1979 was a sandwich of land, the known and the safe; sea, the unknown and dangerous; and then land again, with again a touch of sea in the form of public ferries from Corsica to Italy, and Italy to Greece. On land, the journey investigated the visual means of expression which mankind has used to define places of high spiritual energy. Although these have many forms, they are essentially markers: sacred wells, temples, oratories, standing stone circles, and places of burial and rebirth. These markers can also be, in our own time, various forms of art works, or the places where art is studied, made, or exhibited; or even all things particularly well made which respect the forces of nature: such things as houses, roads, doorways, windows, bridges, tunnels, and all manner of thresholds and places where mankind can work with dignity and be tested by the external elements.

From the Celtic periphery we penetrated the heart of the contemporary art world in Europe, starting in London at the Tate and proceeding to other art centres in France, Italy and Greece. As well as the acknowledged art centres, we visited a number of places, usually churches where the art object is impregnated in the very fabric of the structure, among which were the frescoes of Masolino da Panicole at Castiglioni Olona; Leonardo's 'Last Supper' at Santa Maria delle Grazie in Milan, the tenth-century mosaic floor of the Cathedral of Otranto, the frescoes of Piero della Francesca in Arezzo. We sought out particularly the studios of artists where the whole emphasis was on the process of creation rather than the finished art object: among the many studios we visited were those of Barbara Hepworth and Roy Walker in England, Horia Damian in France, Cioni Carpi and Fausto

Melotti in Italy, Norman and Patience Mommens in Puglia, and Desmond O'Grady in Greece.

As well as the Celtic world, the Journey probed other pre-Renaissance cultures: Corsica, Tuscany, the foothills of the Alps round the Italian lakes, and Puglia. We entered the Greek world at Corfu and went onwards to Athens and the Cycladean islands of Naxos, Paros, and Santorini, where we encountered an older and subtler form of civilization than anything found in the classical world of Greece, the Minoan civilization, the Aegean counterpart of the Celtic.

Islands and coastlines figured largely in the Journey, the 1979 Journey added fourteen more islands to those explored in previous years. The present space of Edinburgh Arts can therefore be now defined as the Hebridean Islands of Eigg and Muck; the Channel Islands of Guernsey and Sark; the Scillonian Islands of Tresco, St. Agnes and St. Mary's; the Breton Belle Île; Corsica, Corfu and the Cycladean Islands of Paros, Gulandris, Antiparos and Santorini added to such islands as Iona, Lewis, Harris, Mull, Inchtavannich, Inchcolm, the Garvallochs, the Island of Women, Arran, Innishmurray, Devenish, Orkney, Rousay, Hoy, St. Michael's Mount, Mont St. Michel, Ilôt St. Michel, Sicily, Torcello, San Francisco del Deserto, Malta, Gozo, and Sardinia.

The Journey begins around midsummer and ends at the beginning of August, the time of Lugus, the Celtic Deity who is the patron of the arts. August is, too, the month when Edinburgh prepares itself for its international Festival of the Arts; the Journey becomes a creative way of approaching the Festival. The fact that the point of departure and the ultimate destination is Edinburgh suggests that the most mysterious far-distant place for anyone living or working in Edinburgh should be Edinburgh itself. For each participant, though, the beginning and ending point is the place where that particular participant began or ended his or her journey. This is best defined for each participant as "home," the place which is nearest to the mystery of each participant's family and forbearers. For all participants the point of origin should also be seen as the ultimate point of destination.

The Journey demands each participant's complete attention and energy. It is a period of reassessment, of stocktaking, of seeing rather than making, and is conducted more in the spirit of a pilgrimage or retreat. It alters the awareness of each participant, deliberately causing a shift in gear. During it the making of art is virtually impossible, and indeed it is designed to make each participant question his motive for being involved in the world of art. Participants continue, more mindful of the attitudes of Darwin or Thoreau, than of any so-called maker of contemporary art. As well as the artists who constitute the majority of the participants, there were professors, lawyers, doctors, artisans, scientists, businessmen, bankers, farmers, sailors, etc. Each Journey is defined in terms of the cumulative energy of the journeys that preceded it: the total distance covered by all eight journeys is approximately 57,700 miles; the total length in time is 466 days; the total number of participants 952.

Artists who influenced the concept of the Journey

The Journey, as I have indicated, grew out of my work with contemporary artists and four artists in particular: Joseph Beuys, Tadeusz Kantor, Dennis Leon and Paul Neagu. None of these artists are strictly Celtic, yet all expressed in their work at that time, whether consciously or unconsciously, something that connected in my mind with the spirit that animates the Celtic and pre-Celtic world. The Celts and their predecessors had left behind a powerful visual legacy, the contemplation of which knocked modern man off balance. In line with this, these artists reacted violently against the visual illiteracy of modern times, a visual illiteracy which I attribute to the mindless repetition of the principles that dominated the classical world of Greece and Rome. Beuys and Kantor participated in the 1973 Journey, and all four artists contributed to the ritual nature of the Journey as it developed.

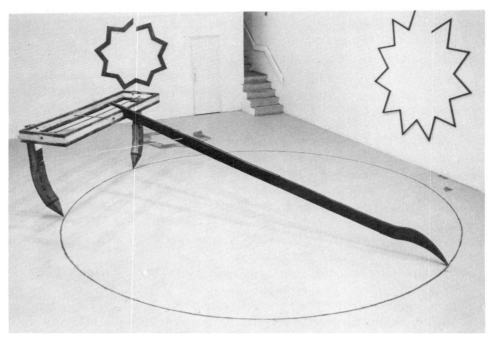

Plate 6: 'Hyphen-Ramp', 1976 and 'Open Fusions', 1979. Paul Neagu writes: "HYPHEN is a generic title for a principle of Connection between triangle, rectangle or square and circle of spiral. As a sculptural device, 'hyphen' could be employed for physically making spirals just as the Compass is used for making circles."

Plate 7: "Hyphen-Fulcrum," 1975-77, and "Open Fusion," 1979, wall. Neagu writes with relation to this and the previous photograph: "With regard to my performance work, its essential meaning is subsumed in the sculptures here photographed."

533

Plate 8: "Fusion and Ramp," by Paul Neagu, 1979. Neagu writes: "A circle-spiral is built up from joining sharp angles (less 90°) with right angles (90°) around a centre. A spiralling collective is suggested, which is related to my early 'Tornado' preoccupations, as in my performance, 'Going Tornado.'"

Paul Neagu, Hyphen-Maker

Since 1969, in an unbroken and developing dialogue, Paul Neagu has helped me to see the artist as the maker of all those objects required for any spiritual journey: the particular compasses and astrolabes which can distinguish the twentieth-century pilgrims. He makes Hyphen-like sculptures, incorporating the forms of triangles, rectangles, and circles. They symbolize the interlocking processes and machinery which link our subconscious and conscious awareness of physical reality.

These sculptural forms are in the tradition of the sculptors of the Irish High Crosses, the Breton Calvaires, and those who keep alive the ancient rituals which are part of our racial memory — the makers of the Padstow Hobby-horse, the Marshfield Mummers, the Morris Dancers, or the Staffordshire villagers of Abbots Bromley who perpetuate ritual ceremonies in their annual Horn Dance on the Monday following the fourth of September. This Horn Dance, which resembles North American Indian Dancing, forms part of the Fair which has been celebrated from a time which cannot be placed easily in history but which surely stems from the Lughnasa Festival.

Paul Neagu's GOING TORNADO "performance" bore a distant resemblance to the form of this Horn Dance. A Paul Neagu performance implies a ritual action, not a theatrical event. It is not about the spoken or written word, the documentation of something past. It is more of a ritual dance, performed not upon a theatre stage but preferably in a place of work or prayer. "Going Tornado" was an exploration of points of balance in a spiral drawn by Neagu on the stone floor of a building which had last been used as a plumber's workshop and which had originally served as the medieval poorhouse of Edinburgh. He first divested himself of all that he brought into the space of the spiral and then, in whirling movements, reminiscent of Dervish ritual dancing, he gathered everything to his person which became the still centre of the tornado, the point of energy which causes all things to change their form, to become restructured and reborn. He is motivated by a sense of events at the periphery of his consciousness and he is compelled to make symbols: out of the food, clothing and the objects he carries as part of his workday life as an artist: paper, pencils, a metronome, chalk, a camera, even his working clothes. All help him to make contact with the metaphysical world. He is a necromancer. He is the artist-craftsman, maker of art objects, tabernacles, jewel boxes, altars, and the doors to the "Sanctum Sanctorum". They are the icons of those ritual spaces which appeal to the serious traveller.

The Hill of Horia Damian and Queen Maeve's Burial Cairn

It is interesting to consider Paul Neagu's Romanian cultural heritage as complementary to that of the Celt. Romania and Ireland both represent peripheral cultures more concerned with metaphysics than scientific facts. Romanian contemporary artists born of a peasant tradition had much to offer Western Europe. In 1977 we sought out the Paris studio of Horia Damian. The expatriate Romanian artist has never been to Ireland and has never seen an Irish prehistoric burial cairn.

Yet he is totally involved in the form of what he calls "The Hill", a breast-like monumental structure made up of countless pellet-like units which could be a precise drawing of the infinite number of stones which constitute any burial cairn in the Bricklieve Mountains. Damian's "Hill" as a sculpture or drawing is an exact perception of Queen Maeve's Burial Mound set high on the sacred mountain of Knocknarea, at one with a Sligo landscape impregnated with memories of rituals honouring the mythological Queen. The work of Horia Damian, like that of Paul Neagu, can clearly be connected to the prehistoric landscape of Ireland: thus the timeless ritual space of the Celts is revealed by the contemporary Romanian spirit.

Plate 9: Detail for Joseph Beuys Performance, "Celtic Kinloch Rannoch — The Scottish Symphony," Richard Demarco Gallery, 1970.

Joseph Beuys and the Scottish Symphony

Joseph Beuys uses art as a means to clarify his ideas on the ancient cultural origins of Europe. He taught me an unforgettable lesson with his fifty-six-hour-long art work called "Celtic, Kinloch-Rannoch — The Scottish Symphony". It was an art lesson par excellence and it recalled forgotten Celtic rituals. Joseph Beuys was then regarded as "Avant Garde" but this work reassured me that he understands and extends the traditional spirit of countless generations of artists. The work was a kind of requiem, suggestive of the ritual of the Catholic Mass, celebrating the permanent living tradition of the artists that Beuys admires. The whole room reverberated with the sound of forgotten European Cultures. The past, present, and future of art activity were brought together. It involved me eight

Plate 10: Detail from Beuys's "Scottish Symphony."

hours each day for a week, ridding me of all the dead wood that I had, until then, been reluctant to cut away from the structure I had built in the name of the Demarco Gallery. A new gallery, or something that went beyond a gallery, had to be created to deal with an artist such as Beuys. Neither exclusively geared to male or female energies, it had to be capable of evoking the experience of all the arts simultaneously, without abstracting them from life, or suggesting that they were in any way "superior" to the common experiences of life. Beuys told me that the ordinary white cube space of the gallery's exhibition rooms was inadequate, that the rooms should retain some evidence of the physical labour of those who have worked there previously. He used the whole space, as if he were a monk working on a page of one of the great illuminated Irish manuscripts. He used the walls of the room, covering them with globules of gelatine: he used the corners, blocking them off and protecting them with wooden boards, thus suggesting that they were not merely physical 'angles' but spiritual presences, key points holding together the mystery of the room as a work space, including the physical reality of every human being who had ever used the room to make art.

He used a grand piano, six tape recorders, two portable tape recorders, two film projectors, a blackboard, electric cables, two long planks of wood, a metal tray, two milk bottles, a walking stick, and his own presence in collaboration with the Danish sculptor-composer, Henning Christiansen, to persuade me that the experience of art does not necessarily happen in the neat, tidy context of a framed art object hanging on the walls of a twentieth-century style art gallery.

Tadeusz Kantor and the Cricot Theatre

Tadeusz Kantor is another major artist to whom I owe much. His use of "performance art", particularly in his Cricot Theatre productions at the 1972 and 1973 Edinburgh Festivals, defined the importance of the Journey as an integral part of artistic activity. The productions involved eighteen members of the Cricot working in collaboration with Kantor, despite the fact that only half of them were professional actors; the remainder were sculptors, painters, art students, technicians and administrators. The "Action" was presented in the same building used by Paul Neagu for his "Going Tornado" performance, Edinburgh's medieval poorhouse.

Within the ancient walls, on medieval paving stones which had at one time been an Edinburgh street open to the sky, Kantor and his company enacted a drama that revealed elements inherent in all human journeys: each character was presented as a traveller laden with what Kantor calls "emballage", an excess of baggage forming a grotesque extension of the traveller's clothing and accoutrements

The productions of "The Water Hen" and "Lovelies and Dowdies" emphasised movements up and down a tunnel-like space with visual points of exit and entry at either end. The audience sat like rows of spectators at a tennis match viewing a constant procession of figures involved in events that took no account of the linear progression of time. Like life itself, the experience they presented was at one and the same time inexplicably comical and deeply distressing.

Plate 11: "Man with suitcases," by Tadeusz Kantor, 1967.

In "Lovelies and Dowdies" one end of the tunnel-like space was dominated by a cloakroom through which all members of the audience had to pass in order to receive long wooden sticks which held high numbers of their cloakroom tickets, or wooden plaques inscribed with the ticket numbers to be worn around their necks. The cloakroom was looked after by two attendants who controlled the movements of the audience, making them resemble at times docile animals herded together with long sheets of cloth round their necks. Doormen guarded the stage area at the other end of the tunnel, opening and closing the sliding screen of the stage which controlled all entrances and and exits made by the players, and which also controlled the movement of forty members of the audience who had been trained during the action of the play to become Jewish mandelbaums or religious fanatics. They represented all closed systems of thought, and were the enemy of Princess Abenceraga who personified not only the spirit of art but the sensual power of the Earth Goddess — the irrational female life-giving force which resists all repressive systems. She appears in the end to be trampled to death by the crowd of mandelbaums, but she reappears with them and all the actors in a final dance of death, reminiscent of Hieronymous Bosch. She continues to taunt and challenge the mandelbaums. Her spirit (call it art if you wish) remains triumphant, continuing its work against closed and non-regenerative systems.

Dennis Leon and the Sutro Baths

Dennis Leon, head of the Sculpture School at the Californian College of Arts and Crafts, is the embodiment of the Californian artist's respect for nature. His art reveals the inherent timelessness and spiritual nature of the landscape. He is a sophisticated master in the use of organic materials. He treats wood and metal with the instinct normally associated with primitive peoples, who make their hunting and fishing gear with their eyes on wind and weather. He knows that the art of today can be a subtle and dangerous form of pollution, as dangerous even as tourism.

In 1976, he showed me a remarkable piece of sculpture he had constructed on a stretch of rocky coast where at one time there had been the luxurious and popular Sutro Baths of San Francisco. Now hardly a trace remains of their former splendour. All that remains are stone foundations, and high on a cliff-face an eye-catching little building which had been a pump house, a shelter for the pumping machinery which controlled the flow of sea water into the baths. It would be very difficult to climb up to the pump house — there is no access — a passer-by would be tempted to climb from the water's edge to observe it as an unsigned Dennis Leon sculpture. There it stands, a concrete 12 foot cube structure, with a semi-circular roofline protecting an open doorway, filled with a pitch black darkness which both attracts and threatens the observer. It is the challenging space of all doorways which are thresholds. It is a black void separating the "outside" of the natural landscape space from the "inside" of a man-made interior. It looks dangerous, and so it is, for not far beyond that doorway is a well-like vertical tunnel shooting deep underground. On either side, there is stamped in large letters, made from special wooden blocks, a reference to the little building's former usefulness and the now exhausted energy of the Sutro Baths. The words constitute a poetic, compassionate statement and a celebration of the mystery of that place and the forgotten generations who were attracted to it. The pump house has been given the spiritual dimension it deserves. It has been released from the time in which we view it. The artist has instinctively worked his magic in the way Nature Herself works upon any ordinary landscape or object with a snowfall, or sunset, or sunrise. The words work as the snow does or the horizontal sunlight, clothing the object of our attention in a timeless space in which the creative imagination can expand. The pump house is a sculpture possessing some of the characteristics we recognise in pre-Renaissance structures. In its own modest way it can be seen as a complement to the work of the Megalith Builders or to works on the same spiritual level as the Egyptian Pyramids, Cezanne's "Mont St. Victoire" paintings, and Brancusi's "Endless Column": all mark entry points into a continuum.

My first sight of the pump house was traumatic because I knew that, unknown to Dennis Leon, it bore an uncanny resemblance to a tiny structure on another rocky coastline, 6,000 miles distant in Pembrokeshire, at St. Govan's Head, a building known as St. Govan's Well, a place of meditation, the point of entry into the continuum for a Celtic saint who may be identified as the adversary of the Green Knight and as a protagonist in the Grail Quest. It was one of the proofs I needed to clinch the argument I had been developing on the Journey: that the work of some contemporary artists is beginning to resemble that of prehistoric cultures and the artifacts of the Celtic world.

Artists Living in Scotland, Ireland, and Wales

Some modern Celtic artists consciously create visual forms of expression reminiscent of prehistoric settlements, dolmens, standing stones, stone circles, Celtic round towers, high crosses, and places of prayer and meditation. The materials and the imagery used, though, are recognizably of the seventies, part of our everyday lives, workable as common instruments as well as ritual objects. It would be incorrect to present these artists as imitators or even defenders of a Celtic tradition. It could even be argued that they only "happen" to live in Ireland, or Scotland or Wales, and that the validity of their art is not found in its Scottishness or Irishness, but in its manner of treating timeless themes.

Alan Smith is an artist who was born and brought up in Edinburgh. He is as much a scientist as he is an artist, regarding the physical world with irrepressible curiosity. He was the first person I ever heard discussing the megalithic theories of Professor Alexander Thom which infused new meaning into Scotland's prehistoric standing stones. In talking about Thom's unit of measurement and lunar observations, Alan Smith was unwittingly revealing his own sensibilities. He is more than the mere mathematical sum of everything that he is: geologist, physicist, chemist, mathematician, archeologist and poet. He is an astronaut in the art world.

In this connection, I should mention Chris Jennings's photographic record of 'The Standing Stones of the British Isles'. The photographs present the ancient stones as being at one and the same time both sculpture and engineering, totally but mysteriously linked to the spirit of the places upon which they stand. The stones are observed as relating directly to distant natural features in the landscape, and, of course, to the complex movements of the sun, moon and stars. Chris Jennings uses the camera as a sculptural tool, respecting the site, evoking the mystery of the stones and that dynamic energy which exists only in a particular landscape, recording this energy at precisely the right moment, when the particular interrela-

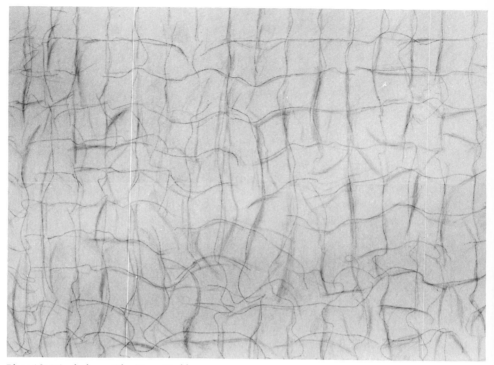

Plate 12: "Ambulance," by Fiona Geddes.

tion of cloud, sun, stone, shadow, or moonglow reflection is right, at the summer or winter solstice, or at other times which are significant to his eyes alone.

Two artists, Fionna Geddes from Edinburgh and Norma Wagner from Montreal, met on the 1978 Journey, and within a year of the meeting exhibited together in Edinburgh under the aegis of the Demarco Gallery. The work that they exhibited made the factory warehouse that was being used temporarily as an art gallery appear as if one were seeing it for the first time. Norma Wagner works with cloth, allowing it to function as a metaphor for life. The materials she uses inherently acknowledges her sense of the fragmentation of human experience in herself and in the world around her, yet through it she attempts, in her own words, to "ritualize the turning points in our experience, the crisis in our lives, the fear of the unknown, the desire for comprehension." Like Norma Wagner, Fionna Geddes works with cloth and string. The patterns in her drawings are created by string, polystyrene, or other fibres that criss-cross, intersect, and move with unexpected tensions. She so understands the weaver's craft that she makes of it a celebration of the art of drawing upon a two-dimensional surface, and by accepting its apparent limitations is able to reveal further dimensions. The way in which she is able to use the energies of her chosen materials, allowing the energies to disperse and reassemble, is close to a spiritual exercise, a form a prayer.

Another artist working in Scotland who exhibits this kind of strength and independence in the use of her chosen materials is Eileen Lawrence. She can be considered as a water-colourist, but few artists would question as deeply as she does the act of enlivening the surface of a sheet of paper with water colour. She questions the very idea of attempting to create an "end product," but identifies completely with the work process, and honours the rituals implicit within that process. Her description of her work methods is worthy of attention:

> I am exploring the way in which my medium, watercolour, fuses with the support paper. I work with a great many different paper surfaces including paper I make myself. Into these handmade papers I incorporate small fragments of my subject matter, real feathers, eggs and reeds; these are laid alongside painted images of the same subject matter. I am now also incorporating the painted image directly into the handmade papers. This somewhat illusionistic device involves a partial destruction of the painted image, in some sense a symbolic act, detailed watercolours of feathers, eggs and reeds are painted then torn up; they are introduced into the basic paper pulp and reprocessed into a sheet of handmade paper; this paper also has in it the real fragments of my subject matter.
>
> By tearing up the painted image I do not consider that I am indulging in a negative act, or an emotional activity, but am making a very serious and positive attempt to expand the traditional limitations of my medium, watercolour on paper. I respect the skill which I have acquired over the years but I have no desire to rely totally upon a certain kind of technical facility. Once one is aware of one's limitations one can do something about pushing the boundaries of those limitations.

Louis le Brocquy has long been regarded as an outstanding Irish artist. Up till about sixteen years ago he was painting the torso as an image of the human presence, and then from 1964 onwards he turned to "the head," producing a remarkable series of Heads of Yeats, Joyce, and Lorca. In Louis le Brocquy's work we have a beautiful sense of the Celtic continuum, for the head to the Celts had, as Helen Hickey says, "the same importance and emblematic significance . . . as the cross was to have in Christianity."[1] The Celts believed that the head contained the soul and they saw it as a symbol of divinity and supernatural power. Louis le Broquy traces his own preoccupation with the head to the Celts, "with their oracular cult of the human head, the mysterious box which holds the spirit prisoner."[2] Or, as Mr. le Broquy suggested in a lecture in Toronto in December 1978, the head to the Celts was "the outer reality of the invisible interior world of consciousness." He himself sees the face as "ambiguous, being at once a mask hiding the human spirit and at the same time an incarnation of that spirit." As well as this, he believes that his paintings emerge from a deeper consciousness than his own: "one disturbs the surface of the canvas or the paper with marks or stains. Some of these marks or stains may suddenly combine by accident to form something which is recognised as being significant as *objet trouvé*. Further marks, further accidents, are then induced to expand around it until eventually a whole image may emerge almost autonomously, in Marshall McLuhan's evocative words, an 'interior landscape.' " Le Broquy likens the process of painting over 200 heads of Yeats, Joyce, and Lorca to a type of archaeology, an archaeology of the spirit.

Plate 13: "Image of Auguste Strindberg," by Louis le Brocquy. Oil on Canvas, 1979.

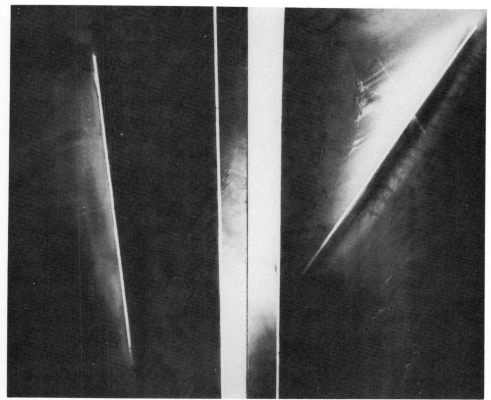

Plate 14: "Alignment," by Anne Madden. Acrylic on Cotton, 1977.

In Louis le Broquy's work, then, we have a contemporary artist using an innate Celtic sensibility to illuminate the artistic consciousness of our time. When I exhibited his heads of Yeats in the 1977 Edinburgh Festival I did so alongside a series of heads carved in Northern Ireland between the third century B.C. and our own time, demonstrating the truth of Henry Moore's statement that art is "a universal continuous activity with no separation between past and present."

Anne Madden finds her inspiration in the megaliths of Ireland and in the landscape of her native land, Connemara stone, and the great storm-tossed Atlantic cloud formations. Yet her paintings are not developments of an abstract concept, but the paints she uses dictate what emerges on the canvas: "what breaks through, emerging from behind the surface of her canvas, is neither dolmen nor menhir, but paint — paint which asks to be recognised as such."[3] She infuses the ancient megalithic forms with a modern consciousness and explosive sensuality, painting as much out of the depths of her own being as out of the depths of the mythological past, creating a "heart of reality" that "craves for light," with the light in turn craving "for further light," light "which isolates every solid mass simply by virtue of its inner living growth . . . Light which is the very limit of our

Plate 15: "Saltmarsh," by Glen Onwin.

Plate 16: "Saltmarsh pond," by Glen Onwin.

being, this limit — whether delible or not — lying with us."[4] I am reminded of André Breton's statement: deeper than the deepest ocean is the heart of a woman.

Brian King is an Irish artist concerned with the mystery of the human presence in the Irish landscape. As a sculptor, he literally plots the ancient pathways of his ancestors, the builders of the dolmens and burial cairns, in an attempt to discover his own identity as a modern Irishman. He works out of doors, often by the water's edge or hill-tops, seeking out the points of balance of ancient sites, knowing that these sites help counter the forces that would confine him to the restrictive spaces of the contemporary art world.

Scotland has also produced artists with the same atavistic instincts. Glen Onwin, with his extraordinary sculpture installation "Saltmarsh", acknowledges the transformation that nature has wrought on an East Lothian shoreline, producing a gigantic piece of what the contemporary critic would call "Land art". His role is to perceive the transformation, and to find an artistic as opposed to a scientific way of presenting a natural phenomenon. Onwin is an artist working with the instincts of the fisherman or hunter who is prepared to lie in wait with great patience for Nature to reveal her secrets.

The art of another Scottish artist, Will McLean, a Hebridean Celt, demonstrates ways in which the contemporary spirit can be wedded to Nature and local landscape. From his youth he was an unlikely combination of fisherman, painter and sculptor. He has received deserved recognition in recent years for his exquisite drawings, paintings and sculpture, often in the form of 3-dimensional collages,

Plate 17: "The Elders," by Will MacLean. Wood, Metal, and Bone, 1978.

sometimes involving *objets trouvés* on a Scottish beach, remnants of the gear and tackle of fishing boats. With the alchemical skill of the artist, Will McLean transforms all ordinary objects, and by juxtaposing them with fish forms and symbols, he reveals the innate respect the Scottish fisherman has for the mystery and magic of the Scottish coasts, particularly the Island of Skye, where his forbearers have for generations fished the waters of the Minch with the instincts of the sailors who manned the galleys of the Lords of the Isles.

Sometimes the modern artist living in Scotland is remarkable not merely for the art work he produces, but by the life style and physical surroundings in which he prefers to live. Such is Gerald Laing. He started his adult life as a professional soldier in the British Army, then went to Art School, after which he experienced a considerable degree of success in the New York art world of the sixties. But he gave up his blossoming career to settle with his newly-wedded wife, Galina, in Scotland, both of them setting themselves the heroic task of rebuilding a medieval castle on the Black Isle, just north of Inverness. Their irrational decision to rebuild a complete ruin was out of keeping with this age but in keeping with the ways of the Goddess. They understood the spirit of the place, the way the building must grow again organically and be once more a part of the unchanging landscape. And so every detail of Kinkell Castle was lovingly restored, as a piece of visual poetry, or a large-scale sculptural form, modern and yet based on age-old methods of construction, and at the same time meaningful as a contemporary work of art. They had the courage to remove that part of the building which had been added in the 18th century. Needless to say, Galina Laing serves to inspire Gerald Laing with her beauty and wisdom, and most of his recent figurative bronze sculpture has been the result of the inspiration that comes when a man is fortunate enough to see a woman as the personification of the Earth Spirit.

Finally I should like to mention two other artists who possess a strong Celtic sensibility: John Latham and David Nash. For at least two decades, John Latham has transcended normal concepts of sculpture, linking it to technical methods of investigation and documentation. In one large-scale work which he called "Niddrie Woman" he endeavoured to reveal the Earth Spirit in the shape of a disused shale-oil bing in the Lothians. Aerial photography showed how the earth underneath had been poluted by industrial waste. The "Niddrie Woman" showed how the Goddess can be regenerated and made triumphant, despite the insensitivity of our technological age.

David Nash works with the decorations which nature has always used to clothe herself in the Welsh mountains; the trees and tree forms which grow in abundance around his Blaenau Ffestiniog studio. He has worked with foresters in the heart of Grizedale in Cumbria in order to reveal the natural sculptural forms inherent in trees and woodland and in the organic nature of the wood itself. He is one of the few artists I know who can give over to nature the power to complete what he has begun in his lifetime, knowing that the work must stretch over many lifetimes in order to come to maturity.

Plate 18: "Cube Cubed," by David Nash. Elm, 1979.

Space has confined my comments to the work of twelve artists, but of course there are many more artists concerned with Celtic and pre-Celtic cultures, or who live and work on the Celtic periphery. Some of them may not believe, with Yeats and Spengler, that the circumference of one civilization becomes the centre of the next, but many have turned away from the neat world of the contemporary art gallery in an attempt to perceive and express a mystery that eluded the classical world of Greece and Rome. What they seek in their work is what we seek in the Journey: something that goes deeper than the individual consciousness; unity of being, the reconciliation of spirit and matter, art and life, and art and technology; human energy working in harmony with the Earth Spirit and the cyclical power of Nature; and the release of consciousness and art from the thin layer of our twentieth-century time space.

NOTES

[1]*Images of Stone* (Belfast 1976), p. 14.

[2]*Studies towards an image of James Joyce* (Genoa 1977), p. 5.

[3]Dominique Fourcade, *Anne Madden* (Paris 1979), p. 5.

[4]*Ibid.*, pp. 7-8.

A CONTEMPORARY QUEST INTO THE CELTIC AND PRE-CELTIC WORLD

Edited by

ROBERT O'DRISCOLL

I

In the foregoing essay, Richard Demarco explores the intuitions and instincts that led him to initiate "Edinburgh Arts," a quest through Europe, or the long way round to the Edinburgh Festival. Using the most ancient form of transportation known to man, a sailing vessel, Demarco fills the *Marques* with artists rather than scientists, and by sailing down the throat of the past he intentionally inverts Darwin's theory of evolution, attempting to bring the modern artist once again into contact with the imagination and mystery at the periphery of our modern world.

When I think back on the two Journeys in which I was participant (1977 and 1979), C. Day Lewis's words float back into my mind: "Poetry was born from magic: it grew up with religion: it lived through an age of reason: is it to die in the century of propaganda?" Demarco's Journey is an audacious, imaginative gesture designed to release human beings from the prison of self and habit, and, relatedly, as he says, to liberate art and consciousness from the thin layer of our twentieth-century time space, to see life and artistic creation once again in the context of the continuum, the multi-layered palimpsest of the past.

The end of imagination is, perhaps, to enable us to see reality as if for the first time, and also to lay bare to ourselves our human frailty and vulnerability. Using the ship as the symbol of exploration, Demarco offers the artist the opportunity of investigating the real world in the spirit of Darwin or Thoreau, and of encountering, in the company of professional sailors (before whom, as in the Greek drama, "appearances" had to be kept up), the full dangers of the physical world, of storms and dangerous currents, where the artist is tested physically as well as spiritually and mentally, sometimes to the breaking point.

On the Journey life was stripped of all pretension and pose and we learned to respond to the beauty and mystery of the real world, and to the ancient sites of the Celtic and pre-Celtic world where the balance between male and female energies is beautifully apparent. What has bifurcated into art and science to modern perception, Demarco suggests, was, in the ancient world, two inseparable parts of a single energy, now incomprehensible to us; and so the Journey was a quest for integrity, wholeness of being, an attempt to understand a female energy which has not often been acknowledged for the last two thousand years, and finally, a realization of the necessity of bringing intuition and reason back into balance again.

During the Journey, too, the floorboards of habit and conscious memory seemed, as Proust or Beckett would say, less firmly placed over the well of the subconscious than during our routine lives; we were constantly placed in touch with our own dark or buried selves, opening ourselves to perceptions and civilizations that offer alternative approaches to experience than those which now dominate the Western world. Most of all, though, we began to observe art in the context in which it was created and we learned to understand that the art object has no value until it enters the soul of the human being, until perceiver and perceived become one, rooted in a particular time and space, yet participating in a timeless spiritual continuum which can be perceived by the imagination.

During the Journey of 1979, the myth of Tristan and Iseult was a recurring motif, insinuating itself again and again into the collective consciousness of the group. This, on reflection, is not strange. The story of Tristan and Iseult has come out of the inappeasable longing of the human heart which knows that there is a love greater than the love of man and woman: love of infinite things which never can be satisfied upon this earth. The myth shows that the invisible bonds of the human heart may prove more powerful than the most carefully-structured edifice of society. In daring to gaze upon one another, Tristan and Iseult become heroic, transcending social conventions and giving themselves up to the quest for an ideal that is impossible; they are, as a consequence, doomed to destruction. The intuition that this is so does not draw them back from their destiny, and perceptions that are very much part of the Celtic approach to the world are embodied in their story: a sense of the fragility and brevity of life; an acceptance of a greater fatality and impetus for action than that suggested by the social order; abandonment to a quest that is born in some impulse or mood and which must inevitably end in death; a realization that the material body is merely the medium of immortal emotion, that, as Yeats says, men are "born and must die with their great thirst unslaked," or, as another poet puts it, our "being's home is with infinitude and only there."

In the same way, the Edinburgh Arts Journey is a spiritual quest in a world which, in its unrelenting search for material ease, is constantly closing in on itself, even to the point of suffocation. Modern man seems to be moving in a mesmeric way more and more towards urban centres. Edinburgh Arts, in contrast, is a Journey outwards from the centre to the periphery, and the thing that most impressed me about the participants on the Journey and the places and people that we visited was that, although many were encountered accidentally, all seemed attuned to the same central source of spiritual energy, and it was the magnetic power of this energy as much as the will or inspiration of any one individual that drew us together. I remember Norman Mommens saying in Puglia, for example, that he expected the Edinburgh Arts group in his studio long before he was aware of their particular existence as a group. As the Journey progressed, there floated into my mind an image of a delicate web of connections and interconnections stretched over the length and breadth of Europe, and I saw our Journey as the instrument by which the web became more finely and intricately interwoven: a delicately wrought web held together by friendship and faith. Then there formed in my mind's eye the apocalyptic prophecies of Celtic visionaries, predicting the formation of an invisible spiritual army, moving like a scythe against the godless materialism of our times.

II

The dialogue and conversations published below took place during the 1979 Journey.* The exchanges were entirely spontaneous, with no eye to publication. The result is varied: certainly not an objective assessment of the Journey, but more a poetic evocation of the atmosphere of an experience which, all of the participants agreed, seemed to defy definition.

It should also be pointed out that the initiator of the Journey, Richard Demarco, is the impressario who, in the words of the Art Critic of the London *Times* "in art terms, has done more for . . . the Edinburgh Festival's image than any other." Yet, Demarco regards his presentations of contemporary art, including his now famous "Strategy Get Arts" Exhibition of 1970, merely as a milestone towards the creation of Edinburgh Arts and the Journey. At the time of that Exhibition, Demarco was disparaged more severely for his presentation of the now internationally accepted Joseph Beuys than he is at present (and there has been disparagement) for his concept of Edinburgh Arts. My last question is: can we afford to ignore, even for a short time, the latest enterprise of one who has for the last two decades been in the vanguard of theatrical and artistic experiment, of one who has done so much to shape our consciousness of European art in the seventies?

NOTE

* The participants in the discussion were as follows: Richard Demarco, Director of the Richard Demarco Gallery; Norman Mommens, a Flemish painter and sculptor living in Puglia; Richard Kline and Richard Janis, painters and art historians teaching in Central Michigan University; Tino Trova, an undergraduate student and son of sculptor Ernest Trova; Pat Yule, a Scottish artist; and Robert O'Driscoll, Director of Celtic Studies, University of Toronto.

Plate 1: H. M. Marques, vessel of the "Edinburgh Arts" Journey.

A CONTEMPORARY QUEST INTO THE CELTIC AND PRE-CELTIC WORLD

Puglia: 25.7.79

Norman Mommens: Our modern knowledge isn't ours any more; it belongs to huge specialized machinery. In the same way, ancient knowledge became specialized and the exclusive possession of a certain group of people, and so it was lost. For as soon as the values which these people depended on for their power changed, they lost the knowledge and it was lost for everybody. Just as today, if the few nuclear scientists were suddenly removed from our midst, nuclear physics would vanish and where would we dig it up again? It is the same with ancient knowledge. It became functional, political, forcing people to act in certain pre-ordained ways.

Robert O'Driscoll: How, then, is man's being renewed?

Mommens: At one time the eclipse was a marvellous opportunity for undergoing periodic regeneration. Why was the ancient world so interested in eclipses? This has puzzled me because a calendar is of very little use to people who are always in the country, who are living in nature, because everything is obvious; what season it is, when to do things — it's part of their own rhythm. So a calendar is not necessary. Why should they want to fix these eclipses? Well, I believe that these people were like dowsers today, very susceptible to all magnetic currents, like animals — a cow will go and lie down to have its calf on a blind spring, or if you leave the gates open to the fields, allowing a current to pass through, the cows will come home of their own accord. People in olden times were similarly susceptible. The moon controls these currents; every fortnight they change; they change direction, one spiral returning to another. The eclipse is catastrophic; it practically cancels out all currents; ancient man felt completely drained, for one moment, and then as the sun appeared again, they felt that all the life-giving regenerative powers were being given to them again after they had undergone this complete loss of vitality.

O'Driscoll: With those energy patterns being as they are, it is, I should think, no accident that you are living here in Puglia which perhaps more than any other part of Europe is a rich palimpsest of many civilizations. In such an area of ancient energy, the individual spirit can be renewed if one tunes into those fields of energy. But are not our modern cities completely cut off . . .

Mommens: No! Nowadays, what we call 'regeneration' is a personal matter. We can only get in touch with huge universal movements personally, and we do that by finding out the thing that gives us the desire to live. You must find it, because that is the sun reappearing from behind the moon. When you begin to discover, in no matter how small a part of your life, the thing that really gives you the zest for life, take notice of it, cultivate it.

O'Driscoll: Even if it seems dangerous?

Mommens: That depends on your character.

O'Driscoll: What do you mean?

Mommens: Some people need danger, initially at least. But the initial thing that you noticed may not be the final thing that makes you want to live. Once you admit the thing that you really like doing, good and evil vanish. The balancing of this can be very tricky: indeed, I doubt whether anybody is capable of consciously balancing good and evil. The thing is to get really interested, absorbed in what makes you feel vital. If it is rudimentary you will, of course, have an awful lot of trouble. But then the pleasure will become more refined; gradually it will become more precise; it will become life giving in every sense, and you will strike your true note. The whole problem of good and evil will vanish: death, discomfort, and boredom are swallowed up in victory.

O'Driscoll: I am reminded of what Nietzsche had to say on the nature of good, evil, and happiness. What is good, Nietzsche asks? Everything that increases the feeling of power in man. What is bad? All that proceeds from weakness. What is happiness? The feeling that power is increasing, that resistance is being overcome.

Mommens: The old ways of regeneration will no longer do. There is no sense in attempting to dig up lost knowledge. People can no longer get in touch with the moon and the sun in the old way. But the moon and the sun still exist: they exist in us and we can encourage the apparition of the sun.

O'Driscoll: Are you suggesting that the knowledge which has been lost may actually be contained or even embodied within ourselves, be there in the darkness waiting to be discovered, or re-discovered? We have been so trained to think in external ways that we tend to visualize lost knowledge as being contained in some secret book or manuscript. It is there then in our own breast, and by following the rhythm which is unique to ourselves, by discovering that frail impulse, by consciously cultivating it, and making it stronger, no matter how it seems to defy present knowledge, we hook into . . .

Mommens: That's it. Call it a mustard seed. But it is never once and for all. It is something one has to discover and develop again and again. All the problems we now have in this world are the result of a wonderful dream we had, offering complete emancipation from all effort: all discomfort, all pain, everything. It has proved a dream, and this is the confinement we are kept in now by the Goddess, whom I call Bridget. She won't let us wriggle out of it, so we have got to get out of it by some other way, and this is what I mean by finding the thing which gives one personally the will to live. Bridget has many manifestations, a thousand names (I sometimes think of the British Isles as the body of Bridget), but the action of the Goddess is always the same action, a forcing of one into the cauldron, the cauldron which leads to regeneration, and it is not always pleasant — far from it.

O'Driscoll: Does Bridget, in one respect, hold the world manacled?

Mommens: We are in the matrix. We have wanted to take possession of Bridget, but we are possessed by her now. The laws of nature have been transgressed to such an extent that the resilience of the whole ecological and biological system is breaking down, and we have to learn to live with it. The rivers are becoming polluted, the seas are dying, the earth is becoming sterile: all of this is the result of our wishing to take possession of the world, of a completely anthropomorphic view. . . .

O'Driscoll: Of looking upon nature as something to be consumed. I see that, but I don't quite see how at the same time we are in a matrix.

Mommens: In being confined to what we have chosen. The Goddess has been punishing us all the time because we have been intent only on expressing our own will and power, on not considering her nature, and part of the consideration of her nature is to know her dark side. When I said that we had this dream of total emancipation from all discomfort and pain, that means to say that we denied the dark side of the Goddess. The dark side has become worse ever since we tried to eliminate it. When we accepted it, it was feared, it was trembling, it was wonder — we could only get over the terrible anguish of being alone in the world, of being aware of it and not comprehending it, by wonder and faith. So the dark side, accepted in that sense, was positive and kept us human. But if we say that we must have no darkness, no fear, no pain, no drudgery, then we will get extraordinary tensions inside of ourselves: diseases, aggressiveness and it will get worse and worse.

O'Driscoll: Part of the reason for so much neurosis in the world, then, is that so many people are leading unnatural lives and not using their powers for the purposes intended by nature. We carry within us the seeds of our own salvation, and what you seem to be saying is that we cannot allow our instinctive fear of the dark to deny us our destiny as truly developed human beings."Why do we praise men who die on the battlefield?" W.B. Yeats asks in one of his lectures, "A man may display as reckless a courage by descending into the abyss of himself." We have to be prepared to descend into that abyss, into the dark lumberyard of our own hearts, so to speak; to undertake a voyage, both spiritual and physical, that will carry us beyond the horizons of familiar thought and leave us vulnerable beneath the heavens. We need something to remind us of our own vulnerability, of our own humanity. And we need a voyage that will expose the dark side of our selves to the light of our own awakening understanding, so that we are complete, two halves, day and night, the turning globe.

Demarco's sailing ship is a splendid symbol as well as being a physical reality: it symbolizes for me the frail barque of the soul caught on the terrifying immensity of the sea which is, of course, symbolic of life. The ship, too, like the body, is a kind of neutral territory where the great symbolic battles between darkness and light, between good and evil, are waged, and a man's destiny can hang in the balance. These battles are waged in those rare moments when we have released ourselves from the bondage of the world. We are asleep so much of the time, dulled, insulated from our own emotions by the habits and demands of cosmopolitan life. As Richard Demarco notes, we are inclined to over-protect what we most love, and so render it soft and vulnerable to attack. Demarco is right then in insisting on the quest: we must, he tells us, move out in the manner of knights of old, and strengthen what we would defend by leaving it open to the elemental forces of the world and, in doing so, strengthen the fibres in our own hearts. We need the ship, then, and we need the Journey, to make us human once again, to take us from a mechanized world and place us among real things, secret and inaccessible things and thoughts, awakening our sensitivity to the beauty and power of nature and to life stirring within us and which has always been there, waiting to express itself. We need to feel the rudder trembling in our hands, reminding us that we can regain control of our own destinies, that the individual human heart still beats.

Mommens: Yes, we need the Journey, both spiritual and physical. The eclipse won't help us much anymore. We're not that sort of people anymore. We need the voyage. It is also necessary for people to be sure of their own place and of the value of that place in relation to the universe. When our ancient ancestors travelled, and they travelled a great deal, they met others who were as equally sure. There was no sameness but a tremendous diversity.

O'Driscoll: All of the world moves towards the same plaster image, one vast Herculean image in which individual idiosyncracies are obliterated. Richard is right when he suggests that modern tourism is not travel at all but the transference of a set of conditions and attitudes appropriate for one place to another place. We must attempt to perceive the uniqueness, the spiritual essence that inhabits each particular place that we visit.

Mommens: Never, it would seem, has there been a greater need for the traditional journey or even the sacred pilgrimage. Only through it can some people know their own soul and their own sacred plot of earth, as if for the first time.

27.7.79

Richard Demarco: It seems appropriate, as we voyage across the sea from Corfu to Patras, that we probe our combined experiences of the Journey. Perhaps I could begin, as we sit on the deck of this overcrowded ferry, by recalling some of the points about Edinburgh Arts '79 which define its reality for me.

1. Edinburgh Arts is about interfaces, thresholds, which are more important than any particular place or thing seen along the way. It is about the spaces between places, and these seem to hold the energy of the Journey.

2. It seems to me that those who are not with us because they happen to be dead, or because they are in another part of the world, are as important as those who are present and they have been brought to us by those who are here. For example: Hugh MacDiarmid was brought to us by James Ferguson; W. B. Yeats was brought to us by Robert O'Driscoll; David Jones by Neil Bartlett; Ezra Pound by Howard Hull; Ernest Trova by his son Tino Trova; Paul Neagu and David Nash by Jonathan Phipps; Henry Thoreau by Cameron Kirchner; Tristan and Iseult were brought to us through the combined consciousness of the whole group and Padre Pio was brought to us by Giovanni Batthyany. We are thus following in the footsteps of artists whose lives represent the journey of the soul voyaging beyond our known horizons.

3. Edinburgh Arts is a sandwich of *land*, the known and safe; *sea*, the unknown and dangerous; and then *land* again, with a touch of sea by the use of public ferry from Corsica to Italy, and Italy to Greece.

4. Edinburgh Arts is about the temptation we know when we are faced with the beauty of this world. To me nothing is more beautiful than the sailing ship, the Marques, or the island of Corsica. Therefore Corsica and the ship represented the two places where I was tempted to reject my responsibilities to the Journey.

5. Edinburgh Arts is about the unexpected rather than the expected or the planned. Consider the unexpected and most difficult journey which led to our friends in Puglia and the expected and easy journey to that horrendous place where tourism thrives which we discovered to be Corfu in July.

6. Edinburgh Arts is essentially about male/female energy — the possibility or impossibility of the dialogue between male and female in all human beings, whether they be male or female.

7. Edinburgh Arts, in its 1979 form, is at its most difficult and innovative phase. This is perhaps because of the element of the ship and because Edinburgh Arts is becoming more establishment. It could easily be used as a means of gaining easy entry into the art world.

8. Edinburgh Arts is about making a journey from Edinburgh, the Athens of the North, to Athens itself; a journey from the Hebrides to the Cyclades and back to the Hebrides: from the Isle of Eigg to the Island of Santorini.

9. Edinburgh Arts '79 is about education and making contact with four particular long-tried and trustworthy places of education for the young: Eton, Marlborough, Dollar and Gordonstoun schools which still resist state control. It is about that corrective educational establishment, which can become the ultimate obscenity and the opposite of the positive learning experience. I refer to Barlinnie Prison, but also to the prison's Special Unit, which educates both prisoners and keepers to reconsider their roles in society.

10. Edinburgh Arts is about the Edinburgh Festival and about the phenomena of festivals and our need to set a time apart for art in all its manifestations. Edinburgh Arts simply concentrates its attention not on the place of Festival but on our journeying towards that place. Our approach to the Festival should be different from the journeys of convenience which we are obliged to make in our 20th century lives. Edinburgh Arts is re-establishing the ritual element which was inherent in the way the travellers to Canterbury or Compostella became recognised as pilgrims.

11. It is about art in its proper place: the Piero della Francesca frescoes, in particular those in the Franciscan church, in Arezzo and only in Arezzo, the Leonardo da Vinci "Last Supper" in the refectory of the Dominican Church in Milan, and only in Milan. It is about artists in their studios, and not anywhere else, where their work can be seen in the process of being formed: Norman Mommens, for example, in his studio at Masseria Spigolizzi, or Fausto Melotti in his studio in Milan. It is about the art which can be seen to exist when John Hale or Cioni Carpi decide to talk about their work in their studios which are also their living spaces. It

is about the unique collection of contemporary art of Dr. and Signora Guiseppe Panza in their home at Varese, where all the art is arranged in order to acknowledge the spirit of the place.

12. Edinburgh Arts cannot be defined by any one year. All the Edinburgh Arts Journeys represent the ritualistic and sacramental attempt of Europeans to celebrate the summer solstice, an annual event in which we acknowledge the sun reaching its summer zenith. It is a manifestation of the human need to make rites of passage when travelling to places held in respect by past generations.

The Edinburgh Arts Journey is about a point of balance: the point between two sources of energy, one associated with the nest, the other with the movement to and from the nest. If Edinburgh Arts emphasises the journey, it is because of the general emphasis on nest-building which we are trying to counter-balance.

Richard Janis: I should like to add two points. Basically, the reasons for the journey are, firstly, to investigate the roots of civilisation as a preliminary in the making of art, which is so different today from the making of art in any other age; and secondly to discover man's environment as the real space in and about which art is created. The Journey represents a search which, by its very nature, represents an act of faith. We don't know if we'll find anything at all. But there is an intuitive motivation for doing the Journey: with the sharing of time and space with others on the Journey, a process of purification takes place. This process is something all of us are experiencing as we are changing our impressions and finding, daily, deeper truer sources which motivate the creative process.

Tino Trova: And a deeper truer understanding of oneself.

Janis: Yes, because the Journey becomes a metaphor for life itself, condensing life's experiences, thus speeding up the consciousness-raising process.

Demarco: It is also for me a search into my origins as a human being, my birthplace in Scotland and the birthplace of my forbears in Italy. This interest in my origins is not a sentimental or academic matter; only by touching the two points, my birthplace and the point from which I was conceived out of previous generations, can I know the full complexity of my being in relation to the earth which produced me.

Robert O'Driscoll: Carl Jung says something to the effect that a man without a sense of his cultural and racial past is like a piece of floating debris. A nation is a many-rooted tree — but if we cut ourselves off from these roots we are thrown onto our own ingenuity and individual resources. The individual resources of any one person are not enough to enable one to face the terrifying complexities of life. One needs the strength of the dead generations, of the past; otherwise one is merely a person stumbling in the all too obvious light of day, incapable of probing the darkness.

Richard Kline: I think this journey is a metaphor. To participate in it in the real sense one has to subjugate the ego to the whole view of the Journey. It is the same kind of thing as creating a work of art. You have to lose consciousness of your own identity for a few seconds, or a few hours or even days. It really requires faith. There is something much deeper in the group than in the ego of any one individual; something we do not understand. In a sense, both Fausto Melotti's studio in Milan and Malevich's painting "Black Square on White" which we saw at Beaubourg, show this depth. All so-called twentieth century innovation in art was embraced by Malevich with this painting in 1912. There was little more innovative if we see history in chronological sequence from the Renaissance to the present day. Art today has gone through a deep crisis because most artists concern themselves with material things. They are conscious of their egos as they work. The work we saw of Fausto Melotti, Cioni Carpi and Norman Mommens is non-egocentric because they are artists taking the old metaphors and adding an extra spiritual quality that is similar to the energy which created the stone circles. The Journey has helped me see the Western world in a more realistic light: by looking back into history one can get a better 'fix' on the present. Materialistic goals dominate the Western world: there is greater need for spiritual direction and for balance. This journey has helped me to define more clearly my own goals.

O'Driscoll: I am reminded of what Norman Mommens said about the Journey. He suggested that the Journey is an expression of the new vortex of energy which is beginning to form in Europe. I look upon the Edinburgh Arts participants as in a way carriers — mediums would be perhaps too strong a word — of that energy, as they move from one point to another. Why has Edinburgh Arts been created? It has been born out of a mood of sadness and profound disenchantment with the modern world, a mood of disillusionment based upon the separation of art from life, the separation of the art object from the spirit of the place which created it, and the separation of the spiritual or artistic from our everyday living.

Edinburgh Arts is a journey to sacred places: to places where art is not allowed to be more important than life, but not less important either. It is a journey to places where the production of a work of art is not an end in itself, where art is not made for the sole purpose of being exhibited in a gallery or published in a poetry anthology. It is to places where art can be seen to grow directly from the life of a community.

The Renaissance cities were not consciously planned to be beautiful or as exemplary forms of townscape, but came into being simply and naturally. They were offering an amenity which the Renaissance city dweller demanded.

But I think that most of the members of our group would agree with Victor Hugo when he says that the Renaissance may have been a sunset rather than a sunrise. In the Renaissance desire to resurrect age-old truths it is unfortunate that most of the artists who followed Leonardo had not his cosmic awareness and were content to look back only to the classical world of Greece and Rome and not to the Celtic world or even the pre-Celtic world of megaliths and mythology. We should not believe exclusively in notions of progress, but rather also in the possibility of the rediscovery of what has been lost. For this reason we have plunged ourselves into the mystery of the past with the same spirit which led to the creation of those sculptural monuments in the form of the Irish passage graves, or the Corsican menhirs and dolmens. That same spirit still moves in the world if we can only purify ourselves to let it express itself. I am reminded of Joseph Campbell's point concerning the quest for the Grail. It is, he says, there before our very eyes if only we could see it. Edinburgh Arts is about seeing those infinite manifestations of the Holy Grail which lie before us, before our very eyes. It is about perception, about seeing.

Janis: Man's unity with nature and with things of the spirit is there whether he is aware of it or not. I found the Journey constructive because it acknowledged and celebrated sites in which this unity has been so strikingly embodied. I am thinking of the Clava circles, the alignments of burial chambers in the Kilmartin valley, the medieval dwellings of Capula and Cucuruzzu, Filitosa, the integrated life style at New Lanark, and the attempts of Marlborough College to stress the importance of visual literacy.

Kline: On the Journey I was hoping to experience some feeling for the mysteries of the stone circles, the ley line and the energy points which outline the magnetic lines of force. Norman Mommens put it beautifully by suggesting that there is hope that we can discover information anew. He said that it was perhaps on purpose that the lost knowledge embodied in the stones was lost, because it was always liable to be used wrongly. The significance of the Journey is that it may simply be re-asserting this truth, that sacred knowledge is bound to be lost if used wrongly.

O'Driscoll: Did Norman Mommens say that lost knowledge may be lost forever or that it can be rediscovered or re-applied? I did not quite understand the process as to how that knowledge can come to express itself again in the consciousness of contemporary man.

Kline: I think that he was saying that it may have been used in the same way that we have used atomic energy or nuclear physics. We have picked out the wrong kind of information and made it into mere technology.

Demarco: He said that if we ever used knowledge for our own sakes, the Mother Goddess will have her revenge on us. He warned us that when the high priest uses sacred knowledge he is using something which belongs to no mortal: it is supernatural. The Goddess could punish the high priest by the oldest law which guarantees the destruction of all mortals who wish to utilise the energy of the heavens for merely earthly purposes. The knowledge of the high priest is, in our time, the knowledge of the artists. But the contemporary artists seem to have forgotten that artistic expression is a state of grace, or in other words, a point of balance. Art is a gift which must be used with gratitude and respect. We should be indeed fearful of its power to work against us.

Kline: We have the responsibility, all of us, to rediscover our own special concept of lost knowledge. We have been able to prove on this Journey, objectively, that lost knowledge does exist. Norman Mommens, through his astronomical calculations, has been able to prove this for himself. The journey is a true art form in itself because it is dealing with rediscovery in the truest sense of the word, the rediscovery perhaps of the nature of art.

Demarco: May I ask you to consider how David Jones saw his work as a search for the "actually known and loved"? Edinburgh Arts is the acknowledgement of that which is actually there; not that which is imagined or intellectually considered to be there. I am speaking of all that we saw, smelt, felt, considered, and in the end loved. So Edinburgh Arts is extraordinary and uncomfortable because many things in the palimpsest which we are endeavouring to investigate are difficult to piece together, daily posing unexpected problems. There is no easy way to juxtapose the experience of Carnac with that of Filitosa or to link comfortably the studios of Fausto Melotti in Milan with that of Barbara Hepworth in St. Ives or Norman Mommens in Spigolizzi, yet we have a deeply felt instinct to make the difficult juxtapositions which the work of all three of these artists demands. So Edinburgh Arts is not about any one thing but is about the comparison not only of the stones of Giurdignano in Puglia with the nearby mosaic floor representing the "Tree of Life" in Otranto but of both of these ancient art expressions in relation to the nearby studios of Norman and Patience Mommens. It is the living artists who give us a sense of pre-history not as something which is past and forgotten, but as something directly related to our own lives. The Giurdignano menhirs tell us that the thoughts of the people who placed them were blessed with a sense of what we call aesthetics, balanced by a technology which could endure over 4000 years, to be physically there in the twentieth century. The Journey should teach us to concentrate on the energy which exists between all the places and people we encounter, particularly what Henry Thoreau called "mind-prints", the thoughts and energy which human beings leave behind them when they know how to treat the Goddess with respect. What David Jones calls "the utile" suggests that the human presence upon the earth is a blessed presence, so what we have been trying to do is not to fall in love with any product of human activity, but with the human presence itself, or to be more precise the divinity of the human presence. It is not enough to fall in love with the work of David Jones. That is easy enough. It will lead you nowhere and in the end you will try to possess it as something beautiful. It is our duty to go beyond the work, to defend the mystery of the presence of David Jones upon the earth and his relationship to every stone and "mind-print" which he used to make his work. As was pointed out by Richard Kline, there was not one art object in the studio of Norman Mommens. Everything was merely a spin-off from his thought processes and his spiritual journey. Edinburgh Arts is a metaphor for the kind of journey which Norman Mommens personifies in his life and work. It is a search for "mind-prints", for the mystery of our own human presence.

Janis: Yes, I think art, I mean specifically visual art, exists in a kind of time-space continuum. If we are talking about an art object, even in contemporary terms, it can mean a piece of conceptual or kinetic art, multi-media art and so forth. What characterises visual art is its distilled quality. It is there. The entire thing is there, and when one looks at it a kind of contemplation takes place. Not quite the same kind of contemplation as we experience while hearing music which carries us off and up somewhere, but one which brings one down to a kind of centre. This is why visual art is more convincing, more reassuring.

Demarco: This certainly makes visual art more durable than music because what you see in ancient cultures endures best in visual terms. We do not have the sound of the builders of Carnac. We have the Carnac stones.

Janis: This in a sense becomes an example of the Journey in which the experiences become condensed into a duration of time. The Edinburgh Arts Journey itself, which takes place within this 63-day period, is a kind of condensation of life itself and so is a metaphor for our own lives. In life we are constantly evolving, whether we are aware of it or not.

Demarco: Life is not static, it is movement.

O'Driscoll: In some ways what we surround ourselves with often reflects the interior geography of the spirit, "psycho-geography" is the term given to it these days. In North America, for example, everything is straight and linear, and because of this, restricting.

Demarco: Angular!

O'Driscoll: Not even angular. I would say rectangular. Last night, for example, in the streets of Corfu, and before in the streets of Siena, we enjoyed the sensuous, free-flowing, mysterious, small and narrow spaces which revealed apertures, threshholds, tunnels and the drama of what we could not see around the carved well-worn corners.

Demarco: We followed the curvilinear lines of the Goddess, the female lines which exist in the earth; not the male, ordered, rational lines of the Romans and, I am sorry to say, the Classical Greeks. If we had really wanted a Renaissance we would have gone much further back than Classical Greece or Rome.

O'Driscoll: I was reminded last night in Corfu, when we finally did escape the hordes of pleasure-seeking tourists into the darkened alleyways and courtyards where Corfu's indigenous population lives, of the interior passages of one's own mind and heart. The simplistic layout or blueprint of the modern city implies that we are progressing in a linear way — that we are square and straight in our thoughts. But we must (and this is another aspect of Edinburgh Arts) summon up the courage to descend into the labyrinthine passages of our own souls, and those of our ancestors which are reflected in the architecture of these ancient cities.

Demarco: This is a very important point, because the ultimate aim of all human understanding is the landscape of the human body. There is nothing more strange to any human being than the landscape of his or her *own* body, which is both male and female energies conjoined. It is not possible within the laws of nature for a male and female to be complete without both the male and female energies conjoined together in love. The human body is the crowning glory of the universe. If you rediscover and respect the energies in yourself, you discover the most foreign, most dangerous landscape in all the world. You discover your mother or maybe even your grandmother. We are born to seek out this landscape — we must know it and indeed we must love it. Everything we see in the universe is merely an extension of the landscape of ourselves. The stars, the sun, the moon, every tree and branch, every leaf and flower, are extensions of our humanity. All the wonders of the universe are as nothing by themselves compared to this mystery. As participants in the Journey, we represent the whole human race. This sounds pretentious, but this is the way it is with any group of people bent on the exploration of their universe. The Journey is, I hope, at least an attempt with the right intentions. We travel further and with more pain, and with more joy than the people on this ferry to Patras or the people in huge tour groups who are searching for Greece and are covering themselves with sun-tan oil, reading *Time* magazine, and listening to disco music. They might as well have stayed at home, because travelling as they are in this floating waiting-room and in such a large group they insulate themselves from contact with Greek culture and the spirit of the Greek shoreline and islands.

Tino Trova: I think that in order to feel and touch upon pure human thought and intention we must directly approach the artist in his or her own space and observe art in the process of being formed.

Demarco: Tino has defined a capacity we have now lost — the capacity to invest energy in the idea embodied in an art work rather than the finished product. We pay too much attention to the artifact. We are afraid to touch it in the heat of creation. The more that we put our energies into art galleries and museums the less we will have a chance of experiencing art.

Kline: I'd like to return at this point to the subject of the ship. I think that the compressed time in the overland journey preceding the experience of the ship was so fast that it was almost like a stream of consciousness viewing. There was no way you could comprehend everything. You just had to see it, try to absorb it, and move to the next almost contradictory or contrasting view.

O'Driscoll: In his play "Not I", Samuel Beckett has a stage direction indicating something to the effect that the words are to be spoken slightly faster than the speed of human comprehension.

Kline: Then suddenly we were on the ship. It involved a sense of interior time. You had more time to absorb the experience of the land journey. And then with the exploration of dangerous shores, of Carnac and so on, the ship represented a vessel that helped to accelerate the land journey.

Demarco: A moving space capsule? Are you suggesting then that the voyage of the Marques and indeed the whole Edinburgh Arts Journey represents a moving space capsule?

Kline: Yes. It is really like a Venturi compressor in a jet engine in the way it compresses our feelings, preparing us for the next land journey — which we are now on. The sea is enduring too in the religious sense. It gives a sense of the all-powerful. Water can destroy land and indeed can destroy anything. We were floating on a most fragile vessel, upon this powerful substance.

Janis: As vulnerable as we ever have been in our lives.

Demarco: We had to give ourselves over. Almost as sacrifices to the Goddess, to do with us what She willed. It was our way of saying our place is with Her and She will take us to whatever it is She must take us to.

Kline: There was all the pain and pleasure of love and hate.

Demarco: Within the Christian conrext, it is the Mother of God who takes you to the love of God and the Son and the Father. The ship became the necessary symbol of the female energy to carry us towards our idea of truth.

Tino Trova: The necessary energy. The ship was creative energy itself which enabled us to reach points of energy on land.

O'Driscoll: Of course there are some practical points too. We must remember that the sites we saw on the coast of Brittany, Cornwall and Ireland were created by human beings travelling not by land, but by sea. There was a tremendous feeling of harmony with the people who built the sites. I don't think that the forms of energy really change. The instinct that we had in approaching the sites may be the same as the instinct of the mysterious people who created them in the first place.

Demarco: We saw the full meaning and purpose of Carnac as we approached it from the sea by moonlight. We were privileged to see things from the sea.

Kline: It was natural that we approached Carnac from Belle Île by ship. Our whole life was there on that moonlit shore. When we had reached our destinations it was moonlight, but we went ashore in small boats across that mile of moonlit sea and then walked two miles towards the actual Carnac alignments. If we had been in a motel we would not have been inclined to go out at that hour of night.

Janis: I think this ties in with the process of purification which the Journey implies. On the ship when you are alone with your own thoughts, and even when you are communicating with others, there are a lot of things from the past which emerge. I call this a preconscious or subconscious type of knowledge — knowledge which is always with us, but which we are not fully aware of. It seems to crop up out of nowhere. We are experiencing a sensory deprivation being surrounded by a large body of water in a small sailing ship, especially when it is under sail. But this very deprivation creates the conditions to enable what is buried in our subconscious to emerge.

O'Driscoll: For me, the process of purification achieved by the Journey implies a stripping from ourselves of what Beckett or maybe Kantor would call "emballage", the twentieth-century material embellishments that sometimes insulate us from the dangerous life of the spirit. In approaching the prehistoric sites in the pure ritualistic way that we do, we are sometimes placed in touch with some currents of energy that stirred the ancient world to create those megalithic and mythological monuments. And not only merely placed in touch with these currents. Is it too much to suggest that we become a medium for this forgotten energy to come again into the consciousness of the world? The transmitter is as essential as the source. We become in short what we truly are: a transparent human barque vulnerable to the impulses of the spirit. The great lesson that Edinburgh Arts confirms in me is the conviction that mankind is not complete, the initiator of action, but merely the foam upon the deep, merely the momentary blossom of some spiritual impulse.

This leads to an important point about the temptation by beauty. We can abandon ourselves to the immensity of the sea and the Goddess as symbolised by a beautiful, romantic, ancient vessel sailing through the water with only the sound of gently creaking timbers and the wind in the sails. We can abandom ourselves to that, but I am afraid that part of the agony and joy of existence is that we have to fix our attention on the inevitable return to the prison of our life of routine after we have known the freedom of pure imagination. Therefore, the ship has two aspects. She is both the Goddess and the enchantress. Part of the agony of this life is that we must face the mundane reality of it as well as satisfy our romantic dreams. This is, I think, one of the main triumphs of the Journey.

Demarco: We witnessed the ship, the perfect instrument of flight from the nest, become itself the all too comfortable nest when we reached the point of having to leave her and face the continuation of the Journey from the Gulf of Morbihan to the city of Paris, and onwards through Europe. But the fact that a group of artists used the ship associated with Darwin is a step in the right direction. The world needs the poetic imagination now because it is so overwhelmingly overweighted by logic and the views of scientists. Obviously we are questioning Darwin's theory by thinking that there is no such thing as a "missing link". We are not being nostalgic, looking back and saying what a great journey Darwin made. Edinburgh Arts deals with reality not make-believe. We are continuing and extending Darwin's journey into our own lives.

Kline: And playing all the possible chords.

Trova: We must keep in mind the non-pure spaces that we touched in our attempt to come in contact with the pure in nature.

Kline: I don't think we can move through Europe without being totally inundated with the impure. Some of the things we encountered were ugly, but that is what is so beautiful. Because we were so well tuned to finding the beautiful we often discovered the ugly.

Demarco: The Journey of Edinburgh Arts, as I have said, is first of all explained by the words "Edinburgh" and "Arts". It is about Edinburgh, the capital of Scotland and the home of the Edinburgh Festival. It is unfortunate that this city, one of the world's most important art centres, has become, at least for me, a not altogether beautiful place. It can become a safe welcoming nest in which artists and lovers of art can afford to be self-indulgent, and self-congratulatory. The Festival is in danger of becoming an extension of the tourist season in Scotland, a money-making, materialistic exercise which is judged by the city fathers by the amount of money it makes or loses. On this journey we are facing the terrifying problem of how to approach any city which is graced by the light of art. Edinburgh is called the Festival City. I know that most people who think of the Edinburgh Festival as an international festival of the arts want to reduce it by increasing the already large amount of festival-goers who are tourists. The whole world of Europe has become one great summer tourist attraction. It is, although we don't admit it, a European equivalent of Disneyland. In certain places you feel this more than in others. London or Paris in summer are perfect examples, as is Edinburgh during the Festival; the Costa del Sol, and Costa Brava, and the Greek Islands being perhaps worst afflicted. Europe in summer has become an obscenity because we have not found a way of allowing it to be itself so that we can go about our daily tasks. We have forgotten that the main purpose is about survival; about how we seek our points of balance between good and evil. We have been given a daily task involving mental, physical and spiritual survival and we ignore it, at our peril, in this false security of tourism. This is a deflection from our function and our purpose. I am not saying this with the instincts of a puritan, but with the instincts of an orthodox Christian. The Journey is horrific because it leads in the end right into tourism; the worst aspects of the Edinburgh Festival and the world of art. There can be nothing more horrific than that. The idea that anyone should imagine that we are running away from anything should consider the fact that we are beginning and ending our Journey in Edinburgh. Of course any nest can be questioned, restated, restructured by the proper use of art as a liberating force which frees us from materialism; even a nest such as Edinburgh, the Festival City, has to be re-thought.

O'Driscoll: Have you not considered other ways, such as yoga or meditation, of finding a solution to the problem that you are talking about?

Demarco: These can become a mere fad. The guru usually represents a ridiculous meaningless detour. The whole responsibility of the European 'psyche' is to face the fact that Europe is the one culture in the world which possesses the dynamic to produce the greatest good and the greatest evil in the twentieth and twenty-first centuries. As Europeans, as the inheritors of the Christo-Judaic tradition, — we who have become the all-powerful carriers of pollution — I am asking us to reconsider the use we have made of our power. We have polluted Russia with Communism and we have polluted the Western World with materialism. This journey is an attempt, whether we like it or not, to redefine the meaning of the medieval Christian pilgrimage.

Tino Trova: I don't know whether this fits into this conversation, but I think that Richard Demarco could experience a terrible nightmare. As he draws people into his journey he will have a problem if these people are not perceptive enough or do not develop the imagination required to understand it.

Demarco: My only answer is that so far I have been spared the desire to make Edinburgh Arts a success in terms of this world. The Journey can never have any popular appeal. It is difficult, and getting on it demands an act of faith. It tends to attract and make sense to those who have a proper respect for its dangers as well as its attractions. I am not sure if there is any strong possibility of the journey happening again. Basically it has been held together by friendship, and this friendship is an aspect of the love that engenders the whole thing and keeps it together. Remember what Archibald MacLeish says: "Acceptance", he says in an essay published in *Christian Century,* "even Dante's acceptance — of God's will is not enough. Love — love of life, love of the world, love of God, love in spite of everything, is the answer — the only possible answer — to our ancient human cry against injustice. . . . Man, the scientists say, is the animal that thinks. They are wrong. Man is the animal that loves. It is in man's love that God exists and triumphs; in man's love that life is beautiful; in man's love that the world's injustice is resolved. To hold together in one thought those terrible opposites of good and evil which struggle in the world is to be capable of life, and only love will hold them so."

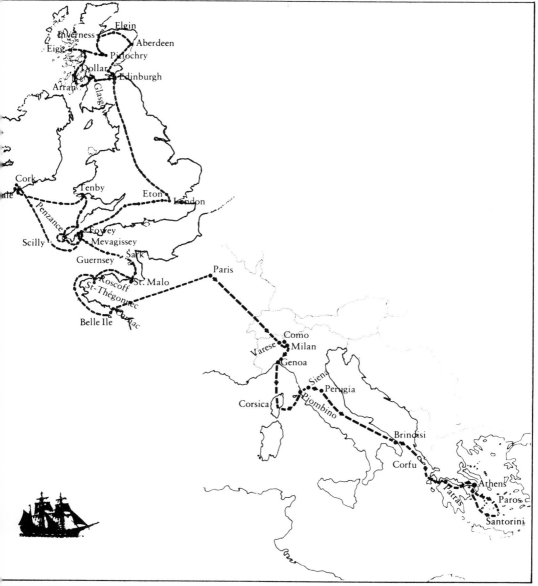

2: Route of the Journey, 1979.

GREEK CODA   2.8.79

Robert O'Driscoll: Perhaps I should begin this Coda by asking Richard Demarco why has he brought us to Greece?

Richard Demarco: Greece represents Athens and Athens is the so-called centre of the classical world upon which Europe has built its idea of the Renaissance. It is the historic centre that we all know. Today, however, and paradoxically, it represents, as Scotland does, the periphery of Europe. The main reason we came to Greece is that we wished to touch the Minoan civilisation, which we did in the last two days when we sailed towards the volcanic island of Santorini. As leader I was taking a risk. I was not playing safe, because I thought that I should add a dimension to the Journey as it is in its 1979 form which would be a surprise to me. I could easily have taken everyone to Malta. And in many ways of course Malta is even more mysterious than Greece because the Maltese civilization — Hagar Qim, Minidjra and Gozo — is even older than the Minoan. I guess the Journey had eventually to come to Greece and to the island of Santorini because Santorini suggests the lost world of Atlantis which is part of our European heritage and is, in a way, the land we long to explore; the land beyond the charted European seas and the known world's end. Since we did go to the Isles of Scilly, which are known literally as the islands of the lost Atlantis, it seems fitting that we took the trouble to acknowledge Santorini. We who are the survivors have a story to tell, which, like "The Rime of the Ancient Mariner", is a long impossible tale but one worth the telling if you can grab hold of a suitable wedding guest to lend his or her ear. It's our responsibility to tell this tale. It would probably be a good idea not to bother with a book, but to rely simply on our ability as bards and storytellers. It would also probably be a good idea if we banned all cameras, all recording machines and all books, and the impressions went directly into our memory and consciousness. We'd maybe all learn again how to become bards, use the spoken word and develop once again our faculty of recalling all things past. Unfortunately we're losing this.

O'Driscoll: I am glad that I continued on the Journey until the end, because it is only now that I am beginning to understand what it is all about; to understand the beginning one must be able to persevere to the end. In this, the Journey resembles Joyce's *Finnegans Wake*, a book built on layer after layer of understanding of the cultural history of the west. Joyce himself says that no man can understand it unless he is willing to devote a lifetime to it. Like the *Wake*, the Journey is built on a palimpsest of experience. In one of our earlier dialogues, we likened ourselves to a space capsule of energy moving from one point to the next — but in order to appreciate the full levels of resonance and association one should really have had the experience of the whole Journey. Nevertheless, we do have one participant, Pat Yule, who was with us for the Greek section only and we should now ask for her reaction.

Pat Yule: I met you all in Athens. One of you said "Carnac in moonlight, approached from the sea, was a spooky and wonderful experience". Another said,

"Do you know what it felt like at the top of the mast?" And another "We had a love affair with a boat — she was called Marques." You all talked a lot about self-discovery, your search for roots, your attempts to reassess the meaning of art, tradition, ancestors. You found links and comparisons between the Celtic and Minoan civilizations. You visited artists and writers, lairds and poets. You asked, sometimes "Do you think that we have been affected by this Journey?" The answers were of course not possible for me to give. I met you at the end of this trip through time and sea. I was looking for people — the kind of people who would want to make such a journey. I know that if this journey could not encompass *me*, a last-minute traveller, then it had nothing to give to anybody. The search had to be about people.

There were, I am glad to say, final experiences to share, some of them extravagantly comforting, and extravagantly stimulating. We went to Paros and met the strange poetic genius called Desmond O'Grady — a man who embodied in his work the ethos of the Celt and the humanity of every man. We sat in a taverna, drank wine, ate figs, and cheese, and listened to the chat and his poetry about voyaging. He talked about sea-gulls, ships, the known and the unknown. He certainly understood the idea of the Journey.

O'Driscoll: Remember what O'Grady had to say about the Journey, that although he is concerned in general with the cultural history of the West, his main intellectual and poetic energy is focussed on making the connection between the Celtic and southern Russian steppes or northern Iran to that fatal bullet in Dallas, Texas, — the last full stop. And so, O'Grady in a remarkable sequence of poems, *The Wandering Celt*, is confronting his own fate and the fate of the Celts by working back from the famine roads of Ireland to the Caucasus from where he believes the Celts originally came, recording under the persona of Riley or the Wandering Celt or the Dying Gaul the experience of his wanderings in an attempt to connect what he left with what he finds along the way. Not an easy journey by any means. Remember O'Grady saying that he feels at times as if he is carrying the whole burden of Celtic history on his back.

Demarco: What O'Grady had to say interests me greatly. Once we understand that the Mediterranean and the whole of that extraordinary womb of Europe is our space, we will inherit once again whatever it was that the Romans misunderstood about the Celtic world. Not being a poet like O'Grady, but having to deal with hundreds of artists, I know now that the only space where I can judge the poet, the artist, or the maker of things — he who makes things well — is to place them into positions of such terror and risk that they are tested to a breaking point, and that space is, of course, the space of the Journey, the interface, the place between the nests. In that space I see them as themselves. In that space they can come to some kind of brotherhood of men, and through their communion with place and space come to understand the thousands of years of wandering as defined by their ancestors.

Yule: There is one thing I'd like to say about the whole thing. I've done a fair bit of travelling, and I think that it would be perfectly possible to walk down that very crowded aisle there, pick out any one individual from the sweaty masses, scratch that individual a little bit on the skin, spend about a week talking to him, no matter how rich or poor, and that same individual would have got just as much out of the Journey as almost anybody. Because that person is a human being, because he relates in a human way.

Demarco: That's an interesting point. There is another element of the Journey which nobody can talk about unless they have been on it, and that is the tough physical strain of it. I think that the Journey will continue to be misunderstood. In this last day, once again I feel, as I always do, that I have got away with something. The one thing that I am sure of is that all those who have remained loyal to it will feel stronger for having done so. The Journey wouldn't exist if I were speaking to myself. You cannot do the Journey on your own. That is the whole point of it. The Journey has to be done in the company of your fellow human beings. They represent the body of man, as it were, and that is what we are examining: the collective consciousness. It's not about the individual ego. You will always find an artist prepared to put his signature on a painting. I think the things that pleased us most were very often the work of totally unknown people who will forever remain anonymous; the stonemasons who carved the sculptures in Corsican churches, for example, the people we met incidentally along the way. At the end of it, I am delighted to know that everyone looks reasonably fit, certainly fitter than they were at the beginning. And as we finish our ordeal I am conscious of the fact that the forces that bind us together are mysterious and much stronger than my own weaknesses and moments of doubt. Edinburgh Arts is about friendship and people mainly with the memory of the occasional standing stone or fresco by Piero della Francesca or Leonardo da Vinci tacked on. But the Journey is basically the people. Edinburgh Arts deals with the unbelievable beauty and magic of reality. For once in my life, looking at the great houses and villages and human settlements on the high volcanic cliffs of Santorini, I realize that we have moved through the world of the imagination, directly into the world of reality under the golden light of the afternoon sun in Greece. In that clarity I realize that the miracle is indeed the human presence doing the right thing. This Journey is a journey from the world of the imagination into the miracle of reality, when we see all real and apparently ordinary things as forever beyond our imagination.

THE PERMANENCE OF THE SPIRITUAL: CELTIC ART AND MODERN ART: BRANCUSI, DAMIAN

RADU VARIA

During his seminar of February 6, 1978, at which he had kindly invited me to speak, Marshall McLuhan asked me the following question: *Is there anything really new in contemporary art?* There has indeed been a fundamental departure, in my opinion — the rediscovery of structures which I shall call *prime* (Brancusi, Damian). They are universally meaningful in themselves, as opposed to the currently fashionable *primary* structures which are no more than abstractions, schematic forms that are reductions within one cultural tradition.

The paper which I should like to present will be very brief. It deals with modern art, but at the same time it throws an unexpected light on the Celtic world.

Here are the facts.

In 1976, I organized an exhibition at the Guggenheim Museum in New York of the work of the Romanian sculptor Horia Damian. That exhibition, in essence, consisted of a monumental sculpture entitled *The Hill*.

By a subtle and indefinable process, this sculpture was unanimously regarded as a sacred object. I must mention here that neither Eliade nor Caillois, who have both studied the sacred, could define it any other terms than the following: "The sacred is what we feel as such, as opposed to the profane."

This unanimous feeling of the *sacred* was confirmed by the reactions of the public in the street when this same *Hill* was, at my suggestion, temporarily installed on the esplanade of the Seagram's Building on Park Avenue in New York. On this occasion, on October 14, 1976, I launched the *New York Manifesto* in order to express the idea of the supremacy of the spiritual over the temporal, in contrast to the predominant directions of contemporary art (Plate 1).

No one will be surprised if I declare that between Damian's *Hill* and the Celtic *tumuli*, there is an obvious similarity (Plates 1 and 2). (I have analyzed that similarity in a text entitled *Damian and the Actual Infinite*, published in 1976 by the Guggenheim Foundation.) Now mounds, we all know, often have a sacred significance;[1] they occur frequently in human imaginings and reveries; and the oldest of religious beliefs, shamanism, has already attributed to them the value of *axis mundi*, the axis of the world. The Celts and the pre-Celtic peoples also used the tumulary form; those of the Boyne Valley in Ireland or the Orkney Isles in Scotland are examples of its use.

There is another fact that I would like to underline. Robert O'Driscoll and Richard Demarco, at the time of their 1977 visit to Europe, mentioned to me in passing the existence of the St. Molaise Chapel in Innishmurray, an island in Sligo Bay. The Chapel is spherical in shape, and was a retreat for Irish Celtic monks (Plate 4). Mention of that form suddenly, and with the force of revelation,

NEW YORK MANIFESTO

Today, October 14, 1976, Horia Damian's *Hill* was installed on the Plaza of Seagram's Building. Its presence has made the vastness of Park Avenue come alive as it emits subtle particles and completely modifies the spatial ontology of the city. If thousands of people have felt and experienced this impact, it is because between this sculpture and the colossal geometry of the city, a new harmony is confirming its presence.

And if this relatively small work loses none of its monumentality, which on the contrary is magnified, it is because it appears as natural as a work which has no author.

It is precisely this point which constitutes a major event in the art of our time. Indeed, for the first time in this second half of the 20th century, here, in the very center of New York, a new view of the artist towards his work and the rest of the world is being expressed.

This new view implies the disappearance of the artist's personality to pave the way for universal sensitivity which animates all things.

And if this constitutes an event it is because the 20th century, imprisoned in its decline and gripped in a crisis of civilization, has replaced art by the cult of the artist's personality, thus creating a void between the creator and that which he creates. The first consequence of this situation is the inversion of the very terms applied to reality, not only have we forgotten that the universal is the very essence of all individuality, but we have even managed to give individuality priority. This confusion is enhanced when we forget that individuality, by its very nature, is subject to the effects of time where as the very essence of art is to be eternal.

Today's event changes this state of affairs and gives art once again its sole chance of being. In the present context, it makes it possible to realize the supremacy of the spiritual over the temporal and at the same time affirms the new revolutionary line of art in the light of the millennium to come.

New York, Thursday October 14, 1976   *Radu Varia*

Plate 2: Mound, Sligo. Photo: Courtesy of Richard Demarco Gallery.

reminded me of a project for a monument that another Romanian sculptor, Brancusi, had been commissioned to make for the Maharajah of Indore, whose wife had just passed away. Ezra Pound made reference to it in his correspondence in the thirties, but there is no description given. And the monument was never constructed.

James Johnson Sweeney, who played a major role in the creation of the principal American museums and who knew Brancusi well, has also assured me that he knew of Brancusi's project for a monument in India, but that he had heard no description of it. Had he done so, and considering his own Irish background, it is unlikely that

Plate 3: The Mandala City by Horia Damian, Gouache on paper.

he would have forgotten it. Accordingly, there has so far been no evidence concerning the form this monument was to take. Information on the subject is, at the same time, of considerable importance since it would have been Brancusi's second great monumental project, together with the one in Târgu-Jiu.[2]

I can now reveal, and for the first time, that to honor his commission, Brancusi intended to construct a *Meditation Temple for one person only.* This temple was to have been more or less spherical, suggesting the shape of an apple. This information was given to me by the architect Octav Doicescu of Bucharest, to whom I spoke about the project some ten years ago, and with whom I consulted again upon seeing pictures of the Chapel of Sligo. He sent me precise details in a letter dated October 31, 1977.

Professor Doicescu had been summoned by Brancusi to construct the monument with him in India. But the project was finally abandoned. "Neither Brancusi nor I myself," writes Professor Doicescu, "ever made a sketch or a model of the monument. He conjured it up; I just listened. The image, as it was orally transmitted to me, was to have been that of an apple. In the center, where the seeds would have been, there was to be a chamber for the sarcophagus, illuminated by daylight coming from the top, from the location of the stem of the apple. Access, possible for only one person at a time, was to have been very simple and situated at the level of the surrounding garden. A few steps would have led to the chamber of the sarcophagus, where man's dialogue with himself would have taken place." "This would have been," the architect Doicescu adds, "a work of art similar to ancient monuments, anonymous, but with great emotive powers."[3]

Thus, two Romanian sculptors, among the greatest artists, moreover, that that country has produced, have created forms related to Celtic forms. Like the Chapel at Sligo, Brancusi's temple allows only one person at a time to enter; it is in the shape of an apple, is situated on a plain and is approached by a few very simple steps.

This proves, at the very least, that such forms are part of the experience of man in the twentieth century. But why precisely were they perceived and expressed by two *Romanian* sculptors and, at that, forty years apart? It is historically certain that neither Brancusi nor Damian knew these Celtic forms. A formalistic hypothesis is automatically excluded.[4] The most plausible hypothesis remains without a doubt that of a very deep Celtic reminiscence. But if this hypothesis seems difficult to prove on an historical level, another explanation is incontestable and even more significant: like the Celts, Brancusi and Damian are manifestly mystical,[5] and with the mystical, we necessarily proceed from multiplicity to uniqueness. At that point, of course, the repertoire of forms is extremely limited.

By way of conclusion to this discussion of Damian's *Hill* and Brancusi's *Temple* in the form of an apple, I come to the legend of King Arthur. The poet Jacques Roubaud has provided some surprising details on the subject. The Celtic hero was said to have arrived at the island of Avalon, an enchanted place, where there would be fruit the whole year round. The Celtic name of this island is Avallach. Avallach or Avalah, that is to say *apple*. Without wanting to draw too hasty a conclusion, I point out that the inhabitants of Brancusi's and Damian's country are Vallachs or Valahs. Their country for a long time was called Vallachia or Valahia. This word, contrary to the accepted etymology,[6] is more than a thousand years older and could perfectly well have been brought or conveyed by the Celts in timeless myths. But this is merely a suggestion for eventual consideration by linguists.

Additional Notes

It is evident that my intention was not to give a talk on linguistics. However, my comments in this area have provoked certain responses. Trusting in the timelessness of certain shapes, which he knows by experience and by intuition, Professor Octav Doicescu, in a letter of April 4, 1978, fully agreed with my remarks, including those touching on the ancient name of the country. Professor Alexandru Rosetti of the Romanian Academy wrote to me on May 24, 1978 that "the medieval word *vlah* does not correspond to Avallach." Agreed. However, if one concedes that there is a certain relationship between *vlah, valah,* and *avalah*, the real question then becomes whether research in this area, based as it is on Latin and Slavic influences, has not ignored the more ancient Celtic element. It is no longer difficult to show that the Celts left important traces in Romania. One need merely recall that in Maramuresh, considered to be the cradle of the entire country, the Celtic cross is used in graveyards to this day. And the cross is not an object usually borrowed from other civilizations, but is rather passed down to us from our ancestors.

The Celtic world has great surprises in store for us. When I first published the analogies of the *Hill* of Damain and the Boyne Valley *tumuli* in 1976, I had no idea of the development of Celtic studies at that time. The same yeaar, Barry Fell, a Harvard professor, published a book entitled *America B.C.* (Quadrangle, The New York Times Book Co.) which included a description of Celtic sites in North America dating from before Christ. The only problem was the lack of explanation as to how the Celts could have come to America. By the early months of 1978, another professor at Harvard, Tim Severin, had published *The Brendan Voyage* (McGraw-Hill). It is an account of a crossing of the North Atlantic by the author and a small party in 1976. Their boat was made of cattle hides according to instructions in an eighth century Latin text, and their route was very close to that taken in the sixth century from Ireland to Newfoundland by an Irish monk named Brendan. They encountered the same landscape, animals and marine phenomena as those in the ancient accounts. Thus, they proved it possible that the Celts reached the new world at least four centuries before the Vikings and nine centuries before Christopher Columbus.

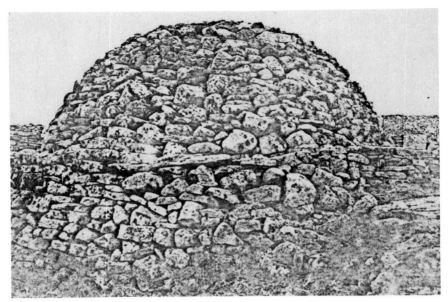

Plate 4: Chapel of St. Molaise, Innishmurray, Sligo, Ireland. Photo: Courtesy of Richard Demarco Gallery.

NOTES

[1] An international syposium organized in June, 1979, at St. John's College of the University of Santa Fe, New Mexico, revealed the existence of hundreds of mounds built along the Mississippi River as early as 300 B.C. and as recently as 1300 A.D., by a civilization whose downfall remains a mystery.

[2] John Russell, commenting on the present article and Professor Doicescu's letter in the *New York Times* of February 17, 1978, writes: "In every generation there is a great work of art that might have been but never was. A prime example of these mooted but never-made masterpieces is the memorial temple that the Maharajah of Indore once commissioned from Constantin Brancusi."

[3] It is interesting to observe that Octav Doicescu describes these anonymous ancient monuments in exactly the same terms as those of my *New York Manifesto* (1976), about which he knew nothing at the time. That also confirms, in and of itself, the profound reality inherent in the notion of *prime structures*.

[4] There is no indication that Brancusi knew anything about Celtic art, or that he was even aware of its existence. As for Damian, he first heard — with great astonishment — about the Celtic *tumuli* from me in 1975, although he had been using this prime shape since 1952. (See Radu Varia, *Damian and the Actual Infinite*, Guggenheim Foundation, 1976, p. 36.)

[5] The word "mystic" should be taken in its universal sense; "I," the artist, am not separate from the Universe, but am the same thing as the rest of the Universe. Hence the *naturalness* of the shapes created.

[6] Slavic, according to the dictionaries of the Romanian Academy.

"PYTHAGORAS PLANNED IT.
WHY DID THE PEOPLE STARE?"

JOHN DAVID MOONEY

Art today seems to be becoming a much more public phenomenon, not only from the experiential viewpoint but also in terms of those who commission the art works. With the increase in governmental patronage for the arts, politicians, art administrators, and to a much lesser extent the artists themselves are being pressed to define the role of the artist in society.[1] As well as this, works which are commissioned are generally supposed to involve the public in some sort of "significant and meaningful manner". There was, of course, public involvement with art in the Renaissance, but the Renaissance world was far removed from our supermarket world of modern art. In contrast to the Renaissance, too, we tend to separate our art galleries and museums from our normal living and working space, both public and private. Art has become separated from life; it has become a narcissistic activity for the young.

Today's artists are becoming more and more geared to the museum environment, and from their early art education they conceive of their works as existing only in the museum or the gallery. This brings the artist to a dilemma which he must face: does he, at the same time as he is forced to watch his environment disintegrate, insulate himself in the private gallery world, producing art objects that as part of a consumer society multiply and become part of the pollution? Or does he dare to face the challenge of his own environment and attempt to turn his vision to the landscape of the modern city?

The city, it seems to me, is a multi-textured thing, and its changing face should have the same drama and joy for its citizens as the changing seasons. In the planning of the spaces that gradually cohere into a city, I believe too that both with regard to the part as well as the whole man's aesthetic spirit must prevail, as is so clear when we look at a Mediterranean fishing village, a medieval town, or Renaissance piazza. It is axiomatic to say that art embodies the spiritual, that it should not be created merely to please the material it is made from: it should be for man and for the body politic. Too often in our modern world of long-range planning, public architecture and transportation, the emphasis is on a mindless perpetuation of the system rather than on the human beings which these systems are supposedly designed to serve. The artist's task is to rescue modern man from the isolation and despair of this mechanistic world by sensitizing his visual awareness and by raising his aesthetic consciousness so that he can again perceive his individual worth in relation to the environmental whole.

One of my own attempts to do this was in a seven-day performance piece, "LIGHT SPACE 77," an environmental light sculpture commissioned by the City of Chicago for the Lakefront Festival in 1977. Because the piece was not concrete in the way that art usually is, it was unusual for a city to commission such a work. In

Plate 1: Hager Qim, Malta. Photo: John David Mooney.

fact it was the first major work that they had ever commissioned from one of their own living artists. It did not last after the taxpayer's money had been spent: there was no object to see, touch, or even discern after the last performance, yet the city carried through the entire concept from start to finish. It should be said, I suppose, that Chicago is a city of Irish politicians who with their pragmatic management skills also possess a sense of poetry, and although the sculpture can no longer be seen, the emotional impact of the patterns of light is stored within the individual and collective psyche of the city and can be stirred by the visual stimuli of the environment which it once transformed.

If the artist of today wishes to speak with immediacy and effectiveness to the public, he must be sensitive to his audience, as well as to the complexities of his creative drive. I drew my inspiration for "LIGHT SPACE 77" from the standing stones and megaliths of the pre-Celtic world; yet, the audience in this case perceived this environmental light sculpture as part of their own space, just as temples were once constructed to achieve a consciousness of time, space, and order extending far beyond the people for whom the temple was built.

Richard Demarco introduced me to those spaces of the ancient world but for many years I had drawn upon the illuminated Irish manuscripts as a source for my painting and sculpture: the energy embodied in those manuscripts is also found in the architectural space of the standing stones. Conversely, the standing stones themselves occupy space which is not just architectural, nor are they merely a

Plate 2: "Light Space 77" Environmental Light Sculpture, Chicago. Photo: Mary Cairns.

collection of objects. They are about fears, mysteries, beliefs, and levels of consciousness which cannot be recorded in a tangible way.

"LIGHT SPACE" was not a static piece, but an open and expansive kinetic light sculpture, stretching along eight miles of shoreline, out over the water and six miles into the sky. At the time this work was being executed, Robert O'Driscoll and Richard Demarco were at the alignments of Carnac. The standing lines of that space and the standing lines of the piece in Chicago were one and the same, a coexistence in time and spirit. Light is about energy; energy derives from light. Place has its own magnetism. There is something magnetic about a location where a Christian church is built on the same spot as a megalithic or pagan temple. Standing stones, those at Hagar Qim in Malta for example, owe their location perhaps to the part they played in certain solar and lunar calculations some 4200 years ago, but they still possess the same mystery and presence and the same sense of being in touch with a spirit beyond ourselves, that they must have possessed in the beginning. In the case of Chicago, it could be said that the series of "Standing Stones" that constitute the city, though built for a different reason, began with the same impulse that stirred the early temple builders. The early French traders came to a sacred space which the Indians used as a source of water and fire and built a city on exactly the same site. However, instead of a group of stones built for a purpose which is mystical and spiritual, the traders and merchants of the past 100 years have built a series of stones, one taller than the next, trying to reach up to the materialistic, "relevant" statement about economics, which only brings us right back down to the ground again. No matter how tall the next building is built, it will never raise one up, and if it does raise the level of a certain type of consciousness, it cannot be a Celtic one.

In my light sculpture I attempted to connect that line of rocks to another line of stones in the universe through what some may call a very ephemeral "material": light. I attempted too to incorporate the same notion of water and rhythm that Daniel Burnham had in mind when he offered his plan for the City of Chicago in 1909. Burnham was in his own way as sensitive as the temple-builders to the space around the stones — in Burnham's case this was a sensitivity to the rhythm and reflection of light on water — but while the movement of people, change of light, and rhythm of the water helps his plan to work by day, at night, as the city glows with thousands of artificial lights, his park plan falls apart. Seldom do architects of today design their buildings using light as it is used in the Mediterranean folk tradition, or with the megalithic stones. Carnac generates an even greater mystery at night and St. Paul's Cathedral in Malta is illuminated at night by burning candles while the same surface by day accepts the sun as natural.

The light beams of "LIGHT SPACE 77" were my solution to a problem given to me by the City of Chicago, which was to do a piece for eight million people and in the process to extend their consciousness of the soul and of the city. Burnham's plan was his temple built to Lake Michigan, symmetrical certainly in the design, but only the design sequence to the north, adjacent to the river, was completed. I first drew small sketches using the extension of line to create light alignments in different positions eight miles to the south. From these sketches a model was built of a piece created to bring an entire city together, able to be seen from land and water, with light beams going six miles into the sky. Even the airlines announced, "Would you please look out your window, there's a sculpture in the sky, as we go by."

The piece actually began with riverboats down the Chicago River and searchlights placed on 350' long barges. The "Light Brigade," the artists and architects who comprised the community, created the sculpture, bringing together, like the temple builders, skills from many walks of life: architecture, engineering, economics, art. They rehearsed with flashlights according to directions which I had formulated in a manual, and they gathered each night to operate the searchlights. This again goes back to stones; two flints, i.e., carbon rods, being struck against each other to make light. Assisting the "Light Brigade" were the union electricians, who, accustomed as they were to operating searchlights, found themselves in a different ambience: out on barges and on land actively participating in the creation of a sculpture.

These standing lines of light moved every eight minutes, so many degrees radial and so many degrees azimuth. They did not rotate, but were a series of kinetic structures. Architects came from all over, saying that this was the perfect complement to the architecture of the city. I was concerned not only with the

Plate 3: "Zagreb Light Lines," Environmental Light Sculpture, Yugoslavia, 1979.

fourth dimension of time and space, but, as well, with two-dimensional activities — when there was a cloud cover, I could execute drawings in the sky. Imagine making a drawing on clouds with everybody able to watch the process. This space and these lines just didn't happen to come about; they evolved from works which I had been doing earlier. "Oriental Interlude" and "Return to the East" are both steel sculptures, line drawings in space — gleaming white, as they transform the ground plane into a kinetic page of their own shadows. "Springflow," also a white steel sculpture, placed at the entrance of the grounds to the Indianapolis Museum of Art, attempts to titillate the sky in the same way that these beams do.

Every night the Chicago sculpture was different. The programs were different; the lights themselves were placed in varying locations along the lakefront on each of the seven evenings, and the space never remained the same. I handled the whole event by radio control, as well as through the manuals: I had, therefore, the opportunity to rearrange the configuration, if I so chose. Sometimes when clouds came in, I would call: "Station 104, would you please move your light from 60 degrees radial to 20 degrees radial, and from 30 degrees azimuth to 90 degrees azimuth," thus beginning a four-mile drawing in the sky. As the light lines changed position, they moved very slowly around each other, creating circles like the temple below them, and the temple above them in the air. In his poem, "The Statues," Yeats wrote: "Pythagoras planned it. Why did the people stare?" There was even an aesthetic relationship between these lines of light and the masts of the sailboats in the harbour. Many of the familiar things of the city were invested with a new luminous presence: for a moment people perceived with an increased visual acuteness, a heightened consciousness of what had always been there.

It is my intention to continue to work with the environment, so that when one looks to land or sky one will perceive an expansion of possibilities, a new horizon, or the old familiar horizon with a new level of consciousness. That is my role.

NOTE

[1] At a recent Congressional hearing on the state of the arts in America, I was one of the two artists out of a plethora of museum directors, art administrators, etc. who were asked to provide material and testimony.

ASTERIX AGAINST THE ROMANS

DERRICK DE KERCKHOVE

Since its first appearance in 1961 in a French children's magazine named *Pilote*, *Asterix* has enjoyed a great success in France and abroad with readers young and old. The recent death of its creator, René Goscinny, was experienced by many Frenchmen as a personal loss. In France Asterix is a national hero, a mini-superman who exhibits specifically French characteristics. But the phenomenal distribution of the comic strips which narrate his adventures in some 20 languages, including Japanese, Chinese, Arabic and Turkish, surely indicates that these good humored Gauls have more to offer than a boost to France's self-respect. The *National Geographic Magazine* itself could not resist the urge to place the tiny Gallic village on the History map in its May 1977 issue, at the end of a remarkable survey of the Celtic world. This must be some sort of consecration.

Asterix and Obelix are more than Frenchmen: they are Gauls, and they are also more than Gauls, they are Celts. As Celts they belong to an order of life which is essentially different from the Judeo-Christian tradition and the Greco-Roman empire which together combine to form what is still known as the Western World. As Celts, not as Frenchmen, they incarnate for every reader, regardless of nationalities, the spirit of the Tribe, which throws everybody, including the Turks and the Japanese, back to a recent or extremely old past, the source of all myths.

The fundamental myth of this comic strip is the reverse of all those which are inspired by the spirit of conquest and aggression typical of the frontier, science-fiction, detective or war stories of the West. The single act of the Gauls is to resist invasion and cultural assimilation by anyone, but especially by the Romans. As in most comic strips based on a repetitive pattern, the formula is very simple: with a few exceptions, every story is made up of a different response to the various ploys attempted by Caesar or his officers to subdue this pocket of resistance to the Pax Romana.

On the surface, the figures of this essential drama are not very sophisticated. Among the Gauls, nobody, apart from the wise old druid, is exceptionally bright. Asterix himself, for all his cleverness, will resort more often to the magic potion which gives him superhuman strength, than to a real strategy. The Romans, on the contrary, are always subtle, crafty, calculating, well prepared, and they always lose. The Gauls are carefree and totally unpremeditated; their behavior and their social attitudes are depicted so as to present an image of freedom and spontaneity unfettered by the constraints of civilization.

As in all plastic expressions of mythical form, the allegorical intent is never far off. The Gauls stand for the eternal values of human community on a human scale, while the Romans project the image of an ephemeral social order imposed from without, and doomed ultimately to failure because of its total disregard for human needs. We are witnessing yet another performance of the Apollonian versus the

Dionysiac, or rather, the contest betwen two types of blends of both.

The figures operate on several levels. Some pertain mostly to the French experience; others have a more universal appeal. For the French, the popularity of Asterix' adventures is certainly rooted in the fact that the centralized Education Nationale, recommends at some point in a child's education the mandatory reading of Caesar's *Commentaries on the War of the Gauls.* The history of France proper starts at the time of Caesar's conquest. Thus the heroic resistance of Asterix' village stands for everything which, in "la France éternelle," escapes the determination of History. The spirit of resistance points to another rather obvious reason for the success of Asterix' saga: the French Resistance to the German occupation during the last War. Surprisingly enough, the Germans who appear in the stories as "les Goths" and speak only in gothic characters, are treated rather gently by the satire. In fact, more often than not, they are made to team up with the Gauls against the Romans, in the true spirit of the Common Market, a Celtic invention.

The attitude of the satirists with regard to basic antagonisms is very consistent; the Germans are not real enemies, they are a tribal rival. Caesar and his ubiquitous troops are another thing altogether. The Romans represent the common ground of grievances shared by all modern peoples from the first to the third World. The Romans, with all their traditional clichés of disciplined bureaucratic order and centralized control, support the insidious models of cultural assimilation, which amounts to a psychological colonisation. The hidden reference, though diffuse and masked by many layers of cultural experience over two millenia, might well be the American way of life. This could be the ground from which the Arab, the Turkish and the Chinese readers of Asterix get their laughs.

The French, of course, did not wait for the American models to try out their own brands of bureaucracy and industrial-military patterns. With the onset of print technology, such forms were given a tremendous amplitude and culminated in the Napoleonic code and in the Neo-Roman way of life fostered by the first and second Empire. The Romans of the Asterix adventures provide the framework for a satire of modern life. Instead of getting the same old story in new clothes, we are given a new story in very old clothes. The best method of discrediting new forms is to show that they are already old hat.

Electronic technology has introduced patterns of decentralization in many aspects of the American way of life which, like the Roman way of life, was based on widespread literacy. The effect of electric media and communications has been to change centralized bureaucracy into its correlative, the multinational corporation whose center is everywhere and whose margin is nowhere.

The historical Caesar used strategy, hardware and brute force to conquer the Gauls and annihilate the Celtic culture. The new Caesar of *Asterix* borrows his techniques from the multinational corporations: market research, development, manipulation of local governments, labor management, advertising and promotion, in fact all the subtle programming of the software revolution.

For example, in one of the best stories, *Le Domaine des dieux*, Caesar plans to gird the village of the Gauls with a modern development complex, with high rise apartment buildings, shopping centers, arenas, theatre, potion-tabernae (drug stores), etc . . . The effect of this strategy is to infiltrate the Gallic village with new fashions and introduce the Roman way of life; in short, by juxtaposition to turn the village into a slum by comparison with the new complex. The Gauls watch the erection of the first apartment building without opposing it too violently because they are amused by the Romans' manoeuvers. Back in Rome, Caesar makes use of modern promotion techniques to persuade a number of his fellow citizens to relocate in Northern Gaul. The new neighbourhood instantly turns every Gaul into a shopkeeper, churning out fish, groceries and antiques to supply the needs of the newcomers. Caesar's plan is working: fierce competition is driving the Gauls against each other in a spirit of hatred. But the old druid, Getafix, senses the danger and its cause, and puts an end to the nonsense by turning loose Cacofonix, the bard, on the high-rise dwellers. His singing is so atrocious that the Romans flee back to the eternal city. Then the druid throws a few magic acorns on the development site. They bloom immediately into fully mature trees. Thus the forest reconquers civilization as it should and as indeed it always did in the good old days.

The sociological analysis does not go very deep, but it reaches far enough to provide a commentary on this war which is waged by new technologies and environmental changes. The nature of such metamorphoses is essentially collective. The Gauls are a community and it is the community as hero which gives weight to the social satire.

The mythical nature of the Gallic Village is obvious: it is the incarnation of a frustration and also of a fulfilled ideal. The frustration leads to the ever-recurring Romantic "return to nature" and it expresses itself in a cheerful resistance against the spirit of organisation whenever it trespasses the "natural law" of brotherhood and tribal order. The ideal is expressed in the harmony of a social order where human proportions are preserved against the lures of fabricated needs. It is worth noting that every *Asterix* story ends in the same fashion, that is with the male population of the village sitting down to a huge collective feast around a round table. Ultimately the story does not lead to the glorification of the hero, but to the return of peace and security for the community. The Asterix Saga resembles that of our oldest folklore and the most ancient epic traditions in that it gives priority to the tribe over the individual figure.

The nature of the comic strip, which is a medium of low definition, is perfectly adapted to give shape to the diffuse tribal feeling people experience today. It is not an individualizing medium because it shuns perspective and is presented as a mosaic of bounding lines in two dimensions. Comic strips do not "hold up a mirror" to their readers, but they provide them with dynamic shapes. In fact one does not so much "read" a comic strip as "immerse" oneself in it. Young Frenchmen who are absorbed in contemplation of a page of Asterix' adventures, retrieve a sense of participation with their tribal past not only because of the heroic figures of Astérix and Obélix, not only because of the obvious tribal content of the stories, but mainly because their own identities melt away in the visual-tactile communion with the coloured page. Even in America, the comic strip turned out to be a tribal medium, dealing as it did for so long with Indians and cowboys, with cats and dogs and ducks and mice, and other species. The international success of Asterix' adventures may be due to the fact that they represent a stage at which the comic strip is coming into its own and finding its "true" nature: of being able to deal with something on the same scale as epic poetry. Indeed worldwide instances of political decentralization and resurgences of regional and local traditions in many countries demand new models and patterns of action. The spirit of rediscovery which, for instance, prompts us to probe our Celtic heritage, must develop for itself new attitudes. The stories of Astérix provide a link with the past because they present as familiar a ground which is in fact very remote. And they reach everybody. The power of the Celtic image as diffused through the medium of *Asterix* among all age groups, and all socio-cultural and linguistic grounds ought to give its creators, Goscinny and Uderzo, a status akin to that of bards in our worldwide tribe. They are the "drawers of tales", having adapted the tropes of the epic song to our visual bias and translated dance into colour. And they have made it fun. Very Celtic.

THE CELTIC SPIRIT IN THE NEW AGE: AN ASTROLOGER'S VIEW

ALEXANDER BLAIR-EWART

The Celt is an original European who has never excelled at most of the things for which European civilization is renowned: the evolution of the state, political and economic refinement, and organized religion. In the beginning of Celtic racial life, its collective spirit was a dominant force in Europe, with Druidic mystery schools at the core of its existence.

Because of its Druidic past, Celtic culture was, of all the cultural groups of early Europe, the most advanced spiritually and the best equipped in an inner sense for the encounter with Christianity. In the Celtic world, Christianity made its first converts from among the best Celts, the living archetypes of the people, the Druids. For the other groups, this was not the case, and a pre-Christian Druidism persisted in a waning form for many centuries, with Christianity making exoteric converts from among the less accomplished members of these peoples.

Through the advanced Christian Druids, the esoteric Celtic Christian Brotherhoods sprang to life, and the whole inner force of the Celtic people became guided by this mystical Christianity. These Druidic initiates withdrew to some extent from the folk life of the people in order to complete the profound transformation that was taking place in their souls. Different brotherhoods had different needs in this respect and so several monastic streams were established with Living Christ initiates at their head. In this way the Celtic people made an immense sacrifice of their racial folk life to the higher embodiment of Christianity, a spiritual path which transcends all racial and national barriers.

The extraordinary energy and courage of the early Celts became focused in a spiritual quest to forge a direct relationship with the Living Christ, and this is an important factor in our understanding of the inner spiritual vitality which the later Celtic missionaries demonstrated in their revitalization of Christian life in Europe. At no time did Celtic missionaries concern themselves with the organizational aspects of the Church in Europe. Working in conjunction with other impulses, which can be traced back to Greek social organization, the Church was re-established as the framework of European civilization. Centuries prior to this period, the Celtic Christian initiates had committed themselves to a higher task: to keep the Living Christ manifest in the world.

When the Celtic Christian missionaries encountered European life in the Dark Ages, many of the followers of their pre-Christian centres of Druidism were now converted to Christianity and pagan Druidism fell deeper into the obscurity of regional tribal life. These pagan societies became the secret Druidic witchcraft cults which are apparently still in existence, but in a completely degenerate form.

From the point of view of the esoteric Celtic Christian initiate, the external form of Christian organization and even its sacred texts are of little importance, except for the Gospel of St. John. The esoteric Christian sees the life of Christ and the mystery of Golgotha not as a teaching to be studied and compared to other teachings but as a series of actions of a divine nature performed by the Christ Being and literally repeated in the life of the esoteric Christian disciple. It need not surprise us that the historical remains of this living tradition are sparse. We see the tradition expressed in the Grail legend and in the much misunderstood Rosicrucian teachings. As distinct from the much more visible Church of Peter or Rome, it is sometimes called the Church of John, the Church of Peter being the outer exoteric church and the Church of John being the inner esoteric church. Esoteric Christians may grow up as devout exoteric Christians: the outer form is essential. While the Church of Peter is an external historical institution, the Church of John is that everchanging vital community of Christ initiates in the world. If the Church of John is not obviously visible in the world, like the Church of Peter, where is it? And in any case, what is esoteric Christianity and what part does it play in a Celtic revival?

The most recent Dark Age (a materialistic one this time) reached its peak in 1850. By 1875, a mystical occult outpouring was taking place in Europe and North America: the activities of the Rosicrucians; the founding of the Theosophical Society, which was to count among its members AE and W. B. Yeats; and the occult societies. Yeats and AE recognized the importance of Theosophical revelation as a source of spiritual inspiration and guidance. It is well known that the Dublin Lodge of Theosophists had a significant influence on the revival of Celtic mythology; also, perhaps, Celts were at the time in a high state of receptivity to spiritual revelation.

The mystical occult outpouring at the turn of the century was largely a replay of all the occult traditions of the world, possible in Europe because Europe had embraced Christianity. It was also a resurgence of the spirit which animated ancient Celtic Druidism before the reception of the Christ mystery. The Church of John in nineteenth-century Europe was to take one more step to ensure the transmission of esoteric Christianity to the new age. For a true esotericism is never merely the preservation of arcane traditions and ritual forms but is the constant rebirth of man's spiritual heart. The reawakening of esoteric knowledge is the response of enlightened initiates to the real spiritual needs of contemporary culture.

One of the ways into esoteric Christianity has been revealed in *Christianity as Mystical Fact* by Rudolph Steiner, founder of the Anthroposophical Society (at Dornach in Switzerland). *Christianity as Mystical Fact* is the first of a series of spiritual teachings which makes clear the same path followed by our Celtic mystical ancestors, but presented in a way which is intelligible to twentieth-century man.

In the twentieth century, in this dark age of technology and materialism, esoteric Christianity has become as elusive as it once was in a former dark age of dying empire and savagery. Esoteric Christianity is the undying Light of the world, the most exalted spiritual revelation, the deepest mystery of the ages. Ancient Celtic man turned to it in complete freedom from a spiritual tradition as rich and profound, though in a different way, as the ancient Judaic life through which Christianity entered the world. There has never been anything compulsive or mandatory about esoteric Christianity. It is the free choice of free individuals, and this is part of the reason why it has a future as the spiritual path of emancipated humanity. A Celtic humanity still knows the meaning of love, and the action of love in culture, which is compassion. A higher light shines in Celtic poetry, language, music, a richer mystical dimension.

The current Celtic revival demands that we know, in modern terms, what a Celt is. If a people are to be defined by the best that is embodied in them, then the definition of a Celt would be — an esoteric Christian. Because Celtic life has been an alternative to everything that has been going on in Western civilization, its revival could be taken as an indication that the spiritual life of the West is about to be revitalized. It may be given once more to Celtic culture to carry a living Christianity out into the world. In the same way as the Celtic missionaries recognized no social or cultural barriers in their resolve to uplift the spiritual life of early Europe, so esoteric Christianity must address itself to the total spectrum of life, and particularly to North America, where the Celtic Revival seems to be gathering momentum.

THE REBIRTH OF THE CELTIC FOLK SOUL

MARIANNA LINES

THE CELTIC SOUL reaches back into the distant past of a golden civilization in tune with the earth and the rhythms of the universe. This folk soul was the channel for ageless, eternal wisdom, and through the early Celtic people and their predecessors the pulse of life flowed. The stones were their altars, their sanctuaries, their sighting points for terrestrial and planetary alignments; the trees, their allies, possessing special properties of strength and healing. The quality of life was enriched by communion with the Goddess, a feminine spirit who dwelt in the rivers, lochs, and hilltops.

People around the earth are now returning to the ancient sites, restoring holy wells, rediscovering the invisible threads and lines that link centres of power, and delving into the unconscious, the etheric worlds beyond the physical. They live in small groups or nuclei within larger communities:

> In celebrating the festivals and through seeking the ancient sites of the standing stones, holy wells, etc., we can reconnect with the living forces of the Earth, and come to feel once again the Earth planet as a living being, revealed as the Earth Goddess.[1]

Many people are feeling this reawakening of a new kind of consciousness, whether it be called Celtic, New Age, or by some other label. But it feels as if a higher state is beginning to be experienced, both on a physical and a spiritual level.

The Findhorn Community is one of those places of awakening. It lies in northeast Scotland in the heart of ancient Pictland, where the early Picts once mingled with the Celts. Findhorn is said to be a power centre where an ancient force was once dominant within a network of crossing ley lines, perhaps where a sacred site may also have stood. It is now a 'reactivated' power point, a living center where new forms of lifestyle, of living cooperatively, of energy, of healing and the arts are being pioneered.

Findhorn forms an important link in a whole chain of activated power centers, and is connected with other New Age centres and groups doing similar work around the world, forming a new network of light. We are integrating the faculty of a more feminine perception into the oneness and wholeness of life. Our greater work is to prepare a soil for the new age to grow, a new womb of the earth capable of nurturing a body of mankind that is fully aligned with the light.

We are beginning to remember: by returning to our roots within the earth, we can renew those links with our primeval mother, and treat her as the Earth Goddess she is, learning to live with her seasons in a cyclical, ritual relationship as one would with a lover. By bringing spirit down into matter, thereby spiritualizing matter, we can work towards healing the Earth, transforming it into a new and good place to live.

The Celtic Renaissance is happening as a subcultural revolution. We are

Plate 1: The Celtic Folk-Soul. Acknowledgement: Alice Rigan and *Celtic Renaissance*, The Thule Press, Findhorn.

beginning to return to the moon to find and nourish our power. We are feeling more rhythmical in our music and art, more meditative in our spiral rituals. The subtle changes in society, as women regain their power and men become more feminine in their sensitivity, are bringing about a renewal of energies that are healing and nourishing to the earth. As Anthony Roberts has written in *Geomancy*:

> The hermetic maxim AS ABOVE, SO BELOW is the key geomantic equation and the complexities thus engendered are only the framework for the complementary spiritual beauties unlocked from within the human soul when it is linked in harmony with the living earth.[2]

Shifts in consciousness can occur only when the energy level is sufficiently heightened to allow communion with another energy. Perhaps with an increased awareness of our intuitive-receptive feminine nature, we shall be able to see more clearly, move so much higher, and develop so many more dimensions of peoples' consciousness that ultimately we can heighten the whole vibration of the earth.

The rebirth of the Celtic folk soul begins in oneself, and in others, when we listen to the earth and then begin to heal ourselves. Only then can we begin to understand ancient wisdom, as we undertake the perennial quest of the Holy Grail towards Wholeness, Light and Harmony with the spheres and the earth.

NOTES

[1] Adam McLean, *The Four Fire Festivals* (Edinburgh 1979).

[2] Anthony Roberts, *Geomancy* (Glastonbury 1981).

THE MYTHIC PAST AND THE PRESENT MOMENT[1]

WILLIAM IRWIN THOMPSON

I did not want to come to this "Celtic Consciousness" festival and read a paper, because I think that Celtic culture is nothing if not oral: to stand here reading a paper and intoning footnotes as if this were the normal academic conference would be, for me, to commit the most grievous of Anglo-Saxon acts. So I would rather talk, and try to present one way in which history is seen from a Celtic point of view.

Although I am an American and am centuries removed from the Celtic homelands, I was raised in an affirmation of the Celtic Consciousness. With Welsh and Scots Irish on my father's side, and Southern Irish on my mother's side, I grew up hearing expressions like "black as Cromwell's heart" or "perfidious Albion," and knew that whatever history was, it was a matter of passionate importance. Of course, as Barry Fell indicates in *America B.C.*, we should not restrict our identification of the Celts to the British Isles, for the Celts were as international in the early days as they are now; indeed Ireland was a rather late discovery of the Celts and certainly not the fountainhead and aboriginal source. What is essential to the Celtic consciousness is the spirit of being an exile on this earth and of being in constant search for the Blessed Isles or the Holy Grail, and it is from this point of view that I would like to look at history.

I think that for an Irishman history is nothing if not the performance of myth, and this is perhaps what separates the Irish from the rest of the world, for in our search for a transcendent reality it's very difficult for us to understand that we're not living in a novel, a legend, or a myth. It's difficult for us to take "reality" very seriously and to believe that the world is made out of matter, a substance which can only be described by weighing, measuring, and calculating. We are continually told that this is the case, but we never can truly accept it, and sometimes we can muscle up rather brilliant rejections of scientific materialism, as, for example, in the case of Bishop Berkeley. For a Celt the world is made out of music, and if he's not listening very hard to the engineer or the stockbroker, it's because he's hearing a different kind of music from the trees or the wind.

If, in the Irish sense of history, history is the performance of myth, then history is the embodiment of transcendence; within the limitations of time and space one hears the fullness of the music of infinity and tries to bear witness to that single instant in every seemingly isolated context. If we begin to look at history as a local context in a much larger one, then the conequences that follow from that shift of perspective are quite profound.

Now if you look at Irish history, or, perhaps, I should personalize it to say when *I* look at Irish history, I see two great dramatic acts that seem to me to be the quintessential examples of history as the performance of myth. One of these is the great period of the Dark Ages when Irish monks created the foundation for the whole civilization of Western Europe. This monastic movement has been beautifully expressed in Irish scolarship by Brendan Lehane in a lovely little book called, *The Quest of Three Abbots.*

I might say in passing that it was this book which inspired me to quit the university and to seek out another way to live the life of the mind rather than in the institutional routines of the academic establishment. Perhaps it's a *fey* and Irish thing to do — to take ideas that seriously that you end up living in a different way, but it's something that every Irish Catholic heretic learns early, for if you're going to quarrel with the Holy Roman Catholic Church, that colossus of Western Civilization with its Sistine Chapel and its Masses by Palestrina, and you know that the stakes are your own immortal soul and that if you're wrong you're going to fry in Hell for all eternity, then you're going to take ideas very seriously indeed. It's simply not enough to do research and add another monograph to the shelf: you have to find a way to bring eternal ideas into our world of time. *The Quest of Three Abbots* captures the mystique of sacred scholarship, and is itself an inspiring book, and had a profound influence on me. His chronicle of the Dark Ages understands how those monks were living a myth, and even in the very writing of the book the scholarship itself becomes a literary embodiment of the spirit of the material he was dealing with, the land of saints and scholars. And that's the ideal for Irish Studies: the writing of our history should always be literary. Let others get caught up in the idolatry and short-lived vanities of the American social "sciences"; let them have their charts and graphs and quantitative measurements of this and that, but for us history should be literature; it should bear witness to the spoken tongue, to the mysteries of language, and if it does it will outlast the idols of the day.

The second movement that seems to me to express history as the performance of myth is, of course, the Irish Literary Renaissance. In my own first book, *The Imagination of an Insurrection: Dublin, Easter 1916*, I tried to show how for the revolutionaries of 1916 local history was seen in the light of romantic myth. The recovery of the past in the romantic scholarship of Standish James O'Grady ignited the imagination of a whole generation. To try to understand this little insurrection which began the process of dismembering the British Empire, you had to do more than talk about the Great Strike of 1913 or Lloyd George's budget; you had to do more than invoke American behavioral science or European dialectical materialism; to understand that insurrection you had to understand the role of the imagination in history. Because it is precisely the Imagination that catches the music of infinity and makes the individual bear witness to it in his own moment of time. Without understanding the Imagination, you cannot even perceive what is going on in history.

So there are these two great movements in Irish history: one lays the foundation for the civilization of Western Europe, the other initiates the dismemberment of the planetary Empire of Great Britain. These two movements which frame the beginning and ending of Western Civilization are quintessentially Irish movements. As AE would say, they are the politics of eternity against the politics of time. We Irish have more energy at beginnings and endings; the stuff in the middle is rather boring, for it's all a matter of running the shop, "the routinization of charisma," and there are other people who can do all that so much better than we can. The Swiss can make better watches and the Japanese can make better cars; it's for the Irish to search for other things to do and be.

Now, in the first movement in the Dark Ages, the Roman Imperial civilization was rejected, and in the other, the British industrial civilization. In each case it is a rejection of Empire, a rejection of *power* by those giving faith to *authority*, a rejection of idolatry in favour of the transcendent. In these two movements of the Celtic Consciousness, I think that another more mystical vision of human culture came close to touching earth. There was a moment when it seemed possible that another vision of culture besides the Imperial vision could come about. But that was only for a moment, for as we all know, despite all the work of the saints and scholars, the Irish Church lost and the Roman Imperial Church triumphed.

In the Synod of Whitby in 664 the Roman ideal of Empire was victorious and the political arguments of Wilfrid won the day. Colman went back to Lindisfarne and then withdrew to that magical center of the Celtic Church, Iona. The mystical Church of John would continue to retreat over the centuries as the Church of Peter consolidated its holdings in the British Isles. In the showdown between these two churches there was more at stake than simply tonsure and the date of Easter. The Celtic Church invoked the mystical and apocalyptic St. John as the source of its authority; it was not a church of cities and bishops, but a rural church of monasteries and abbots. The Celtic Church was decentralized, shamanistic, and simple; the Church of Rome was centralized, hierarchical, complex, and worldly. In the battle between the two churches was the Old Testament battle of the prophets against the priests. But the English king was afraid of St. Peter who was to await his arrival at the gates of heaven, and so he threw his secular power behind Rome. The good guys lost.

Now in the Irish Literary Renaissance the good guys lost as well. The Imperial vision of power and industrial technology triumphed over the visions of the mystics and poets. The British of Manchester and Birmingham got the Americans of Detroit and Pittsburgh to advance their imperial vision all over the world. But failure is quintessentially an Irish experience, so whether we're talking about St. Colman at Whitby or AE and the Cooperative Movement, we're talking about how the good guys lose. The romantic Ireland of AE, Yeats, and Synge fades away like the mystical Church of John, and Dublin strives to become an Irish version of Houston, Texas.

In these two movements, the monastic movement and the Literary Renaissance, the mystical vision of another kind of human culture had to re-ascend. It had come close to touching the earth, but human society was not ready to receive it, and so it had to withdraw and await the end of Western Civilization. In these two movements you have a mythic confrontation of authority against power, mystical vision against worldly empire. A tiny and powerless culture confronts a colossal society in what the anthropologists would call "a nativistic movement." Whether it is Moses rejecting Egypt, or in the cases of the Mahdi, Louis Riel, and Patrick Pearse, the tribal leader confronting the British Empire, it is all a case of an affirmation of community (*gemeinschaft*) and a rejection of the alienation of a technological civilization (*gesellschaft*). From my limited point of view, it's a case of the good guys versus the bad guys, and the good guys always lose.

Even when the good guys win, they end up by defeating themselves and becoming exactly like the enemy they once fought. Moses tries to lead the Hebrews into the promised land, but once there the Hebrews try to build their own little Egypt with their own pyramids. King Solomon becomes another Pharaoh and so the prophets of the desert have to come in to rail against the rich and worldly Jews, as once Moses railed against the imperial Egyptians. In much the same way, Yeats, Synge, and A. E. railed against industrial materialism, but for all that, the modern Irish have become sophisticated and worldly, and now the Harvard Business School is more important to them than all the Irish mist of the Celtic Twilight.

So the good guys always lose, but there is a peculiar kind of revenge built into defeat. Success in this world is failure in another. In triumphing, empire inherits its own contradictions. When the Roman Church triumphed, with a bishop in every city responsible to the bishop of bishops in the city of cities, the Church cashed in its chips to become an empire, and no empire can last. Even Pope Paul said: "It seems as if the Church is destined to die." Something went out of Christianity when it rejected the Church of John in favour of the Church of Peter, and the Church is inheriting the full meaning of that rejection.

If you live like an empire, you must die like an empire. The British Empire is dead, and now New York, the capital of multinational corporate enterprise, is falling apart. I know it well because I live in the decaying heart of the city. The world capital of Empire is bankrupt in more ways than one. Now Dublin is trying to catch up, but that is the pathetic situation of a Dublin or a Teheran. If you're at the bottom or the middle of the ladder, struggling to make it to the top, you think the ladder is secure; but the view from the top is much better, and those who have already made it know that the system is falling, that the person at the top has lost his grip and that the whole thing is about to fall. The most powerful people at the top, say, for example, the Rockefellers, have a good view from the top, but the *parvenus* of Dublin, struggling to make it, cannot see that they have come too late in the history of industrial civilization. When they get to the top they are going to become rather bitter that it's all being snatched away from them right at the moment when they finally made it.

This sort of thing has happened before. In the first phase of the collapse of Mayan civilization the people kept on building pyramids, for the people at the periphery hadn't quite got the news that it was all over at the centre. Eventually, the periphery catches up with the centre: Dublin catches up with New York, and it all comes down together. So whenever I see a new bank going up in Manhattan, like the Citicorp Center, I remember how they built pyramids during the collapse of Mayan civilization, and marvel at the fantasies of those who command "the real world."

It is not surprising, therefore, that the poor Irish are trying to get in on the culture of wealth; it's sad, but not surprising. I suppose before the collapse of industrial civilization, the last freeway probably will be built from Dublin to Shannon, the last Holiday Inn will be built on top of Knocknarea with a lovely view of Yeats's Ben Bulben, and the last Playboy Club and casino will be built on one of the Aran Islands. If we look over Irish history, and see that the good guys always lose, and that loss and failure are basic themes in the Celtic Consciousness, then none of it is surprising at all.

Now in winning at the Synod of Whitby, the Roman Church shut something out of Christianity, something really important, and they would do that again and again: in the Albigensian crusade, in the Inquisition, in the Counter-Reformation. I think the Church of Peter signed its own death warrant when it expelled the Church of John. If you look at the end of the Gospel of John, you'll see that Jesus says to Peter, "Feed my sheep." Peter's is to be the practical job of looking after the flock. Peter then looks over his shoulder and sees John coming along and asks Jesus about him, and Jesus answers him by saying: "If I will that he tarry till I come, what is that to thee? Follow thou me." So we see very clearly in the Gospel that there are two churches, two dispensations. One goes down into history and is responsible for institutionalization and the creation of worldly forms, the other moves to the side of history to bear witness to the truth of myth — always at the edge of the world, never in the centres of power. The relationship between the periphery and the centre is the relationship between the Celtic world at the periphery and Rome at the centre of the world. The Church of John was extremely important, but the tragedy of Christianity is that it was entirely shut out and the esoteric traditions were lost. Christianity, unlike Buddhism, broke the chain in the transmission of the Dharma. In a Zen monastery the monks chant the names of their lineage all the way back to Buddha, and so the chain is unbroken and one illuminated Roshi appoints another illuminated Roshi and so on down through history. In Buddhism the esoteric tradition was not lost; in the West esoteric Christianity was wiped out, first by synod, then by persecution. In Zen Buddhism the head of the monastery is not simply a pious man; he is an illuminated being who has gone through a shamanistic crisis that has torn him apart and put him back together in a wholly new way. Because Buddhism did not sell out its esoteric traditions for worldly power, Buddhist monasticism is still alive and well, and still helping to create culture in much the same way as the ancient Irish monasteries helped to create culture during the Dark Ages. In comparing Buddhism to Christianity, it is hard not to feel the pain of just what Christianity, and all of Christian Civilization, lost. Something came very close to touching the earth with Columba, and Aidan, and Cuthbert. And something came close again with AE and Yeats. But we failed them, and now in the remaining years of this second millennium A.D. we are going to discover just what that loss means.

We failed; we missed our chance, and now we have to wait until the next opening, but in esoteric history the trains only run once every thousand years or so. Another Atlantis must sink before the vision of another kind of human culture can descend within human reach. AE and Yeats could see all this because they were seers; they could see beyond the vanities of societal definitions of reality to what lies behind and beyond history. Voltaire was right when he said that history is the lie commonly agreed upon. Most of the behavior in a society is built upon the common lie, but to see the limits of the lie one has to move out to the edge — from Rome to the Celtic West, from *fin de siècle* Paris to the Aran Islands. To discover that history is the lie commonly agreed upon, it is not enough simply to do historical research. Research will show you that David Hume's history of Ireland is a lie, but what then? Write another lie to fight his? That is certainly what some of the Irish nationalists who disliked Yeats hoped to do. No, if one goes far enough, then the process of discovering the truth is not simply research, it is initiation. The education of a Columba or a Cuthbert, an AE or a Yeats, does not come from research *into* history, but the re-*vision*ing *of* our historical condition.

The seer is a person who sees that most people are like fish caught in pools at low tide. They swim in their puddles and forget that every 5,124 years or so, a new tide comes in and the puddle is reconnected to the immensity of the sea. (I'm taking my numbers from the mystical calendar of the Maya). The task of the seer is to bear witness to the truths of the sea, to keep up the cultural memory, through myth and legend, of the greatness of the ocean. So when you're living in a puddle and have forgotten the sea, and you've built up a nice and tidy world-view on solid things like the Papacy or Wall Street, it's the task of an AE or a Yeats to negate all that, to lift us beyond our puddle-vision to the sea and the stars.

What these artists, visionaries, and saints are all involved in is the resacralization of culture. The sacred reconnects the part to the whole, the part to the universe. The profane is that which has become loose, fallen off, or been broken off from the whole. With those pieces people try to build up a thing called "reality," but it's always a hodge-podge of fragments. Science, Marxism, or any zealous ideological movement, tries to connect fragment to fragment and then tries to hold it together with spit or sweat or other people's blood, but it always comes apart sooner or later. The more mystical way is to realize that you can't force it. The fish with a memory of the ocean cannot reconnect his puddle to the sea. He can only speak of oceans and wait for the tide — and that's quite a different role from the unbending revolutionary who is going to put everything together in an egotistical solution. The impersonal vision of an AE or Yeats is quite different from the viewpoint of a Michael Collins.

In this sense, let us turn our thoughts to the larger sea. What does the Celtic Consciousness, that esoteric tradition that is kept up from one sinking Atlantis to another, have to say about our present moment? It seems to me that if we look at our present moment we can see that our institutions have been built upon a description of reality, and that description is now becoming increasingly inadequate. We are growing aware that our puddles are becoming flooded, that there is a larger ocean beyond our definitions, but we simply don't know what to do about it. The first response is to hold on tight to our institutions and hope that the flood will go away.

In the sixties and seventies the young played with revolution and cultural change, but when their television antics in Chicago were taken seriously at Kent State in 1970, they stopped putting flowers into the ends of the rifles of the National Guard soldiers, cut their hair, and went back to law school. The boom economy of the sixties, which had helped to sustain a mood of Dionysian play, disappeared, taking all sorts of academic jobs and fellowships with it, and a new Apollonian mood of sobriety and resposibility descended on the country. All across North America an entire generation of the young suddenly all wanted to go to law school or med school. The economic recession and energy crisis had sent people scurrying for cover in institutions. When the economy of these institutions collapses, then these people will look to the State to save them and will gladly support any form of emergency authoritarian government which promises to help them make it through the eighties.

When institutions have become monolithic and uncreative, you need cultural enzymes that are small, highly mobile, but effective in bringing larger entities together, or breaking down dead matter. The original Lindisfarne was an enzyme which helped to break down the dead matter of the old Graeco-Roman civilization in order to transform it into a curriculum for a newly emerging civilization. So what you have in entities like Pythagoras's Academy at Crotona, Ficino's Academy at Florence, Lindisfarne in Northumbria, or Yeats's Abbey Theatre in Dublin are not permanent institutions, but cultural enzymes that can interact with the larger institutions of civilization as a whole. (Of course, sometimes when the founder dies or moves on, the enzyme slips out of sight and what remains is a new institution, and such is the case with Yeats's Abbey Theatre.)

If one looks out across the historical landscape of our civilization now, it seems to me that there are many tiny and seemingly insignificant enzymes at work within the organism of culture as a whole. I am going to focus on three such enzymes, not because they are overwhelmingly important, but simply because they are of interest to me. If we look back to the time of AE or Yeats, and consider all the things we have been honoring in this festival, we can see that we are considering many things that would have been seen as rather silly in their own time, things like the occult or the revival of Irish. At the time many of us would have had a good laugh and in doing so have overlooked an interesting historical transformation; we need therefore, to be humble and open enough to realize that many of the things we might be inclined to laugh at now may be having an effect that we cannot now perceive. The three places that I would like to consider are Findhorn in Scotland, the Research Into Lost Knowledge Organization (or RILKO) in London, and my own Lindisfarne Association in New York.

Findhorn is a small spiritual community in the north of Scotland, and one of the things that this community has tried to do is, in effect, to revive animism. They have, in an outrageously anti-materialist fashion that would have appealed to Yeats, begun to talk to the fairies, the little people, the elementals of plants, and angels. But they have not turned their back on technology; in fact, they have their own electronics and recording studio and a rather modern printing shop. They have taken the pre-industrial world view, the Fairy faith in Celtic lands, and combined it with a meta-industrial world view of the age of electronics. I suspect that their combination of the opposites of mysticism and electronics is very likely to be the wave of the future. After all, the Protestant Ethic and the Spirit of Capitalism brought the opposites of religion and technology together in a way appropriate for an industrial society, so perhaps mysticism and electronics are more appropriate for a truly *post*-industrial world. (Certainly, if we look at the case of another Celt, Governor Edmund G. Brown of California, we do seem to see a weird combination of space colonies, computer chip companies, and Zen Buddhism.) Both the atomic physicist and the ecologist are telling us that the world view of the industrial materialist is false and culturally inappropriate, so if we are looking around for another way to look at nature and culture, then Findhorn is a fascinating experiment.

Mysticism is to electronic society what romanticism was to industrial society. In the nineteenth century the technologists cut down the trees to build railroad ties and the poets went out to compose poems about nature. The recovery of nature in romanticism is part of the phenomenology of industrial society. Mysticism provides maps of consciousness for a cybernetic society in which information is more basic than objects or material. When you miniaturize technology down to the scale of a computer chip, you re-adjust the whole relationship between culture and nature, for the trees can once again become larger and louder than our machines. Through the miniaturization of technology, we can dismantle the old industrial factory-system, and return to nature in a "New Alchemy" of science and mysticism. The return of animism in communities like Findhorn is thus a fascinating experiment in the best Celtic tradition.

The second group, Research into Lost Knowledge Organization, is not a community but an association of scholars interested in, most particularly, the megalithic culture of ancient Europe. In the upstairs exhibition gallery of this lecture hall there is a collection of photographs of the standing stones and stone circles of the British Isles.[2] Through the work of the most well-known member of RILKO, Alexander Thom, we now know that the geometry expressed in these circles is quite complex. A good thousand years before Egypt or Sumer, the scientist/priests of Western Europe were constructing ellipses and pythagorean triangles, calculating the positions of the heavenly bodies, and making predictions on forthcoming eclipses: all of this without leaving behind any evidence that they had writing or lived in cities. Since we define civilization in terms of literacy and urban life, it is hard for us to recognize a culture which has little use for either —

hard, that is, for the English, for the Irish can remember that in the Dark Ages there were no cities, only monasteries and the wild countryside. It would seem that this relationship of a priestly élite to an indigenous rural population repeats a pattern set in the West of Europe as early as the fifth millennium B.C. Whoever these priestly astronomers of the megaliths were, their knowledge of the stars was beyond anything we would have believed possible even a few years ago. The archaeological establishment has resisted the work of Thom, but since he is a retired professor of engineering from Oxford, he has known how to amass a wealth of exact measurements, the weight of which has forced the experts like R. J. C. Atkinson to back down on his conviction that Stonehenge had been built by "howling savages."

It is understandably hard for a culture like ours, which is built upon the industrial domination of nature, to understand a more pythagorean culture in which the cultural act is always connected to a cosmological vision. What we see is what we are, and so Professor Atkinson looks at Stonehenge and sees a monument to celebrate the power of a local tribal chieftain and frighten the natives into submission with a little hocus-pocus of the sun peeping through a window. And yet if we are going to move beyond industrial values of domination in our ecological crisis, then the vision of another culture is a most helpful escape from the limits of our own world view. Is there another way of knowing nature, a sacred way in which religion and science are not opposed to one another? Is this "lost knowledge' a once and future heritage? If we learn from the work of Alexander Thom on stone circles or Keith Critclow on Chartres and Glastonbury, then architecture can have more cosmic dimensions than is expressed in the industrial mentality of the international style of the Bauhaus. The architecture of banks dominates the skyline of all our modern cities, from New York to Toronto to Melbourne to London. The World Trade Center sums it all up. If this imperial mentality has its way, then we will all end up inside the tight metal containers of a space colony; but if the Celtic Consciousness has its way, then the ecological crisis will be averted, not by treating the earth as Kleenex to be used once and thrown away, but by the transformation of the earth through the discovery of a sacred lost knowledge.

The last group I wish to consider is another attempt to work for the sacralization of culture in the recovery of lost knowledge, and that is my own experiment in New York, the Lindisfarne Association. When I was a teacher of humanities at M.I.T., it began to be apparent to me that the roots of the ecological crisis were in education. Scientists and engineers were being taught to focus on their problem-sets in class and to forget about the larger philosophical issues. And even the history of science was being distorted in the manufacture of scientists and engineers. No M.I.T. student was told that the Schrödinger of the famous Schrödinger equation had been a Vedantist, that Heisenberg was a Pythagorean, that Einstein was a mystic who proclaimed that the state of contemplative rapture of the divine was the highest state of knowledge. The whole mystical tradition of science, from

Kepler to Einstein, was being erased in an attempt to merchandise science to Washington and the great corporations. History, once again, was becoming the lie commonly agreed upon. It was like a return of the showdown between the Church of John and the Church of Peter, and just as the mystical Church of John was over-run by the imperial ecclesiasticism of Rome, so the mystical and pythagorean science of the West was being over-run by the imperial and worldly orientation of power in that Vatican of technology, M.I.T. I realized that if that vision of science as power were to triumph there would be nothing left of the earth, neither culture nor nature. So I thought it would be worthwhile to set up a special centre for science *and* mysticism within M.I.T. itself; in this special college, the mystical roots of the scientific tradition could be explored. My idea proved but a personal fantasy, totally out of phase with the M.I.T. of the time. The Institute was much more interested in using social science to win the war in Viet Nam, or in celebrating the new power of economics as a science with Nobel laureate, Paul Samuelson; or in preparing new systems of management for the direction of an advanced technological society.

So I quit and began my wandering in search of other modes of life for the humanities. And in that wandering I began to see that the humanists were the new Indians caught in the path of an advancing technological empire. Just as once the tribal Irish had confronted the British Empire, or once the Indians had confronted the railroads, so now the humanist was the atavist. And just as once some Irish or Indians were willing to sell their birthrights for a mess of pottage, so now many humanists were willing to become technocratic specialists of the new behavioral sciences. The forces of modernization, which had been perfected in the Third World, were brought home to bear upon the humanities. Through the power of the professional educational administrator, the humanities were to be subjected to modernization and transformed into relevant social sciences. With behavioral modification practised on children in elementary schools, and with the universities subject to the best post-industrial management techniques, the technological society was shaping up quite nicely.

Who was to say no to all of this? The Church had lost its vision a long time ago; if it raised its voice in protest, it was only heard as the high squeaking peep of an antique maiden aunt. Universities like Harvard, which should have been the places where literature, history, and the love of wisdom (*philosophia*) were strongest, had become the launching pads that put the new generation of politicians into orbit. Rather than being a line of civilized defense against technological empire, Harvard had become the centre of the apologists for the technological society, and men like B. F. Skinner and E. O. Wilson had become the exemplars for all others to copy. Harvard and M.I.T. led the way and York or the University of Toronto struggled to follow.

More than anyone, the humanist, the historian or philosopher, should have been the one to object, for his vision of the whole should have enabled him to see what was going on. Humanists, however, no longer had a vision of the whole; they had become specialists. No one was left to bear witness to the ocean when life had been reduced to a puddle. In the new university, you either were an expert in puddle-research, or you were fired. What was there to do, but swim to the edge of the puddle and wait for the tide?

So, I quit the university and set up Lindisfarne as an affirmation of the archetype of the sacred school in which intellection and meditation were brought together. Since I believed that the esoteric school was a miniaturization of the exoteric civilization, that Sufiism was a miniaturization of Islam; Yoga, a miniaturization of Vedic civilization, and Zen, a miniaturization of East Asian civilization, I thought that by bringing Sufiism, Yoga, and Zen together with esoteric Christianity and Pythagorean science, a new esoteric school could be created that could be the miniaturization for the new global civilization to come. The school could become the seed with its new genetic message packed into a tiny space. But, of course, Lindisfarne wasn't the seed, for only God can create a seed; it was simply an enzyme helping to bring the larger molecules together in new combinations. So Lindisfarne brought together the epistemology of Gregory Bateson with the ecology of John Todd and both with the decentralist economics of E. F. Schumacher. These men became Lindisfarne Fellows and Lindisfarne became a gathering place where individuals from the esoteric traditions (or with credentials from the exoteric world) could come together to re-*vision* culture and relate to the crisis of our civilization by reaching up to try to bring down that vision once again. It was the Church of John confronting the Church of Peter once more, with Harvard and M.I.T. as the Church of Peter.

What it all added up to was, of course, a complete rejection of post-industrial society. Now, obviously, this was rather *fey*, Irish, and hopelessly absurd. It was a Ghost Dance of the Indians against the railroads: little Lindisfarne against the Trilateral Commission. But there it is.

This attempt to bear witness to the esoteric traditions of philosophy in the face of the triumph of the behavioral sciences is, as the Zen abbot and Lindisfarne Fellow, Richard Baker-roshi, would say, "a necessary exercise in futility." Lindisfarne is probably, in the best Irish tradition, bound to fail. So what?

I remember at Toronto airport, on my way down to New York to set up Lindisfarne, meeting my boss at York University, the Dean of Humanities, Professor Sydney Eisen. As we stood in line to fly our separate ways, he said: "You Irish are romantic failures. You've got to go and live out this compulsion to fail, to abandon your success in Toronto, and go follow this absurd Irish fantasy." I remember thinking how similar his words were to what my boss at M.I.T. had said when I had quit M.I.T. to go to Canada. He had said that I was ruining a brilliant career by leaving Cambridge to go to the provinces, and he said it in his best, ivy, Princetonian, Waspish manner. One boss had been an élitist WASP from Amherst and Princeton, the other had been a poor Jewish refugée who had climbed up the ladder of society through the help of public education and the City College of New York, but what the Protestant and the Jew were both agreed upon was that the visions of an Irish Catholic were too transcendentally out of touch with the realities of the modern world. In a way, they were both right. We Irish really are much better at failure than success. Other people seem to know how to be better successes than we are. The English, the Swiss, the Germans, the Japanese: they all can make their cars and watches and bank accounts run quite smoothly. But when the Irish become involved with these things, even if they make money, they fail, for there is something really vulgar and distasteful about Irish bourgeois capitalism. An Irish Houston is even more absurd than a Texas one. We're better at being romantics, mystics, and failures, because then we're truly in touch with our *genius loci* and folk spirit. So if we are truly Irish, success in a worldly thing is an embarrassment; we have to drop it and move on, restless in exile. And certainly that is the archetypal pattern described in Lehane's *The Quest of Three Abbots*.

We drive ourselves to fail, often rejecting success to go on to some other risky opportunity that can finally deliver the romantic consummation we crave. We can't stop, for we're afraid that if we did we might just trade in the ocean for a puddle; and that simply can't be done, for it would break your heart to stop, it would break your heart to wallow in the puddle with memories of the infinite sea (small wonder that many of us take to drink!).

So I have to ask myself whether or not this attempt to challenge the vision of humanities at Harvard, M.I.T., York, or the University of Toronto, is doomed to fail. Perhaps, in a sense, Lindisfarne is not the beginning of "the New Age," but the last of something very old, a part of the Roman Dark Ages that never had its chance, and has now returned in the Industrial Dark Ages to express and release itself. Perhaps it is coming up once more, like a dream-fantasy in the mind of a dying man, just at the moment when the West is about to experience its own finale. There is something to the poetry of finales for it is the moment of death in which life achieves its most consummate expression. Think of Bach on his deathbed: knowing that the great age of contrapuntal music is over and that lesser men are going to write court music for aristocrats, he composes his *Art of the Fugue* and engraves it on copper plates so that it will be found. Think of Thomas Morley saying farewell to the age of the madrigal by writing *The Silver Swan*. So, perhaps, Lindisfarne is the swan song of the humanities, and the contemplative scholars of Lindisfarne, much more than the technocratic specialists of Harvard, are truly sensitive to how the humanities stand in an age of technology in which we have behavioral modification in the elementary schools and Zbigniew Brzezinski in the White House. We can lift our sights to see the whole and understand that the citizen is, as Brzezinski would say, about to be separated from the political system to become a loyal subject, not of Her Majesty, but of scientific management. Think of Robert Heilbronner's *The Human Prospect* and you will get a sense of what the Industrial Dark Ages are likely to be.

Whether it is the Church of John against the Church of Peter, or the Ghost Dance of the Indians against the railroads, it is a case in which a victory for the ego is a defeat for the soul. The technological society will go on, turning its railroads into space colonies, but it is doomed by its own success, for if you live like an empire, you die like one. All the little peoples, whether Irish or Hopi, can only watch Tribe and Empire play it out to the end.

More than any poet, Yeats gave voice to the conflict of opposites. In the face of the advance of everything he was most opposed to, he climbed the winding stair of his tower and expressed his prophecies in verse. So I should like to end with the words of Yeats:

> We Irish, born into that ancient sect
> But thrown upon this filthy modern tide
> And by its formless spawning fury wrecked,
> Climb to our proper dark, that we may trace
> The lineaments of a plummet-measured face.

NOTES

[1]Except for some slight editing, this paper has, for obvious internal reasons, been presented as it was delivered during the Conference. This talk was given as Lindisfarne-in-Manhattan was ending for lack of funds, but in an appropriate mythic fashion, Lindisfarne was reborn and now lives as a solar village in the Sangre de Cristo Mountains of Southern Colorado. The *peregrinatio* from Southampton (1973) to Manhattan (1976) to Crestone, Colorado (1979), is part of the old pattern of Irish monasticism.

[2]Dr. Thompson was referring to Chris Jennings's photographic exhibition, "Standing Stones of the British Isles," which was opened by the Persian Artist, Mitra Naraghi, on 6 February 1978. Richard Demarco writes about Chris Jennings's work in his essay in this volume. *Ed.*

EPILOGUE: THE CELTIC HERO

ROBERT O'DRISCOLL

Idea

The heroic quest has been one of the characteristic and recurring features of the Celtic consciousness. We presented as part of the Symposium "The Celtic Hero" (a production of W. B. Yeats's *At The Hawk's Well, On Baile's Strand, The Only Jealousy of Emer,* and *The Death of Cuchulain*) to demonstrate how that quest has been presented in dramatic terms by the leading poet of the Celtic world.

Yeats, as we know, is one of the great theatrical innovators of the twentieth century. He created new dramatic forms in an attempt to reconcile matter and spirit and to make the stage a centre of vitality and mystery, a place where through the interrelation of the arts — verse, music, mime, song, and dance — a unified image is presented which liberates us from daily experience while at the same time defining that experience. This oscillation between the nobleness of vision and the naked realities of mortal life, this willingness to embrace both as opposing but essential aspects of the same experience, is part of the heroic approach to life.

The hero is one who responds to emotion and the impulses of life, to whatever is most immediate and pressing, and yet he retains control of his destiny in this world. He realizes that man is incomplete, merely the foam upon the deep, and yet he embraces all that is passing in the world, accepting the conditions of life, maintaining self-possession and courage when confronted with impossible odds, gaiety in the face of terror and defeat, indifference to death, whether it be the death of a dream or the death of the mortal body.

Yeats's plays, generally, are built upon a moment, a moment when the antinomies of life come to a crisis. *At The Hawk's Well, On Baile's Strand, The Only Jealousy of Emer,* and *The Death of Cuchulain* dramatise crucial moments in the hero's life: the moment when Cuchulain achieves his heroic stature, the moment when he betrays it, a moment of rebirth, and the moment of death.

At The Hawk's Well presents Cuchulain as a young man seeking the waters of immortality, following an impulse. He confronts at the well an old man who has had a similar impulse fifty years before but who has allowed himself to be betrayed into passivity and abstraction. Ironically the old man views immortality as an extension of the conditions of this life and consequently he shuns the supernatural, which is embodied in the Guardian of the Well. The unmoistened eyes of the Guardian, however, prove more powerful for Cuchulain than the dry stones of the well and under her mesmeric influence he surrenders to the unknown, to action, battle, and the sudden embrace of his sworn enemy in

Plate 1: Sorel Etrog's costume design for The Blind Man in *At The Hawk's Well*.

combat, Aoife. For one moment, at the end of the play, we have the meeting of male and female, of the seen and unseen worlds. In responding to this impulse, in embracing the mortal world which carries with it an acceptance of death, Cuchulain matches desire with action and finds a way to make his noble name live in the minds of those who come after him. In so doing, he ironically achieves an immortality that is denied to the old man who remains nameless because he continues to isolate himself against life and the unknown.

Cuchulain, in *On Baile's Strand*, plays false to his heroic nature and chooses, because he is made to feel "out of fashion," to take the oath of allegiance to the High King Conchubar, who is committed to security and institutional wisdom. Bound by his oath but contrary to his natural impulses, he kills a young man who proves to be his son, thus unwittingly taking away the life he has unwittingly given in *At The Hawk's Well*. Cuchulain, in a rage of passion and remorse, raises his sword again and again against the sea, while the Blind Man, who has in a way manipulated the whole action of the play, capitalizes on the situation for material gain. Thus we have caught in one moving moment at the end of the play the agonized expression of the heroic impulse and the material betrayal of that impulse, a true juxtaposition of incongruities, which is, of course, the absurd.

In *The Only Jealousy of Emer* Cuchulain lies poised between life and death, with a battle for his soul and body being fought between abstract spiritual essences, symbolized by Fand, and the dark powers of this world, symbolized by Bricriu. Body and soul are saved for the world, but only with the renunciation by his wife, Emer, of the thing she prizes most dearly, her love for him. Emer in the process achieves heroic stature and Cuchulain is reborn in the arms of his mistress, Eithne Inguba. The play thus counterbalances *At The Hawk's Well* which also concludes with the embrace of life and the sexual act.

The Death of Cuchulain is set in the circular frame common to many of Yeats's plays, beginning with an uncompromising declaration of dramatic principle, followed by a phantasmagoric procession of characters, mistress, vengeful lover, and finally that emblem of manipulative man, the Blind Man, who severs the dying hero's head because he has been promised twelve pennies, Yeats thereby clearly reducing to absurdity the material capitalization on heroic vulnerability. The hero is reborn as a bird to sing to the coming generations. For a moment in Emer's dance, joy and sorrow are fused in tragic ecstasy. Then the play plunges back into the twentieth century and a ballad singer's vivid perception of what has passed and what may never come again.

Staging

Because Yeats was so influenced by the Japanese Noh, we attempted in our production to combine some of the dramatic techniques of East and West: Wakano Ito, daughter-in-law of Mitchio Ito (who created the role of the Hawk in 1916), danced the part of the Hawk; Grainne Yeats supplied rhythms from the world of Irish traditional music; Robert Aitken combined Irish and Japanese influences in his evolution of the music. Anne Yeats and Liam Miller (who has written the definitive book on Yeats's plays, *The Noble Drama of W. B. Yeats*) supervised various aspects of the production.

One of the most daring aspects of the production was Sorel Etrog's designs for the costumes and sets, some of which are reproduced in this volume. Of his designs Mr. Etrog has written:

> The poetic epic that Yeats created in the Cuchulain plays connects concepts and emotions separated from us by hundreds of years but still pulsating with vitality today. They were structured in the Japanese Noh idiom — a rich encounter of dance, drama, poetry, and a festive occasion. What matters most is their spirit and the visual freedom. I was intrigued by their multi-levelled structure and their potential as a multi-media presentation.
>
> Of all the characters, I singled out Cuchulain and pictured him in modern dress. A Celtic hero confronting an Old Man, his wife, his mistresses, his kingdom, his death and rebirth — a ritualistic man, an ancient hero yet also a contemporary one, his dress does not confine him to any particular time; and so I used the timeless image of the spiral, the contemporary and the mythological running parallel, two points following one another on the same line but separated by time. While this interpretation may provoke controversy, it may also release a typical Yeats audience from the programmed associations of previous productions.
>
> Since the plays take place in the depths of the mind, and since there is no fixed point of reference, I thought it appropriate to create a set which disrupts the solidity of the make-believe, and in so doing I wanted to give to the set a sense of motion. For instance, the columns were not attached to the floor but barely touching it and secured only by a short loose string. Furthermore, the sea was depicted with plastic cut-outs suspended on invisible cords; again movement was suggested. A huge inner-tyre (the well in *At The Hawk's Well*) had a moving light inside the inner cavity and in *The Only Jealousy of Emer* the lovers were lying on a waterbed; this added further to the sense of movement. The few masks which I used were in the spirit of the supernatural dimension of the plays; these added more visual impact and a further contrast between what is here and what has passed.
>
> My approach to the design of these plays is only one of many approaches, and if I were to design them again I might very well do it all differently.

Mr. Aitken wrote of his approach to the music:

> Language and the sound of language have always attracted me more than the meaning behind words. The words in these plays are full of music, the rhythms of speech suggesting every musical innuendo. Because of this and because I felt the plays themselves needed a flexibility of sounds that could vary from one performance to another, I chose improvisation. I felt the actors should be triggered by sounds and vice versa. If I had written the music down I think it would have appeared 'frozen'. . . . When improvisation works it is enlightening, refreshing, and exciting for audience and musicians alike. The production was daring on many fronts: why, therefore, should the music be tame? I had always been fascinated by the element of mysticism and the supernatural, the control that nature has over us, rather than in our control over nature. These were aspects which I attempted to bring into the creation of the music.
>
> Having decided to improvise I chose musicians and singers who were comfortable with this form, people who had the versatility to suggest other strains in the musical background of the plays, while still creating a new, less rooted, more contemporary sound. Because the plays, *At The Hawk's Well* in particular, are strongly influenced by the Japanese Noh form, we used many Japanese instruments, but not in a Japanese way. Yeats's Irish background is manifested in the rhythms of speech and the metre of much of the verse. On some occasions we took Irish traditional folksong and altered one element — a metre, perhaps. On others, we took pitches of Irish music, some

Plate 2: Etrog's costume design for Charmion King as Emer in *The Only Jealousy of Emer*.

Plate 3: Etrog costume designs for David Fox as Cuchulain and Wakano Ito as the Hawk in *At the Hawk's Well*.

modal things, and used entirely different metres. We took indigenous Irish rhythms and changed the pitch, juxtaposing Japanese rhythms with Irish scales and Irish scales with Japanese rhythms.

Another aspect of the production was the integration of music and dance. Contrary to the usual sequence of events, the music was added after the choreography had been done. In these plays the dances reflect the meaning and symbolism of the plays and are an integral part of the whole. This meaning the dancers conveyed to us, inspiring the sounds we created. Thus the dancers were more immediately involved in the action of the plays, the musicians one step further removed. But that was another of the gambles that we took.

The Director, James Flannery, defined his approach as follows:

The directorial approach to "The Celtic Hero" was defined by two primary considerations. First, we tried to develop a production concept and style that expressed both the essential humanity and the vast mythopoeic resonances of the plays. Our second objective was to create a rehearsal environment that enabled each of the distinguished artists involved in the production to express him or herself freely and at the same time to remain fully responsive to the overall dramatic and theatrical intentions of Yeats . . . .

Yeats's theatre is total not merely in its deployment of all the arts to their maximum effectiveness, but in its evocation of a magnificently holistic vision of life. The fundamental purpose of Yeats in writing for the theatre was to provide us with a renewed sense of the spiritual resources available within our own being. Yeats, by celebrating the fully conscious individual as hero, intended the theatre to provide an antidote to the negative forces of greed, cynicism and despair that cause individuals and whole societies to falter. It was by being fully true to himself that Yeats discovered he was most true to his own Celtic heritage. It was through the spiritual riches of that heritage that Yeats found a common bond with the great cultures and civilizations of the world.

The Associate Director and Choreographer, Anna Raphael, expanded on some of these points:

Our problem as directors was to orchestrate and balance Yeats's multiple aggression on the senses and, in rehearsals, to create an environment in which each of the artists involved in the collaboration could function with the maximum amount of freedom while still remaining faithful to Yeats's imaginative concept.

Yeats rejected naturalism as an environment inimical to poetry, and our work with the actors and dancers was directed toward the discovery of a style simple and natural without being naturalistic. We tried to tap their innate capacity for ingenuity by encouraging them to improvise and so explore the mythopoeic resonances of the plays; we then tried to evolve methods of preserving the new energies released, channelling and focusing them toward a mask or figuration of character. We discovered that the mask depersonalizes, forcing the actor to cease to rely on fleeting facial expression and to rely instead on movements of the whole body. This much more organic sense of physical presence and patterns of movement on stage led us back to Craig and further to the acting techniques of the Japanese Noh. Our work with masks challenged us not to try to compete with life, but rather to try to go beyond it, to communicate as directly as possible the unconscious forces at work beneath the surface.

This challenge also influenced our thinking on the nature of the dance sequences. . . . Any attempt to choreograph in the traditional sense by imposing a pre-set pattern of movement on a pre-existing score would have straight-jacketed this response and forced one or other of the dancers to work with a foreign vocabulary. Rather we chose to improvise around the dramatic situation suggested by the text and to build the dance out of the personal movement vocabulary of each dancer. The results were 'programmatic' in the sense that they were danced scenes rather than patterns of abstract movement, and the musicians and singers, triggered by the dancers moving within a context, were free to improvise around them.

Reception

The critical reception for "The Celtic Hero" was, as one might have expected in an age of naturalistic theatre, mixed. A reviewer in *The Toronto Star*, writing under a pseudonym, was totally negative, while the *Toronto Sun* cited the production as something "to challenge the intellect" and as "deeply moving." The reviewer in *The Globe and Mail* wrote: "Yeats's vision is so glorious that it dares others to the impossible — and this production is dressed, danced, sung, and chanted with such splendor that it nearly achieves it. . . . Etrog's astounding sets and costumes as a work of art are worth the price of admission." It was a reviewer, Philip Shepherd, in the small but distinguished Toronto Arts magazine, *Onion*, who seemed to grasp most clearly what the production was attempting: "What I found unmistakably worthwhile in the performance was the delight of being awakened again to the pleasures of music, masks, dance, poetry and song when used as integral elements of tragic theatre. . . . The production was a daring step; perhaps, as Yeats hoped, a first step towards a new form of theatre." The response from the student newspapers at the University of Toronto and Ryerson Polytechnic Institute was encouraging. *Varsity* cited the production as "effective and stunning," while *The Ryersonian* called it "courageous, imaginative and exotic." *The Irish Times* called "The Celtic Hero" an "elaborate impressive production," while a CJRT radio reviewer hit the nail on the head for some when he referred to the opening performance as "rich boulibaisse served to a fish and chip crowd."

Plate 4: Preliminary sketch for "The Celtic Hero" by Sorel Etrog: the Woman of the Sidhe in *The Only Jealousy of Emer.*

Plate 5: Preliminary sketch for "The Celtic Hero" by Sorel Etrog: the fire scene in *On Baile's Strand*.

Plate 6: Preliminary sketch for "The Celtic Hero" by Sorel Etrog: the Blind Man in *On Baile's Strand*.

The credits for the North American premiere of the production were as follows:

Producer:	Robert O'Driscoll
Associate Producer:	Liam Miller
Special Adviser:	Anne Yeats
Director:	James Flannery
Choreographer and Associate Director:	Anna Raphael
Set and Costume Design:	Sorel Etrog
Musical Director:	Robert Aitken
General Manager:	Gully Stanford
Lighting Designer:	Jim Plaxton
Design Co-ordinator:	Nicola Kozakiewicz
Stage Manager:	Maureen Lynett
Assistant Stage Manager:	John Wilbur
Players (in order of appearance)	
The Old Man:	Jeff Braunstein
Cuchulain:	David Fox
Fool:	Douglas Stratton
Blind Man:	Jeff Braunstein
Conchubar:	Wesley Murphy
Old King:	Giulio Kukurugya
Young King:	Rick Clarke
The Young Man:	Tim Leary
Emer:	Charmion King
Eithne:	Maureen McRae
The Old Man:	Wesley Murphy
Servant:	Jeff Braunstein
Aoife:	Nonnie Griffin
Ballad Singer:	Grainne Yeats

Dancers
    Hawk: Wakano Ito
    Guardian/Shape-Changer/Ghost/Morrigu: Jennifer Mascall
    Shape-Changer/Fand: Nancy Schieber

Chorus
    Billie Bridgman   Mary Morrison
    Giulio Kukurugya   Grainne Yeats

Musicians
    Robert Aitken (Flute)
    Russell Hartenberger (Percussion)
    Robert Engelman (Percussion)
    Grainne Yeats (Irish Harp)

NOTES ON CONTRIBUTORS

Christopher Bamford is President of the Lindisfarne Association and the author of a forthcoming study of *The Homily on the Prologue to the Gospel of Saint John* by John Scotus Eriugena.

Neil Bartlett was brought up in West Sussex and has just completed a study of David Jones at Magdalen College, Oxford.

Alexander Blair-Ewart is a practising Consultant Astrologer and a Spiritual Scientist who teaches in the City of Toronto.

Michael Bowles, distinguished Irish conductor and Chairman of the Cultural Relations Committee of Ireland. Author of *The Art of Conducting.*

Joseph Campbell, born in 1904 in New York City, is author, co-author and editor of some 25 volumes on Comparative Mythology, Indology, Literature and Psychology, including *A Skelton Key to Finnegans Wake* (1944), *The Hero with a Thousand Faces* (1949), *The Masks of God* (4 volumes: *Primitive Mythology,* 1959; *Oriental Mythology,* 1962; *Occidental Mythology,* 1964; *Creative Mythology,* 1968); *The Flight of the Wild Gander* (1969), *Myths to Live By* (1972), *The Mythic Image* (1974), the Viking *Portable Jung* (1972), and others.

Salvador Dali, prolific Spanish painter, one of the founders of surrealism and a master of 'fantastic' art.

Kevin Danaher, Lecturer in Irish and Comparative Ethnology in the Department of Irish Folklore, University College Dublin; former Humboldt scholar at the Universities of Berlin (1937-8) and Leipzig (1938-9); guest Lektor in Uppsala University (1952-3). His recently published *Bibliography of Irish Ethnology and Folk Tradition* includes a list of his publications in this field. He has lectured on these and related subjects in Canada, the United States, and several European countries. His other main interest is Irish Military history and he has recently been elected President of the Military History Society of Ireland.

Richard Demarco, artist, co-founder of the Traverse Theatre at the Edinburgh Festival in the early nineteen-sixties, founder and Director of the Richard Demarco Gallery (which has presented almost 700 exhibitions of contemporary art during the last thirteen years), creator of Edinburgh Arts, an annual journey or pilgrimage exploring, among other things, the Celtic roots of Europe.

Derrick de Kerckhove, Associate Professor of French Literature at St. Michael's College, University of Toronto. Author of articles on French literature and modern communications. Translator of several of Marshall McLuhan's books into French. At present engaged on a book on concepts of tragedy in the eighteenth century.

Liam De Paor, archaeologist and historian, University College Dublin; commentator on Irish political events; co-author (with Maire De Paor) of *Early Christian Ireland;* author of *Archaeology* (1967) and *Divided Ulster.* Director of archaeological excavations at Inis Cealtra, Ireland.

Anne Dooley, Assistant Professor, Celtic Studies, St. Michael's College, University of Toronto; author of articles on modern literature and on the early Celtic world; has completed for the press a book on Irish religious poems in the thirteenth century.

Owen Dudley Edwards, lecturer in History, University of Edinburgh; has also taught in the Universities of Oregon, Aberdeen, South Carolina, and California at San Francisco. Broadcaster and Correspondent to *The Irish Times*. Author and Editor of *Celtic Nationalism* (1968), *The Easter Rising* (1968), *The Sins of our Fathers: Roots of Conflict in Ireland* (1970), *Scotland, Europe and the American Revolution* (1976), *P.G. Wodehouse;* currently working on a study of the British Isles and the United States, 1875-1935.

George Eogan, Professor of Archaeology, University College Dublin, and director of the archaeological excavations at Knowth; co-author (with Michael Herity) of *Ireland in Prehistory* (1977); author of many papers for the *Proceedings of the Royal Irish Academy* and other journals on various aspects of archaeological investigation. Chairman of the Archaeological Section of the Royal Irish Academy.

Sorel Etrog, sculptor, painter, poet, dramatist. Illustrator of Ionesco, Beckett, and others. His work is represented in the major capitals of the world.

Fanny Feehan, Irish music critic, author of many articles on different aspects of music.

Jan Filip. Archaeologist and University Professor, University of Prague. Author of *Keltove ve stredni Evrope* (Russian and German Summaries, 1956), *Das Grossmahrische Reich,* and *Celtic Civilization and Its Heritage* (revised edition, 1977), Editor of *Investigations archeologiques en Tchecoslovaquie.*

Hamish Henderson, poet, translator, essayist. Served during the Second World War in the African desert: his *Elegies for the Dead in Cyrenaica* were written between 1942 and 1947 and won the Somerset Maugham Award as well as high praise from T.S. Eliot, Hugh MacDiarmid, Louis MacNeice and C. Day Lewis. Since 1951, Hamish Henderson has worked as a teacher and researcher at the School of Scottish Studies, Edinburgh University.

John Kelly, c.s.b., philosopher and university administrator; Chairman of the Celtic Arts Board and President of the St. Michael's College Foundation.

A.O.H. Jarman, Professor of Welsh at University College Cardiff since 1957; Sir John Rhys Fellow of the University of Oxford and Research Fellow of Jesus College. He edits *Llen Cymru* and subjects on which he has published critical studies include Early Welsh Poetry, the Merlin Legend, Geoffrey of Monmouth, the Mabinogi and Medieval Welsh texts. He is Vice-President of the British Branch of the International Arthurian Society.

Larkin Kerwin, past Rector of Laval University, and Chairman of the Science Council of Canada.

Thomas Kinsella has published many volumes of poetry with the Dolmen and

Peppercanister presses since 1951, and most recently the twin volumes *Fifteen Dead* and *One and Other Poems* (1979). *The Tain*, his translation of the Irish prose epic Táin Bó Cuailgne with a number of associated tales, was published by Dolmen Press in 1969 and is currently in its sixth printing in paperback. He has just completed, in collaboration with Sean O Tuama, *An Duanaire 1600-1900: Poems of the Dispossessed*.

Marianna Lines is Director of Publications at Findhorn.

Sean MacBride, Assistant Secretary General of the United Nations; winner of the Nobel and Lenin Peace Prizes (1974 and 1977); Chairman of the Irish Association of Jurists and one of the founders of Amnesty International; Minister for External Affairs for Ireland, 1948-51.

Proinsias MacCana, Professor of Early Irish Language and Literature, University College Dublin, and at present President of the Royal Irish Academy and Chairman of the School of Celtic Studies of the Dublin Institute for Advanced studies; author of *Branwen, Daughter of Lyr; Celtic Mythology* (1970); *The Mabinogi* (1977); *The Learned Tales of Medieval Ireland* (1978); and other studies of Celtic literature and mythology.

John MacInnes, distinguished scholar and collector, School of Scottish Studies, University of Edinburgh.

Sorley Maclean is regarded as the leading figure and inspiration of the group of poets responsible for the twentieth-century renaissance of Scottish Gaelic poetry. Born Raasay, 1911; schoolmaster; publications include *Dàin de Eimhir agus Dàin Eille*, a book of poems in 1943; contributions to anthologies, notable *Four Points of a Saltire* (1970) and *Nua-Bhàrdachd Ghàidhlig* (1976); *Spring tide and Neap tide: Selected Poems 1932-72* (1977); essays on Gaelic poetry and culture. At present he lives in Skye.

John MacQueen, Professor of Scottish Literature and Oral Tradition, University of Edinburgh; Director of the School of Scottish Studies, University of Edinburgh; his publications include *The Oxford Book of Scottish Verse* (1966), *Robert Hennyson* (1967), *Ballattis of Luve* (1970), *Allegory* (1970), *A Choice of Scottish Verse, 1470-1570* (1972). In the press: *Progress and Poetry*.

Louis Marcus is an Irish writer and film-maker.

Liam Miller. Founder of the Dolmen Press; publisher of the leading Irish authors for the last thirty years; producer, designer, and director at the Abbey and Lantern Theatres; author of *The Noble Drama of W.B. Yeats* and *The Dun Emer Press, Later the Cuala Press;* winner of many international awards for book publishing and design, the most recent being a Bronze Medal at Leipzig for his edition of Holinshed's *Irish Chronicle*.

John Montague, Irish poet and lecturer in literature at University College Cork; has published a volume of stories, *Death of a Chieftain*, and several volumes of poetry, including *The Rough Field* (1972), *A Slow Dance* (1975), *The Great Cloak* (1978), and others. He has also edited *The Faber Book of Irish Verse* (1974).

John David Mooney, American artist based in Chicago; has executed patterns of light in Chicago and Zagreb following some of the megalith configurations.

Pat Musick, an American-born scribe and artist who works in London. Her principal interest is Irish lettering.

Conor Cruise O'Brien, External Affairs, Government of Ireland and United Nations Service, 1944-61; Albert Schweitzer Professor of Humanities, New York University, 1965-9; Minister for Posts and Telegraphs, Government of Ireland, 1973-7; author of *Maria Cross* (1952), *The Shaping of Modern Ireland* (1959), *Conflicting Concepts of the U.N.* (1964), *Writers and Politics* (1965), *The United Nations: Sacred Drama* (1967), *Conor Cruise O'Brien Introduces Ireland* (1969), *Edmund Burke: Reflections on the Revolution in France* (1969), *Murderous Angels* (1969), *States of Ireland* (1972), *The Suspecting Glance* (1972), *A Concise History of Ireland*, with Maire Cruise O'Brien (1972), *Herod: Reflections on Political Violence* (1978), and others. Editor-in-Chief, London *Observer*, 1978-81.

Maire Cruise O'Brien, Irish poet and scholar; studied modern languages and Celtic Studies at University College Dublin, the Dublin Institute for Advanced Studies and the University of Paris. Called to the Irish Bar; entered the Irish Foreign Service and rose to rank of Counsellor before resigning on marriage. Two collections of poetry in Irish; co-author of *Concise History of Ireland;* articles on various subjects.

Robert O'Driscoll, Artistic Director, Celtic Arts Canada, and Director of the Celtic Studies Programme at St. Michael's College, University of Toronto; author and editor of nine volumes on aspects of Celtic and Irish literature, including *Symbolism and Some Implications of the Symbolic Approach* (1975), *An Ascendancy of the Heart: Ferguson and the Beginnings of Irish Literature in English* (1976), *Theatre and Nationalism in Twentieth-Century Ireland* (1971); he has co-edited, with Lorna Reynolds, five volumes in the *Yeats Studies* Series.

Breandán Ó Madagáin, Dean of Arts and Professor of Modern Irish, University College Galway. His publications include *Teagasc ar an Sean-Tiomna* (1974), *An Ghaeilge i Luimneach* (1974), *An Dialann Dulra* (1978), and *Gneithe den Chaointeoireacht* (1978).

Seán Ó Tuama, Associate Professor of Irish language and literature, University College Cork; has lectured at Harvard and Oxford. His books published in the Irish language include four plays, two volumes of poetry, and critical works on eighteenth-century love poetry, *An Gra in Amhrain na nDaoine*. In 1981 he published, with translations into English by Thomas Kinsella, *Poems of the Dispossessed*, a comprehensive bilingual anthology of Irish poetry from 1600 to 1900.

Kathleen Raine, author of many volumes of prose and poetry, her most recent books being *Collected Poems* (1981), *Blake and the New Age, Blake and Antiquity,* and two volumes in the press: *The Inner Journey of the Poet* and *The Human Face of God.*

Lorna Reynolds, Irish scholar and poet, Professor Emeritus, University College Galway. Co-editor, with Robert O'Driscoll, of five volumes in the *Yeats Studies* Series; editor of *University Review* (1954-66); author of several hundred poems and critical articles in periodicals and poetry journals.

Peter J. Reynolds, excavated many sites in West Midlands; at present Director of The Butser Ancient Farm Research Project in Hampshire; has lectured extensively in England, Europe, and North America on Archaeology by Experiment; researches into peasant agriculture in Northern Spain and France.

Anne Ross, Department of Archaeology, University of Southampton; Carnegie Fellow and Senior Research Fellow, School of Scottish Studies, Edinburgh; author of *Pagan Celtic Britain* (1967). *Everyday Life of the Pagan Celts* (1970), *The Folklore of the Scottish Highlands* (1976), *Grotesques and Gargoyles* (1975); and of many articles in *Scottish Studies, Études Celtiques, Archaeologia Cambrenisis, The Listener, Antiquity,* etc.

W.B. Stanford, Emeritus Professor of Classics, Trinity College Dublin; author of many books, including *Ireland and the Classical World, The Ulysses Theme,* and eight volumes on aspects of Greek literature.

Douglas Stewart, Librarian, poet; has published five collections of poems, three of which are on Scottish and Celtic themes: *Glenquaich* (1974), *MacTalla* (1975), *Blessing on Iona* (1981).

Elmar Ternes, Professor of phonetics and Head of the phonetics Institute, University of Hamburg; university studies in Germany and France; linguistic field work in Brittany and the Scottish Highlands; author of *Grammaire structurale du breton de l'Ile de Croix* (1970), *The phonemic analysis of Scottish Gaelic* (1973), and *Probleme der kontrastiven Phonetik* (1976); articles on general linguistics, phonetics, Celtic languages and literatures, Romance languages.

William Irwin Thompson, Founding Director of the Lindisfarne Association; has taught at Cornell, M.I.T., and York University; author of *The Imagination of an Insurrection: Dublin, Easter, 1916* (1972), *At the Edge of History* (1971), *Passages about Earth: An Exploration of the New Planetary Culture* (1974), *Evil and World Order* (1976), *Darkness and Scattered Light: Four Talks on the Future* (1978), *The Time Falling Bodies take to Light: Mythology, Sexuality, and the Evolution of Culture* (1981).

Pamela Travers, close friend of AE during the last years of his life. Author of *Mary Poppins; I go by Sea, I go by Land; The Fox at the Manger; Friend Monkey;* etc. Advisory Counsel of the Threshold Foundation. Consulting Editor of *Parabola - Myth and the Quest for Meaning.*

Radu Varia, international French critic and art historian; member of the International Association of Art Critics since 1967; author of the *New York Manifesto* (1976). In preparation: *The decline of the spiritual and the cult of the personality in twentieth-century art - a crisis of civilization,* for Editions du Chêne, Paris.

Heinrich Wagner, Member of the Royal Irish Academy, Honorary Consul of Switzerland; Professor of Germanic, University of Utrecht (1951-3), University of Basle (1953-8); Professor of Celtic and Comparative Philology, Queen's University Belfast (1958-79); from 1979 onwards Professor at the Dublin Institute for Advanced Studies. Author of *Zur Herkunft der e-Verben in den indogermanischen Sprachen* (1951), *Linguistic Atlas and Survey of Irish Dialects* (4 vols., 1958), *Das Verbum in den Sprachen der britischen Inseln* (1959), *Gaeilge Theilinn* (1959), *Studies in the Origins of the Celts and of Early Celtic Civilization* (1971).

ILLUSTRATIONS

Plate 5: Knocknarea, County Sligo. Aerial photograph looking northeast. Source: J. K. St. Joseph, Director of Aerial Photography, University of Cambridge.

Plate 6: Rathcoran, Baltinglass Hill, County Wicklow. Source: University of Cambridge.

Plate 7: Newgrange, County Meath. Aerial photograph. Source: University of Cambridge.

Plate 8: Knowth, County Meath. Aerial photograph. Source: University of Cambridge.

Plate 9: Tara, County Meath. Aerial photograph. Source: University of Cambridge.

Plate 10: Fourknocks, County Meath. Interior of Chamber of Passage Tomb. Source: Commissioners of Public Works in Ireland.

Plate 11: Loughcrew (Sliabh-na-Caillighe), County Meath. Source: Commissioners of Public Works in Ireland.

Plate 12: Newgrange: Chamber looking out to passage from end recess. Source: Commissioners of Public Works in Ireland.

Plate 13: Newgrange. Entrance Stone. Photograph: M. J. O'Kelly.

Plate 14: Newgrange. Kerbstone, no. 52. Photograph: M. J. O'Kelly.

Plate 15: Fourknocks. Decorated Stone in Chamber. Source: Commissioners of Public Works in Ireland.

Plate 16: Knowth, County Meath. Entrance Stone before Western Tomb. Photograph: George Eogan.

Plate 17: Knowth. Kerbstone to the south of entrance to Eastern Tomb. Photograph: George Eogan.

Plate 18: Knowth. Stone basin in Eastern Tomb. Photograph: Eric Kwint.

The Art of the Celtic Peoples

Plate 1: The Dying Gaul. Source: Museo Capitolino, Rome.

Plate 2: Head of a Celtic warrior from Mšecké Žehrovice, Bohemia. La Tène period. Source: National Museum, Prague.

Plate 3: Gold coin of the Parisii. Source: Bibliothèque Nationale, Cabinet des Medailles, Paris.

Plate 4: Horse-mask mounting from Stanwick, Yorkshire. Source: The British Museum.

Plate 5: Waterloo helmet. Source: The British Museum.

Plate 6: The Battersea Shield. Source: The British Museum.

Plate 7: The Tara Brooch. From Bettystown, Co. Meath. Source: National Museum of Ireland.

Plate 8: The Ardagh Chalice: inner ring of base. Source: National Museum of Ireland.

Plate 9: The Derrynaflan Paten. Source: National Museum of Ireland.

Plate 10: Wine-flagon from Basse-Jutz. Source: The British Museum.

Plates 11 and 12: Gold bracelet and detail of gold torque from Waldalgesheim. Source: Rheinisches Landesmuseum, Bonn.

Plate 13: The Torrs ponycap. Source: National Museum of Antiquities of Scotland, Edinburgh.

Plate 14: A horned god? Source: Armagh Cathedral.

Plate 15: Grave marker, Inis Cealtra, Co. Clare. Source: National Museum of Ireland.

Plate 16: Durham MS A II 10. Source: Durham Cathedral Library.

Plate 17: Dunfallandy sculptured stone. Source: National Museum of Antiquities of Scotland, Edinburgh.

Material Culture, Myth and Folk Memory

Plate 1: Garland Day ceremony, 29 May, Castleton, Derbyshire. Source: BBC TV.

Plate 2: Sucellos, 'The Good Striker,' Arc-sur-Tille, Côte d'Or. Source: National Museum of France, St. Germain-en-laye, Paris.

Plate 3: Head of Celtic Horse, La Bussière-Etable, Haute-Vienne. Source: National Museum of France.

Plate 4: Bronze Gallo-Roman Horse. Source: National Museum of France.

ILLUSTRATIONS

Plate 5: *Terra cotta* Horse, Banassac, Lozère. Source: National Museum of France.

Plate 6: Celtic Mercury, Ile-Barbe, Rhône.

Plate 7: Two St. Bridget's Crosses made in 1977 in Co. Cavan, Ireland. Source: Anne Ross.

Plate 8: Three-headed Grotesque, Bayeux Cathedral, Calvados. Source: J. Roberts, 85 Glenfield Avenue, Bitterne, Southampton.

Plate 9: Bronze Raven Head, Hod Hill, Dorset, eye inlay missing. Source: B. Picard, 164 The Albany, Manor Road, Bournemouth.

Plate 10: Bronze and Iron Lynch Pin, (Paris), France. Source: National Museum of France.

Plate 11: Bronze mount, Malomerice, Czechoslovakia. Source: Moravske Mus., Brno, Czechoslovakia.

Plate 12: Carved stone pillar, Turoe, Co. Galway, Ireland. Source: C. M. Dixon, 21 Ashley Road, London N19 3AG.

Plate 13: Opium Poppy *(papaver somniferum)*, widely grown in prehistoric and later times. Source: Peter J. Reynolds.

Plate 14: Water nymphs, High Rochester, Northumbria. Source: C. M. Dixon.

Plate 15: Tricephalos, Condat, Dordogne. Source: Bordeaux Museum.

Plate 16: Stone figure Euffignieux, Haute-Marne. Source: National Museum of France.

Plate 17: Bronze figure of squatting stag-god, Bouray, Seine-et-Marne. Source: National Museum of France.

Plate 18: Relief of priapic bull-horned god bearing shield and spear, from site of Roman fort Alavna, Maryport, Cumberland (Cumbria). Source: C. M. Dixon.

Plate 19: Hunter God, Touget, Gers; holding hare, naked except for a cloak. Source: National Museum of France.

Plate 20: Esus-Mercury, great stone figure from Lezoux, Puy-de-Dôme. Source: National Museum of France.

Plate 21: Mythical three-horned bronze bull. Source: National Museum of France.

Plate 22: Aristocratic male bnronze head, eye inlay lost, Garancières-en-Beauce, Eure-et-Loir. Source: Chartres Museum.

Plate 23: Two goat heads, La Bussière-Etable, Haute-Vienne. Source: National Museum of France.

Plate 24: Growing Woad. Source: Peter J. Reynolds.

Plate 25: Bronze figurine, male dancer, Neuvy-en-Sullias, Loiret. Source: Musee Historique d'Orleanais, Orleans.

Plate 26: Bronze mythical three-horned bull. Source: National Museum of France.

Plate 27: Bronze cockerel. Source: National Museum of France.

Plate 28: Bronze figurine, Arduina on a boar, Jura. Source: National Museum of France.

Plate 29: Bronze (chariot) mount, deity with raised arms, Waldalgesheim, Germany. Source: Rhein. Landesmus, Bonn.

Plate 30: Oolite head, originally painted red, found when preparing the site for the 'Bon Marche' in Gloucester. Source: Gloucester Museum.

Plate 31: Standing Stones, Clochane, Co. Kerry, Ireland. Source: Proinsias MacCana.

Plate 32: Diagrams of sequence of development of structures at Emain Macha, Armagh, Northern Ireland. Source: R. W. Feachem, 6 Rose Road, Southampton.

Plate 33: Stone relief, Epona mounted, Gannat, Allier. Source: National Museum of France.

Plate 34: Bronze figurine of cockerel. Source: National Museum of France.

Plate 35: Bronze belt plate, Zelkovice, Czechoslovakia. Source: Narodni Muz., Prague.

Plate 36: Spring goddess Coventina in triple form, Brocolitia, Northumberland. Source: C. M. Dixon.

Plate 37: Heads separated by the beak of a raptor, Celtic temple at Roquepertuse, Bouches-du-Rhône. Source: Musée Borely, Marseille.

Plate 38: Phallic stone decorated with head and snakes on one side, a collared serpent on the other, Alavna, Maryport, Cumberland (Cumbria). Source: C.M. Dixon.

Plate 39: Bronze mount for wooden flagon, Durnberg, Austria. Source: Stadtmus, Hallein, Austria.

The Celtic Continuum in Ireland

Acknowledgements for illustrations: Kevin Danaher for Plates 2, 3, 4, 5, 6, 8, 9, 12, 22, 23; Bórd Fáilte Éireann for Plate 1; Office of Public Works, National Parks and Monuments Branch for Plate 7 ; T.W. Mason for Plates 10 and 21; Donal Ó Cearbhaill for Plate 11; Department of Irish Folklore, University College Dublin, for Plates 14, 15, 16, 18; *Illustrated London News* (1852), for Plates 17 and 19; and Liam Ó Danachair for Plate 20.

Plate 1: Irish landscape.

Plate 2: Megalithic monument.

Plate 3: A Christian symbol on a pagan pillar stone.

Plate 4: Farmhouse.

Plate 5: Smaller farmhouse.

Plate 6: Hill farmstead.

Plate 7: Tower house.

Plate 8: Tillage ridges.

Plate 9: Antiquated farm implements.

Plate 10: The old-fashioned horse cart.

Plate 11: The craft of the wheelwright.

Plate 12: Ancient skills in boat building.

Plate 13: An example of folk art.

Plate 14: Evictions after the Act of Union.

Plate 15: Mass in the open air.

Plate 16: Visit to a holy well in Penal times.

Plate 17: The Hedge School.

Plate 18: The blind fiddler.

Plate 19: The dancing school.

Plate 20: Open-air Irish language class in the days of the Revival.

Plate 21: Robin Flower and Tomás Ó Criomthain.

Plate 22: Peig Sayers.

Plate 23: The shanachie and his audience.

The Celtic Continuum in Scotland

Plate 1: Tomb of Alexander MacLeod, St. Clement's Church, Rodil, Inverness-shire.
Acknowledgement: Royal Commission on the Ancient and Historical Monuments of Scotland.

Plate 2: Detail from the Tomb of Alexander MacLeod.
Acknowledgement: Royal Commission on Ancient Monuments.

Plate 3: Detail from Tomb of Alexander MacLeod, "Hunters and Deer."
Acknowledgement: Royal Commission on Ancient Monuments.

Plate 4: Looking south over part of byres to deserted cottage, Smearisary, Moidart, Inverness-shire.
Acknowledgement: Eric G. Meadows and the School of Scottish Studies, University of Edinburgh.

Plate 5: Steading, Letterfearn, Ross-shire. Late nineteenth-century photograph. Acknowledgement: G. W. Wilson and the School of Scottish Studies.

Plate 6: Croft, Eriskay, Outer Hebrides. Photo: August 1911.
Acknowledgement: School of Scottish Studies.

Plate 7: The Interior of a Blackhouse.
Crown Copyright: reproduced by permission of the Scottish Development Department, Edinburgh.

ILLUSTRATIONS

Plate 8: Parliament, St. Kilda. Photo: August 1927. Acknowledgement: School of Scottish Studies, Edinburgh.

Plate 9: Women with 'Fire Balls', Stonehaven, Scotland. Acknowledgement: School of Scottish Studies, Edinburgh.

Plate 10: St. Fillan's Healing Stones, Killin, Scotland. Acknowledgement: School of Scottish Studies.

Seán Ó Riada

Plate 1: Seán Ó Riada. Photograph ᴿ1960 by Lensman, courtesy of Gael Linn. Dublin.

Celtic Calligraphy: From Penstoke to Print
Acknowledgement for all illustrations: Liam Miller and Pat Musick.

Plate 1: Springmount Bog Tablet, late sixth century.

Plate 2: The Cathach, 560 A.D.

Plate 3: The Book of Kells, Trinity College Dublin.

Plate 4: Autograph signature of Michael O'Clery, seventeenth century.

Plate 5: Queen Elizabeth's Irish type, 1571-1652.

Plate 6: Louvrain type 'A', c. 1611.

Plate 7: Rome (Propaganda) type, c. 1675.

Plate 8: Irish Archaeological Society type, Dublin, c. 1840.

Plate 9: Colmcille, designed by Colm O'Lochlainn, 1930.

Plate 10: Stone-cut building sign by Michael Biggs, Dublin, c. 1970.

Plate 11: Lettering on telephone kiosk, Dublin.

The Death of AE: Irish Hero and Mystic

Plate 1: AE drawing, Pamela Travers in paper leggings. Source: Pamela Travers.

Plate 2: AE drawing, a witness to the scene: Pamela Travers in a tree. Source: Pamela Travers.

David Jones: 'Cara Wallia Derelicta

Plate 1: 'Cara Wallia Derelicta. Acknowledgement: Professor William Blissett and the Tate Gallery Publications Department.

Dali, Trajan and the Celtic Consciousness

Plate: Letter from Salvador Dali to Robert O'Driscoll.

Celtic Vision in Contemporary Art

Acknowledgement for Illustrations: Richard Demarco and the individual artists referred to in the course of the article.

Plate 1: Sunhoney, Aberdeenshire. Photo: Chris Jennings.

Plate 2: Sundial on Northleach Church. Photo: Chris Jennings.

Plate 3: Mason's Mark, Minster Lovell. Photo: Chris Jennings.

Plate 4: "Snowfall" Performance devised by Howard Hull, 25 February 1979.

Plate 5: Detail from "Snowfall" performance devised by Howard Hull, 25 February 1979.

Plate 6: Paul Neagu, 'Hyphen-Ramp,' 1976, and 'Open Fusions,' 1979.

Plate 7: Paul Neagu, 'Hyphen-Fulcrum,' 1975-77, and 'Open Fusion', 1979.

Plate 8: Paul Neagu, 'Fusion and Ramp,' 1979.

Plate 9: Detail for Joseph Beuys Performance, "Celtic Kinloch Rannoch — The Scottish Symphony," Richard Demarco Gallery, 1970.

Plate 10: Detail from Beuys's "Scottish Symphony."

Plate 11: "Man with suitcases," by Tadeusz Kantor, 1967.

Plate 12: "Ambulance," by Fiona Geddes.

INDEX